Student Services

❧ ❧ ❧ ❧ ❧

A Handbook
for the Profession

Second Edition

Ursula Delworth
Gary R. Hanson
and Associates

Student Services

A Handbook
for the Profession

Second Edition

 Jossey-Bass Publishers

San Francisco • London • 1989

STUDENT SERVICES
A Handbook for the Profession
by Ursula Delworth, Gary R. Hanson, and Associates

Copyright © 1989 by: Jossey-Bass Inc., Publishers
350 Sansome Street
San Francisco, California 94104
&
Jossey-Bass Limited
28 Banner Street
London EC1Y 8QE

Library of Congress Cataloging-in-Publication Data

Student services : a handbook for the profession / [editors], Ursula
    Delworth, Gary R. Hanson and associates. — 2nd ed.

      p.   cm. — (The Jossey-Bass higher education series)
    Bibliography: p.
    Includes index.
    ISBN 1-55542-148-2
    1. Personnel service in higher education—Handbooks, manuals, etc.
2. College student development programs—Handbooks, manuals, etc.
I. Delworth, Ursula. II. Hanson, Gary R. III. Series.
LB2343.S795 1989
378'.194—dc19   88-46086
                                                       CIP

Manufactured in the United States of America

The paper in this book meets the guidelines for
permanence and durability of the Committee on
Production Guidelines for Book Longevity of the
Council on Library Resources.

JACKET DESIGN BY WILLI BAUM

SECOND EDITION

Code 8923

The Jossey-Bass
Higher Education Series

Contents

Preface

Student Services is for people who help students enter, enjoy, endure, and exit from college. In the time between entrance and exit, those of us who work with students hope the services we provide will help students grow and develop their potential. The ends are clear, but the means of achieving them are not.

For too long, our helping profession has struggled to survive with a shaky philosophical foundation, insufficient conceptual models, and little supporting research with which to evaluate the impact of our services on students. We have not always understood the forces that shape higher education and our roles in it. All too often, we have tried to use theories to guide our actions, only to be disappointed when they did not work. To complicate matters, we have tried to train others even though we have been unable to identify the specific skills that produce effective results or the strategies and techniques that really work. And we have been surprised when our funds and other resources have been severely restricted or even eliminated because we lacked the fundamental management skills to establish our accountability within the college and university system. Clearly, we need to unite theory and practice to understand what we do, why we do it, and how we can be most effective.

For these reasons, we published the first edition of this book in 1980. We commissioned each chapter in an attempt to draw together much of the best thinking in our profession on these critical issues. Other books have described the functions and purposes of student services, and still others have reviewed theoretical approaches and conceptual models. Books in other fields have outlined effective management techniques that have been adopted for use in student services. But few, if any, books have focused on identifying, assessing, and evaluating the ideas and competencies that can influence students. We thought there was great value in integrating these diverse concerns into a comprehensive handbook, one that could be used by the experienced professional as well as by the beginning graduate student. Chief student services officers, middle managers, staff members, and students in college student services and development, as well as those in related graduate programs, have found this integrative perspective helpful. We are gratified by the positive reaction to our efforts and by the opportunity to offer a second edition.

Overview of the Contents

We have organized this edition of *Student Services* into six parts, which can be read in any order. We have added new chapters to cover components that have become more salient over the past decade, and we have deleted or cut back on our coverage of topics that appear less primary. Perhaps most importantly, we have added a sixth component—ethics and standards—to our model for the profession. The part introductions describe the chapter-by-chapter coverage; here, we offer a general overview of the book's contents.

In Part One, we identify the context of current student services by searching its historical roots for the ideas and actions that influence today's service delivery. The philosophy and values that guide our current thinking and practice and our attitudes about students have changed over the years. An understanding of this evolution will lead to a better definition of the role, purpose, and function of the student services profession. Ethics, standards, and legal issues are current arenas in which our values are actualized. It is essential that we understand both the opportunities and the challenges they present. The chapters in Part One proclaim an appreciation for the efforts of our professional pioneers, the philosophical basis of our profession, and the ethical and legal boundaries within which we practice.

As we thought about the importance of theory to the student services profession, we realized that there is really little theory that we can call our own. Instead, we have bought, borrowed, and stolen our theories from such disciplines as psychology, sociology, and business. Nevertheless, these theories help student services professionals organize data about our profession, help us explain what we do for others, guide our day-to-day decisions, and perhaps most importantly, help us dream about the future. Rather than present a wide array of possible theories—each with *some* relevance for the student services professional—we have selected a few theoretical ideas to pursue in depth. In Part Two, these theories stimulate questions of how students grow and develop and how they interact with their college environment in ways that either hinder or facilitate their growth.

Practice in student services is based on models or conceptualizations of the appropriate roles for professionals. Such models are general orientations toward what we should be doing in higher education. Unfortunately, the models are often too general. Part Three explicitly delineates four models to facilitate intentional and knowledgeable choices and commitments. Although few student services divisions or agencies utilize only one model, most operate with one of these models as a predominant orientation for practice. By presenting several different models, we hope to encourage innovation and the development of new approaches to the delivery of student services.

Part Four deals with the major skills and competencies required of student services professionals. To work effectively, we must be well trained in an increasing number of sophisticated competency areas. Each individual cannot be trained in all skill areas, but all these competencies should be represented within a division of student services. Our coverage of these areas in this volume is necessarily less extensive than in our first edition, but it serves to introduce readers to essential competencies for effective practice.

All managers—from the chief student services officer to the staff member responsible for a specific program—are interested in effective coordination. Part Five offers some new ways to organize and manage programs and services. There is no single "correct" way to manage effectively. Each institution is faced with different challenges and has available varying resources to meet them. While one institution may need to focus on developing new staff competencies, another may be able to use bright undergraduates in paraprofessional positions. The chapters in Part Five will help administrators bring about change—effectively and efficiently—through an understanding of sound management and organization.

Every profession must analyze current trends and offer visions for the future. In Part Six, we do this, with specific emphasis on the essential emerging area of outcomes assessment and with attention to models of graduate education.

In shaping the content of *Student Services,* we have intentionally avoided discussing such specific areas or functions as student financial aid, housing, and student activities. The broader scope of the history, ethics, legal issues, theory, models of practice, competencies, and administrative techniques and strategies discussed here will provide student services professionals with the knowledge, attitudes, and skills they need in order to work in many areas. We make some strong statements concerning the student services profession and education for this profession. We hope that our words will facilitate an open dialogue within our field from which a more integrated and effective profession can emerge.

Acknowledgments

The chapters in this book represent the efforts of many people. We are indebted first and foremost to our contributing authors for the long hours they spent thinking and writing in order to bring their ideas to us. Of course, their chapters, prepared for this book by invitation, do not necessarily represent a consensus of opinion. We thank Gale Erlandson, higher education editor at Jossey-Bass, for her skills, patience, and faith in this book. We are also deeply indebted to the individuals who worked with us not only to type and retype manuscripts but also to coordinate and manage our professional lives during the period of rethinking and revision. We thank Reta Litton, Ginny Travis, and Sheena Hickman for excellent computer skills and highly timely work. Gary Hanson expresses deep appreciation to a most understanding family, who resigned themselves to many long evening hours and even more Sunday mornings of his absence while he worked on "the book." Finally, we again dedicate this book to Philip Tripp, a major influence in the professional and personal lives of both editors. Had it not been for his untimely death, we would have included a substantial contribution from him in both our first and second editions. For his wisdom, his philosophy, and his humor, we are most thankful of all.

March 1989

Ursula Delworth
Iowa City, Iowa

Gary R. Hanson
Austin, Texas

The Authors

Ursula Delworth is a student services professional and psychologist who is currently professor of psychological and quantitative foundations at the University of Iowa. She received her B.A. degree (1956) from California State University, Long Beach, in political science and education; her M.A. degree (1962) from California State University, Los Angeles, in counseling; and her Ph.D. degree (1969) from the University of Oregon in counseling psychology.

Author of more than fifty books, monographs, and professional articles, Delworth received the Contribution to Knowledge Award of the American College Personnel Association (ACPA) in 1981. She has also served as a member of the Executive Committee and as chair of Commission VII (counseling) of the ACPA.

Delworth is active in the American Psychological Association (APA) as well; she has served as chair of the Committee on Women in Psychology, president of Division 17 (counseling), and a member of the association's Education and Training Board, Committee on Accreditation, and Committee on

Graduate Education. In the APA, she is a fellow of Divisions 2 (teaching), 17 (counseling), and 35 (women).

Delworth was formerly director of the university counseling service, University of Iowa, and has also been affiliated with the Western Interstate Commission for Higher Education and Colorado State University.

Gary R. Hanson is coordinator of research for the Division of Student Affairs at the University of Texas, Austin. He received his B.A. (1965), M.A. (1968), and Ph.D. (1970) degrees from the University of Minnesota in counseling psychology.

Prior to working for the University of Texas, Austin, Hanson was a psychologist for the American College Testing Program, where he was actively involved in career development research. His current research interests focus on minority student development, retention, and student services program evaluation. In collaboration with Ursula Delworth, Hanson served as co-editor-in-chief of the New Directions for Student Services quarterly sourcebook series and also coedited *Student Services: A Handbook for the Profession.*

David A. Ambler is vice-chancellor for student affairs and courtesy associate professor of counseling psychology at the University of Kansas, a position he has held since 1977. He was formerly a member of the dean of students' staff at Indiana University and vice-president for student affairs at Kent State University.

James H. Banning is associate professor of psychology at Colorado State University. He was formerly chief student affairs officer at Colorado State University and at the University of Missouri, Columbia.

Margaret J. Barr is vice-chancellor for student affairs at Texas Christian University. She previously served as vice-president for student affairs at Northern Illinois University.

Larry G. Benedict is vice-president for student affairs at the University of Southern Maine, where he was formerly dean of academic support services and director of student affairs research and evaluation.

Robert D. Brown is Carl A. Happold Distinguished Professor of Educational Psychology at the University of Nebraska, Lincoln, where he is also assistant dean of Teachers College. He is the current president of the American College Personnel Association (1989–1990).

Harry J. Canon is professor of education in the Department of Leadership and Policy Studies at Northern Illinois University. He has served on the executive council of the American College Personnel Association as senator to the American Association of Counseling and Development.

Jon C. Dalton is vice-president for student affairs and adjunct professor of education at Northern Illinois University. He was formerly dean of student life at Iowa State University, where he taught in the graduate program in higher education.

T. Dary Erwin is director of the student assessment program and associate professor of psychology at James Madison University. He was formerly chair of the Measurement Services Association.

Robert H. Fenske is professor of higher education at Arizona State University in the Division of Educational Leadership and Policy Studies. He is also coordinator of the division's graduate programs, which offer specialization in student affairs administration.

Linda Forrest is associate professor, head of the Division of Counseling Psychology, and on staff at the counseling center at Michigan State University.

H. Jane Fried is director of residence educational programs and research at the University of Hartford.

June Gallessich is professor of educational psychology and former director of the counseling psychology training program at the University of Texas, Austin.

Lois A. Huebner is director of the counseling and consultation center and adjunct associate professor of psychology at Saint Louis University. She has served on the faculties of the psychology departments at the University of Missouri, Columbia, and Virginia Commonwealth University.

Marvalene Styles Hughes is vice-president for student affairs and professor of counselor and human services education at the University of Toledo. She was formerly associate vice-president for student development at Arizona State University. She is immediate past president of the American College Personnel Association.

David H. Kalsbeek is assistant vice-president for student development and director of student life studies at Saint Louis University, where he directs institutional research projects focusing on student enrollment and outcomes and develops information systems for enrollment planning and management.

George D. Kuh is professor of higher education and student affairs in the Department of Education Leadership and Policy Studies at Indiana University.

Oscar T. Lenning is executive vice-president and dean for academic affairs at Waldorf College. Previously he was vice-president for academic affairs and academic design at Roberts Wesleyan College, senior associate at the National Center for Higher Education Management Systems, and assistant director of the Research Services Department of the American College Testing Program.

Dennis L. Madson is vice-chancellor for student affairs at the University of Massachusetts, Amherst.

Weston H. Morrill is director of the counseling center, professor of educational psychology, and clinical associate professor of psychology and of psychiatry at the University of Utah. He was formerly director of the counseling center at Colorado State University.

Scott T. Rickard is senior research associate in the Office of the Dean of Arts and Sciences at the University of Maryland's Baltimore County campus. Previously, he served as the first vice-chancellor for student affairs at the same institution. He has held positions in student affairs at Willamette University; the State University of New York, Stony Brook; and the University of California, Davis.

Robert F. Rodgers is professor of education in the Department of Educational Policy and Leadership at Ohio State University.

Arthur Sandeen is vice-president for student affairs and professor of educational leadership at the University of Florida. He has served as president of the National Association of Student Personnel Administrators.

John H. Schuh is associate vice-president for student affairs and professor of counseling and school psychology at Wichita State University. Previously he was affiliated with Indiana University and Arizona State University.

William H. Weitzer is assistant vice-chancellor for student affairs at the University of Massachusetts, Amherst, where he also served as director of student affairs research and evaluation.

Roger B. Winston, Jr., is professor in the student personnel in higher education program, Department of Counseling and Human Development Services, University of Georgia.

Student Services

A Handbook
for the Profession

Second Edition

Part One

Professional Roots and Commitments

A major purpose of this book is to examine the student services profession in terms of its members: who we are, how we provide services, and for what purposes. This self-examination must be conducted knowing others are vitally interested in our professional business. An examination of the profession should begin with an analysis of our roots—not only in terms of the historical evolution of student services but also in terms of the ideas that have shaped our thinking. History and philosophy shape our professional practice by providing a set of values that help us define what is important. Embracing these values becomes a matter of professional ethics. We need to examine these values when conflicts over them create situations in which students, faculty, and staff may be endangered. These important professional values must be evaluated against community standards as well, for the laws of our country provide guidelines for working with students. We must know the intent of these laws and the implications they have for the delivery of our services.

1

Helping students has not always been the sole responsibility of student services professionals. Long ago, college presidents and faculty members were directly involved in the daily lives of students. As Robert Fenske points out in Chapter One, we have inherited that responsibility by default. How we came to occupy a central role in helping students during their college years is a fascinating story. Understanding it provides an important perspective for evaluating what we do now. By understanding our past, we can improve what we already do well and prevent future mistakes. The first chapter in this book provides just such a perspective.

Each and every day we work, we make value judgments. We hire and fire staff, spend money, make policy decisions, and make mistakes. The decisions we make are influenced by the philosophy we adopt, and when our philosophy differs from that of others in our academic community we must defend what we believe) Although not everyone in our profession subscribes to the same beliefs, we believe that all student services professionals share a common core of ideas. By using these ideas in our daily practice, we can provide a more convincing statement regarding the importance of our existence. Chapter Two, also written by Robert Fenske, attempts to identify the key philosophical ideas that have guided and continue to guide our thinking about the delivery of student services.

/Working within the academic community provides countless opportunities to test our judgment, to examine the fairness with which we implement our policies, and to evaluate whether the rights of students are being protected./Making these judgments is a difficult task that requires the continual review of our ethical values. What principles guide our sense of right and wrong? What standards provide enlightened decision making? To whom do we turn for help in making the many difficult choices among competing priorities? In the first edition of this book, we neglected to include a chapter on ethics. Since 1980, much has been written on this subject, and within our profession our members have made a conscious effort to debate the values that shape our ethical behavior. Chapter Three, written by Harry Canon, is an attempt to capture our professional wisdom as we know it to exist in the 1980s. Our sense of ethical values will undoubtedly change, but keeping those values open to debate will help us refine our practice. This chapter, more than any other chapter in the book, represents a jumping-off place, a new beginning of awareness that our professional values dictate the integrity of the work we do. Others will judge us by the ethical choices we make.

Since the publication of the first edition of this book, legal dilemmas and the possibility of litigation have shaped how we conduct our business. Often, how we deliver student services comes under the scrutiny of the legal microscope. We must uphold the law. We must protect the rights of students. We must represent the best interests of the colleges and universities who pay our salaries. To enter the student affairs profession ignorant of the law is irresponsible. To continue working in ignorance is dishonest—to students, to our academic colleagues, and, most importantly, to ourselves. Margaret Barr presents just the tip of the iceberg of legal issues that confront our profession in Chapter Four. It is the elementary primer, the first reader, so to speak, of what we should know. Much more discussion, research, and practice will be needed before our profession will feel comfortable working within the letter of the law.

Chapter One

Historical Foundations
of Student Services

Robert H. Fenske

In the beginning was the term *in loco parentis*. This term signified that, by acting in place of the parent, the entire staff of the early American colleges was expected to carry out the holistic approach to education inherited from the English residential university system of the seventeenth century. This approach equally emphasized the intellectual, social, moral, and spiritual development of the young men entrusted to the care of the college.

Relatively isolated from developments in higher education on the Continent, American colleges and universities followed this traditional approach from the establishment of Harvard in 1636 up to the last third of the nineteenth century. Specifically, they ignored the exclusive emphasis on intellectualism introduced by German universities with the founding of the University of Berlin in 1810. Most American educators, except for a few like Wayland at Brown University in the 1840s and Tappan at the University of Michigan in the 1850s, condemned the German model as inappropriate. In the German system, only the grad-

Note: I wish once again to acknowledge the fine assistance given to me by Louis Attinasi, Katherine Davis, Elizabeth Fisk, and Paul Zuzich in the development of the original chapter for the 1980 version of this book. At the time, they were all doctoral students in the Higher Education Program at Arizona State University.

uates of rigorous preparatory secondary schools (gymnasia) were admitted to the universities' research-oriented programs. The American educators' disapproval was based largely on the grounds that the American educational system, which lacked the equivalent of the gymnasia, did not adequately prepare students for such laissez-faire treatment.

After the Civil War, however, resistance to German intellectualism broke down. Leading institutions began to embrace avidly the new emphasis and to turn away from paternalism. Students responded by developing a rich and varied extracurricular life consisting of sports, literary associations, dining clubs, and residence halls restricted to members of certain social organizations. Colleges and universities were concurrently increasing their demands that faculty produce research and scholarship along with the intellectual development of students that was assumed to result from classroom teaching. Paternal duties neglected by faculty and academic administrators were assigned to special noninstructional personnel on the college staff. These personnel were charged with the social, physical, moral, and spiritual well-being of students.

Thus, student services emerged and evolved by default, by taking over necessary and sometimes unpopular tasks abandoned by trustees, administrators, and faculty. The field of student services has grown into a ubiquitous but almost invisible empire in virtually every institution of higher education. During a brief period early in this century, it came fairly close to entering the mainstream of the academic program. In general, however, student services as a distinct professional role never became thoroughly integrated into any of higher education's three principal functions of teaching, research, and service. By assuming, over the years, a multitude of student-related roles and activities yet remaining estranged from the vital functions of the academic enterprise, student services has always been in the peculiar situation of being both indispensable and peripheral.

This chapter reviews a number of the historical developments in higher education that have shaped the present role of student services. Three developments are particularly relevant for understanding the historical background of the profession.

These are the shift in emphasis from religious to secular concerns, the expansion of institutions in size and complexity, and the shift in faculty focus from student development to academic interests.

Shift from Religious to Secular Concerns

In the early colonial period, several basic aspects of colleges were established that persist to this day. These include the system of governance vested in citizens (first clergy, later lay citizens) rather than in college faculty, administrators, or government officials; the view of students as immature and in need of guidance and supervision (preferably in college residences); and the assumption that college not only prepared students for civic, professional, and business careers but also somehow made them better, more moral, more humane people.

Many historians, drawing on original documents and testimonials, have developed vignettes of the early colleges. These colleges were established in theocratic colonies that felt the need to preserve their own sectarian Protestantism, "dreading to leave an illiterate Ministry to our Churches, when our present Ministers shall lie in the dust" (Morison, 1935, pp. 423–433). Each of the early colonies consisted primarily of one denomination. The clergy who founded and controlled the colleges on behalf of the colony's congregations thus staffed both the administration and faculty with members of their own denomination. With few exceptions, only the sons of well-to-do colonists were enrolled, in keeping with the rigid class distinctions that were largely preserved before, during, and after immigration (Schlesinger, 1962; Hofstadter, 1973). Because few were allowed to dissent from the predominant sect in each of the colonies (Miller, 1972), there was general support for the practice of permeating the students' social and academic life with piety. This process was facilitated by having the students live under the same roof as the president and tutors—all of whom were ministers (Brubacher and Rudy, 1976).

It is pointless to argue about whether the colonists' colleges were "intended to be theological seminaries or schools of

higher culture for laymen'' (Brubacher and Rudy, 1976, p. 6).
The charters of the three colleges founded before 1745—Harvard
(1636), William and Mary (1693), and Yale (1701)—made it
abundantly clear that they were to be both (Hofstadter, 1955,
pp. 88–89). However, there was no doubt in the minds of the
ministers who constituted the trustees, administration, and faculty
about where the emphasis was to be placed: "They maintained
that college was a religious society whose basic and chief duty
was to train its students to be religious and moral men. The
study of nature was to be subservient to the inculcation of religion: The one was only a threshold to the other, and religious
instruction therefore was to be emphasized" (McAnear, 1972,
p. 264). This pattern of organization, control, curriculum, and
staffing continued well into the 1800s. Brubacher and Rudy
(1976, p. 27) point out that until "the end of the Revolutionary
War college presidents were almost without exception gentlemen
of the cloth. Governing boards, too, abounded with clerics, exclusively at Yale and generally in a majority elsewhere."

        With Christian piety as the unifying aim of college educa-
tion, all functions that might now be called student services were
carried out by trustees, administrators, and faculty in the name
of the colony that nourished the college. The earliest colleges
were cloistered microcosms of their sectarian communities.
Rudolph (1962) describes the essence of the institutional model
that early colonists borrowed from their English roots: "The
collegiate way is the notion that a curriculum, a library, a faculty,
and students are not enough to make a college. It is an adherence
to the residential scheme of things. It is respectful of quiet rural
settings, dependent on dormitories, committed to dining halls,
permeated by paternalism" (p. 37).

        Surely the religiously oriented college that dominated the
American higher education scene for two-thirds of its history
provided a setting in which student services, although not yet
differentiated and professionalized, were at their zenith in the
functional sense—in the sense that they involved all participants
in the college and were inseparable from the academic program.
Contemplation of these early models tempts one to speculate
that only when an absolute unifying principle (such as a specific
orthodox religion) permeates the life and aims of a college can

the field of student services, with its concern for the whole person, become a full partner in the academic enterprise. But that source of unity is gone from all but a small minority of present-day colleges, a minority that constitutes only a tiny fraction of total U.S. enrollment. "Moral purposes, values, the reality of heaven—these were the focus of the early American college, and there can be no denying that they no longer are central to the academic enterprise" (Rudolph, 1976, pp. 32–33).

Given the almost total immersion in religious life of the earliest colleges, the direction of change could only have been toward a decreasing emphasis on religion and piety. The purely sectarian aspect was the first to diminish, especially because colonial and post-Revolutionary society was rapidly becoming more pluralistic in every respect.

In the mid-nineteenth century, higher education began to respond to increasingly secular and technological trends in society. The widespread death and destruction of the Civil War eroded belief in an omnipotent God especially benevolent toward Americans. The publication of Darwin's *On the Origin of Species* in 1859 and the controversy surrounding it after the Civil War (it was banned on many church-affiliated college campuses) undermined the biblical story of creation and the fundamental authority of revealed Scripture; these had supported the view of collegiate education as the transmission of established knowledge to young Christian gentlemen.

By the time of the Civil War, society having become less concerned with religion, many facets of higher education related to religion had also changed. For example, the composition of boards of trustees had changed from predominantly clerical to predominantly lay; administrators had ceased to be drawn primarily from the clergy; and students had become more concerned with higher education as a means to worldly advancement than as a means to spiritual salvation.

Expansion in Size and Complexity

Probably the most significant organizational development in changing the American college student from "theologian to technocrat in three hundred years" (Rudolph, 1976, p. 31) was the growth of the public-sector college as an alternative to the privately supported, church-affiliated college. The public sector of higher education was established on a large scale only after the Civil War by the Morrill Land Grant Act of 1862. The growth in the public sector has been rapid in recent decades. The last year in which enrollments in private institutions equaled those in publicly supported colleges and universities was 1950; there are now nearly four students in public institutions for every student in a private college.

The Constitution had clearly proscribed the use of public funds to support any church; however, the intensely religious society of the early Federalist period had some difficulty in fully accepting this idea. Thus, even though the Northwest Ordinance of 1787 provided for land from the public domain "to be given perpetually for the purposes of a university," the same ordinance included the now familiar Third Article of Compact; "Religion, morality, and knowledge being necessary to good government and the happiness of mankind, schools and the means of education shall forever be encouraged" (Rainsford, 1972, pp. 35–46). Despite the precedent set by the Northwest Ordinance, the various states in the young republic did not move forcefully to establish universities. A number of states chartered universities in the late eighteenth and early nineteenth centuries, but they were generally of collegiate or subcollegiate level and were more private than public in their control (Brubacher and Rudy, 1976, p. 145).

Not until after the Dartmouth College case of 1819 did a publicly supported higher education sector become an attractive alternative to privately controlled colleges. The U.S. Supreme Court ruled that a privately controlled institution of higher education chartered and partially supported by the state could not be taken over or controlled by the state against its will; this would constitute unilateral violation of contract. Under the doctrine of governmental stewardship of public funds, this ruling signaled the end of the use of public funds for private colleges and universities. From that point on, it was inevitable that the states would develop and support an alternative system of colleges and universities controlled by the states for public purposes.

Thomas Jefferson's view of the Dartmouth College case was that, when necessary, the state could and should take control of an institution of higher education—both of its finances and of its governance—because it constituted a public trust, whatever the terms of its charter. Jefferson had earlier been frustrated in his scheme to help his home state of Virginia gain control of his alma mater, William and Mary College. After failing in both Virginia and New Hampshire to engineer state takeovers of private colleges, he set himself the task of establishing the first truly state-supported university in the United States—the University of Virginia, established in 1825. It was distinct from all earlier institutions in several important respects.

First, the University of Virginia was explicitly secular and nondenominational; second, it was a completely public enterprise in its financial and governing structure; and, third, it not only gave more advanced instruction than other colleges but also offered a choice of curricula to its students—a revolutionary concept at that time. The last feature reflected the contemporary need for higher education that was more advanced, practical, and relevant to American society than the standard classical curriculum of the seven liberal arts offered in virtually all other colleges of the time. The year before the founding of the University of Virginia, Rensselaer Polytechnic Institute had been established. The founding of this institute "marked a turning point; it signaled the fact that American life was becoming increasingly complex" (Brubacher and Rudy, 1976).

The founding of these two seminal institutions, as well as George Ticknor's abortive attempt to reform and liberalize the classical curriculum at Harvard in 1825, led to the immensely effective conservative counterattack in the Yale Report of 1828. This document, which was supported by nearly all of the influential church-affiliated colleges of that era, was one of the principal factors in retarding the development of secular, publicly supported institutions of higher education for nearly forty years (Brubacher and Rudy, 1976, pp. 288–290).

The Yale Report convinced the private, church-affiliated colleges that dominated American higher education that they should maintain their narrow, prescribed curriculum and their focus on orthodox Christian piety. Consequently, it ensured that these colleges would ultimately be superseded by institutions more responsive to the needs of a growing agrarian and industrializing society. Parallel and separate kinds of institutions— such as technical institutes of the Rensselaer type, normal schools, and women's colleges—were established during the middle part of the nineteenth century, but the traditional church-affiliated colleges continued steadfastly in their old ways.

The states that attempted to follow the lead of Virginia in establishing a state university encountered massive and effective opposition led by many of the college-educated leaders of society (virtually all of whom were graduates of private, church-affiliated colleges). The state of Wisconsin found little widespread support for the use of its general revenue funds to nurture its new state university, founded in 1848. The struggling institution found that it had to accept poorly educated farm boys to fill out its enrollment, and then had to place most of them in remedial courses to prepare them for college-level instruction (Nevins, 1962, p. 42).

Active political opposition and lack of state-provided general revenue funds were persistent and insurmountable problems for the state universities founded between 1825 and the outbreak of the Civil War. Virtually all of the young state universities had to "cope with a suspicious public in the form of well-defined pressure groups. Prominent among these were the proponents of the various organized religions. . . . Religious leaders often resented the trend toward secularization augured by the university. They might even seek by legislative means to hamper a foundation which harbored alien styles of thought and which at the same time drained students from the local colleges operated by the denominations" (Veysey, 1965, p. 15). Several states came close to losing their universities to these counterattacks. A regent of the University of Michigan warned against sectarianism in 1841: "The history of all collegiate institutions in this country dependent immediately on the State has shown that they have never prospered, as long as they have been subjected to the insolence of desultory legislation. . . . The establishment of a collegiate institution in a free state, and the conducting of its interests, should ever be upon liberal principles, and irrespective of all sectarian predilections and prejudices'' (Hofstadter and Smith, 1961, p. 437).

The slow development of the public sector, the adherence of private colleges to an extremely conservative curriculum, and the effective political resistance within the state legislatures to public support for state universities all built up considerable social and political pressure for federal action. This pressure resulted in the Morrill Land Grant Act of 1862, a landmark federal law that effectively created the basis for a large, significant public sector of higher education. Even though the states failed to capitalize fully and immediately on the opportunity and resources thus provided, the act established the precedent of direct federal intervention in higher education in the United States. Veysey (1965, p. 15) claims that despite the Morrill Act, ''legislatures were always ready to interfere with or curtail the operations of state institutions (as, for example, at Michigan in 1877, when faculty salaries were reduced), and by 1900 only a handful of states had provided outstanding public universities, fit to be compared with the leading private establishments.'' Nonetheless, by 1900 it was clear that nearly all the states would follow the lead of California, Michigan, Wisconsin, and others in building their state universities into high-quality institutions of significant size. By this time, other types of institutions, such as normal colleges, professional schools, and technical institutes, also constituted alternatives to the private sector. Furthermore, in 1901 the first public junior college was established in Joliet, Illinois, heralding the beginning of a new sector of higher education that would ultimately enroll more first-time students than any other.

By the 1920s, the outlines of higher education as it exists today were already formed. Nearly every state had committed itself to significantly upgrading its state university or universities in size and quality. Most of these institutions included research and service as a part of their mission. Most states were also further expanding well-established systems of state teachers' colleges, many of which served as general-purpose regional colleges. Furthermore, most states were committed either to expanding local opportunities for higher education through branch campus systems of the state university or to building public junior colleges through an upward extension of high school districts. Private universities continued in their role as highly selective, prestigious institutions, even though most of them no longer had direct church ties, and private liberal arts colleges still enrolled more students than other institutions.

The massive and rapid expansion of the public sector, especially after World War II, was due to several egalitarian trends. One was expressed by the President's Commission on Higher Education (the so-called Truman Commission), which recommended that racial, ethnic, and financial barriers to opportunity for higher education be removed as soon as possible (1947). It urged the provision of financial aid to students as one way of removing economic barriers. Another egalitarian strategy the commission urged was the development of public junior colleges to provide a network of low-cost commuter institutions.

However, the most direct expression of widening opportunity for higher education was the Serviceman's Readjustment Act of 1944 (the GI Bill). This legislation entitled all veterans to financial support for direct college costs and subsistence upon enrollment in an accredited college or university. The majority of veterans found places at public, rather than private, institutions. Public colleges and universities were better able to accommodate on short notice the hundreds of thousands of young men who wanted higher education and who were reluctant to postpone their opportunity until a later semester or year. A generation later, these veterans turned largely to public institutions to enroll their own children. Thus, while private colleges and universities grew slowly and steadily for the most part, the number and size of public colleges and universities burgeoned, especially from 1950 to the present.

The impending tidal wave of students in the early 1960s caused Congress for the first time since the Civil War to enact legislation providing general assistance to institutions of higher education. There was considerable concern that institutions in the private sector would soon be greatly overshadowed by the mushrooming public colleges and universities. The National

Defense Education Act of 1958 provided for several targeted programs that would help build up the nation's mathematics and science education. Some of its titles provided for student loans and institutional assistance that benefited private as well as public colleges and universities. The Higher Education Facilities Act of 1963, however, explicitly helped both sectors for the purpose of accommodating the rapid enrollment increases. It provided loans as well as nonrepayable grants for construction of classrooms, laboratories, libraries, and dormitories.

The Higher Education Act of 1965 contained many titles that were aimed at expanding opportunities for higher education. This act emphasized financial aid to students, particularly in the form of loans. It also assisted in the rapid expansion of graduate education to help build up the faculties and other staff of colleges and universities.

The 1972 amendments to the 1965 act further expanded the role of federally based financial aid to students in support of higher education. The amendments included the new concept of "entitlement," which was intended to meet the Truman Commission's goal of removing financial barriers to post–high school education. The principal instrument of entitlement was the Basic Educational Opportunity Grant (later renamed the Pell Grant), available to every financially needy high school graduate who was accepted by an accredited public or private postsecondary education institution. Since 1980, the burden of student aid has been shifted to the Guaranteed Student Loan Program.

The 1972 amendments have had two far-reaching effects on higher education as a whole. First, they have carried out the "market model" approach to higher education that was developed during the Republican administrations from 1968 to 1976. Essentially, this model provides for a discontinuance of direct financial aid to institutions in favor of financial aid to students. This shift was expected to impose accountability on institutions by making a student's financial aid "transportable" to any institution the student chooses to attend. Second, the amendments explicitly assist private as well as public institutions by providing for the accommodation of the higher costs of private institutions.

The amount of each student grant depends not only on the financial need of the student and his or her family but also on the cost of the institution the student attends. Since tuition at private institutions is typically at least double that at public institutions, the program channels relatively large amounts of public funds to private colleges and universities. Private colleges and universities that receive public funds through student financial aid programs are subject to federal regulations; they also must be more sensitive and responsive to the wishes of students as ''consumers'' in such matters as determining the selectivity of admissions criteria and tailoring curricula to attract and hold students.

The trends outlined in this section have produced diverse types of institutions, most of which, however, are large and emphatically secular. Their students come from a wide range of socioeconomic and scholastic backgrounds and are enrolled for decidedly utilitarian and vocational purposes.

Changes in Faculty Involvement in Student Services

Historically, the participation of faculty in what are now called *student services* functions gradually changed from total involvement to detachment. In the early colonial period, when many of the precepts of higher education were established, there was considerable agreement among society, trustees, administrators, and faculty regarding the equal importance of the moral, religious, and academic development of students. This section traces the gradual disengagement of faculty concern from all modes of student development other than the academic.

The development of student character and values was originally a central part of the faculty member's role. For the first two centuries of higher education in this country this function had a thoroughly and explicitly religious tone in the vast majority of the colleges. Knapp (1962, p. 292) has called this role the ''*character-developing* function'' and described its metamorphosis thus: ''In many instances, the professor was expected to indoctrinate his students with particular articles of religious belief, according to the prevailing conviction that this would foster their development as total persons. With the passage of time, indoctrination in the narrower sense gave way to a more general function of personal counseling and the inculcation of high moral standards.'' This active, morally prescriptive role in turn gave way to a passive role of "setting a good example for the students" and was finally abandoned altogether by most college teachers. However, "lip service is still given to the proposition that the professor should be a builder of character as well as a transmitter of fact and knowledge" (Knapp, 1962, p. 292).

Knapp summarizes well the dynamic interaction of the three traditional faculty functions of service, research, and teaching: "The evolving role of the college professor in America has been characterized by a progressive decline of his character-developing function along with a strong tendency for the research and the informational functions to part company and form two separate callings" (1962, p. 292).

Many scholars cite certain nineteenth-century developments in higher education and curricula, or the emergence of new institutional forms, as the source of current faculty orientation. However, a good case can be made that the decline of faculty interest in student development had its origins in the colonial colleges. "They developed a peculiar structure which has served as an abiding model, in many respects, for the subsequent development of higher education in America: Administrative control was placed in a nonacademic supervisory body and the president, and the faculty occupied a subservient station. This pattern persisted even after denominational universities and colleges in America became secularized, and . . . has become the almost universal pattern in both public and private institutions" (Knapp, 1962, pp. 292–293).

In addition to its lay Board of Overseers, Harvard in 1650 attempted to set up a parallel policy-making "corporation" analogous to a European university's autonomous guild of scholars. However, the bicameral governance thus established was not adopted in other colonial colleges (Brubacher and Rudy, 1976, pp. 24–25). The ultimate national model was established with the founding of Yale in 1701. Principally because of "sectarian desires to maintain religious orthodoxy, the founders of Yale petitioned for a single nonacademic board of control"

(Duryea, 1972, p. 19). The leading ministers of the local community who composed the early governing boards vigorously
carried out their mandate to oversee and assist the president
in his administrative duties (Leonard, 1956, p. 27).

As American society became more secular and pluralistic,
more administrative control was delegated explicitly to the president. This was due at least partly to the loss of consensus on
absolute standards of morality and a shift from institutional emphasis on piety to diverse views of culture and learning. In the
process, "the development of nonresident control helped to
change the president from being either first among equals or
spokesman or leader of the faculty into something far different—
representative of the governing board and a significant power
in his own right" (Rudolph, 1962, p. 167). The result is a pattern of policy-making in higher education unique to the United
States. Overall goals are not set by governmental agents, as in
a ministry of education, nor are they set by guilds of those most
directly involved in teaching and learning—the faculty and
students. Policy-making power is instead invested in absentee
bodies of lay individuals. Furthermore, it has been the custom
to invest full administrative responsibility as well in the governing boards.

Most scholars of American higher education agree that
this system became less capable of directly carrying out its administrative responsibilities in either public or private colleges
as society became increasingly secular and pluralistic. Powerful and paternalistic presidents came to dominate institutions.
In the twentieth century, faculty gained control of their own
activities, and educational decisions were made on a segmented
and uncoordinated basis within academic divisions, principally
departments.

It is perhaps natural that under these circumstances the
faculty would eventually have a common cause with no other
constituency in higher education, not even students. Their reward system became tied to individual research efforts recognized and evaluated only within each specialized campus department and, on a national scale, within each profession. Effectively
excluded from policy-making both by organizational structure

and by lack of unity and interest, faculty generally are ambivalent toward the administrators who not only "manage" them on behalf of the governing authority but also protect them from outside pressures and obtain necessary resources. Faculty attitudes toward students also have become increasingly ambivalent as the faculty member's role has changed from partner in paternalism to individual entrepreneur.

Thus, faculty reorientation began with the gradual fragmentation of the American college's consensus on the importance of Christian piety, the decline in value of the classical curriculum, and the development of public colleges with their attractive technical and scientific programs. Even the most conservative colleges capitulated during the nineteenth century, forsaking both paternalism toward their students and the unity of their curriculum (Veysey, 1965, pp. 49–55).

In the last decades of the nineteenth century, changes occurred that turned faculty members, especially in universities, more emphatically toward research and away from concern with student academic and moral development. These changes include the development of the elective system in recognition of the irrelevance of the classical curriculum, the formation of academic departments composed of specialists incapable of integrating knowledge with other disciplines, and the development of research-oriented graduate schools superimposed on the liberal arts colleges. The establishment of Johns Hopkins University in 1876 embodied all of these trends. Based deliberately on German models of research universities, it was designed from the beginning as a "faculty-centered institution" (Rudolph, 1962, p. 271). For the benefit of faculty, the best and brightest students were recruited to assist in research. "The ascendance of research also brought about a new and different view of undergraduate and graduate instruction. To a research man, the more mature student is the more useful. . . . To such a professor, the student becomes interesting as he involves himself either in learning the techniques of scholarly research or in working as an assistant to the professor" (Perkins, 1973, p. 7).

American higher education came to embrace, among other characteristics of the German research university, the concept that students should be free of administrative or faculty supervision of their academic and social affairs. Educators were increasingly of "the conviction that American colleges and universities should follow the German philosophy of complete disregard for students outside of class" (Cowley, 1949, p. 19). Thus, the changing values of the faculty, which had "decade by decade narrowed their definition of students until all that was left was their minds," carried the process further until the faculty favored only certain of those minds for their utilitarian value (Rudolph, 1976, p. 31).

Professional societies and specialized research journals were established in great numbers, further balkanizing knowledge and the structure of the university. Scholars soon found that communication across departmental lines was difficult at best and did not foster specialized research. Consequently, "the researcher created a private special world for himself" (Veysey, 1965, p. 14). In this hierarchy of values, concern for students' character development is gone, "teaching comes out badly in a typical professor's maximization criteria," and research "is where the high payoff for academics is now at numerous institutions" (Richman and Farmer, 1974, p. 260). This value system is found especially at the prominent public and private universities that are models to most of higher education; yet it pervades even those colleges that are avowedly devoted to teaching.

This value system has been fostered by a historical accident that ensured that a research degree (the doctorate) would be an almost universal requirement for a teaching position (Brubacher and Rudy, 1976, p. 192) and that the majority of church-affiliated colleges would become secularized in the period from 1910 to 1920 (Knapp, 1962, p. 295). The Carnegie Foundation, in setting up a sorely needed pension fund for college teachers (which later evolved into the Teachers Insurance and Annuity Association), included only those institutions without formal religious affiliations. Furthermore, it demanded that the majority of the faculty at these institutions possess an earned doctorate. Most colleges promptly complied with these requirements.

Finally, even if faculty were to undertake a collective effort to restructure their value system to emphasize concern for students or at least teaching, it would seem most difficult to identify any basis or common cause for action. In some institutions, faculty have taken collective action, but not for the purpose of reintegrating the curriculum or for reorientation toward student development. The process of collective bargaining has instead focused on faculty salaries, fringe benefits, and work load. A review of what has happened to concern for student development in the elementary and secondary schools under collective bargaining agreements does not make for optimism in regard to higher education. The objectives of bargaining have tended toward the greatest possible reduction in every type of contact with students, especially contact outside actual classroom teaching. Given the present reward system for college and university faculty, it is not likely that student services will benefit from collective bargaining. In fact, as a larger proportion of an institution's budget is devoted to salary increases and work load reductions won by faculty, a smaller proportion will be available for student services. This shift is likely to be accompanied by an increase in tuition. The cost to the student in both money and services will probably further estrange faculty and students (Shark, 1975, p. 3).

It would be erroneous to assume that most students need, expect, or desire a return to the unitary college of yesteryear with its emphasis on character development and paternalism. They too have reoriented their value system; they are less concerned with being saved than with being successful (Rudolph, 1976, p. 34). The curriculum of higher education has become resoundingly vocational in response to student demands and expectations and in response to the goals imposed on institutions by funding sources, including government, alumni, trustees, and granting agencies for sponsored research.

Summary

This chapter attempts to lay the foundation for an understanding of the evolution of the student services profession. Study of the historical context of American higher education in the nineteenth century is necessary to interpret the emergence of an educational profession unique to the United States.

The first American colleges were modeled directly on the English residential college system, which assumed that all faculty and academic administrators acted *in loco parentis*. When American higher education belatedly embraced German intellectualism as the sole and proper concern of faculty, nurture of the spiritual and social development of students was delegated to nonfaculty specialists. This occurred gradually over the last half of the nineteenth century as emphasis in higher education shifted from religious to secular concerns and institutions became larger, more complex, and more impersonal. Student services evolved by taking over duties abandoned by trustees, administrators, and faculty. They have remained apart from the main institutional activities of teaching and research. The student services profession's continuing quest has been to convince faculty and academic administration that the student's emotional, spiritual, and social growth is vital to intellectual development.

Bibliographic Note

Leonard (1956) is still the only source that focuses on the profession's development in the nineteenth century. A recent addition to the secondary literature on this topic is the useful overview by Knock (1985). The excellent chapter entitled "Reintegration of Curriculum and Extracurriculum" in Brubacher and Rudy (1976) contains many fine insights, as does Rudolph (1962). Anyone reviewing the secondary literature on the profession will inevitably encounter numerous articles by Cowley, who wrote informative and stimulating works on this topic for over forty years.

References

Brubacher, J. S., and Rudy, W. *Higher Education in Transition: A History of American Colleges and Universities, 1639–1976*. New York: Harper & Row, 1976.

Cowley, W. H. "Some History and a Venture in Prophecy." In E. G. Williamson (ed.), *Trends in Student Personnel Work*. Minneapolis: University of Minnesota Press, 1949.

Duryea, E. D. "Evolution of University Organization." In J. A. Perkins (ed.), *The University as an Organization*. New York: McGraw-Hill, 1973.

Hofstadter, R. *Academic Freedom in the Age of the College*. New York: Columbia University Press, 1955.

Hofstadter, R. "The Colonial Colleges." In M. B. Katz (ed.), *Education in American History*. New York: Praeger, 1973.

Hofstadter, R., and Smith, W. (eds.). *American Higher Education: A Documentary History*. Vol. 2. Chicago: University of Chicago Press, 1961.

Knapp, R. "Changing Functions of the College Professor." In N. Sanford (ed.), *The American College*. New York: Wiley, 1962.

Knock, G. H. "Development of Student Services in Higher Education." In M. J. Barr, L. A. Keating, and Associates, *Developing Effective Student Services Programs: Systematic Approaches for Practitioners*. San Francisco: Jossey-Bass, 1985.

Leonard, E. A. *Origins of Personnel Services in American Higher Education*. Minneapolis: University of Minnesota Press, 1956.

McAnear, B. "College Founding in the American Colonies." In P. Goodman (ed.), *Essays on American Colonial History*. New York: Holt, Rinehart & Winston, 1972.

Miller, P. "The Contribution of the Protestant Churches to Religious Liberty in Colonial America." In P. Goodman (ed.), *Essays on American Colonial History*. New York: Holt, Rinehart & Winston, 1972.

Morison, S. E. *Founding of Harvard College*. Cambridge, Mass.: Harvard University Press, 1935.

Nevins, A. *The State Universities and Democracy*. Urbana: University of Illinois Press, 1962.

Perkins, J. A. *The University as an Organization*. New York: McGraw-Hill, 1973.

President's Commission on Higher Education. *Higher Education for American Democracy*. New York: Harper & Row, 1947.

Rainsford, G. N. *Congress and Higher Education in the Nineteenth Century*. Knoxville: University of Tennessee Press, 1972.

Richman, B. M., and Farmer, R. N. *Leadership, Goals, and Power in Higher Education: A Contingency and Open-Systems Approach to Effective Management*. San Francisco: Jossey-Bass, 1974.

Rudolph, F. *The American College and University*. New York: Knopf, 1962.

Rudolph, F. "The American College Student: From Theologian to Technocrat in 300 Years." *National Association of Student Personnel Administrators Journal*, 1976, *14*, 31–39.

Schlesinger, A. M. "The Aristocracy in Colonial America." *Proceedings of the Massachusetts Historical Society*, 1962, *74*, 3–21.

Shark, A. R. *Current Status of College Students in Academic Collective Bargaining*. Washington, D.C.: Academic Collective Bargaining Information Service, 1975.

Veysey, L. R. *The Emergence of the American University*. Chicago: University of Chicago Press, 1965.

Chapter Two

Evolution of the
Student Services Profession

Robert H. Fenske

No comprehensive history of the origins, development, and differentiation of the student services profession has yet been published. This seems a notable omission for a profession so large and venerable. This brief chapter attempts to fill part of the void by outlining the evolution of the profession and noting many of the salient events in its development. In preparing this chapter, I have drawn on a wide variety of secondary sources, including two recently published collections of selected readings.*

The first professional responsibilities readily identifiable as student services constituted the ''watchdog'' role of the matrons engaged to safeguard the female students enrolled in the first coeducational colleges of the mid-nineteenth century. In the following decades, in many colleges, general disciplinary duties were assumed by specially designated college staff, who

---

*This chapter contains numerous citations from two recent historical collections of selected readings: Belson and Fitzgerald, 1983; and Saddlemire and Rentz, 1986. To convey a sense of the historical evolution of the student services profession, each citation includes the original publication date (in brackets) of the reading in question, followed by the publication date of the collection in which it now can be found. Page numbers for quotations in the text refer to the Belson and Fitzgerald or the Saddlemire and Rentz collection rather than to the original source. In the references at the end of the chapter, the publication date of the original source is given immediately following the title of each reading.

replaced faculty and academic administrators as they gradually relinquished these responsibilities. By the last decades of the nineteenth century, several specialized student services were in place, including health and medical services, spiritual guidance provided by campus ministers, and those functions directly related to student matriculation, such as academic advising, admissions, and student records. Other functions had followed by the first decade of the twentieth century, including guidance and counseling, residence hall supervision, and career placement. Psychological and aptitude testing appeared on the campus as an aftermath of the large-scale testing programs of the armed services in World War I.

The student services profession saw the greatest promise for full integration with the vital functions of higher education, as well as the greatest fulfillment of that promise, between the end of World War I and the Depression of the 1930s. That era coincided with several favorable developments: a supportive educational philosophy had become popular, leading figures in higher education were concerned with reintegrating the academic and social development of students, and student services professionals were developing vigorous, self-confident organizations. A period of some disillusionment and inertia followed during the Depression as hard-pressed institutions drastically cut back student services budgets and staff. These setbacks coincided with the prevalence of a new philosophy diametrically and explicitly opposed to student services. Since then, the profession has resumed its significant growth in size, but it seems to be still searching for ways to become more vitally integrated with the academic enterprise (Mueller, 1961; Brown, 1972; Miller and Prince, 1976).

Several themes are worth tracing in this sketch of the disorderly growth of the diverse and amorphous profession of student services. The genesis of professional activities in the field will be considered first. The profession's adherence to the concept of the "whole person" and the various attempts to synthesize the field with the academic function will then be reviewed. The chapter will conclude with a brief overview of the historical development of the structural aspects of the profession.

Search for Professional Identity

First of all, it is important to note that the term "the student services profession," implying as it does that the field has long had a singular, unified identity and structure, is more a literary convenience than a description of reality. The fact is that almost throughout the field's historical existence it has never had a single functional focus, has never been stable in its role over significant periods of time, and has never had a consensual integrative philosophy. Furthermore, this disunity and instability has been underscored by the lack of a focal professional organization or association or a long-standing coordinating group that could credibly represent the full range of student services.

Perhaps the most striking contrast to this disarray is the medical profession. Ever since the pivotal Flexner report was published in 1910 (Brubacher and Rudy, 1976, p. 207), the medical profession has had a stable, powerful umbrella association and a clear, unambiguous public identity. If the medical profession can be characterized as a mighty oak with a massive trunk supporting sturdy branches, the student services profession resembles a disorderly thicket of stunted saplings, each fighting the others for its place in the sun and the crowded, tangled roots all seeking sustenance from the same inadequate source.

The difficulty of the profession's continuing quest for identity is epitomized by a search of the historical literature for a coherent general description of a student services professional. The best of the descriptions tend to be circular and almost tautological. For example, a typical published definition describes a student services professional as someone whose main salaried responsibility is explicitly in one or more of those functional areas generally recognized as student-oriented services. One of the earliest attempts at definition was in the 1931 report of the Committee on Personnel Principles and Functions, submitted to the Executive Committee of the American College Personnel Association (ACPA): "The Personnel Department is that department of the administration or that group of persons in which initiative and responsibility for the personnel work of the college is vested"

(Clothier, [1931] 1986, p. 11). Five years later Cowley attempted
to dispel the prevailing confusion: "The terms *personnel work,
personnel administration, personnel services, personnel research* and
personnel point of view continue to be bandied about so variously
and carelessly that faculty members cannot possibly be expected
to know what personnel workers are about. Indeed, plenty
of evidence exists to suggest the personnel people do not themselves know" (Cowley, [1936] 1986a, pp. 48–49). Parker proposed in 1969 that it "should be possible to identify a student
personnel worker as one whose occupational tasks enable him
to find membership in one of the COSPA organizations" (Penney, [1969] 1986, p. 288). The Council of Student Personnel
Associations (COSPA) was a coordinating organization that existed from 1963 to 1975 and included up to sixteen associations.
In 1976 Crookston commented that "in the recent literature
the following terms have been used concurrently and at times
interchangeably: student personnel, student affairs, personnel
work, student development and human development. The assumption that these terms refer to the same thing is symptomatic
of the confusion that has been rampant in our field for many
years, particularly the last decade" ([1976] 1986, p. 429).

The central problem of professional identity in student
services is that professionals in this field have always performed
a wide variety of distinct, uncoordinated, and quite specific
roles. Consequently, a survey of the functions student services professionals have actually performed over the span of the
field's history is no shortcut to the discovery of the "tie that
binds." The various student services began their existence
sharply differentiated one from another, remained separate
for a hundred years or more, and continue to be separate
functions even today. Examining any slice of the historical
continuum reveals much more variance within student services
than in either academic or business services, the other two
areas acknowledged to constitute the tripartite division of higher
education administration. Furthermore, student services as
a general area has seen more changes in most of its functional
roles over the last hundred years than either academic or business
services.

Much of the explanation for this difference is structural. Colleges and universities as social institutions are remarkably hardy and resistant to change. They are slow to change because their vital academic and financial processes involve long spans of time. For example, the charter that determines the purpose of the institution is issued essentially in perpetuity; campuses are established at a permanent location; a faculty member makes his teaching specialty his lifelong career, and tenure is awarded for the entire span of that career. Endowments are given to be permanent resources, of which only the interest earned on the investment is to be used for current purposes. When a state establishes an institution and builds a campus, it assumes a financial commitment continuing far into the future. But student services deal with students, the most transient of all the university's constituencies.

In contrast with the academic and financial functions, consider student services' problems in dealing with the 180-degree turn in student attitudes and values during the decade of the 1960s. The 1950s had ended with students characterized as "organization men" in the making. Jacob reported in 1963 that, according to a national survey conducted five years earlier, "the majority of students appear unabashedly *self-centered*. They aspire for material gratifications for themselves and their families. They intend to look out for themselves first and expect others to do likewise" (Feder, [1963] 1983, p. 28). But the end of the sixties saw a complete reversal in the student image. Student values changed to activism, including rioting, to end a distant and obscure war and to pervasive antimaterialism. Just five years after the height of campus unrest in the early 1970s, college students' attitudes turned 180 degrees again; students were now characterized as "the uninvolved generation" that adhered to political conservatism. The student services professional literature and conference programs of the sixties and seventies document the profession's strenuous maneuvering as it tried to stay "relevant" and useful to its student constituency. In contrast, faculty continued, largely unaffected, to teach and research in their disciplines, and the institutional financial specialists likewise continued their budgeting and comptroller functions largely unaffected through the entire metamorphosis of students' attitudinal changes from materialism to involvement to indifference.

Roots of Professional Identity

A whimsical application of the traditional circular definition might identify the first student services professional as "the first tutor at Yale, who was allowed to study for his bachelor's degree, received no salary but subsisted on the fines he collected from the students for presumed disobediences" (Leonard, 1956, p. 29).

The residence halls in the early colleges contained the classrooms and chapel as well as the sleeping rooms accommodating both the students (often as young as thirteen or fourteen) and the clergymen who were their professors and tutors. "To have a student entirely under their control from the five A.M. rising time until lights out at nine gave them the opportunity they sought to minister continuously to the souls' welfare of their charges. . . . If a youngster misbehaved, they believed with certainty that they were exorcizing the devil when they whipped him" (Cowley, 1934, p. 708).

Faculty members and administrative officials abandoned these onerous responsibilities as interest in intense religious indoctrination waned. By the mid-nineteenth century, when faculty were much more interested in academic affairs than in supervising residence halls, dormitories were more and more left on their own by college officials or were replaced by the new fraternities and sororities. The prototypes of deans of women were established somewhat earlier to mitigate the "terrible dangers" inherent in coeducation, which was begun at Oberlin in 1837. The women charged with supervising such daring activities as unmarried young men and women dining together in a campus dining hall were variously called principals, wardens, and matrons. Their diligence succeeded in having the concept of coeducation accepted in most states by the end of the nineteenth century (Woody, 1929).

Like housing, academic and social disciplinary activities were at first the responsibility of all administrative and academic officers of the college. However, a highly visible instance of differentiation occurred in the late nineteenth century. "Harvard claims the appointment of the first college dean, in 1870. He was a personnel administrator who gave his attention to discipline and the routine mechanics of enrollment, in addition to teaching" (Mueller, 1961, p. 52). Despite his multiple duties, the principal reason for his appointment was to take the burden of discipline off newly inaugurated President Eliot's shoulders (Brubacher and Rudy, 1976, p. 335). Other institutions soon followed suit, so that by 1900 nearly every sizable men's or coeducational college or university had a dean of men.

The appointment of the first deans of students late in the nineteenth century should be viewed in the context of contemporary diversification of other administrative functions in colleges and universities. "The proliferation of administrators . . . [resulted in] first a secretary of the faculty, then a registrar, and then in succession a vice-president, a dean, a dean of women, a chief business officer, an assistant dean, a dean of men, a director of admissions." All existed primarily to "free research-minded scholars from the detailed but necessary work that went into the management of an organized institution" (Rudolph, 1962, p. 434–435). Thus, student services were separated from academics, were professionalized, and became, like business affairs, part of "the administration."

The period of the emergence of the student services profession between the Civil War and World War I was one of critical importance to the profession's present role and status. In response to the concentration of both faculty and administrative concern on the academic aspects of collegiate life, students developed their own social and, to some extent, intellectual life. Organizations and activities such as the Greek-letter societies, intercollegiate athletics, drama, student publications, forensics, and literary societies emerged. The common institutional response to this proliferation of student activities was to hire another student services administrator (Knapp, 1969, p. 56). The growing alienation between students and the institution in which they were enrolled extended even to formal religious activities. "By 1880 the various religious denominations were beginning to feel uncomfortable in the new university atmosphere, and from this discomfort developed the university pastorate movement: the assignment of clergymen to work among college students'' (Rudolph, 1962, p. 459). The increasing academic specialization of the faculty and ''learning for its own sake'' seemed more and more remote from the distinctly vocational and utilitarian goals of students around the turn of the century (Brubacher and Rudy, 1976, pp. 332–333).

Among the leading educators concerned about the rift between the purely academic concerns of the institution and the goals and interests of the students were some of the most eminent people in the history of higher education. In 1889, Daniel Coit Gilman of Johns Hopkins University appointed the first ''chief of the faculty advisors,'' stating that ''in every institution there should be one or more persons specifically appointed to be counselors or advisors of students''; ten years later William Rainey Harper of the University of Chicago indicated that the ''scientific study of the student'' would be the next great research field in higher education (Cowley, 1949, p. 20). These pioneers wre followed by Woodrow Wilson at Princeton and by A. L. Lowell, who succeeded Eliot as president in 1909, at Harvard. In Lowell's inaugural address, he ''warned that the recent emphasis upon graduate education and research scholarship was sabotaging the unique function of the American college. Undergraduates must be helped to develop as well-rounded individuals as well as scholars'' (Brubacher and Rudy, 1976, p. 335). Wilson attempted to reconstruct the collegial atmosphere at Oxford and Cambridge in England by developing a quadrangle plan at Princeton.

The disruptions of World War I sidetracked the nascent movement temporarily. After the war, however, ''the personnel movement received a tremendous impetus all over America. Mental testing and counseling had been developed on a large scale by the army, and as soon as peace came they applied their techniques on the campuses. The field assumed more and more of the aspects of a distinct profession, growing out of the stage of 'sentimentalized intuition' and entering that of systematic differentiation and specialization of personnel functions'' (Brubacher and Rudy, 1976, pp. 335–336).

These professional developments were fostered and under-girded by new psychological theories (variously called "organismic psychology," "psychology of the individual," and "the holistic approach") as well as by applications of John Dewey's progressive educational theories to higher education. Such applications included emphasis on meaningful activities, mental and attitudinal testing, and greatly expanded counseling efforts. The thrust of the new approach was summed up in such statements as "Students are developing organisms demanding a personalized learning experience if they are to profit from college" (Wrenn and Bell, 1942, p. 8).

The diversification and professionalization of the student personnel movement during the decade after World War I saw the development of student health services and placement services. The American Student Health Association was formed in 1920, and by 1925, nearly half of all large universities had professionally staffed student placement bureaus. Intramural and intercollegiate varsity athletics also grew tremendously in the "golden age of sports" (Brubacher and Rudy, 1976, pp. 340–346).

The Depression of the 1930s struck a crushing blow to the student personnel movement's attempt to reintegrate academic and character development on the nation's campuses. Because student services not only generated little or no income but were a significant drain on institutional resources, colleges and universities almost invariably cut back or eliminated many student services bureaus and offices in order to save money. These moves not only were consistent with financial survival but also coincided with a new philosophical emphasis on an old theme—that of the overriding value of the intellect, rather than character or personality development, in higher education.

The leading exponent of this philosophy was Robert M. Hutchins. It was of no help to the student personnel movement that he was not only a brilliant thinker but also a facile and prolific writer. He railed against the need for the faculty to "be diverted from its proper tasks to perform the uncongenial job of improving the conduct and the health of those entrusted to it" (Hutchins, 1936, p. 11). He satirically evaluated collegiate life: "Undoubtedly, fine associations, fine buildings, green grass, good food, and exercise are excellent things for anybody. You will note that they are exactly what is advertised by every resort hotel'' (p. 29). He called for a repudiation of the concept of educating the ''whole person'' by claiming that ''we can do so only if some institutions can be strong enough and clear enough to stand firm and show our people what the higher learning is. As education, it is the single-minded pursuit of the intellectual virtues. As scholarship, it is the single-minded devotion to the advancement of knowledge'' (p. 29).

Dewey and his followers retaliated, stating that the ills of higher education were not to be cured by ''monastic seclusion'' (Dewey, 1937, p. 104). The debate was moot in the depths of the Depression, however, because most colleges had few or no resources to revitalize their student services. For example, there was little justification for student placement bureaus when millions were unemployed. At any rate, the debate was interrupted by the upheavals of World War II.

The GI Bill, which created a tremendous need for academic, personal, and financial advising on nearly every campus in the country, exemplified the postwar trends that breathed new life into student-oriented services of all kinds. By 1958, functionally differentiated student services as they are generally known today were listed by the prestigious and influential American Council on Education's Committee on the Administration of Student Personnel Work (Feder and others, 1958, p. 16):

Selection for admission
Registration and records
Counseling (academic)
Health service
Housing and food service
Student activities
Financial aid
Placement
Discipline
Counseling (personal)

Special clinics
   Remedial reading
   Study habits
   Speech and hearing
Special services
   Student orientation
   Veterans advisory services
   Foreign student program
   Marriage counseling
   Religious activities

The historical development of the student services profession has resulted in a large, highly diversified field of student-related activities that suffers from continual identity crises. I have attempted to portray the roots of the trends underlying Brown's assertion (1972, p. 37) that "with historical hindsight, it is possible to say that higher education took the wrong fork in the road when it thrust personnel maintenance upon staff with specialized duties." Whether the direction taken is wrong or not is perhaps a matter of interpretation or perspective. From the point of view of many faculty members, the present arrangement is satisfactory, because it relieves them of many student-related chores. However, there is little doubt that at present most student services professionals view their segregation from primary academic functions as a troubling issue that evades solution.

Concept of the "Whole Person"

The profession's historic yearning to integrate its functions with the academic function and its faithful adherence to the concept of educating the whole person are two sides of the same coin. Ever since the tradition of *in loco parentis* began to fade shortly after the Civil War, reinstatement of the college's full responsibility for all aspects of student development has remained an unattained goal of most student services professionals. In a world full of inconsistencies and rapid changes, the profession's faithful adherence to the goal of educating the whole person is truly remarkable.

The concept of educating the whole person was enunciated in clear pronouncements by leading academic administrators around the turn of the century, and it has endured with unusual consistency. Leading educators, such as Gilman at Johns Hopkins, Lowell at Harvard, and Woodrow Wilson at Princeton, decried the narrow focus on intellectualism even as they set up a faculty reward system based on research and scholarly publication. William Rainey Harper, a graduate of little Muskingum College and Yale (which continued to resist German intellectualism), was given a princely sum by John D. Rockefeller to found the University of Chicago in the early 1890s on the primary policy of "the ceaseless investigation of every realm of knowledge." But Harper also planned to resist impersonal treatment of students by devoting over half of the total building space on the new campus to students' residences. Other midwestern university presidents saw the plan as monastic and a regression to the British wholistic system (Brubacher and Rudy, 1976, pp. 185–186). And, of course, by the mid 1930s Chicago had installed Robert Maynard Hutchins as president on the basis of his leadership in promoting higher education as a purely intellectual enterprise.

In 1931, ACPA accepted the report of a committee chaired by R. C. Clothier that clearly expressed the wholistic philosophy: "In personnel work we are interested in the individual student's development, not in any one phase of his program such as scholarship, intellect, leadership, but from the aspect of his whole personality" (Clothier, [1931] 1986, p. 15). According to Saddlemire and Rentz (1986, p. 3), the Clothier committee's statement of principles and list of functions formed the basis for the first of several American Council on Education (ACE) statements on "the personnel point of view." The first of these, in 1937, asserted that "this philosophy imposes upon educational institutions the obligation to consider the student as a whole—his intellectual capacity and achievement, his emotional make-up, his physical condition, his social relationships, his vocational aptitudes and skills, his moral and religious values, his economic resources, his aesthetic appreciations. It puts emphasis, in brief, upon the development of the student as a person rather than on his intellectual training alone" (American Council on Education, [1937] 1986a, p. 76). In 1949, the first ACE statement made after World War II summarized the philosophy thus: "The student personnel point of view encompasses the student as a whole" (American Council on Education, [1949] 1986b, p. 123). This was echoed about a decade later in the last of the ACE statements on the subject (Feder and others, 1958).

Leaders in the field, among them Blaesser, Crane, and Trueblood, added their voices to the chorus of student services professionals who subscribed to the "whole student" philosophy.

In 1949, Blaesser ([1949] 1986) expressed his view in terms very close to those of the 1937 and 1949 ACE statements, and in 1963 Crane ([1963] 1983) maintained that offering services to students in functionally separated offices defies the logic of treating the student as a whole person. Trueblood pointed out in 1964 that both faculty and student services staff need to understand that "there need be no basic conflict between an interest in the 'whole' student and the scholar-student. Certainly what happens in any facet of a person's life affects other aspects of that 'whole' person including frequently his ability to perform as a scholar-student" (Trueblood, [1964] 1986, p. 226).

Other leaders in the profession also espoused the philosophy during this period, including Wrenn and Bell (1942), Williamson (1949), and Mueller (1961, pp. 64–69). Some observers saw clearly that a college's environment, particularly its size, significantly influenced opportunity to implement the whole person philosophy. Surveying the impending tidal wave of college students in 1961, Cummer pointed out that "one disturbing fact stands out about these principles cited: They are much easier of attainment in the smaller, private college than in the large state university. Yet, it is these large publicly-supported institutions which must bear the larger responsibility in meeting coming waves of students" ([1961] 1983, p. 25). In 1964, Useem tied college environment and size into her blunt questioning of whether "professional status" and "a generalist implementing the whole student philosophy" were simply contradictions in terms: "What is the essence of the developing body of systematic theory in the student personnel profession? Is it concerned with the development of the college student as a whole person . . . with the establishment of a 'home away from home' and acting *in loco parentis?* . . . The profession of student personnel work can contribute partially to all of these goals, but these are society's goals relative to students and are shared with a myriad of other professions and occupations. If these are your primary concerns, then each of you needs to be in a small college and combine within yourself the role of teacher, counselor, academic advisor, policeman, business manager, social arbiter, dietician and parent" ([1964] 1983, pp. 232–233).

Despite such disclaimers, influential books on developing models for the profession perpetuated the historic theme in considerable purity throughout much of the 1970s. For example, consider Brown (1972): "Colleges and universities should establish expectations for students and assess outcomes that cover the broad ranges of human behavior, including the intellectual, personal-social, esthetic, cultural and even the psychomotor dimensions" (p. 44). Tollefson (1975) called for "a resurgence of concern for the student as a person, for how his interests and needs are being served, and for how effectively the institution is educating him to achieve his personal goals and preparing him for his role in society" (p. 7). And Miller and Prince (1976) stated: "The mission of the college is to educate the whole student and not only his or her intellect" (p. 169).

"Education for the whole person," as laudable and comprehensive as it is, is still only a statement of a goal. The statements issued by ACE are, in retrospect, expressions of intentions as unassailably good as motherhood and apple pie. But as mandates for action they revealed the naked truth—that student services were thoroughly balkanized into disparate functions that may perhaps in the aggregate have constituted education for the whole person, and then only if one acknowledged that these functions complemented the intellective function conceded to the faculty. By the end of the 1960s the lack of an integrative philosophy was universally recognized in the profession. Some of its leaders began in the early 1970s to rectify the problem with the formation of what came to be known as student development theory.

Quest for Integration with the Academic Function

Current discussions of an integrative philosophy for student services recapitulate two central problems that have always plagued the profession. First, student services began as specific, separate, and uncoordinated functions. Accordingly, as will be discussed in the final section of this chapter, much of the profession's search for identity has centered on structural solutions to disunity, such as mergers of the separate professional associations or the formation of a coordinating body for the profession. Second, student services have always been separate from the main academic functions of teaching and research. The profession's quest for unity with the academic functions has been at the core of the search for professional identity, an integrative philosophy, and status.

A number of eminent academic leaders around the turn of the century decried the separation between the formal curriculum and the balance of the student's experience during college. However, it was not until the late 1920s that leaders in the student services profession began to suggest systematic ways to reintegrate the formal curriculum with the extracurriculum (or co-curriculum or second curriculum, as it was sometimes called). These suggestions ranged from passive acceptance not only of continued separation but also of secondary status in the educational enterprise to aggressive encroachment on the faculty's traditional domain. In the latter category falls the opinion of L. B. Hopkins, who asserted in an *Educational Record* article in 1926 that college student personnel functions included selection of instructors, curriculum improvement, improvement of teaching methods, objective examinations, and research concerning teaching (Bradshaw, [1936] 1986, p. 41). Similarly, Clothier's Committee on Personnel Principles and Functions reported to ACPA in 1931 that selection of instructors was one of the recommended functions, explaining that "the personnel situation in a college is vitally affected by the type of instructors engaged. Those incapable of taking a sincere and intelligent interest in the individual student should be debarred" (Clothier, [1931] 1986, p. 16). One of the earliest vice presidents for student affairs, E. H. Hopkins of Washington State College (now University), revealed a remarkable level of integration of academic and student affairs in 1946: "Our faculty voted, as a result of their own deliberations, not merely to adopt a deferred-major plan, but to place the administrative responsibility for the entire lower division in the hands of the Dean of Students and his student personnel staff. This plan has been in operation for two years. They are sold on it, and are improving it" (Hopkins, [1948] 1986, p. 102).

D. L. Trueblood, in his 1964 ACPA presidential address, urged student services professionals to move into the "void which appears to be developing in the higher education scene because the pressure for publication, research, increasingly larger classes, and the ever widening base of knowledge seem to force more and more faculty to be less concerned with teaching. . . . [This void] must be filled by the college student personnel leader who perceives himself as an educator" (Trueblood, [1964] 1986, p. 227). Finally, the task force of student services leaders charged with developing Phase II of ACPA's Tomorrow's Higher Education Project in 1975 urged an active student development model that would include faculty and staff equally with students: "It is imperative that the development of all individuals in the academic community be considered. Therefore, the view of student development in higher education must be broadened to accommodate students, faculty and staff" (American College Personnel Association, [1975] 1986, p. 419). Conspicuously absent from all of these aggressive statements are workable plans for cajoling, persuading, or coercing faculty into sharing their control over the formal educational program.

More temperate efforts at integration with the academic function were also made by many student services leaders over the years. For example, Esther Lloyd-Jones pointed out in 1934 that "the teacher as a personnel worker is indispensable in any adequate system of personnel administration. The director of student-personnel administration or dean will succeed only to the extent that he promotes among the teaching faculty the personnel point of view and utilizes every bit of skill and wisdom the teacher may possess" (Lloyd-Jones, [1934] 1986, p. 23). Kathryn L. Hopwood stated in 1961 that "our recognition as full members of the academic community is dependent upon whether or not we possess and thereupon demonstrate a true intellectual commitment" (Hopwood, [1961] 1983, p. 83). Ralph Berdie, in his 1966 ACPA presidential address, carried Hopwood's thought further, maintaining that "student personnel work is different but not apart from other persons and functions in higher education" (Berdie, [1966] 1983, p. 147). He expressed this coequality with faculty another way: "The student personnel worker is the behavioral scientist whose subject matter is the student and whose socio-psychological sphere is the college" (p. 147). In 1974, E. G. Williamson expressed the goal of coequality in terms of academic credentials: "In the future years I believe we will need professional preparation at the doctoral level, at least for the principal staff members. If we are to be accepted as relevant in the educational scene, we must have clearly identified intellectual and professional competence" ([1974] 1983, pp. 138–139). Chandler voiced concern in 1973 that the student development concept, if pushed too vigorously and precipitately, could alarm and alienate both students and faculty; faculty might interpret the concept as encroachment on their turf. Accordingly, he proposed a "transitional model" as "one way to enable student affairs administrators to initiate a student development program on campuses where the complete change to a student development concept would be difficult to achieve in the near future" (Chandler, [1973] 1986, p. 344). Finally, Harvey predicted in 1974 that the force of changing circumstances would blur and ultimately eliminate the distinction between academic and personnel administration: "Student personnel administration will have to merge into educational administration within the university" (Harvey, [1974] 1986, p. 384).

In contrast to these leaders, however, most student services professionals accepted the role of student services as complementary to but distinct from the academic function. The influential ACE statements of 1937, 1949, and 1958, developed by successive task forces of leaders in the profession, are telling. They all described student services as complementary to the academic function but urged that the faculty be converted to the "personnel point of view" to the greatest extent possible. W. H. Cowley, who began his professional career in student services in 1927 as director of the Board of Vocational Guidance and Placement at the University of Chicago, and who published interpretive historical articles on student services over the next forty years, never wavered in his conviction about the distinction between academics and student services. For example, in 1936 he defined student personnel work as "all activities undertaken or sponsored by an educational institution, aside from curricular instruction, in which the student's personal development is the primary consideration'' (Cowley, [1936] 1986a, p. 65). In 1964, nearly thirty years later, he addressed student services with the following admonition: ''You do many different kinds of things, but all of them have one distinctive characteristic, namely, they occur outside the formal curriculum'' (Cowley, [1964] 1983, p. 217). In 1962, Shoben described the origins of the split between the profession and the academic functions and further observed that, ''as is often the case with movements rooted in a reaction to something, personnel services became identified as something apart from instructional activities and even in conflict with them'' (Shoben, [1962] 1983, p. 6). Williamson, in 1967, saw the gap as a ''window of opportunity'' in which the student services professional could devise and control conditions conducive to significant learning outside the classroom. ''The whole extracurriculum is ours. The faculty does not care about it, and does not believe that it really contributes much except distraction to what they consider to be the main mission of the institution, namely, intellectualism'' (Williamson, [1967] 1986, p. 266).

Even a cursory review of the writings and public statements of student services leaders reveals a consistent strain of criticism of the profession's status, much of it self-consciously aimed at the low degree of acceptance by faculty and academic administrators. In 1948, Hopkins lamented that ''the plain truth is that student personnel work *still* is considered by far too many faculty members, deans, and presidents simply as a fifth wheel. And they are not referring to the 'steering wheel''' (Hopkins, [1948] 1986, p. 95). Hardee, writing in 1961, believed that much of the blame for being relegated to ''sideshow'' status lay with the profession itself: ''It is obvious that some personnel workers have been so much concerned with problems tangential to the major concerns of higher education that they have operated on the periphery, circling aimlessly in outer space, with resulting ineffectiveness for the main business of the campus, which is *learning*'' (Hardee, [1961] 1983, p. 103).

Some of the criticism was couched in blunt, even demoralizing, terms. In 1961, Shaffer quoted a professor who referred to student personnel agencies as a "haven for the incompetent" (Shaffer, [1961] 1983, p. 188). Shoben reported in 1962 that the field has occasionally been viewed as anti-intellectual ([1962] 1983, p. 6). Williamson suggested in 1967 that the profession never rose above its lowly origins, namely, as an adjunct or "a repair station for something gone wrong. You know, we began that way, 'something went wrong,' that is, a squeaky axle, and we specialized in repairing and regreasing squeaky axles ever since. One is entitled to ask the question whether or not we have anything unique, or whether or not we are merely a little more relevant in the hierarchy of the academic environment, just a bit above the janitors and the groundsmen" (Williamson, [1967] 1986, p. 263). Greenleaf asked in 1968, "How do we prove that we are more than policemen and disciplinarians?" (Greenleaf, [1968] 1986, p. 275). Penney, in a 1969 article entitled "Student Personnel Work: A Profession Stillborn," concluded that "student personnel workers tend to be relegated to subordinate and peripheral positions as middle-and-lower-level administrators" largely because the profession's functions are viewed as mere housekeeping by others in the academic community (Penney, [1969] 1986, p. 287).

The profession's self-criticism continued unabated into the 1970s. Chandler pointed out in 1973 that "the faculty appear to view student affairs as an academic civil service" (Chandler, [1973] 1986, p. 336). The following year Williamson charged that the faculty continued to view student services professionals as mere "technicians" and repeated his earlier comparison with "groundsmen and janitors" (Williamson, [1974] 1983, p. 140).

Structural Development of the Profession

According to Bloland in 1972, "College student personnel work as a professional field has suffered from a fragmentation and proliferation of organizations, which stems in part from its inability to define itself in concrete and specific terms or to agree on a common definition of student personnel work" (Bloland, [1972] 1983, p. 237). The fragmentation and organizational proliferation cited by Bloland reveal much about the origins of the profession as discrete functions bound only by their

orientation toward the student constituency in higher education. Bloland also points out that the failure to find a common
definition contributes a large share toward the reluctance to
embrace ecumenicalism among the many branches of the profession. As mentioned earlier, perhaps the current vigorous attempts to establish student development as an integrative philosophy will ultimately provide a conceptual framework for the
many functional branches of the profession.

However, the principal remaining problem is one of genesis. The earliest professional associations in the field represented
the most highly specific and unitary functions, and they have
remained among the least enthusiastic in regard to ecumenicalism. Conversely, the most enthusiastic associations have been
the broadest and most diffuse, namely: ACPA; the National
Association for Women Deans, Administrators, and Counselors
(NAWDAC); the National Association of Student Personnel Administrators (NASPA); and the American Personnel and Guidance Association (APGA), which was later renamed the American Association for Counseling and Development. Despite the
relatively high interest level, long-term affiliation and collaboration have never succeeded, even though the history of these associations is laden with numerous attempts. The frequent encounters, withdrawals, rapprochements, and disengagements
have resembled the proverbial mating dance of the porcupine.

The principal sources available on the topic of professional
associations in the field focus on ACPA and NAWDAC. This
is not a particular disadvantage, since these two associations
represent broad interests in postsecondary student services.
Accordingly, this section devotes the most attention to these
organizations.

As Sheeley pointed out, both ACPA and NAWDAC
have been renamed twice. The former began as an association
of placement officers; the latter, of deans of women (Sheeley,
[1983] 1983, p. 179). ACPA originated with the National Association of Appointment Secretaries, founded in 1924, which
became the National Association of Placement and Personnel
Officers (NAPPO) in 1929. To reflect the broadening scope of
the group, its title was changed to ACPA in 1931. NAWDAC,

organized in 1916 as the National Association of Deans of Women (NADW), retained its original name for the first forty years of its history.

The two associations had an on-again, off-again relationship for all the years of their common history. They also negotiated with many other groups in the student services field during this period. In addition, they had various relationships with larger umbrella educational associations, such as the National Education Association and ACE, and were involved in various coordinating groups and councils.

The deans of women may well claim that their occupation was the first student service to emerge as a specific function. As noted earlier, the predecessors of deans of women were matrons hired to safeguard female students in coeducational colleges as early as the 1840s. Cowley pointed out in 1964 that campus chaplains and physicians appeared about the time of the Civil War; the deans of women, however, were the first to meet annually, beginning in 1903, and they formally organized as a professional association in 1916. The following year the National Association of Deans of Men was organized. Members of other student services began to organize at this time, including college chaplains, physicians, directors of student unions, and residence hall directors (Cowley, [1964] 1983, pp. 214–226.) Concurrently, the "guidance movement" began in secondary education and was soon broadened beyond the original emphasis on vocational advising to include academic and personal counseling.

These developments in secondary and higher education, although very significant, were dwarfed by the "personnel movement," which grew from the twin roots of large-scale psychological testing in World War I and the concepts of functional differentiation embedded in the Taylor system of industrial management. The end of World War I thus saw a horde of professionals who had achieved success in psychological testing, placement, and counseling becoming available to implement the new Taylor system in business, industry, and government agencies. The proliferation of student services organizations in higher education therefore should be considered in the context of a massive, socially significant eruption of guidance and counseling movements in education and personnel activities in society as a whole. The student services portion of these activities was remarkable only for the specificity of its constituency and the fragmentation of its professional functions and associations.

Just as remarkable, however, was the unrelenting, persistent effort to offset fragmentation and proliferation through mergers and collaboration among the student services associations. This effort is typified by the alternating courtship and alienation between ACPA and NAWDAC throughout their joint history of over sixty years, traced by Sheeley in his 1983 essay ([1983] 1983, pp. 179–189). After ACPA was founded in 1924, the two organizations exchanged ''observers'' at the national conferences. The next year the two organizations held a joint conference, which was repeated two years later. ''Dialogues'' were also begun concerning possible collaboration beyond the scheduling of joint conferences. By 1929, the two organizations had taken their first tentative steps toward ecumenicalism, participating in joint sessions and open meetings with a total of six personnel organizations.

The following year ''ACE published the programs of ten cooperating organizations, including those of NAPPO and NADW, for the 1930 conference in Atlantic City'' (Sheeley, [1983] 1983, p. 181). Confederation of the various organizations was the goal of many of the associations' leaders in the early 1930s. Their effort culminated in the formation of the American Council of Guidance and Personnel Associations in 1934. According to Sheeley, ACPA and NAWDAC were instrumental in holding the council together through the Depression and World War II until its demise in 1952.

During the council's existence, ACPA and NAWDAC continued their on-again, off-again discussions about closer collaboration or even merger. However, by the early 1950s, these considerations were upstaged by the emergence of the gigantic confederation that came to be called the American Personnel and Guidance Association (APGA). In 1951 the association of deans of women (still called NADW at the time) voted to remain outside APGA, while ACPA voted to become Division One of the new confederation. Sheeley indicates that by 1970 the deans of women's organization was in danger of extinction. It initiated "an ACPA-NASPA-NAWDC Feasibility Task Force organized to consider the viability of a single organization" (Sheeley, [1983] 1983, p. 185). The discussions broke off in 1973 with the decision to "discontinue consideration of a merger" (p. 186).

During the 1960s ACPA became as disenchanted with APGA as it had earlier with the council. During the years of discontent with these affiliations, ACPA looked to strengthen its relationships with larger organizations, such as the National Education Association, as Barry and Wolf recommended in 1959 (Barry and Wolf, [1959] 1983, p. 155). Berdie also indicated in his 1966 presidential address that ACPA's future perhaps lay in affiliation with such disparate organizations as ACE, the Higher Education Association, the American Association of University Professors, and the United States National Student Association. He further commented that "perhaps we have as much in common with organizations such as these as we have with the various professional associations explicitly defined in terms of guidance and counseling" (Berdie, [1966] 1983, p. 155). At the heart of his suggestions was the persistent discontent, shared by NAWDAC, with being submerged in affiliations with personnel confederations that were largely unrelated to the environmental setting of higher education. Sheeley observed in 1983 that over the years, this discontent found expression in various attempts to organize a confederation of all professional groups working at the college level (Sheeley, [1983] 1983, pp. 184–185).

The goal of confederation was echoed by the two succeeding ACPA presidents, William Craig and Melvene Hardee, and later by the leaders Donald Hoyt and William Butler in 1968 and 1969. The desire to form a confederation of college-level student services associations led to the formation of the Council of Student Personnel Associations (COSPA) in 1963. Like earlier confederations, COSPA began to unravel soon after its formation, and it was finally dissolved in 1975. But the need for interassociation collaboration continued, along with the inclination toward ecumenicalism, providing the impetus for the abortive ACPA-NASPA-NAWDAC task force discussions on merger. In 1976, after the dissolution of COSPA, both ACPA and NAWDAC were prominent in meeting with leaders of twelve professional student services organizations to address the need for continued interassociation communication. These efforts ultimately resulted in the chartering of the Council for the Advancement of Standards for Student Development/Services Programs in 1980 (Sheeley, [1983] 1983, p. 188).

One might ask at this point what real difference the failure of the various student services organizations to affiliate, or at least collaborate, makes. One result of this failure, as Craig pointed out in his ACPA presidential address in 1962, is virtually to eliminate the potential for a significant voice in national education affairs. "One needs only to look at the national personnel organization picture to see what fragmentation has done to our profession as an ineffective instrument of national goals. My last count disclosed thirty-one separate national student personnel professional organizations. This represents the uncollected strength of our profession" (Craig, [1962] 1983, p. 211). Craig also pointed out that "ACE no longer speaks for the student personnel field. They have discontinued the Commission on the Student" (p. 211). Hardee made the same observation a year earlier in her ACPA presidential address (Hardee, [1961] 1983, pp. 210–211). Indeed, perusal of the American Council on Education's 1937 (1986a) and 1949 (1986b) statements on the Student Personnel Point of View and the 1958 statement on the administration of personnel programs (Feder and others, 1958) reveals that only the first of the three statements expressed the hope that the various organizations in the field would coordinate their activities (Feder and others, 1958, p. 82).

In her ACPA presidential address in 1968, Greenleaf confronted the question of how academic and financial services on the campus viewed the fragmentation of the student services field. "How does the budget officer look at the request from the dean of students office for travel to meetings of ACPA, APGA, ICPA, IPGA, NAWDC, IAWDC, NASPA, Midwest NASPA, ACUHO, ACU, NASFA, Financial Aids Officers, AAHE, ACE, etc.? Do we today have any professional organization to give us direction as we work with the college presidents? . . . How can we be seen as working together for a common goal?" (Greenleaf, [1968] 1986, p. 277).

Penney, writing one year later, answered these rhetorical questions pessimistically. He maintained that fragmentation into a growing number of student services specialties simply manifests the inescapable conclusion that the "early dreams of a profession of student personnel work cannot be realized" ([1969] 1986, p. 287). The reason is not merely that personnel work is "housekeeping" and hence intrinsically subprofessional; it is simply that there is neither a single philosophy nor enough common interests and activities to constitute a shared professional identification (pp. 287–289). He concluded that "the concept of a single professional entity, student personnel work, is therefore abortive" (p. 288). Most student services professionals obviously did not share Penney's pessimism; they urged their associations' leaders to continue to strive toward ecumenicalism throughout the 1970s. Rhatigan, in 1975, was particularly critical of pessimism such as Penney's, concluding that structural unity of the field is less important than professional identity and competence where it really counts, on the campuses of colleges and universities across the country (Rhatigan, [1975] 1983, p. 167).

Cowley, writing in 1957, provided his usual deep insight into the matter of professional identity. He addressed the question of improving the spirit of cooperation among such disparate student services professionals as student deans, registrars, directors of health services, psychological testers, and clinical counselors. He concluded that cooperation can be attained only by working at it in the full realization that "three kinds of people engage in student services professionally: the humanitarians, the administrators, and the scientists, more especially psychologists" (Cowley, [1957] 1986b, p. 174). The obstacles to cooperation lie not so much in the fact that these three kinds of people do distinctly different tasks, but that they perform their responsibilities from distinctly different and inherently irreconcilable frames of reference and value systems. The humanitarians want to *help* people; the administrators need to *manage* people, as well as other resources; and the scientists want to *study* people. Further, there has never been anything remotely resembling a common base of academic professional preparation in the field.

Summary

Knowledge of its roots will help the profession understand its potential for meeting the challenge of the 1990s and beyond. The quest for organizational ecumenicalism can best be approached by understanding that the profession began as a series of disparate functions progressively abandoned by faculty as they turned their attention away from students' social and spiritual development in the last half of the nineteenth century. Even though the various student services developed separately, they by and large remained steadfast and united in their belief that the proper concern of higher education encompasses the whole student, not just his or her intellectual development or preparation for a career. Student services has persistently striven to reintegrate concern for the whole person with the academic function. Disagreement on how to attain such reintegration and the continued lack of a consensual, integrative philosophy continue to hamper the quest for professional unity.

The profession's disorderly and fragmented organizational history continues to influence efforts to merge associations and even to collaborate on developing an integrative philosophy. These efforts must succeed before the profession can claim and attain equal status with the academic function.

Bibliographic Note

The revision of the 1980 edition of this chapter was aided significantly by two collections of readings recently published by ACPA. Belson and Fitzgerald (1983) comprises twenty-three articles selected, with one exception, from the two journals representing ACPA and NAWDAC. The exception is an excellent article by Sheeley that traces nearly sixty years of relationships between the two associations. The final section of this chapter draws heavily on Sheeley's and Bloland's articles. Saddlemire and Rentz (1986), a collection of forty-two articles, is a revision of an earlier collection. These two collections constitute a valuable resource for the historical development of the profession. However, with the exception of an article published in

1919 and included in Saddlemire and Rentz, none of the articles discusses the profession's history prior to the early 1930s. A collection of articles from earlier years by student services professionals would be a valuable resource; it is to be hoped that such a collection can be made available soon.

References

American College Personnel Association. "A Student Development Model for Student Affairs in Tomorrow's Higher Education." (Originally published 1975.) In G. L. Saddlemire and A. L. Rentz (eds.), *Student Affairs: A Profession's Heritage.* Alexandria, Va.: American College Personnel Association, 1986.

American Council on Education. "The Student Personnel Point of View." (Originally published 1937.) In G. L. Saddlemire and A. L. Rentz (eds.), *Student Affairs: A Profession's Heritage.* Alexandria, Va.: American College Personnel Association, 1986a.

American Council on Education. "The Student Personnel Point of View." (Rev. ed.) (Originally published 1949.) In G. L. Saddlemire and A. L. Rentz (eds.), *Student Affairs: A Profession's Heritage.* Alexandria, Va.: American College Personnel Association, 1986b.

Barry, R., and Wolf, B. "Guidance-Personnel Work: The Near Look and the Far Vision." (Originally published 1959.) In B. A. Belson and L. E. Fitzgerald (eds.), *Thus, We Spoke: ACPA-NAWDAC, 1958–1975.* Alexandria, Va.: American College Personnel Association, 1983.

Belson, B. A., and Fitzgerald, L. E. (eds.). *Thus, We Spoke: ACPA-NAWDAC, 1958–1975.* Alexandria, Va.: American College Personnel Association, 1983.

Berdie, R. F. "Student Personnel Work: Definition and Redefinition." (Originally published 1966.) In B. A. Belson and L. E. Fitzgerald (eds.), *Thus, We Spoke: ACPA-NAWDAC, 1958–1975.* Alexandria, Va.: American College Personnel Association, 1983.

Blaesser, W. W. "The Future of Student Personnel Work in Higher Education." (Originally published 1949.) In G. L.

Saddlemire and A. L. Rentz (eds.), *Student Affairs: A Profession's Heritage.* Alexandria, Va.: American College Personnel Association, 1986.

Bloland, P. A. "Ecumenicalism in College Student Personnel." (Originally published 1972.) In B. A. Belson and L. E. Fitzgerald (eds.), *Thus, We Spoke: ACPA-NAWDAC, 1958–1975.* Alexandria, Va.: American College Personnel Association, 1983.

Bradshaw, F. F. "The Scope and Aims of a Personnel Program." (Originally published 1936.) In G. L. Saddlemire and A. L. Rentz (eds.), *Student Affairs: A Profession's Heritage.* Alexandria, Va.: American College Personnel Association, 1986.

Brown, R. D. *Student Development in Tomorrow's Higher Education—A Return to the Academy.* Washington, D.C.: American Personnel and Guidance Association, 1972.

Brubacher, J. S., and Rudy, W. *Higher Education in Transition: A History of American Colleges and Universities, 1639–1976.* New York: Harper & Row, 1976.

Chandler, E. M. "Student Affairs Administration in Transition." (Originally published 1973.) In G. L. Saddlemire and A. L. Rentz (eds.), *Student Affairs: A Profession's Heritage.* Alexandria, Va.: American College Personnel Association, 1986.

Clothier, R. C. "College Personnel Principles and Functions." (Originally published 1931.) In G. L. Saddlemire and A. L. Rentz (eds.), *Student Affairs: A Profession's Heritage.* Alexandria, Va.: American College Personnel Association, 1986.

Cowley, W. H. "The History of Student Residential Housing." *School and Society,* 1934, *40,* 705–712.

Cowley, W. H. "Some History and a Venture in Prophecy." In E. G. Williamson (ed.), *Trends in Student Personnel Work.* Minneapolis: University of Minnesota Press, 1949.

Cowley, W. H. "Reflections of a Troublesome but Hopeful Rip Van Winkle." (Originally published 1964.) In B. A. Belson and L. E. Fitzgerald (eds.), *Thus, We Spoke: ACPA-NAWDAC, 1958–1975.* Alexandria, Va.: American College Personnel Association, 1983.

Cowley, W. H. "The Nature of Student Personnel Work." (Originally published 1936.) In G. L. Saddlemire and A. L. Rentz (eds.), *Student Affairs: A Profession's Heritage*. Alexandria, Va.: American College Personnel Association, 1986a.

Cowley, W. H. "Student Personnel Services in Retrospect and Prospect." (Originally published 1957.) In G. L. Saddlemire and A. L. Rentz (eds.), *Student Affairs: A Profession's Heritage*. Alexandria, Va.: American College Personnel Association, 1986b.

Craig, W. G. "The Student Personnel Profession: An Instrument of National Goals." (Originally published 1962.) In B. A. Belson and L. E. Fitzgerald (eds.), *Thus, We Spoke: ACPA-NAWDAC, 1958–1975*. Alexandria, Va.: American College Personnel Association, 1983.

Crane, W. J. "Curb Service Administration." (Originally published 1963.) In B. A. Belson and L. E. Fitzgerald (eds.), *Thus, We Spoke: ACPA-NAWDAC, 1958–1975*. Alexandria, Va.: American College Personnel Association, 1983.

Crookston, B. B. "Student Personnel—All Hail and Farewell." (Originally published 1976.) In G. L. Saddlemire and A. L. Rentz (eds.), *Student Affairs: A Profession's Heritage*. Alexandria, Va.: American College Personnel Association, 1986.

Cummer, J. B. "Campus Climate and the Educational Process." (Originally published 1961.) In B. A. Belson and L. E. Fitzgerald (eds.), *Thus, We Spoke: ACPA-NAWDAC, 1958–1975*. Alexandria, Va.: American College Personnel Association, 1983.

Dewey, J. "President Hutchins' Proposal to Remake Higher Education." *Social Frontier*, 1937, pp. 103–104.

Feder, D. D. "Today's Students and Tomorrow's Needs." (Originally published 1963.) In B. A. Belson and L. E. Fitzgerald (eds.), *Thus, We Spoke: ACPA-NAWDAC, 1958–1975*. Alexandria, Va.: American College Personnel Association, 1983.

Feder, D. D., and others. *The Administration of Personnel Programs in American Colleges*. Washington, D.C.: American Council on Education, 1958.

Greenleaf, E. A. "How Others See Us." (Originally published 1968.) In G. L. Saddlemire and A. L. Rentz (eds.), *Student Affairs: A Profession's Heritage.* Alexandria, Va.: American College Personnel Association, 1986.

Hardee, M. D. "Personnel Services for Improving the Campus Climate of Learning." (Originally published 1961.) In B. A. Belson and L. E. Fitzgerald (eds.), *Thus, We Spoke: ACPA-NAWDAC, 1958–1975.* Alexandria, Va.: American College Personnel Association, 1983.

Harvey, T. R. "Some Future Directions for Student Personnel Administration." (Originally published 1974.) In G. L. Saddlemire and A. L. Rentz (eds.), *Student Affairs: A Profession's Heritage.* Alexandria, Va.: American College Personnel Association, 1986.

Hopkins, E. H. "The Essentials of a Student Personnel Program." (Originally published 1948.) In G. L. Saddlemire and A. L. Rentz (eds.), *Student Affairs: A Profession's Heritage.* Alexandria, Va.: American College Personnel Association, 1986.

Hopwood, K. L. "Who's for the Ark?" (Originally published 1961.) In B. A. Belson and L. E. Fitzgerald (eds.), *Thus, We Spoke: ACPA-NAWDAC, 1958–1975.* Alexandria, Va.: American College Personnel Association, 1983.

Hutchins, R. M. *The Higher Learning in America.* New Haven, Conn.: Yale University Press, 1936.

Knapp, R. "Management: Intruder in the Academic Dust." *Educational Record,* 1969, *50,* 55–65.

Leonard, E. A. *Origins of Personnel Services in American Higher Education.* Minneapolis: University of Minnesota Press, 1956.

Lloyd-Jones, E. "Personnel Administration." (Originally published 1934.) In G. L. Saddlemire and A. L. Rentz (eds.), *Student Affairs: A Profession's Heritage.* Alexandria, Va.: American College Personnel Association, 1986.

Miller, T. K., and Prince, J. S. *The Future of Student Affairs: A Guide to Student Development for Tomorrow's Higher Education.* San Francisco: Jossey-Bass, 1976.

Mueller, K. H. *Student Personnel Work in Higher Education.* Boston: Houghton Mifflin, 1961.

Penney, J. F. "Student Personnel Work: A Profession Stillborn." (Originally published 1969.) In G. L. Saddlemire and A. L. Rentz (eds.), *Student Affairs: A Profession's Heritage.* Alexandria, Va.: American College Personnel Association, 1986.

Rhatigan, J. J. "Student Services vs. Student Development: Is There a Difference?" (Originally published 1975.) In B. A. Belson and L. E. Fitzgerald (eds.), *Thus, We Spoke: ACPA-NAWDAC, 1958-1975.* Alexandria, Va.: American College Personnel Association, 1983.

Rudolph, F. *The American College and University.* New York: Knopf, 1962.

Saddlemire, G. L., and Rentz, A. L. (eds.). *Student Affairs: A Profession's Heritage.* Alexandria, Va.: American College Personnel Association, 1986.

Shaffer, R. H. "Student Personnel Problems Requiring a Campus-Wide Approach." (Originally published 1961.) In B. A. Belson and L. E. Fitzgerald (eds.), *Thus, We Spoke: ACPA-NAWDAC, 1958-1975.* Alexandria, Va.: American College Personnel Association, 1983.

Sheeley, V. L. "NADW and NAAS: 60 Years of Organizational Relationships." (Originally published 1983.) In B. A. Belson and L. E. Fitzgerald (eds.), *Thus, We Spoke: ACPA-NAWDAC, 1958-1975.* Alexandria, Va.: American College Personnel Association, 1983.

Shoben, E. J. "A Rationale for Modern Student Personnel Work." (Originally published 1962.) In B. A. Belson and L. E. Fitzgerald (eds.), *Thus, We Spoke: ACPA-NAWDAC, 1958-1975.* Alexandria, Va.: American College Personnel Association, 1983.

Tollefson, A. L. *New Approaches to College Student Development.* New York: Behavioral Publications, 1975.

Trueblood, D. L. "Responsibility for Equal Educational Opportunity for All Youth." (Originally published 1964.) In G. L. Saddlemire and A. L. Rentz (eds.), *Student Affairs: A Profession's Heritage.* Alexandria, Va.: American College Personnel Association, 1986.

Useem, R. H. "Professionalizing an Academic Occupation: The

Case of Student Personnel Work." (Originally published 1964.) In B. A. Belson and L. E. Fitzgerald (eds.), *Thus, We Spoke: ACPA-NAWDAC, 1958–1975*. Alexandria, Va.: American College Personnel Association, 1983.

Williamson, E. G. *Trends in Student Personnel Work*. Minneapolis: University of Minnesota Press, 1949.

Williamson, E. G. "Student Personnel Work in the Future Years." (Originally published 1974.) In B. A. Belson and L. E. Fitzgerald (eds.), *Thus, We Spoke: ACPA-NAWDAC, 1958–1975*. Alexandria, Va.: American College Personnel Association, 1983.

Williamson, E. G. "Some Unresolved Problems in Student Personnel Work." (Originally published 1967.) In G. L. Saddlemire and A. L. Rentz (eds.), *Student Affairs: A Profession's Heritage*. Alexandria, Va.: American College Personnel Association, 1986.

Woody, T. *"History of Women's Education in the United States."* Vol. 2. Lancaster, Pa.: Science Press, 1929.

Wrenn, C. G., and Bell, R. *Student Personnel Problems*. New York: Farrar, Straus & Giroux, 1942.

Chapter Three

Guiding Standards
and Principles

Harry J. Canon

"Fran is residence director of West Hall and Dale is one of eight resident assistants in West. In the last few weeks of the fall semester, it has become clear to both Dale and Fran that they are strongly attracted to each other. How should they proceed?"

The case of Fran and Dale elicits a variety of responses from student services professionals in ethics workshops. Comments and reactions include: "That's not an ethical problem; it happens on our campus all the time"; "What sex are Fran and Dale?"; "If they're both professional in their behavior, it won't be a problem"; "That could really affect the morale of the other resident assistants"; "It's their private business"; "Dale should be moved to another hall"; "Fran had better end the relationship or expect to be fired."

The range of reactions suggests that a series of issues emerges whenever we consider ethical conduct in student services settings. Key issues include (1) identifying ethical issues as they arise; (2) having a set of principles to guide behavior in such situations; (3) having a formal professional ethical code

Note: Portions of this chapter were drawn from an invited address titled "Gilligan, Ethics, and Sin" presented at the Marlin Schmidt Memorial Address, University of Iowa, Iowa City, February 1986.

that addresses such matters; (4) knowing if and how to intervene; (5) the reaction of colleagues when matters of ethical concern arise; and ultimately (6) fostering the kind of environment that will support and promote continuing inquiry into ethical issues.

This chapter addresses these issues and suggests some conceptual models and a series of procedures for giving increased attention to ethical concerns that affect or are affected by student services professionals and student services delivery systems. Because the case method has proved effective in eliciting interest and informing decision-making processes with respect to ethical concerns, ethics cases are scattered throughout the chapter, offset in box form. You are invited to explore and discuss these cases with your colleagues.

It should be kept in mind that any thoughtful exploration of ethical practices in student services settings must have the ethical and moral development of students as a core concern, perhaps as the ultimate objective. Margaret Barr, in her inaugural speech to the American College Personnel Association (1984, p. 10), expressed her conviction that "student services professionals serve as the conscience of the campus." These professionals, more than any other constituent group in higher education, attend to the human needs of students and respond to concerns about individual differences. In doing so, they sustain an awareness of inequities imposed on students by the system, by the fact of individual differences and needs. With such a professional history, student services staff members must address matters of individual dignity and worth, of fairness, and of equity.

That historical mandate calls on us to maintain an ethical environment of the highest possible quality on the campus. Only by doing so can we hope to facilitate the moral and ethical development of our students. The quality of the ethical conduct of faculty and staff has a direct bearing on the quality of ethical conduct that students will demonstrate or aspire to. Other things being equal, the level of ethical functioning on a campus quite possibly determines the upper limits of the ethical sensitivity shown in the conduct of its graduates. The ethical development of staff and that of students, then, are interdependent and wholly inseparable.

Primary Approaches to Promoting Ethical Behavior

There are three common ways of "doing ethics," of achieving acceptable levels of ethical behavior. With the first, a formal ethical code is developed by representatives of a particular professional organization. Such codes most often follow a legal model that offers both prescriptions and proscriptions. These rules and guidelines define what is ethically acceptable and what is not. In its most complete form, this legal model goes on to provide for a trial or hearing when formal charges of a code violation are made, and it describes penalties that may be applied to those found guilty of violating the code.

A second way to promote ethical behavior requires professionals to apply ethical principles to ethical dilemmas. If ethics involves rules of moral conduct, then we can abstract or deduce certain broad principles that underlie these rules. A number of philosophers and ethicists have enumerated either moral laws (not excluding the Ten Commandments) or ethical principles, the latter intended to define abstractions that are very nearly universal in their application to ethical problems. Those who promote the application of ethical principles (as opposed to ethical codes) often note that principles more often express the spirit of the law, while codes are more likely to elicit narrowly based, legalistic responses.

Ethical behavior is fostered in yet a third way by the social environment in which it takes place. The role of the community in supporting (or rejecting) ethical inquiry has long been a part of our folk knowledge. Only recently, however, have we taken formal notice of the critical effect that the peer group, the social-

---

You are a member of a search committee that is to screen and nominate candidates for a position in a student services agency. In the course of a committee interview with one candidate, a colleague member of the search committee asks a candidate how her spouse feels about leaving his job and moving 800 miles to your college town.

psychological environment, or, indeed, an interaction between two individuals can have on the quality of ethical behavior. Gilligan (1982), Delworth and Seeman (1984), and Brown (1985) have argued persuasively that social structures and relationships can be very powerful in their potential for enhancing ethical behavior. More specifically, they have underscored the problems that arise from addressing ethical problems only from the reference points of codes or principles, without considering the human interactions affected by such responses.

Clearly, the three approaches outlined above can and commonly do come into conflict with each other. An ethical principle may not take into account some special professional constraints that are addressed by a more detailed portion of the ethical code. Or the authors of a particular code may have failed to consider circumstances encountered by some of their colleagues in the field. We will explore those conflicts, but we will also review the ways in which the three approaches can complement each other.

Ethical Codes. Ethical codes are usually generated for specific professional groups and organizations and follow a legal model. Certain behaviors are expected of the practitioner; other behaviors are prohibited. The exactness with which the relevant behaviors are described varies widely from one professional code to another. Codes commonly contain provisions for the bringing of charges against members who are alleged to be in violation of the code, and for hearings on the evidence. Penalties for violations are usually defined in the code.

Winston and Dagley (1985) have offered a thoroughgoing review of the development and application of ethical codes by organizations that serve those in the student services professions. Of particular interest is their discussion of the uses of those codes. Codes serve as effective teaching tools for new professionals and assist in socializing students to expected standards of practice and the value structure of their profession. Because a code is commonly developed by representatives of a profession, it also serves as a guide for practical decisions. One has, in effect, a more or less concrete statement to support or reject a proposed course of action. Further, by defining professionally responsible behavior, the code protects the public against incompetence by eliminating ineffective or inadequately prepared persons from the field. Winston and Dagley (1985, p. 51) observe that such a commitment to self-regulation enhances sensitivity to critical issues in daily practice. By being mindful of and sensitive to community standards as set forth in codes, practitioners avoid gratuitous offense to those whom they would serve. Winston and Dagley also note the manner in which codes protect practitioners against unreasonable demands by the institutions that employ them and by clients. Because they are able to present a document representing a consensual statement of professional values, practitioners have an external source of support and thus can avoid appearing petulant or lazy. Finally, most codes provide a series of benchmarks that enable effective evaluation of performance and thus lead to enhanced functioning.

The primary student services organizations that have formulated ethical codes or statements are the National Association of Student Personnel Administrators (NASPA), the American College Personnel Association (ACPA), and the National Association of Women Deans and Counselors (NAWDAC). Our discussion will focus primarily on the codes of the first two, NASPA and ACPA, because they were developed more recently. ACPA's "Statement of Ethical and Professional Standards" (American College Personnel Association, 1981), adopted in 1981, was the product of several rounds of review by various constituencies in the association (Winston and Dagley, 1985). The "Standards of Professional Practice" of NASPA (National Association of Student Personnel Administrators, 1983) was also widely circulated and commented on in its early drafts.

A thoughtful reading of the two documents reveals their differences. First, the design process for each code was distinctly different. Further, whereas the ACPA code tends toward behavioral specificity, the NASPA code is more general. Also, concern for student (client) welfare is differentially addressed. In addition, there is a difference in focus between the two codes. The NASPA code consistently refers to the members' obligation to their employing institutions, while the ACPA code focuses on the rights and responsibilities of students as consumers of institutional services. The implications of this difference will be discussed later; for the moment it is sufficient to note that the potential for conflict between the two documents exists, and that a substantial number of student services professionals belong to both organizations.

Each document reflects thought and concern for ethical obligations to a variety of constituencies. However, a notable gap remains: neither association provides for enforcement, and each seems a long way from doing so. ACPA members have the option of invoking the terms of the ethical code of the American Association for Counseling and Development (AACD), in which ACPA holds divisional status, and thus of using its procedures for hearings and the assessment of penalties. Nevertheless, neither ACPA nor NASPA has put the capstone of enforcement procedures in place. Effectively, their members can refer to a document held to represent the ethical standards of their colleagues, but offenders need not be particularly fearful of retribution. This is obviously a major flaw, since codes are modeled after the legal system, and their effectiveness depends on enforcement. An unenforced law has little effect on transgressors.

Less apparent but equally compelling is the observation that having to initiate enforcement proceedings is in itself probably an admission of failure. It suggests that the offender does

---

A student employee in food services in a campus residence hall looks emaciated, appears to be tired, and has dropped to a minimum course load in the last month. The student rumor mill has it that he has AIDS. There have even been several letters from parents threatening to withdraw their children from school unless ''something is done'' about a food services employee who is said to have AIDS. The campus newspaper, not so coincidentally, has called to inquire about college policy with respect to employees found to have AIDS.

either does not understand the issues involved or does not care. In either instance, little is gained by holding a hearing and applying sanctions. Perhaps the primary gain is ensuring that an offender does not continue to do damage.

The social contexts that produce ethical codes are important. Winston and Dagley (1985, p. 55) show in tabular form the coverage given to a series of topics by the codes of six human service organizations. It is instructive to note that the AACD code identifies the practitioner's primary obligation as being to the client; NASPA asserts that ''members recognize that their primary obligation is to the employing institution''; and ACPA acknowledges responsibilities to both the client (student) and the employing institution. NAWDAC seems to evidence slightly greater concern for the welfare of the practitioner, and much of its code focuses on the rights of professionals.

The origins of these differences in focus become a little more apparent if one looks at the structure of the organizations. NAWDAC, composed almost wholly of women professionals, understandably speaks to the needs of a constituency that has felt the heavy hand of sexual discrimination over the decades. NASPA, which is sustained primarily by institutional membership fees paid directly by colleges and universities, can be expected to generate a document reflecting the rights and expectations of its fee-payers. ACPA, with a constituency largely drawn from middle management and entry-level professionals, is in a better position to speak to the needs of both institutions and students.

So it is that ethical purity is relative, and that the contents of ethical codes are—among other things—the products of social forces operating within the organizations that produce the codes.

Ethical codes are particularly susceptible to literal interpretation and legalistic responses. The greatest danger is that members may respond to the letter rather than the spirit of the law. The ACPA code, by spelling out desired and proscribed behaviors in detail, increases the tendency toward a literal interpretation. On the other hand, the very general statements that make up the NAWDAC and NASPA ethical codes may be too vague or obscure for those seeking guidance.

The fact that discussion and compromise are an essential part of any democratic process also creates a problem in the formation of codes. The very task of drawing up a code may in itself stimulate discussions among professionals that sharpen ethical issues. At the same time, diverse interests and different belief systems not infrequently yield an end-product that reflects the lowest common denominator rather than the loftiest aspirations. Given the complexity of human behavior, it should not then be surprising that the documents generated by all-too-human professional organizations fall short of perfection.

Ethical Principles. While ethical codes may lend themselves to legalistic thinking and a tendency to be unduly doctrinaire, ethical principles are susceptible to vagueness and ambiguity. However, principles afford a helpful degree of flexibility and permit consistency without rigidity. Ethicists have offered arrays of principles ranging from one—the Golden Rule—to a dozen or more. We will consider here the five principles suggested by Kitchener (1985) because they are useful, comprehensive, and thought-provoking when applied to ethics cases by student services professionals. Those principles are (1) to respect autonomy, (2) to do no harm, (3) to benefit others, (4) to be just, and (5) to be faithful.

Respecting autonomy means acknowledging the right of individuals to decide how they live their own lives so long as their actions do not interfere with the rights and welfare of others. Respecting autonomy also serves to protect us against our own paternalistic instincts, however laudable those instincts might be. Students and colleagues are entitled to learn from their own failures, and, following a hearing of whatever caveats we may choose to offer them, they remain free—for the most part—to choose their own courses of action. If, for example, a student organization is permitted to invite a speaker from the Ku Klux Klan to speak on campus, we will very likely find the speaker's racism and anti-Semitism repugnant. At the same time, we will have honored the autonomy of the student organization and upheld the value of maintaining an open forum for the expression of ideas. Kitchener (1985) also notes that the principle of autonomy is related to concerns for the right of self-determination and First Amendment rights. The emergence of exquisitely detailed codes of student conduct on many of our campuses is very probably a consequence of earlier failures to provide for appropriate degrees of student self-determination and self-expression.

In *doing no harm* we honor the obligation to avoid actions that may inflict either physical or psychological injury. Although this principle seems obvious, it may become less so when we consider the requirements imposed on students and on colleagues who aspire to certain goals, where we serve as gatekeepers between them and their goals. For example, a variety of graduate-level programs require students to participate in "growth groups" or in group counseling. The effects of participation in such groups are seldom studied. Little is known of the consequences of disclosing psychologically intimate details to student peers, and certainly the all-too-common use of faculty members as group facilitators poses hazards that ethical codes caution against. In short, in well-intentioned efforts to assist our students and colleagues, we may cause inadvertent harm.

The act of *benefiting others* is at the core of our reason for being as student services professionals. We choose to work in this field in order to help others. Kitchener observes (1985, p. 23), however, that the intent to benefit may conflict with the injunction to do no harm. The potential for such conflict certainly resides in the group process requirement noted above. Furthermore, varying degrees of personal or institutional inertia must be overcome in order to contribute to the welfare of students and colleagues. Many of us can identify institutional requirements that serve only as barriers between students and their reasonable aspirations, as well as organizational processes that interfere with the professional development of colleagues. With sustained effort and a measure of personal risk (institutional change is always a chancy business), one may benefit others by bringing about a change in a regulation, requirement, or arbitrary rule. Even small, thoughtful acts of a colleague or mentor can bring benefits that last a lifetime.

Being just means giving appropriate attention to assuring equal treatment to all those for whom we have responsibility.

An alumnus who graduated some twelve years ago has been appointed as a member of the staff of the newly elected president of the United States. After learning of the appointment on the morning news, a faculty member who also offers his services one day each week in your counseling center comes to the center and starts going through old files. He indicates that he's looking up the MMPI of the presidential appointee, and will share it with you when he finds it.

Just behavior affords each student and colleague a fair portion and, in general, honors the Golden Rule. Paradoxically, assuring equal treatment may involve giving special consideration to those who do not have equal access to the benefits available to most citizens. Affirmative action programs, modification of the structure of the campus to permit access by the physically handicapped, support programs that ameliorate the problems of the educationally disadvantaged, all represent the principle of according justice. Increasing attention is also being given to circumstances—particularly in instructional situations—in which the unequal distribution of power may prevent justice. Thus an ombudsman may serve as an advocate for the student who feels impotent in the face of a disagreement with a faculty member, or call attention to institutional systems that function in an arbitrary manner and thus deny justice. The issues of justice and power are in continuing conflict in every social system, and the college or university campus is not exempt.

To be faithful is perhaps the most exacting of ethical principles. Here we pledge to keep promises, to tell the truth, to be loyal, and to maintain respect and civility in human discourse. Respecting a colleague's personal dignity after he or she has attacked us is exquisitely difficult. The most common response is to counterattack the colleague (or the colleague's integrity) rather than address the idea under consideration. When we yield to that impulse, the cause of human dignity and of faithfulness is abandoned. Keeping a promise can be as simple as devoting adequate time and thought to the preparation of a lecture or topic for class discussion. Few of us who have taught for more than one semester can claim to have kept the implicit promise of always giving our students the best we have to offer. Furthermore, when questioned by an aggressive investigative reporter for the student newspaper about a controversial issue, who of us is not seriously tempted to offer something less than the full truth?

Making exceptions to the rule of strict truthfulness is sometimes necessary. Telling everyone the full truth at all times can result in serious damage to someone's sense of self-worth; in any event, we can tell only our version of what is true. To keep a promise of confidentiality when doing so places a life in danger is nothing more than stupid behavior. The principle of faithfulness deserves more attention than it is generally accorded in relationships with students and colleagues. Faithfulness involves the occasional "caring confrontation," the consistent feedback that gives a colleague the opportunity to attend to shared concerns, and the compliments that make a special effort worthwhile.

Conflicts among ethical principles regularly occur when principles are applied to real-life situations. For example, allowing a student group to bring a Klan speaker to the campus honors the principle of autonomy. The autonomy of that group, however, is placed in opposition to the welfare of students belonging to racial and ethnic minority groups, which is clearly in danger of being harmed. Jews and blacks can reasonably argue that they have the right to be free from harassment and vilification on their own campus. In this instance, the principles of assuring autonomy and doing no harm come into direct conflict with each other; we cannot honor one without sacrificing the other. A solution to this problem may be reached with the introduction of another institutional value or principle—the historical commitment of higher education to an open forum and the free exchange of ideas.

This particular dilemma illustrates a principle for dealing with ethical principles: if one elects to violate or reject one of the five principles in the course of resolving an ethical dilemma, one is obliged to provide a justification or rationale for that rejection. Here, our rationale for violating the principle of doing no harm might be that the search for truth requires free expression—including the expression of outrageous and repugnant ideas—and that provisions for the rebuttal of racist concepts may lead to that truth. At the same time, a rationale for denying the Klan speaker a forum—for rejecting the principle of autonomy—might be that the offensiveness of the Klan speaker's ideas creates a dangerous potential for violence. In this instance the principle of doing no harm prevails. So it is that when a higher moral purpose appears to be served by rejecting a principle, we take on the burden of providing a clear rationale for that rejection.

The details of a behaviorally specific code of ethics are difficult to keep in the forefront of our thinking as we confront daily professional obligations. Kitchener's five principles are easier to keep in mind. If one of our professional goals is to generate an environment in which ethical issues are at the fore, the adoption of a modest array of principles is a promising first step. Professional codes themselves are (or should be) subject to consistent review and revision. Applying principles can enhance the quality of those revisions. At a pragmatic level, principles provide some useful latitude in discussions of real-life ethical dilemmas. Instead of being trapped in the kind of dogmatic

---

A student who is a professed member of the "Aryan Nation" has hung a swastika in the window of his residence hall room. He has been approached by the residence hall director with several appeals to take down the flag, and has responded by saying that he is exercising his First Amendment rights. The president of the university, who has received a host of complaints from people in the community, calls the housing director saying she wants the flag down immediately.

posture that can result from the legalistic application of a particular statement of a code, parties addressing an ethical dilemma by applying principles are afforded a range of possible responses, are less likely to become defensive, and have options that may serve a greater good or a larger moral dimension.

A valuable model for the application of Kitchener's ethical principles has been offered by Krager (1985). Krager looked at two positions commonly assumed by student services professionals—administrator and student development educator—and enumerated the roles incorporated into or assumed by each of those positions. The roles were arrayed on one dimension of a two-by-two table and Kitchener's principles on the other dimension. Krager then filled in the cells that represented the intersection of a particular professional role with each of the five principles. Table 1 presents an adaptation of her analysis of three roles assumed by the student development educator and their intersection with the principles of respecting autonomy and being faithful. For example, in the role of researcher, the educator can respect autonomy by encouraging independent selection of research topics, and can be faithful by keeping promises to collaborate on research. You are invited to list roles of particular interest to you and to follow the Krager model by assigning behaviors associated with each role in accordance with each ethical principle.

Ethical Community. The ubiquitous expression "the campus community" may be an oxymoron. For academic citizens experiencing lonely and cynical moments, the view through the residence hall or office window reveals something other than a community.

Picture, if you will, the last time you crossed your campus. Did a number of students pass you with headphones in place, listening to whatever distant drummer might be on their tape of the day? Was their gaze focused on their feet or over your shoulder? It's usually clear that each has checked into a Walkman cocoon for the trip across campus; human discourse is not invited. This may be the true sound barrier generation, for just so long as stereos are functioning in residence halls, Greek houses, and apartments, and so long as the bars offer

**Table 1. Ethical Principles and the
Student Development Educator's Roles.**

Educator Role	Ethical Principles	
	Respect Autonomy	Be Faithful
Researcher	Support independence in selection of research topics	Follow through on promises of collaboration
Mentor	Relinquish controls over post-graduate placement	Facilitate networking between students and senior professionals
Instructor	Render support without being intrusive in personal lives of students	Assure appropriate rigor in transmitting and assessing essential professional skills

Source: Adapted from Krager, 1985, pp. 39–42.

super-amplified music for dancing, there will be little need to engage a second party in any human or psychologically intimate exchange.

That sense of isolation, of the absence of community, is not limited to students. The very nature of academic pursuit for a faculty member creates a different kind of isolation. Gaining recognition in academic circles commonly depends on pursuing a unique area of study. Good fortune and much hard work may result in the publication of novel findings in that area of specialization. Shared interests are therefore more the exception than the rule, and, as a consequence, all too many faculty members live in ivy-clad isolation from each other. The emphasis on unique, individual achievement does not usually lead to close and regular interactions with colleagues, let alone to the establishment of community.

Student services professionals, by disposition and choice, are more inclined to acknowledge needing the support and stimulation of their colleagues than are their faculty counterparts. Brown (1985) made an eloquent plea for utilizing that incipient sense of community to engender and support an environment that consistently asserts and brings to the fore the importance of human dignity, that nourishes individual growth and achievement, and that insists on civility in interpersonal exchange. His conviction is such that he is willing to insist (along with Barr, 1984) that "the common mission of the student services profession is being the moral conscience of the campus" (Brown, 1985, p. 69). Brown goes on to point out that student services professionals are in a position to act as the campus conscience in light of their collective involvement with the whole student, their virtual around-the-clock contact with students in almost every setting in which students find themselves, and their almost unique awareness of the range of injustices visited upon students by other students, faculty, administrators, and the system itself. Those factors, when combined with the commitment of the student services profession to student development, provide "a cohesive base for a common mission" (Brown, 1985, p. 69).

Brown goes on to outline his model for a community perspective in support of the ethical agenda, the core of which is predicated on the establishment of a community of professionals, much like the germinal community of student services professionals described above. This ideal community incorporates three other levels of community: the community of higher education, the community of our country, and the community of the earth. At each level there are concerns and commitments that address core issues:

- Peace issues and caring relationships: the international arms race; programs for international students; programs fostering multicultural awareness and sensitivity; spouse abuse; conflict resolution
- Careers as vocations: the roles of faculty and of staff members as service providers; career as calling; promoting professional growth and preventing burnout
- Career development for students: integration of vocational preparation and core curricula; integrating values into professional preparation; encouraging volunteerism during the college years
- Theory and research into practice: supporting developmental research; encouraging the testing of applications of developmental theory in real-life settings; providing continuing education to professionals on state-of-the-art research and programming

- Personal development for all: defining developmental needs of students, faculty, and staff; designing programs to meet those needs; integrating such programs into the curriculum (traditional and continuing education); establishing human development goals as a part of the institutional mission
- A humane learning environment: ensuring that practices governing recruitment and retention optimize the chances of success; continuing attention to environmental and institutional variables that affect success (adapted from Brown, 1985, pp. 72–73).

Brown concludes by noting that "taking positions on ethical issues is not easy. . . . At the extreme [doing so] can mean ostracism and loss of job" (1985, p. 75). In a more optimistic vein, he concludes that persistence, prudence, and patience can result in being heard.

Collectively and as they interact with each other, codes, principles, and communities provide a rich and yeasty mix. Codes can lead to literalism; principles may challenge that literalism while concurrently generating a tug-of-war between principles; the agenda of an ethical community may demand more of codes and principles than can be delivered in the real world. As Brown (1985) suggested, taking positions on ethical issues is not easy, but making full use of codes, principles, and the support of a professional community can make the task tolerable and occasionally rewarding.

Asking "Which of the three is most important?" poses the wrong question. We are, it seems, dependent on the interaction of all three. The ethical community—and we shall say more about ethical communities later—supports and encourages our exploration of ethical issues. The process of developing codes challenges our thinking and the premises on which specific articles of the code are to be based. The struggle for primacy among the various principles tests our core notions of right and wrong. Together the three inform, enhance, and elevate the pursuit of moral conduct as it relates to our professional responsibilities and goals.

You are the only student services professional on a panel for a campus forum during Black History Month. Other representatives have been drawn from the student government, the student newspaper, Greek-letter organizations, residence halls, and black student organizations. One of the latter representatives is the last speaker. He launches into an attack on whites, referring to them as "devils" and arguing that the genocide of whites is the only answer to racial conflict.

The Ethical Community and Secular Sin

In some theological circles, sin is viewed not as a violation of one or more of the Ten Commandments, but as a state of separation from God. A theological proposition that often accompanies this view is the assertion that we know God through the actions and behavior of those around us. If those persons with whom we are in daily contact are kind and thoughtful, then we understand God to be kind and thoughtful. If our associates are uncaring and judgmental, then our God is likely to be a punishing, unloving God. It follows that when we feel separated from our friends and associates, we also perceive ourselves to be separated from God. In this manner, we arrive at a state of sin. Even if we eliminate the concept of a Supreme Being, we come to the conclusion that when you and I are not "in community" with our colleagues, when we are separated from them, we are experiencing a state of "secular sin."

Another religious tradition that reinforces the importance of community is the Jewish tradition of the minyan, the minimum of ten persons that must be present before worship services can be held. Traditions such as this did not come about wholly by accident, nor are they retained unless they meet important needs. If there is wisdom in and something to be learned from the tradition of the minyan and from the concept of sin as the state of being separated from our community, it is because they reinforce our daily experience that we are more likely to become what we are capable of becoming, to realize our potential, to be more fully human and humane when we are in community with others for whom we care and who care about us. Being in community affords the nurturance, support, and challenge Sanford (1979) posits as the necessary and sufficient conditions for growth and change. A community, then, that deliberately and intentionally attends to ethical concerns every day provides the support that its members require to carry out the intellectually complex and personally challenging task of addressing the ethical quality of life. Few experiences can leave us feeling more alone, less supported, than attempting to confront an ethical problem as a solitary individual, or being the only one who sees an ethical dilemma in a particular situation. Being part of a community that is committed to moral values increases the likelihood that we will act on ethical matters as they arise, and that we will do so with some consistency.

Brown (Canon and Brown, 1985) provides a thoughtful note on the role of community and relationships as they affect—both positively and negatively—the manner in which we resolve ethical problems. He observes that Gilligan (1982), from her research on how women approach ethical dilemmas, found that the feminine perspective placed a greater emphasis on how relationships would be affected by a given solution, whereas the masculine approach was more closely anchored to general rules and impersonal application of abstract principles. From this, Gilligan proposed an "ethics of care" that attends more to relationships and is less dependent on the impersonal application of rules. Brown notes that an ethics of care is scarcely foreign to student services professionals. It has the potential (Delworth and Seeman, 1984) for supporting our inclination to assert student interests and concerns, often in the face of challenges that suggest we place soft-headed emotionalism over hard-nosed rational judgment. An ethics of care, coupled with the development of an ethical community, may offer new hope for student services professionals who despair of finding solutions to ethical problems.

Being Practical About Being Ethical

In an era that worships pragmatism, we may first have to lay to rest the old canard that one has a choice between being practical and being ethical. Canon and Brown (1985, p. 84) assert that "being ethical is itself a very practical pursuit. Individuals . . . [who] place a high premium on respecting autonomy, avoiding the doing of harm, benefiting others, being just, and being faithful establish a degree of credibility with others that tends to earn loyalty, trust, and respect in return." Our experience and our observations of both the academic and public sectors in the last half of the 1980s tend more to confirm than to reject these words. Recently, a national weekly news magazine printed a cover story that describes how more than 100 Reagan administration officials have "faced allegations of questionable activities" (Stengle, 1987, p. 19). Virtue may not always be rewarded, but a rejection of virtue as part of a "pragmatic" approach clearly carries its own hazards. Brown's ethical community, in the light of the once-mighty-now-fallen, becomes increasingly attractive.

Let us look at some other practical matters that are involved in approaching ethical concerns. First, it is important to distinguish between what is legal and what is ethical. An informed professional cannot afford to be ignorant of the legal constraints on his or her practice or of the legal consequences

---

A director of one of the agencies in your division of student affairs persistently makes ethnic and sexist comments in the course of staff meetings. You have told him on several occasions that you expect the practice to stop, that as vice-president you will not tolerate such comments in your presence. He complies for a week or two but then falls back into his old habits. Just this week, you admonished him in front of the rest of the directors when he made an offhand ethnic slur.

of a professional decision. Happily, most of what is ethical is also legal, and a good portion of all that is legal probably conforms to minimal ethical standards. But the terms are not synonymous. One might, for example, run cautiously through a red traffic light in order to take a passenger having a heart attack to an emergency room. Likewise, there are circumstances in delivering student services where a technical violation of a law serves a greater good than abiding by the letter of the law. The confidentiality of a student's medical record may be protected by state and federal statutes, but the welfare of the student and his or her family may be best served by the disclosure of the details of a serious illness.

One needs to be particularly careful in those circumstances where a colleague (or even the institution's legal counsel) suggests that a lawsuit may follow the proposed course of action. There is often the distinct possibility of being sued for not acting as well as for taking action. An occasionally useful strategy in dealing with such circumstances is to tell college or university legal counsel, "Here is what I'd prefer to do; it seems to be the right (ethical) thing to do under the circumstances. Would you be able to find grounds to defend me should the matter go to court?" This approach reserves for the student services professional the right to exercise a professional, ethical judgment, and offers legal counsel an appropriate situation for a response.

Second, use a trusted colleague for a curbstone consultation when considering the possibility that an ethical problem or dilemma is emerging. The encounter between you and a trusted colleague is where ethical community starts. The principles involved can be viewed from multiple perspectives, support is garnered for acting or not acting, and strategies for intervention—where appropriate—can be devised. The consultation also helps provide insurance against acting in the heat of the moment and decreases the likelihood of an emotional confrontation that leads nowhere.

Third, keep in mind that accepted standards of approach to resolving ethical disputes require that the offending party first be confronted by the person who believes an ethical lapse or violation has occurred. This is the equivalent of contacting your

It has become common knowledge among your group of graduate students that a student colleague is having difficulty in gathering dissertation data because of problems in finding subjects. You and your students have good reason to believe that she has resorted to fabricating data; there certainly is little evidence of any time spent working with subjects to gather such data. All of you are angry that the dissertation supervisor seems totally unaware of the situation.

neighbors about their barking dog before calling the cops. Potential disputes should be resolved at the lowest possible level. For that reason, professional associations commonly request a personal contact with the presumed offender before formal charges are filed and a hearing process triggered.

Fourth, every reasonable effort should be made to structure the initial contact with the presumed violator as a caring confrontation (Brown and Canon, 1978). None of us view an ethical violator as someone we particularly value. It is all too easy to assume that we have all the facts, that we are dealing with someone who is morally deficient. The person in question may in fact be unaware of the ethical implications of the situation and would be horrified to have others see him or her as ethically deficient. It never hurts to assume that the person responsible for your concern also wants to do the right thing. This increases the importance of an approach that shows caring and respect for that person, even if generating a sense of caring requires substantial effort. If nothing else works for you under such circumstances, try to envision how you would feel were you approached by a colleague with allegations of ethical impropriety. "I" statements work best in this context. For example, "I am concerned about a situation where some students have said they feel ridiculed in your classes" is more likely to be heard and addressed appropriately than "Your students are complaining about how you subject them to ridicule." A subtle touch, perhaps, but an important one.

Fifth, as circumstances arise that have ethical implications, seek the reactions of colleagues and students, in both formal and informal settings. It is absolutely crucial to make ethical discourse a legitimate part of our everyday professional conversations. Unless we persist in our pursuit of ethical community, it is not likely to occur. And those who persist prevail.

Finally, remember that we are all sinners. We are all in the process of becoming, and in that process each of us will falter. The avoidance of self-righteousness is critical to the development of an ethical community. Humility with respect to one's personal ethical conduct is always acceptable in the eyes of our friends and colleagues. It will carry us even farther with those who are not our fans.

Conclusion

The scope of issues and circumstances that might be incorporated under the topic of ethics has expanded substantially. We have clearly moved from the consideration of lists of "shalls" and "shall nots" to envisioning a world community in which human worth and dignity define that which is ethical. If ethics do in fact embody moral philosophy, human worth and dignity should rest at the core of ethical discourse. And if there is to be a beginning, it is just possible that ethical inquiry begins with simple civility in human exchanges. That is not a bad place to begin.

References

American College Personnel Association. "Statement of Ethical and Professional Standards." *Journal of College Student Personnel,* 1981, *22,* 184–189.

Barr, M. J. Presidential Address at the annual meeting of the American College Personnel Association, Baltimore, Md., March 1984.

Brown, R. D. "Creating an Ethical Community." In H. J. Canon and R. D. Brown (eds.), *Applied Ethics in Student Services.* New Directions for Student Services, no. 30. San Francisco: Jossey-Bass, 1985.

Brown, R. D., and Canon, H. J. "Intentional Moral Development as an Objective of Higher Education." *Journal of College Student Personnel*, 1978, *19*, 426–429.

Canon, H. J., and Brown, R. D. "How to Think About Professional Ethics." In H. J. Canon and R. D. Brown (eds.), *Applied Ethics in Student Services*. New Directions for Student Services, no. 30. San Francisco: Jossey-Bass, 1985.

Delworth, U., and Seeman, D. "The Ethics of Care: Implications of Gilligan for the Student Services Profession." *Journal of College Student Personnel*, 1984, *25*, 489–492.

Gilligan, C. *In a Different Voice*. Cambridge, Mass.: Harvard University Press, 1982.

Kitchener, K. S. "Ethical Principles and Ethical Decisions in Student Affairs." In H. J. Canon and R. D. Brown (eds.), *Applied Ethics in Student Services*. New Directions for Student Services, no. 30. San Francisco: Jossey-Bass, 1985.

Krager, L. "A New Model for Defining Ethical Behavior." In H. J. Canon and R. D. Brown (eds.), *Applied Ethics in Student Services*. New Directions for Student Services, no. 30. San Francisco: Jossey-Bass, 1985.

National Association of Student Personnel Administrators. "NASPA Standards of Professional Practice." Unpublished document approved by National Association of Student Personnel Administrators Executive Committee, Feb. 1983.

Sanford, N. "Freshman Personality: A Stage in Human Development." In N. Sanford and J. Axelrod (eds.), *College and Character*. Berkeley, Calif.: Montaigne: 1979.

Stengle, R. "Morality Among Supply-Siders." *Time*, May 25, 1987, pp. 18–20.

Winston, R. B., Jr., and Dagley, J. C. "Ethical Standards Statements: Uses and Limitations." In H. J. Canon and R. D. Brown (eds.), *Applied Ethics in Student Services*. New Directions for Student Services, no. 30. San Francisco: Jossey-Bass, 1985.

Chapter Four

Legal Issues Confronting Student Affairs Practice

Margaret J. Barr

Almost every decision that a student affairs administrator must make has legal implications. Thus, student affairs professionals must understand the influence of the law on their work. For example, a parent calls demanding to see a copy of her child's transcript. Should you give it to her? The student newspaper prints an exposé of the financial dealings of a trustee. The chairman of the board of trustees calls to tell you to make the student newspaper desist. Can and should you respond affirmatively to his request? A student parking in the freshman lot is attacked on her way back to her residence hall. She is severely hurt and claims that the institution is not providing proper security. Do you have a legal obligation to her? A fraternity gives alcohol to an underaged pledge; as a result, he falls and is injured. Can you be held personally responsible under the law? The answer to these questions and others will be "it depends." It depends on the status of the institution, state and federal law, the facts of the situation, and what you have or have not done as an administrator.

The legal environment for higher education and student affairs has changed rapidly over the last two decades. Until 1965, there were only thirty-two landmark court cases involving student affairs (Hammond and Shaffer, 1978). Since that time, the amount of litigation, legislation, and regulation affecting student affairs has increased geometrically. In such an environment, prudent administrators must understand the legal implications of their actions as well as of their inaction.

This chapter provides an overview of those points of law that directly influence student affairs. Topics to be covered include the sources of the law, the similarities and differences between public and private institutions, federal and state constitutional questions, liability, and such administrative issues as records and copyright. The chapter concludes with a series of recommendations for practice. It is not intended to be a substitute for sound legal advice; practitioners are urged to seek such advice regularly and consistently. Instead, this chapter is intended to provide a basic understanding of the law so that student affairs administrators can make sound decisions based on all the available facts, including the law. Practitioners should be aware, however, that the law is always evolving in response to new issues, societal trends, and the changing expectations of citizens. The law is one of many forces setting parameters for student affairs work. It is not something to be feared but is a tool to help create institutional climates where fairness and equity may prevail.

Sources of the Law

The law has eight sources that can influence practice in student affairs. These are the federal Constitution; the state constitutions; federal, state, and local statutes; judicial decisions; the rules and regulations of administrative agencies; contracts; institutional rules and regulations; and academic tradition. Each of these sources of the law can influence actions in both private and public institutions; however, the degree of influence may vary markedly from one type to the other.

Federal Constitution. "Constitutions are the fundamental source for determining the nature and extent of governmental powers. Constitutions are also the fundamental source of the individual rights guarantees that limit the power of government and protect citizens generally, including members of the academic community'' (Kaplin, 1985, p. 10). The federal Constitution is the highest source of law in the country. Even so, federal constitutional guarantees influence student affairs practice in public and private institutions differently. Under the law, public institutions operate as an arm of the state and are fully subject to the provisions of the federal Constitution. Private institutions are not subject to the provisions of the federal Constitution except under certain conditions, when the actions of private institutions and their officers may be defined as state action and the federal Constitution will apply (Barr, 1988). A full discussion of these circumstances is provided in the section on constitutional issues later in the chapter.

State Constitutions. The provisions of the applicable state constitution can influence both public and private institutions. Through the residual powers of the federal Constitution, all powers not specifically reserved for the federal government are ceded to the states and their citizens (Alexander and Solomon, 1972, p. 42). Thus, higher education comes primarily under state control. In nine states the state universities are considered constitutionally autonomous and the control exercised by other agencies of the state on these institutions is diminished (Hofstadter and Smith, 1961). Such constitutionally autonomous institutions, however, are not free from all state control, for limitations can be imposed through other state constitutional provisions and state statutes. Private institutions are also subject to some provisions of the state constitution. Not only will the general police power of the state prevail, but individual rights may be protected on the campuses of private institutions (*State* v. *Schmid,* 1980). Careful review of the state constitution is needed to determine the influence of specific provisions on private colleges and universities.

Most public institutions, however, are statutory and are subject to all provisions of the state constitution and state laws. State constitutions may establish a state agency with responsibility for public postsecondary institutions; they may also have provisions that grant ''more expansive individual rights than those guaranteed by parallel provisions of the federal Constitution'' (Kaplin, 1985, p. 10).

Statutes. Three levels of statutes influence higher education: federal, state, and local. Federal statutes govern all citizens of the United States and must be consistent with the powers reserved for the federal government under the U.S. Constitution. Some federal statutes of concern to student affairs administrators are those pertaining to individual privacy, student financial aid, facility construction, immigration, retirement, social security, and antitrust. At all levels of government, laws applying to other entities may also apply to higher education and should be accounted for in policy formation.

By far the greatest number of laws controlling both public and private higher education are at the state level (Moos and Rourke, 1959). Both types of institutions must conform to the general laws of the state and are also subject to regulation by state agencies whose primary function is not education. Private institutions are shielded from much state regulation, but they are not immune from regulations derived from the general police power of the state. Although constitutionally autonomous public institutions do exist, it also should be noted that "the greater part of law defining the status of public institutions of higher education is legislative rather than constitutional" (Moos and Rourke, 1959, p. 17). Private institutions come under additional state control through statutes governing trusts, chartering, licensure, and coordinating bodies. All states incorporate or charter private institutions; approximately two-thirds of the states also require licensing (Education Commission of the States, 1973).

The influence of local ordinances on an institution of higher education is determined by the legal status of the institution, the statutory entitlement of the municipality or county where the institution is located, and the facts of a particular situation. In general, both public and private institutions are subject to local ordinances regarding health and safety, such as fire codes and zoning laws. However, a public institution, as an arm of the state, generally has plenary powers over local government, unless these are restricted by state or federal constitutional provisions (Thompson, 1976). Further, as Meyers (1970, p. 3) notes, "The growing trend for institutions of higher education to become 'involved' with the communities they serve gives rise to even more relationships which have legal implications." For both public and private institutions, the determination of the legal authority of local government on the campus can be clarified only by careful comparison of the legal authority of the governmental body with that of the institution.

Judicial Decisions. All courts have three functions: settling controversies by applying appropriate laws or principles to a specific set of facts, interpreting enactments of the legislature, and determining the constitutionality of statutes (Alexander and Solomon, 1972, p. 8). The force of any judicial decision depends on the jurisdiction of the deciding court.

The federal court system consists of a Supreme Court, the court of appeals, special federal courts, and district courts. In matters related to federal constitutional issues and federal statutes, the decisions of the United States Supreme Court are "binding precedents throughout the country" (Kaplin, 1978, p. 14). Eleven federal districts, or circuits, constitute the court of appeals and serve as intermediate appellate courts in the federal system. Cases may be appealed as a matter of right to the appropriate circuit court. The decisions of the circuit court are binding within all courts and jurisdictions of the circuit unless they are successfully appealed to the United States Supreme Court (Barr, 1988). The decisions of one circuit are not binding on other circuits or on district courts in other circuits. Each federal district court is a one-judge trial court; its decisions are binding only in the district where judgment is rendered. District court decisions may be appealed to the appropriate federal court of appeals and, in some cases, directly to the United States Supreme Court (Kaplin, 1978, p. 15).

Each state court system is unique; in general, however, state court systems are structured like the federal courts. State district courts are usually courts of general jurisdiction and have judicial responsibilities for a geographical area within a state. Most states have separate district courts for civil and criminal matters and maintain this separation at the appellate level. Generally, there is one supreme court, although in some states the appellate court serves as the supreme court in criminal matters.

Although at both state and federal levels court decisions are binding only within the jurisdiction of the court, all decisions should be carefully reviewed. "A knowledge of case law to date gives one knowledge of established legal precedent applicable to one jurisdiction or guidance where litigation may have occurred elsewhere but remains untested in one's own judicial area" (Owens, 1984, pp. 3–4).

Administrative Rules and Regulations. Kaplin (1985, p. 11) indicates that the most rapidly expanding source of post-secondary education law is the directives of state and federal administrative agencies. Like statutes, administrative regulations at either the federal or state level carry the force of law and must be consistent with applicable state and federal statutes and constitutional provisions. Some agencies, such as labor and human rights agencies, also have a legal right to settle disputes on specific issues. In any event, legal advice should be sought before a student affairs administrator deals with any external administrative agency (Rhode, 1983).

Contracts. A contract creates a binding legal arrangement between the contracting parties, enforceable by either party if one party fails to comply with the terms of the contract. "An understanding of the elements of a contract, the authority to contract, and the implications of improper contracting are crucial in student affairs areas" (Owens, 1984, p. 4). As a matter of routine, student affairs administrators sign any number of contracts for goods and services. When disputes arise, the first source of law to be checked is the elements of the contract agreed on by the parties. In addition, an emerging body of case law is redefining as contractual the relationship between the student and the institution.

Institutional Rules and Regulations. Although institutional rules and regulations are subject to the sources of law described above, they are also a source of law in and of themselves. Often the question in litigation will be whether an institution followed its own rules. The keys to sound institutional rules include assurances that the regulations are consistent with other sources of the law, are specific, are enforceable, are known, and are enforced consistently.

Academic Tradition. The most diffuse source of law for higher education is academic tradition: the expectations of members of the academic community for the behavior of the institution and members of the academy. It is also much more informal than other sources of the law. Academic tradition may be documented through speeches, correspondence, media releases, and other interpretations of the way the college or university conducts its business. The use of academic tradition as source of law has been recognized by the courts under specific circumstances (*Krotkoff* v. *Goucher College,* 1978).

Federal Constitution

The federal Constitution's provisions involve a wide range of issues of concern to student affairs. Although it is clear that the federal Constitution applies with full force in public colleges and universities, its influence on private institutions hinges on whether the institution was engaged in state action.

Fourteenth Amendment and State Action. The Fourteenth Amendment of the United States Constitution provides that no person shall be deprived of federally guaranteed rights by a state official acting "under the color of state law." The Fourteenth Amendment states in part that no state shall "deprive any person of life, liberty or property, without due process of law; nor deny to any person within its jurisdiction the equal protection of the laws." It is clear that public colleges and universities and their agents are subject to the provisions of the Fourteenth Amendment. For private institutions, the determination of whether the institution was acting under "the color of state law" depends on the facts of the situation. A symbiotic relationship test has been adopted by the courts to determine if private institutions are really acting as arms of the state.

Grove City College v. *Bell* (1984) has been cited as a landmark case in determining the doctrine of state action. Grove City College, a private institution, asserted that receipt of federal funds in the form of student financial aid did not make it subject to Title IX of the 1976 Higher Education Act barring sex discrimination. The court held that Title IX applied only to the college's financial aid program and other specific federal programs, including grants and contracts. The entire college was not subject to regulation because the symbiotic relationship test had not been met. However, as a practical matter, most private colleges and universities are adopting constitutional guarantees as part of their contract of enrollment with students, although they are not bound to do so under the provisions of the federal Constitution.

First Amendment. The First Amendment of the United States Constitution states that "Congress shall make no law respecting an establishment of religion or prohibiting the free exercise thereof; or abridging the freedom of speech, or of the press, or the right of the people to peaceably assemble and to petition the Government for a redress of grievances." The provisions of the First Amendment are the source of much of the litigation influencing student affairs today.

Public institutions have historically taken the position that the freedom of religion clause of the First Amendment prohibits the use of public university facilities by religious groups. This course of action may be neither prudent nor wise. In *Widmar* v. *Vincent* (1981), the U.S. Supreme Court held that neutral accommodation of student religious groups would not be a violation of the First Amendment. In 1973, in deciding *Hunt* v. *McNair,* the Supreme Court held that the primary effect of any act by the state must be neither to aid nor to inhibit the free exercise of religion. As long as religious organizations conform to applicable institutional policies, they may use the facilities of public institutions. Private institutions, on the other hand, are free to "establish" a religion or to prohibit the free exercise of religion that is not consistent with their stated policies or mission.

The freedom of speech clause of the First Amendment also raises a number of issues of concern to student affairs administrators. Early cases dealt only with outside speakers, and most courts agreed that neither a public nor a private institution was obliged to open its doors to outside speakers. However, if a college or university allows outside speakers and "opens its lecture halls, it must do so nondiscriminately" (*Stacy* v. *Williams,* 1969, p. 971).

Restrictions on the use of campus facilities have been upheld by the courts as long as the regulations are fair and reasonable and are enforced in a fair and equitable manner. *Tinker* v. *Des Moines Independent School District* (1969), although a secondary school case, established the right of students to symbolic free speech and declared that their "constitutional rights were not shed at the schoolhouse gate" (*Tinker*, at 736). Wright (1969) indicates three principles in the regulation of speech that have consistently been confirmed by the courts. First, expression cannot be prohibited because of disagreement with the content expressed. Second, expression is subject to reasonable regulations of the institution regarding the time, place, and manner of such expression. Third, expression can be prohibited if it can be proved that such expression could materially and substantially disrupt the primary educational mission of the institution (*State* v. *Jordan*, 1972; *Harrell* v. *Southern Illinois University*, 1983). The question of commercial free speech has also been litigated. The most noted case is *American Future Systems, Inc.* v. *Pennsylvania State University* (1980, 1982, 1983, 1984). American Future Systems, Inc., sought to sell products in residence hall rooms through telephone solicitation and arranging for demonstrations in residents' rooms. The university prevailed under conditions where its regulations were reasonable and alternate forms of expression existed for the commercial vendor.

Private institutions may, of course, prevent, limit, or refuse to authorize peaceful assembly of any group, including student organizations. Public institutions may not. Private and public institutions must follow their own published rules; such rules should be reasonably specific, not vague or too broad. In *Healy* v. *James* (1972) the Supreme Court upheld the right of a chapter of Students for a Democratic Society to be recognized on a college campus. The college had claimed that the organization adhered to a philosophy espousing the overthrow of the government. The court held that there was a difference between advocacy and action and declared that the nonrecognition was unconstitutional. The *Healy* decision has been tested in the courts many times, most recently in cases involving recognition of gay groups by colleges and universities. In *Gay Students Organization of the University of New Hampshire* v. *Bonner* (1974), *Gay Lib* v. *University of Missouri* (1977), and *Gay Student Services* v. *Texas A&M University* (1984), the judicial system upheld the right of free association by students on the campus of state colleges and universities.

Freedom of the press and the rights and responsibilities of student newspapers and institutions have also been litigated under the First Amendment. *Dickey* v. *Alabama State Board of Education* (1967) was a landmark case involving the college press. Public colleges and universities have been found to be fully subject to the federal Constitution's guarantee of freedom of the press, whereas private institutions have not. Public colleges may not exercise prior restraint on the content of a student newspaper (*Dickey* v. *Alabama State Board of Education,* 1967); *Schiff* v. *Williams,* 1975). Funding cannot be removed because of disagreement with or institutional embarrassment regarding a student newspaper's content (*Antonelli* v. *Hammond,* 1970; *Joyner* v. *Whiting,* 1973; *Minnesota Daily* v. *University of Minnesota,* 1983). Use of obscenity is not a reason for dismissal of a student editor or for using the campus discipline system against the editor (*Papish* v. *Board of Curators of the University of Missouri,* 1973). Student newspapers must, however, conform to applicable statutes governing libel and slander; the university has not been found to be financially responsible for libelous actions by the student press (*Mazart* v. *State University of New York,* 1982).

Fourth Amendment. The Fourth Amendment limits unreasonable search and seizure and is of particular concern to institutions operating residence hall programs. Although *Moore* v. *Student Affairs Committee of Troy State University* (1976) permitted warrantless searches, a more recent line of cases (*Smyth* v. *Lubbers,* 1975) has held such searches to be unlawful. Courts in other jurisdictions have also upheld this rationale (*Piazzola* v. *Watkins,* 1971; *State* v. *Moore,* 1976; *White* v. *Davis,* 1975). In *Washington* v. *Chrisman* (1982) the Supreme Court heard a residence hall search and seizure case and affirmed that the "plain view" doctrine applied to warrantless searches. A secondary school case, *New Jersey* v. *T.L.O.* (1985), has implications for higher education. A high school vice-principal seeking contraband conducted a warrantless search of a student's purse. The court held that a warrantless search under such circumstances was permissible if the school official had reasonable suspicion that contraband would be present. It should be noted, however, that the state of Fourth Amendment law in higher education has not been definitely decided by the courts. Current issues such as mandatory drug testing forecast more Fourth Amendment challenges of unreasonable search and seizure on the campuses of public institutions.

Fourteenth Amendment. The due process clause of the Fourteenth Amendment has also been the cause of many court challenges. The courts have held that students have a right to at least minimal due process standards in disciplinary hearings. Minimal standards include the right to a hearing, notice of the charges, and an opportunity to respond to the charges (*Esteban* v. *Central Missouri State College,* 1969). Nearly two hundred cases have been litigated regarding student discipline and the necessary due process standards. A full adversarial hearing need not be held; the strictness of the due process requirements has been determined by the courts to depend on the severity of the punishment and the protected interest involved (*Goss* v. *Lopez,* 1975).

Private institutions do not need to adhere to the same due process standards as their public counterparts, but they must follow their own rules once they are established (*Harvey* v. *Palmer School of Chiropractic,* 1984). In addition, private institutions must treat students fairly (*Clayton* v. *Trustees of Princeton University,* 1985).

Academic Matters. The courts have also taken a stand of noninterference in academic matters. In general, the courts have deferred to the judgment of professionals in determining whether or not a student has met the required academic standards of an institution (*Board of Curators of the University of Missouri* v. *Horowitz,* 1978). In *Ewing* v. *Board of Regents of the University of Michigan* (1985), the Supreme Court declared in part that courts may not interfere in a genuine academic decision unless "it is such a substantial departure from accepted academic norms as to indicate that the faculty member or the committee did not exercise professional judgment" (*Ewing,* at 507). Faculty, staff members, and others also may have constitutionally protected rights under certain conditions. A discussion of this topic and a full outline of the issues involved in employment can be found in Kaplin's definitive work (1985).

The federal Constitution has a very real and direct influence on the conduct of student affairs at public institutions.

In private institutions, although it is not required by law unless the institution is engaging in state action, federal constitutional guarantees are often honored. University administrators no longer have unbridled discretion in their treatment of students. Minimal standards of due process must be honored and regulations must be specific and precise. Regulation of the student press through prior restraint, loss of funding, or disciplinary proceedings against editors and reporters has not been upheld by the courts. Institutions may regulate the time, place, and manner of public assembly and may take reasonable steps to assure that the primary educational mission of the institution is not disrupted. Discriminatory criteria may not be applied to the recognition of student groups. Religious groups may use the facilities of public institutions on the same basis as other organizations. Private institutions must follow their own rules even if they are not required to do so by the federal Constitution.

State Constitutions

Each state constitution is unique and has the power to influence both public and private institutions. Although there may not be a direct reference to education in the constitution, other provisions, such as a bill of individual rights or financing laws, can influence colleges and universities. In *State* v. *Schmid* (1980), a non-student was charged with criminal trespass for distributing political material on the Princeton campus. The New Jersey Supreme Court held that the provisions of the state constitution did not permit the private institution to deny Schmid's expressional rights. Similar provisions also were applied in Pennsylvania, with the same results. Although the results of these cases are applicable only in the states mentioned, they are illustrative of the power of the state constitution over private institutions under certain circumstances. State constitutions also usually prohibit use of appropriated funds for sectarian purposes. Five states have amended their state constitutions to authorize various forms of aid to students attending private or sectarian institutions. The question has been litigated as to whether students attending religious preparatory schools should receive such aid. The answer depends on the specific provisions of the state constitution. State constitutional provisions may be applicable to both private and public colleges in a given state. Such constitutional provisions may exceed the requirements of the federal Constitution and should be carefully reviewed during policy development and implementation.

Civil Rights Laws

Civil rights legislation at both the federal and state levels can influence the practice of student affairs. The various civil rights laws, prohibiting discrimination against certain protected classes of individuals, can influence virtually all aspects of a student affairs operation. This section will review the applicable federal laws; the reader is cautioned to review state civil rights statutes as well.

Section 1981. The Civil Rights Act of 1866, Section 1981 (42 U.S.C.), is one of the broadest statutes regarding discrimination. The statute, enacted shortly after the Civil War, specifically prohibits racial discrimination. Under Section 1981, a showing of state action is not required for the law to apply to private institutions. It is linked to the Thirteenth Amendment, which prohibits slavery and applies to both public and private acts. In *McCrary* v. *Runyon* (1976), the court held that a private school could not deny admission on the basis of race. Section 1981 has not been widely applied to higher education because the plaintiff must prove that there has been purposeful and intentional discrimination by the defendant (*Williams* v. *De Kalb County,* 1978).

Section 1983. Unlike Section 1981 claims, Section 1983 (42 U.S.C.) claims are commonly used in litigation involving institutions of higher education. Under Section 1983, a plaintiff must prove only that he or she has been deprived of a federally protected right and that the deprivation occurred under color of state law. In *Weise* v. *Syracuse University* (1982), the courts applied a five-part test to determine if the action of the institution was state action. The five tests determined whether the private organization was dependent on government aid, whether it was regulated by the government, whether regulation connoted approval, whether the private organization served a public function, and whether it had legitimate constitutional or statutory claims as a private organization.

Title VI. In 1954 racial discrimination in schools was outlawed by the Supreme Court in *Brown* v. *Board of Education* (1954). Although *Brown* had far-reaching implications, it did not reach into the private sector. Title VI (42 U.S.C. Section 2000d-1) was enacted in 1964 to fill this gap. Title VI prohibits discrimination on the basis of race, color, or national origin in programs receiving federal financial assistance. The most famous case involving Title VI is *Regents of the University of California* v. *Bakke* (1978). In this case Bakke, a white male, alleged reverse discrimination in the admissions process. The court held that Title VI protected only certain classes. Abernathy's analysis (1978) of the opinion of the Supreme Court concluded that race can be taken into consideration as one factor. Affirmative action and numerical quotas can be used to cure specific cases of prior racial discrimination, but race cannot be the only factor in a decision.

Title VII. The provisions of Title VII apply only to employment and prohibit discrimination on the basis of race, color, national origin, sex, or religion in businesses with fifteen or more employees. It has sweeping implications for hiring, promotion, termination, and benefits for all faculty and staff members in the academy. It is not possible to provide a full treatment of the subject here; the reader is referred to *Employment Discrimination Law* (Schlie and Grossman, 1984).

Title IX. This statute, part of the 1972 Education Amendments, prohibits discrimination on the basis of sex (20 U.S.C., Sections 1681–86). Title IX does not apply to educational institutions controlled by religious, military, or merchant marine organizations. *Grove City College* v. *Bell* established that Title IX does not cover the entire institution. It does, however, cover many areas of concern to student affairs, including admissions, housing, athletics, health care, and student organizations.

Section 504. This section prohibits discrimination on the basis of handicap (29 U.S.C., Sections 791–794). The purpose of this act was to make higher education available to all qualified applicants regardless of physical disability. In addition, the act prohibits discrimination on the basis of handicap in employment. The act is broad in its definition of handicap and has the potential to influence almost every area of student affairs practice. As with Title IX, the courts have enforced the prohibition against discrimination only in those programs receiving federal finance assistance (*Doyle* v. *University of Alabama,* 1982).

The interpretation of what constitutes a qualified handicapped applicant under Section 504 has been tested in the courts many times. The Supreme Court held in *Southeastern Community College* v. *Davis* (1979) that a qualified person "is able to meet all of the program's requirements in spite of handicap(s)" (*Southeastern,* at 405–406). Thus, if a student cannot meet the standards of a course safely and effectively, exclusion does not imply discrimination.

Under Section 504, colleges and universities must make reasonable accommodations for the handicapped in housing, admissions, career counseling, and other services. In 1988, the question of whether people with acquired immune deficiency syndrome (AIDS) will be considered handicapped under the provisions of 504 has not been judicially resolved. Monitoring of this emerging area of the law will be critical in the years ahead.

Civil rights legislation at the federal level is far-reaching; public and private institutions may be differently affected under the law. All policies, practices, and procedures should be reviewed to ensure that they do not have an unequal impact on members of protected classes. The laws influence all phases of students' academic careers, from admission through graduation. Understanding and adhering to state and federal civil rights laws ensures both equity and access in institutions.

Contracts

In recent years courts at all levels and jurisdictions have begun to define the relationship between students and institutions as that of a contract. Thus almost every oral and written statement between a student and an institutional representative has the potential to become part of a mutually binding contract. Cases have been litigated involving admissions in both private and public institutions (*Nuttleman* v. *Case Western Reserve University*, 1981; *Hall* v. *University of Minnesota et al.*, 1982). In all cases where the institution had specific language in publication reserving rights to the institution and clearly articulating procedures, the institutions have been upheld by the courts. Institutions that lacked such specific language have not been upheld.

Discipline cases, both academic and behavioral, have also been litigated under the theory of contracts. As in other cases, the courts have been reluctant to interfere in matters involving the judgment of professionals (*Lai* v. *Board of Trustees of East Carolina University*, 1971). If, however, it can be proved that actions by institutional officials were arbitrary and capricious, institutions are subject to judicial scrutiny for their actions (*McDonald* v. *Hogness*, 1979; *Gaspar* v. *Bruton*, 1975). In *Gaspar*, the court held in part that "the court may grant relief as a practical matter only in those cases where the student presents positive evidence of ill will or bad motive" (at 851). The courts have also held that students must be prepared to read and understand the regulations influencing their academic standing (Shur, 1983).

The right of an institution to alter requirements, change fees, and make other adjustments during a student's period of enrollment has also been litigated. When such changes are reasonable, the courts have upheld the institution (*Mahavongsanan* v. *Hall*, 1976). Some have argued that termination, or a change in the accreditation status, of an academic program is a breach of contract. If there has been a legitimate lack of resources to support the program, the institution has been upheld (*Moore* v. *Board of Regents*, 1978). If students' rights have been adversely affected because of a program cancellation, some jurisdictions have seen it as a breach of contract and awarded monetary damages to students (*Eden* v. *State University of New York*, 1975; *Lowenthal* v. *Vanderbilt University*, 1977).

Tuition and fee refund programs have also been litigated under contract theory. The determination of the case depends on the facts of the case. If institutions have included specific

disclaimers in publications regarding costs, they have usually
been upheld by the courts (*Basch* v. *George Washington University,*
1977; *Eisele* v. *Ayers,* 1978; *Prusack* v. *State,* 1986). In all situations involving contract theory, student affairs administrators
would be well advised to place disclaimers in publications,
educate staff about the importance of oral statements, and ensure
that rules and regulations are fair, equitable, and reasonable.

Liability

Many factors have contributed to the growing concern
of college administrators regarding both personal and institutional liability. The courts are being used more frequently as
the arena in which to settle differences, insurance costs have
risen, and the number of contractual disputes has increased;
all of these have contributed to this concern.

The question of whether a public institution, or a private
institution engaged in state action, is immune from suit is difficult to answer. State law is the primary factor that determines
whether an institution is immune from suit. In Pennsylvania
and Kentucky, statutes provide immunity from suit for public
universities. In Tennessee, the charter of the university was the
deciding factor in determining that immunity did not attach (*Soni*
v. *Board of Trustees of the University of Tennessee and Boling,* 1975).
Whether a university is immune depends on state law, whether
the institution was engaged in state action, the charter provisions of the school, and other state statutes. It is clear, however,
that the doctrine of sovereign immunity for public institutions
does not provide blanket protection from liability claims. Further, private institutions must not assume that they are immune
from such claims.

Prevention of and defense against liability claims in colleges and universities are both difficult and complex. Aiken (1976)
identified several major sources of liability claims, including
bodily injury, property damage, civil rights claims, contracts,
the changing status of the doctrine of sovereign immunity, and
the changed legal view of a good-faith defense. The most common form of liability actions fall under the doctrine of torts.

"A tort is broadly defined as a civil wrong, other than a breach of contract, for which the courts will allow a damage remedy" (Kaplin, 1985, p. 55). Tort actions may be brought on claims of either a direct invasion of some legal right of a person or a failure to meet a public duty or obligation to a person.

This section will address the most common forms of liability actions encountered by student affairs professionals: negligence, alcohol liability, defamation and libel, civil rights violations, and contractual liability.

Negligence. There are three legal elements in a negligence claim: duty, breach of that duty, and the breach being the proximate cause of the injury. Courts have held that an institution of higher education owes the duty of ordinary and reasonable care with respect to the conditions of the premises when a person is invited to the campus (*Leahy* v. *State,* 1944; *Sandoval* v. *Board of Regents,* 1965). When a person is on the institution's property for his or her own convenience but with the sufferance of the institution, the institution likewise owes the duty of maintaining the property in a reasonably safe condition. A trespasser is on the property without the legal permission of the owner, and under these conditions an institution may have diminished legal responsibility in claims of negligence.

A number of cases of sexual assault have been tried under claims of negligence. When the assault was not foreseeable, there was no evidence of repeated criminal activity, and adequate security was in place, negligence claims have not been upheld (*Brown* v. *North Carolina Wesleyan College, Inc.,* 1983). In both New York (*Miller* v. *State of New York,* 1984) and Massachusetts (*Mullins* v. *Pine Manor College,* 1983) negligence claims were upheld in sexual assault cases involving female resident students. In both cases the court declared there was a special duty of care owing to the landlord-tenant relationship between the institution and the student.

Accidents are also a source of negligence claims. If the university knew of a dangerous condition and failed to correct it, liability would attach (*Lumbard* v. *Fireman's Fund Insurance Company,* 1974). A mere fall or injury does not by itself establish negligence (*Yost* v. *TCU,* 1962). When a person has knowingly assumed a risk, liability claims against institutions or their agents have not been upheld in the courts (*Rubtchinsky* v. *State University of New York*, 1965; *Dudley* v. *William Penn College*, 1974). In *Mintz* v. *State* (1975), the State University of New York at New Paltz was not found to be liable when two students died on a canoe trip sponsored by a student organization. Weather conditions, rather than any action or inaction on the part of the institution, were cited as the cause of the deaths and liability did not attach.

Alcohol Liability. Four distinct aspects of alcohol use by students are of concern for student affairs administrators. These involve the roles played by the institution as supervisor of student conduct, property owner, seller of alcohol, and social host. Buchanan and Oliaro (1987) cite service to a minor, drunk driving, and establishment of a custodial relationship as the greatest areas of risk. They further indicate that either criminal or civil liability may attach under any of the circumstances. *Bradshaw* v. *Rawlings* (1979) is cited as a leading case in the area of student conduct and liability. In this case a student was severely injured while returning from a class picnic in a car with an intoxicated driver. Class funds supported the picnic, where alcohol was served. The faculty advisor aided in planning the event and publicity was allowed on campus. Although damages were awarded at the trial court level, the decision was reversed on appeal. The appellate court held that there was no duty on the part of the college to keep a student from getting into a car with an intoxicated person. Similar reasoning prevailed in *Baldwin* v. *Zoradi* (1981), where the college was not found to be liable for an injury occurring off campus and involving alcohol illegally consumed in a campus residence hall.

Unintentional injury is often associated with alcohol, and even when there was no intent to harm, liability may attach for both the institution and its agents. State laws vary greatly in this area and should be carefully understood. For example, in a California residence hall, staff members served alcohol to an intoxicated person, who subsequently fell and was injured (*Zavala* v. *Regents of the University of California*, 1981). Although he played a part in his own injury, the institution was held to be partially liable under California law.

Whitlock v. *University of Denver* (1986) is also illustrative of this type of claim. In this case, a student was injured on a trampoline in the yard of a fraternity renting premises from the university. As a condition of the lease, the fraternity agreed to nominal supervision by the university. Trampolines owned by the university were closely supervised, but the fraternity trampoline was not. The lower court upheld a liability claim against the university, which was reduced at the appellate level. Roth (1986) indicates that the lower court held, in part, that the university was negligent in failing to ban unsupervised trampolines; the judgment was reduced at the appellate level because of the student's own negligence. On appeal, the Colorado Supreme Court reversed the judgment, declaring, in part, that the university held no duty of care in *Whitlock*.

Many institutions have established areas on campus where alcohol is sold. This type of facility imposes special liability concerns. In thirty-nine states and the District of Columbia, liability connected with the commercial sale of alcoholic beverages has been imposed through statute or judicial decisions (Roth, 1986, p. 50). The scope of state law varies considerably, as do the criminal and civil liabilities that may attach under the law. It should be noted that negligence claims often arise on "failure to conduct an activity as a reasonably prudent person would under similar circumstances" (Roth, 1986, p. 49). Decisions about what constitutes prudent action are difficult to resolve, however; caution should be exercised. Potential liability connected with the sale of alcohol also extends to student organizations. Events, either on or off campus, where alcohol is sold under the sponsorship of student organizations raise special liability questions. State law will determine who is responsible, if anyone, in liability claims. In addition, state law may require a temporary license to sell and insurance for injury claims associated with alcohol at such events.

Social host liability is a relatively new legal development. Statutes have been adopted in many states assigning liability to social hosts. "A university is likely to be a social host where it, its agents, or employees actually serve alcoholic beverages such as an official reception or ceremony" (Steinbach, 1985, p. 36). Such laws have profound implications for colleges and universities, for social host liability could extend to official social functions held in private homes of university faculty and staff. Careful monitoring of this emerging area of the law is urged.

Alcohol-related liability is clearly an appropriate area of concern for student affairs administrators. The law is rapidly evolving and close monitoring of developments is essential. Institutional policies should adhere to all applicable laws and should be enforced consistently; institutions should caution students that inappropriate behavior associated with alcohol will be confronted. Further, the institution must respond quickly to violations of policy and take corrective measures to deter such violations in the future.

Defamation and Libel. Defamation claims arise when "oral or written publication of material tends to injure a person's reputation" (Kaplin, 1985, p. 61). For defamation to occur, that material must have been published by a third person and must have been capable of ruining the reputation of the claimant. Evaluation of employees (particularly faculty) has resulted in several key cases of concern to student affairs. In *Greenya* v. *George Washington University* (1975) the court held that "educational officers and faculty members enjoy a qualified privilege to discuss the qualifications and character of fellow officers and faculty members if the matter communicated is pertinent to the functioning of the educational institution" (p. 563). For public institutions, a second defense against claims of defamation is possible. Under circumstances where a defendant publishes defamatory material in the performance of official duties, the court held that such material may be published (*Shearer* v. *Lambert,* 1976).

Public figures may have a more difficult time proving defamation. First, the courts have held that a determination must be made whether the person is indeed a public figure (*Avins* v. *White,* 1980). If a person is a public figure, liability will not attach unless the statement made was known to be false or was made in reckless disregard of whether it was true or false (*Garrison* v. *Louisiana,* 1964, at 74). For student publications, the issues of defamation and libel are even more complex because of First Amendment protections governing a free press. Common and constitutional law doctrines indicate it is not enough for the statement to be false and misleading. In addition, nominal injury must be caused and the libelous material must be attributable to some fault of the publisher of the paper or magazine. Policy issues in this area are complex and decisions must be made with regard to the legal relationship with student publications to limit institutional liability (*Mazart* v. *State,* 1981).

Civil Rights Liability. The civil rights statutes previously described can also be a source of liability for the institution and its agents. Section 1983 of the Civil Rights Act specifically provides for liability if it is proven that a person has been deprived of "rights, privileges or immunities" (42 U.S.C.). *Wood* v. *Strickland* (1975), although a secondary-school case, has been viewed as a landmark case regarding personal liability of administrators. Previously, in *Scheuer* v. *Rhodes* (1974), the Supreme Court found that government officials, including a university president, had qualified immunity from suit under Section 1983. In *Wood,* however, the court set both a subjective and an objective test to determine if immunity applied. Did the school official act without malice? Did he know, or should he reasonably have known, that his actions would violate a constitutionally protected right of a student? The court further declared that compensatory damage awards would be appropriate only if the school official had acted with "such impermissible motivation or with such disregard of the student's clearly established constitutional rights that his action cannot be reasonably characterized as being in good faith" (*Wood,* at 1001). Analysis of the decision by both Clague (1976) and the *Harvard Law Review* ("Developments in the Law . . . ," 1977) indicates that it is doubtful that school officials would be held personally liable under Section 1983 claims if their conduct was reasonable given the facts at hand. Institutions, however, have been found to be liable under Section 1983 (*Taliferro* v. *State Council of Higher Education,* 1977). *Harlow* v. *Fitzgerald* (1982), a subsequent Supreme Court case, deleted the subjective question of deciding immunity promulgated in *Wood.* The court held, in part, that "government officials performing discretionary functions generally are shielded from liability for civil damages in so far as their conduct does not violate clearly established statutory or constitutional rights of which a reasonable person would have known" (*Harlow,* at 2738).

Although the law is clearly evolving in this area, ignorance is not bliss. "The state of law under Section 1983 and the Eleventh Amendment taken together, give administrators of public postsecondary institutions no cause to feel confident that either they or other institutional officers or employees are insulated from personal civil rights liability" (Kaplin, 1985, p. 84).

Contract Liability. Contractual liability for institutions can arise from a number of sources. This area of law is very complicated and legal advice should be sought before any administrator enters into a contract on behalf of the institution. Kaplin (1985) states that reduction in contract liability can be achieved by specifically delineating the contracting authority of faculty and staff. Unauthorized contracts by those seemingly acting with institutional authority have been upheld by the courts under specified circumstances (*Brown* v. *Wichita State University,* 1975). Other courts have not so ruled (*First Equity Corp.* v. *Utah State University,* 1975). State law has a powerful influence over contracts. Thus, contracts are another area where administrators should not proceed without sound legal advice.

Other Statutes

There are many, many statutes at the federal and state levels that may influence practice in student affairs. This section will review the most relevant federal legislation; readers are cautioned to review parallel legislation at the state level.

FERPA. The Family Educational Rights and Privacy Act of 1974 (as amended) (FERPA) influences record keeping in all postsecondary institutions. Signed in 1974 and popularly known as the "Buckley Amendment," the law regulates educational records in colleges and universities. FERPA provisions must be followed by all institutions receiving Department of Education funds directly or through students receiving federal financial aid. The records covered by FERPA are defined to include any record that could be identified as that of a particular student.

The primary emphasis of the act is on the right of students to inspect their records, challenge those records, and request formal hearings to resolve disputes. Disclosure of information from records is prohibited without approval by the student except under specific circumstances. Parents may not have access to educational records unless the student is a dependent according to tax law (Janes, 1988). Directory material may be released, but it should be defined, and students have the right to refuse release of some or all of that data. FERPA requirements may conflict with other federal statutes or state laws. Thus, legal advice on policies and procedures regarding educational records is essential.

Immigration. The Immigration Reform and Control Act of 1986 affects all institutions that enroll or hire foreign citizens. Immigration law is clearly under federal control (*Toll* v. *Moreno,* 1982; *Plyler* v. *Doe,* 1982). Very specific requirements for reporting, monitoring, and following foreign nationals must be met. The institution must process documents associated with admissions application, certification of academic ability, mastery of the English language, and assurance that there are financial resources to cover all costs of study for foreign students. The changes in immigration law have brought new requirements for documentation of citizenship for employment. These requirements have the potential for many additional records requirements and must be carefully monitored as the law evolves.

Copyright. The General Revision of the Copyright Law (as amended, 1976) describes what may be copied and under what circumstances. The law covers print, visual arts, music, and computer works and is very specific. Protected material can be copied under a variety of conditions if the "fair use doctrine" applies. Scholarly and research purposes have been seen as legitimate fair-use materials, but restrictions are placed on the number of copies and methods of distribution. For specific advice, the reader is refered to *Guidelines for Classroom Copying* (U.S. House of Representatives, 1976).

Other Laws. A variety of other laws—including those governing employment, occupational safety, and taxes—are also of concern to student affairs administrators. If circumstances warrant, legal advice should be sought regarding the applicability of such statutes in a specific situation.

Conclusions

This chapter has provided an overview of the law of particular concern to student affairs administrators. Not all legal concerns influencing student affairs practice have been covered; a full understanding of the law will require much more extensive reading and study. Several themes, however, emerge that practitioners should understand.

The law changes. The law is always in the process of change. Astute professionals will try to keep informed of changes in the law and seek assistance in determining if those changes will influence their practice. A changing environment requires a high tolerance for ambiguity, for answers to legal questions are rarely simple and are dependent on specific facts and the current state of the law.

Legal challenges will increase. Student affairs administrators are not likely to avoid litigation. The proliferation of statutes and administrative rules, coupled with the litigious nature of society, forecasts increased legal challenges in student affairs.

Every area is influenced. Every area of student affairs practice is influenced by the law. Part of a staff development effort should focus on keeping practitioners abreast of current developments and assisting them in translating those legal constraints into practice.

Sound judgment is still necessary. Lawsuits will be threatened and brought for both frivolous and substantive reasons. Fear of legal proceedings should not, however, be substituted for sound administrative decisions based on the best available facts. Attorneys can provide advice; administrators must make decisions.

The law should not be feared. Although legal requirements and parameters can feel overwhelming and create a burden, the influence of the law is not all negative. Protection of individual rights, concern for the common good, ethical and humane treatment, and responsible action are principles on which the student affairs profession is founded.

Careful decisions are required. Student affairs administrators do not have unilateral authority in their dealings with others. Arbitrary and capricious actions will probably be challenged in the courts. The result can and should be a more thoughtful and careful decision-making process on campuses.

Students, faculty, and staff have legal rights. In both public and private institutions, members of the academic community have legal rights. Their rights may come from very different legal sources, but they do exist and cannot be ignored.

The student-institutional relationship is being redefined. The definition of the relationship between students and institutions is changing to that of a contract. Under contract theory, both parties have rights and responsibilities that can be enforced under the law.

Liability is of concern. Liability questions for both institutions and individuals are becoming pervasive in all areas of student affairs administration. The increase of liability judgments, coupled with rising insurance costs, has created a crisis in higher education.

Institutions are not immune. Colleges and universities are no longer viewed as enclaves where legal issues are not of concern. Statutory and constitutional provisions influence administration on a wide range of issues and must be accounted for in policy formation and development.

The following recommendations are designed to be of assistance to student affairs administrators coping with the legal framework of their profession.

- Student affairs administrators should become more aware of the law through academic study and professional development programs.
- Staff members at all levels should be informed of their legal obligations.
- Policies and procedures should be reviewed at least annually to see if they are consistent with the current status of the law.
- Publications should be reviewed to assure that legal obligations that cannot be met are not included.
- Special efforts must be made to reduce negligence claims through staff training and a risk management program.

- Qualified legal advice should be sought early and often to avoid unnecessary and burdensome litigation.
- If problems arise, do not try to be your own lawyer—seek help.
- Ask questions and do not be afraid to challenge institutional traditions if you feel they are inappropriate.
- Exercise the best judgment you can based on the facts, including the educational mission of the institution.

The law is one of the many tools available to student affairs administrators to meet goals of honesty, fairness, equity, and responsibility. Our legal framework provides a strong foundation for correct actions that meet both individual and institutional goals.

List of Cases Cited

American Future Systems, Inc. v. *Pennsylvania State University,* 618 F.2d. 252 (3d Cir. 1980).

American Future Systems, Inc. v. *Pennsylvania State University,* 688 F.2d 907 (3d Cir. 1982).

American Future Systems, Inc. v. *Pennsylvania State University,* 568 F. Supp. 666 (M.D. Pa. 1983).

American Future Systems, Inc. v. *Pennsylvania State University,* 464 F. Supp. 1252 (1979), 752 F.2d 854 (1984).

Antonelli v. *Hammond,* 308 F. Supp. 1329 (D. Mass. 1970).

Avins v. *White,* 627 F.2d 637 (3rd Cir. 1980).

Baldwin v. *Zoradi,* 123 Cal. App. 3d 275, 176 Cal. Rptr. 809 (1981).

Basch v. *George Washington University,* 370 A.2d 1364 (D.C. Cir. 1977).

Board of Curators of the University of Missouri v. *Horowitz,* 435 U.S. 78, 90 S. Ct. 948 (1978).

Bradshaw v. *Rawlings,* 612 F.2d 135 (3d Cir. 1979); cert. den. 446 U.S. 909, 100 S. Ct. 1836 (1980).

Brown v. *Board of Education,* 347 U.S. 483 (1954).

Brown v. *North Carolina Wesleyan College, Inc.,* 309 S.E.2d 701 (N.C. App. 1983).

Brown v. *Wichita State University,* 217 Kan. 279, 540 P.2d 66 (1975); vacated in part 219 Kan. 2, 547 P.2d 1015 (1976).

Clayton v. *Trustees of Princeton University,* 608 F. Supp. 413 (D.N.J. 1985).

Dickey v. *Alabama State Board of Education,* 273 F. Supp. 613 (1967).

Doyle v. *University of Alabama,* 680 F.2d 1323 (Ala. 1982).

Dudley v. *William Penn College,* 219 N.W.2d 484 (Iowa 1974).

Eden v. *State University of New York,* 49 App. Div. 2d 277, 374 N.Y.S.2d 686 (1975).

Eisele v. *Ayers,* 63 Ill. App. 3d 1039, 381 N.E.2d 21 (1978).

Esteban v. *Central Missouri State College,* 277 F. Supp. 649 (S.D. Mo. 1967); aff'd 415 F.2d 1077 (8th cir. 1969).

Ewing v. *Board of Regents of the University of Michigan,* 742 F.2d 913 (6th Cir. 1984); rev'd (other grounds) 106 S. Ct. 507 (1985).

First Equity Corp. v. *Utah State University,* 544 P.2d 887 (Utah 1975).

Garrison v. *Louisiana,* 379 U.S. 64 (1964).

Gaspar v. *Bruton,* 513 F.2d 843 (10th Cir. 1975).

Gay Lib v. *University of Missouri,* 58 F.2d 848 (8th Cir. 1977).

Gay Students Organization of the University of New Hampshire v. *Bonner,* 509 F.2d 652 (1st Cir. 1974).

Gay Student Services v. *Texas A&M University,* 737 F.2d 1317 (5th Cir. 1984).

Goss v. *Lopez,* 419 U.S. 565, 95 S. Ct. 729 (1975).

Greenya v. *George Washington University,* 512 F.2d 556 (D.C. Cir. 1975).

Grove City College v. *Bell,* 104 S. Ct. 1211, 465 U.S. 555 (1984).

Hall v. *University of Minnesota et al.,* 530 F. Supp. 104 (D. Minn. 1982).

Harlow v. *Fitzgerald,* 102 S. Ct. 2727 (1982).

Harrell v. *Southern Illinois University,* 457 N.E.2d 971 (1983).

Harvey v. *Palmer School of Chiropractic,* 363 N.W.2d 443 (Iowa 1984).

Healy v. *James,* 408 U.S. 169, 92 S. Ct. 2338 (1972).

Hunt v. *McNair,* 413 U.S. 734, 93 S. Ct. 2868 (1973).

Joyner v. *Whiting,* 477 F.2d 456 (4th Cir. 1973).

Krotkoff v. *Goucher College,* 585 F.2d 675 (4th Cir. 1978).

Lai v. *Board of Trustees of East Carolina University,* 330 F. Supp. 904 (E.D.N.C. 1971).

Leahy v. *State,* 46 N.Y.S.2d 310 (Ct. Cl. 1944).

Lowenthal v. *Vanderbilt University,* Davidson Co., Tennessee, Docket No. A-8325; Memorandum Opinion (1977).

Lumbard v. *Fireman's Fund Insurance Company,* 302 So. 2d 394 (Ct. App. La. 1974).

McCrary v. *Runyon,* 515 F.2d 1095 (4th Cir. 1975); aff'd 427 U.S. 160 (1976).

McDonald v. *Hogness,* 598 P.2d 707 (Wash. 1979).

Mahavongsanan v. *Hall,* 529 F.2d 488 (5th Cir. 1976).

Mazart v. *State,* 441 N.Y.S.2d 600 (Ct. Cl. 1981).

Mazart v. *State University of New York,* 109 Misc. 2d 1092 (N.Y. 1982).

Miller v. *State of New York,* 467 N.E.2d 493 (1984).

Minnesota Daily v. *University of Minnesota,* 719 F.2d 279 (8th Cir. 1983).

Mintz v. *State,* 362 N.Y.S.2d 619 (App. Div. 1975).

Moore v. *Board of Regents,* 59 A.D.2d 44, aff'd 44 N.Y.2d 593 (1978).

Moore v. *Student Affairs Committee of Troy State University,* 284 F. Supp. 775 (M.D. Ala. 1976).

Mullins v. *Pine Manor College,* 449 N.E.2d 331 (1983).

New Jersey v. *T.L.O.,* 469 U.S. 325 (1985).

Nuttleman v. *Case Western Reserve University,* 560 F. Supp. 1 (N.D. Ohio 1981).

Papish v. *Board of Curators of the University of Missouri,* 93 S. Ct. 1197 (1973).

Piazzola v. *Watkins,* 442 F.2d 284 (5th Cir. 1971).

Plyler v. *Doe,* 457 U.S. 202 (1982).

Prusack v. *State,* 498 N.Y.S.2d 455 (A.D.2 Dept. 1986).

Regents of the University of California v. *Bakke,* 438 U.S. 265 (1978).

Rubtchinsky v. *State University of New York,* 46 Misc. 2d 679, 260 N.Y.S.2d 256 (Ct. Cl. 1965).

Sandoval v. *Board of Regents,* 75 N.M. 261, 403 P.2d 699 (1965).

Scheuer v. *Rhodes,* 416 U.S. 232, 94 S. Ct. 168 (1974).

Schiff v. *Williams,* 519 F.2d 257 (5th Cir. 1975).

Shearer v. *Lambert,* 547 P.2d 98 (Or. 1976).

Smyth v. *Lubbers,* 398 F. Supp. 777 (W.D. Mich. 1975).

Soni v. *Board of Trustees of the University of Tennessee and Boling,* 513 F.2d 347 (1975).

Southeastern Community College v. *Davis,* 442 U.S. 397 (1979).

Stacy v. *Williams,* 306 F. Supp. 963 (N.D. Miss. 1969).

State v. *Jordan,* 53 Hawaii 634, 500 P.2d 56 (1972).

State v. *Moore,* cert. den. 429 U.S. 1004 (1976).

State v. *Schmid,* 423 A.2d 615 (N.J. 1980).

Taliferro v. *State Council of Higher Education,* 372 F. Supp. 1378 (1977).

Tinker v. *Des Moines Independent School District,* 393 U.S. 503, 89 S. Ct. 733 (1969).

Toll v. *Moreno,* 102 S. Ct. 2977 (1982).

Washington v. *Chrisman,* 455 U.S. 1, 102 S. Ct. 812 (1982).

Weise v. *Syracuse University,* 553 F. Supp. 675 (N.D.N.Y. 1982); 522 F.2d 397 (2d Cir. 1975).

White v. *Davis,* 553 P.2d 222 (Cal. 1975).

Whitlock v. *University of Denver,* 712 P.2d 1072 (Colo. App. 1985), 85 S.C. 391 (Colo. 1986).

Widmar v. *Vincent,* 102 S. Ct. 269 (1981).

Williams v. *De Kalb County,* 582 F.2d (5th Cir. 1978).

Wood v. *Strickland,* 348 F. Supp. 244 (1972), 95 S. Ct. 992, 420 U.S. 308 (1975).

Yost v. *TCU,* 362 S.W.2d 338 (Tex. Civ. App. 1962).

Zavala v. *Regents of the University of California,* 125 Cal. App. 3d 648, 178 Cal. Rptr. 185 (1981).

References

Abernathy, C. "Affirmative Action and the Rule of Bakke." *American Bar Association Journal,* 1978, *64,* 1233–1237.

Aiken, R. J. "Legal Liabilities in Higher Education: Their Scope and Management." *Journal of College and University Law,* 1976, *3* (2), 127–219.

Alexander, K., and Solomon, E. *College and University Law.* Charlottesville, Va.: Michie, 1972.

Barr, M. J., and Associates. *Student Services and the Law: A Handbook for Practitioners.* San Francisco: Jossey-Bass, 1988.

Buchanan, E. T., Jr., and Oliaro, P. M. "Law, Alcohol and Higher Education." in T. Goodale (ed.), *Alcohol and the College Student.* New Directions for Student Services, no. 35. San Francisco: Jossey-Bass, 1987.

Clague, M. "Suing the University 'Black Box' Under the Civil Rights Act of 1871." *Iowa Law Review,* 1976, *62,* 337–379.

"Developments in the Law, Section 1983 and Federalism." *Harvard Law Review,* 1977, *90* (6), 1135–1360.

Education Commission of the States. *Model State Legislation.* Report of the Task Force on Model State Legislation for Approval of Postsecondary Institutions and Authorizations to Grant Degrees, no. 39. Washington, D.C.: Education Commission of the States, 1973.

Hammond, E. H., and Shaffer, R. H. *The Legal Foundations of Student Personnel Services in Higher Education.* American College Personnel Association Monograph Series. Washington, D.C.: American Personnel and Guidance Association Press, 1978.

Hofstadter, R., and Smith, W. (eds.). *American Higher Education: A Documentary History.* Vol. 1. Chicago: University of Chicago Press, 1961.

Janes, S. S. "Administrative Practice: A Day-to-Day Guide to Legal Requirements." In M. J. Barr and Associates, *Student Services and the Law: A Handbook for Practitioners.* San Francisco: Jossey-Bass, 1988.

Kaplin, W. A. *The Law of Higher Education: Legal Implications of Administrative Decision Making.* San Francisco: Jossey-Bass, 1978.

Kaplin, W. A. *The Law of Higher Education: A Comprehensive Guide to Legal Implications of Administrative Decision Making.* (2nd ed.) San Francisco: Jossey-Bass, 1985.

Meyers, J. H. "Conduct of Enterprises." In A. Knowles (ed.), *Handbook of College and University Administration.* New York: McGraw-Hill, 1970.

Moos, M., and Rourke, F. *The Campus and the State.* Baltimore, Md.: Johns Hopkins University Press, 1959.

Owens, H. F. "Risk Management and Professional Responsibility." In H. F. Owens (ed.), *Risk Management and the Student Affairs Professional.* Columbus, Ohio: National Association of Student Personnel Administrators, 1984.

Rhode, S. "Use of Legal Counsel: Avoiding Problems." In M. J. Barr (ed.), *Student Affairs and the Law.* New Directions for Student Services, no. 22. San Francisco: Jossey-Bass, 1983.

Roth, R. A. "The Impact of Liquor Liability on Colleges and Universities." *Journal of College and University Law,* 1986, *13* (1), 45–64.

Schlie, B., and Grossman, P. *Employment Discrimination Law.* Washington, D.C.: Bureau of National Affairs, 1984.

Shur, G. S. "Contractual Relationships." In M. J. Barr (ed.), *Student Affairs and the Law.* New Directions for Student Services, no. 22. San Francisco: Jossey-Bass, 1983.

Steinbach, S. "Student Alcohol Abuse: Who Will Pay the Price?" *Educational Record,* 1985, *66* (4), 32–38.

Thompson, J. *Policymaking in American Public Education.* Englewood Cliffs, N.J.: Prentice-Hall, 1976.

U.S. House of Representatives. *Guidelines for Classroom Copying.* House Report no. 94–1476, 94th Cong., 2nd sess. Washington, D.C.: U.S. House of Representatives, 1976.

Wright, C. A. "The Constitution of the Campus." *Vanderbilt Law Review,* 1969, *22,* 1027–1088.

Part Two

Theoretical Bases
of the Profession

Part One of this book presented the philosophical ideas and historical trends that influence the student services profession. Ideas and thoughts alone, however, are not enough to guide our practice. One idea must be related to another in an organized and systematic fashion if we are to use these ideas in our day-to-day work. Although the models described in Part Three will help us organize our practice, we need theory as the conceptual cement for our ideas.

Organizing and ordering ideas into theory allows us to accomplish several important tasks. First, theory helps us to organize data, the useful facts that we collect. To use data in our programming efforts from year to year, it is best to store them systematically according to theoretical guidelines. If we have a theory that deals with young adults' social development, we can remember what we learned earlier about the social interaction of men and women if we relate those facts to our theory. Theory also helps us organize the facts we know about the differences between the adult learner and the traditional college-age student. This marriage between theory and facts should culminate in a better organization of those bits and pieces of information that we find valuable in our daily practice.

A second use of theory is to better explain to others what we do. A casual observer of our professional activities may have difficulty understanding what we do and, more importantly, why we do it. Theory not only helps explain what we are doing, but also defines our goals and thereby provides a rationale for why we engage in certain activities. When administrators and state legislators ask what we are doing and why we have initiated such services, we should be able to respond more clearly if we use our theory.

Theory also aids our everyday decisions. The details of providing student services raise innumerable questions regarding money, staffing, resources, goals, policies, and politics. Usually, each question will have multiple options, and rarely will there be a right or wrong decison. Value judgments can best be guided by theory, which supplies the boundaries of our options for action and describes the process for achieving our goals.

Finally, theory helps us to dream about the future. Rarely are student affairs professionals content with their current efforts: programs could be improved, costs could be cut, and students could achieve greater satisfaction if only we could design that ideal program or service—an ideal that should arise from theory. Examination of the ideal programs and services that theory suggests will also help us evaluate whether our dreams can become reality.

In the first edition of this book we felt that two areas of theory were important: theories of student development and theories of student-environment interaction. We still feel those two areas are important, but we have come to realize that a third theoretical orientation—theories of how our organizations operate—can broaden our thinking about how to help students.

Because we work with students daily, we must understand how they learn, grow, and develop. In Chapter Five, written by Robert F. Rodgers, three critical questions help us compare various theories of college student development. These theories should help us examine the kind of developmental phenomena that take place while students attend college, how the process of development unfolds, and how we might use theory in our student affairs practice. Each theory reviewed in this chapter provides a slightly different perspective for examining these three central issues. Taken together, these theories stimulate our thinking about the growth and development of college students.

We also realize the importance of a second major theoretical area—educational environments and their impact on students. We sense that certain learning environments have a greater impact on students than others and that we can use theory to design different kinds of environments to meet the needs of students with different kinds of learning characteristics. In Chapter Six, written by Lois Huebner, several major theories are examined with the goal of understanding how environments affect people, why matching people with environments is important, and how we can shift our focus of intervention from changing students to changing how students interact with their environments. Perhaps the most significant contribution of Chapter Six is the strategies that suggest ways to channel the impact of environments on people in maximally effective ways.

The first two chapters in this part focus on how students grow and develop and the beneficial ways in which students may interact with the college environment. In addition, we feel that understanding how our colleges and universities function as organizational entities will help us design more effective student services. We must work within our organizations to get things done. We have to compete for precious financial resources, and we have to convince others that what we do is important. Understanding the institutional context of our work place and how it operates can only help us accomplish our educational goals. Chapter Seven, written by George Kuh, not only reviews a number of traditional approaches to thinking about our organizations but also presents new and emerging conceptual models that force us to look at how our institutions really work. These new and emerging models broaden our vision and provide new directions for alternative ways to help students.

Chapter Five

Student Development

Robert F. Rodgers

Robert Brown, in *Student Development in Tomorrow's Higher Education: A Return to the Academy,* expressed optimism that student affairs was entering a new era. He wrote: "There are signs that theory and research are beginning to converge and that in the future those involved in student development will not only understand student development, but also will be able to specify the conditions necessary to promote positive student development" (Brown, 1972, p. 46). The turning point that Brown thought was approaching had been long in coming. Willey, twenty-three years earlier, had criticized student personnel for not basing their work on "scientific knowledge" and had characterized student affairs staff as being guided by "general insight," "good intentions," and "sympathy" (1949, pp. 7–12). Fourteen years after Brown's hopeful prediction, Bloland (1986b) questioned whether theory was being used to shape practice, even in light of available theories and approaches. He wrote, "In the real world, student affairs staff are carrying out their traditional functions and many new ones but in traditional ways and with staff who still are not well schooled in student development or even in higher education. . . . Many entry-level and not a few seasoned professionals know little of student development theory or practice" (Bloland, 1986a, p. 1). Bloland expressed a common concern that the gap between theory and practice remains large.

This gap can be closed only when student affairs staff obtain and internalize an in-depth knowledge of college student development. Such knowledge is a necessary but not a sufficient condition for using theory in one's practice. Hence, the purpose of this chapter is to make a case for using developmental theory in designing and conducting student affairs practice. First, we will summarize some of the historical, philosophical, and personal issues involved in deciding whether or not to use student development as an approach to student affairs practice. Second, selected formal theories of college student development will be reviewed and related to professional practice.

Ideological History of the Purposes of Higher Education

Higher education in the United States derives its major purposes from three traditions. From the English residential liberal arts tradition, we inherit the idea that the fundamental purpose of higher education is the well-rounded development of college students. This tradition assumes that students are in the process of discovering and deciding who they are and what they want from their collegiate experiences and that the goal of the college is to help this process in prescribed ways, usually by teaching the liberal arts. The focuses are the liberal arts, and the growth of the person and these focuses dictate the primary roles and activities of faculty and staff.

From German universities, we inherit the idea that the fundamental purpose of higher education is to advance knowledge through research and scholarship. The "disinterested pursuit of truth through original investigation" (Brubacher and Rudy, 1968, p. 175) and the preparation of the next generation of researchers, not the well-rounded development of students, are the purposes of higher education. The means to these ends is the in-depth and research-oriented study of specialties in the arts and sciences, law, theology, and medicine. The focus is on ideas and theories, not persons. This paradigm assumes students know who they are and what they want from their education, and that what they want is to become scholars or research specialists. Faculty, in turn, are not concerned primarily with a student's personal growth, moral character, or liberal studies. Faculty are expected to become specialized researchers who push back the frontiers of knowledge. If any attention is paid to well-rounded development, it might be by staff hired to do this auxiliary task.

The United States has contributed its own paradigm of higher education. In this land-grant tradition, the fundamental purpose of higher education is vocational and professional preparation. Colleges and universities are to supply qualified personnel in order to meet the human resource needs of society. The means to this end, therefore, is study in various vocational, technical, and professional fields. The United States, in fact, has added schools of business, education, agriculture, engineering, social work, home economics, nursing, dentistry, optometry, veterinary medicine, and allied medical professions to the university; these fields are often taught in separate schools in other parts of the world. The focus is on skills and competencies, and this tradition assumes that the purpose of higher education is to help students make a mature career choice. Students in colleges and universities must know or be helped to know who they are and what they want out of a career as soon as possible. Qualified staff are needed to help them.

Like higher education, student affairs in colleges and universities is also derived from three major historical paradigms. These may be called in loco parentis, student services, and student development. In loco parentis grew out of our colonial history, when the youth of students (most of whom were between thirteen and sixteen) and prevailing theological assumptions about human nature caused educators to emphasize control of student behavior. The goal of this paradigm is to teach students to control their sinful nature and behave according to prescribed moral values. Faculty act in place of, and as if they were, parents; students are their "children." Faculty seek to inculcate prescribed moral values and to set goals and plan appropriate activities for students, as well as to teach classes. This paradigm is alive and well today, although these parental roles are assumed by staff as well as faculty.

Student services is the name given to a model in which the social and behavioral sciences are used to help troubled students with remedial services and to provide other services and programs that students want as consumers. The services and programs must be affordable and compatible, or at least not in conflict, with the educational mission of the institution. In this model, development per se is not the central focus, although many of the services provided may facilitate maturation. Rather, student services supplement the main enterprise, which is the academic program. The academic program, of course, is often understood in terms of the German or American paradigms. This may well be the dominant model in student affairs today.

Student development focuses on using formal theories of individual and group development in designing environments that help college students learn and develop. Formal theories provide the general and specific criteria for designing physical environments, programs, policies, and services that are appropriate for persons at different developmental levels. The general design criteria are applicable across domains—that is, they are applicable to social, cultural, athletic, spiritual, physical, and academic environments—while specific criteria focus on only one aspect of development or type of environment. Thus, development is defined by scientific theories rather than by theological or philosophical propositions of the colonial period of our history, and these scientific theories and student affairs practice are linked together. The hypothesis is that both learning and developmental outcomes will improve as a result of the linkage.

Advocates of the student development paradigm also assert that formal theories of individual and group development form a knowledge base applicable in principle to all areas of student affairs. This assertion rests on three propositions. First, it assumes that colleges and universities have development as one of their primary goals. Hence, all areas of student affairs, regardless of the particular competencies required in each specialty, should use developmental perspectives in implementing their programs and services, just as a history professor should use them in order to teach better (Widick and Simpson, 1978). Second, it assumes that all areas within student affairs should design programs and services that will help student learning and development. Third, it assumes that the use of formal theories in the process of environmental design will result in better learning and developmental outcomes. While there is support for the second and third propositions, the first is widely debated. From the German perspective, for example, it is possible to reject well-rounded development as a primary goal and to emphasize the student services paradigm and intellectual development. Well-rounded development would be seen as a secondary enterprise, auxiliary to the main purpose of higher education.

Theories of College Student Development

There are at least four kinds of developmental theory (Knefelkamp, Widick, and Parker, 1978; Rodgers, 1980) that may be of use to student affairs professionals: psychosocial theory, cognitive-structural theory, person-environment interaction theory, and typological theory. The term *psychosocial* refers to the developmental issues or tasks and life events that occur throughout the life span, as well as to a person's pattern of responses to issues and adaptations to events. *Cognitive-structural* refers to the sequence of meaning-making structures through which people perceive, organize, and reason about their experiences. *Person-environment interaction* refers to various conceptualizations of the college student and the college environment and the degree of congruence that occurs when they interact. *Typological* refers to phenomena—such as cognitive style, temperament, personality type, and patterns of socialization—that may cause individual variations in the processes and patterns of outcomes in development. Since person-environment interaction theories are covered in depth elsewhere in this book, this chapter will review the other three kinds of theories in light of the following questions:

1. What kind of developmental phenomena does the theory describe? What do these phenomena look like during the college years? To what degree are there gender-related and cultural differences and similarities?
2. How do the processes of development take place? How does developmental change occur?
3. What are some of the uses of the theory for student affairs practice?

Psychosocial Theories

The foundations of psychosocial developmental research were laid by Jung (1954, 1961, 1969, 1971), Buhler and Massarik (1968), Erikson (1950, 1968), Havighurst (1948), and Sanford (1956, 1962a, 1962b). In the United States, Jung and Erikson have been especially influential, while Sanford has addressed student affairs most directly. In contrast to most psychologists of their time, these theorists have argued that human development continues throughout the life span and that a basic underlying psychosocial structure guides this development.

Psychosocial theories attempt to describe the developmental tasks that occupy adults at different phases or times in the life span. The phases, or stages, are initiated by a convergence of biological and psychological changes within the person and environmental demands that represent a given culture's social norms and roles for a given age range. The nature of the convergence defines the issues or tasks that need to be resolved during each stage of life. The stages and their tasks tend to occur in sequence; however, the existence and order of the stages and tasks can vary owing to cultural and gender-related influences. How people resolve or fail to resolve the tasks of a given stage has a cumulative effect on their ability to resolve the tasks of future stages. Erikson's theory illustrates these concepts.

Erikson. Erik Erikson (1950, 1968) regarded psychosocial development as *epigenetic;* that is, there is an underlying structure to development throughout the life span. This structure unfolds in a series of predictable stages. His epigenetic principle states that "anything that grows has a ground plan, and that out of this ground plan the parts arise, each part having its time of special ascendency, until all parts have arisen to form a functioning whole" (Erikson, 1968, p. 92). Development, therefore, occurs due to this epigenetic unfolding. Internal changes, both biological and psychological, interact with environmental roles and other cultural expectations to initiate the changes. Early and late in life, biological changes dominate the initiation of change. During midlife, psychological and environmental factors are more influential. Each stage is characterized by an issue or task that is qualitatively different from the issues or tasks of other stages. The resolution of the issue is conceptualized as one of two opposed outcomes. These polar outcomes and the approximate age ranges of the stages are summarized in Table 1.

Table 1. Polar Outcomes and Age Ranges
of Erikson's Developmental Stages.

Polar Outcome			Age Range
Basic Trust	vs.	Mistrust	Birth to 2 years
Autonomy	vs.	Shame, Doubt	3 to 6 years
Initiative	vs.	Guilt	6 to 10 years
Industry	vs.	Inferiority	10 to 14 years
Identity	vs.	Role Confusion	14 to 20 years
Intimacy	vs.	Isolation	20 to 40 years
Generativity	vs.	Stagnation	40 to 65 years
Integrity	vs.	Despair	65 + years

Source: Rodgers, R. F. "Theories of Adult Development: Research Status and Counseling Implications." In S. D. Brown and R. W. Lent (eds.), *Handbook of Counseling Psychology.* New York: Wiley, © 1984.

Students at the traditional age for college are in the stage of identity versus role confusion. From puberty until about age twenty, young adults face identity issues that require them to experiment with roles and life-styles, make choices and experience the consequences, identify their talents, experience meaningful achievement, and find meaning in their lives. A person who has these experiences and thereby achieves an inner sense of identity is prepared to deal with the issues of the next stage, intimacy versus isolation. Since intimacy issues occur at their assigned time regardless, the person who has not resolved the issue of identity is handicapped in, if not prevented from, developing the capacity for mature intimacy. Developing the capacity for intimacy is a prerequisite for resolving the issues of generativity versus stagnation, which begin in the early forties. Generativity is characterized as learning to be a caring, teaching, contributing member of one's society. Finally, if identity, intimacy, and generativity have been resolved in satisfactory ways, people are prepared for the final stage, integrity versus despair. If people can look back on their lives and find achievement, meaning, and integrity, the wisdom of their later years may be integrated into a sense of satisfaction with life. If not, they may experience disgust, despair, and a deep feeling that they have been passed by.

Psychosocial theories such as Erikson's are valuable to student affairs because they identify the content of the developmental issues or tasks generally relevant for persons at different points in the life span. Traditional-aged college students—at least the males—are preoccupied with issues of identity and need programs and services that assist them with these issues. The problem with Erikson's theory, however, is that his conceptualizations are so broad that it is difficult to find the specificity needed to ground one's practice in his theory. In addition, his work may be biased in favor of the experience of males; it may have serious limitations if used with women students. Hence, we must turn to other psychosocial theories for the specificity and gender balance needed for student affairs practice.

Chickering. The psychosocial theory most useful to student affairs is that of Arthur Chickering. His theory, modified by recent ethnic and gender research, has endured as a work worthy of in-depth study and use. Chickering's (1969) theory of college student development provides the specifics that Erikson's lacks. It elaborates on Erikson's stage of identity, providing details on the vectors or tasks that make up the content of the three broad issues of identity. These issues are:

1. Career development: Who am I? What am I to become?
2. Defining one's sexuality and initiating the development of the capacity for intimacy: Whom am I to love? What does mature love mean anyway?
3. Finding and integrating an adult philosophy of life, morality, and values: What am I to believe? Am I to accept my heritage or do I have to decide what I am really going to stand for?

For student affairs, Chickering's conceptualizations of developmental vectors or tasks can provide a blueprint for program plan-

ning and evaluation. A student union program board planning
future programming efforts, for example, must ask, what content would be developmentally appropriate for freshmen? For
seniors? What do career, sexuality, and philosophy of life look
like for freshmen and for seniors?

Chickering's vectors or tasks provide a response to such
questions. His summary of psychosocial research on college
students indicates that most freshmen are attempting to resolve
three vectors: competence, managing emotions, and developing autonomy. Seniors, on the other hand, are resolving four
different vectors: establishing identity, freeing interpersonal relationships, developing purpose, and establishing integrity. Each
of these vectors is made up of a series of contents, or tasks, and
associated processes. The contents make up the developmental
challenges to be mastered; the processes describe how the tasks
are resolved and their chronological relationships with one
another. Psychosocial tasks are not resolved suddenly. Their
mastery takes place after repeated exposure to appropriate
developmental environments. It may take one or more years
to resolve a single vector.

As we examine Chickering's theory, the vectors will be
summarized and one developmental task for freshmen and one
for seniors will be examined in more depth. These tasks will
then be used to illustrate different programming for freshmen
and seniors. Space does not permit an in-depth reconstruction
of all the vectors; however, if staff members hope to use Chickering to inform their practice, they must take the time to understand the complexity of each vector and its relationship to the
others (Rodgers, 1983).

The first three vectors—competence, managing emotions,
and developing autonomy—preoccupy most students as they
enter college. The positive resolution of these vectors seems to
be a prerequisite for resolving the fourth vector, establishing
identity. The first three vectors represent finding oneself—
determining one's capabilities, integrating self-control and interdependence, and finding sexual-social expression—and finding
that one can negotiate and be competent within the college's
academic and social environments. Partial resolution of these

issues provides the raw material for establishing one's first adult identity, which involves acceptance of body and appearance, integration and acceptance of one's sexuality, and determination of a life-style. Accepting and integrating one's body and appearance, sexuality, and life-style, in turn, provide the necessary framework for juniors, seniors, and graduate students to work on tasks that make up what Levinson (1978) calls one's initial adult life structure. Life structure is made up of the pattern and nature of one's vocational commitment (developing purpose), capacity for intimacy and associated mature roles as lover, friend, and colleague (freeing interpersonal relationships), and integration of and behavior consistent with a set of self-determined values (developing integrity).

The first vector that freshmen must resolve is that of developing competence. Competence is divided into three parts: intellectual competence, physical-manual competence, and social-interpersonal competence. If we focus on intellectual competence, we find that entering college students are preoccupied with how well they will perform academically. This preoccupation involves exploration of one's competencies, knowledge, academic skill, and unrecognized potential, as well as exploration of the intellectual demands of various disciplines and majors. Ultimately, these explorations culminate in either selecting a compatible major or leaving school.

Paraprofessionals such as resident advisers have roles and functions that are appropriate to this vector. For example, resident advisers can attend to the development of intellectual competence by monitoring freshman students' performance on initial midterm examinations, being aware of how much or how little the students study, and expressing concern or encouragement for those who have performed poorly or who seldom study. Resident advisers should also discuss their perceptions with the professional staff since students may need to be referred to the career or learning resources center. Resident advisers can help establish, administer, and refer students to a tutoring service; professional staff should refer students to other professional agencies as needed.

Counseling and career center staff also have roles and functions that are developmentally appropriate to this vector. For example, they can design career exploration workshops or credit classes for freshmen that emphasize exploration of knowledge levels, academic skill levels, known competencies, and hidden potential. The workshops and classes can include environmental exploration of the intellectual demands of selected disciplines and majors. The focus is on differentiating the self and academic disciplines and possible majors, not on integration or making firm commitments. The freshmen explore majors and disciplines but not careers and vocations per se. The developmental goal is a tentative choice of a major course of study compatible with the self, not commitment to a career.

Most college juniors, many seniors, and many graduates are involved in resolving the issue of developing purpose. This vector involves both differentiation and integration tasks. It involves exploring careers and vocations, narrowing toward a commitment to one vocation and career, and finding outlets for other talents in avocational interests. These tasks require the student to know his or her competencies, to be self-regulating, and to have established a consistent identity or sense of self. The problem is that everyone can follow any one of several careers or vocations. How does one decide? How does one give up what one might have been? One's values (integrity) and life-style (identity) often provide the basis for narrowing down and making commitments.

Counseling center staff can use the content of these vectors as a basis for designing a career workshop or class for seniors that is different from the workshop for freshmen. A single design cannot serve both groups. The developmental tasks of seniors require a design that allows students to finish exploring career and vocational areas (not majors) and to narrow toward an initial commitment to a vocational area and work setting. Chickering's vectors suggest that an exploration of mature, internalized values and even spiritual and life-style issues often helps students narrow down and make commitments. It also may be necessary to help students literally grieve over what they give up, at least for a time, as they make these commitments. Finally, if two students have made a commitment to each other, it may be important to design a version of the workshop or course in which the couple explores these issues together. Mutual exploration reinforces interdependent relationships and interdependent decision making.

To sum up, freshmen working on competence and seniors working on purpose need different career development workshops. The contents of their tasks are different, although both broadly relate to career development. Having a freshman participate in a purpose workshop or a senior in a competence workshop would be developmentally questionable. Hence, offering only one version of a career workshop for all students achieves less than is possible and also is questionable professionally.

Chickering discusses developmental change in terms of a series of differentiations and integrations associated with the vectors and challenges and supports appropriate to the tasks within the vectors. It is important not to offer challenges or supports that are behind or too far ahead of the student's developmental level (Sanford, 1967). Chickering also relates global environmental conditions to the resolution of vectors. These environmental conditions include clear and consistent goals, organizational size, curriculum design and teaching strategies, classroom evaluation, residence hall design and programs, interactions between students and faculty and staff, and the influence of peer culture.

Chickering's theory is based on his study of men and women at thirteen liberal arts colleges and all the research on the psychosocial development of college students that was available at the time. In some cases, his generalizations need to be differentiated for men and women. For example, women tend to integrate the management of emotions ahead of men, while men tend to achieve autonomy ahead of women (Straub, 1987; Straub and Rodgers, 1986). Further, there is some evidence that black students' development also deviates somewhat from Chickering's descriptions on some vectors (Branch-Simpson, 1984). For example, black students in our culture may achieve autonomy with less alienation and less need to distance themselves from their families of origin than white students. Hence, the family as well as the college environment may have to be considered in viewing the psychosocial development of black students.

As adults become more and more numerous on college campuses, the need grows to understand and use psychosocial theories that go beyond the stage of identity. Levinson (1978), Havighurst (1953), Chickering and Havighurst (1981), Neugarten

(1976), and many others have published theories and research that meet this need. Space limitations do not allow these theories to be reviewed; however, staff who work with adults should investigate this literature widely and in depth (see Rodgers, 1984).

Cognitive-Structural Theories

The foundations of cognitive-structural development were laid by Piaget (Inhelder and Piaget, 1958; Piaget, 1948, 1952, 1954), who defined the basic concepts and assumptions of this family of thought, and Kohlberg (1981, 1984), who refined and extended Piaget's work on moral development. Both Kohlberg's (1981, 1984) and Perry's (1970) works have been used extensively in college teaching and student affairs, while the recent theories of Gilligan (1982a), Kegan (1979, 1982), and Kitchener and King (1981, 1985) also have broadened and deepened our understanding of this kind of development.

Cognitive-structural theories attempt to describe the development of how we make sense or meaning of our experience with the world. Their concern is with the structure of meaning-making rather than the content of the meaning itself. Structures, therefore, are the tacit assumptions by which we make meaning of our experience. They influence what we perceive, how we organize what we perceive, and how we evaluate and make decisions on those perceptions. Cognitive-structural theories attempt to describe the stages of the development of meaning-making in various domains of our experience.

Both psychosocial and cognitive-structural theories use the concept of stages; however, the meaning of the concept is different in the two schools of thought. In psychosocial development, stages are sequential but both the order of appearance and the nature of the stages may be influenced by cultural experiences. Cognitive-structural stages seem to follow invariant sequences that are not defined by culture. Psychosocial stages are cumulative; the accomplishment of one stage affects one's ability to resolve subsequent stages. Cognitive-structural stages are hierarchical and each successive stage incorporates the functional parts of the previous stages. Finally, people are conscious of their psychosocial preoccupations during each stage, but one's highest cognitive-structural stage is largely unconscious; we are our highest stage of making meaning.

Generally, cognitive-structural theories postulate that developmental change results from cognitive conflict. That is, a person's current way of making meaning is challenged, perhaps in a college classroom or a residence hall discussion, by different and structurally more complex ways of making meaning. Cognitive conflict results and this conflict often leads to confusion and disequilibrium. Developmental change therefore comes from learning how to deal with the confusion and disequilibrium.

When faced with confusion and disequilibrium, cognitive-structural psychologists postulate, a person may assimilate or accommodate in order to deal with the situation. If a person assimilates, the conflict and confusion are handled by forcing the challenge to fit into the person's current way of making meaning. The current structure is not changed. Instead, conflict and confusion are eliminated by interpreting the challenge in terms of current ways of making meaning and explaining it away. If a person accommodates, the conflict and confusion are resolved by beginning the process of changing the current way of making meaning to accommodate the challenge. Accommodation, therefore, is the name of the process of transition from one stage to a new stage of meaning-making. It is important to note, however, that accommodations happen only when the student is ready to receive the challenge and when the environment provides appropriate challenges repeatedly.

What, then, are appropriate challenges? Why do some environmental events or conflicts facilitate change and others result in assimilation? Briefly, environmental challenges are more likely to facilitate an accommodation when four conditions are met. First, if the environmental challenge is about issues that are important to the individual person, accommodation is more likely. Thus, there is an affective or involvement element in cognitive-structural development. Unless the person has an affective investment in the issue, accommodation is unlikely. Second, if the environmental challenge is presented one stage above a person's current way of making meaning, accommodation is facilitated. If the challenge is two or more stages above the person's level, assimilation is usually the outcome. People apparently do not understand and cannot make meaning of challenges more than one stage above their current way of making meaning. Third, other aspects of personality, such as personality type, also can facilitate or hinder assimilation or accommodation. In principle, if challenges are presented in ways consistent with one's personality type, accommodation is facilitated. Finally, cognitive-structural research suggests that environmental challenges will have more impact if they are processed in an atmosphere of support and feedback as soon as possible after the challenge (Blocher, 1978). Many experiences in our lives lose their developmental and learning impact because we do not take the time to reflect on their meaning. Hence, if a student affairs staff member is attempting to facilitate cognitive structural development, he or she will try to provide an opportunity for students to process environmental challenges in an atmosphere of support and reflection.

Kohlberg. Since the 1950s, Lawrence Kohlberg has been developing and refining a theory of moral development built on Piaget's work. His theory attempts to describe justice reasoning—how people reason about what they should do when faced with a moral dilemma. In order to understand Kohlberg's theory and its use in higher education, it is important not to confuse the structure of reasoning with the content of the issues involved or a particular course of action. Kohlberg's theory concerns the structures of meaning that define what one should do, not the content; different contents—different solutions to a dilemma—can be obtained with the same structure of reasoning. For example, student A observes student B, who lives in A's residence unit, stealing books from the unit's study lounge. Student A must consider whether to report student B to residence hall authorities. A knows that B has severe financial problems because of the recent death of B's father. A also knows that B is an honors student and is usually a good citizen. Finally, B is A's good friend. Student A may reason about the situation in either of the following ways:

1. Student B is my friend. You don't report friends. Besides, B is usually a good citizen and only took the books because of an urgent need for money. I should make an exception in this case. I will not report my friend B.
2. Even though B is my friend, so are the rest of the people on the floor. We're a group. B stole from our group, not some other floor! What will the group think of me if I do not report B? I have to remain a loyal member of the group and report B.

The actual decisions that result from these two paths of reasoning are different. The structure of the reasoning, however, is the same. In this way of making meaning one should live up to what is expected by one's primary social group; it is important to be seen as a good person by one's peers and oneself. Both illustrations are examples of Kohlberg's third stage of moral development, the morality of interpersonally shared norms (Kohlberg, 1984). The social perspective of this stage is the perspective of an individual in relationship with certain other individuals; it does not consider a generalized system perspective (Kohlberg's fourth stage), which is an abstraction beyond specific groups' expectations. Hence, different conclusions can be obtained from the same situation using the same reasoning structure. It is the structure of making moral judgments that is the focus of Kohlberg's work.

Kohlberg (1984) derives his justice reasoning stages from a longitudinal study of eighty-four males over a twenty-year period and cross-section studies of an international sample of urban and rural persons from different cultures. The theory distinguishes three levels of moral development—preconventional, conventional, and postconventional—and two stages of reasoning within each level. A summary follows in Tables 2, 3, and 4.

Kohlberg not only has sought to build a theory of moral justice reasoning, he also has designed educational programs in order to facilitate moral development. His educational models require that a moral dilemma, real or hypothetical, be encountered by students and discussed, with arguments at various stages challenging the adequacy of reasoning at lower stages (see Galbraith and Jones, 1976; Blatt and Kohlberg, 1975; Straub and Rodgers, 1978). In one-on-one or group formats, once a dilemma has been presented and defined, the facilitator (for example, a student affairs judicial officer) should attempt to start the dialogue of challenges and rebuttal at the lowest stage of reasoning presented by an individual or a member of a group and work upward through the stages in sequence.

For example, Student B might defend his stealing of books from the residence unit lounge with a Stage 2 argument, citing the immediate need created by his father's death. He might also mention his history of and belief in good behavior among a group of friends and describe this one slip as understandable, if not justified—a Stage 3 defense. The judicial officer can challenge the Stage 2 justification at the same level by arguing that the needs of those from whom B stole books are just as pressing as those of B himself. She can then challenge the Stage 2 justification with a Stage 3 position by suggesting that B has responsibilities to his residence unit friends regardless of his immediate pressing need. Finally, she can make the argument from Stage 4 that a community cannot function and uphold the rights of all members if exceptions to the rules are made for individual circumstances. Besides, the university has social agencies to meet such financial needs; a responsible citizen uses the social services of the university and does not break the rules even in emergencies. The Stage 3 defense similarly could be challenged at Stages 3 and 4.

Galbraith and Jones (1976) have designed group processes that attempt to maximize the interaction of the natural stage diversity in a group in order to facilitate challenges from one stage above. The facilitator guides the steps in the process and may provide such challenges himself. Kohlberg (Hickey and Scharf, 1980; Higgins, Power, and Kohlberg, 1984; Ignelsi, 1988) has also experimented with "just communities" as an educational model. Briefly, a just community is a group with an ongoing life (such as a student government group) that governs

Table 2. Kohlberg's Preconventional Stages of Moral Reasoning.

	Stage 1: Naive Moral Realism	Stage 2: Morality of Concrete Individual Needs
What is just?	Justice is defined by self-centered perspective; other perspectives do not exist. Justice is inherent in events. What one should do is self-evident and requires no justification beyond a label. Good happens to those who are right; bad happens to those who are wrong.	Justice is defined from the perspective of a particular individual and an awareness that each person pursues his or her self-interest and that the self-interests of two people may be in conflict. What is right and just is maximizing one's needs and desires and minimizing negative consequences. The focus is on concrete needs, not intentions.
Norms	There are inherent absolute categories of right and wrong for actions and people.	There are no fixed norms for balancing mutual exchange. One gets what one can to maximize meeting one's concrete needs.
Reciprocity (mutual exchange)	Give same for same, an eye for an eye.	One meets one's needs by striking mutual exchange agreements, and it is fair to bargain to try to get the exchange to go in one's favor. Instrumental exchange is emphasized.
Correction	Punishment follows automatically as a consequence of a transgression.	One recognizes that one may modify one's needs in light of another's specific needs or intentions.

Note: Interested readers should consult Appendix A in Kohlberg, 1984, for additional information regarding these stages.
Source: Adapted from Kohlberg, 1984.

Table 3. Kohlberg's Conventional Stages of Moral Reasoning.

	Stage 3: Morality of Interpersonally Shared Norms	Stage 4: Morality of the Codes and Procedures of a Social System
What is just?	Justice is defined by an integration of individual perspectives into a general social agreement on what a good member of society should do; this may not always be in accord with an individual's self-interest. Justice is defined by living up to the shared norms of people in relationship with each other. Justice is primarily focused on being a good group member. Social approval and loyalty are very important.	Justice is defined from an abstract, generalized perspective and is the same for any member of a social system—regardless of whether one is in personal relationship with him or her. A social system is just if it has a consistent set of codes (laws) and procedures that are impartially applied to members. Formal codes, roles, procedures, and rules are used to mediate conflicts and promote the common good of the social system as a whole. Individuals who reason using Stage 6 cannot adjudicate a social system.
Norms	Norms are defined by the expectations shared by people in relationship; they apply only to group members. Their purpose is to maintain trust, loyalty, and care among members.	Norms must promote social cooperation and contributions to social systems and avoid disorder and disagreement.
Reciprocity (mutual exchange)	Being in a group or relationship gives members a sense of belonging, loyalty, identity, trust, and care; members owe the group these things in return.	How individual and society (collective) are linked is often expressed as a balance between individual action and society's standards.
Correction	Corrective action is applied by degrees; it depends on the degree to which one's motives were "bad" or to which one did not behave as a "good" person should.	Laws, roles, and procedures protect society through deterrence; this is the basis for corrective action. One must pay one's debt for breaking society's laws and norms.

Note: Interested readers should consult Appendix A in Kohlberg, 1984, for additional information regarding these stages.

Table 4. Kohlberg's Postconventional Stages of Moral Reasoning.

	Stage 5: Morality of Human Rights and Social Welfare	Stage 6: Morality of Universal, Reversible General Ethical Principles
What is just?	Justice is defined from a perspective prior to society and from the perspective of a rational moral agent who is aware of universal values and rights that anyone would choose to build a moral society. These universal rights and values are used to judge societies and institutions and their laws or procedures. Just societies must be freely entered, protect universal rights, and promote welfare of all members. The primary focus is on human rights and the social welfare of all members. Members are obliged to uphold universal human rights even when these are in conflict with society's laws. Human rights protect minorities. Social welfare means rule-utilitarianism and evaluations are made in terms of the long run.	Justice is defined from a perspective prior to society and by the moral point of view that ideally all should take freely and autonomously. The moral point of view generally means equal consideration of the claims of every person affected by a situation. Procedures should ensure fairness, impartiality, reversibility in role taking. Many concrete interpretations or formalized procedures are consistent with the above.
Norms	Norms maximize and protect human rights and social welfare through contractual agreements entered into freely.	Norms are manifest in attitudes of care and respect for persons; persons are not regarded as means for achieving ends no matter how lofty, such as "the good of society," or even human survival. Norms are manifest as general principles and not as rules or rights; they apply to all persons in all situations and can override social rights of Stage 5.

		Some general principles are respect for personality, action to benefit all involved, universal human care (agape), maximum liberty consistent with liberty of others, fair distribution of assets.
		These principles can be expressed in the language of justice or the language of care and responsibility, as well as in terms like *intrinsic worth, dignity of all persons,* and *equality.*
		Completely reversible mutual role taking, especially considering least powerful person in a moral dilemma.
		Strong or socially useful persons are not favored.
		Correction is not retribution.
		Incarceration may be needed to protect the life, rights, or welfare of others, but it is not used to punish immorality.
Reciprocity (mutual exchange)	Focus is on equivalence in contracts entered into freely.	
Correction	Correction is not retribution.	
	Social justice is obtained by interpreting laws and agreements in terms of human rights.	

Note: Interested readers should consult Appendix A in Kohlberg, 1984, for additional information regarding these stages.

itself through Kohlberg's version of participatory democracy. Just communities use moral discussion groups to establish a sense of community, goals, expectations, and rules of conduct; they also deal with grievances in community forums. Kohlberg's just community ideas have been tested in high schools, prisons, and college residence halls, and there is some evidence to support the effectiveness of this approach. Governance, cross-cultural enhancement, and residence life are areas where higher education especially can use Kohlberg's ideas.

In addition to these formal one-on-one and group interventions, there are many other opportunities to facilitate students' encounters with moral decisions. These occur in the day-to-day interactions between students and staff. Students often discuss issues such as sexual conduct, the use of illegal substances, abortion, sexual orientation, and racial issues among themselves and sometimes with staff. These discussions are opportunities to use Kohlberg's ideas. In order to use any of Kohlberg's educational models, student affairs staff must have internalized Kohlberg's theory to the point where they can roughly assess a student's arguments by ear. They must know how to use and process structured experiences such as those defined by Galbraith and Jones (1976). Finally, they must be able to facilitate moral dialogue in one-on-one and informed group discussions. In short, both moral development knowledge and skills must be internalized if one is to be a moral development educator.

Gilligan. Carol Gilligan's (1982a) work on the development of women grew out of her work with Kohlberg's theory. While studying the relationship between moral reasoning and moral behavior with women who were involved in a real rather than hypothetical dilemma concerning abortion, Gilligan discovered a phenomenon she called "the different voice." Many women in her study appeared to reason in ways that had different basic assumptions from those of Kohlberg's men. She called this different way of reasoning the Care and Responsibility voice and labeled Kohlberg's theory the Justice voice.

In reasoning about moral dilemmas, the Care voice emphasizes the connection between self and others and sees others in their own specific situations (Lyons, 1981). Care is concerned with understanding what others need and with responding to others on their terms, not our own. Moral problems are usually seen in terms of issues or relationships and are resolved through actions of Care. Maintaining or restoring interdependent relationships is emphasized along with promoting the welfare of others and preventing physical or psychological harm.

In contrast, the Justice voice emphasizes effects on the self rather than others. This voice sees others in terms of how we would like to be seen by them. Justice rests upon principles of fairness and relationships of reciprocity rather than relationships of care. Moral problems are often analyzed in terms of issues and conflicting claims among competing individuals. These claims need to be fairly and objectively adjudicated by impartial rules or principles of fairness. Obligation and duty are emphasized along with the impartial rules and principles of justice. The voices can be compared thus:

Justice	Care
autonomy	interdependence
reciprocity	responsiveness
rational	affective and esthetic
seeing a situation as if one were in it oneself	seeing a situation as the other sees it
"stepping back" from a situation	"entering into" a situation
mediating conflict, making decisions, and solving problems by using fair rules	mediating conflict, making decisions, and solving problems through a concern for caring for others and alleviating their burdens, focusing on the interdependence of persons

Gilligan is careful to point out that all people, both men and women, use both voices; however, individuals prefer one voice to the other and use that one more often. In her research, about 70 percent of all women preferred the Care voice, and about 70 percent of all men preferred the Justice voice. Some women, however, preferred Justice and some men preferred Care. Since the majority of each sex prefers the same voice, there may be a gender bias built into any theory whose constructs and relationships among constructs are derived from research on only one sex. Hence, Gilligan argues that since Kohlberg's theory is based on an exclusively male sample, his work may have a Justice-voice bias and may systematically rate Care-voice persons (most women and some men) lower than Justice-voice persons (most men and some women) in moral development. In fact, she argues, adult women have been rated one stage lower than men in conventional stages of development.

Gilligan argues that neither voice is better than the other; they are merely different. They stand in tension whenever a moral dilemma occurs. They offer complementary sets of assumptions for analyzing what we ought to do. Sometimes Justice may benefit from the connectedness of Care, and sometimes Care may benefit from the objective fairness of Justice.

Kohlberg has accepted some of Gilligan's arguments and rejected others. He claims that his justice reasoning stages are universal and are applicable to both men and women. He sees no grounds for postulating two separate structures of moral reasoning. Instead, he argues (1984) that there is one structure with two styles of making meaning within it. His substage A corresponds roughly to Gilligan's Care voice and his substage B to the Justice voice. He also claims that research (Walker, 1984; Gibbs, Arnold, and Burkhardt, 1984; Denny, 1988) does not support the conclusion that men systematically score higher than women if educational experiences are held constant. Only when educational levels are not controlled have previous studies revealed a gender difference in outcomes. On the other hand, Gilligan (1986; Haan, 1985; Baumrind, 1986) indicates that in two recent studies where education was controlled men scored higher than women on Kohlberg's measure of moral development.

Hence, there are unsettled theoretical issues between Kohlberg and Gilligan. Are there two structures for making meaning in moral situations, or is there only one structure and two stylistic (nonstructural) ways of expressing it? Current research has not yet clarified these issues. Nevertheless, Gilligan's work has broad implications for practice in student affairs.

Whether stylistic or structural, the systematic differences between the Justice and Care voices indicate that many student affairs programs may need reexamination. These differences have led Gilligan (1982a, 1982b; Johnston, 1985) to postulate that there may well be two ways of expressing oneself in a relationship, two ways of reasoning about moral dilemmas, two ways of developing identity during college, two ways of resolving psychosocial tasks throughout the life span, and two ways of solving problems, making decisions, and resolving conflict. If one of these voices goes uneducated owing to the fact that classrooms and student affairs programs are designed primarily for the Justice voice, the historic goal (American Council on Education, 1937, 1949) of student affairs—the well-rounded, holistic development of college students—cannot be realized.

Student affairs programs and services should serve both voices. For example, in attempting to resolve roommate conflicts in a college residence hall (Rodgers, 1983), staff members are often taught to meet with both parties in the staff member's room in order to negotiate and attempt to resolve their differences. The hoped-for outcome usually is either the control or the resolution of the conflict (Walton, 1969; Rodgers, 1983). Often a new agreement for living together is expressed in a written contract. *Conflicting issues, contract*—the very language and processes seem to assume the Justice orientation. From a Care perspective, the desired outcome would be the restoration of the relationship, the trust, the mutual care, the interdependent consideration needed to live together. A contract misses the point entirely. Anything less than reconnection would be painfully unacceptable.

Perry and Kitchener and King. Both William Perry (1970, 1978, 1981) and Karen Kitchener and Patricia King (King, 1982; King and others, 1983; Kitchener, 1985; Kitchener and King, 1981, 1985) have theories of intellectual or epistemological development. This kind of cognitive-structural development refers to how we cognitively perceive, organize, and evaluate questions of knowledge and valuation; that is, these theories attempt to describe our natural epistemologies. Perry calls this intellectual development; Kitchener and King call it reflective judgment.

Questions of knowledge and valuation in principle can include any content from history and mathematics to career choice and religion. Like Kohlberg's theories, these theories are not concerned with content per se but with the structure of how students make meaning of questions of knowledge, whatever the content. These two theories are presented together because there is a question as to whether the two are different theories or one theory (Perry's) clarified and extended by the other (Kitchener and King's). Rather than describe both theories in detail, a comparison of the two will be presented here. The interested reader may consult Perry (1970) and Kitchener and King (1981) for a more detailed discussion of each theory.

Perry's (1970) theory proposes nine stages or positions of intellectual development, the first five of which are considered to be cognitive-structural and the last four of which are considered to be existential and psychosocial (Rodgers, 1980; Broughton, 1975; King, 1982). Hence, Perry's work mixes or confounds cognitive-structural development and psychosocial development without making it clear that this is the case. As a consequence, if the two kinds of development are differentiated, two questions emerge: What does the psychosocial development of college students look like prior to Perry's Stage 6? What does their intellectual cognitive-structural development look like after Perry's Stage 5? Chickering's (1969) vectors and Kitchener and King's (1981) work provide responses to these questions. Chickering describes psychosocial developmental tasks prior to Perry's Stage 6; Kitchener and King carefully focus only on cognitive-structural epistemological development and extend and define intellectual development beyond Perry's Stage 5. Kitchener and King's theory and the first five stages of Perry's theory are summarized and contrasted in Table 5.

The two theories appear to coincide from Stage 1 through Stage 3. The differences begin to appear at Stage 4. Perry's Stage 4 seems to combine Kitchener and King's Stages 4 and 5. Perry's

Stage 5 may include Kitchener and King's Stages 6 and 7. Perry (1981) believes that Kitchener and King have misrepresented his Stages 4 and 5 by including within Perry's Stage 5 structures from his Stage 4 and by failing to acknowledge that his Stage 5 contains structures similar to their Stages 6 and 7. Kitchener and King have accepted Perry's first argument but disagree with him on the second (personal communication). They acknowledge that their Stage 5 is not the same as Perry's; however, they believe that they have been able to differentiate Perry's Stage 4 into two separate stages, their Stages 4 and 5. Kitchener and King disagree with Perry's contention that they have differentiated his Stage 5 into two stages (their 6 and 7) but contributed nothing new beyond his Stage 5. They believe that their Stage 7, at least, is a new and unique contribution. Regardless of one's opinion on these issues, Kitchener and King have clearly focused their work only on the cognitive-structural phenomena and have not confounded their work with psychosocial content. Furthermore, they seem to have differentiated Perry's Stage 4 into two stages and probably have extended the scheme with Stage 7.

As indicated previously, intellectual development is central to the primary purposes of higher education in the English, German, and American traditions. It is an aspect of well-rounded development; it is related to performance in complex vocational and professional careers; and it is central to research and inquiry. It is the one form of development in which faculty and student affairs staff may have a common commitment, and it has wide application to practice in both domains.

The educational use of intellectual development derives from the fact that students at different stages of epistemological meaning-making learn best in different environments. The general criteria for designing these different environments were first formulated and tested by Widick, Knefelkamp, and Parker (1975) and refined and extended by Knefelkamp and Slepitza (1976), Rodgers (1980), Schmidt and Davison (1981, 1983), and Baxter-Magolda (1987, 1988a, 1988b). Appropriately designed environments allow students at the earlier and later stages of meaning-making to do the following things (Widick, Knefelkamp, and Parker, 1975):

Table 5. Perry's and Kitchener and King's Theories.

Stage of Cognitive-Structural Development		Characteristics of the Stage	What Students Are Learning	What They Can Do Cognitively	Appropriate Challenge
Dualism/Absolutism	Stage 1	Knowing is observing, hearing, etc. without evaluating	What to learn	Memorization Awareness Identification	Break away from absolute view of authority
	Stage 2	What is known must be right (early) or either right or wrong (later) No tolerance for diversity		Knowledge of facts Learning to compare and contrast	See various points of view as legitimate Tolerate diversity
	Stage 3	Knowing is observing, hearing, etc. without evaluating or searching for what we don't know yet When we know, it must be right; if we don't know yet, how do we search? Authorities are important to tell us what is right and how to search correctly for what we don't know yet Tolerance for diversity when we don't know yet		Comparing and contrasting Analysis Seeing multiple points of view	Deal with areas of uncertainty Lose category of absolute certainty Support positions with evidence

Relativism	Stage 4 (Perry)	My "knowing" is my truth	How to learn	Inference	Find and use nonabsolute criteria for making judgments Synthesize points of view Relate learning in one context to another context Develop judgment and critical appraisal of competing ideas
	Stages 4 and 5 (Kitchener and King)	Truth is internal coherence for me Knowing is subjective Diversity is all there is There is no real "authority"	How to think	Comprehension Analysis Application Positive and negative critiques Use of supportive arguments	
Context	Stage 5 (Perry); Stage 6 (Kitchener and King)	Knowledge is relative to the context The truth depends on a particular context or perspective, time, and issue Perspectives need to be defended with evidence	Competence in building a case and choosing	All of the above across domains of knowledge Synthesis Relating learning across contexts	Develop commitment in face of uncertainty Solve complex problems within or across domains Generate new ways of looking at a domain Complex application of thought within or across domains

Table 5. Perry's and Kitchener and King's Theories, Cont'd.

Stage of Cognitive-Structural Development		Characteristics of the Stage	What Students Are Learning	What They Can Do Cognitively	Appropriate Challenge
Reflection	Stage 5 (Perry); Stage 7 (Kitchener and King)	Knowledge is result of ongoing process of reasonable inquiry about objective reality Knowledge approximates truth Knowledge is probabilistic Criteria for evaluation may vary from domain to domain	How to know, apply, and inquire critically	Evaluation Problem solving within and across domains Generation of new questions within and across domains Generation of new ways of looking at domain Application across or within domains	Generate new ways of looking at a domain or across domains Resolve apparent paradoxes Find new way to inquire

Stages 1, 2, and 3	Stages 4, 5, and above
Encounter two or three points of view on the topic under consideration	Encounter two, three, or more points of view on the topic under consideration
Use direct experiential learning when encountering these points of view	Use abstract or experiential learning when encountering these points of view
Process the encounters analytically, emphasizing cognitive skills	Process the encounters through both differentiation and integration, emphasizing the narrowing toward a personal stand or commitment on the topic under consideration
Use highly structured processes, with authorities providing the structure in advance	Students structure their own learning, with authorities providing little structure and extensive freedom
Build and maintain trust and a personal atmosphere in the environment, especially early in the relationship	Build and maintain a personal atmosphere of collegiality in the environment

Rodgers (1980, 1983) and Schmidt and Davison (1981, 1983) have refined these general criteria and provide stage-specific suggestions. Baxter-Magolda (1987) has identified some gender-related style differences applicable to some of the stages, while Knefelkamp and Slepitza (1976) have related the stages to several trait dimensions. These refined criteria can be used to increase the individuality of program or classroom design in situations where groups of students are at the same stage of development or in situations where individualized learning and feedback can be accommodated.

Theories of intellectual development have been used to

redesign instruction in history (Connell, 1979; Widick and Simpson, 1978), English (Bliss, 1986; Burnham, 1984; Haisty, 1983; Hays, 1983; Reid, 1986), mathematics (Buerk, 1985; Copes, 1982; Glasby, 1985), engineering (Culver and Hackos, 1981), agriculture (Froberg and Parker, 1976), anthropology (Gibbs, 1981), foreign languages (Jacobus, 1985), biology (Kimmel, 1985), religion (Meyer, 1977), health education (Nowakowski, 1980), teacher education (Stuck, 1984), and psychology (Van Hecke, 1985). Perry's scheme and Kitchener and King's theory have been used to redesign student affairs practice in counseling (Cooper and Lewis, 1983; Knefelkamp, Widick, and Stroad, 1976; Perry, 1978), career development (Touchton, Wertheimer, Cornfeld, and Harrison, 1977; Gordon, 1981; Knefelkamp and Slepitza, 1976; Rodgers and Widick, 1980; Schrader, 1982), conflict resolution (Rodgers, 1983), and residence life (Rodgers, 1985).

Evaluating the two theories of intellectual development is a complex task. Perry initially studied three groups of students—mostly men—over their four years of college. Questions of cultural differences in intellectual development are currently being investigated by Perry's associates, while Alishio (Alishio and Schilling, 1984), Clinchy (Clinchy and Zimmerman, 1981), Benack (1982), and Baxter-Magolda (1987) are investigating gender differences. Kitchener and King (1985) have followed their original sample of men and women longitudinally for over ten years and have refined both their method of assessment and the structures of their stages of reflective judgment. King is currently investigating the question of whether there are cultural differences in reflective judgment. Literally hundreds of intervention applications have been made, only some of which have been published.

Other Theories. Robert Kegan's (1979, 1980a, 1980b, 1982) theory of ego development and Janet Fowler's (1981) theory of faith development are new and important cognitive-structural theories. Staff members interested in counseling applications of developmental theory or in faith development should refer to their theories; space limitations do not permit their presentation here.

Typological Theories and Models

Typological theories have no unifying theoretical heritage. Some have been derived from behavioral work on learning styles (such as Kolb, 1976). Others were generated from Jung's work on personality type (Myers, 1980). Another grew out of the reflective practice of a college counselor (Heath, 1974), and yet another from temperament theory (Kiersey and Bates, 1978). What these theories have in common is an attempt to describe permanent or semipermanent stylistic or type preferences. These styles or preferences are important because they can be used to facilitate both learning and development by informing program and workshop design about stylistic differences, informing team building and delegation about task preferences, and focusing attention on the fact that stylistic differences need to be taken seriously if teaching is to be taken seriously at colleges and universities.

Typological theories can be examined at four levels (Claxton and Murrell, 1987): personality type, information processing, social interaction, and instructional methods. Since information processing, social interaction, and instructional methods can be subsumed under the broader category of personality type, the Jung/Myers-Briggs theory will be used to illustrate the basic characteristics of this family of theories.

In 1923 Carl Jung wrote that the apparently chance variations in human behavior are not due to chance but are the logical result of differences in mental functioning. For Jung and other typological theorists, therefore, type or style is a preferred or habitual pattern of mental functioning; that is, it consists of preferred ways of taking in information, classifying information, making judgments, reflecting or interacting, and moving toward judgment or staying open to taking in information (Lawrence, 1982). In turn, these preferred patterns lead to *dispositions,* tendencies toward attending selectively to elements in a learning environment, seeking out learning environments compatible with one's type and avoiding or leaving incompatible environments, and using certain learning tools and avoiding others (Lawrence, 1982, 1984). For the Jung/Myers-Briggs theory, these preferences consist of four dimensions: extraversion-introversion, sensing-intuition, thinking-feeling, and judgment-perception.

Extraversion-Introversion. Extraversion *(E)* and Introversion *(I)* are complementary attitudes that describe whether one prefers to spend time and energy interacting with people, places, and things or reflecting on one's experience internally with ideas and concepts (Myers and McCaulley, 1985). Everyone does both but prefers one attitude to the other. The preferred attitude usually is used more often and is better developed. Students preferring Extraversion are disposed toward interactive external activities, breadth of involvements, acting first and reflecting on the action afterward, and reflecting out loud with others. They are verbal "after-thinkers." Introverted students prefer private internal activities, depth in fewer involvements, thinking before they act (if they ever act at all), and reflecting silently and alone. They are silent "fore-thinkers."

Given these preferences and dispositions, Extraverts are drawn to learning environments where there are action-oriented activities and group interactions. They like verbal communication, opportunities to explore their thoughts out loud with others, and application of ideas. On the other hand, Introverts are drawn to environments that emphasize private study and reflection, individual effort, written communication, and depth of comprehension.

Sensing-Intuition. Sensing *(S)* and Intuition *(N)* are two opposite ways of perceiving or taking in information. All students use both forms of perceiving; however, people prefer one to the other and use the preferred method more often. Sensors rely primarily on the concrete information provided by their five senses. They are disposed toward focusing on the present situation and being aware of components of that situation. They trust their experience and may distrust their inspirations. They try to figure out how to do things efficiently. Intuitives rely primarily on their less obvious preconscious processes of perceiving meanings, relationships, and possibilities (Myers and McCaulley, 1985). They are disposed, therefore, toward finding general patterns and new ways of doing things, formulating or mastering theories, engaging complex problems, and generating alternatives.

Given these preferences and dispositions, Sensors are drawn to learning environments that stress application in realistic and practical ways. They like clear and specific instructions. They prefer to have specific, concrete learning experiences prior to dealing with generalizations, theories, or overviews. Intuitives, in contrast, are drawn to learning environments that involve theoretical understanding, opportunities to create something new, and open-ended assignments. They dislike routine and highly detailed activities.

Thinking-Feeling. Thinking *(T)* and Feeling *(F)* are two opposite ways of making judgments on the basis of one's perceptions. Everyone uses both judgment functions in everyday and academic life; however, people prefer one to the other and use the preferred method more often. Students who prefer Thinking rely primarily on impersonal, analytic, cause-and-effect reasoning in making decisions; as a result, they are disposed toward organizing and manipulating facts or ideas, considering the logical flow of ideas, and being objective when weighing alternatives. Their gift is their ability to be critical and to consider both pleasant and unpleasant data. They prize competence and productivity. Students who prefer Feeling rely primarily on their personal or social values in making decisions. They check objective data with their hierarchy of values and make decisions on the basis of their values. These students are disposed toward focusing on how decisions affect people, maintaining and restoring personal relationships, being charismatic in supporting their decisions, and supporting and caring for others.

Given these preferences and dispositions, Thinkers are drawn to learning environments where a logical rationale is presented for activities and where their competence is respected. They prefer approaches that help them understand the cause-and-effect systems at work. Feeling types, on the other hand, are attracted to learning environments that give personal encouragement, use logic to examine and prioritize values, and focus on the "people" aspects of the topic under consideration. They have difficulty criticizing others or accepting critical feedback themselves. They give their best when there is harmony in the interpersonal environment, not conflict.

Judgment-Perception. Judgment *(J)* and Perception *(P)* indicate complementary ways in which people—both extraverts and introverts—interact with the external world. Whether a student is an *E* or an *I,* when the student is extraverting, does the student prefer to use Judgment or Perception? Students who prefer to extravert with their Judgment function (*T* or *F*) are disposed toward living an organized, planned life-style. They set goals and meet deadlines. They often seek to control situations; they are decisive. Students who prefer to use their Perception function (*S* or *N*) when extraverting have different dispositions. They prefer to remain open to their experience; they are more spontaneous and more open to changing their plans. They work in bursts of energy and often are late with assignments. They are slow to make commitments and prefer to remain open to additional experiences.

These dispositions often mean that *J* types are achievement-oriented and need to complete tasks. They prefer more structured learning environments and want clear expectations. On the other hand, *P* types prefer learning situations that are more free, open, and flexible. They care less about deadlines than about how they do what they do. They want freedom rather than structure. They prefer to do what interests them rather than what authorities define as important.

A student's type, therefore, is the sum of his or her preferences for one of each of these pairs of mental functions or attitudes. An *ENFP,* for example, prefers Extraverted experiences, Intuitive perception, Feeling judgment, and Perception (*N* in this case) when dealing with the extraverted world.

Type Characteristics. The Jung/Myers-Briggs types and the other typological or type preferences appear to have the following characteristics. First, preferences, which may be genetic, stabilize early in life and appear to remain stable over a lifetime. Second, types have the character of "handedness." If one is born right-handed, one uses the right hand more and trusts it more than the left, and the right hand is better developed. Nevertheless, one uses the left hand often, even though it is less developed. Similarly, one uses one's type preferences more often and trusts them more than their opposites, and they are better developed, but one uses the opposite preferences as well. Third, preferences are only "zip codes," describing areas of tendencies that people have in common; they do not account for the uniquenesses of our individual selves. Further, type is not static; it is dynamic. Types are various tracks to wholeness, "zip code" areas within which we grow and develop.

Type development research indicates that people should seek to maximize experiences consistent with type preferences during the first half of life (perhaps until one's early forties) and then work on developing opposites or other styles in the second half of life. Hence, an *ENFP*, for example, would facilitate her development if she sought the following during the college years and in a career:

> *E:* experiences interacting with the real world; experiences of learning ideas in order to use them in the world and testing thoughts out loud in group contexts; broad involvements
>
> *N:* experiences requiring creative imagination and complex problem solving rather than detailed precision and repetition
>
> *F:* experiences where judgments are made about people, requiring sensitivity to feelings and values; experiences of supporting or caring for others rather than experiences requiring impersonal and logical judgment concerning objects
>
> *P:* flexible environments that do not require precise deadlines or rigid schedules

If an *ENFP* seeks such environments and experiences, it is easy to see how her type development might interact with other forms of development. Different types may need different environments in order to resolve psychosocial vectors or to stimulate cognitive-structural development. Extraverts, for example, would profit more from direct experiences with social-interpersonal competence or managing sexual emotions in order to resolve these vectors, while Introverts could more easily learn from vicarious or indirect experiences (such as literature). Feeling types may have an easier time with managing emotions than Thinking types because *F*'s are more at ease expressing feelings and relying on values than *T*'s. On the other hand, *T*'s may have an easier time becoming autonomous than *F*'s because *T*'s have an easier time dealing with conflict, more often take an independent stand based on logical principles, and do not have as high a need for harmony in their lives.

Since almost all experiences in higher education involve the use of perception and judgment, type interacts with almost everything we do at colleges and universities. As Myers and McCaulley (1985, p. 4) and Provost and Anchors (1987) indicate, type can be used to:

- develop different teaching methods
- understand differences in motivation
- analyze curricula or program design
- build administrative teams
- understand staff and supervise interactions
- form ad hoc groups with preferences suited to working together and to the nature of the task at hand
- design different environments for psychosocial development and cognitive-structural development
- cope with personal problems
- choose majors, careers, and work settings
- conduct meetings
- assign roommates in a residence hall
- understand and respond to attrition problems
- help academic advising
- aid psychological counseling
- analyze policies and procedures

Roy Heath's (1973, 1974) model of ego styles and Kolb's (1976) learning styles also describe different ways of learning or patterns of functioning. Kolb's model has been used in education at all levels, Heath's less so. Both, however, are assimilable into the Jung/Myers-Briggs theory. Kiersey's (Kiersey and Bates, 1978) theory, on the other hand, is a rival to Jung/Myers-Briggs and deserves serious consideration for use in student affairs practice.

Conclusion

Our knowledge of the development of college students, both those of traditional age and older adults, has improved in the past few years. We know more about cultural influences, gender differences and similarities, how developmental change takes place, and how to use multiple theories in understanding our students. The gap between theory and practice remains large, however, partly because too few staff have learned theory in depth. Brown's (1972) dream of a profession using theory-in-practice cannot be fulfilled nor Willey's (1949) criticisms silenced until this changes. Staff must know the constructs and propositions of theory in depth in order to use theory to understand and explain student behavior, environmental influences on behavior, and student-environment interactions. Staff must know how developmental change takes place in order to set appropriate goals and design practice. We can close the gap. This knowledge can be used to create environments that help students to learn and mature. In this chapter families of theory and selected specific theories have been introduced. The reader must take the next step and learn specific theories in depth. Then and only then can theory inform our practice.

References

Alishio, K. C., and Schilling, K. M. "Sex Differences in Intellectual and Ego Development." *Journal of Youth and Adolescence,* 1984, *13,* 213–224.

American Council on Education. *The Student Personnel Point of View.* American Council on Education Studies, series 1, vol. 1, no. 3. Washington, D.C.: American Council on Education, 1937.

American Council on Education. *The Student Personnel Point of View.* American Council on Education Studies, series 4, vol. 13, no. 13. Washington, D.C.: American Council on Education, 1949.

Baumrind, D. "Sex Differences in Moral Reasoning: Response to Walker's (1984) Conclusion That There Are None." *Child Development,* 1986, *57* (2), 511–521.

Baxter-Magolda, M. B. "Measuring Gender Differences in Intellectual Development: A Comparison of Assessment Methods." Paper presented at annual convention of the American College Personnel Association, Chicago, Mar. 1987.

Baxter-Magolda, M. B. "The Effective Dimension of Learning: Faculty-Student Relationships That Enhance Intellectual Development." *College Student Journal,* 1988a, *21,* 46–58.

Baxter-Magolda, M. B. "Experiential Learning and Student Development Theory as Guides to Developing Instructional Approaches." *International Journal of Social Education,* 1988b, *1* (3), 28–40.

Benack, S. "The Coding of Dimensions of Epistemological Thought in Young Men and Women." *Moral Education Forum,* 1982, *7,* 3–23.

Blatt, M., and Kohlberg, L. "The Effects of Classroom Moral Discussion upon Children's Moral Judgment." *Journal of Moral Education,* 1975, *4,* 126–161.

Bliss, F. W. "Intellectual Development and Freshman English." Paper presented at Project MATCH conference, Davidson College, 1986.

Blocher, D. H. "Campus Learning Environments and the Ecology of Student Development." In J. H. Banning (ed.), *Campus Ecology: A Perspective for Student Affairs.* Columbus, Ohio: National Association of Student Personnel Administrators, 1978.

Bloland, P. A. "Student Development: The New Orthodoxy? Part I." *ACPA Developments,* 1986a, *13* (3), 1, 13.

Bloland, P. A. "Student Development: The New Orthodoxy? Part II." *ACPA Developments,* 1986b, *13* (4), 1, 22.

Branch-Simpson, G. "A Study of the Patterns in the Development of Black Students at The Ohio State University." Unpublished doctoral dissertation, Ohio State University, 1984.

Broughton, J. M. "The Development of Natural Epistemological Childhood." Unpublished doctoral dissertation, Department of Policy and Leadership, College of Education, Harvard University, 1975.

Brown, R. D. *Student Development in Tomorrow's Higher Education: A Return to the Academy.* Washington, D.C.: American College Personnel Association, 1972.

Brubacher, J. S., and Rudy, W. *Higher Education in Transition: A History of American Colleges and Universities, 1636–1968.* New York: Harper & Row, 1968.

Buerk, D. "From Magic to Meaning: Changing the Learning of Mathematics." Paper presented at ISEM Workshop on Teaching and Learning Mathematics, St. Paul, Minn., 1985.

Buhler, C., and Massarik, F. *The Course of Human Life.* New York: Springer, 1968.

Burnham, C. "The Perry Scheme and the Teacher of Literature." Paper presented at Conference on College Composition and Communication, Las Cruces, N.M., 1984.

Chickering, A. W. *Education and Identity.* San Francisco: Jossey-Bass, 1969.

Chickering, A. W., and Havighurst, R. J. "The Life Cycle." In A. W. Chickering and Associates, *The Modern American College: Responding to the New Realities of Diverse Students and a Changing Society.* San Francisco: Jossey-Bass, 1981.

Claxton, C. S., and Murrell, P. H. *Learning Styles: Implications for Improving Educational Practices.* ASHE-ERIC Higher Education Report, no. 4. Washington, D.C.: Association for the Study of Higher Education, 1987.

Clinchy, B., and Zimmerman, C. "Epistemology and Agency in the Development of Undergraduate Women." In P. Perun (ed.), *The Undergraduate Woman: Issues in Educational Equity.* Lexington, Mass.: Heath, 1981.

Connell, C. W. "Attitude and Development as Factors in the Learning of History: The Work of William Perry." *American Historical Association Newsletter,* 1979, *17,* 6–8.

Cooper, T. D., and Lewis, J. A. "The Crisis of Relativism: Helping Counselors Cope with Diversity." *Counselor Education and Supervision,* 1983, *22,* 290–295.

Copes, L. "The Perry Developmental Scheme: A Metaphor for Learning and Teaching Mathematics." *For the Learning of Mathematics,* 1982, *3,* 38–44.

Culver, R., and Hackos, J. "Perry's Model for Intellectual Development: Implications for Engineering Education." Paper presented at annual conference of American Society of Engineering Education, University of Southern California, Los Angeles, Calif., June 1981.

Denny, N. "Sociomoral Development Variability: Comparisons of Kohlberg's Moral Reasoning Stages for Jung's Thinking-Feeling Judgment Process, Educational Level, and Gender." Unpublished doctoral dissertation, Department of Policy and Leadership, College of Education, Ohio State University, 1988.

Erikson, E. H. *Childhood and Society.* New York: Norton, 1950.

Erikson, E. H. *Identity: Youth and Crisis.* New York: Norton, 1968.

Fowler, J. *Stages of Faith.* New York: Harper & Row, 1981.

Froberg, D., and Parker, C. A. *Progress Report on the Developmental Instruction Project.* Minneapolis: College of Agriculture, University of Minnesota, 1976.

Galbraith, R. E., and Jones, T. M. *Moral Reasoning: A Teaching Handbook for Adapting Kohlberg to the Classroom.* Minneapolis, Minn.: Greenhaven, 1976.

Gibbs, J. C., Arnold, K. D., and Burkhardt, J. E. "Sex Differences in the Expression of Moral Judgment." *Child Development,* 1984, *55,* 1040–1043.

Gibbs, J. L. "Anthropology." In A. W. Chickering and Associates, *The Modern American College: Responding to the New Realities of Diverse Students and a Changing Society.* San Francisco: Jossey-Bass, 1981.

Gilligan, C. *In a Different Voice.* Cambridge, Mass.: Harvard University Press, 1982a.

Gilligan, C. "New Maps of Development: New Visions of Maturity." *American Journal of Orthopsychiatry,* 1982b, *52,* 199–212.

Gilligan, C. "Reply by Carol Gilligan." In *"In a Different Voice: An Interdisciplinary Forum." Signs: Journal of Women in Culture and Society,* 1986, *2,* 304–333.

Glasby, M. K. "An Analysis of Cognitive Development and Student Profiles over Three Levels of Mathematics Courses at a Selected Community College (Perry Scale)." Unpublished doctoral dissertation, Curriculum and Instruction, University of Maryland, College Park, 1985.

Gordon, V. N. "The Undecided Student: A Developmental Perspective." *Personnel and Guidance Journal,* 1981, *59,* 433–439.

Haan, N. "With Regard to Walker (1984) on Sex Differences in Moral Reasoning." Berkeley: Institute of Human Development, University of California, Berkeley, 1985. (Mimeographed.)

Haisty, D. B. "The Developmental Theories of Jean Piaget and William Perry: An Application to the Teaching of Writing." Unpublished doctoral dissertation, English Department, Texas Christian University, 1983.

Havighurst, R. J. *Developmental Tasks and Education.* New York: McKay, 1948.

Havighurst, R. J. *Human Development and Education.* New York: Longmans, Green, 1953.

Hays, J. "The Development of Discursive Maturity in College Writers." In J. Hays, P. Roth, J. Ramsey, and R. Faulte (eds.), *The Writer's Mind: Writing as a Mode of Thinking.* Urbana, Ill.: National Council of Teachers of English, 1983.

Heath, R. "Form, Flow, and Full-Being." *Counseling Psychologist,* 1973, *4,* 56–63.

Heath, R. *The Reasonable Adventurer.* Pittsburgh, Pa.: University of Pittsburgh Press, 1974.

Hickey, J., and Scharf, P. *Toward a Just Correctional System: Experiments in Implementing Democracy in Prisons.* San Francisco: Jossey-Bass, 1980.

Higgins, A., Power, C., and Kohlberg, L. "The Relationship of Moral Atmosphere to Judgments of Responsibility." In W. Kurtines and J. Gerwitz (eds.), *Morality, Moral Behavior and Moral Development.* New Work: Wiley-Interscience, 1984.

Ignelsi, M. G. "Ethical Education in a College Environment: The Just Community Approach." Paper presented at national convention of American College Personnel Association, Miami, Fla., Mar. 1988.

Inhelder, R., and Piaget, J. *The Growth of Logical Thinking from Childhood to Adolescence.* New York: Basic Books, 1958.

Jacobus, E. F., Jr. "The Developmental Hypothesis in Foreign Languages Learning: Implications for Proficiency." Paper presented at Project MATCH conference, Davidson College, 1985.

Johnston, K. "Two Moral Orientations—Two Problem Solving Strategies: Adolescents' Solutions to Dilemmas in Fables." Unpublished doctoral dissertation, School of Education, Harvard University, 1985.

Jung, C. G. *The Development of Personality.* In H. Read, M. Fordham, G. Adler, and W. McGuire (eds.), *Collected Works.* Vol.
17. (R.F.C. Hull, trans.) Princeton, N.J.: Princeton University Press, 1954.

Jung, C. G. *Memories, Dreams, and Reflections.* (A. Jaffe, ed.; R.
Winston and C. Winston, trans.) New York: Pantheon Books,
1961.

Jung, C. G. *The Stages of Life.* In H. Read, M. Fordham, G.
Adler, and W. McGuire (eds.), *Collected Works.* Vol. 8. (R.F.C.
Hull, trans.) Princeton, N.J.: Princeton University Press, 1969.

Jung, C. G. *Psychological Types.* In H. Read, M. Fordham, G.
Adler, and W. McGuire (eds.), *Collected Works.* Vol. 6. (R.F.C.
Hull, trans.) Princeton, N.J.: Princeton University Press,
1971.

Kegan, R. "The Evolving Self: A Process Conception for Ego
Psychology." *Counseling Psychologist,* 1979, *8,* 5–34.

Kegan, R. "Making Meaning: The Constructive-Developmen-
tal Approach to Persons and Practice." *Personnel and Guidance
Journal,* 1980a, *58,* 373–380.

Kegan, R. "There the Dance Is: Religious Dimensions of a
Developmental Framework." In R. Kegan, *Toward Moral and
Religious Maturity.* Morristown, N.J.: Silver-Burdett, 1980b.

Kegan, R. *The Evolving Self: Problems and Process in Human Development.* Cambridge, Mass.: Harvard University Press, 1982.

Kiersey, D., and Bates, M. *Please Understand Me: Character and
Temperament Types.* (3rd ed.) Del Mar, Calif.: Prometheus
Nemesis Books, 1978.

Kimmel, D. L., Jr. "Use of the Perry Model in an Introductory Biology Course." Paper presented at Project MATCH
conference, Davidson College, 1985.

King, P. M. "Perry's Scheme and the Reflective Judgment
Model: First Cousins Once Removed." Paper presented at
annual conference of Association for Moral Education, Minneapolis, Minn., Nov. 1982.

King, P. M., and others. "The Justification of Beliefs in Young
Adults: A Longitudinal Study." *Human Development,* 1983,
26, 106–116.

Kitchener, K. S. "The Reflective Judgment Model: Characteristics, Evidence and Measurement." In R. A. Mines and K. S. Kitchener (eds.), *Social-Cognitive Development in Young Adults.* New York: Praeger, 1985.

Kitchener, K. S., and King, P. M. "Reflective Judgment: Concepts of Justification and Their Relationship to Age and Education." *Journal of Applied Developmental Psychology,* 1981, *2,* 89–116.

Kitchener, K. S., and King, P. M. "The Reflective Judgment Model: Ten Years of Research." Paper presented at Beyond Formal Operations Symposium, 1985.

Knefelkamp, L. L., and Slepitza, R. "A Cognitive-Developmental Model of Career Development: An Adaptation of the Perry Scheme." *Counseling Psychologist,* 1976, *6,* 53–58.

Knefelkamp, L. L., Widick, C., and Parker, C. A. (eds.). *Applying New Developmental Findings.* New Directions for Student Services, no. 4. San Francisco: Jossey-Bass, 1978.

Knefelkamp, L. L., Widick, C., and Stroad, B. "Cognitive-Developmental Theory: A Guide to Counseling Women." *Counseling Psychologist,* 1976, *6,* 15–19.

Kohlberg, L. *Essays on Moral Development.* Vol. 1: *The Philosophy of Moral Development: Moral Stages and the Idea of Justice.* New York: Harper & Row, 1981.

Kohlberg, L. *Essays on Moral Development.* Vol. 2: *The Psychology of Moral Development: The Nature and Validity of Moral Stages.* New York: Harper & Row, 1984.

Kolb, D. A. *Learning Styles Inventory Technical Manual.* Boston: McBer, 1976.

Lawrence, G. D. *People Types and Tiger Stripes.* (2nd ed.) Gainesville, Fla.: Center for Applications of Psychological Type, 1982.

Lawrence, G. D. "A Synthesis of Learning Style Research Involving the MBTI." *Journal of Psychological Type,* 1984, *8,* 2–15.

Levinson, D. J. *The Seasons of a Man's Life.* New York: Knopf, 1978.

Lyons, N. P. "Two Perspectives: On Self, Relationships, and Morality." *Harvard Educational Review,* 1981, *53,* 125–145.

Meyer, P. G. "Intellectual Development: Analysis of Religious Content." *Counseling Psychologist,* 1977, *6,* 47–50.

Myers, I. B. *Gifts Differing.* Palo Alto, Calif.: Consulting Psychologists Press, 1980.

Myers, I. B., and McCaulley, M. H. *Manual for the Myers-Briggs Type Indicator: A Guide to the Development and Use of the MBTI.* Palo Alto, Calif.: Consulting Psychologists Press, 1985.

Neugarten, B. L. "Adaption and the Life Cycle." *Counseling Psychologist,* 1976, *6,* 16–20.

Nowakowski, L. "Developing a Nursing Conceptual Framework for Directory Practice." In B. Redmond (ed.), *Patterns for Distribution of Patient Education.* East Norwalk, Conn.: Appleton-Century-Crofts, 1980.

Perry, W. G., Jr. *Forms of Intellectual and Ethical Development in the College Years.* New York: Holt, Rinehart & Winston, 1970.

Perry, W. G., Jr. "Sharing in the Costs of Growth." In C. A. Parker (ed.), *Encouraging Development in College Students.* Minneapolis: University of Minnesota Press, 1978.

Perry, W. G., Jr. "Cognitive and Ethical Growth: The Making of Meaning." In A. W. Chickering and Associates, *The Modern American College: Responding to the New Realities of Diverse Students and a Changing Society.* San Francisco: Jossey-Bass, 1981.

Piaget, J. *The Moral Judgment of the Child.* New York: Fres Press, 1948.

Piaget, J. *The Origins of Intelligence in Children.* New York: International Universities Press, 1952.

Piaget, J. *The Construction of Reality in the Child.* New York: Basic Books, 1954.

Provost, J. A., and Anchors, S. (eds.). *Applications of the Myers-Briggs Type Indicator in Higher Education.* Palo Alto, Calif.: Consulting Psychologists Press, 1987.

Reid, G. B. "The Use of the Perry Scheme in the Teaching of Freshman English." Unpublished doctoral dissertation, Memphis State University, 1986.

Rodgers, R. F. "Theories Underlying Student Development." In D. G. Creamer (ed.), *Student Development in Higher Education: Theories, Practices, and Future Directions.* Cincinnati, Ohio: ACPA Media, 1980.

Rodgers, R. F. "Using Theory in Practice." In T. K. Miller,

R. B. Winston, and W. R. Mendenhall (eds.), *Administration and Leadership in Student Affairs.* Muncie, Ind.: Accelerated Development, 1983.

Rodgers, R. F. "Theories of Adult Development: Research Status and Counseling Implications." In S. D. Brown and R. W. Lent (eds.), *Handbook of Counseling Psychology.* New York: Wiley, 1984.

Rodgers, R. F. "The OASIS Project: Applying Developmental Theory to Residence Life." Paper presented at annual conference of American College Personnel Association, Baltimore, Md., Apr. 1985.

Rodgers, R. F., and Widick, C. "Theory to Practice: Uniting Concepts, Logic and Creativity." In F. B. Newton and K. L. Ender (eds.), *Student Development Practices.* Springfield, Ill.: Thomas, 1980.

Sanford, N. (ed.). "Personality Development During the College Years." *Journal of Social Issues,* 1956, *2,* 1-71.

Sanford, N. (ed.). *The American College.* New York: Wiley, 1962a.

Sanford, N. "Developmental Status of the Entering Freshman." In N. Sanford (ed.), *The American College.* New York: Wiley, 1962b.

Sanford, N. *Where Colleges Fail: A Study of the Student as a Person.* San Francisco: Jossey-Bass, 1967.

Schmidt, J. A., and Davison, M. "Does College Matter? Reflective Judgment: How Students Tackle the Tough Questions." *Moral Education Forum,* 1981, *6,* 2-14.

Schmidt, J. A., and Davison, M. "Helping Students Think." *Personnel and Guidance Journal,* 1983, *61,* 563-569.

Schrader, D. E. "Intellectual Development: Myers-Briggs and Perry Scheme Applications in Career Development Seminars." Unpublished master's thesis, Ohio State University, 1982.

Straub, C. "Women's Development of Autonomy and Chickering's Theory." *Journal of College Student Personnel,* 1987, *28,* 198-205.

Straub, C., and Rodgers, R. F. "The Student Personnel Worker as Teacher: Fostering Moral Development in College Women." *Journal of College Student Personnel,* 1978, *29,* 430-436.

Straub, C., and Rodgers, R. F. "An Exploration of Chickering's Theory and Women's Development." *Journal of College Student Personnel,* 1986, *27,* 216–224.

Stuck, A. "Cognitive Development: A Perspective for Teacher Development." Paper presented at annual conference of American Educational Research Association, New Orleans, La., Apr. 1984.

Touchton, J. G., Wertheimer, L. G., Cornfeld, J. L., and Harrison, K. H. "Career Planning and Decision Making: A Developmental Approach to the Classroom." *Counseling Psychologist,* 1977, *6,* 42–47.

Van Hecke, M. "The Work of William Perry, Part II: Teaching Psychology to Dualistic Level Students." *Illinois Psychologist,* 1985, *24,* 15–20.

Walker, L. "Sex Differences in the Development of Moral Reasoning: A Critical Review." *Child Development,* 1984, *55,* 667–691.

Walton, R. E. *Interpersonal Peacemaking: Confrontation and Third Party Consultation.* Reading, Mass.: Addison-Wesley, 1969.

Widick, C., Knefelkamp, L. L., and Parker, C. A. "The Counselor as a Developmental Instructor." *Counselor Education and Supervision,* 1975, *14,* 286–296.

Widick, C., and Simpson, D. "Developmental Concepts in College Instruction." In C. A. Parker (ed.), *Encouraging Development in College Students.* Minneapolis: University of Minnesota Press, 1978.

Willey, M. M. "The University and Personnel Work." In E. G. Williamson (ed.), *Trends in Student Personnel Work.* Minneapolis: University of Minnesota Press, 1949.

Chapter Six

Interaction
of Student and Campus

Lois A. Huebner

Interactionism is a theoretical perspective that posits that behavior is best understood and predicted through the transaction of individuals and their environment. Campus ecology is an application of this interactionist perspective that focuses on the student-college transaction. Campus ecology is largely pragmatic, sometimes political, and nearly always a participative enterprise. As such it is generally atheoretical, although it draws on theoretical and empirical work from several intellectual traditions. This chapter will highlight major theories of person-environment interaction that have provided the academic rationale for campus ecology applications, as well as elucidate major concepts involved in campus ecology. A final section looks at promising future directions.

The Interactionist Perspective and Campus Ecology

The idea that people are influenced systematically by their environment is not recent; it has, in fact, been discussed in the psychological and sociological literature for years. Historically, three theoretical positions have been used to explain person-situation variance—"personologism," "situationism," and "interactionism" (Ekehammar, 1974). Personologism explains behavior in terms of individual attributes (or traits) that allow or cause people to act in a fairly consistent fashion in a variety of situations. Behavior is seen as largely internally directed. The opposing view, situationism, views behavior as chiefly influenced by the environment or context in which it occurs. Thus, individuals are expected to behave inconsistently (or discriminately) in differing situations. The third position, interactionism, hypothesizes that a person's attributes interact with situational variables to motivate and direct behavior. Behavior is thus a function of both the individual and the environment.

For a variety of reasons (including a lack of appropriate research and statistical methodologies), the interactionist perspective failed to produce substantiating empirical studies and, in fact, dropped from the forefront of psychology until the mid 1960s. In the interim, opinion was divided about whether behavior is best understood through the situationist perspective (for example, through behaviorism) or through the personological perspective (for example, by focusing on the explanatory power of personality, demographics, or other individual variables). Development of analysis of variance techniques made the study of the relative contributions of person, environment, and $P \times E$ interaction possible (Ekehammar, 1974), and between 1960 and 1980 a number of important studies documented the superiority of the interactionist perspective in accounting for human behavior (for example, Bishop and Witt, 1970; Bowers, 1973; Ekehammar, Magnusson, and Ricklander, 1974; Endler, Hunt, and Rosenstein, 1962; Endler and Hunt, 1966; Mischel, 1973; Moos, 1968, 1969, 1970; Sandell, 1968).

One attempt to apply this interactionist perspective to practical problems occurs with the campus ecology model. Campus ecology is an outgrowth of the more general movement called social ecology. The social ecological approach conceptualizes behavior as a function of the person-environment relationship and seeks to "investigate the intricate relationship between human beings and their environments without needing to invoke the limiting and dysfunctional metaphor of mental health (Blocher, 1981, p. 71). According to this perspective, constructive as well as dysfunctional behaviors (disorders) are best understood and most effectively promoted, treated, or prevented within (as a part of) the environments where they occur.

Thus, besides acknowledging that dysfunctional student behaviors may be an expression of a dysfunctional environment or student-environment relationship, the campus ecology approach also directly posits that student growth and development are best fostered by intervention in this interactional relationship. Thus the ecosystem approach "is concerned with the creation of campus environments which potentiate students as physical, mental, social and spiritual beings" (Western Interstate Commission for Higher Education, 1973, p. 2).

The approach is proactive rather than reactive and is focused more on designing (or redesigning) campus environments to meet the needs of members than "adjusting" or "treating" students so that they will fit into existing environments. The campus ecology approach also acknowledges the usefulness of helping or teaching students to make better use of existing environments (resources), adjust to some unmodifiable aspects of the environment, choose environments that facilitate or enhance their own functioning, and make decisions about leaving environments that do not facilitate their growth.

Models of Person-Environment Interaction

Interventions from the campus ecology perspective generally rest on the constructs and propositions of several theoretical models of person-environment interaction (Walsh, 1973; Huebner, 1980; Huebner and Corazzini, 1984; Kalsbeek, 1985). In a 1973 review Walsh noted that then-current models of P × E interaction did not meet the rigorous criteria of formal theory, but were at best "only hypotheses, partial theories, or theoretical orientations" (p. 5). This evaluation still seems largely accurate today. A similar situation also exists with regard to theories within environmental psychology. Nevertheless, the theoretical underpinnings of environmental change efforts are embedded within these models of person-environment interaction, and they have proven to have heuristic value. Five models will be reviewed: the behavior setting approach, the need-press model, the transactional approach, the human aggregate model, and social climate.

Behavior Setting Approach. Roger Barker's (1968) approach to the study of person-environment relationships is based on the premise that environments select and shape the behavior of people who inhabit them through the operation of "behavior settings." That is, individuals within the same environment may behave in highly similar ways despite their individual differences. Behavior settings are defined as basic and naturally occurring environmental units, consisting of "one or more standing patterns of behavior," with the surrounding environment (milieu) similar in form to the behavior (Barker, 1968, p. 18). Examples of behavior settings might be a football game, a monthly residence hall floor meeting, or a classroom lecture.

Originally, Barker believed that behavior settings had great and direct coercive power over the behaviors occurring within them. However, later formulations noted that the effect of any behavior setting was related to the proportion of the number of people in the setting to the physical size and essential functions of that setting (Wicker, 1973; Wicker and Kirmeyer, 1976; Willems, 1967, 1969). Behavior settings have thus been defined as potentially "undermanned" or "overmanned," depending on the number of people available to perform essential functions. This "manning" status affects the functioning of those in the setting and can be used to predict behavior, especially that of marginal individuals (Willems, 1967, 1969).

Barker and his colleagues make only minimal reference to the psychological environment. In their theory the "psychological habitat" refers to what individuals see and the meaning of their observations. The psychological habitat is defined in terms of observed behavior, the sequential context of the behavior, and the characteristics of present settings and objects (Wright, 1978).

Need-Press Model. A second useful model is Stern's (1970) "need-press" model, which is an extension and elaboration of theory presented by Murray (1938) and Lewin (1936). A central tenet of this model is that person and environment must be studied in commensurate terms as part of one situation. The key concepts are (personal) needs and (environmental) press. These concepts are related through three primary assumptions of the model (Stern, 1964; Walsh, 1973). First, behavior is a function of the individual and the environment: $B = f(P,E)$. Second, the person is represented in terms of needs (organizational tendencies that seem to give unity and direction to a person's behavior), which are inferred from self-reported behavior. Third, the environment is defined in terms of press, which is inferred from the aggregate of self-reported perceptions or interpretations of the environment.

Within this framework, behavior is studied as a function of the congruence of need and press, or of the congruence between explicit press (stated purposes of an institution) and implicit press (perceived policies and practices as reported by constituents). Stern discusses relevant dimensions of the person-environment relationship. One dimension—congruence-dissonance—refers to whether there is a stable and complementary combination of need and press. Stern hypothesizes that a relatively congruent person-environment relationship would result in positive outcomes, such as a sense of satisfaction or fulfillment. A dissonant relationship, on the other hand, would likely result in negative outcomes, such as discomfort or stress. Thus, if a student reported a high need for achievement and the campus environment was consensually identified as exerting a press for achievement, a congruent situation would exist, leading to satisfaction and good functioning. If the student had a low need for achievement and was in this high-achievement setting, an incongruent situation would develop. The student would become dissatisfied and perhaps leave the environment.

Transactional Approach. A third model for studying person-environment transactions is that set forth by Pervin (1968). According to Pervin, for each individual there are both interpersonal and noninterpersonal environments that are suited to, or fit, that individual's personality characteristics. A match between an individual and the environment is viewed as contributing to the (good) outcomes of higher performance, greater satisfaction, and less stress, while poor fit is viewed as related to the (negative) outcomes of decreased performance, greater dissatisfaction, and more stress. Pervin further hypothesizes that an ideal environment for any given individual is one in which the congruence of individual and environment is not exact, but presents opportunities for change and personal growth.

Pervin defines both the individual and the environment subjectively, according to the self-reported perceptions of setting inhabitants (for example, scholarly or nonscholarly, sociable or unsociable, moral or amoral) and the reactions to those perceptions (such as satisfaction). According to this theory, behavior is explained best in terms of interactions (cause-effect relationships), or "objects in a causal interconnection of one object acting upon the other," and transactions (reciprocal relations), or "objects relating to one another within a system" (Pervin, 1968, p. 58).

A main focus of Pervin's work has been the discrepancies that exist between the individual's perceived actual and ideal selves. Assumptions about how persons relate to their environment revolve around this issue. Specifically, Pervin makes three assumptions (Pervin, 1968; Walsh, 1973). First, individuals find large discrepancies between their perceived actual and ideal selves to be both unpleasant and painful. Second, individuals are positively attracted to objects in the perceived environment that have the potential of moving them in the direction of their ideal selves; conversely, individuals are negatively disposed toward stimuli that have the potential of moving them away from their ideal selves. Third, when individuals have a low actual self–ideal self discrepancy, they perceive themselves as similar to important objects in the environment. Pervin's main tenet is that individuals will perform better and report more satisfaction in environments that tend to reduce the amount of discrepancy between their perceived actual selves and their ideal selves.

Pervin's approach has been used to study congruence between student and college outcomes such as academic performance and satisfaction with college (for example, Bauer, 1975). In addition, studies have compared perceptions and satisfactions among different settings within the same college or among different colleges (Pervin, 1967; Walsh, 1973).

Human Aggregate Model. Holland (1966, 1973) puts forth a model in which the influence of the environment is related to the composition of the "human aggregate"—that is, the characteristics of the people inhabiting the environment. In particular, the relationship (congruence) between an individual's characteristics and characteristics of the aggregate determine important outcomes, such as satisfaction, achievement, and so on.

In line with his interest in vocational development, Holland uses variables such as the self-reported vocational preferences, academic majors, or occupations of members of the population to describe the environment. This reflects Holland's view that people within a given occupational group "will create characteristic interpersonal environments" (1973, p. 9). More specifically, Holland employs a six-point code to describe an environment's similarity to each of six model or primary environments. Thus, campus environments are described in terms of codes that reflect the mix of students claiming majors or vocational preferences belonging to each of the six models.

In an analogous fashion, Holland describes individuals according to their vocational preferences or choices. This decision rests on Holland's belief that members of a vocational group have similar personalities and histories of development and therefore should respond to given situations in similar ways. Like Pervin, Holland is concerned with the degree of fit or congruence between individuals and environment. He hypothesizes that a good fit is predictive of vocational satisfaction, stability, and achievement.

Holland states four formal assumptions. First, individuals may be described by their resemblance to one or more personality types (that is, clusters of personal attributes), which can be used to measure the person. The six basic types, corresponding to vocational choices, are: Realistic, Investigative, Social, Conventional, Enterprising, and Artistic. Second, environments may be characterized by their resemblance to one or more of six model environments (which correspond to the six personality types). Third, each personality type (that is, each person) searches for a congruent environment. Fourth, congruent person-environment relationships lead to predictable and understandable outcomes with respect to vocational choice, vocational stability, vocational achievement, personal stability, creative performance, and personal development.

Thus, students described as Investigative-Social types would be expected to prefer and seek out aspects of the campus environment (such as an academic department or major, a residence hall floor, an extracurricular activity) consistent with their personality style; they might, for example, be drawn to majors such as pre-med or psychology. In addition, Holland's theory suggests that such congruent student–major or student–residence hall floor matches should lead to higher productivity and a more stable vocational choice. Pairings involving greater (or lesser) degrees of discrepancy will lead to other predictable outcomes.

Holland uses two additional constructs, consistency and differentiation, in making predictions from the model. Consistency in an environment or person is said to exist when the primary and secondary characteristics are similar to each other. For example, Realistic-Investigative types are considered to be consistent types, while Artistic-Conventional types are considered inconsistent types. Differentiation refers to the degree to which a person or environment resembles only one type rather than several types. According to Holland, people having more consistent and more highly differentiated personality patterns are generally more satisfied than others.

Social Climate. Moos (1976) initially hypothesized that the environment affects the individuals who inhabit it via the "social climate." This aspect of his approach is grounded in the theoretical work of Murray (1938), Lewin (1936), and Stern (1964, 1970) and parallels the study of organizational climate (Gavin and Howe, 1975; James and Jones, 1974; Murrell, 1973). In his study of social climate, Moos has been interested primarily in the consensually perceived climate, which he measures by having respondents describe both the usual patterns of behavior that occur in their environment and their own subjective impressions of the environment.

Moos and his colleagues identified three clusters or broad categories of social climate dimensions (Insel and Moos, 1974;

Moos, 1974). These clusters are relationship dimensions (how people affiliate together, their involvement and mutual support), personal development or goal orientation dimensions (the available opportunities for personal growth or task performance), and system maintenance and system change dimensions (the extent to which the environment is orderly and clear in its expectations, maintains control, and is responsive to change). Based on their own data and reanalysis of others' climate scales, Insel and Moos (1974) concluded that each of these dimensions must be accounted for "in order for an adequate and reasonably complete picture of the environment to emerge" (p. 186).

More recently, Moos and his colleagues (Moos, 1984) have formulated a conceptual framework that broadens the approach to measuring the environment. They also hypothesize a link between stressful life circumstances and adaptation that is affected by both the environmental system and a personal system as well as by social network resources, appraisal, and coping responses. The environmental system is defined by its physical attributes, policies and other organizational factors, suprapersonal or human aggregate characteristics, and social climate. The personal system is defined in terms of sociodemographic variables, self-concept, health status, and functioning factors.

This environmental systems model is an attempt to elucidate the various pathways of influence among life stress, adaptation, the environmental system, the personal system, and the intervening or mediating factors of social network resources, appraisal, and coping responses. Thus, stress may be buffered (or prevented) by social network resources, which are themselves influenced by cognitive appraisal, which in turn may be influenced by social network resources. In addition, environmental and personal factors can shape social network resources and coping responses and their effectiveness. Furthermore, factors in the environmental and personal systems can interact to produce appraisals that precipitate preventive coping responses that may reduce the probability of future stressful life events.

The model is significant in its methodological integration of several dimensions of environmental assessment (for example,

Moos and Lemke, 1983) as well as its integration of person-environment interaction models with health and stress models to understand a variety of personal outcomes.

Much of the empirical work of Moos and his colleagues has involved the description of environments and study of the impact of various environments and social climate dimensions on inhabitants—that is, with relating various dimensions of the environment to the affect, attitude, and behavior of inhabitants (for example, Moos, 1974, 1979; Moos and Moos, 1981; Cronkite, Moos, and Finney, 1983; Keyser and Barling, 1981; Moos and Van Dort, 1979; Nielsen and Moos, 1978).

More recent research examines the determinants of social climate (for example, Moos and Lemke, 1983). Moos and his colleagues have also used their systems model to explore the relationship between life stress, social network resources, coping resources, and health-related criteria, and the role of personal and social resources in stress prevention (Billings and Moos, 1982a, 1982b; Cronkite and Moos, 1983; Holahan and Moos, 1983).

Territoriality. Although space does not permit analysis of theories related to the impact of the physical environment, the concept of territoriality warrants at least brief mention. Territoriality is a primary mechanism that mediates human social behavior and the physical environment, thereby enhancing environment-function fit (Ardrey, 1966; Bakker and Bakker-Rabdau, 1978; Hall, 1966; Mehrabian, 1976; Mehrabian and Russell, 1974). This complex behavioral system serves a number of functions for both humans and animals, including regulating density and social interaction, organizing behavior, providing areas for privacy and security, reducing conflict and aggression, and ensuring social order and group stability (Altman, 1975; Schroeder, 1981). Heilweil (1973) notes that lack of control over personal space can result in dissatisfaction owing to lack of privacy and the opportunity for solitude, the development of interpersonal conflicts, enforced sociability, and the absence of the ability to change the environment. Schroeder (1980) outlines four basic strategies for the application of territoriality to residence hall environments: personalization (changing the atmosphere of rooms, lounges, and hallways), creating defensible space (marking secondary territory such as hallways and lounges with distinctive painting or locking corridors to restrict access), regulation of social interaction, and group stability and privacy regulation. These concepts have served as the basis for a number of interventions.

Constructs and Propositions in Campus Ecology

Campus-based efforts to intervene in the person-environment interaction and research on student-campus interaction have evolved independently from the theoretical models just described. There has, in fact, been little attempt to use any specific theory to guide the development of assessment or intervention projects. More often the approach has been pragmatic or perhaps implicitly or superficially related to theory. Models of intervention have been based on selective application of various aspects of different theories rather than an explicit translation of a single theory into practice. Nevertheless, it is possible to identify components of theory building in the campus ecology literature (Huebner, 1983).

Constructs. A small number of constructs appear repeatedly in the campus ecology literature. These constructs include environment, campus environment, person, interaction, transaction, match/mismatch, and congruence/incongruence. There are no universally accepted operational definitions of these constructs. While some authors (such as Stern and Holland) provide good operational definitions for one or more of these terms, their views do not constitute standard definitions. In addition, each has failed to adequately define many of the other terms.

In the most general sense, *environment* has been defined by Kaiser (1978) as "a set of stimuli occupying consciousness in any given moment" (p. 24). Environment, in this construction, is active and evocative and calls forth a response from consciousness. The composition of the campus environment was described in an earlier paper (Western Interstate Commission for Higher Education, 1973) as consisting of all the stimuli that impinge upon the students' senses, including physical, chemical, biological, and social stimuli. Environment has been operationally defined in numerous ways in campus ecology studies. Typically, a narrow band of the environment Kaiser described is studied or altered. For example, the environment has been defined in terms of press (Stern, 1964); as the aggregate effect of the persons who occupy it (Holland, 1973); as it is perceived along some specific climate dimensions, such as support (Insel and Moos, 1974); in terms of the actual goals that appear to be pursued (Huebner, 1975); and in terms of the physical attributes (Schroeder, 1976).

There is no consensus about whether the environment is best understood, in Rychlak's (1968) terms, as "real"—actually existing independent of observation—or "ideal"—existing only in terms of perceptions. (This is typically addressed in terms of whether the environment is measured via perceptions of its qualities or via direct measures, such as behaviors, physical characteristics, or observable events.) In addition, there is no consensus about whether the environment is, again in Rychlak's terms, "objective"—transcending any one individual's perceptions—or "subjective"—private, impossible to generalize beyond one's own self. A variety of content areas are also used to represent the environment, including measures of the physical environment, the social environment, and the psychological environment.

These points of ambiguity accurately reflect the lack of consensus about this major variable both within and among models. It is, in part, a reflection of the fact that no theories of person-environment interaction have adequate operational definitions of environment (Walsh, 1973) and that in environmental psychology as well, there is no adequate theory of the environment (Mehrabian and Russell, 1974; Proshansky, Ittelson, and Rivlin, 1970).

Persons constitute another construct used in campus ecology. As with environment, a number of different operational definitions have been employed. Walsh (1973) concluded that both Holland (1973) and Stern (1970) had formally acceptable person definitions. For Stern, the person is represented in terms of needs, which are inferred from self-reported behaviors and refer to organizational tendencies that unify and direct a person's behavior. Holland defines persons in terms of their vocational choices or preferences; he categorizes people according to their similarity to certain personality or vocational types (clusters of attributes). Campus ecology literature does not explicitly define the construct person. In fact, very little is said about the nature of persons, except that they "are viewed as active, choice-making agents who may resist, transform or nullify environmental influences" (Western Interstate Commission for Higher Education, 1973, p. iii), possess capacity for a wide spectrum of possible behaviors, and will attempt to cope with any educational environment in which they are placed. In interventions, persons have been defined by their versions of the ideal environment; their personal and vocational preferences; and their levels of moral, cognitive, or intellectual development.

The relationship between persons and the environment or setting is sometimes referred to as an *interaction* or a *transaction*. The earliest document of the Western Interstate Commission on Higher Education (WICHE) on this topic (1973) indicates that a transactional relationship exists between college students and their campus environment. That is, the students shape the environment and are shaped by it. A more formal description of the term *transaction* is given by Pervin (1968)—"objects relating to one another within a system." Pervin distinguishes transaction from interaction, which he defines as "objects in a causal interconnection of one object acting upon the other" (p. 58). According to Endler and Magnusson (1976, p. 969), interaction means that "not only do events affect the behavior of organisms but the organism is also an active agent in influencing environmental events." No consensual operational definitions exist for the notions of interaction and transaction. Moreover, these terms are often used interchangeably, although they have somewhat different meanings. A large number of studies have operationalized interaction in terms of matching person and environment on one or more variables.

The concepts of *match* and *mismatch* have been central to campus ecology. In general, a match describes the case in which the environment provides what a person needs, desires, or finds pleasing, or demands a response a person is able to provide. A mismatch describes the case in which the environment fails to provide what the person needs, desires, or finds pleasing, or demands a response a person cannot provide. A mismatch may also exist when the environment fails to provide a place for the development or exercise of current competencies or forces interaction with stimuli that are obnoxious or unpleasant. A match is said to refer to a state of *congruence* between certain personal variables and related environmental variables, while mismatch refers to a state of *incongruence*.

Other constructs appear in the campus ecology literature, but they are not as pervasive as the above. *Primary prevention*, for example, is described by Conyne (1977) as the underpinning of campus ecology, which he viewed as a campus community mental health model. Caplan (1964) defines prevention as "lowering the rate of new cases of mental disorder in a population over a certain time period by counteracting harmful circumstances before they have a chance to produce illness" (p. 26). Conyne (1983) identifies key components of primary prevention. These components begin with a proactive orientation in a population-based approach. Other components include anticipating potential disorder for a population at risk and introducing "before-the-fact" interventions that may be delivered either directly or indirectly. The interventions are designed to decrease the incidence of a disorder by counteracting harmful circumstances that contribute to it and by promoting emotional robustness in the population at risk so that population members both are protected and become more fully competent.

The concept of populations *at risk* is also used in campus ecology. Members of a population are at risk when they have a greater than average probability of developing one or more disorders. Bloom (1977) identifies three types of at-risk populations: total populations (at risk, for example, for alcohol abuse); milestone populations (for example, those facing normative life transitions, such as new retirees or college freshmen); and at high-risk populations (for example, those facing nonnormative or sudden crises, such as death of a loved one, natural disaster, or rape). At-risk populations are targeted for study or intervention in an attempt to understand the mechanisms whereby risk is translated into disorder and to reduce the incidence and prevalence of disorder in the population.

From a developmental perspective, Blocher (1977, 1978) introduces another set of constructs relative to campus ecology. He abstracted from numerous research reports the essential ingredients for growth or learning—that is, for structural change in thinking, feeling, and acting. These essential environmental ingredients include involvement (psychological engagement with the learning environment), challenge (an optimal mismatch between demands and present coping behavior), support (experiencing a degree of caring, empathy, and honesty from others), structure (the availability of examples of functioning slightly more advanced than one's own), feedback (opportunities to practice), application (opportunities to test new concepts, attitudes, and skills), and integration (opportunities to review, examine, and evaluate experiences in a safe environment).

Blocher (1978) also defines three major subsystems of a learning environment: *opportunity, support,* and *reward.* The opportunity subsystem provides task structure or enabling experiences. It is related to three previous constructs: involvement, challenge, and integration. The support subsystem provides both structure and support. The structure comes from cognitive frameworks that reduce the stimulation the individual experiences. Support is provided by a relationship network. The reward subsystem provides for feedback and application opportunities.

Several classification constructs also have been defined in order to describe interventions with different purposes. *Remedial interventions* are those in which the environment is designed to compensate for deficits within individuals, groups, and communities. That is, they aim to bring persons up to a level where the deficit is no longer a deterrent to optimal functioning. In *preventive interventions,* individuals who are at risk are the target of person-centered or environment-centered efforts to keep "dysfunction" or distress from occurring. In *developmental interventions,* the environment is designed to enhance the functioning of individuals, groups, and communities so that they may more fully realize their objectives. Finally, *potentiating interventions* are those in which environments are designed so that they expose individuals, groups, and communities to new stimuli that enable them to develop potentials of which they may not have been aware.

Propositions. Several overarching theoretical propositions have also appeared in campus ecology literature. The most basic concern is the interactional-transactional relationship between persons and the environment. Mead and Davis (1979) cogently present an interactional paradigm, which holds that the "organism and environment are engaged in a *continuous* process of mutual feedback" (p. 11; emphasis added). Behavior, then, is determined by this continuous process of interaction. In Stern's (1964) terms, $B = f(P, E)$; that is, behavior is a function of the interaction of person and environment.

According to this proposition, dysfunction is viewed as systemic, making intervention in the system a legitimate mental health function. More emphatically, student problems can be treated most effectively not through treatment of the student individually but through treatment of the environment and the person-environment relationship.[1] Paul and Huebner (1977) explicitly develop the possibility of intervention at the interaction or intersection points of environment and person. Pursuing a similar thought, Aplin (1978) hypothesizes that changes in organizational structure and process (enabling mechanisms) should have a direct and immediate impact on both input and output variables. By contrast, changes in behavior, without accompanying structural change, would probably have a less direct impact on organizational performance. Aplin also makes the assumption that structural inadequacies are manifest in behavioral symptoms. This is similar to Huse's (1978) formulation that many "personality clashes" are the direct result of improper organizational design.

A second major proposition is that the individual is an intentional, active agent in this interactional process. The indi-

[1] These concepts bear much similarity to those underlying family therapy and other systemic approaches (see, for example, Becvar and Becvar, 1982).

vidual "has an impact on the environment *and* is an active rather than passive receiver, organizing the world, the stimulus field, in a unique . . . fashion" (Mead and Davis, 1979, p. 9). Students shape the environment and are shaped by it. They are active, choice-making agents who may resist, transform, or nullify environmental influences (Western Interstate Commission for Higher Education, 1973).

Mead and Davis (1979) present two related propositions that describe ways in which the individual contributes to the interaction effect. Taken from Endler and Magnusson (1976), these propositions are: (1) cognitive factors are important in the interaction of person and environment, and (2) the psychological meaning of the situation to the individual is an essential determinant of behavior. Mischel (1973, p. 276) states: "The meaning and impact of a stimulus can be modified dramatically by *cognitive transformations*" in such a way as to make the individual's response to a situation idiographic. Thus behavior is not generalized across situations because the person "always behaves within a context which provides some *information* to the person about the meaning of a given behavior within a contextual frame" (Mead and Davis, 1979, p. 11).

On a more pragmatic level, three hypotheses concerning students' involvement in influencing the environment have been identified. First, psychological well-being requires self-esteem, which may in turn depend on a belief that one's own behavior can affect the environment (Lewis and Lewis, 1977). Second, a successful campus design intervention is a function of the participation of all campus members. Finally, opportunities for achieving an optimum environment are significantly enhanced when students have information about environmental effects.

A third major theoretical proposition, emanating from the belief that individuals will attempt to cope with any environment in which they are placed, concerns the effects of various types or levels of person-environment congruence. Generally, if the environment is not basically compatible with the student, the student may react negatively or fail to develop desirable qualities. It is also noted that each student will have an idiosyncratic response to an environment because of his or her unique characteristics and perceptions, and thus will require an idiosyncratic matching environment. These responses and underlying characteristics/perceptions may also change from time to time.

Some theorists have failed to define explicitly the optimal degree of fit for individuals or groups. In most of these instances, the informal theory implies that an increasingly close person-environment fit is related to increasingly positive outcomes for all individuals. However, other theorists more explicitly state that optimal fit is not absolute, perfect, or similar for all individuals. Rather, some amount of incongruence (such as challenge) amidst a generally congruent situation (such as support) will stimulate development. Adjusting the degree of fit to an optimal level for an individual or group, then, is a potential method of intervention. This type of intervention decreases dysfunctional stress and promotes growth and development. These assumptions imply that environments can be modified to increase the availability of features or dimensions that are optimally or facilitationally congruent and to reduce or change features that are seriously or disruptively incongruent.

Finally, as noted earlier, Blocher (1977, 1978) has identified seven ingredients for growth in a learning environment. He set forth the proposition that these elements—involvement, challenge, support, structure, feedback, application, and integration—constitute the essential environmental ingredients for growth and that students differ widely in their need for each of these elements.

Conceptual and Process Models
for Assessment and Intervention

Based on the constructs and propositions just presented, practitioners and theoreticians have developed a variety of models for intervening in the university system. Several of these models focus primarily on the *process* of assessment and the design and delivery of an intervention. These models generally offer guidance regarding political and participation issues, delineate stages of the assessment/intervention process, and specify important types of activities. *Conceptual* models, on the other hand, have primarily addressed the relationship of variables in the person-environment system, and they focus on ways of understanding what must be assessed or changed to create a successful intervention.

Four process models have been fairly widely acknowledged. The first was presented by WICHE in its 1973 monograph and has been among the most influential. This model identifies seven steps in the ecosystem system design process: "1. Designers, in conjunction with community members, select educational values; 2. Values are then translated into specific goals; 3. Environments are designed that contain mechanisms to reach the stated goal; 4. Environments are fitted to students; 5. Students' perceptions of the environment are measured; 6. Student behavior resulting from environmental perceptions is monitored; 7. Data on the environmental designs' successes and failures, as indicated by student perceptions and behavior, are fed back to the designers in order that they may continue to learn about student-environment fit and design better environments" (Western Interstate Commission for Higher Education, 1973, p. 7).

Aulepp and Delworth (1976) present a simpler model that focuses on specific steps an intervenor would need to follow. Their monograph provides detailed instruction in the implementation of this model, which has generated significant applied efforts. Step 1 is to obtain sanction and establish a planning team. Step 2 is to generate assessment topic areas. Step 3 involves developing assessment instruments. Step 4 is the administration of assessment instruments, and step 5 is the introduction of the redesign intervention and reassessment.

A third process model is presented by Huebner and Corazzini (1978). Their eco-mapping model involves ten steps, based on a general theoretical framework in which the student has a variety of needs, desires, wants, and so on that must be met in large measure through the environment and its resources. Person-environment interaction is then defined in terms of the congruence between needs, desires, and so on and resources.

The student is conceptualized as "mapping" the environment for the presence of resources, especially as they relate to his or her needs. Professional intervenors also have a "mapping" function as they develop a map or chart of the characteristics of the environment. Huebner and Corazzini (1978) emphasize the importance of using multimethod assessment procedures to gather data from several domains (physical features, perceptions, behaviors, and so on) and then to integrate those data. Their steps are: (1) obtain sanction and establish an on-site planning team, (2) chart the actual environment; (3) identify subgroup needs and goals, (4) identify matches and mismatches between needs and environment, (6) examine how students have coped with the mismatches, (7) return data to the design team, (8) implement design activities, and (9) reassess to ensure that mismatches are reduced. This model, like that of Aulepp and Delworth, pays explicit attention to the political nature of this process and to the need for broad representation on the planning or design teams.

Several conceptual models have also been presented, but they appear to have had somewhat less impact on practice. For example, Huebner (1975, 1979, 1983) presents an organizational interactional model, based on the work of the industrial-organizational psychologists Howe and Gavin (1974). This model is based on the notion of person-environment fit and employs nine categories of variables. Briefly, the first variable consists of the organizational environment or system, including, for example, physical properties, academic offerings, behaviors, norms, channels and modes of communication, maintenance functions, rewards, and punishments. Environmental characteristics are seen from an ''objective'' perspective and are also identified as potential stressors.

The second variable consists of characteristics such as psychological, demographic, and other descriptors of persons and groups, including personality constructs, goals, needs, values, probable areas, and psychological vulnerability or strength. Person and environment are both construed as independent variables, which then interact to create a ''person-in-environment'' variable. This, the third variable, is actually a unique constellation of variables associated with a particular person in a particular role.

The fourth variable, the perceived environment, is a function of the interaction of the first three variables. It is compared with the ideal environment, the fifth variable, which is a function of person characteristics. The comparison produces a certain degree of person-environment fit, the sixth variable. The state of person-environment fit is equated with "stress," such that poor person-environment fit is the equivalent of a state of high systemic stress, while good person-environment fit is equated with low systemic stress. Fit and stress are thus intervening variables.

Attributes of the person and of the environment, plus the perceived degree or quality of person-environment fit, interact and produce outcomes—including affective outcomes for the person (the seventh variable), behavior outcomes for the person (the eighth variable), and outcomes for the organization (the ninth variable). These outcomes may be more or less positive or negative. The goal of the system is to create an optimal level of stress and fit. In situations of poor person-environment fit, person outcomes are conceptualized as strain. Both positive and strain effects for person and environment are the dependent variables. Numerous feedback loops are also acknowledged, although not delineated.

Dohrenwend's (1978) community stress model has provided the basic conceptualization scheme for at least one major campus ecology intervention (Paul and Morrill, 1982) and appears to have considerable potential. In this model, individual and environment interact in a way that may lead to the occurrence of a "stressful life event." For example, a student planning to go to medical school may fail chemistry and be dropped from the pre-med curriculum. A temporary disequilibrium or transient stress reaction is the student's natural reaction to this stressful event. During the time of the stress reaction, situational mediators (such as material supports or handicaps, social supports or handicaps) and psychological mediators (such as aspirations, values, coping abilities or disabilities) may be activated to buffer the experience of stress. The outcome of this transient stress reaction may leave the student as she was, improve her psychological functioning, or result in a more chronic adjustment problem (such as a prolonged and disruptive depression).

Dohrenwend does not spell out specific operational methods for defining the variables in each of these categories.

She does define realms of intervention, however, noting that "political action" is a major way to change environmental situations; general education and socialization can change the person; community and organizational development can affect situational mediators; individual skill training can affect psychological mediators; crisis intervention can respond to transient stress reactions; and corrective therapies can respond to psychopathology, if it develops. The campus ecological perspective encompasses a number of these types of intervention and hopes to speak to environmental changes and the provision/strengthening of situational mediators, as well as to general education and socialization and skill training (to a lesser degree). It is considerably less concerned with crisis intervention and corrective therapies.

Conyne (1983) presents an adaptation of the public health model, which he calls the "stressful life variables model," as a way to conceptualize the process of prevention. He notes that the biologically oriented public health model does not work as well for multiply determined psychological and social problems as it does for biologically rooted medical problems. In the public health model, the process of illness development is conceptualized as host × environment × agent = disease. This model focuses on undesirable end-states and suggests that identification of the causal linkages among host, environment, and agent, followed by intervention, will result in reduced incidence and prevalence of the targeted disease.

The modification suggested by Conyne approaches prevention through the following sequence: "Identify a stressful life variable (situation, transition event, or social indicator), intervene, lower incidence" (Conyne, 1983, p. 333). In this model, a central task is to identify the potential stressful life variables in the environment that may contribute to undesirable outcomes (end-states). Strategies that may be used to prevent the negative effects of stressful life variables include competency enhancement and environmental change. Competency enhancement (such as increasing knowledge and skills) is used to bolster the hosts' (students') resistance to the future effects of certain causal agents or stressful life variables. Environmental change strategies are used to remove or to alter noxious elements or sources of stress in the environment itself. Additionally, environmental change may be initiated to promote a better "ecological match" between a population and its environment.

An important implication of this model is its assumption of multifactorial causes and effects in problems and illness development. Thus, one end-state (such as attrition) is not usually a direct result of just one stressful life variable (an indifferent adviser), and the existence of a stressful life variable (severe grade competition) does not necessarily result in any one specific outcome. Thus, interventions ought to include not only specific components targeted at hypothetical causal connections, but also nonspecific intervention components that provide general psychological and social support and promote the development of competencies.

Paul and Huebner (1977) present a model for reviewing the process of person-environment interaction. Their model does not adopt any particular theoretical position but can serve as an "integrative framework for existing concepts as well as a heuristic vehicle for . . . new ideas" (Paul, 1980, p. 71). The model conceives of the person as a problem solver and delineates a series of eight steps (based on the model of D'Zurilla and Goldfried, 1971) that the person initiates in order to gather information and to act, with the aim of producing outcomes that are satisfying, need-reducing, or self-sustaining. The model is prescriptive rather than literal, in that it acknowledges that not all individuals under all circumstances will go through this process.

In this model, the individual is defined by physical, affective, motivational, personality, interpersonal, social/cultural, and cognitive variables. The first step involves this individual taking in information from the environment, causing arousal. Based on interpretations (step 2) of the information, a problem may be recognized, which may give rise to some expression (step 3). If the problem is intense and persistent enough, the individual then performs an internal (step 4) or perhaps external (step 5) search to generate alternative solutions. The alternative solutions are then evaluated (step 6) and one of them may be chosen (step 7). The final step is evaluation of the outcome of the preceding process (step 8) with the option of cycling through again if the outcome has not been satisfactory.

The model suggests an environmental process parallel to and interactive with the personal process. Environmental features of interest are adapted from Moos (1973) and James and Jones (1974) and include physical features, organizational structure, personal characteristics of inhabitants, reinforcement properties, organizational climate, organizational tasks, administrative style, and organizational goals. At the most passive stage of the process, the environment furnishes an existing arrangement of elements as a context for human behavior. Moving toward greater activity, agents of the environment may allow for the expression of perceptions or reactions or may even solicit such expressions. At this point, the activity of the environment becomes more intentional; agents of the environment may deliberately inform community members about some features of the environment, train members in new skills, or attempt to change perceptions or attitudes about the environment. More active yet, the environment may modify itself, creating a new constellation of environmental features. Finally, the environmental process is evaluated with respect to the outcomes produced.

Person-environment interaction occurs as the two processes overlap and contribute to each other. For example, a person searches for information in the external environment; simultaneously, the environment attempts to make information available. Intervention can take place with either component at any step. For example, a person can be trained to do a better search, or the environment can be helped to be clearer and less ambiguous in its presentation of information. The most important implications of the model are that interventions can be directed at both elements simultaneously and that their intersection (literally the person-environment interaction) can also be a target of intervention.

There is an additional type of "model" that also deserves attention here. Several practitioners of campus ecology have created classification systems for identifying and organizing possible interventions. Banning (1980) created the management template for campus ecology, which aids its user in identifying opportunities, supports, and rewards present in the campus environment to support student development along the seven vectors described by Chickering (1969). Thus, campus managers can identify the ways in which development along these vectors is and is not facilitated in the environment (see Chapter Twelve for more detail).[2]

Hurst (1980) also designed a two-dimensional chart describing the activities of a student affairs division. The chart crosses intervention programs (both for the general university and for specific subgroups) with content areas that the intervention programs may relate to, including: the management of basic resources (such as food, housing, health, and finances), student development (defined along the seven dimensions described by Drum, 1980), and environmental development (design and modification along physical, social, cultural, academic, and administrative dimensions). In addition to facilitating a description of services, this chart also leads to the identification of needed programs that do not exist and aids in future program planning.

Finally, Hurst and McKinley (forthcoming) developed a diagnostic classification system for counseling that allows for an interactional analysis of student problems. Adapted from the Missouri Diagnostic System (Apostal and Miller, 1959), this system defines three broad categories of potential "sources" of problems: the person (who may suffer from lack of information about self, conflict within self, and personal deficit), the environment (where there may be a lack of information in the environment, conflict within the environment, and environmental deficit), and the person-environment interaction (in which both person and environment are healthy, but there is a lack of congruence between them). Three problem content areas (personal-social development, career development, and educational development) are crossed with the above problem sources to produce a 3 × 7 matrix. This system allows counseling centers to develop meaningful ecological data bases through the tracking of prob-

---

[2]This model could be strengthened through the addition of a search for the *obstacles* to development that also are present in the campus environment. Thus, a force field analysis type of process would be generated. This could be a final column in the template, which would call for interventions that might enhance opportunities, supports, and rewards or decrease or diminish obstacles.

lems brought into the counseling center. Such data should suggest fruitful areas for intervention as well as provide a base line for evaluation of various planned and unplanned environmental changes. The system also encourages counselors to consider nonintrapsychic (and even noninterpersonal) sources of client problems, which should be useful in increasing options for effective treatment.

Evaluation and Conclusions

A number of specific criticisms can be made of the theory and practice of campus ecology. First, the theoretical postulates are not very explicit and they generally lack adequate operational definitions of the critical terms. For example, we still lack an adequate definition of environment, and definitions of persons are often makeshift. Studies in campus ecology are especially deficient in defining the physical environment and relating it to the perceived or psychological environment. For this reason it might be useful to consult the work of environmental psychologists, such as Mehrabian and Russell (1974), who proposed a model of environmental impact in which the environment is represented by sensory stimulus components (such as color, pitch, texture, temperature) and the concept of "information rate" (which subsumes concepts such as complexity, novelty, crowding, harmony). The person is represented as an intervening variable, measured by characteristic and current emotional responses to the environment (pleasure, arousal, dominance, and their combinations). The outcome or behavior is measured in terms of the concept of approach-avoidance (which includes physical approach, performance, affiliation, preferences, and so on). Briefly stated, their theory is that "physical or social stimuli in the environment directly affect the emotional state of a person, thereby influencing his behaviors in it" (p. 8).

Another shortcoming in campus ecology efforts is that the concept of interaction is seldom explicitly or carefully spelled out. Often it is limited to operational definition as a literal match between group members' responses to sets of items (such as goals and perceptions or real and ideal environments) or as a match between an individual and the group on some dimensions. In many cases, there is no attempt to define the process or nature of interaction but only to observe how people react when placed in environments with certain features. In addition, explications of the model have presented a superficially interactional picture. While some relationship is hypothesized to exist between certain personal and environmental variables, the model (as judged by the majority of interventions and research) has tended to be static, addressing single points of person-environment interaction and not addressing the ongoing, continual, and mutually adaptive nature of the changes experienced by persons and environment.

Also, the rich concepts of cognitive mediation and cognitive structures are dealt with in only one manifestation—as perceptions of the environment. The way individuals use such cognitive structures to organize events, transform the meaning and impact of a stimulus, or give some consistency to their own behavior is generally ignored. Further, person-environment fit is typically explored with reference to subgroups rather than individuals and along a handful of personal or environmental dimensions. More careful attention should be paid to the choice of variable for which "fit" is examined—perhaps variables related to more substantial theories of human development, learning, health and illness, and so on should be included. Possibly a new and more realistic paradigm is needed to consider the fact that fit between person and environment is multifaceted, changeable, and influenced by a variety of cognitive and perceptual variables.

The literature on campus ecology has generated only a meager set of related theories. Furthermore, most studies have not adequately researched the question of the usefulness of the theories or postulates in predicting important outcomes. Most ecosystems studies, if they include an evaluation of the outcome at all, look at variables such as change of perception (for example, the student union is perceived more positively in x dimensions, or ideal and real descriptions of faculty advisers are more congruent). Lacking is the step of relating these outcomes to other outcomes of either more theoretical or more practical interest, such as achievement, productivity, moral development, retention, illness, and so on. Schroeder (1976), Mayer and Butterworth (1979), Rodgers (1984), and Banning (1985) are four noteworthy exceptions: Schroeder reports changes in residence hall occupancy, building damage, and semester-to-semester retention; Mayer and Butterworth report a decrease in vandalism; Rodgers reports changes in intellectual development; and Banning reports a decrease in vandalism, alcohol abuse, and sexual harassment. Other researchers outside the campus ecology paradigm have documented the relationship of P × E intervention to these types of outcomes.

The interventions reviewed do not make explicit use of the person-environment interaction theories of Holland, Stern, Pervin, Barker, Mischel, or Moos or of theories based on environmental psychology. In fact, although many of Moos's assessment instruments are used in ecosystem assessments, little explicit attention is given to the concepts that underlie the development of these scales. In addition, little direct use has been made of the systems approach, applied to campus ecology by Meade and Davis (1979) and Hamilton and Meade (1984), to the public health model by Conyne (1983), and to the organizational model adapted by Huebner (1979).

For the most part, interventions have been based on the variables that were initially chosen for assessment, without much theoretical justification for the choice of those variables. Lacking is the use of an overarching theory to guide the researcher or change agent in the choice of intervention and assessment targets or desired outcomes. Some theories exist that could be used for this purpose. For example, the developmental theories (Blocher, 1977, 1978; Chickering, 1969; Drum, 1980; Erikson, 1959, 1968; Gilligan, 1982; Kohlberg, 1969; Loevinger, 1976; Perry, 1970) provide a rich source of information about how development should (and, under appropriate circumstances, does) proceed, suggesting numerous important questions about college environments and the extent to which they foster or even allow development to occur. Increasingly, those writing in the field have been calling for such an integration of developmental and interactional methods and perspectives.[3] However, interventions have not yet caught up with this suggestion. One of the few studies to implement such an approach is that by Parker and Lawson (1978), who describe a consulting project in which Perry's theory of cognitive development was used as a guideline for the collection of data about faculty teaching styles and student and faculty expectations about the teaching and learning process.

Research in the area of stress and health also offers some promising concepts for the campus ecologist. Several important predictor variables have been linked empirically with both positive and negative outcomes in stressful situations. For example, Kobassa, Hilker, and Maddi (1979) have found that the ability to withstand the potentially deleterious effects of stress could be related to the concept of "hardiness." In their definition, hardiness is a perceptual set or attitude toward life, consisting of openness to change ("challenge"), involvement in one's activities ("commitment"), and a moderate sense of power over one's life ("control"). Finkel and Jacobsen (1977) present data that reinforce the notion of the importance of perception and attitude in coping with stress and turning stressful situations into growth-producing ones. Moos (1984) has also developed a useful model for examining the multiple influences of personal and environmental characteristics, stressful life events, appraisal, social support, and coping responses in the determination of health status. This model, reviewed briefly earlier in this chapter, may be useful in generating future campus studies.

Explicit Suggestions for Future Direction

Several issues appear repeatedly in the literature (Albee, 1986; Danish, D'Augelli, and Ginsberg, 1984; Long, 1986). These include the importance of personal competencies and personal efficacy or power, social support, and the damaging conse-

[3]Several authors (for example, Banning, 1980; Hurst, 1987; Sullivan, 1987) have made tentative steps in this direction in terms of models and heuristics.

quences of excessive and unmediated stress. These variables are generally believed to relate to the development or prevention of psychopathology and to the enhancement of human potential. (Other variables, such as poverty and emotionally damaging childhood experiences, are also identified as significant, but they do not have as much relevance to our population.) These concepts relate to recurring themes in student development literature as well, particularly to the notion that the amount of challenge an individual can tolerate is related to the support available, and to the central importance of involvement in making college a meaningful experience. These concepts should be the focus of campus intervention efforts.

Data appear to suggest that mental health problems may be at least partially prevented by decreasing the level of psychosocial stress (or minimizing its impact when it is excessive). At the same time, positive development may be fostered by making use of predictable or unexpected stress, by supporting individuals in their effort to contend with or make meaning of it. Increasing individual psychosocial competence and enhancing the social support available to individuals are two additional strategies for prevention of mental health problems. Both also may be effective in promoting development, such as when competencies form building blocks for developmental progression, or when social support provides the necessary context for risk, tolerance of challenge, and change.

To reduce stress, the practitioner can take several steps. First, identify the predictable times (such as the first six weeks of the freshman year and final exams) of increased stress that may prove overwhelming to some and disruptive for many. Second, identify who is most likely to suffer disabling stress reactions at these times—those for whom the change is greatest, the transition most disjunctive; those who have fewer needed competencies to deal with the stress, other concomitant stressors, or insufficient social support to counteract the effects of the stress. Third, once high-risk groups and times (and perhaps places) are identified, consider whether the stressors can be directly decreased, perhaps by altering the amount of information presented, the complexity of information presented, or the number of decisions required. Fourth, look for ways to provide additional supports—such as the option to bring along more items of personal relevance from home, help from an older student to "learn the ropes," or a small group with whom the student spends considerable periods of time during the first weeks, so that friendships are fostered—and to increase stress management competencies.

Since social support appears to directly enhance psychological well-being and may buffer the effects of severe stress as well, the practitioner should increase the availability of social support. First, form small groups based on common interests or common personal attributes for freshmen during the first weeks of school that will meet regularly over some period of time and engage in meaningful activities. Second, pair new students with older students (or more experienced students) according to some shared interest. Third, make available residence halls (or floors) composed of students with some similar interests or personal orientation. Fourth, involve all students in face-to-face interactions with faculty advisers or advising groups that meet regularly. Fifth, promote clubs, organizations, and interest groups that may appeal to and be convenient for a variety of types of students. Sixth, teach one or more students per residence hall basic "good communication skills" or "helping skills" as well as provide information about resources and critical processes (such as registration or financial aid) on campus. Since social support may be particularly critical during times of high stress, training students to be "natural helpers" in the dorms or in programs, structuring organizational events to "take the pulse" of students during critical times, and clearly publicizing sources of personal help on campus may be helpful. In addition, some data suggest that social support may be more important for women than for men; it may be especially important to attend to this variable in women's dorms, in colleges and programs where there is a preponderance of women, and in "programmatic activities" that are likely to attract women.

For the variable of psychosocial competence, it becomes important to define those variables that appear to have the most salience for college students. Some competencies whose significance has been confirmed in several university studies are the ability to solve both everyday and major problems effectively; the ability to do long-range planning about one's life direction (including the ability to adapt and change); personal skills, such as coping with feelings, differentiating feelings, exercising self-control, taking care of one's physical health (including exercise and diet), managing anxiety, and managing the experiential aspect of stress; interpersonal skills, such as effective communication, assertiveness, interpersonal problem solving, intimacy, asking for help or support, and dealing with conflicts; and academic competencies, such as reading, writing, public speaking, logic, reasoning, and so on.

Competencies may be partitioned into those necessary for survival and those that can be conceptualized as "developmental"—those expected to be acquired during college. For those competencies or levels of competency that are necessary for survival or satisfactory progression, the task seems to be to ensure that all students attain proficiency. This may be done via competency-based orientation courses or through the use of "developmental transcripts." For those competencies or levels of competency more related to development, it would be useful to create an expectancy that these will be achieved, and to create appropriate opportunity-support-reward structures, such as courses, credits, action and experience opportunities, and information. Finally, it is important to find out how students view their efficacy and power on campus—personally, interpersonally, and within the system. To increase the sense of efficacy, we might provide opportunity-support-reward structures for leadership (in student organizations, through college work-study or other jobs, through offices, through honoraries or student activism), as well as invite and pay attention to student opinion and initiative.

Identification and design of effective interventions may be facilitated by using the intervention classification scheme presented in Figure 1. The grid identifies three sources or loci of concern and of intervention—person, environment, and person-environment interaction—and four goals of intervention—compensation/treatment, prevention, development, and management. This intervention classification scheme may be

Figure 1. Intervention Classification Scheme.

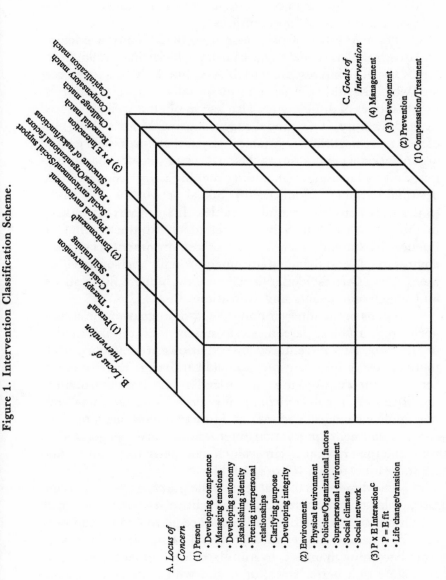

A. *Locus of Concern*

(1) Person
- Developing competence
- Managing emotions
- Developing autonomy
- Establishing identity
- Freeing interpersonal relationships
- Clarifying purpose
- Developing integrity

(2) Environment
- Physical environment
- Policies/Organizational factors
- Suprapersonal environment
- Social climate
- Social network

(3) P x E Interaction[c]
- P = E fit
- Life change/transition

B. *Locus of Intervention*

(1) Person[a]
- Therapy
- Crisis intervention
- Skill training

(2) Environment[b]
- Physical environment
- Social environment/Social support
- Policies/Organizational factors
- Structure of tasks/functions

(3) P x E Interaction
- Remedial match
- Challenge match
- Compensatory match
- Capitalization match

C. *Goals of Intervention*

(1) Compensation/Treatment
(2) Prevention
(3) Development
(4) Management

[a]*Source:* Adapted from Chickering, 1969.
[b]*Source:* Adapted from Moos, 1984.
[c]*Source:* Adapted from Cross, 1976.

used to clarify thinking about problems and facilitate consideration of a diversity of interventions.

Possible types of person-sources of difficulty are legion
and diverse. This model suggests using Chickering's (1969) vectors. Of special interest are variables within the competency vector, which should be assessed individually. Types of environ-
ment-sources of difficulty are also legion but less well explicated
in the literature. This model suggests using Moos's (1984) list
of relevant categories of variables: physical features, policies and
organizational factors, suprapersonal (or aggregate) characteristics, and social climate (including the three dimensions and individual variables within them). Social network is also added
to the list of environmental variables. It is important to keep
in mind that there may be several subenvironments that influence the student, such as the work environment, classroom
environment, and living environment. Finally, person-environment sources are divided into person-environment fit, or stress,
and life-change events and transitions.

Locus of the intervention may also range over these categories of variables: person, environment, and the interaction
of the two. Person-centered interventions are categorized as
therapy, crisis intervention, and skill training. Environment-
centered interventions are categorized as physical environment
modifications, social environment interventions and social support, policy changes, and task and function modifications. Person-environment interaction interventions are categorized as
remedial match, challenging match, compensatory match, and
capitalization match (Cross, 1976).

The dimension of goal reflects the purpose of the intervention, which may be to treat an already distressed person; to create
conditions that will temporarily or more permanently compensate for a deficit; to prevent a potential or anticipated problem
from becoming manifest; to stimulate development from a current state to a better state; or to aid with management goals
(such as decreasing attrition, decreasing vandalism, or increasing
use of certain facilities).

To design interventions, the student development intervenor could begin by specifying a general area of concern, such
as academic competence. Then a specific problem must be iden-

tified, such as an unacceptably high failure rate of nursing students of a certain demographic/socioeconomic status description. Following this, the goal must be specified. In this case, the goal might be to work with incoming students who fit this description to ensure their academic success. Next, potential interventions can be considered. For example, are there specific skills that can be taught prior to matriculation or in the first week of classes (such as study skills, test-taking skills, or assertion skills)? Is a policy or curricular change appropriate to alter the sequence or pace of courses? Would changes in the suprapersonal configuration help? For example, would study groups of a single personality type (as determined by the Myers-Briggs Type Indicator, or MBTI) add needed support, or would MBTI groupings based on complementary combinations provide mutual aid for blind spots? In terms of person-environment interaction, would changes in the method of teaching and testing help—with a focus on a better match between student learning style and faculty teaching and testing style?

This process may be further aided by the generation and use of guides to developmental principles, environmental principles, and interactional principles. These guides would summarize accepted findings about stimulating specific types of development (such as factors that aid dualistic students in moving toward a relativist position). They would also summarize findings about the kinds of effects known to be generally produced by various kinds of environments or arrangements of physical features (such as what dimensions of the perceived social climate are related to increasing students' academic achievement or their creativity). Finally, they would present the findings about person-environment interaction in a usable fashion (such as the effects on an individual who is congruent with the aggregate of living in an environment that is fairly homogeneous on features related to the incongruence). These guides could then provide theoretically or empirically solid guidelines for initiating a variety of person-, environment-, and interaction-oriented interventions. While such guidelines could not be definitive or complete, they would go a long way in helping student development staff members design more powerful and more appropriate interventions. Such a technology is just within our reach.

References

Albee, G. W. "Toward a Just Society." *American Psychologist,* 1986, *8* (41), 891–898.

Altman, I. *The Environment and Social Behavior.* Monterey, Calif.: Brooks/Cole, 1975.

Aplin, J. C. "Structural Change vs. Behavioral Change." *Personnel and Guidance Journal,* 1978, *56* (7), 407–411.

Apostal, R. A., and Miller, J. G. *A Manual for the Use of a Set of Diagnostic Categories.* Columbia: University of Missouri Testing and Counseling Center, 1959.

Ardrey, R. *The Territorial Imperative.* New York: Atheneum, 1966.

Aulepp, L. A., and Delworth, U. *Training Manual for an Ecosystem Model.* Boulder, Colo.: Western Interstate Commission for Higher Education, 1976.

Bakker, C., and Bakker-Rabdau, M. *No Trespassing: Explorations in Human Territoriality.* San Francisco: Chandler, 1978.

Banning, J. H. "The Campus Ecology Manager Role." In U. Delworth, G. Hanson, and Associates, *Student Services: A Handbook for the Profession.* San Francisco: Jossey-Bass, 1980.

Banning, J. H. "Using the Ecosystem Design Process to Redesign a Macrolevel Campus Event: A Case Study." Paper presented at the third annual Campus Ecology Symposium, Pingree Park, Colo., June 1985.

Barker, R. G. *Ecological Psychology: Concepts and Methods for Studying the Environment of Human Behavior.* Stanford, Calif.: Stanford University Press, 1968.

Bauer, G. E. "Performance and Satisfaction as a Function of Person Environment Fit." Unpublished doctoral dissertation, University of Missouri, 1975.

Becvar, R. J., and Becvar, D. S. *Systems Theory and Family Therapy.* Lanham, Md.: University Press of America, 1982.

Billings, A., and Moos, R. H. "Social Support and Functioning Among Community and Clinical Groups: A Panel Model." *Journal of Behavioral Medicine,* 1982a, *5,* 295–311.

Billings, A., and Moos, R. H. "Stressful Life Events and Symptoms: A Longitudinal Model." *Journal of Health Psychology,* 1982b, *1,* 99–117.

Bishop, D. W., and Witt, P. A. "Sources of Behavioral Variance During Leisure Time." *Journal of Personality and Social Psychology,* 1970, *16,* 352–360.

Blocher, D. H. "The Counselor's Impact on Learning Environments." *Personnel and Guidance Journal,* 1977, *55* (6), 352–355.

Blocher, D. H. "Campus Learning Environments and the Ecology of Student Development." In J. H. Banning (ed.), *Campus Ecology: A Perspective for Student Affairs.* Cincinnati, Ohio: National Association of Student Personnel Administrators, 1978.

Blocher, D. H. "Human Ecology and the Future of Counseling Psychology." *Counseling Psychologist,* 1981, *9* (4), 69–77.

Bloom, B. *Community Mental Health: A General Introduction.* Monterey, Calif.: Brooks/Cole, 1977.

Bowers, K. S. "Situations in Psychology: An Analysis and a Critique." *Psychological Review,* 1973, *80,* 307–336.

Caplan, G. *Principles of Preventive Psychiatry.* New York: Basic Books, 1964.

Cassell, J. "The Contribution of the Social Environment to Host Resistance." *American Journal of Epidemiology,* 1976, *104,* 107–123.

Chickering, A. W. *Education and Identity.* San Francisco: Jossey-Bass, 1969.

Conyne, R. K. "The Campus Change Advocate." *Journal of College Student Personnel,* 1977, *18* (4), 312–316.

Conyne, R. K. "Two Critical Issues in Primary Prevention: What It Is and How to Do It." *Personnel and Guidance Journal,* 1983, *61* (6), 331–333.

Cronkite, R., and Moos, R. H. *The Role of Predisposing and Mediating Factors in the Stress-Illness Relationship.* Palo Alto, Calif.: Social Ecology Laboratory, Stanford University, 1983.

Cronkite, R., Moos, R. H., and Finney, J. "The Context of Adaptation: An Integrated Perspective on Community and Treatment Environments." In W. A. O'Connor and B. Lubin (eds.), *Ecological Models in Clinical and Community Mental Health.* New York: Wiley, 1983.

Cross, K. P. *Accent on Learning: Improving Instruction and Reshaping the Curriculum.* San Francisco: Jossey-Bass, 1976.

Danish, S. J., D'Augelli, A. R., and Ginsberg, M. R. "Life

Development and Intervention: Promotion of Mental Health Through the Development of Competence.'' In S. D. Brown and R. W. Lent (eds.), *Handbook of Counseling Psychology*. New York: Wiley, 1984.

Dohrenwend, B. S. ''Social Stress and Community Psychology.'' *American Journal of Community Psychology*, 1978, *6*, 1-14.

Drum, D. ''Understanding Student Development.'' In W. H. Morrill, J. C. Hurst, and Associates (eds.), *Dimensions of Intervention for Student Development*. New York: Wiley, 1980.

D'Zurilla, T. J., and Goldfried, M. R. ''Problem Solving and Behavior Modification.'' *Journal of Abnormal Psychology*, 1971, *78*, 107-126.

Ekehammar, B. ''Interactionism in Personality from a Historical Perspective.'' *Psychological Bulletin*, 1974, *81*, 1026-1048.

Ekehammar, B., Magnusson, D., and Ricklander, L. ''An Interactionist Approach to the Study of Anxiety.'' *Scandinavian Journal of Psychology*, 1974, *15*, 4-14.

Endler, N. S., and Hunt, J. McV. ''Sources of Behavioral Variance as Measured by the S-R Inventory of Anxiousness.'' *Psychological Bulletin*, 1966, *65*, 338-346.

Endler, N. S., Hunt, J. McV., and Rosenstein, A. J. ''An S-R Inventory of Anxiousness.'' *Psychological Monographs*, 1962, *76* (entire issue 17).

Endler, N. S., and Magnusson, D. ''Toward an Interactional Psychology of Personality.'' *Psychological Bulletin*, 1976, *83*, 956-974.

Erikson, E. H. *Identity and the Life Crisis: Psychological Issues*. New York: International Universities Press, 1959.

Erikson, E. H. *Identity: Youth and Crisis*. New York: Norton, 1968.

Finkel, N. J., and Jacobsen, C. A. ''Significant Life Experiences in an Adult Sample.'' *American Journal of Community Psychology*, 1977, *5* (2), 165-175.

Gavin, J. F., and Howe, J. G. ''Psychological Climate: Some Theoretical and Empirical Considerations.'' *Behavioral Science*, 1975, *20*, 228-240.

Gilligan, C. *In a Different Voice*. Cambridge, Mass.: Harvard University Press, 1982.

Hall, E. *The Hidden Dimension.* Garden City, N.Y.: Doubleday, 1966.

Hamilton, M. K., and Meade, C. "Implications of Natural Ecology for the Campus Ecologist." Paper presented at the second annual Campus Ecology Symposium, Pingree Park, Colo., June 1984.

Heilweil, M. "The Influence of Dormitory Architecture on Resident Behavior." *Environment and Behavior,* 1973, *5,* 377–411.

Holahan, C. J., and Moos, R. H. *Life Stress and Health: Personality, Coping, and Family Support in Stress Resistance.* Palo Alto, Calif.: Social Ecology Laboratory, Stanford University, 1983.

Holland, J. L. *The Psychology of Vocational Choice: A Theory of Personality Types and Model Environments.* Waltham, Mass.: Blaisdell, 1966.

Holland, J. L. *Making Vocational Choices: A Theory of Careers.* Englewood Cliffs, N.J.: Prentice-Hall, 1973.

Howe, J. G., and Gavin, J. F. *Organizational Climate: A Review and Delineation.* Technical Report no. 74-02. Fort Collins, Colo.: Industrial Psychological Association of Colorado, 1974.

Huebner, L. A. "An Ecological Assessment: Person-Environment Fit." Unpublished doctoral dissertation, Department of Psychology, Colorado State University, 1975.

Huebner, L. A. "Emergent Issues of Theory and Practice." In L. A. Huebner (ed.), *Redesigning Campus Environments.* New Directions for Student Services, no. 8. San Francisco: Jossey-Bass, 1979.

Huebner, L. A. "Interaction of Student and Campus." In U. Delworth, G. Hanson, and Associates, *Student Services: A Handbook for the Profession.* San Francisco: Jossey-Bass, 1980.

Huebner, L. A. "The Status of Theory in Campus Ecology." Paper presented at the first annual Campus Ecology Symposium, Pingree Park, Colo., June 1983.

Huebner, L. A., and Corazzini, J. G. "Ecomapping: A Dynamic Model for Intentional Campus Design." *Journal Supplement Abstract Service,* 1978.

Huebner, L. A., and Corazzini, J. G. "Environmental Assessment and Intervention: Current Trends, Future Directions."

In S. D. Brown and R. W. Lent (eds.), *Handbook of Counseling Psychology*. New York: Wiley, 1984.

Hurst, J. C. "The Target of Intervention." In W. H. Morrill, J. C. Hurst, and Associates (eds.), *Dimensions of Intervention for Student Development*. New York: Wiley, 1980.

Hurst, J. C. "Student Development and Campus Ecology: A Rapprochement." *National Association of Student Personnel Administrators Journal*, 1987, *25*, 5–18.

Hurst, J. C., and McKinley, D. L. "An Ecological Diagnostic Classification Plan," forthcoming.

Huse, E. "Organizational Development." *Personnel and Guidance Journal*, 1978, *56* (7), 412.

Insel, P. M., and Moos, R. H. "Psychological Environments—Expanding the Scope of Human Ecology." *American Psychologist*, 1974, *29* (3), 179–186.

James, L. R., and Jones, A. P. "Organizational Climate: A Review of Theory and Research." *Psychological Bulletin*, 1974, *81* (12), 1096–1112.

Kaiser, L. R. "Campus Ecology and Campus Design." In J. H. Banning (ed.), *Campus Ecology: A Perspective for Student Affairs*. Cincinnati, Ohio: National Association of Student Personnel Administrators, 1978.

Kalsbeek, D. H. "Environmental Assessment: A Review of Related Conceptual and Methodological Approaches." In C. Schroeder and others, *Student Development Through Environmental Management: New Perspectives for Residence Educators*. Student Life Studies, St. Louis, Mo.: St. Louis University, 1985.

Kalsbeek, D., and others. "Balancing Challenge and Support: A Study of Degrees of Similarity in Suitemate Personality Type and Perceived Differences in Challenge and Support in a Residence Hall Environment." *Journal of College Student Personnel*, 1982, *23* (5), 434–442.

Keyser, V., and Barling, J. "Determinants of Children's Self-Efficacy Beliefs in an Academic Environment." *Cognitive Theory and Research*, 1981, *5*, 29–40.

Kobassa, S. C., Hilker, R. J., and Maddi, S. R. "Who Stays Healthy Under Stress?" *Journal of Occupational Information*, 1979, *21*, 595–598.

Kohlberg, L. "Stage and Sequence: The Cognitive Developmental Approach to Socialization." In D. Goslin (ed.), *Handbook of Socialization Theory and Research*. Skokie, Ill.: Rand McNally, 1969.

Lewin, K. *Principles of Topological Psychology*. New York: McGraw-Hill, 1936.

Lewis, M. D., and Lewis, J. A. "The Counselor's Impact on Community Environments." *Personnel and Guidance Journal*, 1977, *55* (6), 356–358.

Loevinger, J. *Ego Development: Conceptions and Theories*. San Francisco: Jossey-Bass, 1976.

Long, B. B. "The Prevention of Mental-Emotional Disabilities." *American Psychologist*, 1986, *7* (41), 825–829.

Mayer, G. R., and Butterworth, T. W. "A Preventive Approach to School Violence and Vandalism: An Experimental Study." *Personnel and Guidance Journal*, 1979, *57* (9), 436–441.

Meade, C., and Davis, C. "Person-Environment Interaction: A Systems Approach." Unpublished paper, Department of Counseling Psychology, University of Iowa, 1979.

Mehrabian, A. *Public Places and Private Spaces*. New York: Basic Books, 1976.

Mehrabian, A., and Russell, J. *An Approach to Environmental Psychology*. Cambridge, Mass.: MIT Press, 1974.

Mischel, W. "Toward a Cognitive Social Learning Reconceptualization of Personality." *Psychological Review*, 1973, *80*, 252–283.

Moos, R. H. "Situational Analysis of a Therapeutic Community Milieu." *Journal of Abnormal Psychology*, 1968, *73*, 49–61.

Moos, R. H. "Sources of Variance in Responses to Questionnaires and in Behavior." *Journal of Abnormal Psychology*, 1969, *74*, 405–412.

Moos, R. H. "Differential Effects of Psychiatric Ward Settings on Patient Change." *Journal of Nervous and Mental Disease*, 1970, *5*, 316–321.

Moos, R. H. "Conceptualizations of Human Environments." *American Psychologist*, 1973, *28*, 652–665.

Moos, R. H. "Systems for the Assessment and Classification of Human Environments: An Overview." In R. H. Moos and P. Insel (eds.), *Issues in Social Ecology*. Palo Alto, Calif.: National Press Books, 1974.

Moos, R. H. *The Human Context: Environmental Determinants of Behavior.* New York: Wiley-Interscience, 1976.

Moos, R. H. *Evaluating Educational Environments: Procedures, Measures, Findings, and Policy Implications.* San Francisco: Jossey-Bass, 1979.

Moos, R. H. "Context and Coping: Toward a Unifying Conceptual Framework." *American Journal of Community Psychology,* 1984, *12,* 5–23.

Moos, R. H., and Lemke, S. "Supportive Residential Settings for Older People." In I. Altman, J. Wohlwill, and P. Lawton (eds.), *Human Behavior and the Environment: The Elderly and the Physical Environment.* New York: Plenum, 1983.

Moos, R. H., and Moos, B. *Family Environment Scale Manual.* Palo Alto, Calif.: Consulting Psychologists Press, 1981.

Moos, R. H., and Van Dort, B. "Student Physical Symptoms and the Social Climate of College Living Groups." *American Journal of Community Psychology,* 1979, *7,* 31–45.

Murray, H. A. *Explorations in Personality.* New York: Oxford University Press, 1938.

Murrell, S. A. *Community Psychology and Social Systems.* New York: Behavioral Publications, 1973.

Nielsen, H. D., and Moos, R. H. "Exploration and Adjustment in High School Classrooms: A Study of Person-Environment Fit." *Journal of Educational Research,* 1978, *34* (9), 740–754.

Parker, C. A., and Lawson, J. M. "From Theory to Practice to Theory: Consulting with College Faculty." *Personnel and Guidance Journal,* 1978, *56* (7), 424–427.

Paul, S. C. "Understanding Student-Environment Interaction." In W. H. Morrill, J. C. Hurst, and Associates (eds.), *Dimensions of Intervention for Student Development.* New York: Wiley, 1980.

Paul, S. C., and Huebner, L. A. "Multiple Perspectives: Intervening with People in Their Contextual Systems." Unpublished manuscript, Department of Counseling Psychology, University of Missouri, 1977.

Paul, S. C., and Morrill, W. H. "Prelude to Prevention: An Overview of Theory and Method." Paper presented at annual meeting of the American Psychological Association, Washington, D.C., 1982.

Perry, W., Jr. *Forms of Intellectual and Ethical Development in the College Years.* New York: Holt, Rinehart & Winston, 1970.

Pervin, L. A. "A Twenty-College Study of Student *x* College Interaction Using TAPE: Rationale, Reliability, and Validity." *Journal of Educational Psychology,* 1967, *58* (5), 290–302.

Pervin, L. A. "Performance and Satisfaction as a Function of Individual-Environment Fit." *Psychological Bulletin,* 1968, *69* (1), 56–58.

Proshansky, H., Ittelson, W., and Rivlin, L. (eds.). *Environmental Psychology: Man and His Physical Environment.* New York: Holt, Rinehart & Winston, 1970.

Rodgers, R. F. "Student Development Through Campus Ecology." Paper presented at the second annual Campus Ecology Symposium, Pingree Park, Colo., June 1984.

Rychlak, J. F. *A Philosophy of Science for Personality Theory.* Boston: Houghton-Mifflin, 1968.

Sandell, R. G. "Effects of Attitudinal and Situational Factors on Reported Choice Behavior." *Journal of Marketing Research,* 1968, *5,* 405–408.

Schroeder, C. S. "New Strategies for Structuring Residential Environments." *Journal of College Student Personnel,* 1976, *17,* 386–390.

Schroeder, C. S. "Territoriality: An Imperative for Personal Development and Residence Education." In D. DeCoster and P. Mable (eds.), *Personal Education and Community Development in College Residence Halls.* Washington, D.C.: American College Personnel Association, 1980.

Schroeder, C. S. "Student Development Through Environmental Management." In G. Blimling and J. Schuh (eds.), *Increasing the Educational Role of Residence Halls. New Directions for Student Services,* no. 13. San Francisco: Jossey-Bass, 1981.

Stern, G. G. *"B = f(P,E)." Journal of Personality Assessment,* 1964, *28* (2), 161–168.

Stern, G. G. *People in Context: Measuring Person-Environment Congruence in Education and Industry.* New York: Wiley, 1970.

Sullivan, C. E. "Developmental, Ecological Theories and Wellness Approaches: A Synthesis for Student Life Programming."

National Association of Student Personnel Administrators Journal, 1987, *25* (1), 18–27.

Walsh, W. B. *Theories of Person-Environment Interaction: Implications for the College Student.* Iowa City, Iowa: American College Testing Program, 1973.

Western Interstate Commission for Higher Education. *The Ecosystem Model: Designing Campus Environments.* Boulder, Colo.: Western Interstate Commission for Higher Education, 1973.

Wicker, A. W. "Undermanning Theory and Research: Implications for the Study of Psychological and Behavioral Effects of Excess Populations." *Representative Research in Social Psychology,* 1973, *4,* 190–191.

Wicker, A. W., and Kirmeyer, S. "From Church to Laboratory to National Park: A Program of Research on Excess and Insufficient Populations in Behavior Settings." In S. Wapner, B. Kaplan, and S. Cohen (eds.), *Experiencing the Environment.* New York: Plenum, 1976.

Willems, E. P. "Sense of Obligation to High School Activities as Related to School Size and Marginality of Student." *Child Development,* 1967, *38,* 1257–1258.

Willems, E. P. "Planning a Rationale for Naturalistic Research." In E. P. Willems and H. L. Raush (eds.), *Naturalistic Viewpoints in Psychological Research.* New York: Holt, Rinehart & Winston, 1969.

Wright, H. F. "Psychological Habitat." In R. G. Barker and Associates, *Habitats, Environments, and Human Behavior: Studies in Ecological Psychology and Eco-Behavioral Science.* San Francisco: Jossey-Bass, 1978.

Chapter Seven

Organizational Concepts and Influences

George D. Kuh

Many student affairs professionals have studied theories about personal adjustment, personality functioning, individual motives and aspirations, and small-group behavior. Individual development is one focus of student development theory—the theoretical cornerstone of student affairs work. Student development theories have raised the quality of professional preparation in student affairs. However, these theories are based on models of individual psychology that do not explicitly examine the relationship between individuals and organizational structures and governance processes.

Organizational theory is a window through which to view the behavior of individuals (students, faculty members, student affairs professionals) and groups in relation to the college as a complex organization. In addition, organizational theory informs interpretations of processes such as resource allocation, policy-making, personnel management, leadership, institutional renewal, reorganization of administrative units, and termination of programs.

The purposes of this chapter are to provide an overview of organizational theories and to illustrate the utility of organizational theory for student affairs. A rationale for using organiza-

Note: I acknowledge, with great appreciation, the comments made on earlier drafts by John Bean, John Schuh, and Elizabeth Whitt.

tional theories in student affairs work is presented, followed by descriptions of four conventional models and three emergent, nonorthodox perspectives of organizational behavior. Some suggestions are offered for using organizational theory in student affairs work.

Organizational theories are abstract representations of experience. No single model or perspective on organizational behavior can account for or explain everything that takes place. Just as student development theories (psychosocial, cognitive-intellectual, moral-ethical) illuminate certain aspects of students' growth and behavior but cannot explain other aspects, so it is with organizational theories. Therefore, using multiple models and perspectives to analyze organizations and individual behavior increases the number of meaningful insights into student affairs work that can be generated. The terms *model* and *perspective* reflect different levels of familiarity with the concepts common to the categories. *Model* connotes a definitive structural design, while *perspective* implies a distinctive view or impression. Conventional models are based on traditional assumptions about behavior in colleges and universities. The assumptions on which emergent, nonorthodox perspectives are based are less familiar but often generate richer, more accurate descriptions of experiences in institutions of higher education.

In practice, theoretical concepts from various models and perspectives are mixed with experience in a practitioner's mind and become theories-in-use (Argyris and Schön, 1978)—highly personal, unique patterns of understanding. Familiarity with varied interpretations of organizational behavior increases the possibility that an individual practitioner's theories-in-use will enable her or him to generate more complicated interpretations of events and actions than are possible using any one organizational perspective or any single theory based on the psychology of the individual (Kuh, 1984a).

Conventional Organizational Models and Emergent, Nonorthodox Perspectives

Conventional models of organizing emphasize hierarchical structures, clear communication channels, top-down expertise, control, and authority, and reliability and predictability (Clark, 1985; Kuh, Whitt, and Shedd, 1987). The emergent, nonortho- dox models, in contrast, emphasize unstructured organizations in which the flow of information is indirect and diffuse; power and influence may reside with a given individual regardless of title or position; and the relationships among people, events, and ideas are ill defined. Table 1 presents a comparison of con- ventional and nonorthodox assumptions about organizational behavior.

Conventional and emergent assumptions are disjunct (Clark, 1985). That is, the two sets of assumptions do not an- chor ends of the same continuum but represent different con- tinua. Expectations consistent with bureaucratic behavior, such as waiting for instructions from a supervisor before taking ac- tion or following communication channels outlined on the or- ganizational chart, can be thought of as one continuum. Be- havior compatible with emergent assumptions is qualitatively different. In the emergent perspective, information may flow in many different directions; mutually shaping interactions be- tween individuals within and across organizational units in- fluence (but not in a causal manner) the behavior of others, as well as institutional processes such as policy-making and pro- gram implementation.

Conventional Organizational Models

Hierarchical structures are common to most colleges and universities. The title and position of institutional agents deter- mine and describe their responsibilities and authority. A chain of command is implied; those near the top of the hierarchy, such as a chief student affairs officer (CSAO), are expected to be more knowledgeable and to have greater expertise in most matters than those who are lower in the organizational hierarchy, such as an assistant dean or resident assistants. Staff believe that the organizational structure also dictates who is responsible for shar- ing what kind of information with whom. For example, resi- dent assistants (RAs) convey information about residence hall policies and practices to students and report problems to super- visors. The director of residence life reports information from

Table 1. Conventional and Emergent
Assumptions About Organizations.

Conventional Models	Emergent, Nonorthodox Perspectives
Hierarchical structures are normal, necessary, functional, and desirable.	Heterarchical interactions are uninhibited by hierarchical structures and facilitate organizational learning and effective administration; organizational structures evolve over time.
Communication channels are clearly delineated and consistently used.	Information is available from many sources and flows in many directions.
Expertise, control, and authority are commensurate with position and exercised by superordinates.	Any person at any level has the potential to influence organizational behavior in an effective, positive, creative manner.
Goals and means to attain goals are clear, are shared, give direction to behavior, and are tied directly to outcomes.	Relationships among events, individual behavior, technologies, and outcomes in institutions of higher education are ambiguous.
Intentions are directly linked to actions.	Intentions and actions, by units or individuals, are loosely coupled, and can be understood only in retrospect.
Reliability and predictability of organizational processes are hampered only by factors such as knowledge and technology.	Qualities of indeterminacy, morphogenesis, action learning, and self-organizing compromise expectations for reliability and predictability.

Source: Adapted from Kuh, Whitt, and Shedd, 1987, p. 58.

RAs to the CSAO. In turn, the CSAO informs the campus chief executive officer (CEO) about events in the residence halls and usually speaks for student life when communication is required with external audiences, such as parents and community leaders. Through centralization and coordination, information can be monitored for accuracy and dissemination to the appropriate audiences.

Conventional organizational models assert that the quality of decision making and policy formulation is a function of accurate information and appropriate ''technology,'' or the means by which the organization gets work accomplished. Ineffective or inefficient management is attributed to inadequate information or flawed technology. For example, tardy financial aid awards may be explained by obsolete or poorly conceived computer software that does not accommodate recent changes in federal aid programs. Flawed technology can also include cumbersome communication networks or human errors, such as a decision-making process that fails to obtain input from legitimate stakeholders—for example, parents—when residence hall visitation policies are being changed.

Despite the increasing influence of external forces, conventional organizational models (with the exception of the political model) generally portray the institution as a "closed" system. That is, all the most important variables (including people) and conditions are considered open to purposeful manipulation and control by institutional agents (Katz and Rosenzweig, 1974). A closed system's approach to addressing alcohol abuse in residence halls would focus on students' behavior and the hall environment but ignore societal drinking habits, drinking customs common to ethnic groups, family histories of alcohol use, and so on.

Much of the student affairs literature (Borland, 1983; Dutton and Rickard, 1980; Foxley, 1980) is based on assumptions of control, predictability, and hierarchical authority compatible with a closed-system interpretation of organizational behavior. These assumptions are congruent with the four conventional models—rational, bureaucratic, collegial, and political—of understanding behavior in institutions of higher education described below.

Rational Model. Logic and order are preeminent values in the rational model (Chaffee, 1983). More specifically, organizational rationality implies that behavior is not random but purposeful, behavior is directed toward end-states or goals agreed upon in advance, and action is prospective rather than retrospective—that is, behavior is guided by intended or anticipated outcomes rather than understood after the fact (Pfeffer, 1982). Table 2 presents the advantages and limitations of the rational model, as well as of the bureaucratic, collegial, and political models.

**Table 2. Advantages and Limitations
of Conventional Organizational Models.**

Model	Advantages	Limitations
Rational	Compatible with academic values (such as fairness, purposeful behavior). Appeals to reason and logic.	Constrained by information-processing limits. Expectations for goal consensus and control often are not met. Oversimplifies complex problems.
Bureaucratic	Clearly defined roles, functions, responsibilities, scope of authority, and relationships. Expertise is acknowledged by position. Performance is standardized. Prospective approach. Emphasizes productivity.	Incompatible with certain values of the academy (such as autonomy, multiple areas of expertise, decisions by peers). Resistant to change. Measures of productivity not well suited to purposes of higher education.
Collegial	Consistent with traditions of academy. Responsive to persuasive argument of colleagues. Based on democratic principles. Ensures representation.	Inefficient (labor-intensive and time-consuming). Insensitive to power differentials, resource availability, and policy implementation issues.
Political	Acknowledges importance of power and conflict resolution. Emphasizes policy as vehicle for issue management. Encourages involvement of disparate stakeholder groups.	Incongruent with certain values of the academy (such as openness, fairness, peer governance). Reinforces status quo. Exchanges achievement and merit for influence in decision making.

The rational model is appealing because it emphasizes qualities valued in the academy: fairness and objectivity in decision making, deliberate and purposeful action, and predictable outcomes. Indeed, the rhetoric of the rational model is quite compatible with characteristics traditionally associated with an educated person, especially the primacy of reason and the intellect over intuition and emotion (Kuh, Whitt, and Shedd, 1987).

One limitation of the rational model is "bounded rationality" (Simon, 1957)—constraints on the amount of information an individual can assimilate at one time. Because the information-processing ability of humans is imperfect and limited, no one can be aware of everything that takes place in a complex organization. Another limitation of the rational model is the assumption that goals are shared by all members of the unit. Everyone agrees that high-quality education for all is an important goal; consensus begins to unravel when we try to define quality in a physics laboratory, in a writing assignment, in a residence hall, in a Greek-letter house, or in the financial aid office.

The limitations of the rational model do not imply that reasoned judgment or logical analysis are irrelevant, or that reason never prevails. In fact, most actions in a college or university are rational—to someone! That fatal flaw in the rational model is the assumption that managers can and should anticipate, account for, or control all the possible contingencies that may bear on a decision, an expectation that cannot be met by any individual or organization.

Bureaucratic Model. Organizational charts, job descriptions, and detailed policies and procedures abound in business and industry, government and social service agencies, and institutions of higher education. Indeed, the bureaucratic model probably has had more influence on how we think the institution is supposed to operate than any other view of organizations (Kuh, 1981, 1983a).

Hage (1980) listed seven characteristics of a bureaucracy: (1) hierarchical authority—every person in the institution is responsible to someone in a higher office; (2) limits on authority—specific persons in specific roles are responsible for certain areas of performance; (3) division of labor—efficiency is maximized and duplication of effort minimized by assigning responsibility for specific functions to certain persons and groups; (4) technical competence—workers have requisite training; (5) standard operating procedures—procedures to perform tasks are carefully prescribed; (6) rules for work—requirements and competence levels for various positions are specified; and (7) differential rewards—salary and perquisites are tied directly to seniority and position in the hierarchy. Examples of these characteristics are readily available in most divisions of student affairs (Strange, 1983): the chief student affairs officer is ultimately responsible for what occurs in student life; job descriptions describe activities for which incumbents are responsible; those with more responsibility, such as the CSAO and unit directors, make more money than those below them in the hierarchy, such as RAs.

The principles of scientific management (Taylor, 1911) are often associated with the bureaucratic model. Scientific methods, such as time and motion studies, task analysis, and assembly-line processes, have been used to identify the most efficient and precise manner in which work can be performed, to select the best person for the job, to train workers efficiently, and to monitor performance (Morgan, 1986). Bureaucratic principles coupled with scientific management concepts are the foundation for many modern management techniques, such as management by objectives (MBO), planned programming budgeting systems (PPBS), and other hyperrational planning and control mechanisms (Clark, 1985).

Certain characteristics of colleges and universities are incompatible with bureaucratic technologies. For example, faculty and professional staff expect autonomy, not close supervison. Standardization is difficult when activities are not similar across jobs or units of analysis. Although many bureaucratic elements, such as organizational charts and routinized payroll processes, can be found in all colleges and universities, some anomalies almost always exist. For example, it is not unusual for a medical school faculty member to have a higher salary than the president of the institution, or for academic departments to use something other than standardized processes to make decisions about curriculum or admission of students. Most student affairs staff would argue that their jobs in residence life, student activities, and career planning are not easily routinized.

Although Max Weber is the father of modern bureaucracy, he was skeptical about the desirability of pervasive implementation of bureaucratic principles because of their dampening effect on the individual's imagination and capacity for spontaneous action (Weber 1947). Bureaucratic assumptions encourage specialization and isolation and foster conditions—such as standardization, regularity, and repetition—that inhibit organizational flexibility (Strange, 1983) and evolutionary change (Morgan, 1986). As a result, changing organizational structures is usually time-consuming and costly (Morgan, 1986). Behaviors characteristic of workers in high-performing organizations, such as individual initiative, innovation, and risk taking (Peters and Waterman, 1982; Vaill, 1984), are discouraged when staff have little latitude in making decisions about matters that exceed the responsibilities of their role. In addition, some of the traditions of the academy, such as academic freedom and collegial governance, are incompatible with many bureaucratic principles of organizing.

Collegial Model. The collegial model of organizing underscores the assumption that participatory governance is the most appropriate way to pursue institutional goals (Chaffee, 1983). Participants in a collegial system are assumed to share fundamental beliefs about the purposes and processes that guide the institution and are assumed to have equal opportunities to influence decisions about priorities, allocation of resources, conditions of work, selection of peers, and standards of quality (Baldridge, Curtis, Ecker, and Riley, 1977). Devices are created to solicit community input for making decisions. For example, virtually every campus has a governing body composed of faculty and students responsible for establishing and monitoring academic policies. The democratic principle of self-governance through representation is usually replicated throughout the institution in academic departments and student residences.

For collegial processes to be effective, participants must be open to new ideas, share and clarify their positions through discussion, and change their positions when presented with compelling reasons to do so. While some roles and processes are delineated, such as the role of the president pro tem of the faculty senate and the use of Robert's rules of order, specific procedures are not necessarily prescribed but emerge from reasoned dialogue among peers.

The collegial model is attractive because it is consistent with enduring values of the academy, including enlightened debate and governance by peers. Professional covenants, such as the tenure statement of the American Association of University Professors, reinforce the importance of shared decision making. Collegial processes also are consistent with the principle that the more people feel that they can influence their destiny and shape the ethos of the work environment, the more committed, satisfied, and productive they will be (Kanter, 1983).

However, collegial governance processes, such as decision making and policy formulation by groups of peers, are labor-intensive and time-consuming, even for what seem to be minor decisions. In recent years, faculty have reduced the amount of time they spend in institutional governance (Bowen and Schuster, 1986). The increasing influence of external agencies and such factors as the economy, sunshine laws and threats of litigation, parents' wishes, and demographic shifts in the number and characteristics of college students have further complicated decision making and reduced the utility of the collegial model for certain types of decisions, such as resource allocation and physical plant expansion.

Decisions or policies that favor the interests of certain groups or individuals invariably disappoint—and sometimes anger—one or more groups. Many important initiatives deserve support: recruitment of minority faculty and students, scholarships for superior students, and aid for educationally disadvantaged students, to name a few. Faculty usually wish to spend more money for such initiatives than is available. Commitments can outstrip resources if information about needs and resources is not gathered and analyzed in one location, usually an administrative office. The collegial model does not explicitly address conflict resolution or the influence of power in decision making, issues that are emphasized in the political model.

Political Model. When powerful stakeholders compete for limited resources or differ in opinion on important issues, conflict is inevitable. Some student affairs staff view conflict as a dysfunctional condition triggered by regrettable circumstances, such as personality problems, rivalry, and role dissonance. Conflict associated with self-interest cannot be avoided, however. Staff may disagree on how funds for professional development or programming are allocated, who will remain on duty during spring break, or the formal position adopted by the division concerning student activism. The political model acknowledges the uneven distribution of power within increasingly pluralistic colleges and universities. It challenges the "myth of organizational rationality" (Morgan, 1986, p. 195), including its expectations for rational decision making and goal-directed, functionally interdependent units.

Conflict resolution can take the form of negotiations between coalitions of persons with similar interests and may evolve into formulation of policy (Baldridge, Curtis, Ecker, and Riley, 1977). The policy-making process allows those interested in the resolution of tensions to work together to create a process to cope with future conflict. Often, coalitions are formed to advocate a particular alternative. Policy alternatives may be proposed to respond to the interests of groups participating in the process. Lobbying and debating take place in public forums and in private. Some form of ratification (such as voting or formal acknowledgment by institutional leaders) usually affirms the policy option adopted (Baldridge, 1971). When implemented, however, a policy may look very different from the one that was proposed (Lipsky, 1980). On some occasions, decisions are made without the knowledge of the persons they affect, which leads to feelings of alienation and problems in implementing decisions or policies.

Differences between groups may also be exacerbated rather than ameliorated by the debate and lobbying activities. Often, things are said that create more tension. For example, when faculty and students learn that funds have been allocated for additional no-need scholarships for students with certain talents, such as athletes and musicians, one or more groups are likely to challenge the wisdom of such decisions.

Although the political model suggests a high degree of involvement on the part of stakeholders, not all those with an interest in the relevant issues become actively involved in the process. Few issues are of sufficient importance to stimulate active involvement by large numbers of stakeholders. Unless an issue is of particular salience, faculty or student affairs staff are not likely to invest their limited energy and time in the deliberations.

Faculty and student affairs staff who think of their institution as a community of equals may reject or feel threatened by actions described in the assumptions of the political model. Conflict and competition are antithetical to the traditions of collegial decision-making and governance processes. Some associate campus politics with Machiavellian behavior and ruthless self-interest. Nevertheless, as resources decline and the number of special-interest groups increases (Education Commission of the States, 1980), colleges and universities will experience more, not less, competition. Acknowledgment of the political nature of colleges and universities is essential to identifying the relevant actors both on and off the campus, and to maximizing the potential benefits of conflict resolution and policy-making.

Implications of Conventional Models. Conventional models consider organizational behavior to be goal-directed. Either clear goals must be consensually validated and agreement must be reached on how to attain the goals, as in the rational, bureaucratic, and collegial models, or the preferences of some persons or coalitions must supersede the goals of others, as in the political model. Logic and reason are paramount in problem solving, planning, and policy-making, although power also influences decision making. Student affairs managers who rely on conventional models of organizing believe they are responsible for articulating what must be done and when, how, and by whom it must be done. Because they are assumed to have the most expertise, persons at or near the top of the hierarchy are expected to measure, evaluate, and reward efficiency and effectiveness.

Leadership tasks and tactics are driven by assumed responsibility for control. Control is exercised from the top downward, a process that often erodes trust and motivation and places persons lower in the hierarchy on the defensive (Morgan, 1986). The CSAO and department heads send directives through formally approved channels, such as chains of command, collegial governance structures, and institutional policy-making bodies. Staff at lower levels expect leaders to provide direction. Success is measured by the accuracy of predictions, the comprehensiveness of plans, and the degree to which predetermined objectives are attained. To the extent that staff fulfill supervisors' expectations and the unit runs smoothly, the student affairs department is judged to be effective.

For more than fifty years, the machine metaphor has dominated thinking about organizations. When used in concert, conventional models—which are based on beliefs about how institutions of higher education should work (Kuh, 1983a)—account for many important aspects of college and university life. However, when people do not behave as they are supposed to, conventional models are not very helpful.

Emergent, Nonorthodox Organizational Perspectives

Within the last two decades, different ways of thinking about organizational behavior have evolved that challenge many of the assumptions on which conventional models are based. Critical examination of conventional assumptions has stimulated experimentation with different metaphors for organizations, such as "flying seesaws" (Hedberg, Nystrom, and Starbuck, 1976), "garbage cans" (Cohen, March, and Olsen, 1972), and "rainforest tribes" (Schroeder, Nicholls, and Kuh, 1983). The interpretations generated by these and other metaphors seem to describe more accurately everyday experiences in institutions of higher education.

The enthusiasm for alternative organizational views is buttressed by challenges to conventional models in other fields. In disciplines such as history, law, economics, psychology, and physics, discoveries have been made that question the efficacy of conventional assumptions for giving meaning to experience and indicate a shift to qualitatively different perspectives (Capra, 1983; Gleick, 1987; Howard, 1985; Lincoln and Guba, 1985). Emergent organizational perspectives are based on alternative assumptions that suggest different interpretations of commonplace events and behaviors. The three perspectives on organizing that follow are based on assumptions compatible with the emergent, nonorthodox view of organizations. Table 3 presents the advantages and limitations of these perspectives—organized anarchy, culture, and holographic image.

**Table 3. Advantages and Limitations
of Emergent Organizational Perspectives.**

Perspective	Advantages	Limitations
Organized Anarchy	More descriptive of life in institutions of higher education. Images are intuitively appealing and evocative. Compatible with academy values (such as autonomy, minimal supervision). Acknowledges retrospective understanding rather than prescriptive models.	Information not always available to those who need it. Legitimates and encourages divided loyalties. Hinders coordinated response to issues and crises. Does not suggest implications for staff and leader behavior. Challenges basic assumptions about effective organizing.
Culture	Acknowledges context as important variable in understanding behavior. Explains unusual and routine behavior. Accommodates different behaviors (subcultures) within institution or student affairs units. Acknowledges validity of subjective views. Emphasizes importance of mutual shaping.	Lacks conceptual specificity. Insights gleaned from one experience or culture not transferable to others. Organizational properties cannot be manipulated or controlled. Requires different expectations for leader behavior.
Holographic Image	Compatible with ecological and cybernetic principles (such as mutual shaping, evolutionary change). Acknowledges importance of all members of organization. Deemphasizes formal structures and procedures, which encourages innovation, creativity, and organizational change. Encourages personal and professional development of staff through role expansion and involvement in problem solving and changing of norms.	Based on unfamiliar concepts that are counterintuitive. Contradicts conventional wisdom about organizations. Emphasizes complexity and paradox over simplicity and search for correct solutions. Encourages policies that many institutions are not prepared to adopt.

Organized Anarchy. The term *organized anarchy* (Cohen, March, and Olsen, 1972) describes events in colleges and universities that contradict the expectations for order, structure, and rational goal-directed processes that characterize ideal bureaucratic organizations. Although virtually every campus has a chief executive officer, in most colleges and universities, people pursue tasks and interests without coordination or control by a central authority. Institutional goals usually lack specificity, and decisions seem to be by-products of a tenuous marriage between intentions and serendipity. Leaders are relatively weak and serve primarily as catalysts, not so much leading the institution as channeling activities in subtle ways. "Problems, choices, and decision-makers *happen* to come together in temporary solutions" (Baldridge, Curtis, Ecker, and Riley, 1977, p. 15; emphasis added).

Seven characteristics (described in this perspective as *anarchistic* qualities) peculiar to institutions of higher education severely strain conventional assumptions about organizing: ambiguous, conflictual goals, exchange of incentives, unclear technologies, loose coupling, fluid participation, a professional work force, and clients who participate in institutional governance (Baldridge, Curtis, Ecker, and Riley, 1977; Weick, 1976).

Colleges and universities have multiple, sometimes contradictory, goals (Gross and Grambsch, 1968). Research universities are committed to knowledge production as well as undergraduate instruction; not enough resources are available to fund all the requests related to teaching and research that merit support. Individual faculty members experience conflict about apportioning time to teaching, research, and service activities. Administrators must weigh the need to raise faculty and staff salaries against requests for new equipment and student aid. Each of these preferences reflects legitimate priorities (Hull, Hunter, and Kuh, 1983), but finite resources impose constraints on the institution's ability to accommodate the desires of all.

Performance is not always a function of traditional, formal incentives such as salary or promise of promotion. Instead, individual needs for personal recognition and satisfaction may be more important than institutional goals or unit objectives.

Consequently, individuals "barter" with informal or personal incentives, such as reciprocal favors, to obtain other "commodities," such as satisfaction, advantages, and influence (Georgiou, 1973). Over time, a complex, dynamic web of incentives is created among staff, students, faculty, and others, all of whom are attempting to make the most of the rewards and satisfaction they derive from their involvement with the student affairs unit (Hull, Hunter, and Kuh, 1983).

Unclear technology (Cohen and March, 1974) refers to the inability to accurately describe and replicate important processes, such as teaching and learning, relationship therapy in the campus mental health unit, and theory-based residence hall programs. In almost every field, professionals use tacit information, experience, and enlightened judgment, in addition to formal theory or research evidence, when working with clients (Schön, 1987). When many different people exercise professional judgment in an organization, a variety of approaches or responses to situations is inevitable. Student affairs staff, like faculty and other professionals, rely on "theories-in-use" (Argyris and Schön, 1978), guidelines for behavior based on assumptions and beliefs developed from experience with recurring problems and circumstances. The complexity of any task, such as student development programming, and the absence of reliable, comparative data about the efficacy of various approaches contribute to unclear technology in student affairs (Hull, Hunter, and Kuh, 1983; Kuh, Whitt, and Shedd, 1987).

Coupling refers to the strength of the relationship between or among elements in an organization (Clark, Astuto, and Kuh, 1986; Weick, 1976). For example, residence life may be affected by the performance of admissions and financial aid staff; rooms might be vacant if enough students do not apply or if financial aid awards are not made promptly. Conventional organizational models typically depict functional elements in colleges as tightly coupled (Kuh, 1981, 1983a). That is, communication is direct and immediate and the links between units such as admissions, financial aid, and residence halls are responsive and predictable. According to Weick (1976), however, tight coupling is the exception, not the rule, in most educational institutions. Loosely coupled units lack one or more characteristics of conventional, tightly coupled bureaucratic organizations (Clark, Astuto, and Kuh, 1986).

Loose coupling can lead to problems. Student affairs units are complex organizations that perform diverse, specialized activities with disparate goals and objectives. In most organizations, there are simply too many events and activities for one person to monitor. Consequently, information does not always flow to the persons who are in the best position to take action. If the counseling center staff are not aware of a student's conflict with a roommate, the student may perceive the institution or student affairs unit as inefficient, poorly managed, or—worse—uncaring and unresponsive.

A loosely coupled student affairs division has some advantages, however. Staff may operate with minimal supervision and assume greater responsibility for their work (Weick, 1976). If the union film series is not successful, its failure is not likely to interrupt work in financial aid or residence life. Because failures in one area are isolated from other parts of the system, staff may be more likely to seek their own solutions to problems or respond to opportunities, thereby encouraging more risk taking and innovation.

The challenges presented to student affairs staff by ambiguous goals, unclear technology, and loose coupling are further complicated by fluid participation (Cohen and March, 1974). Fluid participation means that persons who might ordinarily participate may not be present to make the decision or available to implement it; either absence may affect the quality of the decision. Predicting when and in what setting a decision will be made is difficult. The absence of the director of student activities, who is off campus attending a professional conference, may delay a decision about next year's student activity fee. Or a decision may be made to raise the fee without the input of the student activities office, which could have a deleterious effect on student morale.

These anarchistic qualities of colleges and universities are exacerbated by the presence of highly autonomous professionals who expect to work without supervision and to control important aspects of the work environment, such as work load and availability to students. Many faculty, particularly at prestigious institutions, have a stronger allegiance to a national network of peers than to the employing institution (Clark, 1985). Obligations to professional associations sometimes conflict with institutional expectations and create tension (Baldridge, Curtis, Ecker, and Riley, 1977).

Because enlightened citizenship is a characteristic of an educated person, students have been encouraged to participate actively in institutional governance (Baldridge, Curtis, Ecker, and Riley, 1977). But student participation increases the amount of time needed to make decisions. New student representatives must be oriented to governance structures and processes, and meetings must be scheduled when students are available. In the past few decades, the number of constituents who expect to have input into institutional decisions has expanded to include alumni, corporate and philanthropic sponsors, local and federal government officials, and parents (Education Commission of the States, 1980). As the number of stakeholders seeking a voice increases, decision-making processes become more complicated and time-consuming.

The organized anarchy perspective is descriptively rich and intuitively appealing. However, organized anarchy concepts create dissonance because they do not reflect the prescriptive, predictive qualities that people have come to expect from theories and models. The playfulness with which structural elements of organizations are addressed seems incongruent with serious social science.

Nevertheless, every day student affairs staff have experiences that are more accurately depicted by one or more organized anarchy concepts than by conventional models (Kuh, 1981, 1983a). We forget the rules used last year to allocate student activity fees to student groups and must develop new procedures (unclear technology). The assistant dean who was the architect of the recently reorganized student government decides to pursue a doctorate at another institution (fluid participation), and someone unfamiliar with the new structure becomes the student government adviser. These experiences are not necessarily random or without meaning, as the term *anarchy* suggests. Certain patterns and themes emerge out of annual events and daily interactions; some are even predictable. For example, students arrive in late August, class schedules for the spring semester must be prepared in early fall, the annual spring weekend fling will irritate faculty, test the patience of student affairs staff, and bring great pleasure to students and merchants. Therefore, student affairs staff should not forget the first word of the term— *organized* anarchy—when thinking about events and actions in institutions of higher education.

Culture. For decades, anthropological concepts have been used to interpret life in colleges and universities (Clark and Trow, 1966; Clark, 1985; Becher, 1984; Ouchi, 1981; Peters and Waterman, 1982). As a result of these studies, hundreds of definitions of culture exist (Peterson and others, 1987), but none is both comprehensive and specific to the degree that social scientists require to test hypotheses and experimentally control or manipulate variables. This is understandable, since culture is a complex, elusive web of assumptions, beliefs, and behaviors that represent learned products of group experience (Kuh and Whitt, 1988; Schein, 1985).

Culture is context-specific and context-bound. That is, behavior cannot be understood without taking into account the context within which it occurs, nor can the behavior or its meaning be generalized to other settings. Culture cannot be imposed by any individual or group but evolves through social interaction. As an "unconscious infra-structure" (Smircich, 1983, p. 341), culture encourages, supports, and rewards certain behaviors. Because people impose their own subjective constructions on what takes place, multiple interpretations of behavior are legitimate.

Schein (1985) divided culture into three levels. The first level is composed of artifacts, some of which, such as the rituals of orientation or recognition banquets at the end of the year, are obvious (Trice and Beyer, 1984). Other artifacts are less tangible; these include the philosophy of the institution, stories and symbols that transmit important values from one generation to the next, and our professional language (Kuh, Whitt, and Shedd, 1987). Examination of the artifacts of a culture— ceremonies, rituals, and language—reveals what is important to a group of people.

The second level of culture is composed of values asserted to be important by members of the institution or student affairs division. A strong core of values enhances stability (Masland, 1985). Values often take the form of exhortations about what is right or wrong and may be demonstrated by encouraging or discouraging certain behaviors. For example, the CSAO believes that student affairs should be the institution's conscience and expects staff to articulate and model acceptable community standards by discouraging discrimination in every form and advocating the rights of all students, faculty, and staff (Lyons, 1987).

The third level, the core of culture, consists of basic assumptions consistent with the culture's values and artifacts. Although core assumptions are rarely made explicit, they exert a powerful influence over what people think about, what they perceive to be important, how they feel about things, and what they do. An example of a core assumption on many campuses is that students are not trustworthy, as is evidenced by the rules that have been developed to control student behavior.

The strength of an institution's culture depends on several factors, including the size and age of the institution, the convictions of its founders, the conditions under which the institution or division of student affairs was founded or reorganized, and any heroes, rituals, and symbols associated with the stories told about the institution or the division of student affairs (Clark, 1972; Kuh and Whitt, 1988; Masland, 1985). Familiarity with the institutional saga (Clark, 1972), the story of how the college came to be what it is today, is integral to understanding why certain values are important.

The corporate culture literature is grounded in conventional assumptions of determinism and control (Deal and Kennedy, 1982; Kilmann, Saxton, Serpa, and Associates, 1985), which suggest that culture can be managed, changed, or manipulated. Intentional manipulation or management of culture implies predictability and linear causality, which are conventional expectations for organizational behavior. However, such expectations are anathema to emergent perspectives. Certain properties of culture, such as holism, mutual shaping, and context-bound and context-specific interpretations of behavior, suggest culture is not controllable. Therefore, attempts to manipulate deeply held assumptions and beliefs—the core of culture—are ill-advised.

Whether the culture perspective has utility depends on what one hopes to gain. If the purpose is understanding and explanation, the culture "window" will be useful. For example, culture may explain why the goals of student affairs are sometimes perceived as inconsistent with the expectations of faculty or with the way student affairs are perceived by others. By examining values and beliefs, events may be understood that otherwise might seem mysterious, out of place, debilitating, or irrational.

As an analytical tool, culture is best used as an interpretive lens for understanding and appreciating nuances of behavior in a particular subculture or institutional context (Kuh, Whitt, and Shedd, 1987). For example, it is customary in some social fraternities for new initiates to demonstrate their equality by throwing the pledge father (fraternity "whip") into the shower (Leemon, 1972). This "celebration," marking the completion of a rite of passage, differs markedly from the firm handshakes, hugs, and use of the title "Doctor" by the initiate that often characterize the successful defense of a doctoral dissertation, or from the party for victorious candidates in a student government election. The interpretations of these events depend on the context in which the events occurred and the meaning given to the events by the actors or "culture-bearers" (Allaire and Firsirotu, 1984).

The culture perspective cannot explain everything that takes place in a division of student affairs. Culture concepts lack semantic precision, which reduces their analytical power. Because meaning is context-bound, insights from one setting will not necessarily be applicable to other settings; thus, those who hope to develop a set of generalizable guiding principles will not be satisfied with the contextual restrictions imposed by the cultural perspective. However, student affairs professionals will find appealing the emphasis on holism, history, tradition, evolving circumstances, and individual motives implicit in the culture perspective. The culture perspective also is consistent with the assumption about individual differences valued by the student affairs field.

Holographic Image. In conventional models of organizing, the division of student affairs is represented by the sum of its parts—departments, offices, individual staff members. The holographic image perspective suggests that by developing an integrative capacity, the division of student affairs becomes more than the sum of its parts. In a hologram, each part reflects the whole. In this sense, each staff member reflects the qualities of the entire division of student affairs at any given point in time. Therefore, any person in the student affairs organization can shape the actions of others and help the organization learn how to do things differently. To understand one aspect of an organization requires information about other aspects of the organization. Thus, student affairs staff must synthesize and integrate information and probe below the surface of events to examine motivations and desires of others grounded in "tacit assumptions (unquestioned beliefs behind all decisions and actions) and hidden cultures (shared but unwritten rules for each member's behavior)" (Kilmann, Saxton, Serpa, and Associates, 1985, p. 8).

A holographic interpretation of organizational behavior is compatible with cybernetics, an interdisciplinary approach to understanding the relationships of information, communication, and influence. Cybernetic systems are characterized by four abilities: the ability to sense, monitor, and scan internal and external environments; the ability to compare information from the environment with the norms that guide behavior in the organizational context; the ability to detect significant deviations between organizational norms and environmental conditions; and the ability to change norms that are incompatible with the environment (Morgan, 1986).

Consistent with cybernetic principles, goals and objectives do not drive behavior; rather, staff are encouraged to avoid undesirable outcomes. "It is no coincidence that most of our great codes of behavior are framed in terms of 'thou shall not'" (Morgan, 1986, p. 106). Pursuit of a specific goal and avoidance of the worst-case scenario are qualitatively different modes of action. Pursuing specific goals invariably leads to narrowly circumscribed views of environmental conditions and desirable responses. In contrast, conscious decision to avoid undesirable outcomes uses only the most important constraints—such as budget deficits or violation of human rights—as limits, which allows staff the freedom to pursue other options (Kuh, Whitt, and Shedd, 1987).

Cybernetic systems have a capacity for self-organizing (Caple, 1985; Prigogine and Stengers, 1984), which requires four conditions: redundancy, requisite variety, minimum critical specification, and action learning (Morgan, 1986). Redundancy is excess performance capacity acquired by adding responsibilities to a staff member's portfolio so that each person engages in a range of functions rather than a narrowly focused, specialized activity. Thus, when the institution, division, or specific area faces a crisis, redundancy ensures that several staff members are prepared to respond. Some degree of redundancy is necessary for organizational flexibility and action learning, and to encourage evolution of the organization to the next stage of development.

Financial and human limitations make it impractical, if not impossible, for every person to have the skills required to perform every function in a division of student affairs. To secure the benefits of redundancy, student affairs units should have requisite variety, that condition of the organization in which the internal diversity of the organization matches the variety and complexity of its environment (Morgan, 1986, p. 100). For example, as the number of minority students going to college increases, student affairs staff should reflect the values of a more pluralistic student body. In this sense, the values and attitudes of student affairs staff are compatible with important characteristics of the external and internal environments.

By assembling only the minimum number of staff and resources needed to begin a task or project, a student affairs division meets the condition of minimum critical specification (Kuh, Whitt, and Shedd, 1987). Thus, actions of staff and students are not bound by prescriptive structures or rules but can be shaped by evolutionary circumstances—whatever it takes to get the job done. For example, by adhering to only a few community governance principles, such as a representative hall governing body and roommate selection policy, students have the freedom to become responsive and responsible rather than being told what to do by staff (Schroeder, Nicholls, and Kuh, 1983). Students are encouraged to identify and learn to deal with problems when they arise without being unduly constrained by detailed procedures or ever-present residence hall staff who "solve" problems for students.

The fourth condition required for self-organizing is action learning, or "learning to learn." Action learners take risks, are skeptical about what their experiences teach them, and never assume they have discovered the "best" way or "correct" answer (Kuh, Whitt, and Shedd, 1987). By asking questions like "What are we doing?" and "Why are we doing it this way?" staff can test whether routine practices are responsive to the changing needs and interests of students and institutional conditions.

Holograms and action learning may seem nonsensical to student affairs staff expecting (or hoping for) predictability and reliability. Avoiding undesirable outcomes instead of pursuing predetermined goals seems to defy common sense. However, "sensing direction through variety, action and involvement of many persons throughout the student affairs division is quite compatible, humane, and even sensible in the ambiguous, loosely coupled context of colleges and universities" (Kuh, Whitt, and Shedd, 1987, p. 67).

The holographic perspective encourages student affairs professionals to exploit their autonomy and capitalize on relationships with students and faculty, behaviors that encourage the institution to evolve toward novel and increasingly progressive solutions to complex problems. Even though the institution has hierarchical structures, the relationships between subsystems, such as the department of residence life or a particular residence hall, and higher-order systems, such as the division of student affairs or the institution, are allowed to evolve into new forms through experience (Morgan, 1986).

An obvious limitation of the holographic perspective is that concepts such as action learning and minimum critical specification are unfamiliar to most student affairs staff. The implications of allowing students to determine their own policies and rules may be impossible to accept or implement in many institutions. However, some concepts characteristic of the holographic image can be applied to student affairs. Action learning principles, for example, are helpful in thinking about ways to encourage experienced staff to acknowledge and adapt to evolutionary changes in the organization. Requisite variety provides a rationale for expanding a staff member's portfolio while introducing the staff member to the diversity of activities in which the student affairs division is engaged.

Implications of Emergent Organizational Perspectives. Emergent perspectives share several qualities. First, each institutional context is believed to be unique. Therefore, behavior that is effective in one setting may not be effective in another institution or at a later date in the same setting. Second, emergent perspectives recognize that people construct reality for themselves. Student affairs staff interpret and give meaning to everything they encounter. The illusion of a single objective reality, which permeates the conventional models of organizing, is replaced by the acknowledgment and legitimation of subjectivity and multiple realities. What people see is filtered through a lens colored by past experiences, current circumstances, and personal agendas. Sense-making is influenced not only by externally verified factors, but by shared beliefs and organizational values that shape activities and behaviors. Faculty, student affairs staff, students, and others are influenced through mutually shaping interactions; each individual interprets events differently but, like a hologram, each interpretation reflects the whole of the institution from a unique perspective. The "collective unconscious" or culture that bonds people is continually evolving, but it cannot be directly, intentionally manipulated by any person or group.

Third, emergent perspectives suggest that all members of an organization have expertise, power, and responsibility. Contrary to conventional models, in which those near the top of the hierarchy have more expertise, emergent perspectives suggest that persons closest to the effective point of action should be directly involved in the resolution of issues and development of policy (Kuh, 1985). Many resident assistants, for example, are competent—perhaps uniquely qualified—to help students deal with problems and to advise on residence life policy.

Concepts associated with emergent, nonorthodox perspectives are compatible with an ecological view of colleges and universities (Banning, 1980). The campus is a web of physical structures and spaces, relationships, activities, and behaviors shaped by the interpretations that people give to places, events, actions, and processes. Ecological systems evolve over time through mutual shaping—the numerous interactions among individuals and groups that are associated causally with changes in organizational structures and processes. Changes in form may be spontaneous or cumulative and incremental. People, events, and actions influence one another and are related to outcomes; however, it is impossible to link specific causes with specific effects (Kuh, Whitt, and Shedd, 1987).

Emergent perspectives require new assumptions about leader behavior, such as the capacity to think and act in paradoxical ways (Huff, 1985). Students, staff, and faculty expect the CSAO to reduce the ambiguity inherent in complicated situations. The CSAO (and other leaders in the student affairs division) must provide a historical context for current issues and demonstrate the connections between one situation and other events and activities (Neustadt and May, 1986). Through the contradictory processes of simplifying and complicating, ambiguity is reduced through explanation and the complexity of constituents' understanding of organizational issues is increased. The process of simplifying and complicating contributes to an information-rich environment. Thus, as participants learn more about the organization, understandings between members and knowledge about the organization as a whole are increased.

Using Organizational Theory in Student Affairs

Conventional and emergent organizational concepts are important enough to be systematically examined, challenged, and applied in professional preparation programs, staff development activities, and student affairs research. Three types of student affairs preparation programs have been approved by the Council for the Advancement of Standards: counseling, student development, and administration. The conceptual framework for the three program tracks was developed from the results of a study of preparation program curricula conducted in the mid 1970s (Rodgers, 1977). Many counseling-based student affairs preparation programs do not include formal study of organizational theories. Students who do not have work experience often perceive organizational theory as irrelevant to their future role in student affairs. Most master's-level students have an affinity for human development models that stimulate personal revelations and help the students, many of whom are just out of undergraduate school, to organize and understand what they experienced as undergraduates.

Human development courses are important and necessary. But master's-level students must also be introduced to conventional models and emergent perspectives on organizing to understand the context within which student development occurs. Without at least a formal overview of organizational theory, student affairs professionals will be hampered by an underdeveloped capacity to analyze the relationships between relevant factors and actors in the external and internal environments. Doctoral-level students who aspire to leadership positions should be expected to have at least one organizational theory course and one or more advanced seminars in education, business, or sociology that examine in greater depth one or more organizational theories (Kuh, Whitt, and Shedd, 1987).

Both conventional models and emergent, nonorthodox perspectives on organizing can serve as useful frameworks for staff development activities. By contrasting the assumptions on which conventional and emergent perspectives are based, "the 'sacred totems' of the student affairs rainforest" (Schroeder, Nicholls, and Kuh, 1983, p. 53), the assumptions that guide student affairs work, can be identified. Concepts such as loose coupling and fluid participation, when discussed openly, can increase tolerance for error and help staff appreciate the importance of interacting face-to-face with colleagues (Kuh, 1983b).

The process of addressing these ideas is an opportunity to practice action learning (Argyris and Schön, 1978) and to test the assumptions about student affairs held by persons throughout the institution.

Much of what is reported in the student affairs literature does not stimulate the imagination of practitioners nor accurately describe what they experience in their workplace (Kuh, Bean, Bradley, and Coomes, 1986a). Empirical descriptions of student affairs organizations are grounded primarily in conventional assumptions about organizations and reinforce expectations for control, linear causality, and tight coupling, which contradict the actual experiences of student affairs staff.

Studies about student affairs organizations grounded in assumptions congenial to emergent organizational perspectives are likely to be of interest to practitioners as well as scholars (Kuh, Bean, Bradley, and Coomes, 1986b). Such studies will require methodological approaches, such as naturalistic inquiry (Lincoln and Guba, 1985) and case studies using qualitative techniques (Miles and Huberman, 1984), that are different from those typically found in student affairs journals (Kuh, Bean, Bradley, and Coomes, 1986a). Thoughtful essays about leadership that are compatible with emergent perspectives would also be welcome. No comprehensive work exists on leadership in student affairs, except for unpublished dissertations (such as Halstead, 1980).

Conclusion

The shapes and colors seen through a prism depend upon contextual factors—environmental conditions and the position from which the prism is viewed. Using organizational models and perspectives to understand behavior in an institution of higher education is similar to looking through a prism. What is perceived depends on many factors, all of which are influenced by the viewer's assumptions.

No single perspective can accurately account for the predilections, feelings, thoughts, and actions of all the individuals and groups that compose a division of student affairs. Each perspective emphasizes different aspects of the work environment and is grounded in some different assumptions about power, control, causality, and how change occurs.

Although conventional organizational models, particularly the collegial and political models, are helpful in understanding and appreciating certain aspects of life in colleges and universities, they also impose unnecessary and undesirable psychological limits on the actions of leaders and followers that obfuscate action learning and evolutionary change processes. The concepts associated with emergent organizational perspectives seem messy when compared with concepts characteristic of conventional models. Yet life in institutions of higher education is messy (Kuh, 1984b). Ambiguity and surprise are commonplace. To accommodate emergent organizational concepts, student affairs staff must learn to think differently. Expectations for authority, control, and predictability are worth questioning; ambiguity should be embraced, not merely tolerated. Playfulness and a capacity to celebrate anomaly and paradox should be emphasized when seeking new staff (Cohen and March, 1974; Kuh, 1983b, 1984c; Kuh, Whitt, and Shedd, 1987).

The conditions facing institutions of higher education in the next decade will be different from those of the past. Conventional models of organizing will not be useful in understanding events and actions in uncertain, turbulent times. Student affairs professionals cannot afford to conform blindly to convention, impeded by familiar, time-honored assumptions inadequate to the transformational tasks they face. By integrating multiple perspectives on organizing with insights from human development and person-environment models, student affairs professionals can develop richer, more evocative mini-theories for understanding behavior. Staff members who are open to multiple perspectives are institutional treasures. Support them; they will make your life more interesting.

References

Allaire, Y., and Firsirotu, M. E. "Theories of Organizational Culture." *Organization Studies*, 1984, *5*, 193–226.

Argyris, C., and Schön, D. A. *Organizational Learning: A Theory of Action Perspective*. Reading, Mass.: Addison-Wesley, 1978.

Baldridge, J. V. *Power and Conflict in the University: Research in the Sociology of Complex Organizations.* New York: Wiley, 1971.

Baldridge, J. V., Curtis, D. V., Ecker, G. P., and Riley, G. L. "Alternative Models of Governance in Higher Education." In J. Baldridge and T. Deal (eds.), *Governing Academic Organizations.* Berkeley, Calif.: McCutchan, 1977.

Banning, J. H. "The Campus Ecology Manager Role." In U. Delworth, G. Hanson, and Associates, *Student Services: A Handbook for the Profession.* San Francisco: Jossey-Bass, 1980.

Becher, T. "The Cultural View." In B. R. Clark (ed.), *Perspectives on Higher Education.* Berkeley and Los Angeles: University of California Press, 1984.

Borland, D. T. "Organizational Foundations of Administration." In T. Miller, R. Winston, and W. Mendenhall (eds.), *Administration and Leadership in Student Affairs.* Muncie, Ind.: Accelerated Development, 1983.

Bowen, H. R., and Schuster, J. H. *American Professors: A National Resource Imperiled.* New York: Oxford University Press, 1986.

Caple, R. B. "Counseling and the Self-Organization Paradigm." *Journal of Counseling and Development,* 1985, *64,* 173–178.

Capra, F. *The Turning Point: Science, Society, and The Rising Culture.* New York: Basic Books, 1983.

Chaffee, E. E. *Rational Decision-Making in Higher Education.* Boulder, Colo.: National Center for Higher Education Management Systems, 1983.

Clark, B. R. "Organizational Saga in Higher Education." *Administrative Science Quarterly,* 1972, *17,* 178–184.

Clark, B. R. "Faculty Culture." In M. Finkelstein (ed.), *ASHE Reader on Faculty and Faculty Issues in Colleges and Universities.* Washington, D.C.: Association for the Study of Higher Education, 1985.

Clark, B. R., and Trow, M. "The Organizational Context." In T. Newcomb and E. Wilson (eds.), *College Peer Groups: Problems and Prospects for Research.* Hawthorne, N.Y.: Aldine, 1966.

Clark, D. L., Astuto, T. A., and Kuh, G. D. "Strength of Coupling in the Organization and Operation of Colleges and Universities." In G. Johnston and C. Yeakey (eds.), *Research and Thought in Educational Administration.* Lanham, Md.: University Press of America, 1986.

Cohen, M., and March, J. G. *Leadership and Ambiguity: The American College Presidency.* New York: McGraw-Hill, 1974.

Cohen, M., March, J. G., and Olsen, J. P. "A Garbage Can Model of Organizational Choice." *Administrative Science Quarterly,* 1972, *17* (1), 1-25.

Deal, T. E., and Kennedy, A. A. *Corporate Cultures: The Rites and Rituals of Corporate Life.* Reading, Mass.: Addison-Wesley, 1982.

Dutton, T. B., and Rickard, S. T. "Organizing Student Services." In U. Delworth, G. Hanson, and Associates, *Student Services: A Handbook for the Profession.* San Francisco: Jossey-Bass, 1980.

Education Commission of the States. *Challenge: Coordination and Governance in the '80s.* Report no. 134. Denver, Colo.: Education Commission of the States, 1980.

Foxley, C. H. (ed.). *Applying Management Techniques.* New Directions for Student Services, no. 9. San Francisco: Jossey-Bass, 1980.

Georgiou, P. "The Goal Paradigm and Notes Toward a Counter Paradigm." *Administrative Science Quarterly,* 1973, *18,* 291-310.

Gleick, J. *Chaos: Making a New Science.* New York: Viking, 1987.

Gross, E., and Grambsch, P. *University Goals and Academic Power.* Washington, D.C.: American Council on Education, 1968.

Hage, J. *Theories of Organization: Form, Process, and Transformation.* New York: Wiley, 1980.

Halstead, J. R. "A Time Allocation Study of Chief Student Affairs Officers at C.I.C. Institutions." Unpublished doctoral dissertation, Department of Educational Administration, Ohio State University, 1980.

Hedberg, B., Nystrom, P., and Starbuck, W. "Camping on Seesaws: Prescriptions for a Self-Designing Organization." *Administrative Science Quarterly,* 1976, *21,* 41-65.

Howard, G. S. "Can Research in the Human Sciences Become More Relevant to Practice?" *Journal of Counseling and Development,* 1985, *63,* 539-544.

Huff, A. S. "Managerial Implications of the Emerging Paradigm." In Y. Lincoln (ed.), *Organizational Theory and Inquiry:
The Paradigm Revolution.* Newbury Park, Calif.: Sage, 1985.

Hull, D. F., Jr., Hunter, D. E., and Kuh, G. D. "Alternative
Perspectives on Student Affairs Organizations." In G. Kuh
(ed.), *Understanding Student Affairs Organizations.* New Directions
for Student Services, no. 23. San Francisco: Jossey-Bass, 1983.

Kanter, R. M. *The Change Masters.* New York: Simon & Schuster,
1983.

Katz, F. E., and Rosenzweig, J. E. *Organization and Management:
A Systems Approach.* New York: McGraw-Hill, 1974.

Kilmann, R. H., Saxton, M. J., Serpa, R., and Associates.
Gaining Control of the Corporate Culture. San Francisco: Jossey-
Bass, 1985.

Kuh, G. D. "Beyond Student Development: Contemporary
Priorities for Student Affairs." *National Association of Student
Personnel Administrators Journal,* 1981, *18* (1), 29–36.

Kuh, G. D. "Guiding Assumptions About Student Affairs Orga-
nizations." In G. Kuh (ed.), *Understanding Student Affairs
Organizations.* New Directions for Student Services, no. 23.
San Francisco: Jossey-Bass, 1983a.

Kuh, G. D. "Tactics for Understanding and Improving Student Affairs Organizations." In G. Kuh (ed.), *Understanding
Student Affairs Organizations.* New Directions for Student Services, no. 23. San Francisco: Jossey-Bass, 1983b.

Kuh, G. D. "A Framework for Understanding Student Affairs
Work." *Journal of College Student Personnel,* 1984a, *25,* 25–31.

Kuh, G. D. "It's More Complicated Than That. . . . " *Journal of College Student Personnel,* 1984b, *25,* 37–38.

Kuh, G. D. "Suggestions for Remaining Sane in Institutions
That Don't Work the Way They're Supposed to." *National
Association of Student Personnel Administrators Journal,* 1984c, *21*
(1), 55–61.

Kuh, G. D. "What Is Extraordinary About Ordinary Student
Affairs Organizations." *National Association of Student Personnel Administrators Journal,* 1985, *23* (2), 31–43.

Kuh, G. D., Bean, J. P., Bradley, R. K., and Coomes, M.
D. "Contributions of Student Affairs Journals to the Literature

on College Students." *Journal of College Student Personnel,* 1986a, *27,* 292–304.

Kuh, G. D., Bean, J. P., Bradley, R. K., and Coomes, M. D. "Is One Galaxy Enough?" *Journal of College Student Personnel,* 1986b, *27,* 311–312.

Kuh, G. D., and Whitt, E. J. *The Invisible Tapestry: Culture in American Colleges and Universities.* ASHE-ERIC Higher Education Report. Washington, D.C.: Association for the Study of Higher Education, 1988.

Kuh, G. D., Whitt, E. J., and Shedd, J. D. *Student Affairs Work 2001: A Paradigmatic Odyssey.* Alexandria, Va.: American College Personnel Association, 1987.

Leemon, T. A. *The Rites of Passage in a Student Culture.* New York: Teachers College Press, 1972.

Lincoln, Y. S., and Guba, E. *Naturalistic Inquiry.* Newbury Park, Calif.: Sage, 1985.

Lipsky, M. *Street Level Bureaucracy: Dilemmas of the Individual in Public Services.* New York: Russell Sage Foundation, 1980.

Lyons, J. Keynote address to the Indiana University Undergraduate Life Symposium, Bloomington, Ind., May 1987.

Masland, A. T. "Organization Culture in the Study of Higher Education." *Review of Higher Education,* 1985, *8,* 157–168.

Miles, M. B., and Huberman, A. M., *Qualitative Data Analysis: A Sourcebook of New Methods.* Newbury Park, Calif.: Sage, 1984.

Morgan, G. *Images of Organizations.* Newbury Park, Calif.: Sage, 1986.

Neustadt, R. E., and May, E. R. *Thinking in Time: The Uses of History for Decision-Makers.* New York: Free Press, 1986.

Ouchi, W. A. *Theory Z: How American Business Can Meet the Japanese Challenge.* Reading, Mass.: Addison-Wesley, 1981.

Peters, T. J., and Waterman, R. H., Jr. *In Search of Excellence: Lessons from America's Best Run Companies.* New York: Harper & Row, 1982.

Peterson, M. W., and others. *The Organizational Context for Teaching and Learning: A Review of the Research Literature.* Ann Arbor, Mich.: National Center for Research to Improve Postsecondary Teaching and Learning, 1987.

Pfeffer, J. *Organizations and Organizational Theory.* Boston: Pitman, 1982.

Prigogine, I., and Stengers, I. *Order out of Chaos.* New York: Bantam Books, 1984.

Rodgers, R. F. "Student Personnel Work as Social Intervention." In G. Knock (ed.), *Perspectives on the Preparation of Student Affairs Professionals.* Alexandria, Va.: American College Personnel Association, 1977.

Schein, E. H. *Organizational Culture and Leadership: A Dynamic View.* San Francisco: Jossey-Bass, 1985.

Schön, D. A. *Educating the Reflective Practitioner: Toward a New Design for Teaching and Learning in the Professions.* San Francisco: Jossey-Bass, 1987.

Schroeder, C. C., Nicholls, G. E., and Kuh, G. D. "Exploring the Rain Forest: Testing Assumptions and Taking Risks." In G. Kuh (ed.), *Understanding Student Affairs Organizations.* New Directions for Student Services, no. 23. San Francisco: Jossey-Bass, 1983.

Simon, H. A. *Administrative Behavior.* New York: Free Press, 1957.

Smircich, L. "Concepts of Culture and Organizational Analysis." *Administrative Science Quarterly,* 1983, *28,* 339-358.

Strange, C. C. "Traditional Perspectives on Student Affairs Organizations." In G. Kuh (ed.), *Understanding Student Affairs Organizations.* New Directions for Student Services, no. 23. San Francisco: Jossey-Bass, 1983.

Taylor, F. W. *The Principles of Scientific Management.* New York: Harper & Row, 1911.

Trice, H., and Beyer, J. "Studying Organizational Cultures Through Rites and Ceremonials." *Academy of Management Review,* 1984, *9,* 653-669.

Vaill, P. B. "The Purposing of High-Performing Systems." In T. Sergiovanni and J. Corbally (eds.), *Leadership and Organizational Culture: New Perspectives on Administrative Theory and Practice.* Urbana: University of Illinois Press, 1984.

Weber, M. *The Theory of Social and Economic Organization.* London: Oxford University Press, 1947.

Weick, K. E. "Educational Organizations as Loosely Coupled Systems." *Administrative Science Quarterly,* 1976, *21,* 1-19.

Part Three

Roles and Models
for Practice

Our identity as student services professionals is clearly a mix
of many components—the context of higher education, the
theories that undergird our work, and the specific skills and
knowledge we bring to our mission on campus. A key component, perhaps the crucial one for defining our identity, is the
use of general models for practice, or role orientations, in student services. In most of our literature, as well as in our preparation programs, these roles are vaguely defined or only briefly
explored. The jump all too often is from theory to specific competency. The glue that holds context, theory, and skills together
is a model of practice, a guide that is more tangible than theory
and yet more general than skills. Such models of functioning
provide general orientations for our work in higher education.

Each student services professional harbors a sense of role,
a model that holds together all the various activities that fill each
day. And from time to time thinkers in our field have called
either for a recommitment to an existing model or for a change
to a newer model. Yet rarely is it clear just what models pre-

dominate in our field. Such models are often not explained in a way that leads to a choice among them by the individual student services professional or by a division of student services. The four chapters in this section represent an effort to label the predominant models, explain and clarify each, and illustrate the relevance of and need for each in student services.

In our literature and practice of the past thirty years, three models stand out: surrogate parent and disciplinarian, administrator, and counselor. Although the first role, that of surrogate parent, was predominant in early periods (see Part One), it is no longer relevant for our profession. Changes in higher education and in society, as well as our own growing distaste for this role, have produced a milieu in which students are expected (and generally themselves expect) to be treated as adults. There is no doubt that a flavor of this surrogate parent model remains in our field, expressed sometimes by parents who hope we will take over their role as their son or daughter enrolls on our campus, sometimes in institutional policy or procedure, and sometimes in our own need to nurture or control. But even though remnants of it exist, the model is no longer central and viable.

The other two traditional models, administrator and counselor, remain viable today. In Chapter Eight, David Ambler develops the administrative model, emphasizing the current challenges in this role. Some readers may think this chapter does not apply to them because they do not have official administrative responsibilities. Yet Ambler addresses several issues that all professionals in the field will find useful. The counselor role, on the other hand, is one with which many student services personnel identify but also one that many find difficult to explicate. Linda Forrest, delineating this role in Chapter Nine, briefly reviews the historical roots of this orientation and specifies its current relevance for a wide variety of professionals in our field.

In Chapters Ten and Eleven, Robert Brown and James Banning present the newer models of student development educator and environmental manager. Both models assert the need for new ways to look at ourselves, our students, and our campuses. Brown sees student services professionals as educators who bring a solid background in theory and concept to helping students develop personally, intellectually, physically, and esthetically. Banning advocates actively assessing our campus environments and providing routes (such as programs or organizational changes) to enhancing the fit between students and various aspects of campus communities.

None of these four models or orientations claims exclusive adherence. Each offers a unique, important perspective for understanding and articulating our role. How much of each role or model we adopt depends on individual perceptions and philosophy, specific interests, talents, and jobs, and, certainly, the nature and mission of the institutions and agencies in which we work. In presenting and explaining these central models, we hope to help each student services professional understand them and intentionally select those portions of the models that fit his or her own practice.

Chapter Eight

Designing and Managing Programs: The Administrator Role

David A. Ambler

Throughout its history, the student affairs profession has been plagued by an identity crisis: Are its primary functions administrative or are they educational? Is its allegiance to the academic mission or to the management of the university environment? The debate centers on the question of whether student personnel workers are educators, with a systematic body of knowledge based on theoretical constructs, or administrators of ancillary—but necessary—services for students. The debate is unfortunate because the arguments are always presented as extremes; the dichotomy is unnecessary because—as this chapter will argue—it is possible and desirable to be both.

The administrative model, which this chapter explores, is based on the premise that the student services profession is an administrative, service-oriented unit in higher education that provides many facilitating and developmental activities and programs for students. A historical perspective on the debate surrounding this administrative model and the forces that have shaped the managerial aspects of student services can help improve the understanding of the substance of this role: its rationale, function, and elements.

History: A Debate About Models

The dichotomy in the student services profession between administrator and educator has become deeper in recent years with higher levels of specialization, greater utilization of technology, diminishing resources, and increasing emphasis on student outcomes measurement and organizational accountability. But it is also reflected in the historical factors and movements that gave rise to the student personnel field (see Fenske, Chapter One, for a fuller exploration of these factors). Appleton, Briggs, and Rhatigan (1978, p. 13) trace the split to the early battles between deans of men, deans of women, and personnel and mental health workers. They assert that the struggle has continued and is reflected in the more recent efforts to merge the organizational vestiges of these movements: the National Association for Women Deans, Administrators and Counselors (NAWDAC), the National Association of Student Personnel Administrators (NASPA), and the American College Personnel Association (ACPA).

The time-honored positions of these organizations reflect the major source of the debate. Early deans of men and women were identified with the administration of colleges and universities and with the enforcement of institutional regulations. Personnel workers were not; they came from a variety of academic movements—educational psychology, measurement and testing, vocational guidance, and mental health—and they were perceived less as disciplinarians and more as counselors and advisers of students.

Fenske, in Chapter One of this book, traces the history of student affairs in the context of higher education. The diversity and numbers of students, the assumption of responsibility for extracurricular services, and the growth of institutional bureaucracy thus describe how the complex portfolio of student services emerged. Concern for their impact on the educational environment and the need for efficient management of these rapidly expanding services tied the profession to the administrative structure and introduced the position of the chief student services officer.

A number of more contemporary authors suggested that the dichotomy between education and administration was unreal and unnecessary and asserted that the profession—like a political party—was broad enough to accommodate various concerns and viewpoints. It could be open, they suggested, to the behavioral scientist's developmental concerns as well as the personnel dean's desire for effective management of services. In summarizing his objections to what he perceived as Clyde Parker's (1970) reconceptualization of student personnel work, James F. Penney (1970, p. 5) noted that "most campuses need the kinds of functions and the kind of competencies that the student development center and its specialists propose to make available. Most campuses *also* need effective personnel program administration."

In 1972, the Commission on Professional Development of the now defunct Council of Student Personnel Associations in Higher Education (COSPA) outlined a philosophy encompassing both the service and developmental aspects of student affairs. In diplomatic language, the council introduced "student development services in higher education" as an inclusive term for the many areas usually included in student personnel programs (Commission on Professional Development, 1972, p. 2). It defined the purposes of student services work in terms of behavioral and developmental goals but conceded that they are accomplished through administrative, instructional, and consultative roles. Different members of the profession perform their responsibilities through one or a combination of these roles. Through this document, COSPA recognized the need for a multidisciplinary curriculum in training new professionals, whose demonstration of basic educational values, consistent with those of the profession, is as important as any skills acquired in training.

Yet the dichotomy continues today. Don G. Creamer (1980, p. 1) asks, "Is student development different from student services? Not surprisingly, the answer is mushy or fuzzy— yes, maybe, no, sometimes." Gary H. Knock (1985, p. 36) notes that the most important development in the era following World War II was the creation of student services divisions as separate administrative bureaucracies: "This approach to organizational management provided clear identity for student personnel services, but also limited educative efforts to the out-of-class life of students." And Louis C. Stamatakos (1980, p. 287) believes that the contemporary interpretation of student development divided the profession anew: "It split into three groups . . . , those who initiated and gave direction to the student development movement . . . those who opposed it (chiefly administrative types) . . . and . . . those who were relatively disinterested, uninformed, uninvolved and preoccupied with other more provincial concerns." Creamer (1980, p. 2) contends that the debate will necessarily continue. It is the intent of this chapter to demonstrate that the debate is unnecessary.

Rationale of the Administrative Model

The rationale for the administrative model of student services can be stated in five assumptions that reflect both the historical roots of the profession and current realities.

First, the effective development and delivery of services and programs are the historical and legitimate basis of the profession and its only viable means to accomplish its educational goals for students. To abandon our role of providing essential services and of managing them to achieve desired institutional outcomes would result in our demise. Colleges and universities could not afford us or—worse yet—tolerate us if we were not related to their basic service functions.

Second, there is no inherent conflict or dichotomy between the profession's administrative orientation and its educational and developmental goals. Resolving conflict between society and the individual is an important function of democratic leadership—on or off the campus. Tension between the individual and the group is in itself educational. In his efforts to focus higher education on individual student development, Parker (1971, p. 405) says, "I have become less concerned with whether this becomes the new identity for student personnel, is contained within the framework of student personnel, or is part of the larger system of the university." I hope he is wrong. Students see us as administrators, but they also see us as models. The fact that they do not recognize us as teachers is testimony to our current lack of effectiveness in that role.

Third, in order to effect desired educational outcomes, student services must be effectively managed and coordinated with academic programs and services. If student services cannot be justified by their contribution to the educational mission, they should probably be abandoned to private entrepreneurs, or the students should be allowed to fend for themselves. By linking the classroom and the campus, student services provide the students with some reality referents to test their scholarly constructs. This assumption about the relationship between academic programs and student services was noted by Miller and Prince (1976) in their principles for a student development organization. They state that "collaboration among student affairs staff members, faculty members, and students is essential to the success of the student development program. . . . The institution's commitment to student development is directly proportional to the number of these collaborative links between the student affairs staff and the faculty" (Miller and Prince, 1976, p. 155).

Fourth, identification with the administrative structure permits student services to influence policy formulation and resource allocation to effect its educational goals. Policies, procedures, and resources are the lifeblood of any institution; the ability to influence their development and use is real power. The involvement of the chief student services officer in policy decisions can affect the climate for inquiry, create or enhance factors that contribute to student persistence, and protect and advance student citizenship rights. As a member of the central administrative staff, the chief student services officer can help keep the institution honest in its obligations to students.

Fifth, the administrative model provides the student services profession with the greatest flexibility for responding to student and institutional needs and with the ability to reach large segments of the student population. Because the administrative model relates to the management function of directing resources to achieve desired outcomes, it does not prejudice the needs or the process. It can alter, abandon, or add services according to contemporary educational trends, societal demands, or student characteristics.

Historically, we have claimed that each student is unique, with special needs, and that students are responsible for their own development. It follows that not all students have the same need of our assistance. The administrative model recognizes that fact while permitting the student services worker to specialize in satisfying needs identified in the total student population. Under this arrangement, we are not limited by a prescribed set of developmental tasks or predetermined solutions.

Functions of Administration

Concern for the efficient management of the educational enterprise is a legitimate aspect of the administrative model. The concern dates back to the early part of this century, although the systematic study of higher education gained prominence only after World War II. Management functions, however, had been analyzed in a number of ways for years prior to their application to higher education. Luther Gulick dissected the management process into the functions of planning, organizing, staffing, directing, coordinating, reporting, and budgeting with his "POSDCORB" (Gulick, 1937). Edward H. Litchfield (1959), former chancellor of the University of Pittsburgh, wrote of the management process in higher education as consisting of programming, communicating, controlling, and reappraising.

Planning, programming, and budgeting systems (PPBS), management by objectives (MBO), management information systems (MIS), and other planning schemes hit the campuses in the late 1960s and early 1970s as enrollments and resources peaked and began to decline. Calls for economies, long-range planning, and better use of resources gave these new management systems some degree of credibility on campus. Although some people touted these industrial and government systems as saving higher education in the latter quarter of the century, others continued to resist any efforts to quantify educational outcome or measure educational "productivity." Saner administrators recognized these evaluation systems as useful new adaptations of the management systems adopted in business, government, and education after the industrial revolution and believed that the conscious and systematic application of these systems to higher education in general and student services in particular held great promise for the profession (see chapters in Part Five of this book for a detailed analysis of these approaches).

All of these management techniques, however, pale when juxtaposed with the impact of the application of computer technology to student services administration that has occurred over the past fifteen years. In the early 1970s, most chief student affairs officers would have been pleased if their budget reports were computerized while they continued to handle increased admissions, enrollment, financial aid activity, and other student services functions by antiquated hand methods. Today, computer applications are utilized in every aspect of student affairs management. Garland (1985, p. 44) identifies two major uses of information technology: "First, through the collection and analysis of student and program data, student affairs professionals are able to learn more about students' needs, characteristics, program use and effectiveness. . . . Second, information systems assist labor-intensive work. . . . Automated office systems in admissions, financial aid, room assignments and placement offices, to name a few, are reducing the amount of time spent by professionals and support staff on routine activities." It is evident that we have only scratched the surface of the contributions that computer technology holds for student development and the administration of student services. We are constrained only by the fact that few student affairs managers have fully equipped themselves to utilize creatively this powerful educational tool.

We have changed the nomenclature, redefined some of the procedures, applied new technologies, and become more conscious of their daily applicability, but the basic management functions remain unchanged. In one manner or another, any effective chief student services officer undertakes the basic management functions of planning, organizing, motivating, executing, and controlling. They are the standards for the daily routine of a chief student affairs officer. These management activities apply at every level in the administrative structure and are found in every activity or program in the taxonomy of student services. They are most evident in such service units as admissions, records, and financial aid, but they are equally useful and necessary for the effective administration of such services as counseling, career guidance, and student activity programming.

Elements of the Student Services Program

Every good student services staff member knows that administration is a process, not an end in itself. The effective student services administrator uses the basic management functions of planning, organizing, motivating, executing, and controlling to integrate various program elements in order to achieve the goals of the student affairs program. The development of students as self-reliant, functioning individuals and the realization of their own personal and academic goals are the desired outcomes of all we do as educators and managers.

Certain elements needed to achieve those outcomes are common to all student services programs regardless of size, scope, purpose, or organization of the college or university. From the perspective of the administrative model, these elements are students, services, structure, staff, and sources.

Students. Ever since student services emerged as an organized unit in higher education, students have been an integral part of the program. They have never been viewed as "customers" or the end-product of our bureaucratic machinery. Almost everything we do, we do with students. The high regard for and the devotion to students that have characterized this profession are perhaps its most significant contribution to the unique character of higher education in the United States. They have served to keep higher education aware of its special role of educating the individual in and for a free society.

This is the historical commitment and mission of student services. The original statement of the "student personnel point of view" by the American Council on Education in 1937 and its restatement in 1949 made it clear that the student was seen as an active participant in the educational process: "The concept of education is broadened to include attention to the student's well-rounded development—physically, socially, emotionally and spiritually, as well as intellectually. The student is thought of as a responsible participant in his own development and not as a passive recipient of an imprinted economic, political, or religious doctrine, or vocational skill. As a responsible participant in the societal processes of our American democracy, his full and balanced maturity is viewed as a major end-goal of education" (American Council on Education, 1949, p. 1).

Those who criticize the identification of student services with the administrative elements of higher education accuse the profession of often neglecting its commitment to the student's education for the sake of institutional order and harmony. They point to the lack of educational theory, the poor record of assessing student needs, and the hodgepodge of unrelated services that constitute student services programs. There is some merit to their criticisms. Harpel (1978, p. 22) noted, "Given that the institution's purpose is derived from the needs of its constituents, the lack of attention to needs analyses within higher education is astonishing. Even when someone tries to find out what students need, subjective judgments and public opinion are often substituted for systematic inquiry."

A dynamic administrative model of student services, however, provides for constant reassessment of student characteristics and needs. Parker (1971) doubted that such assessment was possible in the traditional organization of student services, yet it is encouraging to note the more recent incorporation of student development concepts and research programs within the administrative organization of student affairs. Knowing student needs is essential to an effective student services program; it is compatible with institutional goals and essential to the administrative model.

There are several different organizational models for structuring a student services research program. Which model is used depends on such factors as staff competencies, available resources, and the institution's structure and commitment to organizational research. Three possible arrangements for student research would be within each office of the division of student services, as a separate office of the division, or as a part of or in cooperation with an institutional research office.

Each arrangement has its own problem and promise. There is some merit in creating an ethic in which each office is responsible for researching its own effectiveness. Yet such research may be biased, may lack coordination with other units, or may fail to assess student development from a broad perspective. A separate office for research within a division of student services can promulgate a comprehensive student assessment program as well as an effective management and program evaluation system. It frequently is unable, however, to secure institutional resources and commitment. Teaming up with an institution-wide research effort has two major advantages: resources as well as credibility are easier to secure, and the assessment program can command the attention of academic programs, student services, and other university elements that affect student development. The major disadvantage of this approach is the danger that the research on students and program effectiveness may not be used for measuring educational outcomes but may be used strictly for cost-benefit analysis.

Services and Programs. The student services administrator is frequently asked a sometimes embarrassing question: "What do you do?" What we do is not always readily apparent. Because we are neither exclusively teachers nor administrators, student services workers frequently respond by enumerating the various kinds of services and programs we offer, hoping that the educational role will be implicit if not self-evident. "What we do" follows logically after identifying student needs; student services and programs are the primary means by which the profession accomplishes its goals and organizational assignments.

Some models of student services are based on complete professional control of the scope and definition of its function in the university. In the administrative model, however, the content and assignments of the student services unit are determined by the institution's purpose, philosophy, and organizational structure. The student services unit is viewed as one of many subdivisions, related to the organizational whole and institutional goals. Indeed, this model frequently shows a variety of functions shared among units. Examples include housing, shared with the business office; financial aid, shared with the comptroller; and admissions and records, shared with academic administration.

Because the content of the student services program in this model is controlled by institutional rather than professional considerations, it provides the greatest latitude in defining the scope and extent of the services offered. Student services may have activities assigned to it that are somewhat foreign to the profession or distasteful to the staff, such as intercollegiate athletics, alumni affairs, and the university security program. And, as in most political systems, the skill and effectiveness of the student services leadership—more than professional requirements—dictate whether the unit has a limited or comprehensive role in the institution's mission.

Developing a comprehensive service taxonomy is vital to the functioning of the administrative model; structuring or clustering services promotes program and management effectiveness. In a major survey for the federal government, Ayers, Tripp, and Russell (1966) identified the primary student services and programs under four main functions: (1) welfare functions—such as counseling, testing, health services, financial aid programs, placement, and alumni relations; (2) control functions—such as admissions, records, discipline, and living arrangements; (3) activities functions—such as cocurricular and extracurricular programs, student government, student publications, student unions, and cultural programs; and (4) teaching functions—such as orientation programs, foreign student programs, remedial clinics, and other special informal educational services in residence halls and elsewhere in the college community.

Others have designed different but useful program classifications. Hershenson (1970) suggested four different function categories: internal coordinating, orienting, supportive, and educational. But perhaps the most useful taxonomy of student services comes in the program classification structure (PCS) of the National Center for Higher Education Management Systems (NCHEMS) of the Western Interstate Commission for Higher Education (Myers and Topping, 1974).

The PCS system provides for eight major functional units in higher education. In the original definitions of student services, six categories are identified: student services administration, social and cultural development, counseling and career guidance, financial aid administration, student auxiliary services, and intercollegiate athletics (Myers and Topping, 1974). Recent modifications have added student recruitment and admissions and records. The PCS system is the most widely used system for comparative studies because its categories and definitions are sufficiently broad, yet specific enough, to permit inclusion of virtually every defined student service. It is also useful for planning organizational structures, strategies, and evaluation.

If services and programs follow the identification of student needs, then evaluation is the logical next step in the process. Yet the lack of systematic evaluation of student development and program effectiveness continues to plague the profession. It remains to be seen whether contemporary theories and models will substantiate our achievements. One thing is sure: The coming decades of diminished resources will demand that student services demonstrate their contribution to the institution's goals and welfare.

Structure. Bureaucratic organization is an American way of life. Although the size and complexity of contemporary corporate life may seem negative, it is successful (or lacks any equally successful substitutes). Many have criticized the corporate model for higher education; nevertheless, it has allowed us to provide advanced education to most Americans.

Student services must be effectively organized to accomplish their mission. They must be appropriately clustered, staffed, and supervised. Lines of authority and communications must be established and operational guides and parameters identified. Staff titles, training, and compensation must properly motivate people to work together on the unit's programs and services. Through effective coordination of administrative efforts, student services helps achieve the institution's goals. (See Sandeen, Chapter Seventeen, for a more detailed discussion of this area.)

Kuh (this volume and 1983) demonstrates the need for more systematic study of the traditional organizational structures in student affairs. Increased size and institutional complexity combined with the expanding diversity of student services are forcing changes in organizational structures and decision making. Kuh (1983, p. 35) recommends "that student affairs staff be eclectic in their approach and use multiple perspectives to understand the organizational environment. Using multiple perspectives can decrease the amount of error associated with organizational sense making.''

The most common structure for student services has been the horizontal or ''flat'' organizational pattern, in which all major services report to the chief student services officer. This pattern has worked well for small colleges and in situations where the program is limited or the unit head is not considered a major institutional officer. Unfortunately, this pattern is also found in many large, complex universities where the unit is expected not only to direct the student services program but also to serve as an institutional leader. Clearly, some other pattern is needed if the program is to be an integral part of the institution. No one organizational pattern can be imposed on student services programs. However, Sandeen (this volume) suggests factors to be considered in organizing or reorganizing a program.

Staff. Operating with students through the structures and services of the student services program is the staff of competent professionals. Nothing is accomplished without them. Their degree of effectiveness, availability to students, morale, and personal welfare must be a daily concern of the chief student services officer.

The administrative model calls for a wide variety of professional specialists to perform its various tasks. Unlike other models, it welcomes people from a large array of disciplines and professions; mobility within the structure depends more on the level of training and performance than on the kind of training. Although specialization is a chief staff characteristic, common attributes such as organizational commitment, behavioral modeling, and interunit cooperation and collaboration are encouraged and rewarded. The specialized training of staff members notwithstanding, in this model each person performs his or her task through administration, instruction, consultation, or some combination of these roles.

Regardless of the structure, scope, or size of the student services programs, three levels of staff are evident in the administrative model: administrative, managerial, and program. These three classifications refer to what is commonly called the ''professional'' staff. In addition, there are many technical, clerical, paraprofessional, student, and skilled and semiskilled workers.

The category of administrative staff is reserved for the chief student services officer and middle-level administrators who coordinate major program areas in the larger, more complex programs. The title of vice-president for the chief student services officer usually signifies institution-wide involvement and responsibility. Some deans of students with corresponding duties, however, report directly to the president. A more recent development has been personnel deans with specialized responsibilities for administering a cluster of services. Titles used with this category of administrative staff include dean of admissions and records, dean of student development, and dean of student life. The chief administrative officer and the middle management personnel come from diverse specialties. Some come from traditional counseling or student services training programs, while a growing number are graduates of higher education or educational administration programs. And some come from disciplines unrelated to student services, having been selected for personal qualifications or circumstantial reasons.

Most service units within the student services division are headed by people who carry the title of director or coordinator. They are the management staff: a diverse group of middle managers who frequently share little with respect to professional training and interests. They range from the medical doctor who directs health services and the business manager who supervises housing programs to the more traditionally trained student services worker who coordinates student activities or runs the admissions program. In the administrative model, however, these people share common management responsibilities in terms of personnel policies, budgeting procedures, and program management and evaluation. It is the responsibility of the chief student services officer to achieve a high degree of administrative effectiveness and functional interdependence within this group.

Undergirding the organization are the program or professional staff, who deal in direct instructive, consultative, or administrative service to students. These people also reflect a wide range of training and specialization. They are usually the youngest and most energetic workers in the organization. Many of them enter student services out of some positive experiences as an undergraduate with either service staff or campus life. Certain student services require a high degree of specialization in the program-level staff, while others can effectively use people from student services training programs or other related disciplines. Still other people enter the profession as much because of personal skills they possess as because of the degrees or training they have received. Services requiring specialized training at this level include health services, counseling programs, psychological testing, food services, and legal and consumer advising programs. Most other services attract generalists and provide much on-the-job training.

Staff development is most crucial at this level. Young staff members can easily get locked into a position if concern for their professional mobility is not expressed early. It is easy to become tagged as a residence hall specialist or an activities person if opportunities to explore other career options are not provided on the job. In his chapter in this book, Jon Dalton explores staff development programs.

Entry-level workers are the backbone of the profession. Yet they are frequently asked to carry the burden with little experience or supervision. They often have titles that do not reflect what they do and are branded bureaucrats or cogs in an unresponsive system. They are usually the most poorly paid members of the team in both dollars and attention. Chief student services officers need to make regular contact with these people.

Sources. Volumes have been written about the financial and other resources for higher education. Not much, however, has been said about the funding of student services in its own literature. However, we do not here intend to explore the complexities of finance for higher education and student services, although it is extremely important to the effective functioning of the administrative model. This subject is covered by Schuh and Rickard in Chapter Eighteen.

It is a major responsibility of the chief student affairs officer to secure the necessary financial and other resources for the services and programs. The chief student affairs officer must be skilled in budgeting and finance and must demonstrate those competencies to others in the administrative structure. A good student services officer knows how to skillfully blend the different kinds of funds available to ensure the maximum level of service delivery.

One piece of advice: Chief student services officers must be well versed in higher education finance. Only in recent years have we included courses on this subject in training programs. Staff members are well advised to enroll in business, finance, and economics courses to supplement their other training.

Summary

Student services has traditionally and historically been an administrative unit in higher education. Yet its role has been unique; while providing essential services in support of the academic mission of the institution, it contributes significantly and directly to the student's education and development. Thus, there should be no real or perceived dichotomy with respect to the role of student services work in higher education. Its service-oriented function should be as clear to the practitioner today as it was to the authors of *The Student Personnel Point of View* in the 1930s (American Council on Education, 1937).

Functioning within the administrative system gives the student services worker the greatest latitude for responding to both student needs and institutional purpose. The survival of the profession depends most heavily on its ability to deliver these essential services in a manner that clearly demonstrates that they make a difference to the students and the institution. This unique, historic, and valuable aspect of American higher education can best be accomplished through the administrative model of student services.

References

American Council on Education. *The Student Personnel Point of View*. American Council on Education Studies, series 1, vol.

1, no. 3. Washington, D.C.: American Council on Education, 1937.

American Council on Education. *The Student Personnel Point of View.* American Council on Education Studies, series 4, vol. 13, no. 13. Washington, D.C.: American Council on Education, 1949.

Appleton, J., Briggs, C., and Rhatigan, J. *Pieces of Eight.* Portland, Ore.: National Association of Student Personnel Administrators Institute of Research and Development, 1978.

Ayers, A., Tripp, P., and Russell, J. *Student Services Administration in Higher Education.* Washington, D.C.: U.S. Department of Health, Education, and Welfare, 1966.

Commission on Professional Development. *Student Development Services in Post Secondary Education.* Commission on Professional Development, Council of Student Personnel Associations in Higher Education, 1972.

Creamer, D. G. (ed.). *Student Development in Higher Education: Theories, Practices, and Future Directions.* Cincinnati, Ohio: ACPA Media, 1980.

Garland, P. H. *Serving More Than Students: A Critical Need for College Student Personnel Services.* ASHE-ERIC Higher Education Report no. 7. Washington, D.C.: Association for the Study of Higher Education, 1985.

Gulick, L. "Notes on the Theory of Organization." In L. Gulick and L. Urwick (eds.), *Papers on the Science of Administration.* New York: Institute of Public Administration, 1937.

Harpel, R. L. "Evaluating from a Management Perspective." In G. R. Hanson (ed.), *Evaluating Program Effectiveness.* New Directions for Student Services, no. 1. San Francisco: Jossey-Bass, 1978.

Hershenson, D. B. "A Functional Organization of College Student Personnel Services." *National Association of Student Personnel Administrators Journal,* 1970, *8,* 35–37.

Knock, G. H. "Development of Student Services in Higher Education." In M. J. Barr, L. A. Keating, and Associates, *Developing Effective Student Services Programs: Systematic Approaches for Practitioners.* San Francisco: Jossey-Bass, 1985.

Kuh, G. D. (ed.). *Understanding Student Affairs Organizations.* New

Directions for Student Services, no. 23. San Francisco: Jossey-Bass, 1983.

Litchfield, E. H. "Organization in Large American Universities." *Journal of Higher Education,* 1959, *30,* 353–364, 489–504.

Miller, T. K., and Prince, J. S. *The Future of Student Affairs: A Guide to Student Development for Tomorrow's Higher Education.* San Francisco: Jossey-Bass, 1976.

Myers, E. M., and Topping, J. R. *Information Exchange Procedures Activity Structure.* Technical Report no. 63. Boulder, Colo.: National Center for Higher Education Management Systems, Western Interstate Commission for Higher Education, 1974.

Parker, C. A. "Ashes, Ashes. . . . " Paper presented at American College Personnel Association Convention, St. Louis, Mo., Mar. 1970.

Parker, C. A. "Institutional Self-Renewal in Higher Education." *Journal of College Student Personnel,* 1971, *12* (6), 405–409.

Penney, J. F. "Who's Minding the Store? Reactions to 'Ashes, Ashes. . . . '" Paper presented at American College Personnel Association Convention, St. Louis, Mo., Mar. 1970.

Stamatakos, L. C. "Pre-Professional and Professional Obstacles to Student Development." In D. G. Creamer (ed.), *Student Development in Higher Education: Theories, Practices, and Future Directions.* Cincinnati, Ohio: ACPA Media, 1980.

Chapter Nine

Guiding, Supporting, and Advising Students: The Counselor Role

Linda Forrest

The development of the student affairs profession can be understood from many perspectives, but the oldest and most enduring approach originated in the field of counseling. An in-depth comprehension of the student affairs profession requires an understanding of the history, context, and applications of counseling models.

Many senior professionals in the field of student affairs completed their education prior to the development of professional preparation programs. Consequently, many received their advanced training in other disciplines, often counseling and guidance, counselor education, or counseling psychology programs. These leaders identify with a counseling perspective, understand its benefits, and recognize the importance and uniqueness of a counseling approach in their interactions with students. Furthermore, student affairs faculty have required counseling courses within their curricula and encouraged students to gain practical experience with counseling models. Likewise, many students enter the field of student affairs because of a special interest in serving students from a counseling perspective.

There are numerous counseling models and theories. In this chapter, terms such as *counseling perspective, counseling approach,* and *counseling model* are used interchangeably in a generic sense to connote a set of broad-based values, knowledge, methods, and skills rather than a specific theory or model. This set of basic values, knowledge, methods, and skills permeates many student affairs professionals' work with students and can be used alone or in conjunction with the other approaches and models discussed in this book.

The first section of this chapter presents a brief history of the philosophical and structural developments in student services, counseling, and psychology over the last six decades that have influenced the development of a counseling approach to student affairs. The second section covers the components of a counseling approach as it is practiced today, including some basic assumptions underlying a counseling perspective, the knowledge base required to use a counseling model, and the distinction between direct and indirect professional training in counseling. The final section covers the benefits of a counseling approach and presents examples of its application to student services today. The distinction between direct and indirect professional training in counseling and the corresponding roles played by the different professionals within student affairs are emphasized throughout the chapter.

Historical Background

The purpose of this book is to examine the student affairs profession by asking such questions as Who are we? What do we do? and How do we provide services? These questions cannot be answered without a historical perspective and an examination of the ideas that shaped the thinking within the profession (see Fenske, Chapter One). The counseling perspective or role orientation is a building block of student services and has had profound influence on the overall development of the profession (American Council on Education, 1937; Cowley, 1937).

Counseling was recognized early as a large and significant component of student personnel work (Lloyd-Jones and

Smith, 1938; Strang, 1962; Williamson, 1939). Cowley (1937) saw counseling as the coordinating force that integrated the various personnel services. He believed that without counseling, the various services might split students into many parts (for example, emotional, vocational, educational) and make it difficult for students to organize these parts into a whole. Lloyd-Jones and Smith agreed that counseling "coordinated the various personnel services" on students' behalf (1938, p. 103).

During the 1930s and 1940s, questions were emerging within the field about counseling models and the roles of counselors. Some authors proposed that counseling be carried out by faculty, especially faculty who showed an inclination to be counselors (Paterson, 1928). Others advocated that faculty receive general training in counseling to handle normal developmental concerns of students, and that professionals respond to students with difficult psychological problems (Lloyd-Jones and Smith, 1938; Strang, 1932). Still others argued for specialized, professional training for those who counseled (Paterson, Schneidler, and Williamson, 1938; Williamson, 1939). Confusion existed about who should practice counseling. The specific responsibilities of the counselor as well as the amount and specificity of counselor training were also under debate (Strang, 1940; Tyler, 1969; Williamson, 1939). Leaders in the fields of student affairs and counseling were formulating positions and influencing how a counseling model would develop within student services.

From the 1930s through the 1960s, as the purpose and structure of higher education were changing, additional changes were occurring on three fronts: in the population of students, in student services, and in counseling and psychology. All of these changes are important to understanding the counseling model today and its influence on the student affairs profession.

Changes in the Population of Students. During this period, larger numbers of students were attending college and the diversity apparent in our society was beginning to be represented in the student population on our campuses. Numerous factors influenced this change. Most public universities were opening their doors to a wider segment of the population (Aubrey, 1977). Education was no longer primarily a privilege of the white upper class. After World War II, many veterans took advantage of government educational support and flooded onto college campuses. The Veterans Administration (VA) provided financial support to universities to assist veterans in their personal adjustment and vocational planning. Public universities, aided by the VA's commitment to serving veterans, developed their counseling services for all students.

Barriers to higher education for racial and ethnic minorities were recognized and altered. As the role of women in our society gradually shifted, many more women entered institutions of higher education—not only eighteen-year-olds, but also older, returning students. The federal government developed programs to assist students financially, removing a major barrier to entry for many middle- and lower-income students.

Consequently, the population of students after World War II represented a greater diversity than universities had traditionally experienced, often creating a mismatch between faculty expectations about student behavior and the reality of students' adjustment and success. This increased diversity also provided a much more complex and elaborate social and cultural life. Students and faculty were interacting with others who did not share a single value system or cultural heritage. Finally, there was increasing acceptance by the general public, and especially by the student population, of the value of counseling and psychological services. With this increased acceptance came a heightened demand. These changes in the student population affected the philosophy and functions of student services and were integrally linked with concurrent changes occurring in the field.

Changes in Student Services on Campuses. During the great expansion, when students were flooding onto campuses across the country in greater and greater numbers, new staff and faculty positions were created. Student services evolved into a set of distinct services offered by staff with a diversity of professional expertise.

The expansion of services to students created opportunities for specialization and diversification of staff responsibilities. No longer were all services provided by a dean of students or the office of a dean of men or women. Students could go to health centers for medical care, placement bureaus for assistance in gaining employment, and counseling centers for testing, advising, and counseling. The professional staff developed new skills and techniques for handling the specific problems students brought to their service units; this in turn created a greater need for specialized training. Not only were protocols developed about the specific functions associated with a service unit, but different philosophies of service developed. In this diversification and professionalization of student services, a counseling perspective remained the solid base on which new services and professional skills for staff were developed.

Changes in Counseling and Psychology. While changes occurred in the field of student affairs, concurrent changes were taking place in the fields of counseling and psychology. Specifically, the growth of the vocational guidance movement and the mental health movement in the early 1900s was affecting the field of counseling (Aubrey, 1977; Whiteley, 1984). The desire of colleges to select students with the capacity for academic success and to advise students effectively about courses of study and career directions created a need for valid and reliable means of measuring abilities and interests (Williamson, 1939). The psychometric movement was integrally linked to the development of counseling techniques and methods.

Psychological theories—including learning theories, developmental theories, personality theories, and counseling theories— also grew in number and complexity from the 1930s on. With the development of these theories and the increased sophistication of personality and vocational tests came an increased understanding of assessment, diagnosis, and treatment. Techniques for intervention and treatment were described extensively in the professional literature (for example, Rogers, 1961) and distinctions were increasingly being made among remedial, developmental, and preventive strategies for therapeutic involvement (Morrill, Oetting, and Hurst, 1974). Like student services, counseling and psychology were being affected by the trends toward specialization, professionalization, and a greater knowledge base.

In psychology, distinctions were made between master's and doctoral degrees. Efforts to monitor the minimum level of training and experience of those who practiced psychology and called themselves psychologists were under way. State licensing laws and credentialing guidelines were passed by state legislatures. Supervised experience and degree requirements were outlined within the licensing statutes of most states.

A similar movement to specify minimum standards was emerging at the training level. The growth in the size and status of the American Psychological Association (APA) drew many counseling people involved in service and training into the organization's fold. Counseling psychology as a distinct field developed in the 1950s (Whiteley, 1984); as it grew, and as APA developed accreditation guidelines for training programs (American Psychological Association, 1986), counseling training programs reached a crossroads. The influence of APA encouraged a focus on doctoral-level applied psychological training, the establishment of curricular requirements, and criteria for practicum and internship experiences. The American Association for Counseling and Development also developed accreditation and credentialing guidelines for training programs (American Association for Counseling and Development, 1986).

What had started out as a generalist training program for professionals who wanted to work with college students in all aspects of their development was slowly shifting toward more specialization and professionalization. Yet the basic underpinnings of a counseling perspective remain valuable to all of student services. The benefits of the model suggest the value of general training in counseling as part of professional preparation programs in student affairs, as well as of the use of a counseling model in student affairs professionals' work with students (Brammer, 1977; Egan, 1975; Parker, 1966; Strang, 1962).

Thus, over the last six decades, the people who practice counseling and the settings in which it is practiced have changed gradually. The cumulative effect of these changes make the concept of a counseling approach within student affairs a complex one. There are different levels of training in counseling, different functions and responsibilities, different methods and techniques, and sometimes different goals, depending on where we practice within student services. Consequently, the com-

monalities and distinctions among the student services professionals who use a counseling model need to be clearly defined.

Components of the Counseling Approach

Different types of professionals use different aspects of the
counseling model in different settings in student services, yet
we all share basic assumptions and knowledge. These common
ideas will be explored in this section. Distinctions among different professionals using a counseling model will also be delineated.

Basic Assumptions. The basic assumptions underlying the
counseling perspective are shared by student affairs professionals
who were trained in various professional preparation programs,
including student affairs, counseling psychology, and counselor
education. Two of these assumptions are that we should focus
on the "whole" student and that we should see the student as
an individual. These ideas can be traced back to the early days
of personnel and counseling work. The focus on the whole student acknowledges that development occurs on many dimensions—emotional, interpersonal, physical, and spiritual—during
the college years and that these developmental dimensions are
related. For example, attending to a student's emotional concerns can increase the student's ability to enjoy and succeed in
academic work.

The focus on the individual embraces a respect for the
great diversity among students and an appreciation, not just
tolerance, for individual differences. The desire to understand
a situation from the individual student's perspective means a
recognition of and sensitivity to the uniqueness of each person.
This belief requires attending to the student in a nonjudgmental and inquisitive manner that includes listening to the student's
perspective rather than directing the student from one's own
perspective. This high regard for the individual incorporates
a commitment to democratic and egalitarian methods of interacting with students (Cosby, 1966).

A third assumption underlying the counseling model is
that we should recognize the importance of the affective domain

to students' overall development. A counseling model suggests that special attention be paid to the feelings and personal meanings students convey through their conversations and behavior. The counseling process provides a framework in which feelings and personal meanings are a regular part of the professional's interactions with students. This assumption also implies an appreciation of the significance of the affective domain in students' interactions with others. A counseling approach helps students understand themselves and their influence on others better.

A fourth basic assumption of the counseling model is the value of a developmental perspective. This perspective includes a focus on normative rather than medical or pathological approaches to human development, facilitation of growth in normally functioning people, and emphasis on developmental and preventive interventions rather than remediation. Counseling is committed to facilitating psychological growth. The counseling model is concerned with the effect of the campus environment on students' growth and development, and it recognizes explicitly the basic interdependence between students and their environment (Parker, 1966).

The counseling model also rests on a set of assumptions about the importance of the personal characteristics of the person providing the counseling. Both Rogers (1957) and Tyler (1969) considered such qualities as warmth, responsiveness, genuineness, openness, integrity, and sincerity to be necessary for counselors. Carkhuff (1969) delineated the separate dimensions of an effective counselor so that such characteristics could be both measured and taught. The attributes of self-awareness and self-understanding are also basic and critical components of an effective counselor. Knowing and understanding one's own inner life of feelings and personal meanings as well as the effect one has on others is an important quality for those who practice from a counseling model.

People who use the counseling approach share a belief in the value of counseling to students and universities. Counseling is seen as helping students to benefit from the rigors of academic life, make better vocational and educational decisions, and be more responsible for their social and emotional behavior.

Counseling is also viewed as decreasing both the occurrence of discipline problems and the need for extensive remediation.

Knowledge Base. When a counseling model is used, a certain level of knowledge and training is assumed. The basic beliefs and assumptions of the counseling perspective are developed and sustained in the context of a shared knowledge base. New understanding in counseling and psychology about human development and behavior has created a tremendous amount of knowledge for which student affairs professionals are now responsible. To provide services to college students from a counseling perspective, we must obtain an understanding of these developments through a general course of study.

To ensure that students of counseling receive proper training, professional organizations have outlined standards of preparation or accreditation for training programs in counseling psychology, counselor education, and other student services (American Association for Counseling and Development, 1986; American Psychological Association, 1986; Forster, 1977). These organizations recognize ten major areas of study: human development, including learning theories, personality theories, and abnormal psychology; biological bases of behavior, including physiological psychology; social and cultural foundations of behavior, including ethnic and cultural knowledge, gender differences, urban societies, and the effect of social class; the counseling relationship, including listening skills and intervention strategies; group dynamics and process; career and life planning, including vocational theories and career decision making; psychological appraisal, including individual and group testing; research and evaluation, including statistics, research design, and program evaluation; professional orientation, including ethics, history, professional standards, and current professional issues; and practicum and internships, including supervised practical experience in various counseling settings, case conferences, individual and group supervision, and didactic seminars. (See American Psychological Association, 1986, and Forster, 1977, for more information.)

Professional Background. Many student affairs professionals use a counseling model in their work. Some professionals use this perspective throughout their day in almost every interaction they have with students, staff, faculty, and administrators. Others use a counseling model regularly, especially when their job responsibilities lend themselves to a counseling perspective. Still other professionals rarely use a counseling model, even though there are tasks within their job that would allow them to do so.

The type of training professionals receive affects whether and how they use a counseling perspective in their student affairs work. Many receive their professional training in student affairs programs that require courses from the ten categories listed above. Some elect to take additional courses because they want to use a counseling approach as a regular part of their job. These people use a counseling perspective when assisting students with concerns about making friends, problems with friends or family members, handling academic demands, and planning a career direction. They use a counseling approach in a variety of settings within student affairs, such as residence halls, student activities, career services, admissions, financial aid, health centers, and academic advising.

Others receive their professional training in counselor education or counseling psychology programs. In these programs the general introductory course work may be the same as in student affairs training programs. However, people receiving their professional training in counseling or counseling psychology take more advanced courses in the ten areas mentioned above. They also complete several practica and an internship in a supervised psychological setting working with students who present psychological concerns. The number of courses, the amount of supervised practice, and the depth of coverage depend on whether a person is completing a master's or doctoral degree.

Psychologists and counselors, unlike other student affairs professionals, are governed by codes of professional ethics and standards for providing psychological services (American Association for Counseling and Development, 1981; American Psychological Association, 1977, 1981, 1985). They may also be licensed at the state level as psychologists or credentialed at the national level as counselors. Licensing and credentialing requirements for counselors vary from state to state; most states do not provide for counselor licensure (American Association for Counseling and Development, 1986). People who select this route for their professional training use a counseling model as the framework for organizing their job. They are more likely than others to work in college counseling centers. These professionals focus on the psychological aspects of student development and keep abreast of new developments in psychology relevant to their therapeutic interactions with students.

Professionals from student affairs training programs and counseling training programs often behave in a very similar manner when working with individual students. There are major factors that distinguish their work, however. Psychologists and many professional counselors are more likely to consider the work they do to be psychotherapy, more involved in diagnosis and assessment, better informed about theories of abnormal behavior and psychopathology, more likely to administer and interpret psychological tests, more likely to receive referrals or to consult about seriously disturbed students, and more likely to be considered the mental health experts on campus than other student affairs professionals. This suggests that student affairs professionals who are not trained in counseling or psychology are limited in their use of a counseling model.

Many people who have completed a master's degree in counseling have chosen to work, not in counseling centers, but in other student affairs offices, such as academic advising, career development, and residence halls. These people link the worlds of student affairs professionals and counseling professionals. They often select positions within student affairs that allow them to work with preventive and developmental rather than remedial interventions. They prefer to work with normally functioning students on concerns common to students' age cohort. Because these professionals have completed counseling degrees, they often have a deeper understanding of and greater experience with a counseling model than their colleagues with professional training in student affairs. Their presence in many offices in student services indicates that a counseling perspective can be used beneficially in many different settings.

Benefits and Applications of the Counseling Model

Many tasks and responsibilities of student services professionals correspond well with a counseling perspective and allow this approach to be used with ease. Initially, the counseling approach focused on the individual and was used mainly with individual students. Over the years, the concepts of the counseling model expanded to include work with students in groups and a focus on prevention. These changes have made a counseling approach more versatile and useful in a wide range of activities undertaken by student affairs professionals, such as serving as a role model to students, providing direct support, developing direct programs, facilitating groups, referring students to professional counselors, consulting with counselors, and advocating changes in student services.

Serving as Role Models. The beliefs, personal characteristics, knowledge, and skills described in the previous section are integrated into the student affairs professional's work with students. These beliefs and skills are observed by students and can have powerful effects on their ideas and attitudes about their own development.

Students observe the professional's ability to listen carefully and ask thoughtful questions, interest in the affective domain, commitment to understanding the student's perspective, skill in handing conflict, and respect for individual differences and diversity. Because students learn in part by observing others, particularly those whom they admire and respect, the presence of professionals working within a counseling model can have a profound effect on students' growth and development.

Providing Direct Support. Many student affairs professionals work closely with students on a daily basis. These interactions provide many opportunities to offer informal support and encouragement. During these daily contacts, students can be encouraged to share their personal concerns. A supportive environment offers students opportunities to clarify their feelings and thoughts, expand their perspectives, and understand themselves better. This support can be an impetus for students to address and handle the normal developmental issues of college life. This contribution of support can create a nurturing environment in which students can tackle difficult and often painful problems.

Student affairs professionals who work informally with students on a daily basis also have the added advantage of observing students in interaction with their peers. This provides a broader context in which student affairs professionals may give students helpful insight and suggestions about their effect on others.

Developing Direct Programs. Many introductory graduate counseling courses provide student affairs professionals with basic communication skills for their work with students. Such skills can be translated into direct psychological and educational programs for students (Ivey and Alschuler, 1973). These programs assist students with normal developmental concerns and vary from basic programs on attending and listening skills to more sophisticated programs on empathy skills, group facilitation skills, and conflict resolution skills. These basic interpersonal communication skills are also built into programs focused on developmental topics, such as developing intimate relationships, career decision making, and stress management. Student affairs professionals working with a counseling perspective are ideally suited to developing and providing these educational programs (Ivey and Alschuler, 1973; Morrill, Oetting, and Hurst, 1974).

Training and experience in the counseling model also help student affairs professionals determine what programs would fit current student needs. Assessing needs by listening to students' concerns enhances decision making about the selection of topics, the methods and techniques for presenting information, the timing of programs, and the evaluation of programs (see Chapter Sixteen). Working from a counseling perspective, the student affairs professional contributes special skills to creating, presenting, and evaluating direct programming on a broad spectrum of students' developmental concerns.

Facilitating Groups. Many students share concerns about their development during the college years. These common concerns offer an ideal framework for structuring programs for students using a group format. Exposure to a counseling perspective provides student affairs staff members with a set of skills and attitudes on which they can rely for facilitating groups. A counseling model, with its roots in psychology, offers a solid base for understanding how people learn and develop in interaction with one another. Attention to the affective responses of individuals in groups provides an additional body of information about the topic under discussion. A focus on emotional interchanges can add great richness, insight, meaning, and complexity to people's understanding of their own and others' development.

Referring Students to Professional Counselors. Student affairs professionals who understand and use the counseling model in their work are in an ideal situation to help students who need a referral to counseling services. For example, students may be afraid to go, uncertain about what it will mean if they go, uncertain about whether they need to go, or afraid of the consequences if they go for counseling. These students can benefit from talking through their fears and uncertainties with student affairs staff members.

The staff member can describe what happens in the counseling center, how students with normal problems go there for help, and what it will be like if the student goes for counseling. The staff member furnishes information that dispels the student's unrealistic fantasies and creates realistic expectations about counseling. Sometimes student affairs professionals will share the fact that they have sought professional help for their problems at key times in their lives, and that they found it useful. This sharing provides a model for students of a person who seeks help and remains competent and respected by others.

In their discussions with students about seeking help, student affairs professionals who use the counseling model work to improve students' readiness for counseling. Students arrive at the counseling center better prepared to utilize what counseling has to offer. Good referrals to counseling go a long way toward ensuring that students begin counseling with realistic ideas about the process.

The student affairs professional can explain to a student the counseling profession's obligation of confidentiality that protects and respects the student's privacy. Knowing about confidentiality alleviates students' concerns about having their problems become known to others. Because student affairs professionals who work from a counseling model understand the issues of confidentiality, they are less likely to make referrals that convey inaccurate information or create misunderstandings among the student, the referring staff member, and the counseling center staff member. Good referrals enable students who need the special help of professional counselors to receive it, whereas students with normal developmental concerns may profit from the more general counseling help of student affairs professionals.

Consulting with Professional Counselors. Situations arise in student services offices in which the psychological expertise of a professional counselor may be helpful. In requesting consultation with a professional counselor, the student affairs professional can use the perspective and set of skills that the counseling model offers in making an initial assessment of the situation. The student affairs professional can describe the behavior of the people involved in the situation, the observable conflicts, and the plausible explanations for the conflicts using language and assumptions that the counselor shares.

For example, recent changes in federal laws have caused many students who were receiving financial aid to become ineligible for aid. Financial aid staff members must deal with more students who are hostile and angry, often at them. Staff members working from a counseling model have a basic understanding of human behavior that includes understanding normal and unusual expressions of anger and hostility, as well as possible interventions. These staff members also recognize the limitations of their ability to handle students whose angry responses are outside the normal range of reactions and the need to seek advice from a mental health consultant. The request for consultation includes an assessment of the staff's current understanding of human behavior—specifically, the affective domain of anger—and the staff's ability to intervene. The staff member making the request may also provide the consultant with a sense of how he or she might be helpful to the financial aid staff.

Advocating System Change. Sometimes the functions and

structure of the system, or the attitudes and behavior of key people within the system, create an unhealthy environment for students. Professionals using a counseling approach listen and observe carefuly students' reactions to the campus environment. From this watchful perspective, the student affairs professional may observe a situation that is harming not just one student, but a group of students. An unhealthy situation for large numbers of students suggests the need to analyze the system; it may need to be changed to create a healthier environment for student growth and development. For example, student affairs professionals using a counseling model might listen to complaints about the unfair practices of faculty who change the times of final examinations from those posted in university documents. Such changes often create scheduling conflicts with other exams or other responsibilities, such as jobs. These complaints may be heard from numerous students over a period of several years; during this time, the student affairs professional listens carefully to reports of the consequences of these practices on students' lives (such as poorer performance on exams, emotional stress, and an increased sense of powerlessness). Eventually, the student affairs professional may accumulate sufficient evidence to document these harmful consequences for students and to support changes in the rules governing the scheduling of final exams. The student affairs professional might take the lead in developing an environment more attentive to the well-being of both students and faculty.

Summary

A counseling model has been an integral part of student affairs since its inception, and counseling remains basic to all student affairs functions. In this chapter the historical changes during the last six decades in the population of students, in student services, and in counseling and psychology were reviewed. Over the decades, increasing diversification and professionalization of student services and psychology created changes and complexity in the use of a counseling model in student services.

To understand better the current uses of a counseling model in student services, one must understand the basic assumptions and knowledge base of a counseling approach, as well as the distinctions among professionals who use a counseling model. During their graduate training, some professionals select student affairs programs that include general courses in counseling, and these professionals now use a counseling perspective as a regular part of their work in student services. Others select graduate training in counseling, receive extensive course work in psychology, and now work in counseling centers serving the psychological needs of students and providing mental health expertise to a university community. People from different training backgrounds often work in similar ways with students. However, differences in professional training and responsibilities dictate how a counseling model is implemented by various student affairs professionals.

A counseling model can be useful and beneficial to all student affairs professionals. Acting as role models, providing direct support to students, developing and providing preventive psychological programs, facilitating groups, making referrals to mental health experts, requesting psychological expertise from professional counselors, and advocating system change are activities in which a counseling model can be used by student affairs professionals to benefit students and the university environment.

References

American Association for Counseling and Development. *Ethical Standards*. Alexandria, Va.: American Association for Counseling and Development, 1981.

American Association for Counseling and Development. "Accreditation and Credentialing Information." *Journal of Counseling and Development*, 1986, *64*, 358–363.

American Council on Education. *The Student Personnel Point of View*. American Council on Education Studies, series 1, vol. 1, no. 3. Washington, D.C.: American Council on Education, 1937.

American Psychological Association. "Standards for Providers of Psychological Services." *American Psychologist,* 1977, *32,* 495–505.

American Psychological Association. "The Ethical Principles of Psychologists." *American Psychologist,* 1981, *36,* 633–638.

American Psychological Association. *Standards for Educational and Psychological Testing.* Washington, D.C.: American Psychological Association, 1985.

American Psychological Association. *The Accreditation Handbook.* Washington, D.C.: American Psychological Association, 1986.

Aubrey, R. F. "Historical Development of Guidance and Counseling and Implications for the Future." *Personnel and Guidance Journal,* 1977, *55,* 288–295.

Brammer, L. M. "Who Can Be a Helper?" *Personnel and Guidance Journal,* 1977, *55,* 303–308.

Carkhuff, R. R. *Helping and Human Relations: A Primer for Lay and Professional Helpers.* 2 vols. New York: Holt, Rinehart & Winston, 1969.

Cosby, B. "Professional Preparation for Student Personnel Work." *Journal of the National Association for Women Deans and Counselors,* 1966, *29,* 14–18.

Cowley, W. H. "Preface to Principles of Student Counseling." *Educational Record,* 1937, *18,* 217.

Egan, G. *The Skilled Helper: A Model for Systematic Helping and Interpersonal Relating.* Monterey, Calif.: Brooks/Cole, 1975.

Forster, J. R. "An Introduction to the Standards for the Preparation of Counselors and Other Personnel Services Specialists." *Personnel and Guidance Journal,* 1977, *55,* 596–601.

Ivey, A. E., and Alschuler, A. S. "Psychological Education Is. . . . " *Personnel and Guidance Journal,* 1973, *51,* 588–589.

Lloyd-Jones, E. McD., and Smith, M. R. *A Student Personnel Program for Higher Education.* New York: McGraw-Hill, 1938.

Morrill, W. H., Oetting, E. R., and Hurst, J. C. "Dimensions of Counselor Functioning." *Personnel and Guidance Journal,* 1974, *52,* 354–359.

Parker, C. A. "The Place of Counseling in the Preparation of Student Personnel Workers." *Personnel and Guidance Journal,* 1966, *45,* 254–261.

Paterson, D. G. "The Minnesota Student Personnel Program." *Educational Record,* 1928, *9,* 3–40.

Paterson, D. G., Schneidler, G. G., and Williamson, E. G. *Student Guidance Techniques: A Handbook for Counselors in High Schools and Colleges.* New York: McGraw-Hill, 1938.

Rogers, C. R. "The Necessary and Sufficient Conditions of Therapeutic Personality Change." *Journal of Consulting Psychology,* 1957, *21,* 95–103.

Rogers, C. R. *On Becoming a Person.* Boston: Houghton Mifflin, 1961.

Strang, R. *The Role of the Teacher in Personnel Work.* New York: Bureau of Publications, Teachers College, Columbia University, 1932.

Strang, R. *Pupil Personnel and Guidance.* New York: Macmillan, 1940.

Strang, R. "Communication in the Counseling Process." *Journal of the National Association for Women Deans and Counselors,* 1962, *26,* 11–15.

Tyler, L. F. *The Work of the Counselor.* (3rd ed.) Englewood Cliffs, N.J.: Prentice-Hall, 1969.

Whiteley, J. "Counseling Psychology: A Historical Perspective." The Counseling Psychologist, 1984, *12* (1), 1–125.

Williamson, E. G. *How to Counsel Students: A Manual of Techniques for Clinical Counselors.* New York: McGraw-Hill, 1939.

Chapter Ten

Fostering Intellectual and Personal Growth: The Student Development Role

Robert D. Brown

A student development educator, by definition, is knowledgeable about theories and practices in learning, development, and assessment that relate to the intellectual, emotional, cultural, moral, physical, interpersonal, and spiritual dimensions of student life. He or she works with individual students, groups of students, and people who interact with students to establish institutional goals, policies, and programs for student development; to assess students' developmental status and diagnose their developmental needs; to help students determine appropriate goals and experiences; to design and implement programs to foster development; to evaluate students' developmental progress; and to record student attainments. Student development educators serve numerous educational roles in fulfilling their educational mission. These include roles as adviser, mentor, instructor, curriculum builder, evaluator-assessor, and scholar-researcher.

This chapter examines the meaning of student development, describes how institutions fail to operationalize their student development goals in comparison to their goals for the intellectual-academic development of students, presents a model of how student services professionals can promote student development, and compares student development educators' roles to those of academic faculty.

The Meaning of Student Development

The term *student development* in the preceding definition of a student development educator's role refers to the goals that institutions have for students. What do we want students to be like when they have completed their degree programs? College catalogues state that we want students to become alert, sensitive, ethical, knowledgeable, and capable citizens. A few decades ago, student services professionals referred to these characterizations as the "whole" student. As Fenske (Chapter One) notes, since their founding, student services professional associations have asserted their interest in the social and personal growth of students, particularly in development influenced through participation in student activities, student government, and residence hall life (American Council on Education, 1937). More recently, cognitive and personal development have been viewed as highly interlaced (Barrow, 1986) and the whole student has been considered more than the sum of educated parts. Student development is the goal of promoting the growth of the whole student—intellectual development in the classroom as well as social-personal development outside the classroom—and the student development educator is one whose role is to make that growth possible.

The educator role is an important dimension of the professional activity and identity of student services providers. As educators, staff members purposively work with students to help them become the kind of persons our institutional goal statements hold out as the ideal. Their "educational moments" with students often occur outside the classroom, such as in counseling, when they help a student learn decision-making skills, in financial aid, when they assist students to become autonomous, in residence hall life, when they help students learn new group skills, and in campus activities, when students acquire leadership competencies. Though we expect the educational role of student affairs staff to occur in informal, nonacademic, outside-the-classroom activities, it may also occur in formal, academic, classroom settings and may include traditional academic subjects. The educational moment may be in the hallway, in a cafeteria, in an office, or in a classroom.

The student development educator role rests on several assumptions. First, it is assumed that student development educators know how students learn and develop. Student services evolved from attempts to meet the needs of students by providing individualized services; these services remain the cornerstone of professional activities. To best meet these needs, staff must also understand how students think, solve problems, make decisions, respond to crises, and resolve personal problems, as well as how different kinds of students (for example, older and part-time students, females, males, members of different ethnic groups) vary. Second, intentionality is an important element of the educator role. Students and the educator, through collaboration, determine needs and ways to meet those needs. Development is not left to chance. Third, directionality is also an important educational element. The student development educator educates students *in* a subject and *for* a purpose.

The specific content of student development emphasizes interpersonal skill development and autonomy, but not exclusively. The dimensions of student development suggested earlier (Brown, 1980) continue with slight variations to be sufficiently descriptive and comprehensive. These dimensions are (1) personal identity, which includes having a sense of purpose, a value system, a spiritual perspective, and a vocational purpose; (2) interpersonal development, which includes communication skills, ability to understand and empathize with others (including people of different cultures and races), being able to give others emotional support, and possessing group interaction skills; (3) intellectual and academic skills, which permit the person to engage in lifelong learning; (4) esthetic development, which includes an awareness and appreciation of the arts and possession of personal skills in creative arts and crafts; and (5) physical recreation skills, which includes knowledge, appreciation, and integration of physical activity into a life-style.

Though personal development goals have a long history in higher education, they have never been defined and fostered as those for intellectual-academic goals have been. Personal and intellectual-academic development are part of every college's rhetoric in the first few pages of its catalogue, but the similarities stop there. Most colleges strive to fulfill systematically their goals for intellectual-academic development with well-defined policies and expectations, but this is seldom true for personal development. Most colleges have admission requirements and entrance examinations regarding intellectual-academic skills, but few require more than a letter of reference regarding personal characteristics. Numerous colleges put students through an extensive process of program planning for intellectual growth that includes testing, prescribed course requirements, and performance expectations as indicated by grade point averages. Faculty advisers are available to assist students in planning their programs and selecting course options, but no comparable processes or expectations exist for personal development. Cocurricular opportunities are available but are not required, nor necessarily strongly encouraged. No comparable advisers are readily available, though individual counseling for deficiencies is accessible. A student's academic progress is monitored in each course and recorded at regular intervals. Colleges often require a comprehensive final examination for assessment of the student's competency level upon graduation. The student's academic progress is recorded on an academic transcript, and the process culminates in the awarding of a degree. Again, no real counterpart exists for personal development. No formal or informal assessment occurs, no exams are given, and no record is kept nor certificate awarded.

The rest of this chapter presents a model for how the student development educator might interact systematically with students for the purpose of promoting student development. It also describes the important parallels between the developmental educator role and traditional faculty members' roles as educators.

Student Development Educator Model

The student development educator model assumes that the students' personal-social development is an acknowledged goal and that the institution has a strong commitment to providing programs and resources to promote student development. The student development educator's interactions with students in this model occur systematically as students proceed through their college experience. Just as students take college entrance examinations assessing their intellectual and academic skills, the student development educator assesses their developmental status. After assessment, the student development educator works with the student on goal setting, program planning, evaluation, and record keeping. In a formal system, certain competencies would be required for graduation and the institution and the student would maintain a developmental transcript (Brown and Citrin, 1977). Each task of the system has its corresponding activities:

Institutional Goals	Institutional goals for personal-social development are translated into achievable goals for individual students.
Assessment	Student's developmental status is assessed in key developmental dimensions: personal identity, interpersonal skills, intellectual-academic skills, esthetic development, and physical-recreational development.
Goal Setting	Student and student development educator mutually establish student's goals congruent with personal interests and needs and institutional expectations.
Program Selection	Student and student development educator map out programs (courses, workshops, readings, exper-

	iences) related to student's goals.
Evaluation of Progress	Students and student development educator assess progress toward goals and establish new goals.
Recording Accomplishments	A developmental transcript maintained by student or institution records student attainments.

This section will illustrate the assessment and goal-setting activities of the model.

Assessment. The student development educator uses a rich variety of assessment tools and procedures to determine the developmental status of each new student and constructs a profile of each student's strengths and weaknesses. Assessment may take many forms, ranging from paper-and-pencil tests and surveys to proficiency tests that require the student to give a speech, lead a group, or demonstrate competency in swimming. The student development educator administers several paper-and-pencil assessment instruments. These include a complete vocational inventory, a career maturity index, and several values inventories for the purpose of assessing the students' *personal identity*. Assessment of personal development is primitive and remains a challenge. This is particularly true for domains like spiritual and moral-ethical development. Ethical development has received attention through the work of Kohlberg (1971), but spiritual development has been almost a taboo subject and has received limited attention in the student development literature (Collins, Hurst, and Jacobson, 1987; Styles, 1985). Failure to explore assessment possibilities creatively in this challenging domain will certainly not lead to progress. More risk taking will perhaps lead to some successes as well as a share of failures.

Results from inventories of learning style and study skills and habits, along with traditional achievement and aptitude test data, provide the developmental educator with information about the student's *intellectual and academic skills*. Paper-and-pencil inventories, as well as other aptitude measures, can be used to assess historical and factual knowledge and proficiencies related to *esthetic development* and *physical-recreational skills*.

The student development educator also uses several other assessment techniques. Group processes can be used for *interpersonal skills* assessment. Students may be assigned, for example, to work with a team to develop a short-term program to meet the needs of persons in the community (for example, the elderly, handicapped, or retarded). Selected group meetings can be videotaped and analyzed. Similar groups can be designed for the purpose of focusing on multicultural awareness. The assessment process is clearly ongoing, rather than a single event. The student development educator is concerned with how well students communicate their ideas, understand the ideas of others, facilitate the group's decisions and actions, and provide support for others in the group.

As part of the assessment process, the student development educator may lead group discussions on moral-ethical issues and dilemmas in a manner that encourages students to explain their positions and to learn how to listen well to the positions of other students. After these explorations, the student development educator may ask students to write brief essays describing themselves, how they compare themselves to others, the rationale for their beliefs and life-styles, the possible implications for change, and topics or issues they wish to explore. Students may be encouraged to ask themselves, "What are my strengths and weaknesses?" "How do these relate to the goals and challenges I face?" and "How do I move toward my goals?"

Student development educators work more intensely with students at key times during the student's college career to prepare profiles that reflect the student's developmental status at that time. Key time periods are early in the college experience, as the student makes decisions about academic concentrations and career choices, and near graduation. Assessment of progress may be formal or can be primarily a self-assessment process (Brown and DeCoster, 1982). More formal programs may require certification of specific accomplishments prior to graduation.

Goal Setting. After the student's current developmental status is assessed, the student and the student developmental educator collaboratively arrive at long-range and short-range goals. Long-range goals include making a career choice, acquiring key interpersonal skills, and making progress on understanding other cultures and ethnic groups. Short-range goals focus on delineating the steps necessary to acquire these skills and competencies. An integral part of short-range goal setting is determining available institutional resources (for example, courses, reading, workshops, volunteer groups), setting priorities, and deciding on the next steps. Students continually change their personal goals and reorder their priorities, just as they do their academic and career goals. This means that, like the developmental assessment process, goal setting is ongoing. Through this continuous process of self-assessment and goal setting, the student becomes what Weinstein (1981) refers to as a self-scientist.

Implementation of this student development educator model can involve all students or a volunteer group of students who select the program. Brown and DeCoster (1982) describe several programs that tie this model to a developmental transcript program. Cosgrove (1986) notes the variety of programs that exist and discusses the success of one program. Formal transcript approaches can take several different forms, ranging from letters of reference to student-maintained portfolios (Tilden, 1985).

Selecting programs or courses, doing reassessments, and recording progress are the next steps in this model. Some of these steps are illustrated in the next section, which compares the role of the student development educator to the roles that faculty members play as educators.

Student Development Educator Roles and Faculty Roles

Being an educator is more than tutoring students or leading classroom discussions. It is more than lecturing or grading papers. The most prominent campus educator is the professor who serves multiple roles that make up what we consider to be a faculty member. These are the roles of adviser, mentor, curriculum builder, instructor, evaluator-assessor, and scholar-researcher. The professor is an educator not only when lecturing, but also when advising students, grading assignments, helping the institution make curriculum decisions, and conducting research. The student development educator serves in analogous roles on campus.

It is helpful to examine each role independently, though we know the roles overlap. This analysis does not mean student development educators must become faculty members or behave like faculty members. The comparisons and descriptions demonstrate that the educational missions of faculty and student development educators are similar, their goals are compatible, and their means are comparable. The comparisons provide insights into how we might broaden our image, our roles, and our educational activities. Table 1 presents a succinct comparison of faculty and student development educators in these educational roles.

Adviser. The academic adviser helps students translate the requirements of the college's catalogue into a planned program of study, usually on a semester-to-semester basis. Advisers help students match their interests and time-lines with the course requirements and sequence demanded by different academic majors. Usually a student's adviser teaches in the field in which the student intends to major. There has been a growing interest in improving academic advising and looking at the academic advising role from a developmental perspective (Winston, Miller, Ender, Grites, and Associates, 1984).

Like the academic adviser, the student development educator interprets institutional expectations regarding personal growth in the developmental dimensions and explores with students the alternative paths to meeting these expectations and sequencing their program. If the institution expects students to demonstrate leadership competencies, the student development educator explains to students what the criteria are for successful demonstration of these competencies and what campus resources (for example, courses, workshops, volunteer activities) are available. In this role, the student development educator advises students on how to sequence their developmental experiences.

Table 1. Comparison of Faculty and Student
Development Educators in Educational Roles.

Role	Faculty Member	Student Development Educator
Adviser	Interprets institution's academic, course, and graduation requirements. Approves registration at semester meetings.	Interprets developmental expectations, criteria, and avenues open to obtain and demonstrate competency.
Mentor	Serves as role model in student's academic major. Meets regularly with student. May help student establish academic career goals.	Serves as role model as a professional and as a person. May not be in same field as student. Works collaboratively with student to establish personal-social and career goals.
Curriculum Builder	Designs individual courses and courses of study for students. Develops policies regarding requirements and standards. Keeps curriculum relevant to field and student career needs.	Designs workshops, programs, and courses related to cognitive and personal-social development. Provides options that reflect current societal concerns, student needs, and responses to preventive, remedial, and developmental issues.
Instructor	Teaches courses in area of expertise.	Teaches workshops, programs, and courses in area of expertise.
Evaluator-Assessor	Assesses student achievement in courses and sometimes overall through comprehensive examinations.	Assesses developmental task achievements and competency. Assesses ability to integrate knowledge and skills.
Scholar-Researcher	Conducts research in academic discipline and integrates latest research into course content.	Conducts research on student development and how students learn, evaluates programs, and integrates theory with practice.

Since students do not major in a developmental dimension, the developmental adviser does not have to be from a particular field. The adviser views students as growing persons rather than as potential math or history majors. Academic and career development would be one likely focus, but not necessarily the sole one, for the advising relationship.

Mentor. The role of mentor is more encompassing than that of adviser (Brown and DeCoster, 1982) and therefore merits discussion as a distinct role. The mentoring role includes facilitative and prescriptive functions and cognitive and affective developmental domains (DeCoster and Brown, 1982). As Cross (1976) notes, "Mentoring involves dealing with individuals in terms of their total personality in order to advise, counsel and/or guide them" (p. 205). Lester and Johnson (1981) comment that "the mentor must care enough about the student to take time to teach, to show, to challenge, and to support" (p. 51). These expectations for mentors clearly go beyond the expectations we usually have for faculty advisers and even beyond what we might expect of the student development educator as adviser.

The mentoring role is also distinct from the advising role because it includes an informal dimension as well as a formal dimension. The mentor serves as a consultant-friend rather than solely as a prescriptive programmer, and the mentor must be a respected role model for the student as well as a good provider of advice. Students' portrayals of mentors as contrasted to academic advisers are quite distinct (Baack, 1982). They see mentors as friends and people who know them and can help them. Students may see both advisers and mentors helping them achieve particular goals, but they are likely to see mentors as persons they would like to emulate in at least one dimension of their life: career, personal characteristics, or skills.

Another important distinction between the advising and mentoring roles is time investment. The advising role can be fulfilled periodically at key points in the academic semester, but the mentoring role is more likely to be ongoing throughout the semester and to require the mentor to be readily available and even to seek out the student for informal contacts. A student development educator might serve more students as an adviser than he or she could possibly serve as a mentor. The logistics of providing every student with an adviser are probably more achievable than those of providing every student with a mentor.

Curriculum Builder. The curriculum is a domain that college faculty protect with a vengeance. Designing programs, determining academic major requirements, and establishing individual courses are traditionally faculty responsibilities. Faculty committees discuss and deliberate about the level of difficulty of courses, appropriate sequencing and prerequisites, and graduation requirements. Individual faculty members, however, often have extensive autonomy in deciding what they teach and how they teach a particular course, and as long as they can garner adequate enrollment, they are free to offer specialty seminars and courses.

Faculty members' usual jurisdiction, in descending order of influence, is their own department, their college, and finally the entire university. They have the most freedom to act on their own courses, but they also react to the courses of other departments when there are issues of overlapping content or when they serve on a college- or university-wide curriculum committee. The student development educator is also a curriculum builder. The students' personal development needs must be met by more than an individual course or experience. Issues of requirements, options, and sequencing also need to be considered.

Each institution usually has at least four curricular options available for students to attain the necessary skills, competencies, and perspectives for personal development. These are academic course offerings, courses in human development for credit or no credit, experiential field learning, and informal campus options. The student development educator may be involved in designing and implementing any or all of these options.

Academic courses provide students with the opportunity to understand themselves, as well as the world, better. If the course content is to have its fullest impact on how students think and behave and on their attitudes and skills, a history lecture, for example, must be presented so that it prompts students to think about how they might have behaved and what they think about the issues now. Some course content lends itself more to developmental perspectives than others, but all instructional activities have the potential to influence student development by the way they are taught and the behavior that is modeled and reinforced.

Student development educators may work with faculty as consultants on course development (Simpson, 1981). They can assist faculty in organizing course content and in using instructional methodologies that enhance personal, as well as academic, development. Student development educators can help faculty integrate field experiences into academic courses, such as by having students in a child development class participate in volunteer work for child-care centers (Dail and Dickson, 1983). They can also help faculty integrate developmental experiences and course assignments, such as by having students in English composition write essays on developmental topics like career education (Brock and Yerian, 1986; Pinkney, Deters, and Bizzaro, 1986).

Faculty can benefit from assistance in developing new instructional strategies, practicing group processes skills, and discovering how to individualize assignments. Neither their naivete nor their resistance to help from "nonacademics," however, can be overestimated. Having an impact on the academic curriculum requires cunning, patience, and a thick skin. Until a significant transformation takes place in higher education, student development educators have to rely on informal associations with faculty, occasional participation on curriculum revision committees, modeling good practices when teaching, and responding when educational moments appear in relationships with faculty.

Courses related to human development provide opportunities for the student developmental educator to offer content directly related to student needs and interests. This can be done through courses on such topics as marriage and the family, human relations, adolescent and adult psychology, ethics, and basic psychology. These courses often represent missed opportunities for faculty to have an impact on how students think about themselves. Student development educators might teach these courses if they have the academic credentials. As an alternative, the faculty teaching these courses may be more responsive than others to co-teaching and consultation on instructional methodology.

New freshman seminar courses have evolved over the past several years that combine academic and orientation goals (Gordon and Grites, 1984). Though these course options are often motivated by efforts to increase retention (Prola and Stern, 1984), they provide excellent opportunities for the student development educator to collaborate with faculty in planning programs and co-teaching. Many faculty involved in these courses are respected scholars who are also interested in and concerned about improving their teaching and finding new ways to have an impact on students. Nevertheless, a student development educator might be best advised to support good ideas as they emerge from the planning group and to facilitate the process, rather than using the collaboration opportunity as a platform for propounding his or her own ideas on student development.

Student development educators are increasingly involved with organizing and presenting workshops, short courses, and in-service training experiences for staff and students. This is the curriculum over which the student development educator has the most control. It is important that these offerings be responsive to student needs, which are likely to shift with societal trends and upheavals, and it is essential that the instructors be knowledgeable and skilled. It is important as well that these efforts not be limited to remedial or crisis topics. The organizational framework for developmental courses can take various forms, centering on topics such as life skills, themes, and transitions (Drum, 1980), cognitive development issues (Barrow, 1986), and the developmental dimensions described earlier.

Off-campus learning experiences continue to be an important part of student learning in many academic programs. Field experiences are a vital part of programs for sociology, political science, psychology, health services, and a host of other academic programs. If the interest in volunteerism among college students continues to regain popularity, the possibilities for developmental growth experiences for students will also increase.

Classroom Instructor. Classroom instruction is the traditional educator role, but the student development educator's classroom behavior should be observably different from that of the typical college professor. Perhaps it is unwarranted to expect developmental educators to be among the best, if not the best, classroom instructors in a college setting. Unfortunately, we do not always find educational psychologists to be among the best, so why should we have higher expectations for student development educators? At least we should hold this expectation up as the ideal.

Student development educators who are also classroom instructors are different from college professors in several ways, depending upon the subject being taught. The development educator probably has different instructional goals, or at least a different emphasis. The focus is more on changing how the students think about a subject, how they learn about the subject, and their attitudes toward it, and less on the specific facts they acquire. The student development educator spends more time assessing what the students are like—their learning styles, cognitive levels, and developmental task accomplishments. As much as is practical, the student development educator individualizes instruction to match the learning styles of the students and also individualizes assignments and expectations according to student interests. The instructor does not cater to students' wants, but assesses their needs, and on this basis prescribes and expects certain outcomes or products. The student development educator involves the student in self-assessment of progress, as well as providing the student with an independent assessment. Group presentations and discussions are a major instructional tool, since the instructor serves as a resource person more often than as a lecturer.

Evaluator-Assessor. Faculty members rarely think of themselves as evaluators or as measurement experts, and some resist this role or are uncomfortable in it. For educators, however, the role is unavoidable. Faculty must observe and make comments to students about whether or not they are going in the right direction. It is possible for students to discover this themselves (for example, when their computer program does not work), but there are times when it is better to inform them during the process (for example, when a chemistry experiment is about to explode).

Evaluation and assessment are also important dimensions of a student development program. We noted earlier that assessment in a student development program is an ongoing activity; judgments are made by the students and their mentors as to what progress is being made and decisions are made about what to do next. Faculty are, for the most part, used to giving examinations and assigning grades, however distasteful or inappropriate they may find the task. This is perhaps an unusual role for student services staff and it will require special training and skills. It is critically important that evaluation and assessment be viewed by the institution, the student development educator, and the student as a process aimed at helping the student attain his or her goals. As evaluator-assessor, the student development educator recognizes the value of accurate and complete feedback for student learning and development.

Scholar-Researcher. Student development educators need to have special expertise and to be continuously pursuing new knowledge for themselves and for their field. The scientist-practitioner model (Berdie, 1966) remains a viable but perhaps as yet unfulfilled model for student development educators. Practitioners recognize the value of theory (Strange and Contomanolis, 1983), though perhaps they still need help in translating theory into practice (Heineman and Strange, 1984). As a minimum, student development educators must use current research findings and theoretical perspectives to develop their own theories of practice. It is only when educators know why and how a practice works, not just that it works, that they are able to validate their knowledge and skills with other students and in other situations.

Many disciplines (for example, psychology, sociology, education) contribute to understanding how students learn and develop and how educators can assist students' learning and development. The academic backgrounds of student development educators may also reflect these disciplines. Student services professionals traditionally have had extensive training in counseling or in administration. The skills developed in these training programs remain important; student development educators need to know how to help individual students, supervise people, and operate within a bureaucracy. The special expertise of student development educators, however, is in college students; how they learn and develop and how the college environment—what occurs in and out of the classroom—can be used to promote students' personal development. These educators need an understanding of cognitive psychology and developmental psychology. If they are going to be involved in assessment, they also need a good understanding of measurement theory and an awareness of assessment tools and techniques (Brown, 1985).

Scholar-researchers do more than repeat what they have read or learned; they also try to find new meanings and applications, and to share these speculations with colleagues. Perhaps not all student development educators can be active researchers who publish, but as a minimum they should continue their professional development through reading, attending workshops and conventions, and trying out and evaluating new practices. Their colleagues in these endeavors can easily include faculty in education, organizational development, psychology, and sociology, as well as their student services colleagues as co-researchers.

Conclusion

This model for the student development educator role assumes that student development is a required dimension of the collegiate experience. Some forms and elements of this model already exist on college campuses (Brown and DeCoster, 1982; Cosgrove, 1986). Implementing the proposed role as a viable one for the student services professional has significant implications for the training of student development educators. This role demands broad and perhaps deep knowledge of human learning and development. Measurement and evaluation are also a critical knowledge base for the student development educator. Student development educators must be fully aware of the available assessment instruments and techniques. They need to be able to adapt and devise procedures that fit their unique institution and their students.

Fighting for developmental programming is an uphill battle, despite public support for its concepts and goals, especially if new programming calls for new funds. The exciting research efforts that are leading to refinements of developmental theory, to finding out more about how students learn, and to discoveries of new techniques for assessing student development are beginning to provide new perspectives for theorists and new techniques for practitioners (Baxter-Magolda and Porterfield, 1985; Winston and Polkosnik, 1986; Wise, 1986). It is important to remain patient in our expectations for changes in higher education but persistent in the pursuit of promoting student development.

References

American Council on Education. *The Student Personnel Point of View.* American Council on Education Studies, series 1, vol. 1, no. 3. Washington, D.C.: American Council on Education, 1937.

Baack, J. E. "Evaluation of Mentoring-Transcript Systems." In R. D. Brown and D. A. DeCoster (eds.), *Mentoring-Transcript Systems for Promoting Student Growth.* New Directions for Student Services, no. 19. San Francisco: Jossey-Bass, 1982.

Barrow, J. C. *Fostering Cognitive Development of Students: A New Approach to Counseling and Program Planning.* San Francisco: Jossey-Bass, 1986.

Baxter-Magolda, M., and Porterfield, W. D. "A New Approach to Assess Intellectual Development on the Perry Scheme." *Journal of College Student Personnel,* 1985, *26,* 343–351.

Berdie, R. F. "Student Personnel Work: Definition and Redefinition." *Journal of College Student Personnel,* 1966, *7,* 131–136.

Brock, S. B., and Yerian, J. M. "Integrating Career Planning into the Academic Fabric: A Model Project." *Journal of College Student Personnel,* 1986, *27,* 176–177.

Brown, R. D. "Student Development and the Academy: New Directions and Horizons." In D. DeCoster and P. Mable (eds.), *Personal Education and Community Development in College Residence Halls.* Cincinnati, Ohio: ACPA Media, 1980.

Brown, R. D. "Graduate Education for the Student Development Educator: A Content and Process Model." *National Association of Student Personnel Administrators Journal,* 1985, *22,* 38–43.

Brown, R. D., and Citrin, R. S. "The Student Development Transcript: Assumptions, Uses, and Formats." *Journal of College Student Personnel,* 1977, *18,* 163–168.

Brown, R. D., and DeCoster, D. A. (eds.). *Mentoring-Transcript Systems for Promoting Student Growth.* New Directions for Student Services, no. 19. San Francisco: Jossey-Bass, 1982.

Collins, J. R., Hurst, J. C., and Jacobson, J. K. "The Blind Spot Extended: Spirituality." *Journal of College Student Personnel,* 1987, *28,* 274–276.

Cosgrove, T. J. "The Effects of Participation in a Mentoring Transcript Program for Freshmen." *Journal of College Student Personnel,* 1986, *27,* 92–119.

Cross, K. P. *Accent on Learning: Improving Instruction and Reshaping the Curriculum.* San Francisco: Jossey-Bass, 1976.

Dail, P. W., and Dickson, W. P. "A Model Program for Student Volunteer Experience in a Child Development Course." *Journal of College Student Personnel,* 1983, *24,* 84–85.

DeCoster, D. A., and Brown, R. D. "Mentoring Relationships and the Educational Process." In R. D. Brown and D. A. DeCoster (eds.), *Mentoring-Transcript Systems for Promoting Student Growth.* New Directions for Student Services, no. 19. San Francisco: Jossey-Bass, 1982.

Drum, D. J. "Understanding Student Development." In W. H. Morrill, J. C. Hurst, and Associates (eds.), *Dimensions of Intervention for Student Development.* New York: Wiley, 1980.

Gordon, V. N., and Grites, T. J. "The Freshman Seminar Course: Helping Students Succeed." *Journal of College Student Personnel,* 1984, *25,* 315–320.

Heineman, D., and Strange, C. C. "Use of Developmental Theory by Entry-Level Practitioners in Student Affairs." *Journal of College Student Personnel,* 1984, *25,* 529–533.

Kohlberg, L. "Stages of Moral Development." In C. M. Beck, B. S. Crittenden, and E. V. Sullivan (eds.), *Moral Education.* Toronto: University of Toronto Press, 1971.

Lester, V., and Johnson, C. "The Learning Dialogue: Mentoring." In J. Fried (ed.), *Education for Student Development.* New Directions for Student Services, no. 15. San Francisco: Jossey-Bass, 1981.

Pinkney, J. W., Deters, S. H., and Bizzaro, P. "Self-Oriented Writing Development and Integrative Career Assessment." *Journal of College Student Personnel,* 1986, *27,* 567–569.

Prola, M., and Stern, D. "The Effect of a Freshman Orientation Program on Student Leadership and Academic Persistence." *Journal of College Student Personnel,* 1984, *25,* 472–473.

Simpson, D. "Instructional Consultation." In J. Fried (ed.), *Education for Student Development.* New Directions for Student Services, no. 15. San Francisco: Jossey-Bass, 1981.

Strange, C. C., and Contomanolis, E. "Knowledge Perceptions of Human Development Theory Among Student Affairs Masters Students." *Journal of College Student Personnel*, 1983, *24*, 197–201.

Styles, M. "Effective Models of Systematic Program Planning." In M. J. Barr, L. A. Keating, and Associates, *Developing Effective Student Services Programs: Systematic Approaches for Practitioners*. San Francisco: Jossey-Bass, 1985.

Tilden, A. "A New Approach to the Co-Curricular Transcript." *Journal of College Student Personnel*, 1985, *26*, 361–362.

Weinstein, G. "Self-Science Education." In J. Fried (ed.), *Education for Student Development*. New Directions for Student Services, no. 15. San Francisco: Jossey-Bass, 1981.

Winston, R. B., Jr., Miller, T. K., Ender, S. C., Grites, T. J., and Associates. *Developmental Academic Advising: Addressing Students' Educational, Career, and Personal Needs*. San Francisco: Jossey-Bass, 1984.

Winston, R. B., Jr., and Polkosnik, M. C. "Student Developmental Task Inventory (2nd Edition): Summary of Selected Findings." *Journal of College Student Personnel*, 1986, *27*, 548–559.

Wise, S. L. "The Use of Ordering Theory in the Measurement of Student Development." *Journal of College Student Personnel*, 1986, *27*, 442–447.

Chapter Eleven

Creating a Climate for Successful Student Development: The Campus Ecology Manager Role

James H. Banning

The management of the campus ecology continues to emerge as a role for the student services worker. The concept of ecological management extends traditionally accepted management activities. Historically, the elements of the campus ecology that student services programs have primarily attempted to manage are the people who constitute the student body. Surveys by Morrill and Banning (1975) and Huebner and Corazzini (1984) found that nearly all the reported intervention strategies were targeted to the individual student.

This concentration of effort on the individual student stems directly from the conventional perspectives that have guided and, for the most part, continue to guide student services. Banning and Kaiser (1974, p. 371) described these perspectives as the removal of the student from the environment, or the "unenlightened perspective," the counseling of the student, or the "adjustment perspective," and the adding of skills to the student, or the "developmental perspective." Although these three perspectives overemphasize working with the individual student, they are not without merit. Not all students belong on campus, some students need individual psychological attention, and certainly many students are involved in a number of critical developmental tasks while on campus. However, all three perspectives are one-sided. They all focus on the necessity for the individual student to adjust, and they fail to address the broader need for the campus to change.

The failure to address broader change strategies implied in the campus ecology manager role is related to three factors: the adoption of the medical model by the helping professions, the universities' perception of their role in loco parentis, and the failure to understand the role traditional services may play in maintaining the status quo (Banning, 1980).

The ecological perspective, on the other hand, focuses on the relationship between individual and environment; the potential role for student services in helping to manage the campus ecology thus emerges. See Huebner, Chapter Six, for an extended presentation of the theory underlying the ecological model.

An ecological approach helps correct the overemphasis on working with individual students. The correction called for by the ecological approach reflects a *paradigm shift*. A paradigm shift is a distinctly new way of thinking about old problems. The ecological perspective promotes the shift from viewing students as individuals to viewing students as a part of an ecology. Catalano (1979), in writing about the helping professions, clearly points out the necessity for this shift: "This 'person' oriented paradigm is of little help in measuring or explaining the economic and political forces which shape the larger environmental determinants of emotional stability" (p. 10). The ecology management role strives to foster the shift from person to ecology for the campus student services personnel.

This chapter discusses the use of the ecosystem design process in designing and managing the campus ecology. Four applications of the ecological model to the campus environment are presented, and the use of the model in managing events on campus is illustrated in a case study. Finally, the ethical issue of participation in the intentional design and management of the campus ecology is discussed.

Ecological Designs

Student services managers who apply the ecological perspective as a design model help ensure that a campus encourages maximum growth and development of the students. The practitioner who intends to employ the ecology perspective as a design model will find the ecosystem model helpful. It was developed by the Western Interstate Commission for Higher Education (1973) and expanded by Huebner (1979). The ecosystem design process is based on the ecological perspective and provides a methodology to design and manage the campus ecology. The seven basic steps in the process are these (Western Interstate Commission for Higher Education, 1973, p. 7): "(1) Designers, in conjunction with community members, select educational values. (2) Values are then translated into specific goals. (3) Environments are designed that contain mechanisms to reach the stated goals. (4) Environments are fitted to students. (5) Students' perceptions of the environment are measured. (6) Student behavior resulting from environment perceptions is monitored. (7) Data on the environmental design's success and failures, as indicated by student perceptions and behavior, are fed back to the designers in order that they may continue to learn about student-environment fit and design better environments."

The steps of the design process are interdependent, so the process can begin at any of the steps. If the campus has yet to be constructed, the process of campus design would start with step 1, the selection of educational values, and continue through the final step, feedback. Such an opportunity is quite rare, because most campuses have been established for a number of years, and the goals and values of the institution have been published in various institutional documents. Therefore, the design process would more probably begin at step 5, measuring students' perceptions of the campus, and then move from these perceptions to the next step in the process in order to map the existing ecological relationships between the environment and the students. It should be noted, however, that even in a step 5 beginning, the choice of what to measure will be influenced by the values and goals associated with the earlier steps.

The technology available to carry out the measurement and monitoring in steps 5 and 6 is developing rapidly. Walsh and Betz (1985) outline a number of available environmental assessment instruments that can aid campus administrators at these steps. It may also be desirable for campus personnel to design their own instruments in order to obtain information peculiar to a particular campus environment. Aulepp and Delworth (1978) also suggest a number of assessment strategies that can be used in a team approach to environmental assessment. The role the paraprofessional can play in environmental assessment is presented by May and Rademacher (1980).

The importance of this assessment information, whatever its sources, is that it can be used to map specific elements in the ecology that cause students to be distressed or dissatisfied. By managing the troublesome environmental referents (specific elements in the environment), we can develop an ecology that will promote maximum growth and development of students. The assessment process may also lead to the conclusion that the original values and goals selected by the institution no longer are appropriate; selecting new values and goals becomes the management task. Or it may be found that the original goals and values remain appropriate but that the programs and policies related to these goals need revision. If so, the management task becomes the development of new programs and policies to attain the original institutional goals. Successful management of the campus ecology under any condition depends on how well the managers carry out the seven steps in the design process.

The design and management processes can be implemented at different levels of the campus ecology. The macro-level design is concerned with the ecology that includes large numbers of individuals; the micro-level design focuses on specific campus groups; and the life-space design is concerned with the individual imbedded in the total campus ecology.

Campus Applications of the Ecological Model

Interest in the campus environment is not new (see Banning, 1980, for a brief history). But as the role of the ecology manager has emerged, not only has there been an increasing number of publications documenting the use of the ecological perspective, but the diversity of the applications has also increased. The perspective can be applied in four ways: to creating an organizational and research framework for student services, to the study of particular groups on campus, to the work of specific departments within student services, and to the study and management of special campus issues and events. An illustration of the model's application in managing a campus event will appear later in this chapter.

Creating an Organizational Framework. Interest in campus environments and their impact on students has been well documented, but the utility of the concept of ecology as an organizational framework for student services continues to emerge (Helsabeck, 1980). A campus design center has been suggested as one method for organizing the informational and analytical functions needed to manage the campus ecology (Fawcett, Huebner, and Banning, 1978). The presentation of the campus design center by Fawcett and his colleagues is very structured and detailed, but the important point is not the structure of the center but the fact that the concept allows for the development of a mechanism to assist in the student services role as manager of the campus ecology. Hurst and Ragle (1979) present a similar model that uses the ecosystem design process as an organizing concept within a dean of students' office.

An approach similar to a design center has been implemented at the University of Southern Illinois (Coffman and Paratore, 1987). In 1984, the Campus Environment Team was established by the office of the vice-president for student affairs. The team comprises people on campus who are knowledgeable about the ecological perspective and committed to student development and student services research. To begin its work, the team utilized the ecosystem model to translate the ecological perspective into practice. The efforts of the Campus Environment Team have produced a new student services mission statement, an exploration of the values inherent within the student services organization, renewal in the area of staff development, and the establishment of an ongoing research and evaluation program.

If the ecology model is to be used as an organizational framework for the management of student services, information about students, environments, and their relationships is of critical importance. It is this information that is central to a campus design center or a campus environment team. Hanson (1985) outlines the importance of researching the campus ecosystem and provides a discussion of the characteristics of effective ecosystem research. He notes the following characteristics: the research should be needed, timely, carefully planned, and based on multiple data sources; the data should be communicable; and the results should be simple, brief, and understandable.

Studying Specific Groups. The ecological model has also been useful in the study of issues of specific groups on campus. These studies focus on issues of group "fit" to the campus environment and the need to redesign the ecosystem to produce a better fit. Banning and Hughes (1986) write about the implications of the campus environment for commuter students and illustrate the application of ecosystem design to developing programs for commuters. Kubick (1985) illustrates the concept of "fitting" by addressing the problems of time, communications, transiency, and diversity of needs experienced by commuting students.

The freshman student has also received attention from the ecosystem model. Banning (1989) suggests that the concept of ecological transition (Bronfenbrenner, 1979) is applicable to the freshman year experience, in that students usually experience a change in role and setting. Stress produced by this transition for freshmen can be reduced through an ecosystem assessment and redesign model (Barrow, Marsicano, and Bumbalough, 1987).

Gender differences have been explored from the ecological perspective. Follett, Andberg, and Hendel (1982) find significant differences in men's and women's perceptions of five areas in the college environment: peer relationships, gender role expectations, perceived sex discrimination in the college, attitudes on self-disclosure, and general competitiveness. Forrest, Hotelling, and Kuk (1984) utilize the ecological model to address the issue of eliminating sexism in university environments. They conclude that the ecosystem design model, coupled with the integration of male and female values and attributes, could serve as an approach to redesigning the campus in order to maximize the growth and development of all students. McCann, Sieber, and Scissors (1985) combine the concepts of gender voice and ecosystem design to illustrate the redesign of a university judicial system. The use of the ecology model to change the campus environment in order to support the lesbian and gay experience is presented by Nicoloff (1985). The use of the ecological perspective in eliminating racism and sexism on the college campus is discussed by Harrell and Nayman (1984).

Working in Student Services Departments. The ecological approach has been used by departments within student services. Conyne (1975) illustrates the usefulness of environmental assessment in mapping consultation activities for campus counseling centers. Conyne (1985) also integrates the ''counseling cube'' and the ecological model to form what is referred to as ''counseling ecology,'' where the emphasis is on both helping people and changing environments.

Environmental assessment and management strategies in residence halls have also proved useful (Schroeder and Freesh, 1977; Schuh, 1980; Null and Hull, 1982; Latta, 1984; Waldman, 1985; and Schroeder and Jackson, 1987). These studies illustrate a variety of assessment and design strategies to enhance and foster student development within residence halls.

Other student services departments have also been viewed from an ecological perspective. Hobson-Panico, Ahuna, and Hobson-Panico (1985) discuss how an ombudsman's office can influence organizational effectiveness through the practice of campus ecology. The role of environmental assessment is suggested as an important tool for departments of orientation (Justice and Barr, 1980). Perry (1980) presents the role the college union plays within the campus environment.

Studying Events and Issues. A variety of campus concerns and issues have been addressed by the ecological model and the ecosystem design. The topic receiving the most attention is the issue of ''fit'' between student and environment and its relationship to the following areas: enrollment management (Williams, 1986), retention (Clarke, 1987; Pascarella, 1984; Banning,

1984a), and stress (Tracey and Sherry, 1984; Witt and Handal, 1984).

The study of college outcomes has also been addressed from the ecological perspective (Banning, 1987). The ecological version of the outcomes question is, "Under what environments have what kinds of students changed in what kinds of behaviors?" Academic dishonesty has been viewed from an ecological perspective. Academic integrity is seen as resulting from an interaction between personal variables and environmental conditions (Banning, 1984b). The ecological approach has also been used to analyze the activism of the 1960s, as well as current and future conditions for student activism on campus (Banning and McKinley, 1988).

Finally, the role that the physical environment plays on campus is receiving attention. The influence of the physical environment on university commencement programs is suggested by Banning (1983). He illustrates the physical environment's role of nonverbal communication within the commencement setting. Iwai, Churchill, and Cummings (1983) discussed the physical design characteristics of college and university counseling centers and the possible impact these characteristics have on the sense of security, relaxation, and privacy, as well as a sense of acceptance and humanness. Banning and Cunard (1986) point out that the renovation of a physical space within a college union can encourage the process of student development and that student participation in the design process can promote the acquisition of important life skills.

In sum, the ecological model has shown great versatility in its applications. As the model continues to emerge, other applications will appear in the practice of student services work.

Management Applications of the Ecosystem Model

The management task for student services can be seen as involving two major areas: managing the campus environment for student development and managing the campus environment in terms of services, events, programs, and policies that may enhance the educational climate on campus but are not directly related to a specific student development outcome. The planning of major campus events, the development of admissions and financial aid programs, the delivery of food services, and the development of a campus alcohol policy are all examples of general management tasks. While this type of task is important to the concept of student development, student development may not be the key issue.

Ecosystem Model and Student Development. The ecosystem model is greatly enhanced when it is coupled with the concept of student development. Of particular importance to this coupling is the work of Blocher (1974, 1978). Blocher points out that there is increasing evidence that developmental processes are not automatic but must be purposefully triggered and carefully nurtured by the environment if full growth and development are to be reached. Blocher suggests that the ecology related to individual development can be characterized as containing three subsystems or structures: opportunity, support, and reward. The opportunity structure is represented by the set of tasks, problems, or situations in the environment that the person negotiates to exert mastery or control and thereby gain competency. The support structure is the set of environmental resources available to people for coping with the environment. For Blocher, the support structure includes two kinds of resources: ''These are the affective, or relationship, resources and the cognitive structures available. Relationship networks that touch the student allow stress reduction to occur through the operation of factors of warmth, empathy, acceptance and involvement of others. . . . In addition to relationships, there are important cognitive structures that allow for improved coping with stress. These involve understanding, assessing, predicting, and labeling'' (Blocher, 1974, p. 364).

The reward structure refers to those properties and contingencies of the environment that reward effort. For example, if the rewards offered in an environment are arbitrary and unrelated to effort, the growth-sustaining ecological balance may be destroyed. When coupling the concepts of ecology and student development, student services must design and manage the opportunities, resources, and rewards within the campus

ecology that affect student development. The utility of this merger and a step-by-step illustration of managing for student development are presented by Banning (1980). Further discussion of
the combining of the ecological and developmental perspectives
is given by Banning and McKinley (1980), Rogers (1984), and
Hurst (1987).

*Ecosystem Model and Event Management: A Case Illustra-
tion.* The ecological perspective, in addition to assisting the
management of student development, can also be useful in
managing other student services tasks. To illustrate this utility,
a case study is presented that focuses on the redesign of a macro-
level campus activity called "College Days" on the Colorado
State University campus.

Since 1907, Colorado State University has held an annual, all-campus spring event. It began as an afternoon picnic
to celebrate the coming of spring, but the "College Days"
festivities deteriorated over the years, eventually including significant alcohol abuse and "wet T-shirt" contests. The contests
were not sanctioned, but were impromptu events that occurred
around a lagoon on the grounds where the annual afternoon
concert was held. During the 1980 event, a number of unwilling female students were forced into the lagoon for the contest.
It was a clear situation of sexual assault. The office of student
affairs began the process of redesigning the event to eliminate
the lagoon wet T-shirt contests.

The design process began with steps 5 and 6, whereby
perceptions of the environment (College Days) were compiled
and studied. In this case, perceptions and observations of behavior were not hard to come by. Angry parents, women's groups,
campus police, and concerned students, faculty, and staff representing various parts of campus offered their views in letters
and reports. A "town meeting" was held by the student government for discussion of the events. In addition to these informal
evaluations, surveys were sent to key groups and persons on
campus to obtain their perceptions and observations. Both the
informal reports and the formal surveys were compiled into a
final evaluation report.

The distribution of the evaluation report was, in effect, the execution of step 7 (feedback) in the ecosystem design process. The report provided data and information on the event's design failures to the university community. A critical point at this stage was avoiding the common impulse to move directly to step 3—designing environments that contain mechanisms to reach the stated goals—rather than to step 1—selecting educational values. There is often a strong desire to ''correct the program'' without feeding back the perceptions and evaluations to steps 1 and 2, where the results of the design can be examined from the perspective of values and goals.

The move back to step 1 after completing step 7 illustrates the distinction between ''single-loop learning'' and ''double-loop learning'' cited by Argyris (1980). Moving from step 7 to step 3 would be a single-loop approach. Such a move would attempt to correct errors without altering the underlying values or goals of an event. Double-loop learning is a correction of error that involves the changing of underlying values. The move from step 7 to step 1 is an example of the double-loop process. If the original values and goals have become obsolete, no longer applicable, or unrepresentative of the environment, a single-loop process will never make this discovery. Step 1 is a critical step for the ecosystem design model.

Step 1 was implemented by the formation of the College Days Evaluation Committee. The committee was jointly appointed by administration and student government, and representatives from both groups served on the committee. The committee had two primary objectives: to study the evaluation report (step 7) in order to determine whether the event should continue or be cancelled, and, if it were to continue, to determine values and goals for the event. The committee was directed not to attempt to ''correct'' the event, but to state values and goals.

The committee developed a statement of values and goals that included the following objectives: to enhance relationships within the university community; to enhance relationships between the university and the city; to develop a thematic approach to programming for the spring event; to involve students, faculty, and townspeople in developing a partnership approach; and to have fun and provide a relaxing, safe environment for all involved. Following the committee's report, a new joint planning committee of staff and students was appointed to implement steps 3 and 4—designing and fitting an environment on the basis of the established values and goals. In designing the new program, the joint programming committee implemented a variety of new programs and removed some old programs. These changes were guided by the values and goals statement. In the implementing of steps 3 and 4, a number of ecological interventions were adopted.

The physical environment of the afternoon concert was altered to support the values and goals. For example, the physical distance between buying beer tickets and obtaining beer was significantly lengthened to enhance symbolically the deemphasis of alcohol and, more concretely, to increase physical activity. The ticket booth was placed in front of the lagoon to reinforce the notion that it was off-limits. The bandstand was repositioned to take attention away from the lagoon. The students also placed a string around the lagoon with such humorous signs as "alligators in water" to reinforce in a "soft" way that the lagoon was off-limits. The temporal environment was also redesigned so that there was no down-time between bands. The time between bands had historically been the time for lagoon incidents. A second stage was provided on which a local band would play during the changing of major bands. Finally, the environment was conceptualized as an opportunity structure (Blocher, 1974) and the redesign effort included opportunities for promoting cultural diversity and fun and for deemphasizing alcohol; for example, ethnic foods and alternative beverages were made available.

The outcomes of the redesign of College Days were several; most important, no wet T-shirt contest has occurred since the redesign effort. It is also important to note that the level of participation among campus groups in the redesigned College Days was much greater than in any previous event. The redesigning of College Days illustrates how the intentional design of events can create environments that are more compatible with the values and goals of their inhabitants.

Participation in the Management of the Campus Ecology

Critical to the concept of ecological management is the question, who designs? Kaiser (1975, p. 36) points out the need for community participation: "Successful campus design depends upon participation of all campus members including students, faculty, staff, administrators and regents. The ecosystem model offers a participatory design strategy. It is based upon the conviction that all people impacted by a space have the moral right to participate in its design."

Full participation of all who are involved in the campus's ecology is also a reasonable response to the ethical questions raised by the intentional management of an environment (Conyne and others, 1977). These authors note that "the notion of intentional campus environmental design for the purposes of prevention and the enhancement of student development, while being mandated from several corners, poses significant changes from traditional counselor functions. And these changes have a number of serious implications for individual counselors and for the field as a whole. Not the least of these is the question of ethics. Applied to environmental design, several complex issues arise, including those of freedom vs. control, privacy, competence, political positioning, value systems, and participation" (Conyne and others, 1977, p. 17). The authors conclude, "If one advocates the intentional design of campus environments, then ethical issues such as the above must be addressed within the context of full participation of environmental members. The satisfaction of this stipulation should hedge against the possibility of a select few controlling the behavior of many. Under these conditions, intentional design should increase the probability of personal freedom" (p. 23). Huebner and Banning (1987) raise similar ethical issues and also conclude that a participation ethic will help reduce ethical conflicts within the design process.

Summary

Campus ecology management calls for a shift in the perspectives and attitudes of student services personnel. The historical concern for individual students must be broadened to include the total campus ecology. The new attitude or "set" should include the utilization of the relationship between students and their environment in the management of both student development programs and other management functions associated with campus student services. Although these endeavors can be carried out in a variety of ways, a systematic framework must be developed in order to analyze information needed for ecological management.

An attitude of participation must accompany the new concern for the total ecology. All campus members must be encouraged to participate to avoid the impersonal manipulation of many by a select or self-appointed few. The campus ecology perspective also calls for new knowledge and skills. We need to examine concepts from a wide range of disciplines for their usefulness in helping to understand the campus ecology. Student services must truly become multidisciplinary.

Even though the ecology management perspective calls for a major shift in the attitude, skills, and training of student services workers, the promise it holds for the development of campus environments that promote optimal growth is substantial.

The ecology of today's campuses holds the key to the quality of all future environments in society, since today's students will ultimately design our society. The ecological approach helps to promote our vision of students as designers who have the capacity to influence, plan, and construct, not just as clients or consumers. The future of the ecological approach will be determined by the degree to which we become competent in moving from understanding the relationship between environment and student to fostering the ability of students to determine, build, and manage their own designs.

References

Argyris, C. "Educating Administrators and Professionals." In C. Argyris and R. M. Cyert (eds.), *Leadership in the 80's*. Cambridge, Mass.: Institute for Educational Management, 1980.

Aulepp, L., and Delworth, U. "A Team Approach to Environmental Assessment." In J. H. Banning (ed.), *Campus Ecology: A Perspective for Student Affairs.* Portland, Ore.: National Association of Student Personnel Administrators, 1978.

Banning, J. H. "The Campus Ecology Manager Role." In U. Delworth, G. Hanson, and Associates, *Student Services: A Handbook for the Profession.* San Francisco: Jossey-Bass, 1980.

Banning, J. H. "The Built Environment: Do Ivy Walls Have Memories?" *Campus Ecologist,* 1983, *1* (2), 1-3.

Banning, J. H. "Retention: An Ecological Perspective." *Campus Ecologist,* 1984a, *2* (2), 1-3.

Banning, J. H. "The Ecology of Academic Integrity in the Classroom." *Campus Ecologist,* 1984b, *2* (4), 1-2.

Banning, J. H. "The Ecology of Outcomes." *Campus Ecologist,* 1987, *5* (2), 1-3.

Banning, J. H. "Impact of College Environments on Freshman Students." In M. L. Upcraft, J. N. Gardner, and Associates, *The Freshman Year Experience: Helping Students Survive and Succeed in College.* San Francisco: Jossey-Bass, 1989.

Banning, J. H., and Cunard, M. "Environment Supports Student Development." *ACU-I Bulletin,* 1986, *54* (1), 8-10.

Banning, J. H., and Hughes, B. M. "Designing the Campus Environment with Commuter Students." *National Association of Student Personnel Administrators Journal,* 1986, *24* (1), 17-24.

Banning, J. H., and Kaiser, L. "An Ecological Perspective and Model for Campus Design." *Personnel and Guidance Journal,* 1974, *52,* 370-375.

Banning, J. H., and McKinley, D. L. "Conceptions of the Campus Environment." In W. H. Morrill, J. C. Hurst, and Associates (eds.), *Dimensions of Intervention for Student Development.* New York: Wiley, 1980.

Banning, J. H., and McKinley, D. L. "Activism and the Campus Ecology." In K. M. Miser (ed.), *Student Affairs and Campus Dissent.* Washington, D.C.: National Association of Student Personnel Administrators, 1988.

Barrow, J., Marsicano, L., and Bumbalough, P. "Adapting the Ecosystem Model for Environmental Assessment and Design." *Journal of College Student Personnel,* 1987, *28* (4), 378-379.

Blocher, D. H. "Toward an Ecology of Student Development." *Personnel and Guidance Journal,* 1974, *52,* 360–365.

Blocher, D. H. "Campus Learning Environments and the Ecology of Student Development." In J. H. Banning (ed.), *Campus Ecology: A Perspective for Student Affairs.* Portland, Ore.: National Association of Student Personnel Administrators, 1978.

Bronfenbrenner, U. *The Ecology of Human Development.* Cambridge, Mass.: Harvard University Press, 1979.

Catalano, R. *Health Behavior and the Community.* Elmsford, N.Y.: Pergamon Press, 1979.

Clarke, J. H. "Improving Student Fit with the Academic Environment." *Journal of College Student Personnel,* 1987, *28* (2), 115–122.

Coffman, J., and Paratore, J. "Operationalizing the Ecological Perspective: The Southern Illinois University Experience." *Campus Ecologist,* 1987, *5* (1), 1–2.

Conyne, R. K. "Environmental Assessment: Mapping for Counselor Action." *Personnel and Guidance Journal,* 1975, *54,* 151–154.

Conyne, R. K. "The Counseling Ecologist: Helping People and Environments." *Counseling and Human Development,* 1985, *18* (2), 1–11.

Conyne, R. K., and others. "The Environment as Client: Considerations and Implications for Counseling Psychology." Paper presented at 85th annual meeting of American Psychological Association, San Francisco, Sept. 1977.

Fawcett, G., Huebner, L., and Banning, J. "Campus Ecology: Implementing the Design Process." In J. H. Banning (ed.), *Campus Ecology: A Perspective for Student Affairs.* Portland, Ore.: National Association of Student Personnel Administrators, 1978.

Follett, C., Andberg, W., and Hendel, D. "Perceptions of the College Environment by Women and Men Students." *Journal of College Student Personnel,* 1982, *23* (6), 525–531.

Forrest, L., Hotelling, K., and Kuk, L. "The Elimination of Sexism in University Environments." Paper presented at second annual Campus Ecology Symposium, Pingree Park, Colo., June 1984.

Hanson, G. "Researching the University Ecosystem." Paper presented at third annual Campus Ecology Symposium, Pingree Park, Colo., June 1985.

Harrell, F., and Nayman, R. "Toward the Elimination of Institutional Racism on College and University Campuses: An Ecological Approach." Paper presented at second annual Campus Ecology Symposium, Pingree Park, Colo., June 1984.

Helsabeck, R. "The Student Personnel Administrator as Milieu Manager: Reducing Destructive Conflict Through Social Science Research." *Journal of College Student Personnel*, 1980, *21* (3), 264–269.

Hobson-Panico, P., Ahuna, L., and Hobson-Panico, S. "Can Ombudsmen Influence Organization Effectiveness Through the Practice of Campus Ecology?" *Campus Ecologist*, 1985, *3* (4) 1–3.

Huebner, L. A. (ed.). *Redesigning Campus Environments*. New Directions for Student Services, no. 8. San Francisco: Jossey-Bass, 1979.

Huebner, L. A., and Banning, J. H. "Ethics of Intentional Campus Design." *National Association of Student Personnel Administrators Journal*, 1987, *25* (1), 28–37.

Huebner, L. A., and Corazzini, J. G. "Environmental Assessment and Intervention." In S. D. Brown and R. W. Lent (eds.), *Handbook of Counseling Psychology*. New York: Wiley, 1984.

Hurst, J. C. "Student Development and Campus Ecology: A Rapprochement." *National Association of Student Personnel Administrators Journal*, 1987, *25* (1), 5–18.

Hurst, J. C., and Ragle, J. D. "Application of the Ecosystem Perspective to a Dean of Students' Office." In L. Huebner (ed.), *Redesigning Campus Environments*. New Directions for Student Services, no. 8. San Francisco: Jossey-Bass, 1979.

Iwai, S., Churchill, W., and Cummings, L. "The Physical Characteristics of College and University Counseling Services." *Journal of College Student Personnel*, 1983, *24* (1), 55–60.

Justice, S. H., and Barr, M. J. "Orientation." In W. H. Morrill, J. C. Hurst, and Associates (eds.), *Dimensions of Intervention for Student Development*. New York: Wiley, 1980.

Kaiser, L. R. "Designing Campus Environments." *National Association of Student Personnel Administrators Journal,* 1975, *13* (1), 33–39.

Kubick, J. "Activities in the Traffic Pattern." *Commuter,* 1985, *10* (2), 6–7.

Latta, W. J. "The Residence Hall Environment Questionnaire." *Journal of College Student Personnel,* 1984, *25* (4), 370–373.

McCann, J., Sieber, C., and Scissors, C. "Using Gilligan's Theory to Redesign University Judicial Systems." Paper presented at third annual Campus Ecology Symposium, Pingree Park, Colo., June 1985.

May, R., and Rademacher, B. "The Use of Paraprofessionals as Environmental Assessors in Student Affairs Agencies." *Journal of College Student Personnel,* 1980, *21* (4), 368–369.

Morrill, W. H., and Banning, J. H. "Counseling Outreach Programs on the College Campus." In B. L. Bloom (ed.), *Psychological Stress in the Campus Community: Theory, Research and Action.* New York: Behavioral Publications, 1975.

Nicoloff, L. K. "Changing Campus Environments to Support the Lesbian/Gay Experience." Paper presented at third annual Campus Ecology Symposium, Pingree Park, Colo., June 1985.

Null, R., and Hull, P. "An Environmental Assessment Study of Purdue Residence Halls." *Journal of College Student Personnel,* 1982, *23* (2), 164–165.

Pascarella, E. "Improving Student Fit with the Academic Environment." *Journal of Higher Education,* 1984, *55* (3), 751–771.

Perry, S. B. "The College Union." In W. H. Morrill, J. C. Hurst, and Associates (eds.), *Dimensions of Intervention for Student Development.* New York: Wiley, 1980.

Rogers, R. "Student Development Through Campus Ecology." Paper presented at second annual Campus Ecology Symposium, Pingree Park, Colo., June 1984.

Schroeder, C. C., and Freesh, N. "Applying Environmental Management Strategies in Residence Halls." *National Association of Student Personnel Administrators Journal,* 1977, *15* (1), 51–57.

Schroeder, C. C., and Jackson, G. S. "Creating Conditions for Student Development in Campus Living Environments." *National Association of Student Personnel Administrators Journal,* 1987, *25* (1), 45–53.

Schuh, J. H. "Housing." In W. H. Morrill, J. C. Hurst, and Associates (eds.), *Dimensions of Intervention for Student Development.* New York: Wiley, 1980.

Tracey, T. J., and Sherry, P. "College Student Distress as a Function of Person-Environment Fit." *Journal of College Student Personnel,* 1984, *25* (5), 436–442.

Waldman, D. A. "Development of a Modified University Residence Environmental Scale." *Journal of College Student Personnel,* 1985, *26* (1), 70–72.

Walsh, W. B., and Betz, N. E. *Tests and Assessments.* Englewood Cliffs, N.J.: Prentice-Hall, 1985.

Western Interstate Commission for Higher Education. *The Ecosystem Model: Designing Campus Environments.* Boulder, Colo.: Western Interstate Commission for Higher Education, 1973.

Williams, T. E. "Optimizing Student-Institution Fit: An Interactive Perspective." *College and University,* 1986, *61* (2), 141–152.

Witt, P. H., and Handal, P. J. "Person-Environment Fit: Is Satisfaction Predicted by Congruency, Environment, or Personality?" *Journal of College Student Personnel,* 1984, *25* (6), 503–508.

Part Four

Essential Competencies and Techniques

Student services professionals are asked to work at increasingly complex jobs that require very sophisticated knowledge and skills. We are asked to design programs, administer services, supervise staff, analyze budgets, evaluate programs, assess students, and consult with faculty. It is nearly impossible to teach all that is needed to perform these many tasks in any professional preparation program. Most in-service staff development training programs can only scratch the surface. That leaves conscientious professionals scrambling to learn what they need to know as well as they can—usually with limited resources.

What is needed is a systematic identification and classification of the competencies essential for effective delivery of services. Not all professionals either want or need to master all these competencies; not all graduate programs teach all of them. Within any given division of student services, however, it is important to have a combination of staff members who possess a reasonably high degree of expertise in the designated competencies. We follow Delworth and Yarris (1978, p. 2) in defining competencies. As these authors point out, "to be competent, the staff member needs certain kinds of knowledge, certain attitudes, emotional qualities, and particular skills. So we might think of competence as a combination of cognitions, affect, and skills." Thus, we view skills as one component of the larger domain of competence.

In organizing this part of the book, we identified four critical basic competency areas: assessment and evaluation, instruction, consultation, and counseling and advising. These four competencies, in varying combinations, constitute an essential and more complex competency area: program development. Together, these five areas represent a fundamental core that is currently necessary to maintain a vital and dynamic division of student services. Crucial management competencies are covered in Part Five.

To help readers understand the importance of these competencies, we have asked the authors of the following chapters not only to identify critical knowledge, attitudes, and skills but also to explain how, when, and why they can be used. Each competency relates to one or more of the models or roles for professional practice described in Part Three. Depending on the chosen model for a given decision or unit, some competencies are more important than others.

Our list of essential competencies, astute readers will note, has changed a bit since the first edition of this book. We have added advising to counseling, seeing a set of generic skills applicable to the work of most student services professionals. While paraprofessional training is still relevant to the field, it is perhaps less central. Those involved in this area should find much that is helpful in the chapters on instruction and counseling and advising. Environmental assessment and redesign are probably best presented through the chapters by Huebner and Banning in Parts Two and Three. Readers who have a particular interest in paraprofessional training and environmental assessment might refer to the chapters on those subjects in the first edition of this book.

In Chapter Twelve, Oscar Lenning examines both assessment and evaluation competencies, with a focus on the former. Lenning considers assessment to be one component of evaluation; it precedes and leads to the judgments made in an evaluation but its role and activities are not the same as those of evaluation, nor are its required competencies necessarily the same. To clarify the distinctions between assessment and evaluation skills, Lenning discusses general procedures for conducting student assessments and presents special issues in doing various kinds of assessments. He also gives an overview of the evaluative process and presents several strategies for evaluating student services.

Teaching and training others has long been an important competency for student services professionals to master. In Chapter Thirteen, Jane Fried examines the process of instruction and the factors that influence it, with the goal of identifying specific skills that help others learn. The diversity of the educational audience, in terms of educational background and preferred learning styles, and the context of the teaching situation are two critical factors that define the boundaries of the teaching or training process.

Counseling has long played a central role in the student services profession, although the specific competencies it requires have not always been clearly defined. The purpose of Chapter Fourteen is to delineate knowledge and skills relevant to the counseling and advising role, discuss their importance, and provide examples of their application. Roger Winston focuses on the core skills needed by allied professionals—student services staff who do not view themselves as professional counselors or advisers, but who must use some of these skills in their work with students.

Since student services professionals can make significant contributions to the educational community, we must understand the process of consultation and the competencies needed to do it well. In Chapter Fifteen, June Gallessich develops a rationale for student services staff consultation; describes various consultation services we can offer to faculty, staff, administrators, and student organizations; differentiates consultation from other student services; and identifies critical consultation skills needed by effective student services consultants. Perhaps the most important aspect of her chapter is her description of strategies to be used in acquiring consultation skills.

In Chapter Sixteen Weston Morrill uses the dimension of counselor functioning (cube) model as a focus for thinking about educational programs for students. His chapter provides a framework for developing and implementing a wide variety of programming experiences. Morrill's model draws heavily on the professional role of student developer proposed by Brown but contains elements of the other three roles as well.

Because of the additions to Parts One and Six in the revised edition of this book, we have had to eliminate some of the material presented in the first edition. We refer interested readers to the first edition for some of the excellent diagrams and extended explanations that it was not possible to include here. We believe that the current chapters are strong basic delineations of essential competency areas.

Our hope is that these competencies will make sense to our readers in terms of the philosophy, theories, and role orientations already discussed. We believe that each student services professional must master the competencies addressed in these five chapters in order to make real contributions to the campus community and provide effective services for students.

Reference

Delworth, U., and Yarris, E. "Concepts and Processes for New Training Role." In U. Delworth (ed.), *Training Competent Staff.* New Directions for Student Services, no. 2. San Francisco: Jossey-Bass, 1978.

Chapter Twelve

Assessment and Evaluation

Oscar T. Lenning

Assessment and evaluation have become dominant themes in American higher education, especially as they relate to educational outcomes. (See Erwin, Chapter Twenty-Three.) Now that state governors have taken the lead in pushing both for a better-educated work force that can compete with the Japanese and for performance-oriented accountability that they perceive to have worked at the K–12 levels, it seems clear that this focus will not be another passing fad but rather is here to stay (Marchese, 1987). Furthermore, from the campus practitioner's perspective—whether in student affairs or some other area of the institution—assessment and evaluation must play the crucial role in determining goal achievement, program effectiveness, and how to bring about improvements.

This chapter begins with a brief conceptual overview, followed by a discussion of what skills and competencies are needed to conduct effective program evaluations. There is an abundance of literature about the measurement and assessment phases of evaluation but little pertaining to the important evaluative (judgment) phase. Both are discussed in the next section of this chapter. The following section refers to the various strat-

Note: Special appreciation is hereby expressed to Philip E. Beal, Roger K. Hadley, and Richard L. Torgerson for critiquing this chapter and providing helpful suggestions.

egies and approaches to program evaluation that one can choose from or integrate in an eclectic manner. Space does not allow an accounting of the procedures used in conducting each approach; suffice it to say that the competencies needed depend on the approach used. Finally, a brief closing section refers the reader to additional literary resources that can be helpful for conducting and using program evaluation.

Conceptual Overview

Traditionally, in a book like this, a chapter on assessment and evaluation would come last in the section devoted to essential competencies and techniques; assessment and evaluation are considered to follow the functions that are discussed in the next chapters. Assessment and evaluation cannot be very effective or have a major impact on improving those functions, however, if they are after-the-fact activities. Assessment and evaluation planning should occur along with the very earliest planning for an operational program, whether it is for student services or some other kind of program, to ensure that all the needed data are collected at the appropriate time prior to and during the development and operational phases.

Before discussing the strategies and procedures involved in assesment and evaluation, several basic conceptual classifications should be made. The activities to be discussed in the later sections can be usefully grouped according to these differentiations.

One component of every type of evaluation is assessment. Assessment precedes and leads to judgment, or the evaluative decision-making component. Assessment refers to gathering evidence: collecting data, transforming data so that they can be interpreted, applying analytical techniques, and analyzing data in terms of alternative hypotheses and explanations. On the basis of such assessment, judgments about value, worth, and ways to improve can be made—the evaluative process. Therefore, for the purposes of this chapter, an assessment study includes measurement and analysis, while an evaluation study includes measurement, analysis, and judgment. One cannot have assessment or evaluation without measurement and analysis of some kind. Another way to say this is to use Popham's (1975) definition of measurement as "status determination" and evaluation as "worth determination." Then, according to the preceding discussion, assessment links status determination to worth determination.

The traditionally accepted form of assessment and evaluation is intended to provide evaluative evidence to suggest whether a program should be continued as is, terminated, or revised. Scriven (1967) coined the term *summative* for this kind of evaluation because it focuses on the program in terms of the end-of-period or end-of-tryout status and is intended to provide a summary value judgment about the worth or usefulness of the program and its activities.

A potentially more useful concept of evaluation was referred to by Scriven (1967) as *formative*. Formative evaluation also results in judgment, but its primary focus occurs during the development and operation of the program. Formative activities focus on a continual assessment and evaluation, suggesting how the program should be modified in order to improve it. Thus, planning for this type of evaluation at an early stage of program development is especially crucial.

Another distinction that should be made is between formal and informal assessment and evaluation. Stake (1967, p. 523) made this distinction well when he wrote that informal evaluation depends on "casual observation, implicit goals, intuitive norms, and subjective judgment," while formal evaluation is very systematic, making use of formalized, concrete goals and depending on "checklists, structured visitation by peers, controlled comparisons, and standardized testing of students." Informal evaluation can provide effective and penetrating insight, but if not conducted with care it can just as often be superficial and distorted. How formal the evaluation activities should be depends on the purpose, situation, and context of the evaluation. For example, if the evaluation users distrust scholarly data collected through standardized instruments, carefully collected subjective data may be called for even if the purpose is to see if goals have been reached or promises kept.

Through evaluation, counselors and instructors appraise individual students' status and readiness and make judgments about needs, progress, and so forth. In contrast to individual evaltion, group evaluation results are used to make decisions about programs. Both types are legitimate forms of evaluation. Because this chapter is on evaluation in relation to student services, however, the discussion here focuses primarily on group evaluation.

Skills and Competencies
Needed for Program Evaluation

There are a number of skills and competencies that student services evaluators should have in order to be effective. Some skills are important for all the approaches to evaluation discussed later in this chapter. These key competencies include the ability to ask the important questions, think logically, and communicate effectively. Other skill requirements vary according to the evaluation strategy endorsed.

Owens (1977) focused on the program evaluation skills needed by a busy administrator, who is far more representative than a professional evaluator of the typical student services worker. The skills Owens emphasizes are similar to the ones emphasized by other authorities, such as Scriven (1971) and the American Educational Research Association (AERA) Task Force (Worthen and Byers, 1970). They cover the following broad array of abilities:

- To identify the purposes and audiences for one's evaluation
- To prepare a basic description of the program and the activities to be evaluated
- To refine educational objectives in terms of who will perform the activity, what the activity is, the criteria for judging successful objective attainment, and the conditions under which the activity will be conducted
- To write worthwhile objectives (clearly, emphasizing important skills and processes, and providing a challenge that at the same time is achievable) and to determine which objectives it is most critical to evaluate
- To describe the resources and processes to be used in achieving one's objectives

- To specify the alternative decisions likely to be made about a program
- To state evaluation questions clearly and concretely
- To establish evaluation guidelines consistent with funding availability, local concerns, administrative policy, and ethical principles
- To identify available resources for conducting the evaluation
- To specify pertinent data sources
- To determine appropriate ways to measure selected processes and outcomes
- To select and apply instruments according to their reliability, validity, and usefulness
- To establish and apply criteria for the selection of an evaluation specialist
- To prepare a basic evaluation plan for collecting, analyzing, and reporting data and transforming them into information
- To make judgments regarding various types and formats for evaluation reporting
- To apply various types of evaluation findings

All these skills and competencies are important for the assessment and evaluation of student services programs. However, the amount of emphasis on each depends on the assessment and evaluation strategy one chooses to guide one's efforts (as mentioned earlier), or on the combinations of strategies and procedures from various strategies that are integrated into one's personal framework.

We do not expect the evaluator to be a statistician. The evaluator needs to know enough about statistics, however, to be able to intelligently choose and communicate with a statistics expert when needed for the project and to appropriately interpret and apply any statistical data that are gathered.

Which assessment and evaluation approaches one chooses depends on many factors, including the evaluator's philosophy and skills. It is quite appropriate to use components from several different models to form one's own eclectic model, as long as it is well thought out and logically sensible in relation to the evaluator, the program, and the context. Furthermore, the same evaluator may often need different approaches for different pro-grams and contexts.

One additional skill that has not yet been mentioned is very important to planning an evaluation study: one should be able to explore the potential costs and benefits of the evalua-tion process itself. This should be done in probable terms and far enough in advance of the evaluation that the evaluation pro-cess can be modified if necessary.

Assessment Strategies and Considerations

Eight uses of student assessment by student services per-sonnel are discussed elsewhere (Lenning, 1977a). Three of them are definitely evaluation functions: grading, promoting, and granting merit awards; evaluating efficiency and effectiveness; and evaluating innovations. The others are less evaluative in nature: planning learning experiences, counseling and advis-ing students, diagnosing student problems, appraising student readiness, and classifying and categorizing students.

Assessments can also be conducted by students—of them-selves, their needs, environments, activities, and achievements. Assessing people other than students—such as staff, graduates, and members of the community—can also be important.

Payne (1974) proposes seven generally accepted stages or steps in assessing cognitive and affective learning that are applic-able to all kinds of assessment. These can be reduced to five proce-dures: specifying detailed goals and objectives, designing the assessment system, selecting measures and data-gathering methods, collecting data, and using the data. Each of these tasks will be discussed from the perspective of a student services worker.

Specifying Goals and Objectives. To be useful, goals must be transformed into concrete, observable, precise terms. Too often student services program goals are broad and vague ab-stractions, such as "to promote maximum development of the total self," "to promote self-actualization," and "to develop realistic and independent decision making."

Conrad (1974) has outlined a number of purposes goals

may have. Although he was talking about university goals, the same points can be made about program goals: they are standards against which to judge program success, they provide a source of legitimacy for the activities of the program, they define and order program needs, they define the units of program outcomes, they identify the program's clientele, and they define the relationship between the program, the institution of which it is a part, and society.

Such goals must be clear and precise to effectively guide actions to accomplish ends for students, a course, a program, or an institution. Transforming goals into concrete ends or objectives to be achieved is difficult. For an example of one way to do it, see Lenning, 1977b, pp. 15–25. Additional, more detailed taxonomies, such as Bloom's (1956), may be needed to get the specificity required at the program level. Another resource (Lenning, 1977c) provides an in-depth review of several dozen detailed classifications in the cognitive, affective, and psychomotor domains that may be useful for this purpose.

The task of reaching maximum agreement among various staff members and constituents concerning goals and priorities is also difficult. It may sometimes call for special consensus-rendering techniques, such as the *Q* sort or the Delphi techniques, if give-and-take discussion does not yield enough agreement.

What we assess must relate to the goals and objectives of the program or individuals being assessed. Two types of program goals exist. The first type, *outcome goals,* focuses on the results that the program is intended to achieve. The other type, *process goals,* refers to how the outcome goals are to be achieved— the personnel, money, time, activities, techniques, methods, and tools used to achieve particular outcomes.

Designing the Assessment System. Once the goals and objectives for the assessment are specified, work can begin on developing the strategy and procedures to be used for accomplishing those goals and objectives. Success rests on an integrated, detailed, well-thought-out assessment design.

First, we must outline the purposes of the assessment and then delineate the context in which the assessment is to take place. The context includes factors within the program, institution, or other environments that either assist or constrain the assessment effort. Examples of such factors are the attitudes and values of staff or students, political pressures and situations, available financial and staff resources, time and space considerations, base-line data already available, the diversity of the students using various student services, and so forth. Next, we must outline the specific questions that need to be answered by the assessment concerning particular problem-solving, decision-making, or other purposes. Decisions should then be made and recorded concerning the information needed to answer the questions, available indicators and measures, relevant and feasible data sources, whether sampling should be used and what kind, data-gathering and analysis strategies and procedures to collect the proper data and convert them into pertinent information, the data interpretation strategy, and feedback procedures for getting the information out to decision makers and other concerned people in an effective manner that promotes use. Finally, factors such as assessment costs and how the entire plan fits into an integrated system should be considered and necessary refinements or modifications made.

The design must be realistic and feasible in terms of the costs and effort required and must effectively generate the information needed to answer the pertinent decision makers' questions. It must provide a rationale concerning which specific groups of students, other people, and entities such as the environment should be assessed. How the assessment strategy and procedures vary by group or area should also be ascertained. For example, assessing older students' academic competencies using a standardized psychometric instrument designed for and normed on teenage college students is clearly inappropriate, unless it has been tested and found to be valid for older students also.

Selecting Measures and Data-Gathering Methods. In selecting measures and indicators, reliability and validity are important criteria. So are such factors as ease and cost of data collection, ease of scoring and tabulating, and appropriateness to the analytical procedures and tests that are planned.

I once heard about a new test battery that had been used with reported success and that seemed to be adequately reliable and valid in measuring "real-life" competencies. I recommended this battery to people who were consulting me on the evaluation of a nontraditional program emphasizing the development of such competencies. Fortunately, they tried it out on a pilot-test basis; even though it admirably met the reliability and validity criteria, it turned out to be extremely difficult for their people to administer and score. Yet I have talked to people on other campuses where the administration and scoring procedures worked quite well. This case illustrates the importance of trying out measures and data-gathering procedures ahead of time with small pilot samples of respondents similar to those in the full assessment study before the final decision is made to use them.

Standardized paper-and-pencil instruments are often used in student and program assessments, and new instruments appear periodically. For example, the American College Testing–College Outcome Measures Program and the Educational Testing Service Academic Profile are relatively new standardized instruments purporting to measure selected general education outcomes in college students. Although they may be reliable and valid for what they purport to measure, they often do not measure what is specifically of concern in the program. When considering a standardized instrument, one should examine an actual copy; supporting manuals; and reviews in Mitchell (1985), the eight earlier editions of *Mental Measurements Yearbook* (which have several reviews of some of the same instruments), and other available review sources (such as the journals *Measurement and Evaluation in Guidance, Educational and Psychological Measurement,* and *NCME Measurement in Education*) for assurance that it is appropriate for local needs.

To get a paper-and-pencil instrument that measures specifically what is desired, one often must construct one's own. There is an abundance of excellent texts on measurement theory and the development of norm-referenced tests and questionnaires, offering variety for both experienced and inexperienced instrument developers. Whenever possible, locally developed instruments should build on similar ones developed elsewhere. Lange, Lehmann, and Mehrens (1967) have shown that revising items takes less time, effort, and expense than developing them from scratch. Great care must be taken, however, to modify the instrument appropriately for the new context. Locally developed criterion-referenced instruments that focus on absolute levels of performance or mastery should always be considered as an alternative to norm-referenced instruments (see Gronlund, 1973, and Berk, 1980 and 1985, for help in developing such instruments).

Qualitative measures can be accurate and effective as an alternative or supplement to quantitative measures if the focus is kept concrete and specific enough so that everyone knows what is to be observed and why. There is a wide variety of effective qualitative measures and methodologies from which to choose; see Berk (1986), Guba and Lincoln (1981), Lenning (1988), Lincoln and Guba (1985), Loveland (1980), and Patton (1987).

Most measures and indicators are more reliable and valid in some contexts than in others. Furthermore, all measures have both weaknesses (some more than others) and strengths. Therefore, whenever feasible, multiple measures and indicators should be used for a particular learning outcome.

Specific precautions must be taken when collecting and using data for various kinds of measures. For example, Thelin (1976, p. 163) emphasizes that unobtrusive measures "have to be considered in clusters and tied to a conceptual framework if they are to be of significance for institutional monitoring." Unobtrusive measures—such as the measurement of attendance at campus plays and art displays after a demonstration program on appreciation of the arts sponsored by the office of student services in the dormitories—can be useful and revealing if such cautions are observed. See Secrest (1973, 1979) and Webb and others (1966) for helpful, in-depth discussions about unobtrusive measures.

Often it is possible to use data collected for other purposes (for example, from student transcripts, administrative files, and community records), which some have called "secondary data." Usually we think we need new data for an assessment study, but they may not be necessary. Boyd and Westfall (1972) provide criteria for determining when particular secondary data are acceptable for a particular situation and use, and they also discuss how to avoid pitfalls in using such data (it is very easy to misuse secondary data).

As is true for indicators and measures, and for the same reasons, multiple data collection methods are desirable whenever feasible. That they can be feasible and cost-effective was shown by the learning assessment system developed and implemented at Empire State College (Palola and Lehmann, 1976). Multiple data collections supplement standardized and local test score data with student self-reports, instructor observations, writing samples, and administrator observations.

Collecting Data. The proper measures and data collection methods are of no avail if one does not plan well and use care in the actual data collection. For example, a poorly worded cover letter sent out with a questionnaire can easily cut the response rate by half or more; so can sending students the questionnaire shortly before midterm exams. Much time, money, and frustration can be saved if one takes pains to have well-designed interview forms, written instructions for test administrators to read, careful selection of samples, questionnaire items free of bias, well-designed pilot tests to try out procedures ahead of time, procedures for maximizing response rates (such as showing the need for such data and promising—and giving—respondents feedback about the results), sensible coding and data-formatting rules, careful editing procedures, and so forth. The appendixes of Micek, Service, and Lee (1975) provide many helpful suggestions in this area.

Using the Data: Analysis, Interpretation, Reporting, and Application. Most assessment studies rely exclusively on the use of simple descriptive statistics, such as means, standard deviations, and tabulations and cross-tabulations of frequencies and percentages. Much useful information can be obtained from such simple statistics, especially if they are profiled graphically and patterns of similarities and discrepancies across information items and across groups are examined. Means by themselves can be quite misleading if the frequency distributions are not also examined. Also, response bias should be analyzed in questionnaire and interview studies.

It is often useful to make comparisons across groups when group differences on other characteristics (for example, input variables) are taken into consideration. Although "eyeballing" across groups and profile analysis can be revealing, such procedures may need to be supplemented with statistical tests such as t tests, chi square tests, analysis of variance, correlational analysis, path analysis, and discriminant analysis. In planning the study, the staff member and the analytical design expert should consider the analytical designs proposed by Campbell and Stanley (1963) and the nine evaluation design types proposed by Oetting and Cole (1978), which have been explained by Hanson and Lenning (1979). In addition, many helpful resources discuss the selection and use of statistical methods (for example, Tatsuoka and Tiedeman, 1963; Siegel, 1956). With today's sophisticated computers, and with adaptable and easy-to-use software packages such as SAS (SAS Institute, 1985) and SPSS-X (SPSS, Inc., 1988) available, along with specialized software, such analysis is relatively easy and straightforward.

In outcome studies, change in status is often of concern. However, most analysts now agree that change scores or average score changes of the same individuals should not be used in such analyses. Rather, they advise comparing students' final status to the final status of other students who have the same initial ability. For comparison across groups, this can be accomplished by random appointment to each group, by group assignment through stratified random paired matching on input level, by comparing across similar initial-level strata, or by sophisticated statistical adjustments to post-test scores that effectively equate initial levels (for example, analysis of covariance).

Interpretation and use of data are crucial in an assessment study, and too often data results are applied ineffectively. If the assessment data are to have any impact, the data users must be identified early in the assessment planning process, before the study is conducted. Input should be solicited from them concerning their specific concerns and what assessment information would help them make decisions. Such input serves a primary role in determining what study groups, data, and analyses are desired for the study. Once analyses are completed, brief, concise reports tailored to each user's information needs should be sent to them. Graphic presentation can often be helpful in such reports. An interesting and potentially useful way of making these reports attention-getting is through a peer group–intergroup model proposed by Alderfer and Holbrook (1973) and used by Hecht (1977). In this model, selected college staff prepare "action-oriented" written and oral responses to the evaluation data for presentation to other college staff at their level.

Special Considerations for Different Kinds of Assessment. The steps outlined above apply to the assessment of both groups and individuals. For individuals, however, they apply in a much more informal, subjective way. Furthermore, for individuals, the instruments used must have much higher reliability coefficients (in the 0.8–0.9 range, versus as low as 0.6 for groups) to be useful.

Different considerations also apply to the assessment of students and nonstudents. Usually, one is interested in assessing different factors for each group. Furthermore, the assessment of students often involves the use of standardized paper-and-pencil instruments, such as achievement and ability tests, whereas most nonstudent assessments of interest to student services workers do not make use of such instruments. For an illustration of nonstudent assessment, see May (1975), where two types of assessment (which he calls evaluation) of staff member competence in the guidance setting are discussed.

In assessing individual students, student services workers (especially personal counselors) have been considered experts for many years. However, the traditional focus on student services personnel assessing students is being replaced in many quarters by helping students assess themselves. As outlined by Miller and Prince (1976, pp. 48–49), the goal of assessment for student development "is to help students understand their current patterns of behavior, emphasizing positively the specific skills they have instead of the ones they lack."

Assessment of certain types of factors has produced separate areas of specialization. A good example is needs assessment, where the discrepancy between what is and what should be is a primary focus. Needs assessment is also noteworthy in that there is a serious problem among assessors in defining a need (Lenning and McAleenan, 1979). Other areas of specialization within assessment include the assessment of ability, achievement, personality, goals, values, interpersonal functioning, and organizational functioning.

The Evaluative Process

Whereas much has been written in the professional literature about the assessment process as it relates to evalaluation, relatively little has been written about the evaluative (judgment) process. Furthermore, what has been written tends to see the latter more as an art (for which procedures would be useless) than a science.

The evaluative process involves taking the synthesis of assessment results and various interpretations of those results and using the interpretations to make judgments or decisions about the value and worth of a service, activity, or program and its possible deletion, replacement, modification, or revision. In addition, the process often involves making a judgment or decision about the best ways to bring about improvement. The evaluative process can be carried out by a single person, the evaluator. Often more effective, however, is a group process involving a judgments team or committee; for example, see Harshman and Reinert (1979).

Positive benefits could accrue to student services if a sound system of evaluation (assessment and follow-up judgment) were implemented. Krumboltz (1974) noted several criteria that such a system should meet that are especially pertinent to the evaluative or judgment process. As suggested by Krumboltz, one's values enter into the evaluative process, and one must thus take care that the goals for process and outcome results have been defined clearly and agreed on by all concerned parties. Similarly, it cannot be overemphasized how important it is to use the evaluative process results to make decisions about program continuation, discontinuation, and improvement rather than to blame, condemn, or punish. Finally, Krumboltz cautions that, in making the judgment about whether the benefits of a student affairs activity outweigh the costs, staff accomplishments must be stated in terms of important student behavioral change, not in terms of staff effort and activity expended (which are costs rather than accomplishments).

Scriven (1971) points out an important role differentiation that should be made about the evaluative process: evaluating the goals of the program must be distinguished from evaluating whether and how well the program goals have been achieved. Formal program evaluation studies have almost always focused on judging the worth of the program or how to improve the program without considering the worth of the goals. However, an evaluator should also evaluate the appropriateness and worth of the program goals. Scriven indicates that the goals should be evaluated prior to evaluating the attainment of those goals; if a goal is poor, it matters little whether it was achieved. Evaluating the appropriateness of goals involves agreed-on, objective criteria for what constitutes a good goal. Unlike the evaluation of goal achievement, goal evaluation does not involve data derived from measurement; goals cannot be measured as achievement can. Instead, according to Scriven, the welfare of the consumer and society should be important criteria in evaluating goals.

Scriven made an additional noteworthy point concerning program goals—that evaluators should not focus so intently on whether the program goals have been achieved that they fail to notice significant unintended program outcomes. According to Scriven, one should look for evidence of unintended outcomes and be open to considering such evidence equally with evidence of accomplishment or lack of accomplishment of the program goals.

In reaction to the commonly accepted strategy of devoting all evaluative attention to the outcomes intended or planned for the program, Scriven (1972) developed a model that identifies significant program impacts of any kind, whether implied by the program goals or not. He called this model "goal-free evaluation." In this model, an outside evaluator is brought in who deduces from his or her observations what appear to be the program's goals. Only then does the evaluator talk to the program staff about their intended program goals. Scriven does not downgrade the importance of program goals for evaluation: "The statement of goal narrows our problem to manageable size. We can't apply all possible tests to every sample in order to look for all possible effects. We check in the general area where the shot was aimed, keeping our eyes open for any side effects" (Scriven, 1971).

The evaluative or judgment process is essentially a logical exercise. The evaluator making an evaluation is much like someone putting a puzzle together; a meteorologist predicting the weather on the basis of information about various conditions; a detective solving a crime on the basis of evidence gathered, analyzed, synthesized, and assimilated; a doctor or mechanic making a diagnosis; or an electronics technician troubleshooting an electronic circuit. The important things are, in an orderly and systematic manner, to consider all the evidence available, and look for patterns; to decide on all the plausible alternatives implied by the evidence; to determine weights and probabilities on the basis of the pattern of evidence and experience and knowledge; and to arrive at a judgment, considering the pattern of evidence, weights, and probabilities.

Related to these activities is a general five-step procedure, taken from Scriven (1971), for conducting the evaluative process. First, identify and rate the value of the intended goals of the project or program, using ratings of such things as social utility, current need for the goals, and the number of people who will benefit if the goals are met. Second, determine the value of the program's effectiveness, where effectiveness is not restricted to the stated or implied goals. Third, relate value to the program costs (here Scriven uses a twelve-point checklist involving installation versus maintenance costs, dollar versus psychic costs, per-student versus per-system costs, and so forth). Fourth, relate value to the program's availability and practicality. Finally, produce an overall summary report regarding judgments, recommended actions, and their justification. Scriven was presenting this list for professional evaluators, but it is also relevant for other evaluators. Note that in this five-step procedure, program benefits are related to both program process and costs.

Evaluative Strategies

In their excellent book of readings and comment on theory and practice in educational evaluation, Worthen and Sanders (1973, p. 1) open with a serious charge that unfortunately may still be true: "Evaluation is one of the most widely discussed but little used processes in today's educational systems. This statement may seem strange in the present social context where attempts to make educational systems accountable to their publics are proliferating at a rapid pace. . . . Yet, despite these trends toward accountability, only a tiny fraction of the educational programs operating at any level have been evaluated in any but the most cursory fashion, if indeed at all. Verbal statements about evaluation and accountability? An abundance. Genuine evaluation of educational programs? Unfortunately rare."

This statement applies at least as much to student services programs as to other areas of education. Student services goals for students often are imprecise, vague, illusory, and difficult to measure. Student services programs usually emphasize affective development, while formal instruction programs usually emphasize cognitive development, which is much easier to measure. Counselors and other student services people also perhaps have a greater aversion to empirical data and analysis than academicians involved primarily in research and scholarship.

However, for their programs to retain support, student services personnel must do a more effective and concrete job of communicating to others the important and central benefits students can gain from their programs and must provide factual evidence of such benefits. Furthermore, they must demonstrate that their activities and programs are both efficient and effective. Only through effective program evaluation can such evidence be developed, and such evaluation must begin with a clear and concrete delineation of activity and program goals and objectives.

A number of evaluation strategies or approaches, developed by evaluation theorists and practitioners in the area of curriculum development, provide alternatives for meeting distinct conditions and situations and have aspects or components that student services program evaluators should consider. Worthen and

Sanders (1973) have reprinted original writings by a number
of these strategy developers that they felt had made important
contributions to evaluation practice and could provide frameworks for such practice. They discuss each strategy in terms of
potentials and limitations and then use a chart to compare the
models on twelve factors or dimensions: (1) definition, (2) purpose, (3) key emphasis, (4) role of the evaluator, (5) relationship to objectives, (6) relationship to decision making, (7) types
of evaluation, (8) constructs proposed, (9) criteria for judging
evaluation studies, (10) implications for evaluation design, (11)
contributions to the design of evaluation studies, and (12) limitations and possible misuses of the approach. Noteworthy evaluation strategies have appeared in the literature since Worthen
and Sanders (1973).

House (1978) differentiated eight categories of evaluation
strategies on the basis of their proponents, their major audiences,
what they assume consensus on, their methodology, their outcome or purpose, and the typical question they use. Popham
(1975) classified them into four more subjective categories: goal
attainment strategies, intrinsic criteria strategies, extrinsic criteria strategies, and decision facilitation strategies. The various
models and literature sources that discuss them are listed here
using Popham's classification, which I have used previously to
discuss most of these models in some depth (Lenning, 1980):

1. *Goal Attainment Strategies*
      Behavioral Objective Approach (Tyler, 1942)
      Modified Behavioral Objective Approach (Metfessel and
          Michael, 1967)
      Multi-Dimensional Structure Approach (Hammond,
          1973)
2. *Intrinsic Criteria Strategies*
      Transactional Analysis Approach (Rippy, 1973)
      Interaction Analysis Approach (Flanders, 1973)
      Responsive Evaluation (Stake, 1975)
      Educational Connoisseurship and Criticism Approach
          (Eisner, 1977, 1979)
      Illuminative Evaluation (Parlett and Dearden, 1977)
      Ethnographic Evaluation (Fetterman, 1984, 1986)

Pluralistic Evaluation as Naturalistic Inquiry (Guba and Lincoln, 1981; Lincoln and Guba, 1985; Williams, 1986)

Qualitative Evaluation (Patton, 1980, 1987)

3. *Extrinsic Criteria Strategies*
Adversarial/Judicial/Jury Evaluation (Wolf, 1975; Tymitz and Wolf, 1977)

Countenance/Preordinate Evaluation (Stake, 1967, 1975)

4. *Decision Facilitation Strategies*
Clarification Approach (Alkin, 1969)

CIPP (Context, Input, Process, and Product) Evaluation (Stufflebeam and others, 1971)

Discrepancy Evaluation (Provus, 1971)

Profile/Pattern Evaluation (Lenning, 1980)

Conclusion

A brief chapter such as this can only introduce the reader to necessary competencies. Many helpful resources have been referred to throughout this chapter, but other resources for conducting and using evaluation should be mentioned. The new *Program Evaluation Kit* (Herman, 1987) from the Center for the Study of Evaluation at the University of California, Los Angeles—an eclectic set of books—can be very helpful. The following "how-to" books are included in the kit: *Evaluator's Handbook; How to Focus on Evaluation; How to Design a Program Evaluation; How to Use Qualitative Methods in Evaluation; How to Assess Program Implementation; How to Measure Attitudes; How to Measure Performance and Use Tests;* and *How to Communicate Evaluation Findings.* Other helpful evaluation resources are Ball (1981), Braskamp and Brown (1980), Ciarlo (1981), Cronbach and others (1980), Cronbach (1982), Deshler (1984), Hanson (1982), Kuh (1979), Loveland (1980), Popham (1988), Rossi and Freeman (1982), Stufflebeam and Shinkfield (1984), Hanson and Lenning (forthcoming), Lenning (1988), and Lenning and Torgerson (forthcoming). In addition, Sage Publications adds regularly to its series of books on evaluation, and each year since 1976 it has published an *Evaluation Studies Review Annual.* There are also journals that concentrate on evaluation, such as *Evaluation*

News, Evaluation Quarterly, and the Jossey-Bass New Directions for Program Evaluation quarterly sourcebooks.

A final point should be emphasized. The comprehensiveness of assessment and evaluation implied in this chapter is an ideal; to attain it often requires more time and money than present resources and political restraints allow. Furthermore, it is crucial for the reader to understand that the total evaluation for a program should not be attempted all at once and that feasibility (with respect to fiscal resources, time, staff expertise, the political environment, and so forth) must be a primary consideration in designing the evaluation plan—along with the needs of the program, the purposes the evaluation is to serve, what methods and activities will be effective, and so forth. An ongoing program evaluation plan should be cyclical, its phases lasting several years altogether before the cycle is repeated. During the year in which a particular segment of the program is being evaluated in depth, simple monitoring techniques such as those discussed by Hecht (1977) should be used to keep one's finger on the pulse and gross health of the other areas of program functioning. If assessment and evaluation activities are well planned and spaced appropriately, such activities can contribute greatly to program improvement, support, and accountability.

References

Alderfer, C. P., and Holbrook, J. *A New Design for Survey Feedback.* Bethesda, Md.: ERIC Document Reproduction Service, 1973. (ED 078 598)

Alkin, M. C. "Evaluation Theory Development." *Evaluation Comment,* 1969, *2,* 2–7.

Ball, S. *Assessing and Interpreting Outcomes.* New Directions for Program Evaluation, no. 9. San Francisco: Jossey-Bass, 1981.

Berk, R. A. (ed.). *Criterion-Referenced Measurement: State of the Art.* Baltimore, Md.: Johns Hopkins University Press, 1980.

Berk, R. A. (ed.). *A Guide to Criterion-Referenced Test Construction.* Baltimore, Md.: Johns Hopkins University Press, 1985.

Berk, R. A. (ed.). *Performance Assessment: Methods and Applications.* Baltimore, Md.: Johns Hopkins University Press, 1986.

Bloom, B. S. (ed.). *Taxonomy of Educational Objectives.* Vol. 1: *Cognitive Domain.* New York: McKay, 1956.

Boyd, H. W., and Westfall, R. *Marketing Research.* (3rd ed.) Homewood, Ill.: Irwin, 1972.

Braskamp, L. A., and Brown, R. D. (eds.). *Utilization of Evaluative Information.* New Directions for Program Evaluation, no. 5. San Francisco: Jossey-Bass, 1980.

Campbell, D. T., and Stanley, J. C. "Experimental and Quasi-Experimental Designs for Research on Teaching." In N. L. Gage (ed.), *Handbook of Research on Teaching.* Skokie, Ill.: Rand McNally, 1963.

Ciarlo, J. A. *Utilizing Evaluation: Concepts and Measurement Techniques.* Newbury Park, Calif.: Sage, 1981.

Conrad, C. "University Goals: An Operative Approach." *Journal of Higher Education,* 1974, *45,* 505–515.

Cronbach, L. J. *Designing Evaluations of Educational and Social Programs.* San Francisco: Jossey-Bass, 1982.

Cronbach, L. J., and others. *Toward Reform of Program Evaluation: Aims, Methods, and Institutional Arrangements.* San Francisco: Jossey-Bass, 1980.

Deshler, D. (ed.). *Evaluation for Program Improvement.* New Directions for Continuing Education, no. 24. San Francisco: Jossey-Bass, 1984.

Eisner, E. W. "On the Uses of Educational Connoisseurship and Criticism for Evaluating Classroom Life." *Teachers College Record,* 1977, *78* (3), 345–358.

Eisner, E. W. *The Educational Imagination.* New York: Macmillan, 1979.

Fetterman, D. M. (ed.). *Ethnography in Educational Evaluation.* Newbury Park, Calif.: Sage, 1984.

Fetterman, D. M. "Conceptual Crossroads: Methods and Ethics in Ethnographic Evaluation." In D. D. Williams (ed.), *Naturalistic Evaluation.* New Directions for Program Evaluation, no. 30. San Francisco: Jossey-Bass, 1986.

Flanders, N. A. *Interaction Analysis: A Technique for Quantifying Teacher Influence.* Bethesda, Md.: ERIC Document Reproduction Service, 1973. (ED 088 855)

Gronlund, N. E. *Preparing Criterion-Referenced Tests for Classroom Instruction.* New York: Macmillan, 1973.

Guba, E. G., and Lincoln, Y. S. *Effective Evaluation: Improving the Usefulness of Evaluation Results Through Responsive and Naturalistic Approaches.* San Francisco: Jossey-Bass, 1981.

Hammond, R. G. "Evaluation at the Local Level." In B. R. Worthen and J. R. Sanders (eds.), *Educational Evaluation: Theory and Practice.* Worthington, Ohio: Jones, 1973.

Hanson, G. R. (ed.). *Measuring Student Development.* New Directions for Student Services, no. 20. San Francisco: Jossey-Bass, 1982.

Hanson, G. R., and Lenning, O. T. "Evaluating Student Development Programs." In G. Kuh (ed.), *Evaluation in Student Affairs.* Washington, D.C.: American College Personnel Association, 1979.

Hanson, G. R., and Lenning, O. T. *Student Outcomes Assessment Handbook.* Forthcoming.

Harshman, C. L., and Reinert, P. C. *A Model for Assessing the Quality of Non-Traditional Programs in Higher Education.* St. Louis, Mo.: St. Louis University, 1979.

Hecht, A. R. "A Summary of the Moraine Valley Community College Evaluation System." Unpublished paper, Moraine Valley Community College, 1977.

Herman, J. L. (ed.). *Program Evaluation Kit.* (2nd ed.) Newbury Park, Calif.: Sage, 1987.

House, E. R. "Assumptions Underlying Evaluation Models." *Educational Researcher,* 1978, *7,* 4–12.

Krumboltz, J. D. "An Accountability Model for Counselors." *Personnel and Guidance Journal,* 1974, *52,* 639–646.

Kuh, G. (ed.). *Evaluation in Student Affairs.* Washington, D.C.: American College Personnel Association, 1979.

Lange, A., Lehmann, I. J., and Mehrens, W. A. "Using Item Analysis to Improve Tests." *Journal of Educational Measurement,* 1967, *4,* 65–68.

Lenning, O. T. "Assessing Student Progress in Academic Achievement." In L. L. Baird (ed.), *Assessing Student Academic and Social Progress.* New Directions for Community Colleges, no. 18. San Francisco: Jossey-Bass, 1977a.

Lenning, O. T. *The Outcomes Structure: An Overview and Procedures for Applying It in Postsecondary Education Institutions.* Boulder,

Colo.: National Center for Higher Education Management Systems, 1977b.

Lenning, O. T. *Previous Attempts to Structure Educational Outcomes and Outcome-Related Concepts: A Compilation and Review of the Literature.* Boulder, Colo.: National Center for Higher Education Management Systems, 1977c.

Lenning, O. T. "Assessment and Evaluation." In U. Delworth, G. R. Hanson, and Associates, *Student Services: A Handbook for the Profession.* San Francisco: Jossey-Bass, 1980.

Lenning, O. T. "Use of Noncognitive Measures in Assessment." In T. W. Banta (ed.), *Implementing Outcomes Assessment: Promise and Perils.* New Directions for Institutional Research, no. 59. San Francisco: Jossey-Bass, 1988.

Lenning, O. T., and McAleenan, A. C. "Needs Assessment in Student Affairs." In G. Kuh (ed.), *Evaluation in Student Affairs.* Washington, D.C.: American College Personnel Association, 1979.

Lenning, O. T., and Torgerson, R. L. *Designing Effective Student Assessment Programs.* Washington, D.C.: Association for the Study of Higher Education and ERIC Clearinghouse on Higher Education, forthcoming.

Lincoln, Y. S., and Guba, E. G. *Naturalistic Inquiry.* Newbury Park, Calif.: Sage, 1985.

Loveland, E. *Measuring the Hard-to-Measure.* New Directions for Program Evaluation, no. 6. San Francisco: Jossey-Bass, 1980.

Marchese, T. "Assessment: Fact or Fad." *Change,* 1987, *19*(1), 36–39.

May, R. D. "Guidance Program Evaluation—The Counselor's Role." Bethesda, Md.: ERIC Document Reproduction Service, 1975. (ED 120 595)

Metfessel, N. S., and Michael, W. B. "A Paradigm Involving Multiple Criterion Measures for the Evaluation of the Effectiveness of School Programs." *Educational and Psychological Measurement,* 1967, *27*, 931–943.

Micek, S. S., Service, A. L., and Lee, Y. S. *Outcome Measures and Procedures Manual.* (Field review ed.) Boulder, Colo.: National Center for Higher Education Management Systems, 1975.

Miller, T. K., and Prince, J. S. *The Future of Student Affairs: A Guide to Student Development for Tomorrow's Higher Education.* San Francisco: Jossey-Bass, 1976.

Mitchell, J. V., Jr. (ed.). *The Ninth Mental Measurements Yearbook.* 2 vols. Lincoln: University of Nebraska Press, 1985.

Oetting, E. R., and Cole, C. W. "Method, Design, and Implementation in Evaluation." In G. R. Hanson (ed.), *Evaluating Program Effectiveness.* New Directions for Student Services, no. 1. San Francisco: Jossey-Bass, 1978.

Owens, T. R. *Program Evaluation Skills for Busy Administrators.* Portland, Ore.: Northwest Regional Educational Laboratory, 1977.

Palola, E. G., and Lehmann, T. "Student Outcomes and Institutional Decision Making with PERC." In O. T. Lenning (ed.), *Improving Educational Outcomes.* New Directions for Higher Education, no. 16. San Francisco: Jossey-Bass, 1976.

Parlett, M., and Dearden, G. (eds.). *Introduction to Illuminative Evaluation: Studies in Higher Education.* Cardiff-by-the-Sea, Calif.: Pacific Soundings Press, 1977.

Patton, M. W. *Qualitative Evaluation Methods.* Beverly Hills, Calif.: Sage, 1980.

Patton, M. W. *How to Use Qualitative Methods in Evaluation.* Newbury Park, Calif.: Sage, 1987.

Payne, D. A. *The Assessment of Learning: Cognitive and Affective.* Lexington, Mass.: Heath, 1974.

Popham, J. W. *Educational Evaluation.* Englewood Cliffs, N.J.: Prentice-Hall, 1975.

Popham, J. W. *Educational Evaluation.* (2nd ed.) Englewood Cliffs, N.J.: Prentice-Hall, 1988.

Provus, M. *Discrepancy Evaluation for Educational Program Improvement and Assessment.* Berkeley, Calif.: McCutchan, 1971.

Rippy, R. M. *Studies in Transactional Evaluation.* Berkeley, Calif.: McCutchan, 1973.

Rossi, P. H., and Freeman, H. E. *Evaluation: A Systematic Approach.* (2nd ed.) Newbury Park, Calif.: Sage, 1982.

SAS Institute. "SAS Statistical Package." Cary, N.C.: SAS Institute, 1985.

Scriven, M. "The Methodology of Evaluation." In R. Tyler, R. Gagne, and M. Scriven (eds.), *Perspectives of Curriculum*

Evaluation. AERA Monograph Series on Curriculum Evaluation, no. 1. Skokie, Ill.: Rand McNally, 1967.

Scriven, M. *Evaluation Skills.* Washington, D.C.: American Educational Research Association, 1971. (Audiotape.)

Scriven, M. "Pros and Cons About Goal-Free Evaluation." *Evaluation Comment,* 1972, *3,* 1–4.

Secrest, L. "Use of Innocuous and Noninterventional Measures in Evaluation." In B. R. Worthen and J. R. Sanders (eds.), *Educational Evaluation: Theory and Practice.* Worthington, Ohio: Jones, 1973.

Secrest, L. (ed.). *Unobtrusive Measurement Today.* New Directions for Methodology of Social and Behavioral Science, no. 1. San Francisco: Jossey-Bass, 1979.

Siegel, F. *Nonparametric Statistics for the Behavioral Sciences.* New York: McGraw-Hill, 1956.

SPSS, Inc. "SPSS-X Statistical Package." Chicago, Ill.: SPSS, Inc., 1988.

Stake, R. E. "The Countenance of Educational Evaluation." *Teachers College Record,* 1967, *68,* 523–540.

Stake, R. E. *Evaluating the Arts in Education: A Responsive Approach.* Columbus, Ohio: Merrill, 1975.

Stufflebeam, D. L., and Shinkfield, A. J. (eds.). *Systematic Evaluation.* Hingham, Mass.: Kluwer-Nijhoff, 1984.

Stufflebeam, D. L., and others. *Educational Evaluation and Decision Making.* Bloomington, Ind.: Phi Delta Kappa, 1971.

Tatsuoka, N. M., and Tiedeman, D. V. "Statistics as an Aspect of Scientific Method and Research on Teaching." In N. L. Gage (ed.), *Handbook of Research on Teaching.* Skokie, Ill.: Rand McNally, 1963.

Thelin, J. R. "Beyond the Factory Model: New Strategies for Institutional Evaluation." *College and University,* 1976, *51,* 161–164.

Tyler, R. W. "General Statement on Evaluation." *Journal of Educational Research,* 1942, *35,* 492–501.

Tymitz, B., and Wolf, R. L. *An Introduction to Judicial Evaluation and Natural Inquiry.* Washington, D.C.: Naro, 1977.

Webb, E. J., and others. *Unobtrusive Measures: Nonreactive Research in the Social Sciences.* Skokie, Ill.: Rand McNally, 1966.

Williams, D. D. (ed.). *Naturalistic Evaluation*. New Directions for Program Evaluation, no. 30. San Francisco: Jossey-Bass, 1986.

Wolf, R. L. "Trial by Jury: A New Evaluation Method." *Phi Delta Kappan,* 1975, *57,* 185–187.

Worthen, B. R., and Byers, M. L. *An Exploratory Study of Selected Variables Related to the Training and Careers of Educational Research and Research-Related Personnel.* Washington, D.C.: American Educational Research Association, 1970. (ED 110 441)

Worthen, B. R., and Sanders, J. R. (eds.). *Educational Evaluation: Theory and Practice.* Worthington, Ohio: Jones, 1973.

Chapter Thirteen

Teaching and Training

H. Jane Fried

Undergraduate education in American colleges and universities is descended from a pair of essentially incompatible parents—the German research model and the British collegiate model (see Fenske, Chapter One). Because of the incompatibility of these ideals and the strength of the research model at the graduate level, there is a profound sense that issues of personal concern and personal development do not belong in the college classroom. This mind-set pervades the traditional academic disciplines and makes the inclusion of student development courses and methods a difficult problem in many institutions.

In order to introduce the academic faculty to the value of including student development education in the undergraduate curriculum, student development educators must communicate with their colleagues on several aspects of the topic. Student development staff can provide accurate descriptions of today's student body: who they are, how they learn, what they expect college to do for them, and how they think about the role of the faculty. They can also help faculty become familiar with the various approaches to explaining learning styles, teaching styles, and experiential education. Student development educators can share with faculty colleagues the content of student development education, information about life stages, transitions, and developmental issues. Finally, the process of assessing student learning and course effectiveness remains an area of common concern, one in which faculty from all of the disciplines can share methods and techniques and in which student development educators, as behavioral scientists, have a key contribution to make.

The debate continues about the integrity of student development education as an academic discipline. In the words of our faculty colleagues, "We know it's worth learning, but is it worth academic credit?" This question is bound into the assumptions that form the German model. There are at least two answers to the question. First, student development as an academic discipline should be considered comparable in worth to any of the other applied behavioral sciences and ought to be taught at the same level of academic rigor. Second, the collegiate model of higher education implies that faculty are concerned about the teaching process as well as the content of their courses. The process of engaging students in discussion about the significant issues that are raised in a particular course has implications for students' character development (Widick, Knefelkamp, and Parker, 1975; Fried, 1981) as well as intellectual development. Student development educators are, or should be, knowledgeable about group dynamics, interpersonal communication, theories of cognitive development, and training design. All of these skills apply directly to classroom interaction.

Joseph Katz (1985) indicates that there are three obstacles to student learning, "lack of individualization, lack of collaborativeness in learning and lack of opportunity for applying ideas in situations for which students have responsibility" (p. 6). These three descriptors could as easily apply to the process of advising student government as to a classroom learning situation. It is clear that Katz's concept of learning is not confined to classroom settings. The process of understanding instruction from a student development perspective is like learning to translate—from training to teaching, from a narrow definition of academic education to a broader approach that includes the discussion of values—the application of general knowledge to personal and global problems and a concern for the development of insight along with intellect.

Traditional methods cannot be assumed to work with nontraditional populations. In higher education today, both the complexion of the student body and its age and attendance patterns have changed so drastically that almost all traditional approaches and methods have been called into question. Hispanic and black birth rates are higher than those of the white, English-speaking population. Immigration from Southeast Asia and Central America has had a drastic impact on many communities. Increased numbers of women are attending college later than the traditional time of life. Adults of both sexes are returning to college periodically throughout their lives to improve their skills, to retrain for new careers, and to enhance their own knowledge. The college classroom is not the same place it was thirty years ago (Garland, 1985). The profession of student affairs emerged from a need to attend to the whole student. Since the life circumstances of many students have changed so dramatically, the contributions that student affairs staff members can make to the educational environment have become extremely important.

The Teaching Process

Most recent graduates of student affairs preparation programs have had some exposure to the process of designing training programs and many opportunities to discuss the various theories of student development. The distinction between training and teaching is an important one. The purpose of training is to help people learn skills to solve problems. Chickering (1976) notes that the purpose of training is to "describe a task and then conform the learner to it" (p. 82). People who have been trained in a particular skill will generally apply the skill in a similar manner. The development of "style" in using a skill—for example, the development of one's personal style of counseling—comes after the skill has been mastered. Training imposes a certain uniformity on the practice of a skill, and this uniformity is the basis on which skill development can be evaluated.

The purpose of teaching is quite the opposite—to broaden a person's understanding, to help the person examine a problem from several different points of view, and to place the problem in a cultural and historical context. Boyer (1987, p. 111) describes "the disastrous divorce of competence from conscience" in American colleges, indicating his concern that the focus on narrow vocationalism, or training, has obscured the broader concerns of higher education.

Student affairs preparation programs generally combine education in the various theoretical bases of the profession with training via internships and practica. Student development courses in higher education should do the same. Many student affairs practitioners are prepared to be excellent trainers, because of a professional preference for practical applications and problems that have solutions, but are less well prepared to be teachers. Many current practitioners are products of the narrow vocational preparation that Boyer describes and therefore do not have the broad education themselves that is necessary for good teaching. In addition, the standard format for college teaching is generally the lecture, supplemented by an occasional film, videotape, question, or brief discussion. College teaching typically involves an active teacher communicating information to a relatively passive group of students.

The challenge that student affairs administrators face is to become well educated in areas that pertain to any course they teach, and then to find ways to present educational information in a manner that actively engages the students. Student development education should combine information from a variety of disciplines with the training techniques that engage students in applying knowledge to problems that concern them. Student development education is an applied behavioral science. Theory is essential to understanding the problems under discussion, and skill is essential to solving them, or at least to addressing them at a reasonable level of competence.

Learning and Teaching Styles. The processes of cognitive development and adult learning styles have been the subject of much research in the past twenty years (Messick and Associates, 1976; Perry, 1968; Chickering and Associates, 1981; Belenky, Clinchy, Goldberger, and Tarule, 1986; Kolb, 1981). Researchers have discovered that learning style has little to do with intelligence level (Cohen, 1969), but that people who are taught in a style that is incompatible with their own often have difficulty succeeding in the courses where the incompatible style is used

(Kolb, 1981; Witkin, 1977). Witkin (1977) has discovered that cognitive style categories also apply to categories that describe various dimensions of personality. Since people seem to teach in a style that matches their learning style, instructors should understand their own learning style preferences and be able to assess their students' learning styles as well. The Myers-Briggs Type Indicator (MBTI) (Myers, 1962) has great utility for assessing learning style. It has the advantage of being an instrument with which many student affairs practitioners are familiar because of its applications to interpersonal communication, supervision, conflict resolution, and decision-making issues. *People Types and Tiger Stripes* (Lawrence, 1979) explains in detail the learning style preferences of people who fit the sixteen MBTI categories.

A second approach to understanding differences in learning styles is embodied in Witkin's research (1981) on field dependence and field independence in personality attributes and cognitive style. Messick (1976) describes the field independence/field dependence variable as a contrast between an analytical and a global way of thinking that also involves differences between the tendency to see objects as discrete from their background or embedded in it. Witkin (1977) has discovered that child-rearing styles affect the field independence/field dependence variable in learning styles. Girls and women, probably because of gender variations in child-rearing practices, are more likely to have field-dependent styles than boys and men. Cultural values also affect the development of cognitive style according to this dimension. Cultures that emphasize "conformity, 'tight' role definitions and social control seem to encourage field dependence; 'loose' cultures, with more emphasis on self-control and independence, encourage field independence" (Cross, 1976, p. 118). Finally, many people in all cultures seem to move toward field dependence after the age of fifty. Cross (1976) compares personality characteristics of field-dependent students to those she terms the New Students—those who are older than the traditional group or who are members of minority groups in the United States—and finds numerous similarities.

Field-independent and field-dependent students have different personality characteristics, different approaches to learning new information and solving problems, different attitudes toward authority, and different types of preferred classroom behavior. Field-independent students are characterized by the ability to learn increasingly larger amounts of concrete data as they mature, to think at increasingly abstract levels, to analyze information logically, to sit still and pay attention to impersonal learning stimuli (books, films, lectures), and to value their own ability to organize their time (Fried, 1985). These aspects of field independence seem to be correlated with a preference for receiving information from the teacher and a low opinion of the value of class discussions with peers. A sense of competition related to the ability to learn more information, present abstract generalizations, and generally outsmart one's peers seems to be valued. Classroom dialogues resemble debates.

Preferences and behaviors of field-dependent students present a distinct contrast. These students pay attention to the overall characteristics of stimuli and enjoy looking for patterns and discussing ideas with peers. They prefer essay exams to objective tests. They enjoy being with other people and are sensitive to the needs and reactions of others in their social setting. They tend to be "sensitive to the judgments of others . . . guided by authority figures . . . dependent on others for self-definition . . . extrinsically motivated [and] responsive to social reinforcement" (Cross, 1976, p. 123). Classroom discussion may tend to overlook details in favor of broad generalizations, to rely on intuitive judgments, and to take on the joint inquiry approach, with students building on each other's points, rather than competing with one another.

The overlap between the field independent/field dependent factor and gender-role socialization and cultural background is now becoming apparent. In the United States, female gender-role socialization has been heavily directed toward sensitivity to the needs of others, an awareness of the feeling component of relationships, and the ability to be the nurturer in relationships. Carol Gilligan (1982) has commented on the development of a value system predominant in females, one that focuses on an ethic of caring, in distinct contrast to the ethic of justice described by Lawrence Kohlberg (1969) in his work on the moral development of males. The caring ethic is thought to focus more on the complexities of relationships and the desire to hurt no one, while the ethic of justice focuses on abstract principles of right and wrong and solves human dilemmas by analysis according to those principles. The latter approach could be characterized as a field-independent approach.

Belenky, Clinchy, Goldberger, and Tarule (1986) have described ''women's ways of knowing'' in field-dependent terms. The women in their study began their lives intimidated by authority, assuming that, if they could learn at all, it would be from men who were, by virtue of their gender, smarter than they. As women progress in their development, they become more and more confident about their ability to learn, to create knowledge, and to absorb facts. They are able to learn objective information as they gain confidence, but they generally do not value this activity as much as they value insight and the application of information to the resolution of life's real problems. The most advanced stage of female intellectual development on the scale developed by these authors is one in which objective facts are integrated with a sense of personal meaning and purpose, an approach that could be described as field-dependent dominant, field-independent subordinate.

The field independence/dependence paradigm can also yield some insight into culturally derived differences in learning style. Cultures that value ''tight'' role definitions and obedience to authority and place strong emphasis on sensitivity to the needs of others and the community at large will, theoretically, produce more people who have a field-dependent learning style. Although there is danger in relying on stereotypical descriptions of ethnic groups, a knowledge of the value systems and behavior patterns within specific ethnic groups can yield insight into the probable learning styles of members of those groups, as well as the types of classroom activities with which they would be likely to be comfortable.

Cognitive Complexity. William Perry (1968) was the first person to apply the tools of cognitive-structural development to an analysis of the intellectual development of college students. Perry's work with Harvard undergraduates is presented largely in the form of anecdotes, which flesh out a conceptual scheme of cognitive development that has been applied in college classrooms, residence halls, counseling sessions, student group activities, and almost every other activity in which college students are involved. Excellent summaries of this scheme are widely available (Perry, 1981). The Perry model provides a format for assessing students' attitudes toward authority, specifically knowledge authorities or teachers, and students' beliefs about their proper role: to memorize the "facts," to compare sets of "facts," to develop opinions that can be supported by "facts," and so forth. Perry also provides guidance in understanding the amount and type of structure that a student needs to feel comfortable in a classroom, as well as the types of teacher responses that provide an appropriate mix of challenge and support to encourage continued intellectual growth.

Lee Knefelkamp (personal communication, 1975) has developed a clear format for applying knowledge of students' level of cognitive development to classroom methodology. Students at levels 1 through 4+ expect the teacher to act as an authority and have not yet developed the ability to understand that any given problem or question might have more than one acceptable answer. These students have not developed the ability to examine an issue from more than one point of view, or to compare and contrast different theoretical positions. They benefit from assignments that challenge their assumptions about the world, expose them to a variety of points of view, and encourage them to participate in role-taking activities. Class discussions should avoid problems that have a single right answer. Values clarification exercises that are ambiguous and open-ended can be helpful. Widick, Knefelkamp, and Parker (1975) suggest that two elements are critical if dualistic students are to be challenged effectively: "diversity of viewpoint in course content and instructional methods and . . . experiential learning models" (p. 291). The supporting emotional tone of the classroom is personal and safe. When students are being challenged to question their basic assumptions about the nature of knowledge and the values by which life is to be lived, they must be supported by the knowledge that they will not be intellectually deserted or scorned after they give up their anchors.

Students in the more advanced stages are considered relativists. They no longer assume that Authority knows all or that there are right answers. They are at the stage of learning to make commitments. They need to find new ways to anchor themselves and to make commitments based on their own values. These students must be encouraged to take a point of view and support it with facts. They need to make choices despite the lack of clear external confirmation about the validity of any one of them. Relativists expect the teacher to lead them in inquiry, but they are less comfortable with the request that they choose a position and defend it. This process is not simply one of cognitive development. It is also existential. Relativists are more comfortable with abstract discussions than dualists. Class activities require less structure and can be introduced by general questions. Personal support is still necessary for students to benefit from this approach. If giving up an anchor is difficult, choosing a new one with no guarantees from family or faith is equally so. An awareness of students' level of cognitive complexity gives an instructor guides for managing the classroom, but it is the instructor's counseling ability that must be used to appreciate the emotional strains that development provokes and to develop the supportive atmosphere that encourages progress.

The Perry scheme was normed on male students. *Women's Ways of Knowing* (Belenky, Clinchy, Goldberger, and Tarule, 1986) presents a scheme for describing cognitive development in women. Their work is guided by the belief that there are themes in women's ways of understanding "self, voice and mind" that Perry's work has not uncovered. Women's cognitive development is traced from silence, the first stage, to received knowledge, the second stage, which involves listening to the voices of others for guidance. Subjective knowledge, the third and fourth stages, involves learning to listen to one's inner voice and to define oneself without reference to role or the conceptions of others. During stages five and six, the stages of procedural knowledge, women learn to use reason in articulating their positions and develop a preferred mode of learning, either separate knowing (comparable to field independence) or connected knowing (field dependence). The final stage in this scheme is termed constructed knowledge, the stage at which "all knowledge is constructed and the knower is an intimate part of the known" (p. 137). This stage is analogous to Perry's stages of commitment in relativism. Detailed comparisons of the Perry scheme and the scheme developed by Belenky, Clinchy, Goldberger, and Tarule have not yet been made. Recent research by Marcia Baxter-Magolda (1987) indicates that the structure of cognitive development is similar in males and females, but that the content of the issues seems to differ. The authors of *Women's Ways of Knowing* suggest a form of connected teaching that offers general guidelines for classroom activities and process that are supportive of women and men who function in the feminine mode.

Classroom Management. Much more attention is given to the subject of classroom management in primary and secondary education than in higher education. However, Widick, Knefelkamp, and Parker (1975), Kolb (1981), Bernard (1981), Fleming (1981), and many others have shown that classroom climate continues to be a critical element in student learning throughout the college years. Student development instruction is based on the process of integrating facts and feeling, knowledge and its applications and implications. Students are generally expected to become involved in experiential learning and to examine their values and their behavior in the light of information that is discussed in class. In order to increase the likelihood that this self-disclosure and self-examination will occur honestly, the classroom environment must be one that builds trust and conveys a sense of respect for each individual student.

The notion of challenge and support should govern decisions about classroom management. What type of environment will make the students sufficiently comfortable to take risks? What kinds of activities at the beginning of the semester will give students the self-confidence to ask difficult personal questions and accept new ideas about issues from people who were strangers when the course began? If the class has both field-independent students and field-dependent students, how will the instructor manage discussions to achieve an effective balance between a "debate" atmosphere and a "joint inquiry" atmosphere? What are the ground rules that must be followed in the classroom behavior so that all students feel respected by their peers as well as the instructor?

Issues of classroom management are similar to the issues that apply to training management. Instructors who outline the trust-building questions before beginning to teach will find that they have the skills to answer them within their own training experiences. The major difference between teaching and training in this domain is in the area of grading. This will be discussed in a later section of this chapter.

Clinical Teaching. Almost all student personnel professionals have some counseling and group facilitation training in their educational background. These skills are as effective in a classroom as they are in any other setting. The traditional role for instructors is one of giving information. In student development courses the instructor gives information to students, but plays many other roles as well. "Depending on the nature of the relationship with the student(s) the teacher could be expert, catalyst, critic, facilitator, mediator, consultant, negotiator, counselor, collaborator and contractor for developmental learning contracts" (Crookston, 1973, pp. 59–60). In the classroom, the effect of using these skills is to build trust between teacher and students and among students. Access to counseling, consulting, mediation, and group facilitation skills is one of the advantages that student personnel professionals have as instructors. A conscious effort should be made to use these skills in classroom applications.

Course Content

The content of student development courses generally falls into three categories: topics derived from developmental psychology, topics derived from expressed student needs, and topics of social or institutional concern. David Drum (1980) has developed a three-part description for these types of courses: life themes, life skills, and life issues. Life issues are generally existential concerns, such as loneliness, anxiety, morality, and developing a sense of personal meaning. Developmental topics, or life themes, generally focus on issues that are salient for the students because of their particular developmental status. Students of the traditional age for college are concerned about initial career decision making, establishing intimate relationships, discussing sexuality and establishing sexual identity, and family dynamics, especially issues relating to parent-child communication. Older students are also concerned about family dynamics, but their perspective is different if their role in their immediate family includes being a spouse, parent, or caretaker of their own parents. Both groups are also concerned about identity issues, traditional students about forming and articulating an identity, nontraditional students about changing a self-image that may be defined primarily by family role to one that has a broader focus. Whatever the focus of developmental courses, a person's age, gender, and cultural background inform the kinds of questions that that person must address and the types of resolutions that are acceptable to him or her. Any course that discusses developmental issues must include consideration of these factors as they are represented in the group.

Topics derived from expressed student needs, or life skills, include such areas as time management, stress management, and the skills associated with a job search, such as résumé writing, interviewing, and assertive communication. Students who are peer counselors or group advisers also need instruction in counseling, group dynamics, leadership, supervision, and the many other aspects of effective communication. Instruction in these areas most closely approximates training and frequently does not carry academic credit.

Topics of social or institutional concern are probably the most complex and require the broadest knowledge base of the instructor. These are also the courses that benefit most from team teaching or the presence of many guest lecturers who are experts on the problems under discussion. Subjects addressed by courses of this type include racism, sexism, understanding cultural differences, responsible use of the environment, and the future in a nuclear world. These courses require a broader examination of "facts"—impersonal information that pertains to the subject—than the other types of courses. Methods for relating facts to personal meaning and values apply as effectively in these courses as they do in the courses that focus on more personal issues. An example of one such program is the "I Curriculum" offered at Miami-Dade Community College. The curriculum is designed to provide "an interdisciplinary approach to general education requirements, combining affective and cognitive approaches to education" (Watkins, 1981, p. 79). The course is organized around the question "How can each of us be the person she or he wants to be?" (p. 80). It requires students to examine data from the natural sciences, the social sciences, and communication and the behavioral sciences in their attempts to answer that basic question.

Assessment and Evaluation

At the very beginning of any course it is desirable to assess the students' learning style and get a sense of the expectations that they have for the course. Assessment can range from the formal to the informal and impressionistic. The Learning Context Questionnaire (Griffith and Chapman, 1982) is a paper-and-pencil assessment of students' cognitive development measured according to the Perry scheme. It can give the instructor some initial guidance on methods and styles that will be effective in working with a specific group. The MBTI (Myers, 1962), described elsewhere in this chapter, is also an effective tool for assessing learning style. Finally, the author has found an assignment based on the early work of Perry (1968) to be useful. Students are asked to write approximately two pages in response to the question, "Looking back over the past year, what stands out for you?" An informed reader can make some useful predictions about the developmental stages of the students in a class and learn something about their current life experience as well.

Assessing Student Learning. Since students have different learning styles, it is to their advantage to be given opportunities to demonstrate what they have learned in different ways. Field-independent students seem to perform better on "objective" or factually oriented exams, while field-dependent students prefer to write essays in which they can connect facts to theories and projections. Some students may perform more effectively when working on group projects, while others prefer to research an issue or problem and present the results either orally or in writing. Each of the sixteen MBTI personality types has a series of preferred learning activities and assessment methods (Lawrence, 1979). For example, it is easier for Extraverts to perform well in class discussion, since they tend to speak their developing thoughts. Introverts will have more difficulty in these discussions because their thought processes precede their oral presentation.

Student learning style should be assessed early in the educational process. When tests are given, they should include options for each area of knowledge that is being tested. For example, in assessing a student's knowledge of behavioral approaches to counseling, one question might ask for the names of four behavioral counselors, the types of methods that they introduced, and the types of situations in which they were most effective. A second question in the same area might ask for the general principles underlying behavioral therapy, some examples of this type of therapy, typical applications, and the ethical issues that this approach to counseling raises. The first question asks the student to list and discuss a series of facts about behavior therapy. The second question asks the student to describe the broad perspective into which these facts can be placed and then allows the student to return to some general ethical concerns that stimulate the imagination and allow intuition to come into play.

Testing is the most widely used form of assessment, but it is clearly not the only means. Papers or journals that require students to report on experiential learning or to react to subjects discussed in class, as well as research papers and "reaction" papers that require students to respond to a book, an article, a videotape, a film, and so forth, are also widely used. Class presentations and demonstrations are especially relevant to student development courses because so much of what is discussed and learned falls into the area of life skills. Giving students a wide range of methods by which they can demonstrate what they have learned increases the likelihood that each student will find a way that suits his or her learning style.

Many practitioners in student affairs and student development education have been trained in counseling. This training implies a Rogerian heritage of nonjudgmental approaches to students. Such a background often makes assessment and evaluation difficult, since confusion may arise between judging the student's educational products and judging the student's human worth. This is a particular problem in courses like peer counseling because much of what the student presents in class and on paper is an integral part of the student's life. The key to resolving this dilemma is to make the standards clear and justifiable before any particular assessment is given or any piece of work is judged. Standards can be related to course content, quality of thought and logic, timeliness, honesty, originality, class participation, attendance, literacy, or any combination of these factors. Whatever the evaluation standards, they must be administered equitably, keeping in mind that people who conduct instruction are functioning as part of the faculty. In this capacity they must be able to explain evaluation criteria to the faculty at large in comprehensible terms.

Course Evaluation Formats. Many institutions have standard course evaluation formats. These standard instruments may not provide meaningful feedback in student development courses. In evaluating courses, just as in evaluating students, it is useful to provide a variety of methods by which students can respond. A simple but very useful method is to write statements about the course and ask students to indicate their degree of agreement with them using a Likert type of scale. A similar approach is to list the significant components of the course—for example, class organization, subjects in the syllabus, movies, additional assignments, and library resources—and ask each student to evaluate each component on a scale of 1 (excellent) to 5 (poor). Providing a statistical method of evaluation is a useful shorthand for summarizing student opinion.

In addition to asking students to rank their responses, they should also be asked for less structured feedback. The simplest mode is to provide a section entitled "Comments" on the evaluation sheet. More structure in the questions yields more information in specific areas: "Please comment on the teacher's style of presenting information; of managing class discussions," or, more generally, "Feedback for Jane." Another sort of question inquires, "What were the three most satisfying (or stimulating, or useful, or interesting) classes this semester? The three least?'' Returning to the structures that the learning style assessments provided, an instructor can shape questions designed to discover whether students felt comfortable with course methods, whether they felt accepted in the class atmosphere, whether they had a fair opportunity to present what they had learned, and so forth. These types of questions can be presented in the agree/disagree format or as open-ended questions.

A Final Thought

Since student development education necessarily puts student affairs staff in contact with faculty on faculty turf, approaching the communication process with a cross-cultural model in mind can be very helpful. Cross-cultural communication implies differences in background, life experience, and values that must be acknowledged if mutual understanding is to occur. At its best, the model does not make any value judgments about which culture is "better." Student affairs practitioners who instruct are working in a new culture and can be compared to immigrants. Learning the language and values of the new culture is important as a means to achieving full participation in the society (Fried, 1981). We have observed a search for ethnic roots in this generation and have seen the affirmation that people experience when they once again assert their "hyphenated American" status; student affairs and student development must also hold true to their roots of working with each student as a whole human being, in class and out, and helping students address significant questions in their own lives, regardless of the context in which the questioning occurs.

References

Baxter-Magolda, M. "Measuring Gender Differences in Intellectual Development: A Comparison of Assessment Methods." Paper presented at annual meeting of American College Personnel Association, Chicago, Mar. 1987.

Belenky, M. F., Clinchy, B. M., Goldberger, N. R., and Tarule, J. M. *Women's Ways of Knowing: The Development of Self, Voice, and Mind.* New York: Basic Books, 1986.

Bernard, J. "Women's Educational Needs." In A. Chickering and Associates, *The Modern American College: Responding to the New Realities of Diverse Students and a Changing Society*. San Francisco: Jossey-Bass, 1981.

Boyer, E. *College: The Undergraduate Experience in America*. New York: Harper & Row, 1987.

Chickering, A. W. "Commentary: The Double Bind of Field Dependence and Independence in Program Alternatives for Educational Development." In S. Messick and Associates, *Individuality in Learning: Implications of Cognitive Styles and Creativity for Human Development*. San Francisco: Jossey-Bass, 1976.

Chickering, A. W., and Associates. *The Modern American College: Responding to the New Realities of Diverse Students and a Changing Society*. San Francisco: Jossey-Bass, 1981.

Cohen, R. "Conceptual Styles, Culture Conflict and Nonverbal Tests of Intelligence." *American Anthropologist*, 1969, *71*, 828–856.

Crookston, B. "Education for Human Development." In C. Warnath and Associates, *New Directions for College Counselors: A Handbook for Redesigning Professional Roles*. San Francisco: Jossey-Bass, 1973.

Cross, K. P. *Accent on Learning: Improving Instruction and Reshaping the Curriculum*. San Francisco: Jossey-Bass, 1976.

Drum, D. "Understanding Student Development." In W. H. Morrill, J. C. Hurst, and Associates (eds.), *Dimensions of Intervention for Student Development*. New York: Wiley, 1980.

Fleming, J. "Special Needs of Blacks and Other Minorities." In A. W. Chickering and Associates, *The Modern American College: Responding to the New Realities of Diverse Students and a Changing Society*. San Francisco: Jossey-Bass, 1981.

Fried, J. (ed.). *Education for Student Development*. New Directions for Student Services, no. 15. San Francisco: Jossey-Bass, 1981.

Fried, J. "Equity in the Classroom: A Discussion of Male and Female Learning Styles." *UConn Journal*, 1985, *3*, 14–17, 32.

Garland, P. *Serving More Than Students*. ASHE-ERIC Higher Education Report no. 7. Washington, D.C.: Association for the Study of Higher Education, 1985.

Gilligan, C. *In a Different Voice*. Cambridge, Mass.: Harvard University Press, 1982.

Griffith, J., and Chapman, D. "Learning Context Question-naire." Unpublished paper, Davidson College, 1982.

Katz, J. (ed.). *Teaching as Though Students Mattered*. New Directions in Teaching and Learning, no. 21. San Francisco: Jossey-Bass, 1985.

Kohlberg, L. "Stage and Sequence: The Cognitive Developmental Approach to Socialization." In D. Goslin (ed.), *Handbook of Socialization Theory and Research*. Skokie, Ill.: Rand McNally, 1969.

Kolb, D. "Learning Styles and Disciplinary Differences." In A. W. Chickering and Associates, *The Modern American College: Responding to the New Realities of Diverse Students and a Changing Society*. San Francisco: Jossey-Bass, 1981.

Lawrence, G. *People Types and Tiger Stripes*. Gainesville, Fla.: Center for Application of Psychological Type, 1979.

Messick, S., and Associates. *Individuality in Learning: Implications of Cognitive Styles and Creativity for Human Development*. San Francisco: Jossey-Bass, 1976.

Myers, I. B. *The Myers-Briggs Type Indicator*. Palo Alto, Calif.: Consulting Psychologists Press, 1962.

Perry, W. *Forms of Ethical and Intellectual Development in the College Years*. New York: Holt, Rinehart & Winston, 1968.

Perry, W. G. "Cognitive and Ethical Growth: The Making of Meaning." In A. W. Chickering and Associates, *The Modern American College: Responding to the New Realities of Diverse Students and a Changing Society*. San Francisco: Jossey-Bass, 1981.

Watkins, N. "The Individual in Society: The Interdisciplinary Studies Program." In J. Fried (ed.), *Education for Student Development*. New Directions for Student Services, no. 15. San Francisco: Jossey-Bass, 1981.

Widick, C., Knefelkamp, L., and Parker, C. "The Counselor as Developmental Instructor." *Counselor Education and Supervision*, 1975, *14*, 286–296.

Witkin, H. "Field Dependence and Field Independence in Cognitive Styles." *Review of Educational Research*, 1977, *47*, 1–64.

Witkin, H. "Cognitive Styles: Essence and Origin." *Psychological Issues*, 1981 (entire issue 51).

Chapter Fourteen

Counseling and Advising

Roger B. Winston, Jr.

As E. G. Williamson (1939) observed almost fifty years ago, all students have problems that the college or university can and should help them address. Likewise, C. Gilbert Wrenn, another pioneer in the student affairs field, argued that ''the only justification for student personnel services is that they can be shown to meet the needs of students. . . . These include both the basic psychological needs of all young people and the specific needs that are the direct results of the college experience'' (1951, pp. 26–27).

There probably is no student affairs division in the country that has sufficient staff who specialize in counseling and advising to address the plethora of student needs, wants, and legitimate expectations for assistance. If a student affairs division is to satisfy Wrenn's (1951) raison d'être, then all or most of its staff must possess basic helping skills and utilize them in their daily interactions with students. This chapter is based on this premise. It addresses counseling and advising competencies from the perspective of the student affairs professional who may work in a wide variety of settings, such as student activities, housing, financial aid, international student services, and admissions. To use Delworth and Aulepp's (1976) conceptualization, this chapter is addressed to allied professional counselors and advisers—that is, those who are called on to provide counseling or advising assistance, but who do not view themselves, by reason of either academic preparation or the responsibilities of their position, as professional counselors or professional academic advisers.

Counseling skills are essential to the effective functioning of student affairs professionals at a variety of levels and settings. Entry-level professionals have opportunities to use counseling skills as they interact daily with students, generally in rather informal—that is, not structured or planned—counseling situations. To the extent that entry-level professionals are involved in the training and supervision of student paraprofessionals, they are called on to model and teach basic helping skills and strategies (Upcraft and Pilato, 1982; Ender, 1984; Winston, Ullom, and Werring, 1984). Surveys of student affairs leaders about their expectations of entry-level professionals' skills and competencies have consistently found that they expect knowledge and skills in counseling and advising (Newton and Richardson, 1976; Ostroth, 1981).

As student affairs professionals' careers advance, they tend to spend less time in direct contact with students and more time in interaction with staff members. The basic helping skills, however, are still needed; only the clientele changes. Several well-known leadership theorists (for example, Hersey and Blanchard, 1977; Blake, Mouton, and Williams, 1981) emphasize the essential skills of communicating care and concern to people, creating a supportive atmosphere, and sharing decision making as the foundations of effective organizational leadership. A working knowledge of basic helping skills and interventions greatly increases the leader's ability to create these kinds of relationships and social environments.

This chapter addresses the basic helping skills that all student affairs staff members should be expected to possess through presentation of the basic components of helping and models for understanding the helping process and for determining appropriate interventions (including making effective referrals). Developmental academic advising is defined and the roles and skills it requires are outlined. Ethical issues of particular pertinence to allied professional counselors and advisers are identified.

Components of the Helping Relationship

Carl Rogers (1957, 1961) initiated the great debate that has continued for thirty years about the necessary and sufficient conditions for assisting people in changing their behavior and attitudes. He argued that it is the character and attitudes of the helper that are crucial to facilitation of constructive change—much more so than the helper's knowledge and expertise. He asserted, "If I can provide a certain type of relationship, the other person will discover within himself the capacity to use that relationship for growth and change, and personal development will occur" (Rogers, 1961, p. 33). He identified three personal characteristics or necessary conditions that he considered to be of supreme importance: genuineness or congruence, unconditional positive regard or acceptance, and accurate empathic understanding.

Genuineness is the extent or degree to which the helper is nondefensive and authentic in the interaction with the person seeking help. Genuine helpers do not play roles, do not attempt to change or conceal their values from the help seeker, and are sincere.

Unconditional positive regard, or nonpossessive warmth, refers to the extent to which helpers communicate an attitude of nonevaluative caring and respect for the help seeker as a person. Rogers (1967) asserted that because it is likely that helpers will often encounter persons who hold contrary value systems, it is important that helpers be aware of their own values and beliefs and not to try to conceal them. To pretend acceptance interferes with the helping relationship; pretense can seldom be concealed from the person seeking help for extended periods of time (and destroys genuineness). Helpers, however, must be careful not to attempt to impose their values on the help seeker and not to communicate disrespect or disapproval for his or her values.

Empathy refers to the degree to which helpers communicate their awareness and understanding of another person's frame of reference and feelings in a language that is attuned to that person. Empathy involves two processes. First, helpers must understand the inner world (values, attitudes, and feelings) of the other person; next, they must communicate that understanding by using the other person's frame of reference in the dialogue. Branner and Shostrom (1982, p. 160) maintain that responding empathetically means trying to "think with, rather than for or about the client. It is also the capacity to respond to another's feelings and experiences as if they were your own."

Other theorists (Carkhuff, 1969; Egan, 1975; Ivey and Authier, 1978; Gazda and others, 1984) have also described the necessary conditions for creating a helping interaction. They depart somewhat from Rogerian philosophy by maintaining that effective helpers intentionally utilize specific, identifiable skills and that these skills can be taught and explained in a behavioral frame of reference. Unlike Rogers, who emphasized the primacy of being a certain kind of person, they argue that successful helping involves behaving in certain ways and employing certain techniques. These skills and techniques include concreteness, self-disclosure, immediacy, and confrontation.

Concreteness refers to the helper assisting the help seeker in identifying specifically the feelings that are associated with the experiences being described. The helper's task is to assist help seekers in converting vague statements about themselves and their concerns into concrete expressions.

Self-disclosure involves the judicious revelation of the helper's past or present situation as a means of communicating understanding of the help seekers' concerns and of offering reassurance about the help seekers' ability to deal with problems. There is the danger, however, that the helper through self-disclosure may begin to focus on his or her needs rather than those of the help seekers. As Gazda and his colleagues (1984, p. 16) noted, "When helper self-disclosure is premature or irrelevant to the [help seeker's] problem, it tends to confuse the [help seeker] or put the focus on the helper. The helper steals the spotlight." Self-disclosure, if used appropriately and timed sagaciously, can model behaviors that the help seekers may find useful in changing their attitudes and behaviors.

Immediacy is a form of self-disclosure that deals with what is going on between helper and person seeking help at the present moment. Its principal value is to facilitate the help seekers' becoming more aware of their behaviors in the relationship and to assist them in bringing into the open unverbalized thoughts and feelings associated with the helper. It is a powerful tool that can be effective only after a trusting relationship has been developed. If inappropriately timed, immediacy may frighten help seekers and lead to premature termination of the relationship.

Finally, confrontation is viewed as an action tool that invites help seekers to examine their behaviors and attitudes more carefully and to become aware of discrepancies between affect or words and behavior. Its purpose is to assist help seekers in coming to grips with the reality of the situation. To be effective, confrontation must be preceded by the establishment of a caring and trusting relationship. Corey (1982, p. 90) asserted that confrontation is an invitation to look at the "discrepancies between attitudes, thoughts, or behaviors. Confrontation that is done in a tentative (yet direct and honest) manner can be an extension of caring and respect for clients. It can encourage them to examine certain incongruities and to become aware of . . . ways that they might be blocking their personal strengths." We must emphasize that confrontation can be effective only after helpers and help seekers have established firm relationships committed to solving problems. If used prematurely, it can often be perceived by the person seeking help as either an attack or a personal rejection, and it will usually lead to termination of the relationship without resolution of the problems.

Carkhuff (1969) proposed a four-phase model of the helping relationship, shown in Figure 1. Although somewhat oversimplified, this model has proven effective as the basis for initial training of professional, paraprofessional, and allied professional counselors.

The initial phase, Pre-Helping, calls for the helper to *attend* to the help seeker as she or he begins to talk about concerns. Attending requires the helper to assume a posture that reflects concentration on and concern for what the person seeking help is saying and feeling, "to observe the context, appear-

Figure 1. Basic Helping Model.

Phases of Helping:	Pre-Helping	Phase I	Phase II	Phase III
Helper:	Attending	Responding	Personalizing	Initiating
Helpee:	Involving	Exploring	Understanding	Acting

Source: Anthony and Vitalo, 1982, p. 70.

ance, and behavior of the [help seeker] for cues to the [help seeker's] physical, emotional, and intellectual state," and to listen for content, feeling, and meaning—"the reason for the [help seeker] feeling as he or she does" (Anthony and Vitalo, 1982, p. 70). This *involves* the helper and the help seeker in a mutual effort to deal with the help seeker's concerns or problems and clearly communicates the helper's interest and desire to be of assistance.

Phase I calls for the helper to use *responding* skills to communicate to the help seeker that the helper understands the content, feeling, and meaning of the help seeker's message. The Carkhuff training model involves using the now familiar "You feel_____because_____" type of statement. This assists the help seekers in *exploring* themselves and their problems more fully. Often help seekers develop important insights into themselves when they hear a concerned person orally expressing what they had been feeling but either were unaware of or were unwilling to acknowledge to themselves. Responding may also help troubled persons discover feelings that they have been attempting to suppress or deny.

In Phase II, the helper attempts to *personalize* the problem—to make the help seeker *understand* his or her responsibility for the state of affairs that she or he is experiencing. "Personalizing the problem means developing the response deficit or vulnerability that the [help seeker] experiences by making the [help seeker] directly accountable for the problem he or she is having" (Anthony and Vitalo, 1982, p. 72). Typical statements include "You feel_____because you_____" or "because you cannot_____." For example, "You feel disappointed in yourself because you didn't take preparation for the test seriously enough." This may be expanded to responses such as, "You feel_____because you cannot_____and you want to_____." For example, "You feel confused because when you asked Mary for a date after she seemed so friendly, she not only refused but 'put you down' as well, and you want to know why you misread her interest in you so badly." The latter kind of response can bring about the help seeker's transition from understanding his or her problem to actively beginning to establish goals and make plans for accomplishing them. As Anthony and Vitalo (1982, p. 73) comment, "The ultimate test of the helper's personalizing skills is the level of self-understanding the [help seeker] achieves concerning what he or she wants to achieve in the world."

Phase III calls for *initiating,* or assisting the help seeker in specifying goals, making plans for accomplishing them, and moving toward *acting.* It is important that the helper remain aware that the goals are the help seeker's, not the helper's; if a goal is to be accomplished, the person seeking help must "own it" and must approach its accomplishment in ways that fit into his or her typical life pattern. The helper is in something of a teaching role but nevertheless must assist the help seeker in moving to act in ways the help seeker feels most comfortable with, even if they are not the most efficient ways.

Most effective helpers possess these basic skills, whether or not they subscribe to this particular model. Some people are somewhat offended by use of "formula" phrases such as "You feel_____because_____." On the other hand, one can appreciate the importance and therapeutic benefits of establishing a relationship between helper and help seeker, as advocated by Rogers, without accepting all the baggage Rogers attached to it. There is substantial research, however, that documents the effectiveness of this type of model for teaching would-be helpers basic helping skills (Carkhuff, 1969; Kasdorf and Gustafson, 1978; Lambert, 1982). We contend that basic helping skills are learned (through extensive practice accompanied by critical feed-back) and that student affairs practitioners should master them as part of a repertoire of essential student development and administrative-management interventions.

Application of Helping Skills

One of the essential tasks the allied professional counselor must accomplish when dealing with issues or concerns that a student has been unable to resolve satisfactorily is to make an assessment of the person and the situation or context. The counselor must determine the nature of the student's problems and then decide whether he or she can and should offer assistance or whether more expertise is required.

Central to the process of making an assessment is how students' problems and concerns are conceptualized. As shown in Figure 2, students' concerns can be arrayed on a continuum, one end of which is anchored by developmental concerns and the other end by remedial concerns (Ender and Winston, 1982).

Developmental Concerns. Developmental concerns are issues or problems that basically effective persons encounter. They may have one or several of the following clues or charac-teristics: they have been predicted by developmental theory, they are related to the student's present situation, they center on in-terpersonal relationships or a skill or knowledge deficit, they do not incapacitate the student, and the student is willing to address the concerns.

The concern may be predicted by developmental theory as one that is appropriate or expected for a student of a given age or level of educational experience. For instance, an enter-ing freshman at a residential college who is homesick the first few days or weeks of the first term is experiencing appropriate feelings that are shared by many classmates.

The concern may be directly or indirectly related to the present environment; its genesis is in the present. In other words, the student has encountered a situation that requires new re-sponses, and he or she is in the process of analyzing the situation and deciding on or trying out new ways of coping or reacting.

Figure 2. Conceptualizing Students' Concerns.

Range of Students' Concerns

| Developmental Concerns | Unclear Concerns | Remedial Concerns |

<---------------------- ============= ---------------------->

Characteristics or Cues | *Characteristics or Cues* | *Characteristics or Cues*

Developmental Concerns

- Behavior or issues predicted by developmental theory as appropriate to age, stage, or level

- Concern is directly or indirectly related to present environment

- Problem is interpersonal or skill/knowledge-oriented

- Student is basically coping with the situation, though not to his or her satisfaction

- Student is able and willing to initiate action

Unclear Concerns

- Problem appears to be a mixture of developmental and remedial concerns

- Student is unable to identify source of problem or concern, which may be expressed as general dissatisfaction with life or the institution

- Presenting problem is incongruent with level or intensity of emotion expressed or with nonverbal behavior

- Student is unable to analyze own behavior realistically

- Student is unable to formulate realistic, coherent plans of action

- Student shows lack of motivation to address problems

- Student blames others excessively

- Student pours out confused or rambling monologue

Remedial Concerns

- Behavior is not consistent with developmental theory's projections for student of that stage, age, or educational level

- Student is dysfunctional in meeting daily responsibilities

- Problem is centered in past or basically unrelated to present environment and current experiences

- Concern is intrapersonal

- Persistent pattern of self-defeating or self-destructive behavior is evident

- Student indicates intention to do harm to self or others

- Student reports persistent, chronic depression, anxiety, physical illness, pain, or discomfort, or has experienced trauma

- Student has highly unrealistic self-image or self-assessment

Source: Adapted from Ender and Winston, 1982.

For example, a sophomore who has not yet crystallized a decision about academic specialization is facing the college's requirement that he specify a major field of study. The environment has imposed a decision on him.

A developmental problem may also concern interpersonal relationships or be caused by deficits in skill or knowledge. If a student's difficulty in mastering the content of a history course can be addressed by acquiring more information, spending more time on assignments, or acquiring new academic skills, the concern is developmental in nature. Likewise, a student's difficulties in an interpersonal relationship—such as with her boyfriend or roommate—can be classified as developmental if they are not chronic and are identifiable with a particular issue or incident that occurred in the immediate or short-term past.

The student may be coping with the situation, although not to his or her satisfaction. Blocher (1987) describes coping as having control over large segments of the long-term transactions with the environment, although there may be a lack of satisfactory control over short-term transactions. "Behavior is purposeful and largely goal-oriented. . . . Problems and difficulties tend to be readily identifiable in terms of specific roles or relationships" (p. 155). For example, Juan is considering getting married, but his parents disapprove of his chosen mate and think that he is too young to get married. Juan is torn between a desire to comply with his parents' wishes and a desire to be autonomous and make his own decisions. Juan's problem can be classified as developmental if Juan is able to listen to his parents' concerns and appreciate their point of view, while not allowing it to interfere with his meeting academic demands or force him to terminate the relationship. While the situation is not comfortable, Juan is able to cope as he searches for a solution.

Finally, the student must be able and willing to initiate action to deal with the concern. The student recognizes the demands that the environment makes and is willing to face those demands by altering her or his behavior, seeking assistance from someone, or initiating a project to deal with the situation. For example, Helen is having difficulty in an English course, even though she has used the same study techniques and routines that she has found effective in other English courses. She recognizes that she is not doing well and searches the environment for sources of help. A critical element that makes this a developmental concern is that she wants to take action; she does not attempt to deny the problem in the hope that it will disappear or seek unproductive ways of reducing the stress associated with it, such as cutting class.

Remedial Concerns. At the opposite end of the continuum from developmental concerns are remedial concerns. Several characteristics or cues help define or identify concerns as remedial: the student's behavior is inconsistent with developmental theory, the student is dysfunctional in daily life, the problem is centered in the past, the student has chronic psychological or physical complaints or has suffered trauma, the problem appears to be based on intrapersonal conflicts, or the student is suicidal.

Behavior or reported feelings may be inconsistent with developmental theory's prediction for a person of that age or educational level. For example, Bob, a college junior, has been unable to establish a dating relationship with anyone in either high school or college. He is not performing as developmental theory predicts for someone his age in terms of interpersonal relationships; his concern is remedial in nature. (The same concern encountered by Bob as a high school sophomore, however, would probably be developmental.)

The student may be dysfunctional in meeting daily responsibilities. Students who are unable to function well enough to eat regular meals, sleep at night, attend classes, and maintain personal hygiene are operating in a remedial condition. Often this dysfunctional behavior is obviously accompanied or caused by excessive use of alcohol or other drugs. It is generally not wise, however, for an allied professional counselor to attempt a "diagnosis" of the causes of these dysfunctional behavior patterns.

Problems that are centered in the past or are basically unrelated to the current environment are clues to remedial concerns. Students whose present unproductive behavior is an extension of past dysfunctional behavior are operating in a remedial mode. For instance, Bob's inability to establish dating relationships predated his entry into college and is basically unaffected by the college environment. His problem is not simply lacking a date this term. His problems in interpersonal relationships have a long history and are evidence of a persistent pattern of ineffective or self-defeating behavior.

Other clues that a student is functioning in a remedial mode include reports of persistent, chronic depression, anxiety, or physical illness, pain, and discomfort that do not seem to have an organic, medical explanation. Students who hold highly unrealistic self-images or self-assessments often act in a highly eccentric or alienating fashion that may be the result of developmental deficiencies. Likewise, students who are frequently involved in acrimonious or hostile interactions (sometimes even physical assaults) with peers are operating in a remedial mode. Students who are addicted to alcohol or other drugs or who experience eating disorders such as bulimia or anorexia are dealing with remedial concerns; they require the assistance of professionals skilled in treatment of those specific illnesses. Likewise, students who have been attacked or sexually molested or have experienced other highly traumatic events generally require professional psychological services. These behaviors or events are outside the typical developmental pattern for most college students.

A problem that is basically intrapersonal in nature is another clue to remedial concerns. Such problems involve deep-seated internal conflicts that interfere with students' ability to be purposive in their behavior or to find personal satisfaction in any activities. Long-standing feelings of inferiority, low self-esteem, and anxiety attacks fall into this category. Treatment of this kind of problem is generally lengthy and requires intensive therapy by highly skilled professionals.

Students who report the intention to harm others physically or who threaten suicide exhibit behaviors that result from remedial concerns. Bernard and Bernard (1985) suggest a number of indicators that identify students who have a relatively high or increased likelihood of attempting suicide: a family history of suicide; previous attempts at suicide; having lost a parent through death, divorce, or separation, especially if the loss led to destabilization of the family; reports of feelings of being a burden, useless, or hopeless; giving away prized possessions or putting personal affairs in order, especially after the loss of a loved one, pet, or job; and a prolonged state of agitated depression.

Unclear Concerns. Unfortunately, most encounters with students and their concerns do not obviously fall at either extreme of the continuum; they are not easily classified as developmental or remedial. When allied professionals listen to students talk about their concerns or problems, they typically hear a mixture of both remedial and developmental concerns and considerable confusion and ambiguity. A number of clues alert the helper to the unclear nature of the student's concerns. First, the student is unable to identify the source of his or her concern; the student expresses a vague or pervasive dissatisfaction with life or the total educational experience without naming specific problems. Second, there is a lack of congruence between the presenting problem and the intensity of emotion or nonverbal behavior. For example, a student may complain about making a poor grade on a minor test, while behaving in a highly emotionally disturbed manner. The importance of the concern expressed is obviously incongruent with the level of emotion evident.

Third, students seem unable to analyze their own behavior realistically. For example, Frank may complain about hallmates being unfriendly, while he rejects their invitations to eat in the dining room or to engage in informal bull sessions on the hall. Fourth, students are not motivated to address concerns or are unable to formulate realistic plans of action. They talk about their problems, but when encouraged to try various approaches to dealing with them, they seem reluctant or make excuses to justify inaction. Fifth, students blame others excessively. Whatever the issue, the student finds the responsibility belongs to someone else; it is never the student's fault. Finally, one of the most frequently encountered clues that a student's concerns are unclear (both to the student and to the helper) is a confused and rambling monologue that cannot be focused. The student pours out a mass of issues, concerns, problems, fears, and seemingly irrelevant facts, accompanied by a relatively high level of emotion.

Assessing the Nature of Students' Concerns. The allied professional counselor needs to assess the nature of students' concerns as a means to formulating an appropriate response or plan of action. Blocher (1966), however, has cautioned that assessment or diagnosis is most effective when it is continuous and tentative. He also asserts that assessment is not a distinct stage in the helping process but rather is continuous. Assessments must be altered, checked, revalidated, and revised often as the helper carefully listens to the student, thereby gaining a better understanding of the student's ways of viewing the world and the context or environment of his or her concerns. Blocher also warns that helpers must always view their assessments as hypothetical and therefore tentative. If the model of the student and the student's concerns becomes frozen and new observations are shut out, the helper's responses become inappropriate and can lead to premature termination of the relationship or inappropriate (unhelpful) action by the helper.

Gazda and others (1984) suggest that students come to a helper with four basic requests: for information, for appropriate action, for inappropriate action or interaction, or for understanding and involvement. The first, a request for information, is relatively simple. The helper tells the student what he or she wants to know or informs the student where the information is available. The second request, for appropriate action, is also relatively straightforward. The helper does what is requested. These two requests, however, can also present themselves in less straightforward ways. For instance, students are sometimes embarrassed because they do not know something. Rather than simply ask for information, they hint around the subject in the hope that the helper will volunteer the information. The same is true for a request for action; students will sometimes describe their needs to the helper rather than simply request assistance. For example, a student wanders into a residence hall office and begins talking about waiting for her roommate to return with the key to the room. She is describing her need to get into her room in the hope that the helper will volunteer to unlock her door without the student having to ask (which might result in being turned down or being called "irresponsible").

On some occasions students will seek out a helper with a request for inappropriate action. This may take a number of forms; students may ask the helper to excuse them from a college regulation, to overlook a rule, or to "solve" their problems for them—"Tell my mother the college requires me to stay here this weekend." Helpers must discriminate between requests for appropriate and inappropriate action. When the helper encounters an inappropriate request, the helper must tactfully explain why the request is not appropriate, while also reassuring the student that the helper cares about the student's welfare. The helper must communicate clearly to the student that the refusal of a request is not a rejection of the person making the request.

Finally, students often seek out allied professional counselors with a request for understanding and involvement. Sometimes this is explicit—"I have a problem that is really bothering me. Will you help me?" More often, however, students approach their important concerns gradually, testing the helper's receptiveness and skill as they move closer to the real issues. Often students bring a "safe" presenting problem to an allied professional helper—which may appear simply as a request for information—as a means of establishing contact with the helper and gauging the helper's openness to helping, trustworthiness, and competence. When they become convinced that the helper can handle the issues, the students will reveal their more significant concerns. The helper, however, must first earn the right to be of assistance. The helper earns the right to help by communicating a willingness to become involved in addressing the student's problems, by listening carefully to both the content and affect of the student's "message," and by demonstrating an understanding and appreciation of the student's situation and perspectives.

When an allied professional counselor encounters a student who requests information or action, either directly or indirectly, the counselor should listen carefully to assess the nature of the concern. As Figure 1 shows, the counselor first engages the student in self-exploration and problem exploration. The nature of the concern must be determined; this is best accomplished by attending and using interchangeable responses.

If the concern is simply a straightforward request for information or action, the counselor complies with the request. If there is uncertainty or the nature of the concern is unclear, the counselor assists the student in exploration as the counselor attempts to understand the concern and to see where it falls on the continuum (see Figure 2). If the concern is developmental, the allied professional counselor should be able to assist the student in initiating action to deal with the issues. If the concern is remedial, the allied professional counselor will need to make a referral to someone with greater expertise or more time to devote to the student.

Counseling Interventions. Once the allied professional counselor and the student have explored the student's concerns, there comes a time for action. Figure 3 summarizes actions that may be initiated, depending upon the assessed nature of the student's concerns and the skills and knowledge of the counselor.

If the concerns are basically developmental in nature, the counselor generally should be able to offer a variety of helpful interventions. These include: (1) further self-exploration or problem exploration, (2) identification of possible goals and alternative means of addressing them, (3) identification of resources available on the campus or in the community, (4) provision of information or identification of information sources on the campus, (5) referral to agencies that have programs already established to address the student's concerns, (6) providing encouragement, reassurance, and support, and (7) teaching specific skills or strategies, such as simple study techniques, time management strategies, goal-setting processes, stress reduction (relaxation) techniques, or social skills. These interventions may be offered informally, one-to-one, or through programs, such as intentionally structured groups (Winston, Bonney, Miller, and Dagley, 1988).

The allied professional counselor needs to act as a sounding board for the student if the concerns are unclear as a means of facilitating further exploration. This is done primarily through showing the student empathy, respect, and genuineness and a commitment to helping the student bring clarity to the present situation. Encouraging the student to become active in the

Figure 3. Conceptualizing Advising
and Counseling Interventions.

Range of Advising and Counseling Interventions

If Concern Is Developmental	If Nature of Concern Is Unclear	If Concern Is Remedial

◄———►

• Assist in self-exploration	• Act as a sounding board as a means of facilitating exploration of the concern	• Show concern and willingness to listen
• Explore alternatives		• Explore alternatives for addressing concern
• Assist in identifying desired goals	• Respond to student in ways that communicate empathy, respect, genuineness, and concern	
• Assist in devising a plan of action to accomplish goals		• Describe available resources for dealing with concern
• Identify resources and services	• Encourage active problem solving	• Offer information and assistance in initiating contact with appropriate referral source
• Provide information	• Confront student about incongruence between behavior or talk and actions	
• Teach specific strategies or techniques		• Offer encouragement and support
• Refer to established program especially designed to address issue	• Decide whether concerns are basically developmental or remedial in nature and proceed appropriately	• If there appears to be danger to self or others, take extraordinary measures to assure that student receives assistance from appropriate professionals
• Provide encouragement, reassurance, and support		
• Provide positive feedback		

Source: Adapted from Ender and Winston, 1982.

problem-solving process, expressing reassurance, and confronting incongruence (only after a firm, trusting relationship has been established) may be appropriate strategies for helping to clarify issues and associated feelings. These techniques, if applied with patience and sincerity, will usually allow both the student and the helper to determine the nature of the concern—whether developmental or remedial. If the concern is developmental, the counselor then may adopt one or more of the intervention strategies described previously; if it is remedial in nature, the counselor has the responsibility to assist the student in making contact with a campus or community agency that has the resources and staff expertise to help. It is important that the student be assisted in getting help, not just told to "see Dr. X" or "call Office Y for an appointment."

Referral. Allied professional counselors should refer students when (1) the concerns are clearly remedial in nature, (2) the student's need for attention far exceeds the time available, (3) the counselor knows or interacts with the student on a personal basis, (4) after considerable effort, the student seems unable to verbalize his or her own problem, (5) there is evidence that the student plans to do harm to himself or herself or to others, (6) there is reason to believe that the problem is at least partly due to a medical condition or illness, or (7) there is no progress toward behavior change after a reasonable period of time. Even more important than knowing when to make a referral is knowing how to make a referral.

The first goal in making a successful referral is to communicate two things to the student. First, the referral is suggested because the helper cares and wants the student to get help, not because the helper wants to get rid of the student. Second, referral does not mean that the student is "sick," abnormal, or in serious trouble. Specificity is highly desirable when making referrals; that is, the student needs to know exactly where to go, whom to contact, and what to request. If the person making the referral is mistaken or misinformed and the referred students are unable to locate the appropriate source of help, they may give up because they feel like they are getting the "old college runaround." Many students, especially first-generation college students, are reluctant to seek help because the system appears intimidating. They do not know what to expect when they enter an office and will avoid dealing with their concerns because they have visions of having to tell a receptionist all their personal problems. It may be helpful to explain to students exactly what they will encounter when they first set foot in the office and help them work out what they will say to the receptionist. If the agency is structured to handle it, a referral to a particular person is most desirable, especially when the counselor can cite personal observations about that professional's qualifications and personality. When appointments must be made, the allied professional counselor may offer his or her telephone as a means of supporting the student through the initial steps of taking action.

Both ethically and legally, student affairs professionals have the responsibility to take action when they have reason to believe that a student is suicidal or intends to harm another person (American College Personnel Association, 1981). In such instances, the allied professional counselor must take whatever steps are necessary to ensure that the student receives the help required. Each campus should have a suicide response plan that is disseminated to all staff members (professional, paraprofessional, and support). Likewise, the campus should have a plan for dealing with situations when a college representative learns of threats to others' safety or property.

Academic Advising

Many of the skills and competencies required of the allied professional counselor are also needed by the academic adviser, if the academic advising process is conceived of as more than completing class schedules and other administrative forms. Academic advising has received renewed attention in the 1980s, owing in large measure to the need to address the problem of student retention. Academic advising has been the single most frequently utilized strategy to increase student retention (Beal and Noel, 1980; Forrest, 1985; Crockett, 1978, 1985). Anderson (1985) has argued that one of the most powerful positive influences on student persistence in college is individual attention. He asserts that this attention can be expressed through helping students identify and clarify their reasons for attending college, affirm themselves as persons who possess the potential to be successful, deal with anxiety and patterns of self-defeating behaviors, and find reinforcement of their determination to persist. Given the current organizational structures and political realities on most campuses, the academic advising process seems to be the only existing structure available to address these goals in large-scale, systematic ways.

Academic advising belongs to the academic sector in most institutions, especially four-year colleges and universities. Crockett and Levitz (1984) found that on 80 percent of the campuses surveyed, academic advising is provided by faculty members who are uncritically selected (or not selected at all—everyone does it), who receive little or no training, who are not systematically evaluated, and who are generally unrecognized and unrewarded for good performance. There continues to be steady movement toward creation of advising centers (predominantly at public institutions) that are staffed totally or in part by personnel with educational preparation and experience as student development specialists. However, there is a truism about academic advising: no one but students cares about academic advising until someone shows an interest in making changes.

It has been argued, however, that academic advising can and should be viewed as a potent intervention for influencing positively the educational and personal development of students (Walsh, 1979; Ender, Winston, and Miller, 1982, 1984). This kind of advising has been called ''developmental academic advising'' to distinguish it from the mechanical, clerkish activities presently identified as ''academic advising'' on many campuses. ''*Developmental academic advising* is defined as a systematic process based on a close student-advisor relationship intended to aid students in achieving educational, career, and personal goals through the utilization of the full range of institutional and community resources. It both stimulates and supports students in their quest for an enriched quality of life. . . . Developmental advising relationships focus on identifying and accomplishing

life goals, acquiring skills and attitudes that promote intellectual and personal growth, and sharing concerns for each other
and for the academic community" (Ender, Winston, and Miller,
1984, pp. 18–19). The goals of developmental academic advising are indistinguishable from the goals of most progressive student affairs divisions. In order to be realized, however, they
require active collaboration between academic affairs and student affairs; neither can accomplish these goals alone (Grites,
1979; Winston, Grites, Miller, and Ender, 1984).

Ender, Winston, and Miller (1984) propose seven conditions or principles that are essential in the developmental
academic advising process. First, advising is a continuous process with an accumulation of personal contacts that have a synergistic effect. Second, advising must concern itself with quality-
of-life issues; the adviser's responsibility includes attention to
the student's total experience in the institution. Third, advising is goal-related; that is, the advising process should include
identification of academic, career, and personal goals as they
relate to the college environment. Fourth, advising requires the
establishment of a caring relationship, which the adviser has
primary responsibility for initiating. Good academic advising
is intrusive. Fifth, advisers are models for the students with
whom they have contact. Sixth, advising is a focal point for the
integration of the services and expertise of both academic and
student affairs professionals. Seventh, advisers should encourage
students to utilize the full range of resources, services, and learning opportunities available within the institution.

Unfortunately, on many campuses the focus has often
been on who provides advising (and therefore has control of it),
rather than on what goes on in advising or how effectively it
is addressing the needs and concerns of students. Some advocates
of developmental advising have met resistance from academicians who charge that the advocates of change are attempting
to make advising into counseling or psychotherapy. This is untrue, or at least should be. Academic advising is not and should
not be viewed as "counseling." As Walsh (1979, p. 447) noted,
advising "should not be confused with either psychotherapy or
personal counseling. The focus of advisement remains a student's

academic self, not simply in the narrow sense of one who absorbs knowledge, takes courses, and completes requirements, but in the broader sense, which includes the integration of the academic self with one's other selves.'' While advising should not be equated with counseling, successful advisers need to understand and use some basic interpersonal communications and counseling skills.

If we change our focus from who advises and look instead at the skills, knowledge, and competencies developmental advisers need, we see considerable overlap with those needed by allied professional counselors. Identified below are the minimum skills and knowledge both allied professional counselors and academic advisers need.

Counselors and advisers need a clear understanding of the institution's philosophy and mission and should be able to articulate it to students. Ironically, we often assume that students enter our institutions with a full understanding of the purposes of higher education and with a commitment to the ideals on which it is based. It is unrealistic to expect students to take full advantage of the opportunities for intellectual, esthetic, moral, and psychosocial growth without some assistance and direction from the institution. Advisers and counselors should educate students about the opportunities available in the college environment and should promote the ideals of an educated person. They have the responsibility to encourage and assist students in making personal meaning of their educational experiences.

Both counselors and advisers need a working knowledge of college student development theories. They need to understand both themselves as developing persons and the students with whom they work (Thomas and Chickering, 1984). It is essential that they know what would be expected for a person of a particular age and educational experience level; it is particularly important that counselors and advisers be able to classify behavior patterns within a theoretical framework.

Advisers and counselors need to understand the student population with whom they have contact. As Wright (1987) has pointed out, most theories of student development have not taken adequate notice of the unique environments from which many minority students come and the forces that influence their development. Likewise, Gilligan (1982), Straub and Rodgers (1986), and Straub (1987) have demonstrated that women have some unique perspectives and that their development is not identical to that of men. Chickering and Havighurst (1981) have also pointed out the importance of understanding the older, returning adult students as well. These differences need to be understood by counselors and advisers.

Students have a right to expect both counselors and advisers to be knowledgeable about the institution's rules, regulations, and policies. From a student's point of view, the only thing worse than not knowing is being given incorrect information. Even in small institutions, remaining informed and current is a task that requires constant attention. Conscious efforts must be made to seek out information; it is very easy to assume that nothing outside one's own department changes.

Advisers and allied professional counselors should not be expected to be measurement experts. However, they need to have a command of informal assessment techniques that allow them to make decisions about whether they should attempt to address a student's concern or make a referral. They should also be intelligent users of standardized assessment information. For example, advisers should understand and be able to interpret to students academically related measures such as standardized test scores and scores on any achievement or placement tests used by the institution.

Both advisers and counselors need to understand the basics of creating a helping relationship, described previously. Most professionals cannot predict or choose when they will be called upon to be a "helper." Opportunities are presented daily.

Counselors and advisers can provide valuable services by helping students identify their needs, offering support in addressing them, and making effective referrals to the appropriate campus or community services or programs. Most institutions have many potentially effective programs designed to assist students that are underutilized; students are simply unaware of them or are reluctant to initiate contact, owing to either a misconception about the program's services or resources or the perception of a stigma associated with the program ("only dumb or sick people go there").

Counselors and advisers need a repertoire of interventions appropriate to their functions. Advisers should be able to assist students who are having nonchronic problems managing their time, making decisions about majors, and employing effective study techniques, for example. Counselors should also be able to help students overcome nonchronic problems related to stress and anxiety and work through interpersonal relationship problems with peers, parents, and authority figures. Both counselors and advisers need to be knowledgeable about the career development process and to be skilled in assisting students in initiating activities that can lead to making satisfying decisions about academic majors and careers.

Ethical Issues

Student affairs practitioners and academic advisers outside the designated centers for providing psychological services (counseling, career, and mental health centers) who act in the role of counselor to students encounter several troubling practical ethical problems. Particularly important are issues related to confidentiality and determination of competence. The American College Personnel Association's statement of ethical standards (1981, p. 184) specifies that students should be informed about the limits that are placed on confidentiality. The problem, however, often comes in the way that students approach staff for help; students often present a problem that may not appear to have implications for confidentiality. Once the relationship is established, however, the student may make a radical, unanticipated shift in the content of her or his concerns and place the student affairs practitioner in a vulnerable position. For example, the student may acknowledge breaking rules that the staff member is required to enforce, or even committing serious criminal acts.

Another major ethical issue centers on the helper's competence. It is not uncommon for lonely, socially isolated students to "latch on" to a staff member, especially in residence halls, and to consume many hours talking about their feelings of alienation, rejection, and isolation. They often resist attempts to initiate action to change their situation and refuse referral to other agencies. The allied professional counselor or academic adviser may feel that these students have definite remedial concerns and that his or her counseling competence is not adequate to address the students' problems. What is the staff member to do, however, when a student refuses referral and continues to hang around the staff member's office or living quarters?

Academic advisers who also teach often encounter thorny ethical issues. For example, when a student seeks help from an adviser, in the course of their interaction the adviser may learn of personal problems or academic irregularities that cause conflict for the adviser when the time comes to make evaluations in terms of grades. Adviser-teachers may be caught in a conflict of roles before they can take action to avoid it.

These problems do not have simple answers. It is generally desirable for staff members who have frequent, informal contact with students (especially in residence halls, student organizations, student unions, or academic classes or advising sessions) to make a point in group presentations about the limits of confidentiality students can expect and about the parameters of action and the responsibilities of each role the staff member plays. Allied professional counselors and advisers should seek consultation with mental health professionals and with their supervisors when they encounter problems. Alerting students to the limits of action and confidentiality inherent in the professional position is an important first step. This is an ideal, however, that is often difficult to realize, given the pressures of time and the peripatetic way that students often choose to initiate counseling relationships.

Summary

We have difficulty defending student affairs practice as a profession that requires specialized education and warrants minimum standards for entry (such as graduate degrees) and recognition as a specialty in higher education unless it can be demonstrated that the practitioners contribute directly to the education and personal enrichment of students. Well-developed skills and extensive knowledge in the areas of counseling and advising are essential tools in student affairs professionals' repertoire of responses and interventions, no matter what the primary responsibilities of their positions.

These skills, however, require development and constant attention. While some people have "natural helping skills," those native skills are seldom sufficient to meet the myriad concerns of college students—concerns with which they have a right to expect assistance and support. Only through extensive education and practicum, followed by periodic evaluation and feedback, can student services professionals hope to learn and maintain the counseling and advising skills they need to serve students well.

References

American College Personnel Association. "Statement of Ethical and Professional Standards." *Journal of College Student Personnel*, 1981, *22*, 184–189.

Anderson, E. C. "Forces Influencing Student Persistence and Achievement." In L. Noel, R. Levitz, D. Saluri, and Associates, *Increasing Student Retention: Effective Programs and Practices for Reducing the Dropout Rate*. San Francisco: Jossey-Bass, 1985.

Anthony, W. A., and Vitalo, R. L. "Human Resource Development Model." In E. K. Marshall, P. D. Kurtz, and Associates, *Interpersonal Helping Skills: A Guide to Training Methods, Programs, and Resources*. San Francisco: Jossey-Bass, 1982.

Beal, P. E., and Noel, L. *What Works in Student Retention*. Iowa City, Iowa: American College Testing Program, 1980.

Bernard, M. L., and Bernard, J. L. "Suicide on Campus: Response to the Problem." In E. S. Zinner (ed.), *Coping with Death on Campus*. New Directions for Student Services, no. 31. San Francisco: Jossey-Bass, 1985.

Blake, R. R., Mouton, J. S., and Williams, M. S. *The Academic Administrator Grid: A Guide to Developing Effective Management Teams*. San Francisco: Jossey-Bass, 1981.

Blocher, D. H. *Developmental Counseling*. New York: Ronald Press, 1966.

Blocher, D. H. *The Professional Counselor*. New York: Macmillan, 1987.

Branner, L. M., and Shostrom, E. L. *Therapeutic Psychology: Fundamentals of Counseling and Psychotherapy*. (4th ed.) Englewood Cliffs, N.J.: Prentice-Hall, 1982.

Carkhuff, R. R. *Helping and Human Relations: A Primer for Lay and Professional Helpers*. 2 vols. New York: Holt, Rinehart & Winston, 1969.

Chickering, A. W., and Havighurst, R. J. "The Life Cycle." In A. W. Chickering and Associates, *The Modern American College: Responding to the New Realities of Diverse Students and a Changing Society*. San Francisco: Jossey-Bass, 1981.

Corey, G. *Theory and Practice in Counseling and Psychotherapy*. (2nd ed.) Monterey Calif.: Brooks/Cole, 1982.

Crockett, D. S. "Academic Advising: Cornerstone of Student Retention." In L. Noel (ed.), *Reducing the Dropout Rate*. New Directions for Student Services, no. 3. San Francisco: Jossey-Bass, 1978.

Crockett, D. S. "Academic Advising." In L. Noel, R. Levitz, D. Saluri, and Associates, *Increasing Student Retention: Effective Programs and Practices for Reducing the Dropout Rate*. San Francisco: Jossey-Bass, 1985.

Crockett, D. S., and Levitz, R. S. "Current Advising Practices in Colleges and Universities." In R. B. Winston, Jr., T. K. Miller, S. C. Ender, T. J. Grites, and Associates, *Developmental Academic Advising: Addressing Students' Educational, Career, and Personal Needs*. San Francisco: Jossey-Bass, 1984.

Delworth, U., and Aulepp, L. *Training Manual for Paraprofessionals and Allied Professionals Programs*. Boulder, Colo.: Western Interstate Commission for Higher Education, 1976.

Egan, G. *The Skilled Helper*. Monterey, Calif.: Brooks/Cole, 1975.

Ender, S. C. "Student Paraprofessionals Within Student Affairs: The State of the Art." In S. C. Ender and R. B. Winston, Jr. (eds.), *Students as Paraprofessional Staff.* New Directions for Student Services, no. 27. San Francisco: Jossey-Bass, 1984.

Ender, S. C., and Winston, R. B., Jr. "Training Allied Professional Academic Advisors." In R. B. Winston, Jr., S. C. Ender, and T. K. Miller (eds.), *Developmental Approaches to Academic Advising.* New Directions for Student Services, no. 17. San Francisco: Jossey-Bass, 1982.

Ender, S. C., Winston, R. B., Jr., and Miller, T. K. "Academic Advising as Student Development." In R. B. Winston, Jr., S. C. Ender, and T. K. Miller (eds.), *Developmental Approaches to Academic Advising.* New Directions for Student Services, no. 17. San Francisco: Jossey-Bass, 1982.

Ender, S. C., Winston, R. B., Jr., and Miller, T. K. "Academic Advising Reconsidered." In R. B. Winston, Jr., T. K. Miller, S. C. Ender, T. J. Grites, and Associates, *Developmental Academic Advising: Addressing Students' Educational, Career, and Personal Needs.* San Francisco: Jossey-Bass, 1984.

Forrest, A. "Creating Conditions for Student and Institutional Success." In L. Noel, R. Levitz, D. Saluri, and Associates, *Increasing Student Retention: Effective Programs and Practices for Reducing the Dropout Rate.* San Francisco: Jossey-Bass, 1985.

Gazda, G. M., and others. *Human Relations Development: A Manual for Educators.* (3rd ed.) Newton, Mass.: Allyn & Bacon, 1984.

Gilligan, C. *In a Different Voice.* Cambridge, Mass.: Harvard University Press, 1982.

Grites, T. J. *Academic Advising: Getting Us Through the Eighties.* Washington, D.C.: American Association for Higher Education–Educational Resource Information Center, 1979.

Hersey, P., and Blanchard, K. H. *Management of Organizational Behavior: Utilizing Human Resources.* (3rd ed.) Englewood Cliffs, N.J.: Prentice-Hall, 1977.

Ivey, A. E., and Authier, J. *Microcounseling: Innovations in Interviewing, Counseling, Psychotherapy, and Psychoeducation.* (2nd ed.) Springfield, Ill.: Thomas, 1978.

Kasdorf, J., and Gustafson, K. "Research Related to Micro-training." In A. E. Ivey and J. Authier, *Microcounseling: Innovations in Interviewing, Counseling, Psychotherapy, and Psychoeducation.* (2nd ed.) Springfield, Ill.: Thomas, 1978.

Lambert, M. J. "Relations of Helping Skills to Treatment Outcome." In E. K. Marshall, P. D. Kurtz, and Associates, *Interpersonal Helping Skills: A Guide to Training Methods, Programs, and Resources.* San Francisco: Jossey-Bass, 1982.

Newton, F. B., and Richardson, R. L. "Expected Entry-Level Competencies of Student Personnel Workers." *Journal of College Student Personnel,* 1976, *17,* 426–430.

Ostroth, D. D. "Competencies for Entry-Level Professionals: What Do Employers Look for When Hiring New Staff?" *Journal of College Student Personnel,* 1981, *22,* 5–11.

Rogers, C. R. "The Necessary and Sufficient Conditions of Therapeutic Personality Change." *Journal of Consulting Psychology,* 1957, *21,* 95–103.

Rogers, C. R. *On Becoming a Person.* Boston: Houghton Mifflin, 1961.

Rogers, C. R. *Person to Person: The Problem of Being Human.* New York: Pocket Books, 1967.

Straub, C. A. "Women's Development of Autonomy and Chickering's Theory." *Journal of College Student Personnel,* 1987, *28,* 198–205.

Straub, C. A., and Rodgers, R. F. "An Exploration of Chickering's Theory and Women's Development." *Journal of College Student Personnel,* 1986, *27,* 216–224.

Thomas, R. E., and Chickering, A. W. "Foundations for Academic Advising." In R. B. Winston, Jr., T. K. Miller, S. C. Ender, T. J. Grites, and Associates, *Developmental Academic Advising: Addressing Students' Educational, Career, and Personal Needs.* San Francisco: Jossey-Bass, 1984.

Upcraft, M. L., and Pilato, G. T. *Residence Hall Assistants in College: A Guide to Selection, Training, and Supervision.* San Francisco: Jossey-Bass, 1982.

Walsh, E. M. "Revitalizing Academic Advisement." *Personnel and Guidance Journal,* 1979, *57,* 446–449.

Williamson, E. G. *How to Counsel Students: A Manual of Techniques for Clinical Counselors.* New York: McGraw-Hill, 1939.

Winston, R. B., Jr., Bonney, W. C., Miller, T. K., and Dagley, J. C. *Promoting Student Development Through Intentionally Structured Groups: Principles, Techniques, and Applications.* San Francisco: Jossey-Bass, 1988.

Winston, R. B., Jr., Grites, T. J., Miller, T. K., and Ender, S. C. "Improving Academic Advising." In R. B. Winston, Jr., T. K. Miller, S. C. Ender, T. J. Grites, and Associates, *Developmental Academic Advising: Addressing Students' Educational, Career, and Personal Needs.* San Francisco: Jossey-Bass, 1984.

Winston, R. B., Jr., Ullom, M. S., and Werring, C. J. "Student Paraprofessionals in Residence Halls." In S. C. Ender and R. B. Winston, Jr. (eds.), *Students as Paraprofessional Staff.* New Directions for Student Services, no. 27. San Francisco: Jossey-Bass, 1984.

Wrenn, C. G. *Student Personnel Work in College: With Emphasis on Counseling and Group Experiences.* New York: Ronald Press, 1951.

Wright, D. J. "Minority Students: Developmental Beginnings." In D. J. Wright (ed.), *Responding to the Needs of Today's Minority Students.* New Directions for Student Services, no. 38. San Francisco: Jossey-Bass, 1987.

Chapter Fifteen

Consultation

June Gallessich

Student affairs professionals have generally overlooked possibilities for increasing their impact on students through consultation with campus organizations. The purpose of this chapter is to develop a rationale for student services staff consultation and to identify and explore related issues and problems. Underlying the discussions in this chapter is the assumption that the basic responsibility of student services professionals is to provide direct services to students and that consultation should not be regarded as a substitute for these primary functions but rather as an expansion of them.

As the student services profession develops and continues to reexamine and redefine its roles and functions, new possibilities for serving students through consultation are being discovered. Some members of the profession are finding that, at times, they can help students most by going beyond the roles of "adjuster," "parent," and counselor to collaborate with faculty, staff, and administrators who are in continual contact with students and who have a profound impact on student welfare and development. The profession has always acknowledged that the major sources of many student problems are environmental; yet its philosophy, knowledge base, and skills have emphasized student adjustment rather than environmental adjustment and change. Student services staff members might greatly increase their impact by thinking in terms of multiple sources of problems and, prior to allocating resources, considering the advantages and disadvantages of an array of services, including consultation, to meet identified needs.

The profession has many competencies that can be valuable in helping other campus organizations serve students. First, it has a great store of substantive knowledge. Student affairs professionals are experts on students and are knowledgeable in such areas as adolescent development, student and campus characteristics, and students' personal and academic problems. Members of this profession know how to create, implement, and evaluate programs. They have research skills and are knowledgeable about campus administrative structures, political issues, and on- and off-campus student resources. They have also learned helping skills from work with students. These skills are useful in consultation. Student affairs professionals are also experienced in problem solving and conflict management and in organizing and leading student groups. These competencies can enhance consultation services to student-related organizations.

But consultation offers more than a means of helping other people and organizations serve students more effectively. As a result of collaborative interactions with other staff and faculty, student services professionals can gain enriched and expanded perspectives on the campus as a total system, important data for the planning, administering, and implementing of student services.

The chapter begins by describing consultation services that might be offered to faculty, staff, administrators, and student organizations. Next, consultation is defined and differentiated from other forms of service and other professional relationships. The special problems of the in-house consultant and their implications for student affairs professionals' consultation are followed by descriptions of crucial consultant skills and methods by which student affairs professionals can attain these skills. Legitimization, entry, contractual, and ethical issues are addressed.

Types of Consultation

Consultation can be a medium through which student services staff help others. In case consultation regarding individual students' problems, the major objective is to help consultees cope more effectively in a specific case; a second objective is to increase consultees' knowledge and skills in future work. For example, an engineering professor may ask the dean of students' office for assistance in understanding and responding to the special needs of a physically handicapped student who is having trouble taking lecture notes and performing laboratory and library assignments. Student services professionals can provide useful information about handicapped students' needs and resources that is potentially valuable to both student and professor. This consultation might also increase the professor's confidence in working with this student and others with special problems. Similarly, a resident assistant in a first-year residence may seek guidance from counseling center staff in working with a homesick, unhappy student who refuses to seek counseling. In the consultative process, the counselor's training and experience can help the young resident assistant understand the troubled student. The assistant's guidance skills may be increased through learning more about adolescent development, peer counseling techniques, campuswide resources, and methods for creating a healthful residence environment. As a result of consultation, the resident assistant would be better prepared for future work with students.

In either of these situations, consultation regarding individual students may lead to consultation regarding groups of students. The engineering professor may ask for assistance in managing several handicapped students or perhaps in helping foreign students or female students adjust to the department and its demands. The professor might ask colleagues to join conferences in which the consultant works with them regarding common student concerns. The resident assistant may ask for assistance with other troubled students or in managing entire groups of residents or for information regarding programs, activities, and other resources of interest to students. Subsequently, the residence staff might ask for group consultation regarding student problems and development.

Student affairs professionals also may be asked to consult by providing systematic information or training to faculty or other on-campus or off-campus student-concerned groups.

Included here are those workshops, discussion groups, seminars, and so forth that are held not for students but for those who serve students. Workshops and informal seminars led by student affairs professionals can contribute to the effectiveness of departmental faculty, campus community religious organizations, heads of student organizations, and the staff of YMCAs and foreign students' centers. The content might be drawn from numerous areas, such as the needs of special student groups, the "senior syndrome," stages in student development, optimal conditions for growth, indices of poor mental health, how to interview troubled students, changing student mores, and campus community resources.

The extensive experience of student affairs staff in the planning, implementation, and evaluation of their own programs is especially valuable in another service—program consultation. This service, which involves advising other groups on the development of their programs, is different from student services program development, which involves working within a student services division to plan and staff varied programs. The leaders of a student society may want help, for example, in surveying its members' needs or in designing, implementing, and evaluating programs to meet identified needs. Similarly, residence staff may want help in developing recreational programs for their residents. Departmental faculty may ask for help in planning a career advising program. A graduate school might ask for help in planning activities to include students' spouses as a means of alleviating marital tensions related to graduate school experiences. Some student affairs professionals have extensive expertise not only in evaluation but in research and can help other campus groups design methods for gathering and analyzing data to answer important questions.

Yet another consultative service is organizational consultation—working with groups and organizations with the objective of improving their functioning. The focus of the consultation may be on processes—such as leadership, team development, conflict management, goal setting, or decision making—or on organizational objectives, structure, and roles. Organizational consultation may be requested by the governing body of an organization, such as a cooperative housing council, a fraternity, the student senate, a minority students' association, or the Young Democrats or Republicans club.

On some campuses, student affairs professionals may at times be asked to serve at an even more abstract level through policy consultation. Their opinions may be sought by administrators of various campus organizations in formulating or revising policies affecting students. For instance, the executive committee of an academic department may consult with the dean of students' office regarding creation of a policy regarding academic dishonesty. A Panhellenic group may want to discuss membership and discipline policies with this office. An academic dean may seek input from the student dean regarding proposed changes in the limits on academic and job work loads. An official may want consultation with student services staff in regard to curfew hours, restricting student organizations' use of certain areas for meetings, or policies favoring disadvantaged groups. A dads' or moms' club may want help in formulating criteria for scholarship awards.

These examples illustrate some consultative activities in which student affairs professionals might be involved. While diverse, these services share several generic characteristics distinguishing them from our other services. All are indirect ways of serving students. Although the ultimate objective of consultation, as of all student services, is to foster students' development, in the consultant role the student affairs professional does not work directly with students but through consultees, other professionals, or members of campus groups. Thus, the student services consultant interacts with faculty, staff, and student leaders with the objective of increasing their effectiveness with students.

The consultative relationships described are quite different from other work relationships. Unlike administrative or supervisory relationships, in which one person has authority over the work of the other, consultant and consultee relate as coequals, and the consultee's participation is voluntary. Although either consultee or consultant may initiate the relationship, the consultee retains the right to reject the consultant's ideas and may terminate the relationship at any time. Furthermore, responsibility for decision making and implementation belongs to the consultee. The consultant cannot require disclosure of information and does not evaluate the consultee's work. Consultation appears similar in some ways to teaching and indeed often includes explicit educational objectives, but the material covered in consultation is either information specifically requested by the consultee or information the consultant thinks might be relevant and useful in the consultee's learning. Consultation differs from counseling in that the focus is limited to the consultee's work situation. Problems of personal life are outside the boundaries of consultation. The focus may be on a number of levels, ranging from individuals to groups, programs, organizations, and policy.

In-House Consultation Issues

So far, these definitions of consultation are compatible with other student services roles and functions. But in some ways, consultative involvements create special conflicts. Typically a consultant is not a member of the consultee's organization but is externally based and assumes a neutral stance in intraorganizational conflicts. The student services consultant, however, is internal or in-house, an integral part of the consultee's system. Furthermore, internal consultants are members of a particular subsystem with values and priorities that may, at times, conflict with those of other subsystems. These memberships complicate the consultative process.

The perceptions of the internal student services consultant are probably more constricted or system-bound than those of external consultants. Although the internal consultant's background may provide extensive, valuable information related to the consultee's concerns, membership in the system imposes perceptual limitations similar to those of the consultee. The student services consultant therefore lacks the objectivity that physical, psychological, and social distance can bring and may not be able to serve the important function of bringing to consultees a fresh, objective view of their system.

Moreover, as a member of a particular subsystem of the university, the student services consultant views campus phenomena from a particular perspective. Student services professionals are trained and employed to serve students; a student-oriented perspective, as opposed to an academic or general administrative orientation, pervades the profession's values, attitudes, and behaviors. When consulting with other members of the university, student affairs professionals appropriately view the problems in terms of students' needs, while consultees often have greater concern for maintaining standards associated with their particular sectors. Thus, all student services consultation inherently contains the potential for conflict. The assumption of consultant neutrality does not hold in these situations. The extensive implications of this subgroup membership for value conflicts in intracampus consultation are little understood and confuse both consultants and consultees. For example, in a consultation about the problems of a failing student, the academic constituency might place the highest value on preserving performance standards, while the student services person would be likely to place the highest priority on the student's need for growth and for educational opportunities. Even in consultation with other student services organizations, a student services consultant discovers conflicting priorities. Efficient management of student residence halls, for instance, is at times incompatible with certain student needs, such as for self-expression and self-government.

The student services consultant must be alert to such conflicts and prepared to make difficult decisions as to his or her priorities. A choice must be made between student and consultee needs. In some cases, the student services professional may decide to abandon the consultative role and become a student advocate. In other cases, the prospect of long-term gains for students through consultation may persuade the student services person to continue to work within the bounds of the consultant role. In either case, confidentiality will be an especially sensitive issue. One of the major characteristics of consultation is the confidentiality of all information emanating from the client organization. Decisions related to value conflicts within consultative relationships are crucial and should be carefully considered by the entire student services staff involved. It is hoped that as student services professionals increase their contact with other campus organizations, the different values, perceptions, and needs will be better understood. The increased information may facilitate more satisfactory compromises or integrative solutions that incorporate the needs of all constituencies.

Ideally, consultants are economically, socially, and emotionally independent of the consultees' system and may take risks that their consultees cannot. But, because student services consultants receive their incomes from the university and, in addition, are embedded in its social system, they may feel restricted in speech and actions. Service to consultees may be limited to those issues that do not threaten social and professional relationships and job security.

Complications related to the in-house consultant's role conflicts can be reduced by early, frank acknowledgment of their existence and by thoughtful confrontation and working through of issues. Student services professionals can minimize biases related to their system membership by periodically bringing in external consultants and by increasing their competencies in some of the areas described later in this chapter. Moreover, not all of the effects of the consultant's in-house status are negative. Consultees benefit from the student services consultant's in-depth knowledge of the campus and continuity of commitment.

Critical Consultation Skills

Student affairs professionals can greatly increase their effectiveness as consultants by developing competencies that are not included in most traditional training programs. First, however, it is necessary to broaden the framework used to formulate problems. Student services people tend to perceive campus phenomena from a limited perspective, consistent with their training, experience, and skills. They are likely to see problems in terms of student adjustment, development, or deficits and to view the external sources of problems as beyond their influence. If they wish to collaborate with other campus agencies, they must understand from a systems viewpoint the complex and interacting variables affecting student life. This approach can facilitate the identification of general issues and relationships among variables that are not apparent from one domain or from a situation-specific perspective. Temporal patterns can be observed that are useful in understanding the sources and histories of current problems and in predicting long-range problems. The systems approach can help in interpreting the reciprocal interplay of campus and community forces.

An example illustrates the systems approach to understanding students' problems. A faculty member contacts a counseling center staff member regarding the failing performance of several minority students. The professor expects to refer these students to the reading and study clinic for what are perceived to be student deficits. Instead of stopping with this definition, the counselor can collaborate with the professor to study the situation in a more systematic way, to discover contextual forces that might be contributing to the failures. For example, the counselor may help the faculty member understand the students' backgrounds, goals, and reasons for enrollment in college. It is important to identify not only academic pressures on these students but social and financial stresses as well. Pressures on faculty might also be relevant. The background of this particular faculty member might be of importance. The counselor can use a systems approach to help the professor integrate and interpret information gathered from these and other domains.

To be most helpful in consultation with other organizations, student affairs staff members need to be able to go beyond their usual perspectives to comprehend problems from diverse viewpoints and from a gestalt. Therefore, to consult effectively, these professionals need to add to their existing competencies a knowledge of social systems and of organizational processes such as communications, conflict, and decision making. They need to understand the bases, uses, and implications of formal and informal power. They need to be aware of the campus's cultural and educational history and of the trends affecting life on campuses today, as well as those that will be salient tomorrow.

They need knowledge of the local, state, and national forces affecting campus life. They need to learn how to organize and interpret large quantities of information in the context of a larger system.

Student services professionals can learn broader concepts for assessing student concerns from a variety of courses available on most campuses. Courses related to social systems, general systems theory, organizational sociology, and organizational psychology are found in many management, educational administration, sociology, psychology, and government departments. Independent study through readings can supply the needed background (see, for instance, Deal and Kennedy, 1982; Katz and Kahn, 1978; Meyer and Associates, 1978; Schein, 1985).

Student affairs professionals' roles are constricted by limited intervention concepts and strategies, which, of course, complement the traditional diagnostic framework. A systems approach to understanding student problems is of little value if one is unable to think in terms of systemic change; one also needs a conceptual framework for interventions that includes an array of possibilities, strategies not only for changing students but for changing some of the organizational behaviors that have harmful consequences for students. In the example of the failing minority students, the most likely diagnosis might be student "maladjustment" or "deficit," and this diagnosis is probably an accurate, although partial, explanation of the problem. Given the traditional orientation toward intervention, the remedy would be individual counseling or tutoring. With a systems interpretation, one might still want to provide direct remedial services to these students; in addition, however, it might be possible to open up a wide range of interventions for consideration, emanating from a careful review of the problem's sources. It might be useful to suggest that university recruitment activities in the high schools from which these and similar students come be monitored to ensure that realistic information is provided. Student affairs professionals might help faculty establish summer tutorial programs for incoming students with weak academic backgrounds or consult with faculty regarding curricular modifications in the first semester for disadvantaged students. They might intervene to reduce the social shock and isolation often experienced by minority students. They could, for example, work with minority student leaders to establish networks of advanced students to contact entering first-year students prior to their arrival on campus in order to arrange needed social support.

It is easier to find resources for the diagnosis of systems than for extending intervention skills. Most training programs and publications stress direct services. Some campuses, however, have courses in consultation theory and process and include supervised field placements in which graduate students practice case and organizational consultation with human service agencies. The National Training Laboratories offer workshops in consultation and organizational development. National, state, and regional professional organizations—such as the American Personnel and Guidance Association, the American Psychological Association, and the Association of College Unions International—sometimes schedule workshops on consultation at their conventions. Student services staff can also arrange for their own in-service training in different types of interventions.

Readings can help student services professionals extend their conceptual frameworks for intervention. A number of writers have compared the theoretical bases of contrasting intervention strategies (Blake and Mouton, 1976; Brown, Pryzwansky, and Schulte, 1987; Caplan, 1970; Gallessich, 1985; Mannino and others, 1986). Other writers describe the application and underlying concepts of singular intervention approaches (Schein, 1969).

In addition to a systems approach to diagnosis and intervention, consultants need competencies in building and maintaining cooperative relationships with peers. Student services staff have high levels of skill in traditional vertical helping modalities. The interpersonal skills required for consultation are not easy to learn and apply. Many student services staff members are accustomed to working from a position of authority, based on office, status, control of information and sanctions, and age and experience. Consultants cannot be successful if they are parental or judgmental. In this capacity, therefore, it is necessary to shift from the role of an expert to that of an equal; and this shift from a vertical to a horizontal position often involves difficult unlearning. It is usually easier to work in the role of an expert and from a controlling position. Collaborative skills cannot, like the competencies described in the preceding sections, be acquired through readings or attending seminars or brief workshops. Well-learned advice-giving and directive behaviors tend to persist. Laboratory training and supervised experiences in ongoing consultation activities are most helpful in establishing and supporting needed behavioral changes.

Another area of competency needed for successful consultation is that of evaluation. In serving students directly, student services staff members have measures for at least rudimentary evaluations of their impact, such as the number of students using services, their follow-up ratings of these services, the persistence in school of student-clients, and the number of new programs offered. The impact of consultation, although it may affect greater numbers of students and have a deeper and more extensive influence than direct services, is more difficult to measure. It may be necessary to seek assistance from professionals who have the critical skills for evaluation of consultative services.

Finally, even if student services professionals have skill and knowledge in systems concepts and a wide range of intervention skills, they are unlikely to be successful in sustained consultation efforts without a strong support system. Consultation requires a shift from the security of one's own office and the traditional modes of operation to settings and services that are less familiar and in which the consultant has little control. This involves the risk of rejection and failure. Even when consultants are highly successful, they do not receive the immediate gratification that comes from direct service. Rewards in consultation are more remote not only in space but also in time; they are usually vicarious and long-term, at best. Consultation is often intellectually stimulating but emotionally draining, so consultants need emotional support. They also need conceptual support from peers who can join in discussing systems analyses and critiquing consultation processes and underlying assumptions. Would-be consultants also need time allocated to pursue consultation. The home base—student services staff—must decide whether or not consultation will be an integral part of the service delivery program. If the decision is to move in this direction, there must be a corresponding commitment to incentives, guidance, encouragement, and training for the professionals involved.

Student services staffs that decide to offer consultative services may want to obtain knowledge and skills by arranging their own in-service consultation training. Curricular topics and methods of preservice and in-service consultation training have been described (Gallessich, 1982; Gallessich and Ladogana, 1978; Gallessich, Long, and Jennings, 1986). Training methods and related issues are discussed in other publications (Alpert and Meyers, 1983; Parsons and Meyers, 1984).

Legitimization Issues

Attaining critical skills and home-base support does not assure student services professionals of consultation opportunities. Sanction for the consultant role must come from consultees and is not as readily earned as sanction for student support services. Obtaining credibility for in-house consultation is especially difficult. Student services professionals are much more likely to be recognized and used as consultants on other campuses than on their own. Part of the difficulty with legitimization comes from the interagency tensions described earlier. Each agency promotes its own unique values and is alert to conflicts of interest with other groups. Competitive, territorial attitudes may block cooperative efforts. Therefore, student services' consultative overtures may be regarded with suspicion. Status barriers present another set of problems. Academicians on some campuses prefer to discuss problems only with other academicians. Given the realities of campus politics, the first sanction for consultation is most likely to come from other service organizations or from student organizations rather than from the academic sector.

Even the "external" professional is not always granted immediate sanction as a consultant but must demonstrate usefulness and trustworthiness in other roles first. Gerald Caplan (1970) observed that the legitimization of consultative roles typically occurs in stages. In the first stage, consultants work in traditional referral or liaison roles and, with their agencies, provide direct assistance to people whom consultees refer for services. Later comes the role of staff educator; still later, the consultant is trusted with the cases of individual students, then with programs, and finally with organizational and administrative concerns. The legitimization of consultant roles, according to this view, does not occur until acceptance in familiar direct service roles is established. Student services professionals may find Caplan's notion of sequential steps of legitimization helpful. Rather than seeking entry into campus agencies as consultants in the more advanced stages, student services professionals need first to review their performance in traditional roles. If they are not successful and visible in direct student services and as resources for referrals from other campus professionals, their capacities for helping other people solve student-related problems will be suspect.

Consultation Entry

On-campus consultation by student services professionals should always be conducted under staff auspices. There should be weekly opportunities for consultants to discuss their work with other student services staff members to ensure that activities are carefully reviewed and that consultation remains a staff commitment rather than an individual one. Team approaches are preferable to individual consultation; they increase the consultative information base, objectivity, and psychological support.

Entry into the various campus organizations should be the culmination of extensive planning and clarification of consultative goals and priorities by the student services staff. Background information should be gathered about potential consulting agencies, including their goals and operations, current issues and problems, and past and present uses of student services. Newspapers, journals, university documents, and the experiences of long-term, senior staff members can supply helpful background material. The appropriate contact person, the organizational "gatekeeper," should be identified and an appointment made for specified purposes and a specified time. A pre-interview letter confirming the appointment's time and objectives is helpful.

Establishment and maintenance of rapport are critical to the effectiveness of consultation. The consultant is, in a sense, a guest in a foreign land and must be especially sensitive to the host organization's norms and procedures. The consultant should be punctual and reliable in keeping appointments and must observe organizational protocol. The consultant's behavior as well as speech gives consultees cues on what to expect from the relationship. The collaborative dimension that is basic to consultation should be clearly communicated in words and behavior; consultees often misunderstand this aspect of consultation. Ideally, consultative interviews are collaborative and interactive.

Consultant and consultee should participate in setting the agenda for each interview. In initial conferences, information exchange is the major task. The objectives of the interview are a typical topic in preliminary phases of consultation. First, the consultant should acquaint the consultee with the various services available from student services. A brief overview might be accompanied by illustrations of services that might be little known and that might be useful in this particular organization. Next, the consultant should explore the extent to which student services, and consultation services in particular, might be useful to the consulting organization, as well as the extent to which the consulting organization is interested in these services. The consultant needs to get a notion of the concerns of the organization and the degree of support within the organization for a consultation approach to problem solving. The consultant needs to identify any people in addition to the "gatekeeper" who should be contacted before decisions are made on the use of student services consultation.

Definitions of the consultative role and relationship should also be made in the initial interviews. The consultant should describe major dimensions of consultation, such as an indirect service to students, a focus on helping consultees solve work-related problems, a collaborative relationship between consultant and consultee, and any special commitments the consultant has that might either enhance or interfere with the consulting organization's goals. The consultant's background of training and experience and qualifications for consultation with the consulting agency should also be described.

The information exchange phase may be concluded in a few minutes, or it may require several interviews. If at the end of this preliminary stage both consultant and consultee are interested in consultation, a second phase of the entry process begins. During this period, the consultee's concerns are extensively explored. Potential consultative services are more thoroughly elaborated. Various ways of fitting services to the consultee's needs are discussed. Successful progress through this phase culminates in a "contract," an informal agreement for consultative services.

Many consultants fail to explicate the "contract." Consequently, both consultant and consultee are uncertain as to the exact objectives and boundaries of the relationship; all concerned are then likely to be confused and dissatisfied. Furthermore, in the absence of specified goals, the impact of consultation cannot be evaluated. This problem is associated with the general failure of human service organizations to clarify goals and priorities and the bases on which decisions are made. Some of the consultation dimensions on which explicit agreement is needed are the following:

1. A definition of the consultee's problem or concern to be addressed through consultation.
2. Clearly stated objectives (for example, to increase the skills of resident assistants in leading fall orientation activities; to help leaders of a social organization work together more effectively; or to help administrators determine the consequences of current policies regarding student work load and course load limits).

3. Strategies to be used in consultation. Strategies should be stated, including procedures and expected outcomes; any expected risks should be clarified.
4. Criteria and methods for evaluating consultation. In addition to a final evaluation, it is often helpful to set a date for a midpoint review and evaluation with the possibility of renegotiating the contract.
5. The identity of the people who are to work with the consultant.
6. The duration of the contract and the time to be allocated weekly or monthly by consultant and by consultee.
7. The responsibilities of each party in implementation and evaluation of services.
8. The location for consultation activities.
9. Conditions and limitations of confidentiality.

Contracting is usually a continuous process because objectives and strategies may change as the data base generated from consultation increases. The consultant is responsible for the explication and maintenance of a feasible, ethical contract. Consultants should not accept contractual conditions that appear to be inappropriate or in contradiction to the consulting organization's goals and interests.

Ethical Issues

Ethical problems are inevitable in consultation practice. Even with knowledgeable and careful planning, all contingencies and issues cannot be anticipated. Often the surface concerns first encountered in consultation obscure deeper organizational problems. However, ethical dilemmas can be greatly reduced by awareness of common pitfalls and by continual surveillance for potentially sensitive situations. Professional codes provide helpful guidance to consultants. Probably the best single means of preventing ethical problems is to exercise great care in making the contractual agreements described above. The consultant should be certain that his or her behavior is congruent with the contract. Regular monitoring of consultation activities through discussions with consultees should prevent serious ethical problems from arising.

The Challenge

Because they possess unique knowledge and competencies, student affairs professionals have the potential to help other staff members, as well as faculty, administrators, and student organizations, serve students more effectively. The consultative approach offers a medium through which these resources may be brought to bear on a wide range of problems. Moreover, consultation with others on campus offers student affairs professionals an opportunity to deepen their understanding of the complexities of the system within which they work.

References

Alpert, J. L., and Meyers, J. *Training in Consultation.* Springfield, Ill.: Thomas, 1983.

Blake, R., and Mouton, J. *Consultation.* Reading, Mass.: Addison-Wesley, 1976.

Brown, D., Pryzwansky, W. B., and Schulte, A. C. *Psychological Consultation.* Newton, Mass.: Allyn & Bacon, 1987.

Caplan, G. *The Theory and Practice of Mental Health Consultation.* New York: Basic Books, 1970.

Deal, T. E., and Kennedy, A. A. *Corporate Cultures: The Rites and Rituals of Corporate Life.* Reading, Mass.: Addison-Wesley, 1982.

Gallessich, J. *The Profession and Practice of Consultation: A Handbook for Consultants, Trainers of Consultants, and Consumers of Consultation Services.* San Francisco: Jossey-Bass, 1982.

Gallessich, J. "Toward a Meta-Theory of Consultation." *Counseling Psychologist,* 1985, *13* (3), 336–353.

Gallessich, J., and Ladogana, A. "Consultation Training Program for School Counselors." *Counselor Education and Supervision,* 1978, *18* (2), 100–108.

Gallessich, J., Long, K. M., and Jennings, S. "Training." In F. V. Mannino and others (eds.), *Handbook of Mental Health Consultation.* Washington, D.C.: National Institute of Mental Health, 1986.

Katz, D., and Kahn, R. L. *The Social Psychology of Organizations.* (2nd ed.) New York: Wiley, 1978.

Mannino, F. V., and others. *Handbook of Mental Health Consultation.* Washington, D.C.: National Institute of Mental Health, 1986.

Meyer, M. W., and Associates. *Environments and Organizations: Theoretical and Empirical Perspectives.* San Francisco: Jossey-Bass, 1978.

Parsons, R. D., and Meyers, J. *Developing Consultation Skills: A Guide To Training, Development, and Assessment for Human Services Professionals.* San Francisco: Jossey-Bass, 1984.

Schein, E. *Process Consultation.* Reading, Mass.: Addison-Wesley, 1969.

Schein, E. *Organizational Culture and Leadership: A Dynamic View.* San Francisco: Jossey-Bass, 1985.

Chapter Sixteen

Program Development

Weston H. Morrill

Concerned staff members at a college prepared and presented a two-hour workshop designed to educate students about the danger of AIDS and teach safe sex practices. The workshop was held in the university union and utilized videotape presentations with a specially trained psychology graduate student as discussion leader. The overall response to the workshop was small—only fifteen students participated, despite its being held in a high-traffic area. The workshop was highly rated by the students who attended, and measures before and after demonstrated that the workshop was successful in teaching the information and attitudes deemed important by the workshop planners. Should the workshop be repeated or should it be changed so that it will reach more people?

At another institution, through newspaper and class announcements, students were invited to participate in group sessions of systematic desensitization and directive counseling to overcome test anxiety. Thirty-two students expressed interest in the program, but only ten eventually participated. The program effectively reduced their measured anxiety and increased their grade point averages. How can staff time be better used to meet this evidently infrequent but nonetheless serious need among students?

The dean of students on another campus fostered the implementation of several innovative student development programs that were considered nationally to be in the forefront of the profession. During this period of activism, conservative elements in the community called for stricter control over students; the dean was eventually replaced and several of the programs were eliminated. Yet these innovative programs have been widely accepted and implemented on other campuses.

On another campus, a "study skills circus" was held; it was based on the observation that the typical student's life is like a three-ring circus of study, occupation, and family or social life. Over a two-day period, counselors and faculty presented sessions with circus-like names on ways in which students can develop consistently rewarding study strategies. The sessions resulted in significantly higher grades for participating students and increases in the amount of academic work they completed. However, students who participated in a program involving parallel series of achievement training groups, designed to help them economize on time and effort in organizing their work and play for the greatest payoff in grades, made no improvement over a control group that received no training. Why the difference?

These examples illustrate the ways that student services administrators are utilizing available resources to promote student development through programming. Programs are planned, structured learning experiences designed to meet the needs of students. These needs may be remedial, developmental, or even preventive in nature, and interventions planned to meet these needs may be aimed at both individuals and environments (Morrill and Hurst, 1971; Morrill, Oetting, and Hurst, 1980; Conyne, 1979). Barr, Keating, and Associates (1985, p. 3) add to the definition the notion that programs must be based on theory and operate within the context of their host institutions.

It is becoming increasingly apparent that we can no longer afford to design programs that meet low-priority or nonperceived needs, to deal with all student needs on an individual basis (Cannon, 1982), or to ignore institutional context or politics when planning programs. Barr, Keating, and Associates (1985, pp. 5–6) propose that all student services programs are designed for one of three overarching purposes: "to provide essential institutional services, to teach life management skills, and to provide links through which students can integrate knowledge gained in both the curricular and cocurricular settings.'' Many authors suggest that there are common developmental experiences from which most students could benefit. These can be provided more economically, more efficiently, and perhaps more effectively by designing programs for groups of students rather than for individuals. Lewis and Lewis (1977, pp. 11–12) raise these provocative questions about the purpose and design of such interventions: (1) To what extent is the individual student capable of resolving an issue through personal change? What resources in the environment are available to help the individual student grow? (3) To what extent does the solution really rest in the environment instead of the individual? (4) How can the counselor and the counselee act to bring about the necessary changes in the environment?

This chapter focuses on the development of programs designed to benefit students in those situations where it has been determined that their problems can be resolved through personal change, through the use of resources, or through attention to the environment. By using a systematic behavior change approach, it is possible to anticipate in a program some of the developmental needs of students and to do so in a way that provides information that can be used to make decisions regarding the utility, maintenance, or elimination of the program. This chapter will present the important issue of context and discuss in detail a model of program development adapted from Moore and Delworth (1976).

Context of Program Development

Barr, Keating, and Associates (1985, p. 3) define a program as ''a theoretically based plan, under which action is taken toward a goal within the context of institutions of higher education.'' They assert that even with the best theory and plan, a program may fail if the context within which it is to operate is not carefully considered. The context must be the template that guides all phases of program planning and implementation. To ignore historical precedents, the organizational structure of the institution, the philosophical leanings of the administration and faculty, and the current political environment invites failure. Student services exist to contribute to and support the intentions and goals of the institution within which they operate; therefore, in setting priorities and goals, we must consider implicit and explicit institutional values as part of the planning process.

Barr (1985) asserts that while many student services professionals recognize the political environment operating within and outside our institutions, we seldom translate this abstract understanding into our daily work. The idealistic view often taken that what we do is above politics is, according to Barr, "a naive view at best" (p. 63). She asserts (p. 64) that "the astute student services professional should be knowledgeable about the political environment and use that knowledge to develop, maintain, and implement quality student services programs." In fact, offering of a new program is in reality a political act, as a result of which those "in authority may feel threatened, those with power may feel neglected, and the issue of territory is bound to arise" (p. 70).

Barr suggests several ground rules for responsible political behavior that should be considered carefully by anyone who is offering programs. The rules recognize the importance of considering timing, building alliances and bridges, involving the decision makers, not surprising your boss, not ignoring established committees, and exercising an extraordinary amount of patience. Politics is not a bad word, but a reality that must be responsibly considered. The issue of context must be considered in the stages of program development.

A Program Development Model

While student affairs professionals in many if not most institutions plan and implement a variety of programs, little attention has been given in training programs or the literature to program development. In their work on this topic, Hurst and Jacobson (1985) suggest the importance of a theoretical/conceptual foundation for program development. Two major contributions in the area of program development are those of Barr, Keating, and Associates (1985) and Moore and Delworth (1976). Barr, Keating, and Associates (1985, p. 3) propose that many programs fail because practitioners do not attend to three equally important components of program development. These components are the societal and institutional context within which the program is implemented, the goal of the program, and the plan or method of implementation. Moore and Delworth (1976) present a systematic approach for considering the goal of a program and the plan or method of implementation. Each stage of their approach concentrates on an aspect of program development, one stage leading to the next. The program that results has been carefully planned to ensure that it is needed, has specific objectives that can be monitored to determine if desirable results are being achieved, and can supply data for decisions about continuation or modification. The stages of the program development model adapted from Moore and Delworth (1976) are as follows:

Stage I: Initiating the program

Step 1. *The germinal idea.* The idea for the content area of a program is identified through contact with members of the target population or formal assessment of individuals or environments.

Step 2. *The planning team.* A small group of people interested in or concerned about the idea being considered are brought together to begin the initial planning.

Step 3. *Assessing needs, resources, and constraints.* This stage involves collecting data regarding the need for a program, searching the literature for research and program data, and identifying resources and constraints in the environment.

Step 4. *Identifying alternative program targets and purposes.* This is a process to generate alternatives through brainstorming.

Step 5. *Program selection.* After considering the assessment data and the identified alternatives, a program direction is selected.

Stage II: Planning program objectives, delivery system, and evaluation methods

Step 1. *Selecting program goals and specifying behavioral objectives.* The goals of the program are stated explicitly and the specific behavior change objectives specified.

Step 2. *Developing the training methods or delivery system.* This step involves planning the training procedures and tasks that the planning team thinks will best achieve the program objectives with the available resources.

Step 3. *Planning the method of intervention.* On the basis of the planning in step 2, the planning team must determine who will deliver the training and how the training will be offered.

Step 4. *Planning for program evaluation.* This step involves developing the evaluation instruments, methodology, and design to determine if the program meets its objectives.

Stage III. Presenting and evaluating a pilot program

Step 1. *Program publicity.* This task involves acquainting potential consumers of the program with the pilot program.

Step 2. *Implementing the pilot program.* This step involves carrying out the selection of participants and offering the program.

Step 3. *Assessing evaluation data and making decisions about the program's future.* On the basis of subjective feedback and objective data about the effects of the pilot program, decisions about the future of the program are made.

Stage IV: Program refinement

Step 1. *Refining training procedures and materials.* On the basis of feedback data from the pilot program, the training materials and procedures are reviewed and refined.

Step 2. *Planning for continued evaluation.* Continued evaluation is necessary because of changing conditions and circumstances.

Step 3. *Training trainers.* Many mature programs may use peers, volunteers, paraprofessionals, or allied professionals as trainers. A process for selecting and training these people is needed.

Step 4. *Offering the program on a regular basis.* The program is continued with the target population and an ongoing evaluation is conducted of the program's needs, effectiveness, resources, and priorities.

Stage I: Initiating the Program

The first stage of program development, initiating the program, involves five steps: identifying the germinal idea for the program; creating a planning team; assessing needs, resources, and constraints; identifying alternative program targets and purposes; and selecting a program. The steps are generally consecutive, but planners often move back and forth between steps as they plan.

Step 1: The Germinal Idea. The idea for a program may come from the experience of professionals, who, on the basis of their contacts with many people over a long period of time, subjectively feel that a need exists. It may also be generated through a formal assessment of the needs of served populations (Kuh, 1982).

Forquer (1982) presents a model for planning primary prevention programs that requires practitioners to evaluate the coping skills and support systems of groups as they relate to certain risk and stress factors. Forquer (p. 71) notes that the "life span of every human being is characterized by a series of progressive, predictable developmental stages" that can be anticipated for program development. Lewis and Lewis (1977) recognize the existence of common crises that are particularly stressful for people, around which programs can be developed. Following the steps of this program development model provides the means for translating the germinal idea into productive programs.

Step 2: The Planning Team. Once an idea has been identified that has potential for program development, a small group of people who have interest in or concern for the area of the program are brought together to begin the initial planning. A team, rather than an individual, approach is recommended for a number of reasons. A team can represent a number of viewpoints and stimulate creative planning. If people affected by a new program are included on the team, they are in a position to support ideas they have helped create, rather than resist ideas imposed by others. Also, a planning team can bring together a number of individuals with different competencies and skills needed in the program development process.

Step 3: Assessing Needs, Resources, and Constraints. One of the first tasks of the planning team is to carry out three phases of an assessment process. The first phase involves the clear demonstration that a need exists (Kuh, 1982; Beard, Elmore, and Lange, 1982). Many professionals spend hours developing and presenting workshops only to find that there is not much response to the offering. The second phase of the assessment process involves searching the literature for research and program data related to the germinal idea. These data are essential for specifc planning of program delivery methods and for evaluation in later stages of development. The third phase of the assessment process consists of identifying available environmental resources and constraints. Are similar programs already being offered? If so, is another one needed? Does the program create territorial concerns? If another program seems needed, are resource people available who are expert in the area of the program idea and who would be useful additions to the planning team?

Step 4: Identifying Alternative Program Targets and Purposes. Once the program team has determined that a clear need exists, it undertakes a brainstorming process to generate ideas about the delivery of a relevant program. Many program suggestions can be generated for any germinal idea. Professionals tend to develop programs aimed at individual students who are defined as having problems. Although appropriate in many instances, this is a limited perspective. The intervention model presented by Morrill, Oetting, and Hurst (1974, 1980) can stimulate different kinds of thinking about what type of program might be developed. The model presented in Figure 1 suggests alternative targets, purposes, and methods of intervention that are useful in developing program suggestions. The first two

Figure 1. Dimensions of Counselor Functioning (Cube).

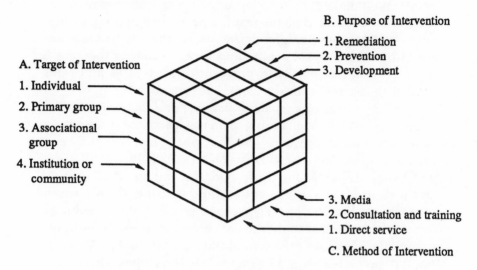

B. Purpose of Intervention
1. Remediation
2. Prevention
3. Development

A. Target of Intervention
1. Individual
2. Primary group
3. Associational group
4. Institution or community

3. Media
2. Consultation and training
1. Direct service

C. Method of Intervention

Source: This figure © 1974 by Weston H. Morrill, Eugene R. Oetting, and James C. Hurst, and is reproduced with their permission.

dimensions of the model are of primary importance in this stage of planning; the third dimension is important in the second stage and is discussed later.

Brainstorming at this level may identify the need for more than one program to address different targets or purposes. For example, the team should consider remedial, preventive, and developmental program possibilities. Remedial programs address deficits or problems of people or negative aspects of the campus environment. Preventive programs are aimed at teaching people the skills they will need to meet future environmental demands; if the environmental demands are expected to be counterproductive, the programs may be aimed at reducing the demands. Developmental programs suggest activities that enhance or enrich people and their environments. The brainstorming team should recognize the possibility of several program ideas in each of these dimensions.

The target dimension of the model also suggests a number of alternatives for program development. The focus can be on individuals or environments (Conyne, 1979). Programs developed for primary groups focus on two or more people in an ongoing, close, interdependent relationship, such as couples, roommates, or families. Programs developed for associational groups are aimed at people associated with one another because of similar interests, needs, or goals. Programs developed for an institution or community are designed for all people who perceive themselves to be affected by the institution or who have the power to influence or change aspects of the institution. Table 1 presents an example of various programs that can be aimed at different targets and constructed for several purposes (Moore and Delworth, 1976).

Step 5. Program Selection. The program selection step requires the integration of the data and ideas generated in Steps 3 and 4. Planners make decisions about the specific program direction and about the program's future. At this point, the planning team has created a proposal that a program be developed in a specific area for a specific target and a specific purpose. The decision to continue is based on the availability of required resources, a supportive political climate, and the willingness of some individual, agency, or group to sponsor the program. At this point it is often useful to add new members to the planning team who possess the skills necessary for completing the program development process. With the decision to continue, the planning process moves into the second stage.

Stage II: Planning Program Objectives, Delivery System, and Evaluation Methods

The activities of Stage II involve four steps: selecting the goals and specifying the behavioral objectives of the program, developing the training methods or delivery system, planning the method of intervention, and planning the method of program evaluation.

Step 1. Selecting Program Goals and Specifying Behavioral Objectives. An extremely important but often overlooked process in developing programs is making explicit the goals that are implicit in the program's purpose. This is accomplished with

Table 1. Examples of Programs to Raise the Level of Academic Achievement Among Students Who Live in Campus Housing, Suggested for Various Combinations of the Cube's Target and Purpose Classifications.

Target	Purpose		
	Remediation	Prevention	Development
Individual	Teach learning skills for students with less than a 2.0 grade point average	Offer a series of learning skills workshops at each residence hall for identified high-risk students	Offer in residence halls special learning modules for advanced writing and reading skills
Primary group		Prepare and distribute to couples in married student housing a manual on "How to Set Up a Study Corner"	Offer workshop on helping your partner graduate
Associational group	Teach learning skills that utilize group interaction for members of a residence hall whose average has fallen below a 2.0 grade point average		
Institution or Community	Train residence hall assistants on how to better identify and refer marginal students to learning skills programs	Train residence hall assistants about study environments and how these can be implemented in residence halls	Training program also achieves this purpose

Source: Adapted from Moore and Delworth, 1976, p. 14. Reproduced with permission.

a version of a three-step procedure developed by Weigel and Uhlemann (1975) to set behavior change objectives for therapy groups. The first step of this procedure is to identify the broad general goals for the program. These are obtained by asking the question "What is (are) the broadest mission(s) of the program?" Moore and Delworth (1976) recommend brainstorming to identify goals. They give the following example (p. 23): "What is the broadest mission for a high-risk freshman learning skills program?" This question obtains the general goal: "To improve skills that freshman students need to succeed academically in college."

The second step of the goal-setting process involves restating each general goal in terms of the behavior that students would display if they had achieved the general goal. Often there are several behaviors that the students could display if they had achieved one general goal; each becomes a behavioral objective of the program. Using the brainstorming process, the second step is achieved by answering the question "How would program participants behave differently if they achieved the general goal?" From the preceding example, Moore and Delworth (1976, p. 23) generated the following answers to the question "How would program participants in a freshman learning skills program behave if they gained the skills needed to succeed academically in college?"

1. Participants will be able to organize their time so that they can get enough studying done and still have some social and recreational time.
2. Participants will be able to give their professors regular positive and negative feedback.
3. Participants will be able to take objective examinations without blocking anxiety.
4. Participants will be able to write term papers in an organized and clear fashion.

The third step of the goal-setting process is critical to the specific planning of the program delivery system. In this stage, the planning team should restate each general goal as several behavior change objectives. These latter objectives are increasingly specific and are obtained by answering the question "What specifically will be happening if participants accomplish the general objective?" According to Moore and Delworth, the task here is to define the scope of the desired behaviors by specifying as many of the following as possible: the time, the place, the person, and the context or setting of the accomplishment. The following examples of behavior change objectives for the second general objective—giving positive and negative feedback—are given by Moore and Delworth (1976, p. 24):

1. Participants will speak up in a designated class every day at least twice to give their reactions about the lecture.
2. Participants (after class) will orally give one of their professors some specific . . . feedback about some aspect of the lecture or lab.
3. Participants will at least once every day ask a lecturer to clarify some point that was not clearly presented.

This three-level process for identifying goals and behavioral objectives is critically important yet deceptively simple to implement. Planners tend to express goals in vague, nonbehavioral terms. Developing clear behavioral objectives greatly enhances the probability of success, facilitates the planning of evaluation, and enhances the ability of the delivery system to achieve the program goals.

Step 2. Developing the Training Methods or Delivery System. This step involves designing the specific training procedures and tasks that the planning team thinks will best achieve the program objectives with the available resources. The behavior change objectives identified in Step 1 provide the basis for selecting and developing the training tasks necessary for their achievement. The information gathered as part of the literature search in the first stage is also important in this step. The planning team can evaluate previously developed training programs in light of the behavior change objectives identified for the cur-

rent program and can determine for which objectives they will
need to develop their own unique training tasks. Again, a number
of training tasks are brainstormed; the final selection of the tasks
is based on a judgment by the planning team about which tasks
are most likely to achieve the objectives with available resources.
The following examples of training procedures were developed
for the behavior change objectives presented earlier (Moore and
Delworth, 1976, p. 27):

1. A didactic presentation outlining the difference
    between assertive and aggressive behavior.
2. A small group exercise where class members
    practice *discriminating* between assertive and ag-
    gressive reactions to professors.
3. A role-playing exercise where class members
    verbally practice giving assertive feedback to
    mock professors (positive or negative) in a wide
    range of situations.
4. Diary or log of each student's progress kept
    on behavior objectives.

Step 3. Planning the Method of Intervention. On the basis
of the planning in Step 2, the planning team must determine
who will deliver the training and how the program will be offered. The method dimension of the cube model presented in
Figure 1 (Morrill, Oetting, and Hurst, 1974) is useful in this
step of the planning. Although the specific goals and training
plans may dictate to a large extent the method of intervention,
the dimensions of the cube suggest that, in addition to offering
the program themselves, student services professionals might
consult with others or train them to conduct the actual training.

The first classification in the method dimension, direct
service, involves the professional staff personally offering the program. This is the preferred method of intervention when training requires the expertise, credibility, and status of professionals.
However, professionals are not always the trainers of choice.
Limited professional resources and the potential multiplier effect of training and consulting with others often suggest the

use of carefully trained and supervised peers, paraprofessionals, or allied professionals to deliver the training to consumers. This is preferred when training is enhanced by the special rapport or influence that peers can establish. Another method that should be considered is the use of media (television, computers, audio recorders, programmed textbooks, or written materials). Many training programs or modules can be presented through the use of media, thus allowing greater dissemination, easier continuation, and less use of professional time.

Step 4. Planning for Program Evaluation. The critical step of designing program evaluation is often overlooked in program planning (Morrill and Banning, 1973), yet it is possibly the most important (Oetting, 1980). If the goals of the program have been carefully stated and translated into behavior change objectives, this step is relatively easy. If this has not been done, this step is difficult if not impossible. Instruments must be developed or identified to measure the behavior change objectives. These may be directly administered instruments, such as attitude tests, self-reports, or personality or behavioral tests, or they may be more indirect or unobtrusive measures, such as observer reports or dropout rates. Once the measures have been selected, a research design that allows control of enough variables to provide confidance that changes are the result of the program must be selected. Applied program evaluation does not allow the strict controls that experimental research provides; however, the design should be as stringent as possible. At this point, a sample is identified and the team prepares to present the pilot program.

Stage III: Presenting and Evaluating a Pilot Program

The goal of the planning team in this third stage is to make an informed decision about continuation or modification of the program after a pilot test. In the examples of programs presented earlier, the decision after the pilot test was to continue the study skills circus program as it had been developed, to modify the AIDS workshop, and to eliminate or reassess the achievement training groups. It was failure to consider the context or political climate, not the results of pilot testing, that contributed to the elimination of the innovative student development programs. From these few examples, it is obvious that considering the context and pilot testing are critical. Without pilot testing, programs are continued when they need to be either extensively revised or eliminated. In addition, there cannot be as much confidence and support for successful programs without evaluation. The three steps of this stage describe tasks concerning publicity, pilot testing, and making decisions about the future of the program on the basis of evaluative data.

Step 1. Program Publicity. The most carefully devised program will not be successful if the potential consumers are not aware and do not take advantage of it. The AIDS workshop and the test anxiety desensitization groups described at the start of the chapter did not attract enough consumers. This may have reflected incomplete assessment of need, but it may also have resulted from inadequate publicity or lack of awareness of the critical need for the program by the intended consumers. The publicity should inform intended consumers why the program is important to them and tell them some of the specific benefits they might derive from their participation, as well as the time and place of the program.

Step 2. Implementing the Pilot Program. Actually selecting participants and offering the program on a pilot basis is the culmination of all the planning to this point. There are three major tasks at this stage of the program. These are recruiting and selecting the participants for the pilot test, establishing the controls dictated by the evaluation research design, and administering the evaluation procedures.

Step 3. Assessing Evaluation Data and Making Decisions about the Program's Future. After the pilot test, the planning team will need to consider the evaluation data and decide whether the program should be continued and, if so, what changes or modifications should be made. The team should review both subjective and objective data in relation to each specific goal and behavioral objective and should decide whether the program should be continued or discontinued. The evaluation data may suggest needed changes or modifications. Thus, the program development model branches at this point, depending on the decision. If the decision is to continue, then the process moves on to Stage IV; if the decision is to abort, the process moves back to the first stage to develop a new idea or to Stage II to develop an alternative delivery system.

Stage IV: Program Refinement

Stage IV involves retooling—that is, making changes and arranging for the program to function on an ongoing basis. This stage consists of refining procedures on the basis of feedback, planning for continued evaluation, and training trainers who in turn will help others learn how to offer the program. The last step in this stage is clarifying responsibility for ongoing coordination of the program.

Step 1. Refining Training Procedures and Materials. Using feedback from the pilot program, the team should review and, where necessary, refine and polish training materials. Data may suggest modifying some procedures or adding audio, written, or visual materials to strengthen the program. Some procedures may be superfluous and can be dropped from the program with little impact on outcomes.

Step 2. Planning for Continued Evaluation. Continued evaluation is necessary for a number of reasons. Changing conditions and circumstances may alter the need for the program or even alter program outcomes. Any redevelopment or modification of the program may change outcomes; therefore, continued assessment must be planned. As a program matures, different personnel may affect program outcomes; also, the newness of a program, the involvement of the planners, and the excitement may produce spurious evaluations because of the special attention the program receives at first. All these issues make it important that the planning team develop plans for continued evaluation, using as powerful a design as is feasible.

Step 3. Training Trainers. Eventually, many mature programs may use peers, volunteers, paraprofessionals, or allied professionals as program leaders so that professional staff are free for other purposes. Often professionals are the trainers during the pilot testing and the early life of programs, but others may be incorporated into the program as time goes on. When this occurs, careful consideration must be given to selecting and training nonprofessional trainers: What skills do they need to have? How are they to be given these skills? Who is to train them? Who is to supervise the continuing program?

Step 4. Offering the Program on a Regular Basis. When all of the preceding tasks have been completed, the planning team is ready to offer the program on a regular basis. Some individual or group must assume responsibility for ongoing coordination and supervision with continuous attention to publicity details, selecting and training trainers, room scheduling, and collecting and disseminating evaluative data. The need and support for the program must be continuously monitored in light of changing priorities. No program remains completely viable over an extended period of time without requiring some changes, modifications, and perhaps reconceptualizations.

Conclusion

This chapter has presented strategies and techniques associated with program development. When professionals carefully consider context or politics in program planning and use an empirically based model, clear and useful results are generally achieved. The planners have the information and support they need to decide whether to eliminate, modify, or fully implement the program. Program development is not unlike good applied research, and the results can be rewarding. While the term *research* creates anxiety for some people, we need to think in research terms in all that we do. Research provides us with a systematic means of answering important questions about what we are doing; for example, What are the needs of those I am concerned about serving? Is there a group of individuals who could profit from a systematic program? Does the program I have developed really make a difference or do I need to seek some other way? And, if the program goals are achieved, is it worth the cost? We cannot avoid the questions, and seeking the answers can be a stimulating and productive experience.

References

Barr, M. J. "Internal and External Forces Influencing Programming." In M. J. Barr, L. A. Keating, and Associates, *Developing Effective Student Services Programs: Systematic Approaches for Practitioners*. San Francisco: Jossey-Bass, 1985.

Barr, M. J., Keating, L. A., and Associates. *Developing Effective Student Services Programs: Systematic Approaches for Practitioners*. San Francisco: Jossey-Bass, 1985.

Beard, S. S., Elmore, R. T., and Lange, S. "Assessment of Student Needs: Areas of Stress in the Campus Environment." *Journal of College Student Personnel*, 1982, *23*, 348–350.

Cannon, H. J. "The Future of College and University Counseling Centers: One Vice President's View." *Counseling Psychologist*, 1982, *10*, 57–61.

Conyne, R. K. "The Campus Environment as Client: A New Direction for College Counselors." *Journal of College Student Personnel*, 1979, *20*, 437–442.

Forquer, S. L. "Planning Primary Prevention Programs: A Practical Model." *Journal of Children in Contemporary Society*, 1982, *14*, 69–78.

Hurst, J. C., and Jacobson, J. K. "Theories Underlying Students' Needs for Programs." In M. J. Barr, L. A. Keating, and Associates, *Developing Effective Student Services Programs: Systematic Approaches for Practitioners*. San Francisco: Jossey-Bass, 1985.

Kuh, G. D. "Purposes and Principles for Needs Assessment in Student Affairs." *Journal of College Student Personnel*, 1982, *23*, 202–209.

Lewis, J. A., and Lewis, M. D. *Community Counseling: A Human Services Approach*. New York: Wiley, 1977.

Moore, M., and Delworth, U. *Training Manual for Student Service Program Development*. Boulder, Colo.: Western Interstate Commission for Higher Education, 1976.

Morrill, W. H., and Banning, J. H. *Counseling Outreach: A Survey of Practices*. Boulder, Colo.: Western Interstate Commission for Higher Education, 1973.

Morrill, W. H., and Hurst, J. C. "A Preventive and Developmental Role for the College Counselor." *Counseling Psychologist,* 1971, *2,* 90–95.

Morrill, W. H., and Hurst, J. C. (eds.). *Dimensions of Intervention for Student Development.* New York: Wiley, 1980.

Morrill, W. H., Oetting, E. R., and Hurst, J. C. "Dimensions of Counselor Functioning." *Personnel and Guidance Journal,* 1974, *52,* 354–359.

Morrill, W. H., Oetting, E. R., and Hurst, J. C. "A Conceptual Model of Intervention Strategies." In W. H. Morrill, J. C. Hurst, and Associates (eds.), *Dimensions of Intervention for Student Development.* New York: Wiley, 1980.

Oetting, E. R. "A Guide to Program Evaluation." In W. H. Morrill, J. C. Hurst, and Associates (eds.), *Dimensions of Intervention for Student Development.* New York: Wiley, 1980.

Weigel, R. G., and Uhlemann, M. R. "Developing Individualized Behavior Change Goals with Clients." *Journal of Contemporary Psychotherapy,* 1975, *7,* 91–95.

Part Five

Organizing and Managing Programs and Services

The job of the administrator and manager in student services has become increasingly complex during the past decade. New tasks and demands have arisen from campus disturbances, increased accountability, and developments in the field. Administrators must deal with the expectations of top-level campus administrators, academic faculty, their own staff members, student services colleagues, governing boards, and student consumers. In addition, these varying constituencies are increasingly better organized and more assertive in expressing their needs and demands. Clearly, student services administrators at all levels need much more know-how to perform their roles effectively. The chapters in Part Five provide an overview of the knowledge and skills administrators need.

Although Chapter Seventeen, written by Arthur Sandeen, is aimed primarily at chief student services administrators in complex systems, we believe middle managers will find it helpful as well. This chapter represents the accumulated wisdom of an experienced administrator writing about the issues involved in organizing and managing a division of student affairs. Both the experienced administrator and the new professional will gain insight into the administration of a division of student affairs by reading this chapter.

The budgeting and planning processes were not included in our first edition, but these administrative skills play an increasingly important role in institutions of higher education. The two processes go hand in hand; effective planning requires a detailed understanding of an institution's budgeting process, and a good budget falls apart without effective planning. In Chapter Eighteen, John Schuh and Scott Rickard present the basic concepts and issues in the planning and budgeting processes and point the interested reader to a professional literature that is broader in scope and provides greater depth of detail for those who must carry out the planning and budgeting processes on their local campus.

Since the first edition of this book was published, the information explosion and the effective use of computers to manage information have confronted nearly all student services administrators, from the entry-level professional to the chief student affairs officer. The art and science of effective administration require a working knowledge and understanding of the use of information to plan and implement student services. Chapter Nineteen, written by David Kalsbeek, introduces the concepts and terminology of information management. Chapter Twenty, by Dennis Madson, Larry Benedict, and William Weitzer, discusses practical applications and offers good advice about getting started. These chapters, when read in combination, provide an excellent overview of the critical skills and knowledge regarding information management that administrators must learn.

In Chapter Twenty-One, Jon Dalton reiterates the concern expressed by Studs Terkel that most people have work that is too small for their spirits. Dalton warns that student affairs work can become too small if staff members do not find ongoing opportunities for growth and development. Staff development is the key to enhancing the growth and learning of our colleagues. Dalton presents a solid rationale and a core curriculum for staff development with specific suggestions for building an effective program.

The blend of concept, models, and practical strategies in Part Five provides a basis for administrative competency. We believe that serious attention to these ideas will result in increased managerial effectiveness and satisfaction, which in turn will increase the impact of student services on campus.

Chapter Seventeen

Issues Influencing the Organization of Student Affairs

Arthur Sandeen

Divisions of student affairs in 1989 often include such diverse departments as child care, campus security, intercollegiate athletics, and the campus bus system. Most of these programs have been added in recent years to the more traditional responsibilities of student affairs, such as admissions, orientation, housing, counseling, student activities, and placement. This has made the administration of student affairs more complex and has resulted in more frequent links to other campus and community services and programs.

This increased scope of responsibility also raises important questions about the appropriate organization of the student affairs division. Among them are the following: Who should determine the organization of the student affairs division? What factors should be considered in deciding how to organize the division? How should specific organizational problems be addressed? These questions and others are discussed in this chapter in an effort to help institutions understand and improve the quality of their student affairs organizations.

Determining the Organization
of the Student Affairs Division

In the great majority of cases, the student affairs organization is already in place when a new chief student affairs officer is appointed. Since relatively few new institutions are now being established, it is unusual to have the opportunity to create a new student affairs division. Most newly appointed chief student affairs administrators have a clear idea of how they want to organize their various responsibilities. There are a number of factors that must be considered as they attempt to put their plan in place.

The institution's president, of course, has the authority to decide what the organizational structure of the student affairs division will be, subject to the approval of the governing board. The chief student affairs officer usually presents a plan to the president, but considerable preparation is needed if the plan is to gain support. Because the responsibilities of student affairs are vital to the institution and are also of concern to many constituencies, any organizational proposal will be carefully scrutinized.

Other than the president, the three major institutional officers for academics, finance, and development are the chief student affairs officer's most important colleagues. These staff members constitute the college's management and leadership team, and most decisions of any consequence will be made with each member of this group present. Thus, it is extremely important that the organizational plan for the student affairs division have the support and understanding of these institutional colleagues.

Functions such as admissions, housing, and placement significantly overlap with the responsibilities of academic affairs, financial affairs, and development. Clear understanding is needed to avoid frequent problems in the day-to-day operations of these programs, and the organizational plan must reflect this. While much of the work of the four major institutional divisions is cooperative, competition for facilities, personnel, salaries, and operating funds is inevitable. The organizational plan proposed by the chief student affairs officer must have the support of the major academic, financial, and development administrators on each of these issues before it is presented to the president. Without such support, the president is unlikely to agree to the plan. Moreover, without the agreement of these major institutional officers, the organizational plan for student affairs cannot work, because it will be met with obstacles and opposition throughout the campus.

Even when the student affairs administrator has secured support for the organizational plan from the major academic, financial, and development officers of the institution, the actual decision to move ahead cannot yet be made. There are three very important groups whose cooperation and understanding must be sought. These are the faculty senate, the major student associations, and the student affairs staff itself. Most institutions have a faculty council or senate that has considerable influence in policy and program development on the campus. Some faculty councils are very powerful, include several standing committees on various matters, and have formal constitutions and by-laws governing their operations. The programs, policies, and services of the student affairs division may be subject to the approval of the council, and its support for the organizational plan is critical. If its members do not agree with the plan, or if they think it is overbureaucratic, it has little chance for success. Many student affairs divisions have experienced difficulty because their basic organization was not understood or accepted by the major faculty council on the campus, or because the division attempted to operate in isolation from the council.

While most students may not be very interested in organizational issues, the representatives of the major student groups certainly will have strong views about how effectively services are delivered and what role they have in helping to decide policies. They will be most interested in where they fit into any proposed student affairs organizational plan. Gaining the understanding and support of major student groups for the organizational plan of the student affairs division is important for its acceptance. Student leaders usually have easy access to all levels of the institution, and if they feel left out of the plan, their opposition can be very detrimental.

A newly appointed chief student affairs officer faces a delicate situation with the existing staff when a new organizational plan is being considered. An autocratic announcement of significant changes is unlikely to be accepted and will certainly result in anger and frustration. On the other hand, an open-ended, democratic discussion of alternatives may take too long and may not result in the kinds of changes that are needed. Many problems faced by newly appointed chief student affairs officers are in need of immediate attention, and solving them often requires real changes in the organization of the division. Indeed, the principal reason the new chief administrator was hired may have been to make organizational changes in a relatively short time. This is particularly true at colleges and universities experiencing financial difficulties and enrollment problems.

The chief student affairs officer must realize that the support and cooperation of the student affairs staff are needed if the changes are to be successful. Careful planning and considerable diplomatic skills are needed to obtain this support. When some student affairs staff are tenured, are part of a civil service classification, or are members of a collective bargaining unit, organizational change may become even more difficult. Ideally, the chief student affairs officer will be so persuasive about the benefits of the new organizational plan that it will gain the acceptance of the student affairs staff on its own merits; indeed, the staff may adopt it as their own. In many situations, it is critical for the staff to know that the new plan has the strong support of the president and the other major administrative officers of the institution.

In some colleges and universities, the governing board has a standing committee on student affairs. If this is the case, the chief student affairs officer will need to present the organizational plan to this committee. If support from the president, the faculty council, the major student organizations, and the student affairs staff can be shown at the same time, it will greatly increase the plan's chances for acceptance. With governing board committees, it is particularly important to present organizational plans that are uncomplicated in their design and understandable in their goals. Some student affairs administrators have failed to persuade board members to accept their plan because they could not effectively articulate it in credible language.

Especially at community colleges, the organization of the student affairs division may be of considerable interest to local agencies and offices that also deliver services to students. Failure to consult with those in charge of community services may cause embarrassment to the college and costly duplication of effort. Careful planning can lead to effective collaboration with community agencies that will certainly improve the overall organization of the student affairs division.

Factors Affecting Organization

As the chief student affairs administrator considers the organization for the division, a number of factors may influence the choice of a plan; among them are the staff's competence, institutional characteristics, characteristics of the student body, institutional resources and facilities, and the goals of the student affairs division.

Staff Competence. The perceived level of staff competence is probably the most important factor for the chief student affairs officer to consider in choosing the organizational plan for the division. Understanding the most effective ways to use available talent is a key to a successful student affairs organization. If the chief student affairs officer inherits a number of key staff members in whom he or she does not have full confidence, this surely will affect the kind of organization proposed. In such a situation, the organizational plan is likely to establish rather tight policy controls and to centralize much of the authority at the top level of the organization. The individual departments in the division would have relatively little autonomy, and their role would be to carry out the plans and policies established by the chief student affairs officer and his or her central office associates. This organizational plan may not be viewed with enthusiasm by the people working in the departments, since it does not encourage initiative or creativity. However, if the chief student affairs officer is not confident of the ability of staff to lead effectively or make good decisions at the departmental level, the more centralized form of organization may be necessary. The chief student affairs officer may prefer to replace existing staff with more competent persons but may be restrained from doing so by various factors at the institution.

It is not unlikely that the chief student affairs officer will receive negative comments from students, faculty, and other administrators about the quality of certain staff members or a specific department. When it is clear that such criticism is justified, yet the chief student affairs officer does not feel persons should be terminated, an organizational change is often made. Usually, the response is to centralize policy-making for that unit, subjecting it to more control. This action may provide some relief in that the critics may be silenced for a while, but it is rarely an effective long-term solution. Placing tighter controls on departmental operations and centralizing decision making most likely will result in low morale, a lower level of dedication to tasks, and less responsiveness to real student needs.

In student affairs divisions where the organizational plan reflects extensive decentralization, there is likely to be a high level of confidence in the ability of the staff, both within and without the division. The autonomy of departments is high, and independence is valued and protected. Staff members' identification with and commitment to the unit are high because they have had a major role in determining policies and priorities there. The chief student affairs officer in this organizational plan is willing to allow considerable flexibility and freedom within the division because he or she is convinced that the results in high-quality programs and staff performance warrant it. When there is a high level of confidence in the quality of the staff and considerable departmental freedom and autonomy, the chief student affairs officer may be more vulnerable to criticism from outside the division. The officer may be accused of not adequately controlling the actions or policies of a particular department. In this kind of organization, the chief student affairs officer must have not only a high regard for the quality of the student affairs staff, but also a firm sense of self-confidence.

Institutional Characteristics. There is considerable diversity in American higher education, and the student affairs organization should reflect the special needs of each institution. The student affairs plan for an urban commuter institution, for example, may be quite different from the plan for a small residential liberal arts college. The particular needs of the students at the institution should be carefully considered in developing the organizational plan.

At older, traditional institutions, where each of the major academic units, or colleges, may be highly autonomous, the student affairs organization may reflect this degree of autonomy. Such services as advising, counseling, and placement may actually be part of the academic organization of each college, while other programs, such as admissions, housing, child care, and financial aid, may be centralized. Where there are large graduate and professional programs, similar arrangements may be made, although admissions services are likely to be placed within each of these specialized programs. At these older, more traditional universities, establishing uniform rules and procedures for dealing with violations of academic standards and codes of conduct may become an organizational issue. The faculty in the school of medicine, for example, may insist on their own standards and judicial system and may object to any participation by university personnel not affiliated with their program. However, the chief student affairs officer may hear pleas for consistency in standards and procedures from students throughout the campus and may also be anxious about the uneven emphasis given to due process if there are several different judicial groups. The organizational plan devised to meet these competing needs will require careful planning and negotiation in order to achieve any success.

At a less comprehensive campus where most students are enrolled in undergraduate programs, the student affairs organization is more likely to be defined as a distinct entity with uniform policies and procedures. While there may be informal links to the major academic programs, the various departments in student affairs are likely to have their own identity. The organization may place a greater emphasis on visibility and distinct roles for the student affairs departments than on the supportive, decentralized approach often found in older, traditional institutions.

Student Characteristics. The academic, economic, and social backgrounds of students may affect the organization of student affairs. Where students live may also be an important factor. Institutions with large numbers of underprepared students are likely to dedicate significant resources to academic development programs and to give these efforts high visibility within the student affairs organization. They also will find it beneficial to establish close organizational ties with academic departments outside student affairs. Colleges and universities with academically talented students may place a high priority within their student affairs organizations on programs that assist students in their preparation for graduate and professional schools.

The financial backgrounds of students clearly affect student affairs organizations. If there is a large percentage of needy students, financial aid programs will be prominent within the organization; often they will be closely linked with admissions and orientation programs to ensure coordinated services. The director of the financial aid program may have more influence within the student affairs organization on such campuses than anyone except the chief administrator.

The age, racial, sexual, and ethnic composition of the student body may also affect how the student affairs division is organized. After needs assessments of these students are conducted, the chief student affairs administrator can establish programs designed to assist them. New facilities, revised programs, and more targeted organizational plans may be required. Giving organizational visibility to a special office for minority students may be an effective action on campuses where minorities need to establish a clear identity. On other campuses, where minorities have been an integral part of campus life for many years, such an organizational action may not be needed, and may actually serve to divide students in an artificial way.

If most students live on the campus in residence halls and similar facilities, the student affairs organization will certainly reflect this. Many colleges and universities have decided to deliver the various programs and services directly to the places where students live, placing counseling, financial aid, recreational, and academic support services in these facilities. Such an organizational design may increase visibility and use of the services, reduce the need for a large central facility, and make staff more responsive to student needs. At campuses where most of the students commute each day, an office is often established to respond to the special needs created by such transient attendance. Because many of these students attend part-time and at different hours of the day and evening, the student affairs organization must respond to their needs when they are on the campus. This may require flexible staffing patterns and "storefront offices" that are placed where the students can use them most conveniently.

Institutional Resources and Facilities. The most important and most costly resource for a student affairs division is its professional staff, and the ability of the institution to provide adequate staff certainly affects the organization. If the college is not well supported financially, salary levels may not be adequate to attract well-qualified staff. In such circumstances, the chief student affairs administrator may have to tighten the organization, centralize more of its responsibilities, and make more use of volunteers or paraprofessional staff. At institutions experiencing severe financial problems, it is sometimes necessary to eliminate certain positions in the student affairs division and combine functions that have been separate entities. It is unlikely that all the services and programs deemed desirable by student affairs administrators will be able to be funded out of institutional resources. As a result, fund-raising activities are now a common part of student affairs organizations. Coordinated with the overall institutional plans to raise private dollars, the student affairs effort is designed to augment the division's ability to deliver high-quality services.

At more affluent institutions, where staff and support dollars are adequate, the student affairs organization is more likely to be decentralized, with considerable flexibility given to the departments to identify needs and develop programs to address them. The organization may also include full-time staff for student affairs research and staff development. Moreover, department heads are more likely to have one or more administrative assistants, who make it possible for them to engage in more planning and creative activities.

When the various offices and departments in student affairs are scattered around the campus in different locations, it is more difficult to achieve organizational cohesiveness. It is also less likely that students, faculty, or other administrators will view the student affairs organization as a unit. In this situation, communication is more difficult, and the chief student affairs administrator may have to spend considerable time visiting the various offices. At larger institutions, the staff in one student affairs office may not even know the names of the staff in another student affairs office on the other side of campus. Such unfamiliarity may result in fragmented services to students, and the chief student affairs officer may need to establish formal organizational links between widely separated offices in order to improve services.

Where there is a student services facility on a campus, the various departments are all located in the building for the convenience of students and the effective coordination of the student affairs departments. This design should result in better visibility and understanding for the student affairs division on the campus. However, such facilities can become liabilities to the organization if they are viewed as isolated entities disconnected from the academic life of the campus. To combat this serious problem, student affairs administrators sometimes establish satellite offices in academic departments, residence halls, or other administrative facilities.

Goals of the Student Affairs Division. The purposes of the student affairs program are largely determined by the goals and priorities of the institution. Although there may be some variation in this principle, student affairs' role is essentially supportive in nature. For example, at an institution whose role is strongly vocational, one would be unlikely to find a student affairs organization whose primary purpose is the development of student values. At a highly selective, research-based university, a student affairs organization is likely to be oriented toward counseling and personal support. At a college characterized by a particular ideological emphasis, the student affairs organization may be oriented toward control of student behavior.

The overall purposes of the student affairs division affect the division's organization. If there is a strong emphasis on control, for example, it is likely that a specific office for judicial affairs will be established and given high visibility. Newly hired staff will be impressed with control as a high priority, and each department will be expected to support it. On other campuses, such an office may not even exist, since the priority for control may be very low. If personal support for students experiencing stress is a priority, psychological counseling services will enjoy high visibility within the student affairs organization and will probably receive a large share of its resources. Finally, if high enrollments are needed for the institution's survival, the organization of the student affairs division will be heavily weighted in favor of recruitment, admissions, and retention.

When the purposes of the student affairs organization are not seen to be in harmony with the priorities of the institution, there are usually serious problems. If the student affairs division isolates itself, uses its own jargon, or pursues programs and policies that are not in accord with the college's goals, it is likely that the organization will be changed, either through student or faculty pressure or by presidential fiat. The ability of the chief student affairs officer to understand the delicate balance between the programs that he or she wants to pursue and those that the institution can support clearly will affect the success of the student affairs organization.

Specific Organizational Problems

Some practical problems faced by chief student affairs administrators in the organization of their divisions are reporting responsibility, divided authority, control of policy-making, mixed messages, breadth of control, participation in decision making, and control of evaluation.

Reporting Responsibility. The chief student affairs officer usually reports directly to the president of the institution and functions at the same administrative level as the chief officers for academic affairs, financial affairs, and development. This reporting relationship is likely to give student affairs issues a high priority on the campus. The chief student affairs officer's easy access to the president often enables programs and services in the division to enjoy sound financial support. On many campuses, the chief student affairs officer reports to the provost or chief academic affairs officer. This reporting relationship may increase academic support and understanding and may even enhance financial support if the provost controls most of the institution's internal resources. However, reporting to the provost may decrease the visibility and priority given to student affairs programs and may encourage a perception of them as merely ancillary to the teaching program. Most seriously, it may remove the chief student affairs officer from the institution's central management group and make it less likely that the needs of students will be a regular part of the decision-making process.

Divided Authority. Most chief student affairs officers are responsible for programs such as student housing, campus unions, and student health services. Sometimes the administrative authority for these departments is shared with the chief business officer. For example, the student affairs division may be in charge of the program and activity functions at the student union, and the business affairs division may handle the financial and maintenance functions. In order for this organizational plan to work effectively, excellent communication must exist between the two divisions, and there must be very good understanding and acceptance of the roles of each area.

There are many opportunities for such an organizational design to fail, or to fall far short of success. Programming staff may not be sure who is in charge, and students and other users may find that when the support of supervisors must be secured before anything can be done, the department is not as responsive as it might be. If there is animosity between the student affairs staff and the business affairs staff at any level, it will most likely have a negative effect on the organization.

Such problems have resulted in many student affairs administrators assuming full control over the programming and financial aspects of these departments. This requires additional staff, increased work loads, and total accountability for the function. All have an impact on the student affairs organization and have resulted in a greater emphasis on management in student affairs.

Control of Policy-Making. The student affairs administrator often has responsibility for departments whose overall policies are mainly decided by persons outside the division, such as admissions and financial aid. Standards and policies in these areas are usually the result of extended discussions by faculty and administrative groups and ultimately are decided by the president and the governing board. Staff working in these offices frequently are the targets of persons dissatisfied with the policies, which may deny them admission or financial support. The staff may not feel as if they are a real part of the organization if they have not had any role in the establishment of the policies they are expected to administer. This organizational problem can sometimes be alleviated by the use of policy-advisory committees that provide for significant participation by members of the working staff.

Mixed Messages. If the chief student affairs officer does not present a clear, consistent, and coherent message to students and faculty about the goals of the division, the organization is likely to experience serious problems. If the staff is confused about what they are expected to do, students and others certainly will not know what the student affairs organization is trying to accomplish. For example, are staff members who act as advisers to student government free to assist the group in any direction it wishes to go, or are there clear limitations? Does the fraternity council really have the authority to decide its own rules, or can it do only what the student affairs administrator allows? Does the faculty understand what the counseling center means when it describes its student development program in highly technical, psychological terms? The chief student affairs officer needs to be keenly aware of the perceptions others have of the division's programs and services. It is the administrator's job to ensure that the messages are not mixed, but are articulated in an understandable, consistent, and persuasive manner.

Breadth of Control. Many chief student affairs officers, in their desire to be involved in all aspects of their divisions, retain direct authority over all of the various functions. On large campuses, this may involve as many as fifteen departments. Except in rare instances, this usually results in difficulties for the chief administrator and keeps the departments from functioning effectively. Moreover, it is inevitable that certain departments will receive much more attention than others and that this attention will be given primarily in response to crises.

The usual organizational response to this problem, of course, is to group the various departments by campus location, functional similarity, or source of financial support and to place senior administrators in charge of each group. The chief student affairs officer then has a much more manageable span of control. It is possible for this organizational design to lead to an unresponsive, multilayered bureaucracy, with the chief student affairs officer far removed from the departments and from the day-to-day lives of students. Vigorous efforts are needed to avoid such serious problems.

Participation in Decision Making. Most student affairs administrators go to considerable lengths to involve students, faculty, and their own staff in the decision-making processes of the division. These may include the identification of campus issues and problems, the selection and evaluation of staff, and the determination of procedures and practices. There often are formal advisory committees for each department in the student affairs division, as well as an overall institutional council on student affairs for the review of policy. While such organizational arrangements are frequently beneficial and usually well received, they can sometimes act as obstacles to change and may be painfully slow. The chief student affairs officer may be keenly aware of a critical need for policy change in the admissions area, for example, in order to meet the institution's enrollment goals for the coming year. However, before any change can be made, lengthy discussions must be scheduled with the appropriate committees set up to review such policies. It is also not unlikely that the advice received from the committee will not support the needed change. The chief student affairs officer must be careful to set up an organization that combines ample opportunity for participation in decision making with the need to make timely decisions for the benefit of the institution.

Control of Evaluation. What the student affairs division does is scrutinized on a daily basis by students who use (or do not use) the services and by faculty and others who observe them.

It is often a concern of chief student affairs administrators that their programs or services are evaluated by others on criteria other than those considered useful by student affairs professionals. For example, some faculty may assume that the student affairs organization is doing a good job at the university if they do not see any serious campus disruption and the students are quiet; other administrators may evaluate the student affairs departments on the basis of their financial viability and the absence of negative audits; and some students may think the student affairs division is doing a good job to the extent that they are left alone in their social activities. Student affairs staff members themselves are highly unlikely to agree with any of these approaches to their work. If the disparity is large, significant frustration may result for student affairs staff, and they will probably be unsure about what activities they should pursue. If services, policies, and programs are selected to avoid controversy and to please others who are not familiar with actual student needs and problems, the student affairs organization will be largely ineffective.

It is the responsibility of the chief student affairs officer to articulate the goals of the organization in a manner that is clear and persuasive to all campus constituencies and to help them understand the criteria by which the various programs are to be evaluated. The evaluation process itself affords a positive opportunity to invite faculty, students, and other administrators into the process of deciding these criteria. With such efforts, the base of support for the organization can be strengthened.

Conclusion

Choosing the best method for structuring a student affairs organization depends on many interrelated factors. Multiple constituent groups with varying levels of vested interest must be consulted. The institution's president and chief administrative officers, the faculty and their governing organization, and the student affairs staff and students all have unique perspectives regarding the way in which the student affairs organization should be structured. In addition, the chief student affairs administrator must examine the staff competence, the institutional characteristics and mission, the characteristics of the student body, the institutional resources and facilities, and the goals of the division of student affairs. All these factors play important roles in defining the organizational structure that works best for a given institution. However, even the best designed organizations encounter specific organizational problems. How the administrator deals with the specific problems mentioned in this chapter will influence how the division of student affairs will ultimately be organized.

Bibliography

Appleton, J., Briggs, C., and Rhatigan, J., *Pieces of Eight.* Portland, Ore.: National Association of Student Personnel Administrators Institute of Research and Development, 1978.

Argyris, C. *Increasing Leadership Effectiveness.* New York: Wiley, 1976.

Bennis, W. G. *Beyond Bureaucracy: Essays on the Development and Evaluation of Human Organization.* New York: McGraw-Hill, 1973.

Bolman, L. G., and Deal, T. E. *Modern Approaches to Understanding and Managing Organizations.* San Francisco: Jossey-Bass, 1984.

Etzioni, A. *A Sociological Reader on Complex Organizations.* New York: Holt, Rinehart & Winston, 1980.

Hersey, P., and Blanchard, K. H. *Management of Organizational Behavior: Utilizing Human Resources.* (4th ed.) Englewood Cliffs, N.J.: Prentice-Hall, 1982.

Herzberg, F. *The Managerial Choice: To Be Efficient and to Be Human.* Homewood, Ill.: Dow Jones–Irwin, 1976.

Keller, G. *Academic Strategy: The Management Revolution in American Higher Education.* Baltimore, Md.: Johns Hopkins University Press, 1983.

McGregor, D. *The Professional Manager.* New York: McGraw-Hill, 1967.

Walker, D. E. *The Effective Administrator: A Practical Approach to Problem Solving, Decision Making, and Campus Leadership.* San Francisco: Jossey-Bass, 1979.

Chapter Eighteen

Planning and Budgeting

John H. Schuh
Scott T. Rickard

Various voices continue to call for increased accountability within higher education. Constituent pressures and demands for accountability come from the "general public, alumni, donors, federal and state government officials, state educational coordinating commissions, boards of trustes, institutional presidents, deans of students, student affairs staff, student government associations, and students themselves" (Barnes, Morton, and Austin, 1983, p. 11). The public has raised questions about the amount of resources employed (Bowen, 1977). The reputation that student affairs officers have, especially among their colleagues on the business affairs side of their institutions, is that they do not manage resources well. Pembroke (1985) commented that it is not uncommon to find a general lack of experience and expertise in financial management among student services professionals. This, in turn, often results in a lack of appreciation of the institution's financial management structure and all too frequently leads to either inappropriate planning or no planning at all.

The need for and importance of planning and budgeting are reflected in the student affairs literature. Knowledge about budgets ranked second in importance among forty-four areas of expertise in a national survey of chief student affairs officers (CSAOs). Moreover, the CSAOs indicated that they spent the

461

most time on goal setting and strategic and long-range planning (Lunsford, 1984). A survey of the needs of mid-level professionals in student affairs indicated that the three most important areas were effective management, the interaction of academic affairs and student affairs, and accountability (Career Development and Professional Standards Divison, 1984). A national survey of college presidents' perceptions of issues of importance to CSAOs and of their abilities to effectively gain the skills needed to resolve deficiencies underscored the importance of planning and budgeting. Presidents ranked future enrollment and planning for change as their third problem and financial difficulties as the fifth. Presidents also mentioned future enrollment, financial aid, and fiscal management as the three areas where chief student affairs officers most often lacked the necessary skill or expertise (Kinnick and Bollheimer, 1984).

Numerous authors from diverse perspectives have identified planning and budgeting as major management functions (Richman and Farmer, 1974; Koontz and O'Donnell, 1972; Deegan, 1981). Related functions in the management process are organizing, staffing, directing, and evaluating. Planning has been described as the most basic of all management functions because it engages staff at all levels in the organization (Koontz and O'Donnell, 1972; Dutton and Rickard, 1980).

Higher education has experienced a managerial transformation in the 1980s characterized by an increased emphasis on financial planning, enrollment management, marketing, strategic planning, and computer technology. The revolution in academic management involves four major movements (Keller, 1982). These are the movement from administration to management, the shift of political power from faculty to administration, the change from long-range planning to strategic planning, and the creation of new forms and approaches to governance. The renewed emphasis on planning results from the increasing importance of financial issues at all levels within institutions of higher education. Current and projected declines in the number of students heighten concern with maintaining enrollments because institutional budgets are enrollment-driven.

In a climate of fiscal restraint, every decision becomes a budget decision.

The shift in emphasis from administration to management evolved during the 1970s, resulting in major changes in job duties and performance. The differences between the two concepts have been noted by Richman and Farmer (1974, pp. 14–15): "Management involves strategy, innovation, initiating and bringing about change, creative problem solving and decision-making, actively seeking other alternatives and opportunities, negotiating, resolving conflicts, dynamic or active leadership, diplomacy, statesmanship, and a high degree of risk taking and entrepreneurship. Administration implies more routine decision-making and operations, and the implementation of goals, priorities, and strategies, usually determined by others. It is more concerned with following predetermined policies, procedures, and regulations. It tends to be much more adaptive, passive and reactive than management, and it is much more of a closed system concept primarily concerned with internal efficiency and operations. It is also more concerned with internal monitoring and control than with external environmental change and strategic planning."

This chapter defines various approaches to the budgeting processes and addresses selected issues in planning; it is not meant to provide complete information about these topics. Rather, the purpose is to introduce the topics and suggest resources the reader may wish to investigate to gather additional information. Questions and topics discussed include these: What is strategic planning? How does strategic planning differ from long-range planning? What are the common elements of the strategic planning process? What are the pitfalls or problems in the process? How has student affairs adapted to the increased emphasis on planning? How does the budgeting process operate in higher education? What are the common elements, advantages, and disadvantages of four budgeting approaches: line-item, program, zero-base, and formula? What are the primary uses and problems of cash and accrual accounting? What are the steps and guidelines in preparing budgets?

Planning Approaches

Over the past several decades, various approaches to planning initiated and developed by business and government have been assimilated by institutions of higher education. Many of the more notable models are easily recognizable by catchy acronyms: PPBS, MBO, PERT (for program evaluation review technique), ZBB (for zero-base budgeting), and MIS (Baldridge and Okimi, 1982). Although these approaches represent both theory and practice, no single planning model predominates among over 3,200 institutions of higher education.

Two general approaches have dominated planning for the past several decades—management science and incrementalism. The roots of management science can be traced to the time and motion studies and efficiency engineering of Frederick Taylor. Although management science has never been fully embraced by campus administrators, contemporary forms of this rational-economic approach include operations research, systems analysis, and policy sciences. Incrementalism, according to Keller (1983), contrasts sharply with management science in that it assumes that "the world is not rational and people are often not rational. Life is essentially political" (p. 106).

In 1959 Charles Lindblom, the most noted proponent of the incremental approach, published the classic article "The Science of Muddling Through," in which he argued that what he called the rational-comprehensive approach was irrational because it presumed intellectual abilities beyond the capacity of most people. Lindblom believed the partisan-political approach was more rational because it best reflected the human condition.

The success or failure of planning in student affairs depends in part on perceptions and attitudes about the nature of the planning process. Moreover, the attitudes and behavior of chief student affairs officers and other top-level staff play a key role in the successful execution of planning. Bean (1983) suggests that "many chief student affairs officers believe that they can plan rationally, despite evidence to the contrary" (p. 41). He indicates that plans are influenced more by subjective than by objective knowledge. If the CSAO and other staff assume that planning will follow a logical, rational process, a likely consequence will be disillusionment and disappointment. Consequently, student affairs administrators need to better understand and appreciate subjective aspects of planning. The recent student affairs literature reinforces concern about the compatibility of rational planning and the way organizations function, as depicted by organizational theory (Kuh, Whitt, and Shedd, 1987). It suggests that rational planning, in the context of the ambiguous, conflicting environment of higher education, can have negative consequences for organizational effectiveness.

Strategic Planning

In the early 1980s, strategic planning was the latest term in higher education. In 1983, the readers of *Change* magazine selected *Academic Strategy: The Management Revolution in American Higher Education* (Keller, 1983) as the best book about higher education of the past two years. Strategic planning has been described as an alternative to mechanical and deterministic long-range planning. Kotler and Murphy (1981) define strategic planning as "the process of developing and maintaining a strategic fit between the organization and its changing market opportunities" (p. 471). For each institution, strategic planning encompasses a range of factors: the organizational mission, relationships with a fluid external environment, interactions with other agencies, competitive circumstances, strengths and weaknesses within the institution, opportunities for growth, and the institution's niche in the marketplace of higher education. Strategic planning focuses on connecting the activities of the organization with environmental demands, emphasizes flexibility and responsiveness to changes in the environment, and requires an external rather than internal perspective. Day-to-day operational issues, such as the routine allocation of resources, represent more conventional planning activities that contrast with the external focus of strategic planning.

The distinctions between strategic planning and conventional planning have been summarized by Baldridge and Okimi

(1982). As Table 1 shows, strategic planning emphasizes relating the organizational mission to external market conditions, typically is limited to top-level officers who have the power and perspective to make decisions, shortens the time perspective of traditional long-range planning, and focuses externally in an open-system perspective in contrast to internal, closed systems. Strategic decision making involves art more than science, utilizing qualitative data based on experience, intuition, trial and error, hunches, and value judgments. Planning is viewed as a stream of decisions seeking wise choices in contrast to the "right" plan.

Table 1. Comparison of Strategic
Planning and Conventional Planning.

Activity	Strategic Planning	Conventional Planning
Arena of Planning	Organization's Destiny, Market	Wide Range of Issues, Nonroutine and Routine
Who Plans	Top-Level Officers	Planning Office
Time Orientation	Medium- to Short-Range	Long-Range
System Perspective	External, Environmental	Internal, Organizational
Theoretical Perspective	Open System	Closed System
Decision Data	Both Quantitative and Qualitative	Quantitative
Decision	Complex Art Form	Exact Science
Outcome	Stream of Critical Decisions	Plan, Blueprint

Because planning involves art and intuition as well as science and rationality, metaphors and analogies provide indirect ways of capturing the essence of the activity. Metaphors have been drawn from activities within education, such as counseling and physical education, as well as other activities—among them optometry, matchmaking, mountain climbing, plumbing, and ballooning (Huff, 1980, Bean, 1983). In describing how strategic planning differs from conventional planning, Baldridge and Okimi (1982) suggest that leaders must learn to think less like the desk-bound planners at headquarters and more like the battlefield commander. Conventional and strategic planning can also be compared to photography; long-range planning typically involves a series of normal plans, or prints, made over a period of time, whereas the time frame for strategic planning is more analogous to a series of Polaroid snapshots.

Elements of the Planning Process

The common elements of the planning process have been identified by various authors (Pillinger and Kraack, 1980; Clugston, 1986; Cope, 1981; Kotler and Murphy, 1981; Keller, 1983). These elements include examining critical trends in the environment and assessing threats and opportunities, assessing institutional strengths and weaknesses, determining strategic direction based on the institutional mission and an assessment of opportunities and strengths, establishing program priorities, and reallocating resources from low-priority to high-priority programs.

Examine Environmental Trends. From the perspective of the student affairs division, monitoring environmental trends requires focusing on broader institutional goals as well as divisional goals. Ideally, the two are in harmony, although what is perceived as a threat by student affairs may be viewed as an opportunity by others.

The information gleaned from environmental scanning provides snapshots of the threats to and opportunities for the institution and student affairs. Institutional and student affairs officers continuously assessing external environments are like air traffic controllers observing blips on the radar screen. Student affairs must continuously monitor social, economic, political, and technological trends in the environment. The threats and opportunities represented by changing environmental conditions create challenges that require responses.

Assess Institutional Strengths and Weaknesses. Assessing strengths and weaknesses in academic departments typically involves comparisons of research productivity with peer departments. Although student affairs departments need to identify exemplary programs in peer institutions, the primary focus should be on responding to the threats and opportunities that affect the institutional mission. Campuswide issues that transcend departmental boundaries, such as the quality of student life or enrollment management, will increasingly be priority concerns for student affairs administrators. The process of determining strengths and weaknesses inevitably involves asking questions about what is done, why it is done, and how well it is done, as well as how services are organized and funded. Moreover, who asks the questions will largely determine the credibility and impact of the assessment. Involving students and faculty in the process adds ''noise'' to the proceedings but, more importantly, provides perspectives other than those of student affairs professionals.

Determine a Strategic Direction. Whether one considers a planning decision rational or irrational depends on one's perspective. For example, from the vantage point of a student affairs professional, moving the orientation function from student affairs to academic affairs may seem to be a misuse of power, particularly if the process involves little or no consultation. From the perspective of the decision maker, the decision may be completely logical on the basis of an assessment of the external environment and internal considerations. The increased importance of enrollment management may suggest that one or more student services units be reorganized or moved from student affairs to academic affairs. A number of functional areas, such as admissions, orientation, and financial aid, typically span reporting boundaries. These and other functions could report to academic affairs, business affairs, or student affairs, depending on the institution's history, the turnover in top-level positions, and the philosophy of administrative leaders. Increasingly, decisions to alter the structure of organizations will probably be made after assessing the threats to institutional enrollment and the opportunities to enhance it.

Establish Program Priorities. Determining program priorities, whether for the purpose of reducing expenditures or allocating new resources, requires the careful delineation of criteria. Pillinger and Kraack (1980) identified the following set of criteria:

- *Essentiality*. Is the function essential or peripheral to the university's or the student affairs division's mission?
- *Quality.* Does the program or service consistently maintain a high standard of excellence? This may be measured by peer ratings, faculty recognition, student evaluation, contributions to knowledge or practice, and so on.
- *Availability*. To what degree is the function available outside the student affairs unit or the university?
- *Need or Demand*. What are the student, institutional, and societal demands for this function? These may be measured by the number of students or staff served, the number of visits, the work load, and so on. To what degree does the function meet current and future projections of need or demand? Is there a legal or public mandate for the function?
- *Efficiency*. How effective is the program in providing the most service for the least money? Could the function be performed appropriately with fewer resources? This may involve comparison of units of service produced to resources used.

Effective planning processes involve all planning elements, as the following examples show. The Biennial Planning Process at the University of Virginia is directly linked to budgeting. Each vice-president distills individual reports from the units into an evaluation of the accomplishments and shortfalls of the just-completed biennium. Units and divisions then update their objectives, strategies, and priorities for the next two years. General descriptions of significant proposals extend the planning for ten years beyond the current biennium. Financial and staffing requirements for all proposed changes are also provided in the plans. On the basis of experience with two planning cycles, the vice-president for student affairs reported that the process improved the coordination and communication among schools and departments in the pursuit of institutional goals (Ern, 1986).

At the University of Maryland, College Park, the vice-chancellor for student affairs established a Union into the 21st Century Task Force, which combined elements of long-range and strategic planning. The broadly representative task force, chaired by a faculty member, was given four tasks:

- to develop a set of assumptions about the university's mission, technology in higher education, the demographic complexion of the campus community, and the changing preferences of students and other union patrons, on the basis of a review of planning and evaluation documents and research;
- to develop a scenario of the future for program and service priorities on the basis of the identified assumptions;
- to recommend physical facilities and fiscal management strategies to meet the priorities; and
- to suggest a ten-year schedule for the implementation of the strategies and to identify specific actions for the next two years (Thomas, 1987).

Reallocate Resources from Low-Priority to High-Priority Programs. Because strategic planning requires an institution-wide perspective and the power to make decisions, it is a high priority for the chief executive officer and other top-level managers. The CSAO represents the division of student affairs at the top level of institutional management if the CSAO reports directly to the president. The CSAO and other staff in student affairs have a difficult challenge in avoiding the pitfalls inherent in institution-wide planning processes. In order to be a viable part of the institution, student affairs professionals must participate fully in the planning process even when the outcome results in a steady-state budget, a reduction in staff, or the reassignment of departments or programs to other divisions of the university. These potentially adverse outcomes severely test the caliber of leadership in student affairs. However, if the CSAO and other staff fail to participate fully in campuswide planning, student affairs may be perceived as peripheral to the central mission of the institution. As a result, staff will feel and act like second-class citizens, staff morale will decline, and service to students will be adversely affected.

Planning Problems

Identifying the likely pitfalls prior to beginning the planning process increases the probability of success. The gap between planning and budgeting constitutes a major problem area for administrators at all levels (Hobbs and Heany, 1977). In a study of college presidents, three major problems with planning were identified: the process was too lengthy and complicated, the process became more important than the results, and the plan was not linked to daily operations of the budget and failed to make sense to participants (Baldridge and Okimi, 1982).

Bean and Kuh (1984) identified problems likely to occur during planning in a problem matrix, shown in Table 2. Their typology assumes an adaptive approach to planning, implying that the process is likely to be more valuable than the substantive plan that results. A second assumption acknowledges that "naturalistic" planning occurs on a constant, informal basis through the interactions of administrators, faculty, staff, and students; planning is not limited to formal activities. The limits of logic and rationality constitute a third assumption.

Planning begins by assessing the institution's capacity to undertake planning; this includes identifying participants, purposes, activities, costs, and a time-line. As Table 2 shows, the planning process involves three subsequent phases: initiation, development, and implementation. Five organizational constructs complete the framework of the problem matrix. These are goals, participation, information and communication, interdependence, and resources. The problem matrix provides practitioners with a helpful device for identifying potential problems in advance and thereby increasing the probability of success in planning.

Budgeting

Budgeting in the university setting is a hybrid of the budgeting processes that one might find in business, government, and charitable organizations (Said, 1974). Why is this the case? So many different endeavors are conducted simul-

Table 2. A Typology of the Sources of Potential Problems Encountered in Planning.

Organizational Constructs	Assessment of the Capacity to Plan	Initiation of Planning Activities	Development of the Plan	Implementation of the Plan
Goals	Level of institutional consensus	Purposes of planning are unclear Goals may change during the process Goals differ at different organizational levels Hidden agendas	Unclear expectations for planner behavior Conflicts with vested interests	Goal displacement Limitations of rational processes "Rational means to irrational ends" Adaptability
Participation	Psychological preparedness of participants	Too many or too few people Representative levels Experts Use of new or existing structures	Inadequate representation Anarchistic behavior Technical staff/faculty relationships Authority not commensurate with responsibility for planning	Rewarding participation Understanding change Expecting conflict Incremental adaptation
Information and communication	Access, types available Current patterns of communication	Technical aspects of planning Accuracy and relevance of information Limitations of planning	Clear understanding of planning process Periodic status reports Balanced treatment of unit data	Communicating the plan Appropriate level of specificity Feedback, evaluation, and revision Degree of flexibility of the plan

Interdependence (internal, external)	Relationships between units	Appropriate scope of planning Degree of coupling among subunits Timing relative to external requirements Length of planning cycle	Involvement of units that must carry out plans Relationship to line administrators and faculty	Environmental changes Plan designed for external and not internal audiences
Resources	Time (staff) Expertise Organizational slack	Adequacy for planning process	Commensurate with unit needs Adequacy for implementation	Realistic process expectations Conflict and turf protection Continuation costs

Source: Reprinted by permission from "A Typology of Planning Problems" by John P. Bean and George D. Kuh in *The Journal of Higher Education*, 1984, 55 (1), 38. © 1984 by the Ohio State University Press.

taneously in institutions of higher education that it is difficult
to characterize various budgetary approaches other than with
broad brush strokes. As in the private sector of our economy,
some institutions of higher education have research parks, hos-
pitals, and athletic teams. Other institutions are dependent on
governmental support, but even here dramatic differences exist, such as the difference between a state-assisted research university and a community college that relies heavily on local property taxes. Further, colleges and universities raise millions of
dollars annually through fund drives, capital campaigns, and
the like. The development arm of a college or university, in fact,
may resemble a private charity in its budgeting and fiscal operating policies.

Much of the process of budgeting in higher education,
particularly in that segment that receives governmental support,
is taken from the budgeting process in the governmental sector. The focus of budgeting in the governmental sector is on
control. "Budgets are created to hold expenses within limits and
to avoid a deficit" (Sherwood and Best, 1975, p. 395). Spending in prescribed ways and dollar accountability are stressed.
Accountability in achievement terms is not emphasized (Said,
1974).

Several steps have been developed from the governmental model to ensure budget control. First, when budgets are
prepared, they are subject to rigid and complex legal requirements. There is an appropriate format for the development of
the budget; other forms are rejected. Second, cash or fund accounting systems, described later in this chapter, are used. Cash
accounting is useful in that it provides detailed information about
budget accounts (Said, 1974). Third, line-item budgeting, described in the next section, often is used. With this form of
budgeting, the focus is on controlling spending so that at the
end of the fiscal year the budgetary account is not overdrawn.
In fact, some states have constitutional requirements that make
it unlawful to finish the year with the state budget in deficit.
Fourth, budgets are prepared on an incremental basis; that is,
the budget for next year is based on the allocation for this year.
This approach is very different from zero-base budgeting, for

example, where budgeting starts from scratch. We assume, in the line-item approach, that what we are doing programmatically makes sense, and only minor adjustments are made in the budget from one year to the next.

The focus of budgeting is on increases and decreases. Long-range planning is not a significant part of the budgeting process. Unit or department budget managers attempt to gather adequate resources so that programs and activities for the next year are funded adequately; rarely are they forced to think about what the status of their programs will be in five or ten years. Demographic data, broad economic trends, and other information that might help the long-range planning process usually are not part of this approach. Whether this approach to budgeting is appropriate or not, institutions of higher education tend to budget using these principles, most of which have been drawn from government. The result is that long-range planning and careful examination of mission tend not to be an integral part of the budgeting process.

Budgeting Approaches

Four budgeting approaches will be introduced in this section: line-item, program, zero-base, and formula. These approaches are fairly common in higher education, and most institutions of higher education utilize one or a combination of them.

Line-Item Budgeting. Line-item budgets are commonly used in government; they are also known as object budgets. This type of budget can be defined as a "financial plan of estimated expenditures expressed in terms of the kinds and quantities of objects to be purchased and the estimated revenues needed to finance them during a specified period, usually one year" (Bubanakis, 1976, p. 9). This is the most simplified approach to budgeting (Muston, 1980).

The real purpose of a line-item budget is to make sure that expenditures and revenues are brought into balance at the end of each fiscal year. Among the important features of the line-item budget are the listing of budgetary divisions by departments or agencies and the listing of expenditures by category. This form of budgeting provides for excellent control of resources, makes sure that funds are utilized for the purposes that were originally intended, and protects fiscal resources (Bubanakis, 1976).

Line-item budgets usually are developed according to the previous year's budgetary authorization. In effect, they tend to repeat themselves and they do not supply information that would provide the manager with alternative courses of action. With minor modifications, line-item budgets tend to be employed without an analysis of the value or utility of the expenditures represented by the budget.

Bubanakis (1976) contended that this budgeting approach has a number of disadvantages. First, the orientation of managers is toward increasing what is already being done, rather than raising more fundamental questions concerning what the department should be doing. Basic programs are not analyzed unless new programs are proposed. In short, the budget becomes static in terms of what it proposes to accomplish.

Second, line-item budgets do not encourage long-range planning. Since the budget tends to repeat itself annually, adjustments are made to handle inflation, but the manager is not encouraged to estimate the unit's budgetary requirements beyond the next fiscal year.

Third, line-item budgets encourage competition for funds. Departments attempt to obtain as large a resource allocation as possible, regardless of whether the resources are well spent or duplicated by another department. Each department prepares its own budget request, and there is little enthusiasm or reward for collaboration. Moreover, it is possible that independent departments are not aware of activities in other units.

Why, then, are line-item budgets so common? For one thing, they are easy to understand. It does not take much of an accounting background to understand the concepts underlying line-item budgets. Second, they are easy to construct. Basically, managers make adjustments for inflation from one year to next rather than step back and review the entire operation for which they are responsible. Third, for those who are interested in amassing resources, this approach facilitates that end. New resources are added to a department's budget whenever possible, possibly without serious questions being raised about the other programs and activities that the department undertakes.

Program Budgeting. Program budgeting is not a new concept (Muston, 1980). According to Steiss (1972), a program is a "group of interdependent, closely related services or activities which possess or contribute to a common objective or set of allied objectives" (p. 157). A program budget consists of five components: identifying goals, analyzing current programs, developing a multiyear plan, analyzing and selecting alternative programs, and evaluating the programs.

The first component involves identifying major goals and objectives in programmatic terms. For example, one might determine as an overall goal that all students who are new to the institution will develop an understanding of the programs and services that are available. Objectives in support of that goal might include developing a unique program that will provide for the orientation of international students and a specialized program that will meet the needs of transfer students.

The second component of program budgeting involves analyzing all the programs that are available to meet the goals and objectives defined in the first component. For example, we might find that the international students' office provides special orientation activities for students from outside the United States, as do the health center and the financial aid office. The reading skills center might also have special orientation programs directed at international students. Taking inventory of available programs thus allows us to develop an understanding of the current situation.

In the third component, an extended time frame and a multiyear program and financial plan are developed. An extended time period is used so that a more coherent plan can be developed and costs are projected over several years.

The fourth component, program analysis, is the key to this budgeting approach. A systematic analysis of alternatives is undertaken and programs are selected for the multiyear plan.

In our example, we might decide to undertake a series of new programs for international students, such as sending representatives of our institution to the students' home countries to give them briefings and other information about making the transition to their new educational institution. While we recognize that this might be an expensive activity, our estimate is that we will reduce the attrition of international students. We will start with just a few countries and expand the program if we find that retention improves. In this phase, we decide how to spend our resources and then determine which programs will best meet our objectives.

The last step involves updating and evaluating our programs. In this component we modify and improve our programs and determine whether or not our goals and objectives were met.

Novick (1973) listed three basic reasons for using the program budgeting approach. In the main, he suggested that program budgeting is a useful technique for determining whether or not a department or unit is meeting global expectations rather than dealing with day-to-day issues. In our example, we were primarily concerned with how well students were introduced to the institution so that they could make a quick, meaningful transition to campus life. We were less concerned with whether or not rooms of appropriate size were reserved for speakers and social activities.

More specifically, Novick (1973) suggested that program budgeting provides for a formal, systematic method of improving decisions concerning the allocation of resources. Resources always are finite, and program budgeting forces budget managers to decide what the general goals will be for a specific activity and then to identify specific objectives to be met. Furthermore, program budgeting provides a dose of fiscal realism to the planning process. If the objectives of the program cannot be sustained by the available resources, the objectives have to be retooled. If we decide that sending our orientation representatives overseas simply is too costly, we have to devise other ways of meeting our program goal.

Finally, program budgeting provides a basis on which planners and managers can make choices between alternatives.

Once the choices are made between alternatives, detailed planning can begin. In the main, however, program budgeting is less concerned with specific details than line-item budgeting. It provides a big-picture approach to budgeting and planning and identifies the path and direction of programming for the next several budget cycles.

There are at least three specific advantages to program budgeting. Bubanakis (1976) described the advantages of program budgeting in an evaluation context. First, program budgeting commits its users to long-range planning. By doing so, it permits the evaluation of the efficiency and economy of programs. Second, program budgeting permits the evaluation of alternative programs or alternative ways of implementing the same program. Finally, program budgeting makes it possible to give priority to various programs with an eye to overall effectiveness.

There are at least two difficult issues related to program budgeting. One is that from a conceptual point of view, it can be difficult for managers to understand what a program budget is. It is not a management information system, and it is not a reorganization plan (Novick, 1973). Defining objectives is not easy, and the initial program may take several years of testing (McKean and Anshen, 1967).

Second, there are a number of problems with the operation phase of the program budget. Activities may be scattered through a variety of departments and bringing them together in a coherent way may be difficult. Often, old structures may exist next to new ones. Other operational problems should be considered before moving into this budgeting approach (McKean and Anshen, 1967). While the benefits of program budgeting are numerous, a significant effort is required to put this approach in place and make it work.

Zero-Base Budgeting. The third budgeting approach considered in this chapter is zero-base budgeting (ZBB). "In the most literal sense, zero-base budgeting implies constructing a budget without any reference to what has gone before, based on a fundamental reappraisal of purposes, methods and resources" (Taylor, 1977, p. 3). For a large organization to attempt a zero-base review of all operations within one budget cycle would be an almost impossible task. The realities of ZBB normally dictate a review and justification of selected ongoing programs starting somewhere in the base area that is not necessarily at a zero base (Droms, 1979, p. 134). In a sense, when one adopts the zero-base approach, all the historical information that has been used in constructing budgets is jettisoned, and the budget process starts from scratch.

Taylor (1977) identified three elements in the ZBB process: decision units, decision packages, and the ranking process. Decision units are the basic units for which budgets are prepared. In a college or university, the basic unit would most probably be the department. In our orientation example, if we had a department whose mission was to provide for the orientation of students, the department would become the decision unit. Decision packages are sets of services, activities, or expenditure items that, taken as an aggregate, equal the sum of the budget requests for a decision unit. The ranking of the decision packages is a process by which the priority of each is established by the manager. At times this can be done by a committee, but in other cases it may be done by a single person.

Although the ZBB process may be conducted in several ways, Austin and Cheek (1979) have outlined a five-step process for zero-base budgeting. The first step is to define decision units. Austin and Cheek suggest that the units may be something along the lines of a cost center (like a residence hall) or a group of people all of whom perform the same function (like the resident assistance staff in a residential life department). Step two is to set objectives. Austin and Cheek comment that ZBB draws heavily on the concepts of management by objectives. At this stage objectives are set for the decision units. Developing decision packages is the third step. This process translates the objectives into an operational plan. Step four involves ranking the packages. In this process the manager attempts to sort out the various options that are available through the decision packages. Once the packages are ranked, funding is set, budgets are distributed, and the programs and activities that were proposed are operationalized. In the fifth step, a performance audit is conducted. The performance audit, sometimes referred to as operational auditing, looks at the total operation from an objective perspective. The performance audit examines what the manager is attempting to do, the alternatives considered and the proposed approach, the benefits of the proposed approach, the consequences of not approving the chosen alternative, and some quantitative measures of performance.

ZBB offers several identifiable benefits. First, it integrates planning, budgeting, and decision making. Second, ZBB moves budgeting away from focusing on the raw numbers of a budget and requires more time to be spent analyzing the present situation and making decisions. As the ranking process is developed, contingency plans become available. While it is entirely possible that there may appear to be a best approach to ranking packages, it is also possible that alternatives may need to be sought in the middle of a budget year. Alternatives that were discarded may, in fact, be utilized. Finally, duplication within an organization can be identified and perhaps eliminated (Austin and Cheek, 1979). This in turn may enhance the efficiency of a particular organization.

How well does ZBB work? A study conducted by Boyd (1982) concluded that "zero-base budgeting, used in the state universities of Texas, is no better or worse than the technique that preceded it" (p. 437). There are some major problems associated with ZBB. It requires that more people be involved in the budget process. For many of them, this may be their first exposure to budgeting, and the process may take longer to complete than previous approaches (Leven, 1977). Additionally, there may be resistance to this approach on the part of veteran budget managers. They may be more concerned about what ZBB will do to them rather than what it will do for them. Furthermore, ZBB works best in an open, collaborative environment. If the work environment is competitive and there is not considerable sharing among managers, ZBB will not be effective. It also presupposes that considerable soul-searching will be done by unit heads as they examine their mission of departmental goals. They may find that their work is duplicated in other areas. Austin and Cheek (1979) concluded that managers may simply prefer using other budgeting approaches because they focus on costs rather than all the components of budgeting.

Formula Budgeting. According to Brinkman (1986), as many as twenty-six states use some type of formula budgeting in the budgeting process. Defining formula budgeting precisely is not easy, but Brinkman (1986) provides the following characterizations: "an objective procedure for estimating the further budgetary requirements of a college or university; subjective judgments expressed in mathematical terms; a combination of technical judgments and political agreements; and a mathematical means of relating the workload of a public institution to its state appropriation" (p. 334). Hence, formula budgeting is a way of allocating appropriated funds to the operating budgets of an institution. In some states formulas are critically important in the funding process, while in others they are more a part of the budgetary ritual. Often, formulas are ignored in the decision-making process of state financing (Brinkman, 1986).

How are formulas determined? In a case study described by Maw, Richards, and Crosby (1976), three approaches were used. First, the literature was reviewed in order to make a judgment as to whether or not general levels of staffing patterns had been established. Second, a list of functions and activities for each area was prepared and the assignment of time and resources to each of the functions was determined. Finally, fifty-three institutions of higher education were surveyed, since the literature review had yielded little information about staffing data and the current funding of programs.

Brinkman (1986) identified a number of criteria for evaluating formulas. In a review of the literature, he found that effective formulas should do the following things:

1. Recognize the varying costs of instruction related to disciplines and levels of programs
2. Contain only those factors that are quantitatively definable
3. Facilitate comparisons with other institutions within and outside the system
4. Recognize the diverse financial needs of institutions
5. Be broad-based, recognizing needs in various functional areas, not just instruction

6. Employ methodologies chosen on the basis of their appropriateness to the specific activities to be funded
7. Be able to treat equitably institutions of varying enrollment levels and of varying degrees of maturity (Brinkman, 1986)

There are some obvious advantages to the formula budgeting approach. Many of these revolve around the political process. Because the formula is agreed on as the mechanism for funding, formula budgeting eliminates politics in the decision-making process, reduces conflicts beween institutions and state legislatures, and allows time to be saved and devoted to special issues. Additionally, the use of formula budgeting should improve institutional relationships within a state. It makes it easy to compare programs and activities across institutions, and it makes explicit the factors to be considered in the decision-making process (Brinkman, 1986).

On the other hand, formula budgets have weaknesses and disadvantages. Among the intrinsic weaknesses of formula budgets are the following: they cannot self-adjust for basically improper levels of funding, they are ill suited for activities that are not quantifiable, and they cannot make policy decisions, although they embody policy decisions the ramifications of which often are not foreseen (Brinkman, 1986).

The other weaknesses of formula budgets, which are more avoidable, tend to result from their focus. Formulas often are based on past behavior; thus, there is a tendency to reduce what should be to what has been (Brinkman, 1986). If bold, new initiatives are desired, it is possible that a formula budget approach could be a hindering influence.

Formula budgets tend to have a leveling effect on institutions and their quality (Brinkman, 1986). If diverse institutions are treated much the same within a state, they will become the same. It is difficult for formulas to take into account institutions' historical differences, different missions, and different purposes. During a time when it may make the most sense for institutions to emphasize their distinctiveness, a formula budgeting approach could work in the opposite direction.

Finally, formulas tend to be rigid, since they are based on what has already happened. They do not encourage new approaches, initiatives, or technologies (Brinkman, 1986). Moss and Gather (cited by Brinkman, 1986, p. 337) observed that formulas typically fail to recognize and fund nontraditional learning, continuing education, and efforts to attract older students.

It seems to be certain that formula budgeting will be used more in the future (Brinkman, 1986). In an effort to address the problems of institutional diversity, formulas may need to become more complicated, and new formulas may be developed to encourage institutions to raise funds from other sources. Brinkman (1986) observed, for example, that institutions may be able to keep more of their indirect cost reimbursements as a means of enhancing quality, such as through the development of endowed chairs.

Accounting

Depending on the kinds of accounts for which student affairs officers are responsible, it is highly conceivable that at least two different forms of accounting—cash accounting and accrual-basis accounting—will be used. Cash accounting is defined as a form of accounting "under which revenues are accounted for only when received in cash, and expenditures are accounted for only when paid" (American Council on Education, 1968, p. 277). Accrual-basis accounting recognizes fund balance increments (such as revenue) when the amount is earned and recognizes expenses and other types of deductions when the goods or services have been used up (Meisinger and Dubeck, 1986). Accrual-basis accounting is designed to provide a more satisfactory matching of revenues and other fund balance additions with expenses and other fund balance deductions in the accounting period that financial statements describe (Meisinger and Dubeck, 1986, p. 123).

What are the implications of different accounting approaches for student affairs budget managers? Cash accounting, sometimes referred to as fund accounting, typically might be used for those accounts that are supported out of the institution's general fund (supplied by tuition and state revenues for a state-assisted institution). The accounting process may include encumbrances (commitments for expenditures), but for the most part it is not dramatically different from balancing a checkbook. Funds are deposited in the account on a routine basis at the beginning of the fiscal year or perhaps more often. Expenses are deducted on a monthly basis and the role of the account manager is to make sure that expenditures do not exceed budgeted amounts. When cash accounting is coupled with line-item budgeting, the purpose becomes obvious. Budgets are protected and overdrafts are avoided. The quality of the spending in this approach becomes less of an issue, since the real concern is to make sure that the budget is balanced at the end of the fiscal year.

On the other hand, when accrual-basis accounting is used—as it frequently is in auxiliary accounts, such as student housing, the bookstore, or the student union—the manager has to make sure that revenues meet the target forecast and expenditures are kept within the revenue realized. This form of accounting is more complicated than cash accounting; just because revenues appear on a budget statement, it does not follow that 100 percent of that amount will actually be collected. In fact, accrual accounting forces the budget manager into approaching the budgeting cycle more like the manager of a for-profit business than does cash accounting. Although the purpose of this chapter does not include delving into the subtleties and nuances of accounting practices, it is important for the budget manager to understand the distinctions between cash and accrual-basis accounting and to realize that the accrual basis, while providing a more accurate financial picture, also has additional risks associated with it.

Preparing the Unit Budget

One of the features of budgeting in higher education is that it can be very accommodating. Fincher (1986) observed that "the budgeting process in institutions of higher education is successful because it has many accommodating features. Within hours after the arrival of a new fiscal year, budgeting-in-amendment begins" (p. 76). It will be helpful to remember this as we discuss the process of preparing a budget for a discrete department within a student affairs division. Much of what is described hereafter is based on Robins's (1986) excellent discussion on unit budgeting.

Forms are supplied by the business office of the institution to department heads, usually during the spring. These forms, along with narrative guidelines concerning percentage adjustments that may be applied to salaries and supplies, provide the basis for the department head's work. The guidelines often give a range within which the department head may work in awarding salary increases and will provide guidance on how supply budgets may be amended for the next year. Salary guidelines also might indicate whether or not salary adjustments should include awards for meritorious service. In some instances merit must be recognized, but in other cases merit awards may be added to the basic cost-of-living increase.

The materials that are provided by the budget office will include many of the following expense categories: personal services, which include salaries and wages; supplies, which also may be known as operating expenses; capital, which includes equipment purchases; fringe benefits, which include such items as retirement, insurance, and Social Security costs; and travel expenses. Different institutions organize these categories in different ways, but these items typically are found in the budget preparation material. The information supplied for personal services tends to be the most detailed; such information as position number, rank or grade, percentage of time worked, and length of appointment, along with current salary information, may be provided for every position. The work of the unit head, then, is to apply the budgetary guidelines to the various categories of the budget.

Guidance usually is provided for the various categories of the budget. The budget office will have prepared estimates as to what the costs will be for the next fiscal year for such items as postage, telephone rental, office supplies, and the like. Within these categories, the manager merely applies the adjustments to the budget items. In the area of salaries, as was mentioned earlier, cost-of-living and merit increases may be recommended for each salary line. Merit increases should be linked to performance reviews; if they are not the manager will have a difficult time explaining to the unit's employees why some of them received larger increases than others. Merit increases should not be awarded unless there is a tangible way of justifying unequal increases.

After completing the unit budget, the department head forwards the budget material to the division head for review. The review examines such factors as compliance with the budgetary guidelines prepared by the business office, internal consistency, and compatibility with budgetary plans prepared by other unit heads. The division head has to be concerned with all of the same issues as the unit heads, but also needs to make sure that the budget plans fit nicely with one another. If one department consistently receives larger increases (or smaller decreases) than other units, the division head will have to explain why, not only to his or her supervisor, but also to disgruntled employees. When the division head completes work on the budget, it is forwarded through normal channels for review by appropriate campus offices.

Conclusions

As mentioned in the introduction to this chapter, student affairs officers often are perceived negatively in their ability to prepare and manage a budget. Pembroke (1985) suggested five principles for budget preparation that would be helpful to the student affairs officer.

First, **know the guidelines.** The person responsible for preparing the budget should understand the guidelines for preparation. What happens to money when a vacancy occurs and the salary returns to a base figure? Can we transfer money from salaries to operations? What is the maximum amount that a salary can be increased without special documentation or authorization? These questions and others should be considered before work is done on preparing the budget. It is useful to ask for as much of an increase in the budgetary categories as is allowable, but not more, lest the entire unit budget be called into question.

Second, **know what is possible.** In the midst of a budget crisis, it is probably not wise to propose a new multimillion-dollar program. Rarely do budget problems arise out of nowhere. Such things as an enrollment shortfall, reduced residence hall occupancy, increased insurance costs, and the like are signals that the budget will be tight. The division head can keep unit heads informed about the general state of the campus budget. Rarely will the campus budget be strained while unit budgets are flush. By paying attention to the signals on the campus, the unit budget manager will be able to anticipate events.

Third, **observe deadlines.** One of the ways to draw the fire of the budget office is to be late with budget material. If there is a good reason for the budget material to be late, the unit head should warn the budget office that the material will not be on time. "Perhaps the most simple yet egregious error that academic administrators make is either their carelessness or cavalier attitude in meeting deadlines" (Pembroke, 1985, p. 96).

Fourth, **help forecast potential problems.** The unit budget officer ought to be able to provide assistance to the budget office in predicting where problems will occur. If residence hall occupancy is low, for example, the budgetary ramifications ought to be pointed out. By providing such assistance, the unit head will begin to develop a solid working relationship, establish credibility, and communicate an understanding of the dynamics of the budget office.

Finally, **reexamine the division's mission.** From time to time, the student affairs division will need to reexamine its mission and how it contributes to the institution. We have a real need, in student services, to be sensitive to the changing needs of students and to be flexible in meeting their needs. For example, as we attract more part-time and nontraditional students to our campuses, what can we do in student services to determine their needs? How can we meet these needs? Answers to questions like these imply a periodic review of the functions of the division and will provide the impetus for providing services that meet the needs of a broadening clientele of students.

References

American Council on Education. *College and University Business Administration*. Washington, D.C.: American Council on Education, 1968.

Austin, L. A., and Cheek, L. M. *Zero-Base Budgeting*. New York: AMACOM, 1979.

Baldridge, J. V., and Okimi, H. P. "Strategic Planning in Higher Education." *American Association for Higher Education Bulletin*, 1982, *35* (6), 15–18.

Barnes, S. F., Morton, E. W., and Austin, A. O. "The Call for Accountability: The Struggle for Program Definition in Student Affairs." *National Association of Student Personnel Administrators Journal*, 1983, *20*, 10–20.

Bean, J. P. "Planning as a Self-Fulfilling Prophecy." In G. D. Kuh (ed.), *Understanding Student Affairs Organizations*. New Directions for Student Services, no. 23. San Francisco: Jossey-Bass, 1983.

Bean, J. P., and Kuh, G. D. "A Typology of Planning Problems." *Journal of Higher Education*, 1984, *55*, 36–55.

Bowen, H. R. *Investment in Learning: The Individual and Social Value of American Higher Education*. San Francisco: Jossey-Bass, 1977.

Boyd, W. L. "Zero-Base Budgeting: The Texas Experience." *Journal of Higher Education*, 1982, *53*, 429–438.

Brinkman, P. T. "Formula Budgeting: The Fourth Decade." In L. L. Leslie and R. E. Anderson (eds.), *ASHE Reader on Finance in Higher Education*. Lexingon, Mass.: Ginn, 1986.

Bubanakis, M. *Budgets*. Westport, Conn.: Greenwood Press, 1976.

Career Development and Professional Standards Division. "Survey Results: Mid-Level Professionals." *National Association of Student Personnel Administrators Forum*, 1984, *5*, 1–27.

Clugston, R. M. "Strategic Planning in an Organized Anarchy: The Emperor's New Clothes." Paper Presented at annual meeting of Association for the Study of Higher Education, San Antonio, Tex., Feb. 1986.

Cope, R. "Environmental Assessments for Strategic Planning." In N. Poulton (ed.), *Evaluation of Management and Planning Systems.* New Directions for Institutional Research, no. 31. San Francisco: Jossey-Bass, 1981.

Deegan, W. L. *Managing Student Affairs Programs: Methods, Models, Muddles.* Palm Springs, Calif.: ETA Publications, 1981.

Droms, W. G. *Finance and Accounting for Nonfinancial Managers.* Reading, Mass.: Addison-Wesley, 1979.

Dutton, T. B., and Rickard, S. T. "Organizing Student Services." In U. Delworth, G. Hanson, and Associates, *Student Services: A Handbook for the Profession.* San Francisco: Jossey-Bass, 1980.

Ern, E. H. "1984-1986 Biennial Evaluation Report and Planning for the Period 1986-1998." Office of the Vice President for Student Affairs, University of Virginia, 1986.

Fincher, C. "Budgeting Myths and Fictions." In L. L. Leslie and R. E. Anderson (eds.), *ASHE Reader on Finance in Higher Education.* Lexington, Mass.: Ginn, 1986.

Hobbs, J. M., and Heany, D. F. "Coupling Strategy to Operating Plans." *Harvard Business Review,* May-June 1977, pp. 119-126.

Huff, A. S. "Planning to Plan." In D. L. Clark, S. McKibben, and M. Malkas (eds.), *New Perspectives on Planning in Educational Organizations.* San Francisco: Far West Laboratory for Educational Research and Development, 1980.

Keller, G. "The New Management Revolution in Higher Education." *American Association for Higher Education Bulletin,* 1982, *35,* 3-5.

Keller, G. *Academic Strategy: The Management Revolution in American Higher Education.* Baltimore, Md.: Johns Hopkins University Press, 1983.

Kinnick, B. C., and Bollheimer, R. L. "College Presidents' Perceptions of Student Affairs Issues and Development Needs of Chief Student Affairs Officers." *National Association of Student Personnel Administrators Journal,* 1984, *22,* 2-9.

Koontz, H., and O'Donnell, C. *Principles of Management: An Analysis of Managerial Functions.* New York: McGraw-Hill, 1972.

Kotler, P., and Murphy, P. "Strategic Planning for Higher Education." *Journal of Higher Education,* 1981, *52,* 470–489.

Kuh, G., Whitt, E., and Shedd, J. *Student Affairs Work 2001: A Paradigmatic Odyssey.* Alexandria, Va.: American College Personnel Association, 1987.

Leven, M. "Zero-Base Budgeting." In J. L. Hebert (ed.), *Experiences in Zero-Base Budgeting.* New York: Petrocelli, 1977.

Lindblom, C. "The Science of Muddling Through." *Public Administration Review,* 1959, *19,* 79–88.

Lunsford, L. W. "Chief Student Affairs Officer: The Ladder to the Top." *National Association of Student Personnel Administrators Journal,* 1984, *22,* 48–56.

McKean, R. N., and Anshen, M. "Limitations, Risks and Problems." In D. Novick (ed.), *Program Budgeting.* Cambridge, Mass.: Harvard University Press, 1967.

Maw, I. I., Richards, N. A., and Crosby, H. J. *Formula Budgeting: An Application to Student Affairs.* Washington, D. C.: American Personnel and Guidance Association, 1976.

Meisinger, R. J., Jr., and Dubeck, L. W. "Fund Accounting." In L. L. Leslie and R. E. Anderson (eds.), *ASHE Reader on Finance in Higher Education.* Lexington, Mass.: Ginn, 1986.

Muston, R. A. "Resource Allocation and Program Budgeting." In C. H. Foxley (ed.), *Applying Management Techniques.* New Directions for Student Services, no. 9. San Francisco: Jossey-Bass, 1980.

Novick, D. *Current Practice in Program Budgeting.* London: Heinemann, 1973.

Pembroke, W. J. "Fiscal Constraints on Program Development." In M. J. Barr, L. A. Keating, and Associates, *Developing Effective Student Services Programs: Systematic Approaches for Practitioners.* San Francisco: Jossey-Bass, 1985.

Pillinger, B. B., and Kraack, T. A. "Long Range Planning: A Key to Effective Management." *National Association of Student Personnel Administrators Journal,* 1980, *18,* 2–7.

Richman, B. M., and Farmer, R. N. *Leadership, Goals, and Power in Higher Education: A Contingency and Open-Systems Approach to Effective Management.* San Francisco: Jossey-Bass, 1974.

Robins, G. B. "Understanding the College Budget." In L. L. Leslie and R. E. Anderson (eds.), *ASHE Reader on Finance in Higher Education.* Lexington, Mass.: Ginn, 1986.

Said, K. E. *A Budget Model for an Institution of Higher Education.* Austin: Graduate School of Business, University of Texas, 1974.

Sherwood, F. P., and Best, W. H. "The Local Administrator as Budgeter." In R. T. Golembiewski and J. Robin (eds.), *Public Budgeting and Finance.* Itasca, Ill.: Peacock, 1975.

Steiss, A. W. *Public Budgeting and Management.* Lexington, Mass.: Heath, 1972.

Taylor, G. M. "Introduction to Zero-Base Budgeting." In J. L. Hebert (ed.), *Experiences in Zero-Base Budgeting.* New York: Petrocelli, 1977.

Thomas, W. L. "Union into the 21st Century." Division of Student Affairs, University of Maryland, College Park, 1987.

Chapter Nineteen

Managing Data and Information Resources

David H. Kalsbeek

Information and how it is managed is a critical concern of anyone needing to understand organizations—whether as an academic pursuit or in order to come to a pragmatic understanding of how to succeed or survive in an organizational environment. Information management has become a skill in great demand in most organizations, including colleges and universities. Galbraith (1973) presents an analysis that speaks to why information management skills are increasingly critical in higher education and especially in student services. He suggests that the information requirements in organizations increase in the face of greater uncertainty, higher performance standards, increased competition, diversity of product line, and interdependence between functional units. All of these characterize higher education today—greater uncertainty about the economy and federal support for education, performance standards dictated by state legislatures, competition for increasingly scarce traditional students, a staggering diversity of students, and the interdependence of offices required by enrollment management perspectives. Galbraith suggests that in such an environment information management strategies and skills are essential. The management of information will determine to a large degree how effectively colleges and universities respond to the challenges and opportunities in today's higher education environment.

493

In addition, new tools and techniques for managing organizational information are being developed at a staggering pace. McCredie (1983) compiled case studies of the computing strategies pursued by ten colleges and universities. These institutions may serve as harbingers, precursors of what soon will be commonplace in higher education, and each of the ten trends noted in these case studies poses challenges to student affairs professionals. For example, new organizational structures and executive-level leadership for information resource management determine the organizational or political context for student affairs work. Decentralized, personal computing electronic networks challenge the traditional structures, staffing, processes, and procedures in student services operations. Information-processing literacy and library automation will have real effects on the student experience—which is very much the concern of student affairs staff. These changes in higher education challenge student services professionals in both how they think about what they do and how they in fact do it. Changes in campus computing strategies may make information management a critical skill for student services professionals.

The primary purpose of this chapter is to describe information management as a requisite skill for student services professionals. The chapter offers an overview of four generic levels of administrative information systems using Masland's (1985) descriptive categories: data-processing systems, management information systems, modeling systems, and decision support systems. These categories describe some ways in which organizations manage information and, conversely, some ways in which information manages organizations. One must be descriptive and not overprescriptive in this regard, since the appropriate design, implementation, and use of information systems and information strategies are wholly contingent upon the idiosyncratic nature of the organizational setting and culture. After the initial overview is a brief discussion of some changing roles for student services professionals in light of the emerging importance of information resource management in colleges and universities and some thoughts about the requisite skills for these roles.

Administrative Information Systems

Data-Processing Systems (DPS). Masland (1985) suggests that "data processing was the first administrative application of computer technology in higher education" (p. 179). The focus of data-processing systems is the highly routine tasks characterizing the day-to-day information processing for core functions of operational units.

Clearly, the data-processing challenges underlying student services in higher education are legion. The management of contemporary admissions and recruiting, course scheduling, registration and grading processes, student billing, financial aid packaging and disbursements, housing, and meal plans are all critical student services functions that involve the routine, repetitious information management tasks well suited to DPS.

Such student information systems offer many avenues for substantive improvement in the management of student services. They may offer improved timeliness of information, greater connectivity between functional units, greater efficiency in office operations, and improved consistency and reliability of information on students. Used within a student development context to pursue developmental objectives, data-processing systems can serve more than purely operational purposes in student services (Erwin and Tollefson, 1982).

A DPS directly dictates the quality of the student experience at a college or university. A DPS determines how long students wait in lines for services or wait for refunds, whether students get the runaround from office to office to resolve problems, and whether counselors and advisers have the information they need to appropriately serve students. A DPS also conveys strong messages to students about how the institution views its relationship to them. Consider the following statement praising the successful implementation of an integrated DPS at a major university: "The integrated Student Systems are everything that they promised to be. Student Registration, for example, is integrated with the Bursar to prevent instruction without payment. Financial Aid is integrated with Academic Records to prevent aid to students who are academically ineligible. Housing is integrated to prevent room assignments to students who are not registered. Academic departments are integrated to prevent students from graduating who are not approved by the Dean'' (Blythe, 1987, p. 237). Surely these outcomes of the integrated DPS are desirable and illustrate some of the real benefits of a DPS. The point, however, is that a DPS is, in both intent and effect, a means of institutional control. Financial and accounting systems control budgets; student information systems control students.

The degree to which student affairs staff are divorced from the process of developing, implementing, and evaluating student data-processing systems is the degree to which they are removed from institutional decision making about the nature and quality of student life. Some student services organizations have demonstrated great success in taking the initiative and leadership in their institutions in addressing data-processing needs (Stelter, 1987). Other student services organizations or professionals find themselves distant from the development and implementation of such systems. Without information management skills, student services personnel may not be able to contribute to these very tangible and far-reaching determinants of the student experience.

Management Information Systems (MIS). While data-processing systems are designed primarily to meet operational needs, management information systems are distinguished by their focus on providing information for management decisions. For example, the DPS in a housing office would post the proper room and board assessment to the student's bill and print the student's name, room number, and other relevant data on a dorm roster. The focus is clearly on the routine data management required to operate the housing program efficiently. In comparison, the MIS in a housing office would provide the housing director with building-by-building summaries of room vacancy patterns; month-by-month comparisons of the time lag between the initiation of work requests and their completion by the maintenance staff; retention patterns in the halls by gender, ethnicity, or academic major; and ratios of the cost of staffing a game room to the revenue it generates.

In some ways the distinction between these two systems is negligible, but the contrast illustrates how management needs and operational needs are served differently by information systems. The terms chosen to name these systems are of no small significance; while one system processes data, the other processes information. Some writers illustrate the difference between the systems by offering comparative definitions of data and information; for example, "Data become informative only when we have specific policy questions that need illumination and resolution" (McCorkle, 1977, p. 3).

An MIS can be a valuable tool in improving student services insofar as it enhances a manager's responsiveness to campus needs, provides timely feedback on services provided, and supports the planning process. An MIS can document patterns of student use of services and facilities, compare revenue and expenditure patterns across departments, provide profiles of the types of students most likely to drop out or most likely to apply to the college, illustrate relationships between financial aid packages and matriculation rates, or summarize weekly ticket sales and compare them to year-to-date sales of the prior year. Given specific management problems and concerns, an MIS can provide the information needed to manage.

The design of an MIS inevitably reflects prevailing assumptions about what information is important in the management of the organization. Information systems designed to accept certain kinds of data in response to certain management questions necessarily preclude the asking of other kinds of management questions. In some cases the information system in fact makes the management decisions insofar as it has restricted the range of possible problems to be solved, inquiries to be made, questions to be answered. At what point, then, is the management decision actually made: in the original design of the MIS or in light of the information generated from the system? The point is that the design of the MIS is an integral part of the management process, not one to be left to "technicians."

Student services professionals face two obligations in this regard. First, insofar as they are users of either the campus MIS or a specific departmental MIS, they must be integrally involved in the design, development, and oversight of that system. Second, recognizing that myriad management decisions occur campuswide that have very real effects on the quality of student services and student life, student personnel professionals must be concerned with the MIS fueling those decisions and be intrusively involved in shaping those systems as well.

Modeling Systems. Bloomfield and Updegrove (1981) suggest that implicit models of reality always underlie the decision-making process. Decisions inevitably reflect some basic assumptions about the situation at hand, about the relationships of the variables involved in the decision situation, about viable courses of action, and about the likely outcomes of alternative choices. The process of taking these complex beliefs and assumptions and making them as explicit as possible while reducing them to their most fundamental components is the process of model building. If these components are given numerical values and the relationships among them are expressed algebraically, the outcome is a mathematical model.

Quantitative models permit testing or experimenting on real-world processes or systems without the costs or risks of doing so in reality (Wallhaus, 1969). Models that represent a process that might take years in reality (such as the graduation of an entering freshman class) can collapse that extended time scale for immediate analysis. Models that represent a policy (such as the combinations of financial need and academic criteria considered in awarding scholarships) can simulate the effects of alternative policies without risky "live" experimentation. Models make it possible to forecast and project probable outcomes given certain specified conditions, and they can suggest alternative policy options or combinations of variables to achieve a specified outcome. While such support of decision making is clearly a benefit of quantitative modeling, perhaps its greatest contribution is in clarifying and explicating the problem at hand (Bloomfield and Updegrove, 1981).

In student services, there are many potential uses of such computer-supported mathematical models. A model could be used

- to simulate or to project enrollment patterns in light of anticipated demographic shifts;
- to simulate budgetary effects of alternative staffing decisions in the learning resource center;
- to investigate the relationship between financial aid packaging policies and minority enrollment;
- to simulate the demand for services or special courses under differing assumptions of enrollment patterns of international students;
- to simulate staff turnover in light of retirement policies and age distribution;
- to study the impact on a department's personnel budget of anticipated changes in college work-study policies;
- to ask, ''What if football ticket sales increased by 3 percent each year?''

Regardless of the use of models within student services departments, there is an increasing likelihood that university planners are making use of mathematical models in shaping institutional decisions and strategic plans. Updegrove (1981), for example, reports that the principal users of the EDUCOM modeling system are business officers, academic officers, planners, and institutional researchers. Regardless of the user, the appropriateness of any model depends on the appropriateness of the assumptions guiding it—and these assumptions, if not fully explicit and public, may go unquestioned or unchallenged. Planning models, insofar as they focus on students as either the input (for example, by projecting the effect of enrollment patterns on parking facilities) or the output (for example, by modeling the enrollment effects of reduced scholarship funds), are by that fact alone the concern of the student affairs administrator.

Decision Support Systems (DSS). Decision support systems constitute Masland's fourth generic category of administrative information systems, one that he suggests represents an evolution from both the modeling and the management information systems discussed above. By definition, decision support systems are ''interactive computer-based sets of procedures that assist decision makers in using information to analyze possible implications and contingencies of alternative courses of action" (Rohrbaugh, 1986, p. 5).

One way to appreciate a DSS is to contrast it with its evolutionary predecessor, MIS. Rohrbaugh (1986) suggests that the MIS is a system for providing information about the organization's current state of affairs that is pertinent to management decisions. The MIS generates standard reports, profiles, tables, or statistical summaries in response to some management need; it is geared toward structured problems, toward the routine and foreseen management decisions of an organization.

In many cases, however, an MIS has failed to meet management needs "mainly because insufficient thought was given to the nature of the management decisions [it was] to inform" (Simon, 1981, p. 221). An MIS can put artificial and predetermined constraints on the information provided to management, making the manager a passive recipient of information rather than an active agent in managing the information. Weaknesses in management decisions "stem primarily from the inadequacy of the structures unwittingly imposed on available information rather than from any lack of information per se" (Rohrbaugh, 1986, p. 11).

By definition, a DSS addresses these shortcomings of the traditional MIS. The DSS focuses not on the decisions but on the decision maker. In contrast to an MIS, which presents to a decision maker information relevant to a known decision, a DSS supports the decision-making process by providing decision makers with direct access to institutional information via sophisticated but technically unencumbered processes. A DSS enables the user to work with the institutional information in light of relatively unstructured decisions and ad hoc concerns. The use of graphic data displays to summarize information is a prominant feature of most data support systems.

The intention and design strategies of the DSS movement will shape future developments in information management technologies. Decision makers' access to decision-relevant data through interactive computing technologies with flexible analytic and graphic capabilities characterizes the information management sytems that student services professionals will encounter in years to come.

Information Resource Management

As colleges and universities have acknowledged the management of information resources to be a critical task that cannot be allowed to slip between the cracks of the bureaucratic structure, new organizational structures have emerged that determine to a very real degree the political and organizational environment within which student services function. Information resource management (IRM) is a rubric that captures the manner in which a number of campuses are addressing the types of issues discussed in this chapter.

The purposes of IRM are broader than the organizational consolidation of computing services under a vice-president for information resource management. Central to IRM is the development of information policies and a focus on uses and users of information. Diebold (1985) suggests that information is a capital resource much like an institution's work force, its capital, or its plant equipment. Those organizations that excel in the future will be those that use information as efficiently as their other assets. Effective use of information requires that policies establish the manner in which institutional information is acquired, standardized or categorized, stored, disseminated, and used. Information policies focus on the lateral flow of information among organizational units as well as the vertical distribution of information within the organizational hierarchy. Information policies support the effective management of organizations by "laying guidelines for sharing and distributing information; resolving questions about proprietary rights; handling problems of security and disclosure" (Diebold, 1985, p. 48); and trying to balance the information needs of single departmental units against the needs of the organization as a whole. An information policy provides both hardware and software specifications that ensure organization-wide compatibility and standard communications interfaces. It addresses staff training issues resulting from the automation of clerical functions and from the development of integrated data-base and telecommunications systems that change what, how, and where managers manage and administrators administer.

In many ways, the development of information policies is mirrored in the emergence on some campuses of the "data administrator" (McKinney, Schott, Teeter, and Mannering, 1987). This role has as its primary focus data access, data integrity, data manipulation, data analysis and interpretation, and data dissemination. However, contrary to traditional organizational arrangements, data administration is not likely to be a function of a campus computing center, since the management of information resources is recognized to be not so much a technical issue but an issue of institutional policy and planning.

Diebold (1985, p. 41) argues that successful IRM must have three fundamental components: adequate technologies for managing the organization's information resources; information policies that provide the infrastructure for the management and use of information in the organization; and an organizational climate that is supportive in structure and process of the policies and the appropriate use of the information technology. This includes appropriately trained staff who are, in Diebold's terms, "information literate, . . . aware of the potential of the information resource, . . . [and who know] how to utilize it most effectively" (p. 42). He suggests that organizational support for IRM may create the need for "information specialists" who are not just technical experts with computing systems but experts in the use of information in management and administrative functions.

The implications for student services professionals are apparent and numerous; three will be mentioned here. First, the prevalence of an IRM perspective on campuses will support student services personnel in technology acquisition, ensuring hardware and software compatibility within student services organizations and between student services and other campus units. The challenge in this regard is that in order for the IRM executive to support student services in this way, it is imperative that student services staff be, in Diebold's terms, information literate—that they know how to articulate information needs and envision information solutions to organizational or management problems. Regardless of the extent of institutional support through centralized IRM, there is no alternative to student services personnel being skilled in information management.

Second, information policies in colleges and universities by necessity deal with student information. These policies address the release and distribution of student data both within and without the institution, the standardization and definition of student data across multiple data bases, the identification of what offices need what student information for what purposes, and so on. As asserted earlier in this chapter, the further the student affairs staff is from this realm of policy-making, the further its members are removed from substantive issues affecting the nature and quality of both the student experience at the institution and the services in their own functional units.

Third, whether or not an IRM perspective is prevalent institution-wide, IRM issues apply within student services as much as they do at the institutional level. Student services organizations cannot afford to be negligent as stewards of their information resources. Technical compatibility and functional integration of computing and communications hardware and software are, of course, important issues within student services. More important are policies about lateral and vertical information flow, about information use, about definitions of who needs to know what and why, and about responsibility for maintaining student data bases. The continuing need to upgrade human resources to take advantage of emerging demands for information management skills at clerical and managerial levels is as critical in student services as in any other administrative unit in the college or university.

Information Management Skills

There are perhaps new roles and new requisite skills for student services professionals as information resource management takes hold in colleges and universities. While new roles may emerge for specialists in managing information resources, some institutions may introduce information management as part of the repertoire of requisite skills for all student services professionals. Below are several notions about what such information management skills might entail.

Informatic Spectacles. If, as argued in the literature on organizational analysis and behavior, information is a significant determinant of organizational power and control, then one's understanding of an organization is enlightened as much by an "informatic" view as by the traditional bureaucratic one (Kalsbeek, 1984). In other words, it is as important to understand the structure of the information flow as it is to understand the bureaucratic organizational chart. When one dons "informatic spectacles," one's view of an organization focuses on how data and information are gathered, stored, retrieved, disseminated, restricted, analyzed, synthesized, and used. Viewing organizations informatically allows one to discern critical information management activities from those that are largely symbolic, ritualized, or ceremonial (Feldman and March, 1981; Masland, 1983).

An informatic view of organizations is both descriptive and prescriptive; one must know not only how information is currently managed throughout the organization (and why) but how it should be managed in pursuit of certain objectives or purposes. Donning informatic spectacles reveals points of "infosclerosis" where hardening of information arteries restricts or blocks information flow and the system suffers as a result (Kalsbeek, 1984). An informatic conceptualization of an organization is a fundamental information management skill.

Training. QWERTY is the sequence of letters on the typewriter keyboard that is used to describe the keyboard arrangement that dominates the market. While many believe that this arrangement was designed to optimize the speed, accuracy, or ease of typing, in reality the opposite is true. The original design of the keyboard was intended to slow down typists so that human speed did not jam the mechanisms of the earliest commercial typewriters. Fortunately, the design was erroneous, so the arrangement is almost random and the effect negligible, but the QWERTY design has persisted because the costs and consequences of retraining an entire work force became too great to be overcome by the advantages of superior keyboard arrangements (Papert, 1981). In any organization, QWERTY reasons may be behind the reluctance of staff to change office technologies; concerns for short-term training costs often overpower long-term productivity concerns.

Staff training and retraining may be the most critical ingredient in the successful implementation of information management systems and strategies; information management skills therefore include basic skills in human resource development and training. This includes the design of training materials, the facilitation of training workshops, and the development of ongoing programs for staff development. It also includes the calculation of QWERTY trade-offs between the costs of staff retraining and the benefits of new systems or technologies. If student development professionals know anything about the process of learning, their contributions in the training area can be enormous if those gifts are coupled with other information management skills.

Technical Competence. Since technical aspects of information technologies largely determine what can be done in meeting the information needs in student services, some technical skills must be part of the information manager's repertoire. This does not necessarily imply traditional academic training in computer science or any fluency in programming languages or even information systems—even for an information specialist (Litaker, 1987). In a computing environment increasingly dominated by personal computers (PCs), the requisite technical skills involve more commercial applications software packages and microcomputer hardware. In working with other campus constituencies in the design of campuswide data-processing or management information systems, fluency in the language of computing is certainly advantageous. Information managers must be technically competent with computing technologies.

Data Display. Information management involves information presentation. Information management skills therefore include the ability to use graphs, tables, and text appropriately and effectively in presenting information to decision makers. Technologies like laser printers and color plotters, coupled with powerful applications software on PCs, open avenues for extremely polished data presentation but can also entrap those who value polish over substance.

Much of the impetus behind the development of DSS by commercial vendors apparently is the belief that executive decision makers need to see graphs. While there is certainly evidence of the value of the graphic display of data, it is nevertheless a seductive and potentially dangerous information management strategy. First, it is not true that all decision makers prefer data displayed in graphic form. Certain dimensions of personality may affect the types of information considered usable (Mitroff and Kilmann, 1978; Keen, 1973; McKenney and Keen, 1974); the same dimensions may determine the preferred mode of data presentation. Second, it is clear that graphs can distort data and patterns, exaggerating or minimizing differences in ways that are not immediately apparent to the viewer (Shubik, 1981); graphs can be an extremely manipulative form of information management. Finally, not all information is appropriate for graphic display; it is not uncommon to find graphic data displays that are much more complex or intricate than the information the graph is intended to convey. Tufte (1983) presents a marvelous discussion of the types of information for which graphs are best suited and a definitive guide to the appropriate use of graphic displays for quantitative data.

Communication. Facilitating human communication is a crucial information management skill. It has been suggested that 60 percent of information systems failures are the result of poor communication between people rather than any kind of technical problems (Atre, 1986). The complexity of integrated information systems that cut across bureaucratic boundaries, the politics of information management, new developments in "group-work software" and communication networks all require the information manager to be skilled in human communication, conflict resolution, and group consensus.

Doing Business. The goal of information management is never the management of information for its own sake; the goal is to support the pursuit of the educational objectives of the institution and the more specific objectives of the student services department or division. Therefore, managing information in any student service requires a fundamental understanding of the core operations in that functional area. Effectively meeting the information management needs of a counseling center, for example, requires the person charged with information management either to be familiar with all the functions and needs of the center or to be able to elicit from the center staff accurate and complete flowcharts, process and procedure documents, and summaries of information needs. Information management skills in student services include having a comprehensive understanding of the services themselves.

Appreciating the Complexity of Information Use. Information management skills include the recognition that information systems are not panaceas for management concerns or institutional problems. Even with easily accessible data bases and flexible modeling systems and striking graphs, the answers provided to decision makers are only as good as the questions posed. Even with an elaborate DSS at hand, "the performance of a mediocre manager will not improve much, because his mediocrity consists in being unable to formulate the right questions" (Vtssotsky, 1981, p. 139). Information management skills actually may have less to do with providing answers than with framing questions. What is problematic here is the typical but limited view of what constitutes the appropriate use of information in organizational decision making.

One would assume, given the traditional, idealized view of information's role in decision making, that relevant information is gathered and analyzed prior to making a decision, that information gathered for a decision will be used in making that decision, that available information will be examined before requesting or gathering more information, and that needs for information will be determined prior to collecting information (Feldman and March, 1981). Even a casual observation of how information actually gets used in colleges and universities shows that such behavior is far from typical. Perhaps the more prevalent scenario in most organizations is that much of the information gathered and communicated has little relevance to the decision, much of the information used to justify a decision is collected after the decision is made, much of the information gathered for a decision is not used in that decision, and complaints that an organization has insufficient information to make a decision persist while available information is ignored (Feldman and March, 1981).

Information management skills therefore include a realistic view of what constitutes information use. The traditional imagery is the "direct application" perspective, wherein one judges that information was used if the decision outcome would have been different had the information not been considered. Many have suggested that such a definition of information use is much too narrow. Weiss (1977, 1980a) in particular suggests that a more common and perhaps more powerful image of information use is the "enlightenment model": information is used not so much for problem solving as for defining problems. Information may more often provide perspectives, generalizations, and contexts than be directly applicable to a specific decision. The more common use of information is diffuse rather than discrete, and information is considered to be used as it percolates into the climate of informed opinion in the organization. Information management must address information use—and information use is far from a simple concept.

Information management skills require a sensitivity to the realities of the decision-making process (Weiss, 1980a; Forester, 1984), including the politics of information dissemination and use, the cognitive limitations of decision makers, decision-making styles that dictate information preferences (Mitroff and Kilmann, 1978; McKenney and Keen, 1974; Keen, 1973), and the prevlence of symbolic information rituals in bureaucracies (Feldman and March, 1981). These all confound and complicate the processes of information use in organizations and provide clues to managing information more effectively.

Conclusion

Providing student services in higher education requires information and the management of that information. The question is never whether to manage information but rather how to manage information in order to attain organizational goals. If one accepts the student development perspective in defining the student personnel profession, the importance of information management is in no way diminished. In fact, a concerted information management effort may be the most effective of all professional roles in achieving such broad institutional objectives as enhancing the quality of student life, promoting student development in and out of the classroom, maximizing student involvement, responding to the diversity of learners in today's classrooms, and demonstrating educational and developmental outcomes. Student development through information management is likely to be a dominant rubric for the profession in years to come (Kalsbeek, 1984). Such an approach would incorporate three primary components (Kalsbeek, 1987): information production (the research and evaluation component of information management), information systems (the technical support component of information management), and information dissemination (the educational and leadership component of information management). While the information systems component of an information management effort has been the primary focus of this chapter, this three-pronged conceptualization of information management characterizes the approach to student development through information management.

Information management, so broadly conceived, is a boundary-spanning activity (Silverman, 1971) that builds bridges between student services and academic areas while addressing organizational objectives that transcend the bureaucratic and functional structures of colleges and universities. It is likely to characterize those student services and student development organizations that in the years to come are viable, vibrant, vital, and valued.

References

Atre, S. "Storing Data About Data." *Information Center,* 1986, *2,* 90.

Bloomfield, S. D., and Updegrove, D. A. "Modeling for Insight, Not Numbers." In J. Wilson (ed.), *Management Science*

Applications to Academic Administration. New Directions for Higher Education, no. 35. San Francisco: Jossey-Bass, 1981.

Blythe, K. C. *End-User Computing at the Pennsylvania State University.* Proceedings of the annual CAUSE National Conference, Monterey, Calif., Dec. 1986. Boulder, Colo.: CAUSE, 1987.

Diebold, J. *Managing Information: The Challenge and the Opportunity.* New York: AMACOM, 1985.

Erwin, T. D., and Tollefson, A. L. "A Data Base Management Model for Student Development." *Journal of College Student Personnel,* 1982, *23,* 70–76.

Feldman, M., and March, J. "Information in Organizations as Signal and Symbol." *Administrative Science Quarterly,* 1981, *26,* 171–186.

Forester, J. "Bounded Rationality and the Politics of Muddling Through." *Public Administration Review,* 1984, *44,* 23–31.

Galbraith, J. *Designing Complex Organizations.* Reading, Mass.: Addison-Wesley, 1973.

Kalsbeek, D. H. "Student Development Through Information Management: Spanning Boundaries in the Information Age." Paper presented at the St. Louis Regional Conference "Student Affairs in the Decade Ahead," May 1984.

Kalsbeek, D. H. "Information Management: New Roles, Resources and Responsibilities in Student Affairs." Paper presented at the NASPA Region IV-West Conference, St. Louis, Mo., 1987.

Keen, P. "The Implications of Cognitive Style for Individual Decision-Making." Unpublished doctoral dissertation, Graduate School of Business Administration, Harvard University, 1973.

Litaker, R. G. "Using Fourth-Generation Tools in Information Management." In E. M. Staman (ed.), *Managing Information in Higher Education.* New Directions for Institutional Research, no. 55. San Francisco: Jossey-Bass, 1987.

McCorkle, C. O. "Information for Institutional Decision Making." In C. R. Adams (ed.), *Appraising Information Needs of Decision Makers.* New Directions for Institutional Research, no. 15. San Francisco: Jossey-Bass, 1977.

McCredie, J. W. (ed.). *Campus Computing Strategies.* Bedford, Mass.: Digital Press, 1983.

McKenney, J. L., and Keen, P. "How Managers' Minds Work." *Harvard Business Review,* May-June 1974, pp. 79-90.

McKinney, R. L., Schott, J., Teeter, D., and Mannering, L. "Data Administration and Management." In E. M. Staman (ed.), *Managing Information in Higher Education.* New Directions for Institutional Research, no. 55. San Francisco: Jossey-Bass, 1987.

Masland, A. T. "Simulators, Myth and Ritual in Higher Education." *Research in Higher Education,* 1983, *18,* 161-177.

Masland, A. T. "Administrative Computing in Higher Education." In J. C. Smart (ed.), *Higher Education: Handbook of Theory and Research.* Vol 1. New York: Agathon Press, 1985.

Mitroff, I. I., and Kilmann, R. H. *Methodological Approaches to Social Science: Integrating Divergent Concepts and Theories.* San Francisco: Jossey-Bass, 1978.

Papert, S. A. "Computers and Learning." In M. L. Dertouzos and J. Moses (eds.), *The Computer Age: A Twenty-Year View.* Cambridge, Mass.: MIT Press, 1981.

Rohrbaugh, J. "Institutional Research as Decision Support." In J. Rohrbaugh and A. T. McCartt (eds.), *Applying Decision Support Systems in Higher Education.* New Directions for Institutional Research, no. 49. San Francisco: Jossey-Bass, 1986.

Shubik, M. "Computers and Modeling." In M. L. Dertouzos and J. Moses (eds.), *The Computer Age: A Twenty-Year View.* Cambridge, Mass.: MIT Press, 1981.

Silverman, R. J. "The Student Personnel Worker on the Boundary." *Journal of College Student Personnel,* 1971, *12,* 3-6.

Simon, H. "The Consequences of Computers for Centralization and Decentralization." In M. L. Dertouzos and J. Moses (eds.), *The Computer Age: A Twenty-Year View.* Cambridge, Mass.: MIT Press, 1981.

Stelter, S. "Implementing Student Information Systems: A Case Study." Paper presented at annual conference of American College Personnel Association and National Association of Student Personnel Administrators, Chicago, 1987.

Tufte, E. *The Visual Display of Quantitative Information.* Cheshire, Conn.: Graphics Press, 1983.

Updegrove, D. A. "EFPM: A Two-Year Progress Report." In D. D. Mebane (ed.), *Solving College and University Problems Through Technology: Proceedings of the EDUCOM Annual Conference, 1980.* Princeton, N.J.: EDUCOM, 1981.

Vtssotsky, V. A. "The Use of Computers for Business Functions." In M. L. Dertouzos and J. Moses (eds.), *The Computer Age: A Twenty-Year View.* Cambridge, Mass.: MIT Press, 1981.

Wallhaus, R. A. "Modeling for Higher Education Administration and Management." In C. B. Johnson and W. G. Katzenmeyer (eds.), *MIS in Higher Education: The State of the Art.* Durham, N.C.: Duke University Press, 1969.

Weiss, C. "Research for Policy's Sake: The Enlightenment Function of Social Research." *Policy Analysis,* 1977, *3,* 531–546.

Weiss, C. "Knowledge Creep and Decision Accretion." *Knowledge: Creation, Diffusion and Utilization,* 1980a, *1,* 381–404.

Weiss, C. (with M. Bucuvalas). *Social Science Research and Decision Making.* New York: Columbia University Press, 1980b.

Chapter Twenty

Using Information Systems for Decision Making and Planning

Dennis L. Madson
Larry G. Benedict
William H. Weitzer

Over the past twenty-five years, student affairs professionals have written about the need for research as a tool for planning and decision making (Hardee, 1962; Dutton, 1967; Sandeen, 1971). However, research alone does not adequately address the needs of today's student affairs managers. As Kalsbeek noted in Chapter Nineteen, knowledge of information systems, decision support systems, data-processing systems, management information systems, and modeling systems is necessary for effective information resource management. The ability to use information effectively has become a critical element of student affairs work as we enter the last decade of this century.

An information system is defined as a means of collecting and storing data that are reliable, valid, and readily available. An effective information system therefore includes processes for collecting and storing data, means of ensuring the reliability and validity of the data, and procedures for ensuring that the data are available in a useful, comprehensible form when needed by decision makers.

In this chapter, a rationale for supporting the development and use of information systems will be presented, along with specific examples of how information systems can be used for planning and decision making. In addition, strategies are offered for planning and implementing information systems in a student affairs setting with a minimum investment in resources; when appropriate, methods of developing a more comprehensive program are illustrated.

Rationale for Using Information Systems in Planning and Decision Making

The effective use of information systems in planning and decision making is essential to the maintenance, development, and improvement of a strong, stable, and comprehensive student affairs division. The thoughtful use of student information systems will foster good management, competition for limited resources, student involvement in decision making, outcomes documentation, and effective public relations.

Supporting Good Management. The use of information systems can assist managers in monitoring routine activities, evaluating specific policies and programs, comparing the size and cost of services at a number of similar schools, and identifying trends. Furthermore, proposed policies can be simulated to determine whether they achieve specific targets and contribute to established goals. Cost studies can establish the cost of processing an application, making a placement, or producing a program. This information can contribute to the process of establishing priorities and making difficult decisions involving the allocation of resources.

Competing for Limited Resources. In the competition for limited resources, information is powerful. Decision makers appreciate, understand, and respect data, particularly when they are accurate, carefully analyzed, and concisely packaged with clear graphics. Unfortunately, student affairs leaders of the past often had a reputation for presenting proposals and making decisions based on few or no data. In an age of limited resources and stiff competition for funds, student services administrators must present budget and policy proposals that are based on documented knowledge rather than conventional wisdom. Furthermore, such proposals must represent straightforward, clear-headed thinking that contributes to the basic needs and mission of the institution. Only in this way will credibility with provosts, budget directors, and vice-presidents for administration be enhanced. The use of information systems is essential if resource allocation decisions are to be favorable for student affairs divisions.

Involving Students in Decision Making. Student input and involvement in the decision-making process are essential to decisions that are thoughtful and well supported by the campus community. Although not always recognized as such, student participation in information-gathering processes is clearly one avenue for student involvement in the development of policy on a campus. Such participation is an especially valuable form of involvement in that the information thus obtained is systematically collected, representative of the average student, and highly credible with all segments of the community. Student involvement also encourages further student input; for example, students are encouraged to participate in surveys when they read about the results of a study in the newspaper, or when they hear that a new policy or management practice has been adopted partly on the basis of evaluation data that they helped to provide.

Documenting Outcomes. Many decision makers and critics are putting pressure on college and university faculties and administrators to document the outcomes of their work. Colleges and universities are being asked to provide evidence that what they do makes a difference, that they actually do what they say they are doing, and that they represent a reasonable investment for future generations. Information systems that are already in place or carefully designed new systems can provide valuable information in an outcomes documentation process. Information about class profiles, applicant pools, student satisfaction, graduation and placement rates, and student attitudes and values contributes to reports on the value of our work.

Promoting Public Relations. In the past, public relations efforts in support of an institution or particular programs have been viewed negatively by educators, including student affairs administrators. Such strategies were considered by some to be beneath their professional dignity. In this day, however, a strong public relations program is both useful and necessary for a strong student affairs division. The public relations process is a powerful tool for telling about programs and services in an accurate and straightforward manner.

Used properly, the products of student affairs information systems can have significant public relations value in educating the campus community, and the community beyond, about the processes, issues, and goals of student affairs. Reports should be thoughtfully distributed not only to colleagues but to faculty leaders, student leaders, top administrators, trustees, and legislators. These people provide support to an institution's efforts when they refer to the student affairs department's research or quote information from these efforts.

Using Information Systems

The student affairs professional can use information systems in many different ways. Erwin and Miller (1985) discuss the use of computer applications for the recruitment, referral, and retention of students. Garland (1985) writes about effective information systems as a condition of effective and insightful planning. He notes that effective systems can be used to solve problems, support new program requests, and manage resources effectively. These systems can even help reduce labor and paper-intensive efforts by student affairs staff. MacLean (1986) presents a number of uses of management information systems in student affairs, among them building budgets, mailing materials to newly admitted students, calculating financial awards to students, and providing information to state and federal regulatory agencies.

The uses of information systems fall into five categories: monitoring routine activities, planning short-term strategies, developing new policies, fostering internal communication and education, and planning long-range strategies. Which systems are used and the ways in which they are used depend on the type of decision to be made, the level of the decision maker within the institution, the urgency of the decision to be made, and so on.

Monitoring Routine Activities. One of the most important uses of information systems is in the daily maintenance and management of student affairs units. Different types of student affairs managers use a variety of information systems to fulfill their management functions. A dean of enrollment management or a director of admissions, for example, uses an admissions inquiry system to monitor routinely the operations of the admissions office. This system creates and uses computerized files on all inquiring students. It provides frequent, timely, and individualized responses to inquiries while at the same time controlling the redundant distribution of admissions information. It also provides information on the relative effectiveness of the institution's recruiting methods and materials.

This system can be used in a number of ways to monitor activities. It can, for example, check the turnaround time from a potential student's first inquiry to the institution's response. Quick turnaround is critical in the increasingly competitive marketplace for students. The system can also help in weekly monitoring. If the number of mailings for a given week seems low, the manager can intervene. Another potential problem is that of redundant mailings, a waste of time and material. The creation and monitoring of a single record on each inquiry allow the user to see at a glance which materials have been sent to a student and when.

The student affairs professional can use this system to monitor activities, make evaluative decisions about timely distribution of materials, ensure efficient distribution of materials, monitor turnaround time on the part of staff responding to inquiries, and make effective interventions to increase the chances of certain students enrolling in the institution.

A chief student affairs officer (CSAO), for example, may be concerned about the satisfaction of the student body with various services provided to it. The CSAO can survey students annually to monitor satisfaction levels. While such a survey will not prescribe a specific course of action, it will point to areas for further analysis. For example, if the CSAO notes that after increasing steadily for several years, student satisfaction with health services has declined rapidly over the last year, she might want to investigate this response in detail by gathering additional information from users of the service. In this case, the director of health services might use a telephone polling system. The results of the phone survey can then be used to make interventions to improve the situation in systematic, targeted ways.

Planning Short-Term Strategies. With a telephone survey system, data can be gathered as programs unfold, rather than after the fact, as often happens with many program evaluations. In an actual application of such a system, the director of the counseling center used a telephone polling system to explore student preferences for services in specific topic areas such as study skills, career interests, and family, health, and personal concerns. Students were asked which type of counseling they preferred—one-to-one, workshop, ongoing group of peers, or one-credit colloquium—for different content areas—study skills, career interests, personal and interpersonal issues, family conflicts and loss, and managing stress. The counseling center used their responses to gauge accurately the demand for services and the best means for delivering them. Appropriate decisions were based on these data.

In another example, the director of admissions requested a one-time survey of high school counselors in order to evaluate certain aspects of the visitation program. The survey posed questions about the professionalism of the staff, the quality of the materials, and the effectiveness of the visitation schedules. The results suggested that no changes were necessary in this particular program, that staff were performing excellently, and that the guidance counselors were very pleased with the service. Had the data indicated differently, the director could have made immediate decisions to change staff, retrain certain staff, alter the program or materials, and so on. In both of these examples, the managers had a need to monitor certain programs. A method (the telephone survey) was chosen and implemented, data were gathered, and the appropriate decisions were made. These examples illustrate typical ways this particular system of telephone surveying is used for planning short-term strategies.

Information systems can also help plan new strategies to meet divisional goals and objectives. The health and safety of students, for example, are clearly a priority for the CSAO, the housing director, and the health services director. Fire safety in the residence halls was the focus of another telephone survey. The results in this example showed that the students surveyed were woefully ill prepared to respond to a fire emergency, despite brochures having been distributed, resident assistants and hall directors having informed students about procedures, and so on. In this case, the educational effort was not working and new programming was required. Such programming was developed immediately.

In this situation, the managers took the active step of assessing students' knowledge, rather than assuming that because brochures were distributed the students had internalized the information. The result of this step is better-prepared students and staff. This was not really program evaluation but rather an attempt to determine how well students were prepared to deal with a fire emergency. Indirectly it became an evaluation of the way the brochures and the educational efforts that had been made were working.

In another case, the registrar noticed an increasing number of problems and concerns among students who had dropped out or "stopped out" of school and now were returning. The number of these students was high enough to warrant attention. In order to better understand the readmitted student, a telephone survey was undertaken. Data were gathered on the attitudes and characteristics of these students, their reasons for leaving the university in the first place, their reasons for wanting to return, and so on. The data revealed that these students by and large had withdrawn because they were unsure of their academic plans or had financial difficulties. They also revealed that since these students were not really new, unlike first-time freshman or transfer students, there was no one office to coordinate responses to their issues.

The decision makers used a comparative institutional study to determine which administrative procedures are used to handle readmitted students at peer institutions. This study gathered information from a predetermined group of institutions using detailed written questionnaires. Such studies might be done by a college or university's office of institutional research or even directly by the administrator needing the information, such as the registrar or the director of placement. Taken together, the data gathered from information systems can be used to develop some short-term strategies to attract students who have left school as well as retain readmitted students once they have returned. Finally, they serve as a basis for providing better advising and support to this population.

Developing New Policies. Information systems can be used very effectively to develop new policies, to ensure that they are well formulated and well articulated, and to ensure that they will receive the support of campus decision makers. For example, the trustees of an institution had set a ceiling on the enrollment of out-of-state students of 15 percent of total enrollment. However, given the demographic projections, the administration preferred the more flexible policy of either having no ceiling at all on out-of-state enrollment or allowing it to float above 15 percent. Changing the policy would have been a major shift. To formulate a policy proposal, several systems or parts of systems were called on. Data were gathered from peer institutions, from land-grant schools, using information from the National Association of State Universities and Land Grant Colleges, and from the admissions system. Using the computer-based graphics capability of the student affairs research office, the results were integrated into a comprehensive report that was sent to the board of trustees.

Information systems can also be used to help fend off or alter policies proposed by external regulatory and governmental agencies—local, state, and federal—that may not be the best for students. For example, statewide admissions standards are used in many states and are subject to change. In one case, a regulatory body proposed a set of standards whose impact had not been considered and that in fact were unrealistic. When accurate and up-to-date data were made available to the regulatory agency, the standards were modified in such a way that the goals of the agency were met without harming the state's colleges and university. In this situation, because effective systems were in operation, a rapid response was made and an improved policy resulted.

A similar case involved statewide financial aid policy and tuition policy. Data from the financial aid data base (a large, mainframe computer information system), the American Council on Education/Cooperative Institutional Research Program (ACE/CIRP) data base, the Higher Education General Information Survey (HEGIS), and the Center for Education Statistics of the Department of Education's Office of Educational Research and Improvement were rapidly and readily integrated into a position/profile paper to influence a regulatory agency's planning on financial aid and tuition policy. In both cases, the goal was to influence policy rapidly, effectively, and efficiently, using coordinated, cohesive, "funded knowledge" rather than conventional wisdom or pious hope.

Fostering Internal Communication and Education. The cooperation of deans, faculty, and other administrative staff is crucial to achieving the institution's goals. An example in this category is justifying the enrollment management policies to the campus. At many institutions, enrollment management is seen strictly as an admissions problem. But at those institutions where research and planning have taken place, enrollment management must involve all the constituencies on campus. Communicating this message, however, requires considerable effort and involves the use of many different systems.

To gather the support of different groups, one campus organized a comprehensive presentation that defined enrollment management. The presentation outlined the major areas of concern and discussed common goals such as an effective marketing campaign, admissions standards, access to courses and majors, financial aid packaging, and the cultural and ethnic diversity of the student body. In short, it provided a complete look at enrollment management from a campuswide perspective. Once organized, all the data thus obtained were used in a major presentation to the president and chief administrative officers of the university. Following this, a presentation was made to chief campus officers. More than two years were used to develop

a consensus, to "educate" the campus, to the point that enrollment management came to be seen as a priority by many significant people on campus, including key deans, the provost, and
other members of the executive staff. The result has been an
officially adopted enrollment management plan. Without information systems, the task of assembling such an effective, comprehensive presentation would have been almost unthinkable.

Planning Long-Range Strategies. Beyond daily management is the larger picture of long-range planning. The enrollment management example just described is also a good example
of planning. Each part of the plan resulted from an application
of an information system. A related and complementary system
used to support this effort was the Western Interstate Commission for Higher Education (WICHE) demographic projections.
These projections spurred the enrollment management efforts.
Initially, WICHE data were used exclusively, but the campus
faculty and staff were not impressed. While many concluded
that declines in the number of high school seniors could not affect their university, others suggested a wait-and-see stance.

To address and counter these attitudes, work was begun
on an enrollment projection model that eventually incorporated
some 375 variables, ranging from past application rates, acceptance rates, and enrollment numbers to statewide migration factors and individual high school graduation rates. The model was
made available for use on a microcomputer, so that it has itself
become an information system. It allows the administration to
test various strategies it might employ in enrollment management efforts and to look at the implications of changes in policy.
This system is portable, being contained on a floppy disk, and
can be adapted to community colleges, state colleges, and state
universities. This system can help inform policy and support
decisions on a wide range of variables affecting enrollment
planning.

Developing Information Systems

In today's environment of limited resources, some might
be afraid to embrace this chapter's broad definition of infor-

mation systems. It would be a mistake, however, to back away from the development of information systems because of the cost of some of the more sophisticated systems discussed thus far. The number of examples in this chapter were made possible because of the slow growth over a fifteen-year period of a student affairs research operation on the authors' campus; no institution in the early stages of developing information systems should expect to cover even a fraction of this range of information systems.

The remainder of this chapter focuses on planning the development of information systems regardless of the level of resources and expertise dedicated to the purpose. For only a few hundred dollars it is possible to begin to improve the utilization of information in decision making. In time, the value of information systems having been demonstrated, more resources may be directed toward the development and utilization of information systems. There are four steps necessary to begin planning the development of information systems: identifying key decision areas that require information, inventorying existing resources that have been applied or are available to address the decision area, developing cost estimates and locating resources for implementing the information systems, and locating persons with the appropriate expertise to manage the information systems.

Identifying Key Decision Areas. In beginning to develop a plan for information systems, it is most important to articulate the decision areas that require information. There is no sense in obtaining information that is tangential to the primary purposes of the operation. A comparison of the purpose of an information system and the decisions to be made in student affairs should yield an estimate of the potential benefits of the information system to the institution. It is often useful to simulate the information that might be produced and ponder the potential effects on the institution.

Inventorying Existing Resources. A second step in planning the development of information systems is to conduct an inventory of what is already being done and what resources are already available. Most institutions have data made available to them by the College Board or the American College Testing

Program (ACT), and many have years of data from the ACE/ CIRP survey of entering freshmen. In addition, expertise may be available in offices within student affairs (such as the counseling center), outside student affairs (such as institutional research), and in academic departments (such as education, psychology, sociology, communications, marketing, and so on).

Developing Cost Estimates. While there may be in-house resources that can be contributed to the development and use of an information system, it is likely that additional resources will be required. Once a system has been evaluated on the basis of its utility in meeting institutional goals and the current resources, the costs of proceeding, in relation to the benefits that will accrue, will be critical to the acceptance of a plan.

Locating Persons with Expertise. Last, but not least, the level of expertise required to develop and implement an information system must be considered. Meeting the goals of the institution and having the funds to proceed are not sufficient for the implementation of successful systems if the people assigned the project do not have the technical expertise and equipment to back up their work.

The last two steps form a matrix, shown in Figure 1, that is useful in the development of an information systems plan. This matrix illustrates the relationship between the type of system and the costs and levels of expertise associated with it. It can be instructive as an institution develops a plan for implementing information systems. Each institution will want to develop a plan that fits within budgetary constraints and institutional time-lines. One option is to begin at point A, with a system or systems that are low in cost and require little expertise. This can benefit the institution and help develop the argument for doing more work of this type. Next, an institution can move to point B, with systems that require moderate levels of cost and expertise. In time, the utility of information systems having been demonstrated, the institution can move to point C, where high-cost or high-expertise systems can be argued for and developed. The institution might then move toward point D, the development of a full range of information systems for use in decision making, including systems that require medium to high

Figure 1. Categories of Information Systems
According to Their Associated Levels
of Cost and Expertise.

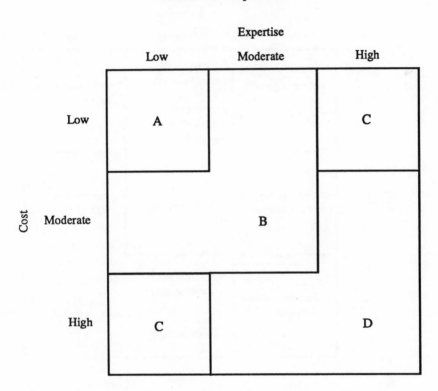

levels of cost and expertise. Figure 2 shows examples of information systems in each category of the matrix.

Initiating Student Information Systems. Using the matrix
in Figure 2 as a guide, it can be seen that there are valuable
information systems that can be instituted immediately because
they involve minimal costs and expertise. The most basic example of a low-cost, low-expertise information resource is a
discussion group on one or more of the decision areas identified
in Step 1. The student affairs manager, working with a few staff
members who are knowledgeable in a given area, might invite
a small group of students to discuss the issues over coffee and
doughnuts. Sometimes selecting a random group of students

Figure 2. Examples of Information Systems
at Various Levels of Cost and Expertise.

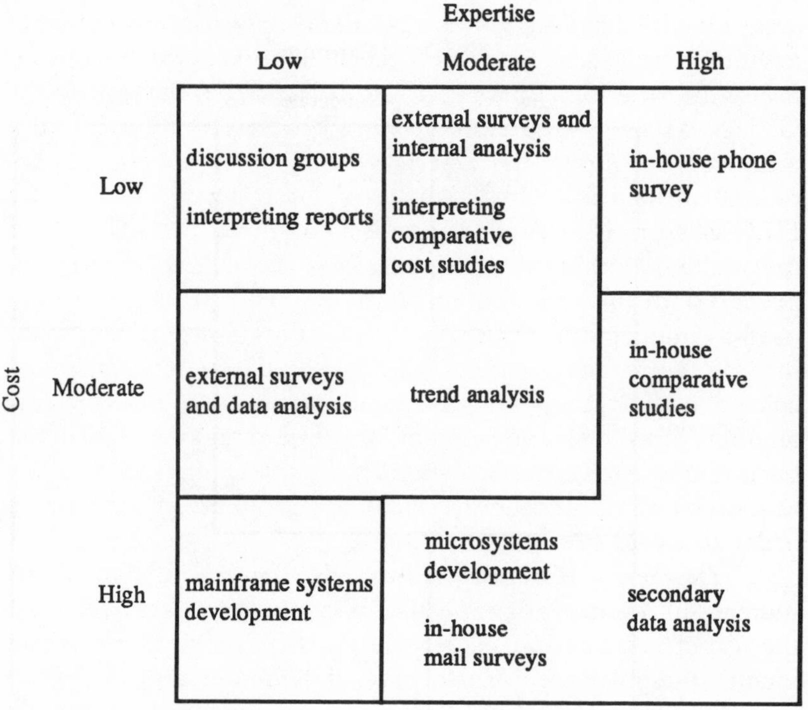

Expertise

	Low	Moderate	High
Low	discussion groups interpreting reports	external surveys and internal analysis interpreting comparative cost studies	in-house phone survey
Moderate	external surveys and data analysis	trend analysis	in-house comparative studies
High	mainframe systems development	microsystems development in-house mail surveys	secondary data analysis

Cost (vertical axis label on left)

is productive (and more ''representative''), but at other times
it may be more appropriate to select students for their knowledge
of a topic or influence as student leaders. One advantage of such
an approach is that the interactive nature of the collection of
information allows for greater flexibility than other information
systems that are set beforehand (such as surveys or computerized
records). Other clear advantages are the rapidity of the collection of information and its immediate utility (since no computer
analysis is necessary) in decision making. A clear drawback of
this method is that because the sample is small, the data are
not representative, and the information is primarily qualitative
in nature.

It is likely that an inventory of existing resources completed in Step 2 will uncover a number of reports that have been filed without further interpretation with respect to the decision areas identified in Step 1. It is a relatively low-cost, low-expertise activity to pull these reports off the shelf and examine them for useful information. Every institution receives reports from the College Board's Admissions Testing Program or the ACT program concerning the characteristics of its applicant pool. In addition, all institutions participate in the collection of data for HEGIS, from which reports are issued for use by colleges and universities. Within the institution, there are often annual reports prepared for the president or board of trustees that are seldom used as information resources for planning and decision making. By taking advantage of what is already an expensive data collection effort, this small investment of time can produce large amounts of valuable information for decision making. The drawback is that care must be taken in the interpretation of information by an office other than the one producing the report in order to avoid misinterpretations.

Developing Moderately Advanced Systems. With a moderate increase in resources or expertise, it is relatively easy to expand the use of information systems in decision making. Examples include the purchase of survey and data analysis services from outside vendors, the purchase of surveys developed externally but analyzed internally, the interpretation of comparative studies of other institutions, and the analysis of trends over time using several years' worth of existing data.

At a moderate cost, surveys can be purchased through a variety of vendors. For example, CIRP, the College Board, and ACT have developed surveys that relieve the institution of the need to have staff with survey expertise. These surveys are analyzed by the vendor, lowering the cost for the institution. In addition to the low level of expertise they require from the manager, these services often produce comparison data from other participating institutions. A drawback is the lack of flexibility in the design of questions suited to a particular institution.

A wider variety of surveys are available for little or no cost if the institution is prepared to administer the survey and analyze the data on campus. Of course, the saving in costs may go to support a higher level of expertise; however, this trade-off is suited to an institution that has the expertise already. This approach retains the advantage of the previous one in that the survey design expertise is already provided and comparison data from other participating institutions may be available. It also provides greater flexibility, since it is easier to add questions of interest to the institution. The danger of this approach is that it is easy to underestimate the level of expertise required to take the surveys, enter the data onto a computer, and analyze the data appropriately.

Institutions continually receive requests for information that involve comparative studies among institutions. At minimal cost, satisfying these requests can result in the return of data about how institutions compare. Expertise is important in order to evaluate the validity of the comparisons (for example, are the comparison groups appropriately defined, or were variables overlooked that invalidate the comparison?). There are obvious benefits to learning about how other institutions handle problems, organize themselves, and allocate budgets. The dangers here are that comparisons are always inexact and require qualification. Therefore, with comparative studies more than any other source of information, these methods should be used to guide decision makers, not to drive the decisions themselves.

Still at moderate levels of both cost and expertise, it is possible to look at information over several years to inform decision making. This is often done with computerized data but overlooked for survey data. For example, the ACE/CIRP survey of entering freshmen may indicate that a certain percentage of the new class wants to pursue a career in business. The percentage alone, however, cannot inform decison making unless information is made available about the percentage of freshmen indicating this preference in past years. This effort requires a greater investment of time and care, but the benefits of having comparison years are high. The danger lies in the fact that a data resource or a means of tabulating data may change without sufficient documentation; in this case, speculation about the reasons behind trends must be cautious.

Developing High-Expertise or High-Cost Systems. Once an institution is prepared to dedicate more resources or a higher level of expertise, there are valuable information systems that can be put in place. For example, an in-house phone survey system is a fairly low-cost, high-expertise enterprise. On the opposite end of the matrix, mainframe systems development carries high costs but requires little expertise from the student affairs staff.

A weekly phone survey of students can cost as little as $750 per survey if expenses are spread out over a number of surveys. The benefits include an ability to accurately gauge student attitudes about specific issues or programs, a higher response rate than most other methods, and an ability to ask questions specifically geared to the institution. The danger lies in not having the necessary expertise to conduct fairly rigorous social science research.

Divisions of student affairs traditionally rely on an independent data-processing unit for the development of mainframe systems. Although there is a high cost to the work associated with mainframe systems development, student affairs can rely on the expertise of the data-processing unit instead of in-house expertise. The benefit of large mainframe systems is that they can accommodate large data bases, multiple users, and a wide variety of purposes (especially research). The danger is the lack of flexibility for a manager's needs, particularly in generating timely reports for use in decision making.

Developing Advanced Information Systems. Often the data-processing center cannot meet the information needs of the decision maker. In this case, the institution may develop its own microcomputer system. The local control over the development of the system and the data collection makes this a useful approach in many cases. Moderately skilled staff are needed to evaluate the application to determine whether there is a fit between the application and the available hardware and software. In addition, moderate expertise is necessary to program microcomputer systems. One major pitfall is that microcomputer systems do not communicate readily with mainframe sources of data; therefore, if up-to-date information on, for example, addresses or student status is required, a microcomputer approach might prove to be inappropriate.

To conduct a major mail survey in-house is a costly enterprise that requires a moderate level of expertise. Expenses include printing, postage, envelope stuffing, response tracking, data coding and entry, data analysis, and report production. At each stage of the project, skilled staff need to be experienced in issues such as anonymity versus confidentiality, response rates, missing data, and so on. If done well, the individualized nature of such a survey can have a high value to the institution. Comparisons with other institutions are difficult if not impossible to obtain when an institution designs its own instrument.

Comparative studies can be designed in-house for moderate costs if a high level of expertise is available. Clearly, there are benefits to tailoring a set of questions to address a specific institution's needs. However, such an individualized survey can be difficult for another institution to complete. In addition, the accurate analysis of data to make valid comparisons is costly, difficult, and always subject to criticism.

An example of a high-cost, high-expertise project is an extensive analysis of large data sets. An institution might want to look back over twenty years of participation in the ACE/CIRP survey of entering freshmen or other sets of tapes provided by the College Board or ACT. While there are potential benefits to such in-depth, high-cost analyses, it is difficult to know how useful the information will prove for decision makers until after the investment has been made.

Conclusions

In this chapter we have tried to show that the effective use of information systems and the establishment of at least a minimal student affairs research and evaluation effort are essential to enhancing the management process, resource allocation, student involvement in decision making, outcomes documentation, and the public relations program of any modern student affairs divison. A viable and relevant student affairs unit must not avoid the development and implementation of a plan for utilizing information systems in decision making.

Furthermore, we suggest that these efforts must be coordinated centrally for all student affairs and maintained separately from the campus institutional research program. Central coordination is important for stimulating research and evaluation activity, limiting redundancy, sharing expertise, promoting work that builds on past research and evaluation, and maintaining a history or catalogue of activity. Over a period of time this may even lead to a comprehensive office of student affairs research.

Although the development, implementation, and use of student affairs information systems must be known to the campus officials responsible for institutional research activities, they also must normally be kept separate for one critical reason. No matter how comprehensive the understanding of institutional research personnel, the pressures of time, limited staff resources, and especially the campus and institutional priorities usually prevent student-life research and evaluation projects from being accomplished by institutional research staff. Institutional research offices, by definition, must place a priority on reviewing, analyzing, and reporting academic budget information and responding to the frequent requests for information from external agencies. They do not have time, even if they have the inclination, to conduct, supervise, or coordinate student affairs information systems projects.

It must be emphasized that information systems are tools, not ends in themselves. Properly used, they can assist student services personnel in meeting their planning responsibilities and in making decisions. Plans and decisions are made not by information but by people. The advantages of information systems are many and these systems will continue to grow as essential tools of modern managers for several reasons. First, they facilitate decision making on the basis of data and funded knowledge rather than intuition and conventional wisdom. Second, the systems improve our effectiveness in working with various constituencies. They help us focus attention on important issues by allowing us to speak with convincing data; they improve credibility. Third, they help us provide the bases on which to improve services to students and faculty. Fourth, they help

us to fulfill our mission by meeting our goals and objectives in
timely, effective, and efficient ways.

Finally, they help us prepare for the future. A manager
familiar with information systems—with their capabilities, their
time limitations, their reliance on graphics and data—need not
reinvent the wheel in every new crisis or emergency. Rather,
he or she can rely on the systems for information and on the
staff for good decisions and plans. Thus, we are able to respond
more rapidly to situations and to increase productivity, allowing better management decisions and improved quality in all
phases of student affairs administration.

It is important to begin. Start by doing. With only a small
amount of money a student affairs division can start to improve
its planning and decision-making processes. It usually takes a
decade or two to build up a comprehensive set of student affairs information systems. A wise person once said: Don't delay;
start today. If you cannot afford to plant a large tree, plant a
small one and you will discover that by the time you can afford
the large tree, you will already have one in your yard.

References

Dutton, T. B. "Research Needs and Priorities in Student Per-
    sonnel Work." *National Association of Student Personnel Adminis-
    trators Journal,* 1967, *5,* 339–343.
Erwin, T., and Miller, S. "Technology and the Three R's."
    National Association of Student Personnel Administrators Journal,
    1985, *22,* 47–51.
Garland, P. H. *Serving More Than Students: A Critical Need for College
    Student Personnel Services.* ASHE/ERIC Higher Education Re-
    port no. 7. Washington, D.C.: Association for the Study of
    Higher Education, 1985.
Hardee, M. D. "Research on College Students: The Student Per-
    sonnel Worker's View." *Educational Record,* 1962, *43,* 132–138.
MacLean, L. S. "Developing MIS in Student Affairs." *Na-
    tional Association of Student Personnel Administrators Journal,* 1986,
    23, 2–7.
Sandeen, A. "Research: An Essential for Survival." *National
    Association of Student Personnel Services Journal,* 1971, *9,* 222–227.

Chapter Twenty-One

Enhancing Staff Knowledge and Skills

Jon C. Dalton

Almost every student affairs organization does something about staff development as an area of professional practice, but few, it seems, do it well. Models of staff development have been offered (Canon, 1976; Parker, 1971), but no single model of staff development is widely accepted among practitioners. Theodore Miller's (1975) study of staff development activities in student affairs programs revealed a surprising lack of research and literature on the subject, as well as an extremely wide range of practices. This diversity of activities and approaches in staff development may simply reflect the particular interests of individual student affairs leaders and the priorities of their organizations and institutions. However, the lack of uniformity in program design and content also may reflect uncertainty about the purposes of staff development, as well as lack of agreement on the essential knowledge and skills necessary for professional practice. This chapter will examine the general purposes of staff development, important program content topics and issues, and practical strategies for organizing effective programs.

There are several compelling reasons for doing staff development in student services. First of all, staff development is an essential aspect of effective personnel management. Management researchers (Halloran, 1986; Cascio, 1986; Schneier and

Beatty, 1978; Albanese, 1978) argue that staff development is a necessary component of comprehensive personnel management programs. Traditional personnel management practice emphasized maintenance functions such as hiring, processing, and keeping records on employees (Schneier and Beatty, 1978). Today, personnel managers recognize the important role of staff development in training and motivating people and in enhancing organizational effectiveness. Staff development simply makes good sense from the standpoint of personnel management in student services.

Staff development is also important because one of the most powerful motivators of people in the work setting is the experience of growth and development. Although great attention is usually given to pay, benefits, and working conditions, these aspects of the work environment may sometimes function as demotivators for staff (Kay, 1974). The most powerful motivators of people on the job are opportunities for responsibility, growth, achievement, and recognition. Staff members need to feel that they are learning and growing on the job and that they are developing as persons (DuBrin, 1978). Student affairs professionals, trained in human development theory, are more likely to recognize the importance of ongoing personal development. Consequently, staff development activities can provide one of the most direct means of assisting student affairs staff in continuing the process of individual growth and development.

Staff development can also provide a direct bridge between graduate education and professional practice. Student affairs staff with graduate training in fields related to student services usually bring to the job a basic understanding of human development theory, research skills, and a general orientation to the organization and administration of student services. What they lack and must learn on the job is how to apply such knowledge and skills in particular work settings. Staff development activities can help staff make the necessary personal transitions from studying a profession to becoming a professional.

Moreover, student affairs organizations frequently employ people with no formal student services training. Some staff members may lack basic competencies in professional knowledge and skills. One of the important functions of staff development is to provide a base line of content and skills training to ensure that all staff possess minimum levels of competency for their job roles and responsibilities.

Finally, staff development can be an important means of personal renewal to help combat burnout and professional obsolescence. Cone (1968) argues that obsolescence occurs when staff lose the technical, interpersonal, and political skills necessary to perform their job roles. Student affairs positions are so demanding in time and pressure that burnout and obsolescence are ever-present dangers. Effective staff development programs can promote self-renewal and help staff to stay current and relevant in the midst of a demanding and ever-changing profession.

Definition of Staff Development

Because there is no commonly accepted model for staff development, the basic purpose of staff development efforts must be defined. Staff development is the intentional and systematic effort to enhance the knowledge and skills of staff members. While activities such as social programs and awards and recognition may be very important for staff morale, they are not designed to promote knowledge and skills and, for our purposes, are not considered to be staff development activities. A narrow definition of staff development enables us to be specific about goals and objectives and to identify essential program content more easily. Much of what goes by the name of staff development in student services programs has little to do with enhancing knowledge and skills. Too often the assumption is made that anything done for employees is staff development and that any such efforts are intrinsically good. This may be one of the reasons that there is so little agreement about content and purpose in staff development programs. Many things may be worth doing for employees but contribute little to staff development as we have defined it.

Surveys (Creamer, 1987; Rhatigan and Crawford, 1980; Miller, 1975) of student affairs staff development programs reveal a very eclectic content. Some programs are primarily social in character, while others are almost exclusively concerned with in-service skill training. Staff development programs can be organized in many ways, but two basic program components should be enhancing knowledge and enhancing skills.

Enhancing knowledge is important because staff must stay current with the latest research and developments in the profession and be given opportunities to reflect on new information and integrate it into their professional roles and responsibilities. Such information helps to provide the big picture of trends and developments in the profession and to keep staff members informed about change. Enhancing knowledge in ways that help the staff member to be a more effective professional should be a basic objective of staff development programs.

Enhancing skills focuses more narrowly on helping people to improve the level of their specific job-related skills and abilities. For some staff positions, skill training involves the enhancement of technical skills. For others, the focus of skill training is in improving technique, procedure, or practice. Delworth (1978) argues that skill development is a necessary aspect of staff competence in specific roles and tasks. Skill development should be an important aspect of staff development programs because it promotes expertise in specific job responsibilities and can be provided close to the job setting. Skill development must obviously be limited to the competencies that student affairs organizations have the leadership and resources to provide.

Purposes of Staff Development

Staff development is an integral part of the student affairs mission of promoting student development. The welfare and development of students are served by promoting the expertise of staff and providing greater quality assurance in student affairs educational services and programs. The purposes of staff development are therefore to benefit students, to improve the individual staff member, and to improve the organization.

Benefiting Students. The ultimate goal of staff development activities should be to benefit students. This goal provides a necessary value framework for staff development activities and should be acknowledged from the outset. Staff development is important for a number of reasons but above all because it helps to further the basic student affairs mission of promoting the welfare and development of students. Staff development should not be viewed primarily as either a personnel fringe benefit or a management tool for enhancing productivity, worthy as these are. Staff development activities should be conducted because they promote the basic mission of student affairs organizations. Competent and highly motivated staff are critical to the accomplishment of student development objectives. Jacqueline Fleming (1984) argues that investing in staff and faculty development may be one of the most effective strategies for achieving student development outcomes. Acknowledging the goal of benefiting students and integrating this goal into the design and content of staff development activities help to keep an appropriate focus on what is relevant and important. Many activities that are worthwhile or enjoyable in their own right may have no direct consequence for the benefit of students.

Improving the Individual. Improving individual staff members should also be a primary goal of intervention strategies for staff development. When the knowledge and skills of individual staff members are enhanced, both the students and the organization benefit. Research (Adams, 1984) on the way people work in organizations indicates that growth and development in the job setting are essential if they are to maximize their achievement and creativity. People look for meaning in their work that far exceeds their job responsibilities. Effective staff development programs can help people enlarge their vision and raise their level of competence. Student affairs organizations that do not give systematic attention to helping staff members grow and develop will underutilize staff potential and artificially limit organizational effectiveness.

From a practical standpoint, staff development programs that meet the needs of individual staff members are most likely to work. Every staff member has certain underdeveloped or underutilized qualities, and most will respond to opportunities for personal development if they feel their involvement is truly valued by the organization and will enhance their effectiveness.

Improving the Organization. Another important objective of staff development activities is to improve the organization. By fostering effective communication and networking among staff members and promoting shared values, innovations, and goals through staff development programs, the student affairs organization is made more effective. Deegan (1979) claims that developing staff is the pillar of any system of management the organization espouses. Effective staff development programs help merge self-interest with organizational interests. Individual staff members who are committed to common organizational values and who share a unity of mission can give the organization extraordinary influence and impact.

People want and need to understand the purpose of their work and how it fits into the broader goals of the organization. Staff will be more motivated and satisfied if they see that their efforts contribute to priorities shared by co-workers in a larger organizational context. Shared goals and priorities help to create a sense of community that provides support and direction for individuals (DuBrin, 1978). A dynamic organization embodies the values and norms of individual staff members, represents their collective ideals, and provides the practical means for achieving them.

Organizing for Staff Development

As noted earlier, one of the difficulties with organizing staff development programs is that there is no commonly accepted model in use in the profession. The most successful staff development programs share the following characteristics: they have clearly defined objectives, they are strongly supported by the top leadership levels, they involve all levels of the organization, they are coordinated by a divisionwide committee that includes representation from many if not all departments, and they have centralized institutional resources and support.

Communicating the goals and objectives of staff development is important to overall program success. The staff manual or handbook can provide an excellent means for accomplishing this purpose, since it provides easy access to employee resources, information, and expectations. Professional development objectives should be included in the staff manual and used regularly in the orientation of new staff. The staff manual should include a compilation of material designed to communicate key information to staff members, such as the statement of mission and goals of the student affairs division, its administrative structure and organization, and pertinent policies and procedures, as well as specific information about staff development opportunities.

Strong leadership from the top is needed to communicate clearly that staff development is a high priority within the organization. Active involvement and support by the chief student affairs officer demonstrate that staff development has divisionwide priority and support. Without commitment from the top, staff participation will almost certainly be uneven. Department heads will vary in their levels of support and some may even oppose staff participation when higher priorities or more compelling obligations exist. In such situations, staff development efforts are seriously jeopardized. Not only is there inconsistent and insufficient support, there is almost always low morale and even resentment among those staff members who feel they are denied opportunities for involvement.

The most important indicator of top leadership support is the extent to which staff development is formally recognized and rewarded. The best-designed staff development programs will have little impact unless they are directly supported by the recognition and reward system in the student affairs organization. If staff development participation is not tied in relevant ways to performance evaluation, salary and promotion, and professional recognition, it is likely to be viewed as a low-priority commitment. Student affairs staff members simply have too many competing priorities to make significant personal commitments to activities that are not judged important enough to be rewarded. Staff development activities should be noted on employee résumés and formally included in performance evaluations. Efforts should be made to give regular feedback to staff who participate in staff development and to publicly recognize their participation.

Staff development efforts must involve all levels of the organization. Since the focus of staff development is on enhancing knowledge and skills to improve the individual and the organization, the issues and concerns of staff throughout the organization must be addressed. Some issues may be unique to the specific work setting of an employee, while others may involve divisional or institutional concerns. To achieve a uniform program of staff development and to ensure that input is secured from all departments of the student affairs organization, a centralized coordinating committee composed of representatives of all departments should be established (Canon, 1980). This accomplishes several goals: the staff development activities of individual departments are integrated into the overall divisional program, needed knowledge and skills are identified through broad staff input and collaboration, program duplication is avoided, and commitment and loyalty to staff development activities are promoted.

A central coordinating committee needs a strong liaison with the chief student affairs leader. The committee should report directly to the CSAO or an immediate associate and include a nonvoting member from his or her office. It is best for the senior student affairs officer not to chair the coordinating committee, since such an arrangement often inhibits participation and may limit the range of ideas generated. Staff development committees need support, but not excessive direction, from the CSAO.

Staff development activities should also have designated budget and staff resources. Moreover, these resource commitments should be clearly communicated to the coordinating committee as well as to all line administrators in the division. Too often staff development activities are "bootlegged" out of various operating budgets; worse yet, staff members are often expected to develop a program with no provision for budget or resources. The message is clear to all staff: these activities are not really important. Strong support from the CSAO is helpful in obtaining specified resources and demonstrates the high level of commitment given to the program.

Core Curriculum for In-House
Staff Development Programs

Miller (1975) found that student affairs staff were typically involved with four kinds of staff development activities: divisional, institutional, academic, and off-campus. Student affairs staff were reported to spend the greatest amount of time in divisional staff development activities, but they also spent significant time in staff development activities outside student affairs. We will talk later about outside opportunities for staff development; here we will focus on staff development activities conducted by student affairs organizations for professional staff.

In the literature on staff development activities, five themes or issues can be identified as especially important for student affairs professionals. These issues are of such enduring and fundamental importance that they should be considered core content in all staff development programs. These five issues are mission and philosophy, communication skills, management and leadership skills, professional ethics, and current professional issues. These core content issues represent recurring themes of professional growth and excellence regardless of level of responsibility or job title. We will use these core content areas as a topical framework for discussing approaches to in-house staff development programming.

Many of the five core content topics are included in the curricula of graduate training programs for college student personnel. However, staff in student affairs organizations often have graduate training in a variety of fields and may have had little or no contact with the core content areas. Moreover, graduate training programs for college student personnel differ widely in curriculum requirements and emphasis. Hence, graduates from different programs often do not have the same competency levels in the core content areas. An important objective of staff development is to ensure that all staff members have minimum competency levels in all five content areas.

Effective staff development programs address these knowledge and training topics from the perspective of a particular organizational context. Consequently, when topics such as communication, ethics, and mission are studied, they should be approached from the context of one's own specific organization and its particular circumstances. This approach serves to link theory and application and increases the likelihood that staff development education will carry over into professional practice. Because of this unique learning context, even people with formal training in the content areas will be likely to benefit from participation in such staff development activities.

While five specific content areas should compose the core curriculum of staff development education, staff members should have some options in selecting the experiences that best fit their immediate needs and interests. Both objectives can be accomplished by designing program activities that allow for some choice within a structured framework. In this cafeteria approach, the coordinating committee determines the "menu," while individual staff members choose the particular "courses" they prefer.

Mission and Philosophy. The importance of a clear sense of mission and organizational values to staff performance and satisfaction has been repeatedly stressed in research on organizational development (Adams, 1984; Albanese, 1978; Franklin, 1978). The efforts of individuals are energized and focused when there is widespread agreement on goals and outcomes (DuBrin, 1978). Adams (1984) claims that effective organizations, like people, operate best as integrated wholes. Understanding the overall mission of the organization helps individual staff members to see their work in the context of broader purposes and meaning. When they experience a commonality of purpose with a network of colleagues engaged in the same essential mission, they will become more motivated and productive. Staff development programs that include components on mission and philosophy provide important opportunities for staff to see the big picture and to integrate their individual goals with those of colleagues.

Increasingly, student affairs staff bring with them to the job some familiarity with student development philosophy. Most graduate training programs in student affairs provide a good orientation to student development philosophy and the associated research literature. Unfortunately, graduate students often do not immediately recognize the relevance of educational philosophy to professional preparation and practice. What they do not value they are not likely to learn well nor retain.

In the past three decades, the student affairs profession has achieved considerable agreement both on a philosophical understanding of the growth and development of college students and on appropriate educational strategies for promoting this development. Student development philosophy is a powerful integrating and motivating force in student affairs organizations because it provides the value framework and outcomes orientation that integrate and give meaning to the efforts of individual staff members. Understanding student development philosophy is just as critical to effective professional practice. Student affairs organizations engage in myriad activities, some of which have little practical value in promoting student development and may even serve to inhibit it. Philosophy, of course, does not define job descriptions and performance objectives, but it is indispensable for defining what is relevant and worthwhile about the work that is done. Without an understanding of philosophy and mission, professional practice is rudderless.

Communication Skills. Perhaps the most popular and directly beneficial aspect of staff development programs is communication skills training. Communication training is a practical necessity in student affairs work. Effective communication skills are critical to the development of both individuals and organizations. The improvement of people in the work setting depends on their ability to give and receive information, to empathize and understand, and to listen and receive feedback. Without these essential skills, staff members will have difficulty relating to others and understanding what is expected of them in the work setting. In a survey of student affairs administrators (Rhatigan and Crawford, 1980), the activities reported to be most beneficial for staff development involved discussions with colleagues, students, and faculty. The high rating of survey items involving verbal activity indicates the importance staff members ascribe to interpersonal communication.

Effective communication skills are also important for the improvement of the organization. Organizational effectiveness depends on the ability of staff members to communicate and relate effectively with one another. Achieving a sense of commonality about mission and philosophy is difficult unless individuals discuss and share perspectives on these issues. Likewise, staff members will not come to know one another as persons and professionals without skills and opportunities for effective communication. From a management standpoint, the most serious and frequent organizational problems result from the inability of staff members to listen, to be courteous, to be empathetic, and to share openly—in short, to be effective communicators. These interpersonal skills can be taught (Delworth, 1978) and should be included as a core content area in staff development activities.

The ultimate beneficiaries of better staff communication skills are students. The skills that serve to enhance personal and organizational development are equally valuable in facilitating the growth and development of students. Staff members who are good listeners, who attend to students' behavior, and who empathize with students' needs are better able to establish relationships of trust and openness that facilitate developmental interventions.

Management and Leadership Skills. Student affairs staff frequently identify management and leadership skills as important areas for staff development and regard these skills as instrumental in professional advancement. Staff members who have jobs with little management responsibility see management and leadership training as a means of qualifying for positions of greater responsibility. Staff members in management roles often feel that management and leadership training will enhance their effectiveness, particularly with complex management tasks.

Training programs in management and leadership skills should include topics on goal setting, conflict management, decision making, and team building. These topics are especially relevant to leadership roles and represent some of the most important and challenging aspects of leadership. All staff members confront these tasks in their professional work and can utilize such training even in nonmanagerial roles. Management and leadership training helps to broaden perspectives on issues in the work setting and to provide insights on the duties and responsibilities of leadership roles. Learning how to set goals, manage conflict, make decisions, and promote teamwork not only prepares staff members for greater leadership roles but also sensitizes them to these issues in the work setting.

Professional Ethics. Understanding the nature of one's responsibilities and moral obligations and being able to make sound ethical choices are among the most difficult aspects of professional practice. Student affairs staff members confront many value conflicts and ethical dilemmas in their jobs and need opportunities to examine the moral implications of how they handle such matters. Staff development programs should include a component on professional ethics to enable staff to examine accepted standards of professional practice and to explore the application of these standards in work relationships and commitments (Canon and Brown, 1985). All work is moral to the extent that every activity occurs within the context of a framework of meaning and values. Some of the values that operate in the work setting are directly promulgated by the organization or professional group. Other values may come from individual belief systems. When these values clash or become confused in work situations, they can create stressful situations of internal conflict or social confrontation. Because staff development is ultimately concerned with benefiting students, professional ethics should also be used to help staff members clarify their obligations to students and understand students' rights.

Although specific ethical issues vary, some ethical problems are enduring for the student affairs professional. These include confidentiality, truthfulness, obedience to authority, fairness and justice, duty and obligation, loyalty and friendship, and the relationship of means and ends. The content of these ethical problems is unique to each situation and individual, but their form and nature as ethical issues are largely unchanging. Student affairs staff everywhere confront dilemmas of confidentiality and truthfulness. At one time or another, they struggle with the problem of determining what is fair and just, whether in administering student conduct, helping to resolve a room-mate conflict, conducting a performance evaluation, or writing a student recommendation. Staff development programs that include discussion of basic ethical problems give staff important opportunities to clarify value issues and resolve moral conflicts.

The topic of professional ethics includes many issues and concerns and because of its great breadth can be difficult to address in staff development programs. One helpful way to approach this subject is to utilize the professional ethics statements of the major student affairs associations. These statements identify the major areas of ethical obligation and professional practice and suggest guidelines for managing ethical issues on the job. While these professional standards do not cover special ethical issues in great detail, they provide a framework of ethical principles that can be readily applied to specific contextual issues.

Discussion of professional ethics has the added benefit of promoting communication and team building in student affairs organizations. As staff members share perspectives on value issues and discuss the obligations of professional work, they give and receive valuable feedback and learn to see their problems in the context of a much broader framework of meaning and shared values.

Current Issues. Student affairs staff members, like other professionals, have an obligation to stay abreast of current issues and developments in their field. Consequently, some attention to current issues is important in staff development programs to ensure that staff are aware of the trends and issues that shape the work of their profession. Professional conferences and journals are excellent sources of information on current issues, but many staff do not have access to them. Further, student affairs staff need opportunities to explore current issues in the context of their particular institutional setting and work environment. This enables staff both to learn about issues and to explore their implications for everyday professional practice.

A good way to identify trend-setting issues is to survey the major topics and themes of annual professional conferences. Conference topics and the themes chosen by major speakers are bellwethers of the current issues that concern many of the profession's leaders. Professional journals are also useful in identifying issues, but they may be somewhat less current because of the time lag caused by the review and publication process. Another important source of current topics and issues is national reports and studies on issues related to higher education. The number of major research reports on higher education published in the 1980s is almost unprecedented. These reports have had far-reaching impact on colleges and universities and, in turn, on college student personnel work. Such "think-tank" efforts of leading educators and professionals provide some of the best sources for the current and future agenda of professional issues.

Other Opportunities for Staff Development

To this point, we have discussed topics and issues that should be included in in-house staff development programs. There are, however, a variety of other resources available that should be considered when a comprehensive staff development program is being devised. Many staff members take academic classes and believe them to be an important means for professional development (Miller, 1975). Academic classes have become popular with student affairs staff as institutions have made tuition waivers more available as an employee fringe benefit. Where it can be demonstrated that academic class work contributes to the purposes of staff development, enhances individual professional development, and does not directly conflict with job responsibilities, staff should be supported and encouraged to take relevant academic classes.

Institutional in-service programs for employees provided by the college or university personnel office are another important resource for staff development. Such programs are usually broad and general in orientation, since they are directed at a large and diverse group of employees. However, they can provide valuable staff development opportunities, particularly on topics pertaining to general knowledge and skill areas such as communications, decision making, and conflict resolution. Institutional programs provide excellent opportunities for student

affairs to interact with staff outside the division and to supplement in-house staff development activities. Institutional programs usually also have the added advantage of being provided
free to employees and thus can help to reduce the costs of staff
development for student affairs units.

Activities sponsored by national, state, and local professional organizations should not be overlooked for staff development purposes. Professional student affairs associations provide
national, regional, and state conferences, drive-in workshops,
and institutes and special programs for new professionals, mid-
level managers, and chief student affairs administrators. These
programs provide an important supplement to staff development
efforts. The staff development coordinating committee should
compile information on the dates, locations, and topics of all
relevant professional meetings, to be circulated and used by staff
and supervisors in planning annual staff development priorities.

There is a variety of other practical means for assisting
staff in developing knowledge and skills. Job rotation and job
enrichment are two staff development strategies that attempt
to promote development through direct changes in job assignment (Kay, 1974). In job rotation, the employee is given an
opportunity to work in another position as a means of gaining
desired experience and skills. Job rotation can be done on a permanent or a temporary basis and can be highly effective, especially for mid-level professionals who wish to explore other job
alternatives. One problem with job rotation is that it may be
difficult to arrange in student affairs because of the specialization of most positions.

In job enrichment, the employee is given additional job
responsibilities that are specifically designed to promote growth
and development. These responsibilities may include leadership
opportunities for departmental or divisional projects and tasks.
They are designed specifically to provide opportunities for
achievement and recognition and to give the staff member
an opportunity to gain valuable leadership experience. Job
enrichment can be one of the most powerful staff development
strategies because it combines direct leadership experience with
personal recognition. It can be used at any organizational

level and can involve job "loading" of both major and minor proportions.

Other strategies for staff development that involve lesser alterations in job roles include temporary staff assignments, project teamwork, and task force assignments. Involvement in such activities, especially if it is coupled with individual recognition, can provide excellent opportunities for promoting staff development.

Finally, two other staff development activities should be briefly mentioned. Mentoring and self-directed training are highly individualized activities that can be effective techniques for staff development in some situations. In a mentoring relationship, the more experienced professional serves as a personal adviser and resource guide for the less experienced staff member. In the initial stages of a mentoring relationship, there is no direct change in job assignment. Swoboda and Millar (1986) claim that the relationship between mentor and protégé must be sufficiently close to sustain a working relationship for up to five years. Mentoring can be a powerful staff development technique, since it links the learner with a personal role model who provides information, recognition, support, and encouragement to grow and develop. In some instances, mentors may even intercede for protégés and provide special institutional support and access to resources. Mentoring may be especially useful as a staff development strategy for advancing minorities and women in order to achieve affirmative action goals. Because special treatment is generally involved in mentoring, other staff members may perceive favoritism in mentoring relationships. Mentoring relationships are also highly dependent on rapport and affiliation between individuals. These characteristics make it difficult to organize mentoring as a formal part of staff development activities.

Self-directed training can also be an effective form of staff development. This approach to development permits the staff member to learn independently and to focus on particular skills or knowledge that may be of special interest or relevance. Self-directed activities also enable individuals to study at their own pace while still participating in an organized educational program.

Conclusion

Studs Terkel (1974) writes that "most people have work that is too small for their spirits" (p. 175). Student affairs work can become too small if staff members do not find opportunities for growth and development. Staff development programs can provide the vehicle for staff renewal by expanding people's knowledge and skills. The education and development of college students are work that presents a constant challenge to the spirit and expertise of student affairs staff. Staff development activities can help us to meet the challenges of such important work and to give powerful meaning and direction to professional growth and practice.

References

Adams, J. D. (ed.). *Transforming Work*. Alexandria, Va.: Miles River Press, 1984.

Albanese, R. *Managing Toward Accountability for Performance*. Homewood, Ill.: Irwin, 1978.

Canon, H. J. "A Developmental Model for Divisions of Student Affairs." *Journal of College Student Personnel*, 1976, *17* (3), 178–180.

Canon, H. J. "Developing Staff Potential." In U. Delworth, G. Hanson, and Associates, *Student Services: A Handbook for the Profession*. San Francisco: Jossey-Bass, 1980.

Canon, H. J., and Brown, R. D. (eds.). *Applied Ethics in Student Services*. New Directions for Student Services, no. 30. San Francisco: Jossey-Bass, 1985.

Cascio, W. F. *Managing Human Resources*. New York: McGraw-Hill, 1986.

Cone, L. M., Jr. "Toward a Theory of Managerial Obsolescence: An Empirical and Theoretical Study." Unpublished doctoral dissertation, New York University, 1968.

Creamer, D. "A Model of In-Service Education: Professional Initiative for Continuous Learning." Unpublished paper, Division of Student Affairs, Virginia Polytechnic Institute and State University, 1987.

Deegan, A. X. "A Management Skill for Improving Individual Performance." In A. X. Deegan (ed.), *Coaching*. Reading, Mass.: Addison-Wesley, 1979.

Delworth, U. (ed.). *Training Competent Staff*. New Directions for Student Services, no. 2. San Francisco: Jossey-Bass, 1978.

DuBrin, A. J. *Fundamentals of Organizational Behavior*. New York: Pegasus Press, 1978.

Fleming, J. *Blacks in College: A Comparative Study of Students' Success in Black and in White Institutions*. San Francisco: Jossey-Bass, 1984.

Franklin, J. L. *Human Resource Development in the Organization*. Detroit: Gale Research, 1978.

Halloran, J. *Supervision: The Art of Management*. Englewood Cliffs, N.J.: Prentice-Hall, 1986.

Kay, E. *The Crisis in Middle Management*. New York: American Management Associates, 1974.

Miller, T. "Staff Development Activities in Student Affairs Programs." *Journal of College Student Personnel*, 1975, *16* (4), 257–261.

Parker, C. A. "Institutional Self-Renewal in Higher Education." *Journal of College Student Personnel*, 1971, *12* (6), 405–409.

Rhatigan, J. J., and Crawford, A. E. "Professional Development Preferences of Student Affairs Administrators." *National Association of Student Personnel Administrators Journal*, 1980, *18* (3), 46–52.

Schneier, C. E., and Beatty, R. W. *Personnel Administration Today: Readings and Commentary*. Reading, Mass.: Addison-Wesley, 1978.

Swoboda, M. J., and Millar, S. B. "Networking-Mentoring: Career Strategy of Women in Academic Administration." *Journal of the National Association of Women Deans and Counselors*, 1986, *50* (1), 8–11.

Terkel, S. *Working*. New York: Pantheon Books, 1974.

Part Six

Emerging Roles and Opportunities

The current times are, curiously, a mix of best and worst. We have expanded our profession and our services to students dramatically during the past two decades. Access to higher education has improved dramatically for underserved populations (although retention has not always kept pace). We have taken student development seriously, both in theory and in practice. At the same time, the 1980s have witnessed a sharp increase in both the financial pressures on our institutions and the related concern over the quality of higher education.

In Part Six, we examine the challenges and opportunities presented by the last decade of the century. In Chapter Twenty-Two, Robert Fenske and Marvalene Hughes bring us a comprehensive picture of the state of the art in higher education and student services. They project a vision of the immediate future in which members of our profession must play a vital role. In their words, "leadership and active involvement in education, including the deliberate response by student services professionals to the reform movement, will result in the new empowerment of the profession and of practitioners" (p. 578).

Part of this leadership role comes in a highly important emerging arena, that of outcome assessment. As our institutions deal with pressures to document the value of higher education, student services professionals are taking the opportunity to be involved in the development and implementation of programs that assess outcomes of the college experience. We see no more essential and powerful involvement than this one for our profession during the next decade. In Chapter Twenty-Three, Dary Erwin informs us about this movement and provides the direction we all need to be involved productively in outcome assessment on our own campuses. Erwin's chapter includes eight highly useful steps for action assessment to aid us in beginning this work.

Finally, we look at the structure of the profession as we believe it to be, the structure around which we have organized this book. To the five components of the first edition we have added a sixth, ethics and standards, since the 1980s were the years in which we saw this area move to a central position in the field. We again make recommendations for the curriculum of professional preparation programs, in light of standards developed by the Council for the Advancement of Standards. As in the first edition, we close with our own visions for the profession.

Chapter Twenty-Two

Current Challenges: Maintaining Quality Amid Increasing Student Diversity

Robert H. Fenske
Marvalene Styles Hughes

American higher education professionals are nearing the end of the 1980s with ambivalent feelings of accomplishment and apprehension. Overall quality has been maintained despite over two decades of relatively open access for hundreds of thousands of students from formerly underserved populations— including women, minorities, and international, low-income, and older students. The vastly increased diversity has not been without cost, however. As Hansen and Stampen (1987) point out: "The massive expansion of higher education enrollments and the broadened mission of higher education institutions that began in the late 1950's and continued through most of the 1960's not only required but also stimulated a substantial increase in resources allocated to higher education. During the 1970's, however, the resources available for instructional programs became relatively less abundant at the very time that institutions were held accountable for increasing access and responding to a host of equity related mandates. By the early 1980's financial pressures on colleges and universities intensified as a result of a resurgence of national concern over the quality of higher education and its key role in enhancing the country's economic strength. How higher education institutions can and will respond to these challenges in the face of tightened resources remains unclear" (p. 1).

As the tension between quality and access escalates, student services professionals are once again in the center of the fray. This chapter reviews some of the salient trends and issues confronting the profession as it enters the 1990s. We begin by focusing on students and the increase in their number, their diversity, and the challenge they present to the profession's resiliency and flexibility. Next we move to the way institutions are meeting the dual problem of maintaining and even increasing academic program quality while simultaneously keeping access open to students from an increasingly wide spectrum of backgrounds and abilities. The current movement toward outcomes-oriented program assessment, variously seen as a threat and an opportunity for improvement, may provide a setting for increased cooperation between academics and student services professionals. We conclude with an overview of how these trends might affect the continuing search for identity, consensus, and ecumenicalism in the profession.

Students

Enrollments. Since 1950, the last year in which public- and private-sector enrollments were equal, "enrollment has increased by more than 300 percent, while the number of institutions has increased almost 80 percent" (Kaufman, 1987, p. 1). Diversity has been the distinguishing feature of this growth, both in student characteristics and in types of institutions. Public two-year colleges proliferated through this period and by 1985 enrolled slightly more than half (51 percent) of all first-time freshmen. By 1985, more than three-fourths of all students were enrolled in the public sector. Trends in enrollment during the 1978–1985 period showed a slight increase despite declines in the traditional college-age population of eighteen- to twenty-four-year-olds. This increase was due to both a higher enrollment rate of this age group and a marked growth in the college attendance of older women. These two factors have forestalled the predicted decline in enrollments. However, the U.S. Department of Education's Center for Education Statistics warns that the effect of these two factors may be transitory. First, because more and more women are attending college at the traditional age, there will be a decrease in the number of women who defer higher education until a later age, reducing the pool of older women enrolling in college. Second, traditional college-age enrollments may decline in general as the proportion of groups with traditionally lower rates of college attendance increases in this age group. Consequently, the long-predicted enrollment declines are more likely than ever to appear by the early 1990s (Kaufman, 1987).

Enrollment trends also follow the general geographical movement of the U.S. population from the North and East to the South and West. California, Texas, Florida, and Arizona have experienced strong growth in college enrollments and will continue to do so, with most of the growth coming at the expense of the northern and eastern sections of the country, especially the upper Midwest.

Student migration is, curiously enough, one of the least studied topics in all of higher education. Students who migrate to institutions in another state clearly have a greater need for various services than local students, yet little is known about the extent of and motivation for such migration. A study in the mid 1970s indicated that the rate of student interstate migration was decreasing owing to the extremely high tuition levied on out-of-state students by public institutions since the 1960s, and that the decrease was greater for students of lower socioeconomic status (Fenske, Scott, and Carmody, 1974). In fall 1984, only 14 percent of first-time students migrated to an out-of-state college, and of these less than half attended public colleges even though the public sector enrolls three-fourths of first-time students (Center for Education Statistics, 1986c). The true migration rates may be obscured by the large number of migrating students who establish legal state residency as quickly as possible. The tuition stakes are high and encourage most migrating students to challenge existing definitions of nonresident status. The regulations and conditions involved in the resulting controversies are so complex and legalistic that many public institutions' student affairs divisions employ professionals who specialize in handling these problems. The situation is likely to persist and consequently will offer attractive professional opportunities.

Women and Older Students. One of the most striking recent phenomena in higher education is the "graying of the campus," the rapid growth in the proportion of the student body that is older than the traditional undergraduate age span of eighteen to twenty-four. The change is widespread, especially in urban areas and wherever large concentrations of older students are available. These increases reflect both the shift in age distribution and societal demands for postsecondary education to meet career requirements.

Colleges and universities are thus participating in the rapidly growing adult education movement in the United States, especially in those educational activities related to career requirements. Older adults have special needs, motivations, and apprehensions that heavily involve student services professionals, and their enrollment rate remains high and may even increase. A significant facet of this trend involves the return to campus of many midcareer professionals and managers responding to new certification and upgrading requirements imposed by professional associations and employers. Urban colleges and universities are becoming accustomed to the phenomenon of two-generation enrollment, with children and parents attending from the same family.

The "graying of the campus" is part of an even broader trend in enrollment that began in the fall of 1974, when the number of women recently graduated from high school who were registering as full-time students exceeded that of men for the first time. The phenomenon has since extended to the full undergraduate student body and includes both traditional college-age and older students. In fall 1978, slightly more men than women enrolled in college (5,580,000 compared to 5,559,000); by fall 1985 there were 712,000 more women than men in the overall total of 12,524,000 students (Kaufman, 1987). The shift in undergraduate college enrollment had been predicted some years earlier (Fenske and Scott, 1973), but it seemed to catch much of higher education by surprise, despite the fact that there had been more female than male high school graduates for more than three decades.

The "quiet revolution" that resulted in a female majority on college campuses contained two trends challenging both academic and student services functions. The first is a predominating trend in the academic aptitude of women compared to men. While both sexes have scored lower on tests over the last twenty-five years, women's scores have shown steeper declines, especially in the math areas. The second trend relates to the continuing difference between the sexes in high school preparation in math and science and in the choice of majors in college.

The complex reasons for gender-related score differences have received intensive study from social, historical, and educational perspectives. For example, at younger ages girls score higher than boys in nationally standardized math exams. Data from the National Assessment of Educational Progress indicate that at the ages of nine and thirteen, girls' math scores are generally higher than boys'; however, by high school (age seventeen), boys score higher (Center for Education Statistics, 1986c, p. 23). For well over twenty years, women have scored significantly and consistently lower than men in academic aptitude tests during high school and college. What is less well known is that the slight edge in verbal scores long held by women disappeared in the early 1970s, and men now also score higher in this area (Rigol, 1987).

One of the primary causative factors consistently identified is exposure to appropriate academic subjects in high school (Harnischfeger and Wiley, 1977). A nationally representative study of the graduating class of 1980 revealed that 39.1 percent of boys graduating from high school that year had completed at least three years of math and 26.5 percent had completed at least three years of science; the percentages for girls were only 28.0 and 18.5, respectively (Center for Education Statistics, 1986b, p. 77). These differences suggest that the choice of college majors would be expected to vary between the genders in a similar and consistent manner. Enrollment statistics bear out this supposition. On average, 72.4 percent of the students enrolled in the physical sciences and 87.4 percent of those enrolled in engineering were men in fall 1980; 27.6 and 12.6 percent, respectively, were women (Center for Education Statistics, 1986b, p. 105). A recent study of the issue of math as a "critical filter" to key majors at one of the largest public universities found that the traditional predominance of men in engineering, the physical sciences, and computer science and technology is continuing, while women continue to predominate in education and the social sciences. Math preparation and aptitude were clearly implicated as a causative factor in these patterns (Whiteley, 1986).

Thus, women have achieved near equality in access to college, yet much enrollment maldistribution among the various fields still exists. Since the completion of degrees in the technically oriented majors and professional fields is highly rewarding in social status and in immediate and long-range earnings, women must still overcome a large deficit in the benefits of a college education. Engineering is a particularly salient example of the economic consequences of maldistribution between the genders in fields of study. It is the top-ranked field in starting salary: the average earnings for bachelor's degree holders in the first year after graduation were $25,100 in 1983–1984 (Korb, 1987, p. 4). The low enrollment rates for women in the engineering and math-oriented fields are counterbalanced by increased enrollment in other professional fields, notably law and medicine (Center for Education Statistics, 1986b, p. 105).

Minority Students. The next generation of high school graduates coming to college will be different from any before it. Its members will be drawn from a school population comprising increasing proportions of minorities, owing to recent immigration and higher fertility rates among some ethnic groups. While Asian elementary and secondary enrollments increased the most rapidly (by 40 percent) between 1976 and 1980, Asians still constituted only 7 percent, or 749,003, of all minority schoolchildren in 1980. In contrast, blacks constituted 60 percent, or 6,418,194, and Hispanics 30 percent, or 3,179,285. Native American schoolchildren accounted for only 3 percent,

their enrollment having dropped from 368,262 to 305,730 between 1976 and 1980. "Part of the increase in enrollment for
Asians and Hispanics came as a result of recent immigration"
(Center for Education Statistics, 1986a, p. 144). A large part
of the increase in Hispanic enrollment continues to come from
the high birthrates of Hispanic women. In 1984, Hispanic
women aged eighteen to forty-four produced 86.1 live births
per 1,000 women, compared to 64.4 per 1,000 for non-Hispanic
women in the same age bracket (U.S. Department of Commerce,
1985a).

The rapid increases in minority school populations are
greatest in what Hodgkinson (1983) calls the "sun belt" states
of the Southeast and Southwest. Few of the "rust belt" states
of the North and East will experience large increases. Texas and
California already have large percentages of minority schoolchildren (45.9 and 42.9, respectively, in 1980), and in the very
near future they will probably find white, non-Hispanic children
making up less than half of school enrollments. These states are
also experiencing a demographic shift; principally, the minority
population is becoming the majority (Western Interstate Commission for Higher Education, 1987).

A large proportion of minority schoolchildren are at risk
of receiving diminished benefits from their educational experience because of economic, family structure, and language factors. "Almost two of every five (39 percent) Hispanic children
and one of every two (47 percent) black children were living
in poverty in 1983" (Congressional Research Service, 1985, p.
2). The traditional family structure of two parents living at home
with the father employed and the mother in residence tending
to the full-time duties of child rearing has been displaced by other
forms. The Center for Education Statistics (1986a, p. 140) summarized these changes and their implications thus: "It has been
estimated that 59 percent of the children born in 1983 will live
with only one parent at some point before reaching the age of
18. . . . This estimate reflects both high divorce rates and an
increase in the number of out-of-wedlock births. There has been
a steady increase in the number of female-headed families, from
9 percent of all families with children under 18 in 1959 to nearly

23 percent in 1984. . . . In 1984 60 percent of black families were headed by a single parent (94 percent of these by the mother).''

Populations of recent Asian and Hispanic immigrants have the highest concentration of non-English-speaking family backgrounds. These populations are located primarily in the Southwest and California (in which over 20 percent of the five-to-seventeen-year-olds belong to minority groups) and also in New York, Florida, New Jersey, and Connecticut (between 10 and 20 percent) (Center for Education Statistics, 1986a, pp. 146, 148). A very large proportion of these families are low-income because of the language barrier and their recent immigration to this country.

A few years ago Astin (1982) used the analogy of a leaky pipeline to depict the progressive loss of students throughout the span of school years from kindergarten through graduate school. The pipeline loses more minority children in both elementary and secondary school. However, rapid increases in the minority population because of immigration and higher birth rates mean that the college-age population from which the nation's campuses will be filled will be increasingly minority. Consequently, ''a large proportion of the children enrolled in the public schools will have one or more of the following characteristics: poverty, non-English-language background, and single-parent families, which may place them 'at risk' in terms of success in the educational system. . . . The increase in the 'at risk' population will not be short-lived but is expected to continue into the 21st century'' (Center for Education Statistics, 1986b, p. 151).

The term *minority* is becoming less useful as a general descriptor of the heterogeneous population not counted in the white population. For example, in the fastest-growing regions of the United States, nonwhite school populations will soon outnumber the ''majority'' white population. Furthermore, there may well be more important differences within the minority sector than between the minority and majority sectors. This heterogeneity among minority groups is particularly vivid in academic aptitude and achievement measures at both the precollege and collegiate levels, as well as at the transition point. Specifically, in most academic aptitude and achievement measures, the two largest minority groups, blacks and Hispanics (constituting 16.1 and 8.0 percent of the total 1980 U.S. school population, respectively), tend to cluster closely with Native Americans (0.8 percent) at a level significantly below the white majority. Asians and Pacific Islanders, however (constituting 1.9 percent of the 1980 school population), not only score markedly higher than the other three minority groups but exceed the scores of the white majority on most measures. Consequently, any score depicting an average of all four minority groups will be inflated toward the white majority score by Asian scores and hence will mask crucial educational deficiencies and problems of the three non-Asian minority groups.

The foregoing comparisons are presented not to extol the educational achievement of any minority group but to highlight the significant variance among the groups that is obscured by aggregating data into a general "minority" category. The remarkable attainments of Asian-Americans, for example, show that numerical minority status does not in itself deny access to the benefits of the educational system at the secondary and postsecondary levels. Notable successes on a smaller scale— such as the high levels of educational achievement in some "model" inner-city high schools and the recruitment of blacks and Hispanics into exemplary engineering programs—clearly demonstrate that the potential for spectacular gains in education is by no means restricted to any one minority group.

Attitudes and Values. In Chapter Two, students' attitudes and values were depicted as changing in a cyclical fashion from materialism and conformity in the late 1950s to selfless involvement in causes and antimaterialism in the 1960s and early 1970s, returning to monetary and selfish goals by the end of the 1970s. Annual freshman surveys conducted by the Cooperative Institutional Research Program since 1966 provide evidence that the "me generation" attitudes that had emerged by 1980 have persisted and even intensified (Hirschorn, 1988, p. A-31). The survey found that the percentage of students interested in a business career has increased almost continuously from 10.5

percent in 1972 to a new high of 24.6 percent in 1987. Meanwhile, teaching, which had attracted nearly 25 percent in 1968, fell to an all-time low of 4.7 percent in 1982 and by 1987 had increased only to 8.1 percent (Hirschorn, 1988, p. A-31).

Materialistic attitudes among the 1987 freshmen rose beyond the already high levels reported in the preceding years of the 1980s. Three-fourths (75.6 percent) reported "being well off financially" as an essential or very important objective, nearly twice the level (39.1 percent) of 1970. On the other hand, the objective of "developing a philosophy of life" was reported by only 39.4 percent, less than half of the 82.9 percent who reported this objective in 1967 (Hirschorn, 1988, p. A-31).

Institutional Challenges and Responses

Current challenges to institutional viability are many and serious. The demographic environment of the 1990s will continue to strain institutional capabilities for maintaining enrollment in the face of the continuing decline in the number of traditional college-age students, especially those of nonminority background, and the potential saturation of postsecondary education demand among older students. The pricing of educational programs will become even more of a problem, especially to nonprofit, privately controlled institutions, owing to sharply rising costs and the leveling off of student financial assistance from the federal government. Higher education will struggle to meet the dual challenge of increasing academic program quality while simultaneously maintaining access for students from a wide spectrum of backgrounds and abilities. Effective responses to these challenges will be necessary to reverse the current trend toward the sharply differentiated clustering of students into various types of institutions according to socioeconomic background and academic ability. Otherwise, societal and governmental interventions to solve these and other problems will inevitably result in continued loss of campus autonomy in decision making.

Older, narrow views of student recruiting, financial aid, academic advising, and student retention as separate functions are being superseded by the global, integrative concept of enrollment management. According to Hossler (1984), this concept encompasses a wide range of activities, including the review of institutional missions and goals, current and future environment scanning, and the assessment of institutional capacity for change and adaptation. The specific functional responsibilities are student marketing and recruitment, pricing and financial aid, academic and career advising, academic assistance programs, institutional research, orientation, retention, and student services (Hossler, 1984, pp. 6-7). By student services, Hossler refers to specific activities such as counseling and residence hall supervision, but student services professionals will recognize that except for institutional research, all of the functional responsibilities he lists involve some part of the domain of the chief student affairs officer.

Marketing and student recruitment have become increasingly sophisticated in recent years to deal with intensified competition for the shrinking pool of traditional college-age students, and also to relate to the expanding diversity in student characteristics described earlier. "Institutions are responding to the decreasing supply of traditional college-age students by competing harder for the students that do exist, recruiting non-traditional students, and expanding the geographical range over which recruiting is conducted" (Breland and others, 1986, p. 47). The surveys on which this conclusion is based show that "all recruiting has increased since 1979" and that virtually every category of recruiting "shows an increase, ranging from relatively moderate increases in formerly heavily-used techniques to doubling and sometimes tripling of formerly little-used devices" (p. 50).

The first annual International Higher Education Marketing Symposium was held in Chicago in April 1986. Specialists from dozens of colleges and universities presented a wide variety of marketing techniques in over fifty sessions. The extreme range of techniques provided stark constrasts in approach. For example, the director of marketing for one of the largest and most prestigious public research universities introduced a dignified concept called "academic promotion," which stressed its marked differences from commercial marketing. The preceding session, however, had shown how a small public community college eagerly embraced the most direct commercial marketing techniques, including placing booths in shopping malls, grocery stores, and factory cafeterias. Future plans featured the rental of advertising on prime-time television, billboards hauled by special vans, and the soliciting of registration at churches after Sunday morning service (Burns, 1986, pp. 62–70).

Student financial aid continues to play a central role in providing access to college, choice of college, and opportunity for program completion (retention). The total for all sources—federal, state, and institutional—of financial aid was estimated at over $20 billion for both 1985–86 and 1986–87 (College Board, 1988). About three-fourths of the total was provided by the federal government. One of the principal concerns about federal student aid in recent years has been the pronounced shift from grants to loans. This shift resulted in large allocations to loan programs (nearly $10 billion in 1986–87) and a decrease in grant dollars. The Social Security program of grants for college students was phased out in 1985–86, and Veterans Assistance is on the verge of a similar fate. Student services professionals are concerned that the levels of student loan debts are excessive, particularly for students who do not complete their degrees and thus lack the earning power of degree holders. A related concern is that the new emphasis on loans is discouraging racial and ethnic minority students from low-income families from going to college or is relegating them to the lowest-cost institutions, generally public community colleges and short-term programs in proprietary schools (Stampen and Fenske, 1988). By the late 1980s, serious questions had begun to arise concerning the decline in real value of federal student aid and the shift from grants to loans (Hansen, 1987). Although the number of recipients jumped 22 percent from 1980–81 to 1985–86, each student received much less in constant dollars. Furthermore, these smaller awards had to meet sharp increases in tuition. Tuition grew by 9.8 percent annually in the 1980s, twice the rate of inflation (4.9 percent) and one-third more than the increase (6.5 percent) in U.S. average annual income (Hauptman and Hartle, 1987).

Student loan burdens are also suspected of unduly influencing choice of major. Students with large debts are selecting high-paying career fields; low-paying fields like social work and education are more often selected by students with light loan burdens. Some scholars worry about the long-term effect of loans on the student's freedom to choose liberal arts and other fields simply for their intrinsic value rather than for how well they pay after graduation (Mohrman, 1987, p. 30).

For all students who enroll despite the daunting prospect of sharply rising costs and heavy loan burdens, the institution has a serious responsibility for budgeting and debt management counseling. This function is a significant new responsibility for student services professionals; it is related not just to student financial aid administration but also to enrollment management in all of its aspects. Ethical considerations come strongly into play when financial aid is involved in recruiting, counseling, and retaining students who are the budgetary lifeblood of the institution. "Many of the same theories and strategies used in the business world are being adopted for use in recruiting students. In this context, student aid is used as an inducement in the same way that automobile manufacturers use cash rebates to recruit customers and the military services use promises of travel and training to recruit enlistees" (Fenske and Huff, 1983, p. 392).

Financial aid probably has as much influence on the student recipient's program completion as on the initial decision to enroll. For example, high debt levels early in the college career are suspected of causing "stopping out" or even permanent program discontinuance.

The prospect of enrollment decline in most colleges and universities has led to a sharply intensified interest in retaining students until they complete their programs. A national survey of campuses in 1987 revealed that all but a small percentage have special programs to increase retention (El-Khawas, 1987, p. 28). Academic administrators have perceived that retaining students already enrolled has much more potential and can be much cheaper than scouring the countryside amid increasing competition for a shrinking number of potential applicants. For example, if the dropout rate is approximately 40 percent over the first three years of an undergraduate program in a college with 1,000 students, the 400 students who fail to graduate will provide less than half of their four-year tuition total to the college. Cutting the dropout rate in half would be equivalent to locating, recruiting, and enrolling 200 new students over the same period. The tuition paid to the college would increase proportionately, and this increase would be gained more efficiently, since programs to retain students already on campus are much cheaper than recruiting efforts off-campus.

Educational Reform, Program Assessment, and Remedial Education

The educational reform movement triggered by the reports of national commissions and task forces in the early 1980s appropriately focuses on long-term solutions, specifically the improvement of elementary and secondary schools through more efficient administration and more effective teacher training. But the ultimate benefits to society in an increasingly complex and "credentialized" world of work result largely from postsecondary programs. Consequently, three national reports on the quality of American higher education were issued within two years of the release of *A Nation at Risk,* the seminal report of the National Commission on Excellence in Education (1983).

The first and most influential of the higher education reports was *Involvement in Learning,* written by the Study Group on the Conditions of Excellence in American Higher Education and submitted to the Secretary of Education in October 1984. "The core recommendations of *Involvement in Learning* were based on a theory derived from empirical research: that the more active engagement of students in both learning tasks and the life of the college will lead to improved rates of retention and higher achievement, and that the most critical period for student involvement occurs in the first year" (Adelman, 1986, p. 1). The thesis of this report restates the student development concept without explicitly acknowledging that the student services profession had been promoting the concept for at least ten years. Nonetheless, the report provides a mandate and a blueprint for massive participation by student services in improving academic effectiveness. For example, one of the four recommendations designed to increase student involvement called for "a strengthening of existing co-curricular organizations, associations, and activities to maximize student involvement by providing opportunities to exercise, apply, and reinforce course-related learning" (Adelman, 1986, p. 1).

Involvement in Learning is, we believe, the first report written by a national non–student services group to express and support either the "whole person" or student development concept since the report of the American Council on Education's Commission on the Student in 1949. The Study Group on the Conditions of Excellence in American Higher Education (1984) identifies three necessary conditions for achieving excellence in higher education: student involvement in learning, high standards of academic performance, and regular and periodic assessment. The last two conditions call for outcome-oriented program assessment to be developed and applied to all of undergraduate education, not just to professional areas such as nursing and accounting. Predictably, these recommendations have revived all of the familiar concerns about applying standardized assessment to liberal arts education, including fears that the existence of performance evaluations would inevitably lead to faculty "teaching to the test" rather than adjusting course content to the learning needs of students. Another basic concern is that the most important goals of a liberal education are often intangible (for example, increased intellectual curiosity and participation in civic affairs) and hence cannot be measured accurately, at least not immediately after the conclusion of the program.

Despite the objections, *Involvement in Learning*'s emphasis on performance assessment strikes a responsive chord in many quarters. State-level agencies in particular seem interested in seeing whether the successes achieved in imposing performance assessment on the secondary schools could be emulated with postsecondary systems. Florida, for example, has imposed on its public baccalaureate programs the "Gordon Rule," which requires a minimum of six hours in math and twelve hours in English, the latter including at least 6,000 words of writing by the student. In Tennessee, the legislature now requires higher education institutions to quantify and report periodically on a number of significant program objectives, including the improvement of the scores of graduating seniors on nationally standardized tests such as the Graduate Record Examination. The state also monitors the pass rates of various professional exams and job placement rates and, like Florida, ties state funding levels to these performance assessments.

The advance of program assessment in public favor, and its advocacy by the Department of Education, deeply concern traditional higher education. If program assessment becomes widespread, institutions will need to pay much more attention to the strategies and determinants of student learning. As Gary R. Hanson pointed out: "Institutions must take responsibility for fostering active student learning. Student affairs administrators have come to recognize that the campus environment has a strong influence on student learning. . . . Yet another barrier to student involvement is lack of knowledge concerning how college students learn" (in Adelman, 1986, p. 3).

Whether the advent of program assessment will usher in a millennium of student services professionals centrally involved in fostering student development in tandem with faculty remains to be seen. It is one thing to perceive that if the basis for funding shifts from the academic credentials of faculty to the actual learning outcomes of students, faculty will need the kind of insights and support that only student services practitioners are trained to provide. It is quite another matter to get faculty to realize the strong influences environmental and affective factors have on cognitive learning. The clearest and most compelling statement of these influences ever written is *The American College* (Sanford, 1962), a collection of the empirical evidence presented not by student services professionals but by the nation's top social psychologists and other researchers. It had virtually no impact and was generally ignored by academic faculty. The "carrot" of empirical evidence worked no better than student services' historic appeal to faculty's instincts for humane concern for the spiritual, ethical, and social development of students—that part of the "whole person" not served by intellectual training. Will the threat of the externally applied "stick" of funding tied to outcomes assessment be enough to

get faculty to see the light of the doctrine of student development? Robert Parelius, professor at Rutgers University,
comments:

> *Involvement in Learning* demands a great deal of
> faculty members. Professors are urged to discard
> their comfortable and familiar (albeit passive) teach-
> ing techniques, to act as intellectual guides and
> mentors rather than mere instructors . . . and to
> end their preoccupations with narrowly specialized
> aras of research and publication. . . . The formal
> systems which organizations use to evaluate and
> reward the performance of their employees are
> critically important. Within American colleges and
> universities, especially the leading ones, it has been
> customary to use scholarly productivity as the pri-
> mary criterion of evaluation and reward. Even in
> less prestigious institutions, where scholarly pro-
> ductivity is not critical, Trow's felicitous phrase
> "Publish and Flourish" applies. . . . *[Involvement in
> Learning]* is much more easily formulated than im-
> plemented. . . . The objective of our doctoral pro-
> grams is not to prepare faculty members to be ex-
> cellent undergraduate teachers. The Ph.D. remains
> a research—not a teaching—degree. Students in
> traditional graduate programs often develop a
> trained incapacity to be excellent undergraduate
> teachers. They are encouraged to identify narrow
> areas of specialization and to focus completely on
> them. They are taught that the only true measure
> of a professor's worth is her or his list of publica-
> tions. . . . The teaching of undergraduate courses
> [is regarded] as dirty work to be avoided whenever
> possible [in Adelman, 1986, p. 11].

Any progress toward implementing student development
concepts that might involve cooperative efforts between academics and student services professionals should realistically

assume a continuation of the present faculty reward system. The program assessment movement optimistically assumes that teaching effectiveness will be more directly measurable and more highly rewarded, but it does not assume that research and publication will be deemphasized.

Even educational technology seems at times to militate against faculty involvement in student development. The use of increasingly powerful personal computers has unquestionably made faculty more productive of research and publications. The personal computer now in the home study of many, if not most, faculty members has the potential for sophisticated analysis of large data sets and for complete desk-top publishing. Thus, it frees the faculty member from dependence on campus resources for data analysis, typing, editing, and printing. As a result, campus faculty offices are increasingly vacant while faculty are busy at home and thus even less available to students.

Hansen and Stampen (1987) noted that the tension between academic quality and access was intense and growing. A key factor is the recent increase in college admissions standards. Breland and others (1986) found in a national survey that between 1979 and 1985, significantly more institutions reported increased requirements for specific high school courses such as English and math, years of such high school courses completed, high school grade point averages, and admissions test scores. Over the same period, fewer institutions offered exceptions to standard admissions requirements for minorities and athletes (Breland and others, 1986, p. 66).

In the light of the increase in admissions requirements, the current emphasis on remedial education is likely to become even stronger. A national survey reported that four out of five colleges offered remedial courses in 1983–84 (Cahalan and Farris, 1986). Remedial education is ubiquitous, but is it popular with faculty? The faculty reward system and standard graduate training militate against involvement in courses aimed at high school–level (and sometimes lower-level) skills. Few activities could be less productive of professional advancement than teaching or tutoring in subcollegiate programs. The Carnegie Foundation for the Advancement of Teaching (1977, p. 220) implied as much when it recommended that the college community be scoured to find personnel for skill development centers; it suggested using unemployed new doctorates, advanced undergraduates, faculty members' spouses, and retired faculty or schoolteachers, but conspicuously excluded regular faculty.

In 1980, we asserted that remedial education seemed to offer an unparalleled opportunity for student services professionals to work in tandem with faculty in an enterprise essential to teaching (Delworth, Hanson, and Associates, 1980). Departmental faculty, like it or not, must be involved with remedial education in their subjects, if only because they must deal with the "remediated" students received from such programs. Since remedial education is by nature developmental, it was hypothesized that a symbiotic cooperation would develop; faculty would be dependent on student services for the necessary diagnostic and remedial work involved in preparing students for regular college work.

An empirical survey of national administrative arrangements for remedial education would be most informative. Perhaps there is yet room for optimism, owing to the incoming flood of underprepared and "at-risk" students, especially minorities with their special needs for adaptation to the academic climate. The financial need to increase retention of students will also underscore effective remediation, and perhaps student services will yet be seen as the key to success.

Implications for the Profession

The debate over the professional status of student services is as lively now as at any time during the past century. Although progress has been made and new developments have elevated the status of the profession in recent years, consensus has yet to be achieved. Salient issues being debated are the exploration of student development theory as an undergirding set of principles for the profession, the examination of the balance between the "service provider" and "student development educator" roles in the profession, the review of the recently identified roles of student services in the total mission of education as presented by the educational reform reports, and the construction and dissemination of professional standards and guidelines designed to standardize the scope and quality of functions within student services. Resolution of these issues is viewed as vital to the attainment of a professional status.

As student affairs progresses toward professionalization, it is important to note the increasing trend of feminization. This feminization is evidenced in the gender composition of the 1988 membership of the American College Personnel Association: 5,137 (58 percent) of its members are female and 3,659 (42 percent) are male (American Association for Counseling and Development, 1988). In the past, the feminization of any profession in a society that values masculine principles has resulted in the labeling of the work as "women's work" (Pfeffer and Davis-Blake, 1987), a label that "includes the idea that work done by women is less valuable and can be paid less than work done by men. [When women are in the majority in a profession,] the work is seen as . . . less valuable, critical, or economically important" (p. 7).

Bose and Rossi (1983) found that the prestige accorded an occupation was negatively correlated with the proportion of women in that occupation. Touhey (1974) found that male and female college students rated professions they perceived to be female-dominated as having less prestige and being less desirable as personal career choices than fields perceived to be male-dominated. Heilman (1979) found similar views among male high school students.

Sex-role attitudes and perceptions are gradually changing in the United States as more women enter the workplace (Lenz and Myerhoff, 1985). Concurrently, values attributed to femininity, such as nurturing and caring, are not only gaining acceptance but are becoming normative in a healthy work environment (Lenz and Myerhoff, 1985). This reevaluation of sex-role attributes places those values of student services that are identified with femininity in a more credible position than in the past.

It is our belief that by labeling practitioners as service providers exclusively rather than student development educators, we exacerbate the devaluation of the profession. The move toward certification within the profession may be seen as a reaffirmation of the profession's commitment to student development. This is reflected, too, in the American College Personnel Association's action in March 1987, when it changed the name of its long-established journal, the *Journal of College Student Personnel*, to the *Journal of College Student Development*.

Overpowered by a renewed emphasis within the profession on gaining a consensual professional identity and increasing the higher education community's understanding of the role of student services, the "whole person" language of the past has died. Despite this, the functions associated with it have reached unprecedented national eminence through *Involvement in Learning* (Study Group on the Conditions of Excellence in American Higher Education, 1984) and Boyer's (1987) report. Boyer, however, does not assign the functions identified in the "whole person" language to any areas in higher education, and so avoids any reference to student services.

The crucial question at this juncture is who will take active leadership for the study of those theoretical and philosophical principles undergirding the profession while the search for an identity continues. A vibrant discussion of student development theory and practice is going on among many professionals in the American College Personnel Association (ACPA), but there is a striking absence of dialogue and debate on the topic with other student services associations. Bloland (1986a, 1986b) and Stamatakos (1987) suggest that active public debates be continued on this topic to catalyze movement toward professional consensus on the theoretical principles and foundations of student services. Both caution that blind acceptance of untested assumptions can lead the profession into an even greater state of inertia. Notable contributions have been made to the literature on student development (Knefelkamp, Widick, and Parker, 1978; Miller and Prince, 1976; Saddlemire and Rentz, 1986). Knefelkamp, Widick, and Parker (1978) offered guidelines for classroom applications of student development theory. Still, we have not gone far enough in this endeavor.

The Council for the Advancement of Standards (1986) made monumental strides in advancing the profession by presenting uniform national standards and guidelines endorsed and collaboratively prepared by scores of student services organizations. While the standards have been widely disseminated, their acceptance and application remain in the embryonic stage of development. They represent, however, the first coherent set of professional standards for most student services. Like other members of the academic community, student services professionals must apply their professional standards, submit to professional review, and conduct rigorous research and evaluation.

Student Services and Ecumenicalism

Ecumenical beliefs challenge the rigid boundaries dividing individuals and groups and encourage tolerance of diversity. Ecumenicalism maintains that dogmatism inhibits growth and promotes values that may be antithetical to the mission and goals of education. This notion is echoed by student services practitioners who are proponents of liberal education and by Bloom (1987). Liberal education, student development, and the historical "whole person" concept share a view of education as a broad, liberalizing process that promotes moral, ethical, social, and intellectual development. As liberal education struggles to sustain its role in higher education, so does student services as a profession risk losing its meaning in the institution of higher education. "The purpose of liberal education has always been to enable students to see things whole" (Rawlings, 1987, p. B-2). Rawlings contends that liberal education is hampered by the organizational structures on campus that force faculty to affiliate with highly specialized academic departments. Bloom's (1987) argument that too much specialization on campus is detrimental to education is worthy of serious examination.

Many challenges face the profession today. The return of students to careerism, the relative weakness of liberal education, and the rise of repressive political and religious dogma suggest that student services professionals must prepare to assume the role that Sanford (1962) described as the need to challenge and support.

Additional resources to respond to new initiatives have not been available, by and large, and some student services professionals lament new stresses in their professional and personal lives. One adjustment strategy employed by some universities has been the introduction of privatization practices. Some counseling centers, career services, and health services, in particular, have either instituted some form of fee-for-service or directly structured a community network for referrals.

Societal and political intrusions into the educational community will continue to escalate. National politics and attitudes trickle down into the educational community. An indication of how strong the trickling influence can be is the resurgence of white supremacy, which includes and extends beyond the tradition of campus racism. Racial brawls, heretofore associated predominantly with campuses in the South, have plagued some of the most prestigious institutions of higher learning during the past five years, defying previous trends of geography. The perpetrators range in group identity from white student organizations to newly formed bigotry cults such as the "skinheads." Their dominant themes are anti-Semitism, racism, white supremacy, and a return to white male dominance. These new cults for white male supremacy challenge the values on which student development is founded, the values of individual rights and human dignity. The challenge facing student services professionals is analogous to but more complex than that of the 1960s, when students rioted in demonstration of their antiwar and other human rights beliefs.

In the United States, higher education espouses the values of human diversity and democratic education. Implicit in these values is the assumption that education is responsive to societal, political, economic, and population trends. Higher education is periodically inundated with new societal intrusions demanding new skills and resources. Most recently the profession has been called upon to harness resources related to such societal problems as new initiatives in substance abuse and AIDS education; education against bigotry; changing financial aid packages; new admissions requirements; student recruitment and retention as related to ethnicity, handicaps, gender, and other protected classes; students' rights to privacy; and the special attention to student athletes. Classroom practices, however, remain largely unaffected as student services practitioners struggle to integrate insightful program responses to societal diseases and symptoms.

Summary

In the 1990s, higher education will be faced with the dual challenge of improving the quality of academic programs while maintaining access for increasing numbers of low-income and minority populations not yet served adequately. Can the nation financially afford to reach both of these goals? It seems clear as the 1980s draw to a close that a strong push will be made to radically improve academic quality, especially in science, engineering, and technology programs, to meet foreign economic competition. But failure to provide wide access to higher education as well will result in millions of educationally disenfranchised young people being trapped in a lower economic structure with no hope of obtaining the credentials qualifying them for productive careers.

Student services will be at the core of the effort to maintain humane, personalized educational programs in the face of pervasive pressure to further vocationalize higher education. Professionals in the field will be pressured to simply provide services aimed at smoothing students' progress through such programs. Where will concern be maintained for nurturing students' social and personal growth in the campus environment emerging in the coming decade?

Never before has the mandate for active leadership by student services been so essential. Leadership and active involvement in education, including the deliberate response by student services professionals to the reform movement, will result in the new empowerment of the profession and of practitioners. Professional empowerment of student services continues to be sorely needed. By viewing ourselves solely as student advocates and service providers, noble as these roles are, we will not achieve partnership in higher education. If we view our role as student development educators as being equal in importance to that of teachers, we will have taken a giant step toward professional empowerment.

Note

An embarrassment of riches is available to anyone attempting to review current trends in higher education that affect the student services profession. Both ACPA and the National Association of Student Personnel Administrators provide newsletters, periodicals, journals, and books of professional interest. The *Chronicle of Higher Education* not only covers professional news but also combs national data sources for its weekly Fact File presentations, most of which are directly relevant to student services professionals.

There are other good publications that abstract and present data; however, it is always best to use original sources if possible. The premier data source on recent and current trends is the newly expanded and reorganized Center for Education Statistics in the U.S. Department of Education. The annual *Digest of Education Statistics* and *The Condition of Education: A Statistical Report* (Center for Education Statistics, 1986a) epitomize the center's penchant for producing both basic statistics and reports that focus on significant trends. One can peruse, for example, the excellent interpretive "Issue Paper" on higher education enrollment trends in *The Condition of Education,* then backtrack to the basic tables supporting the paper, which are presented earlier in the report. A full exploration of any related lines of inquiry can be carried out in the *Digest,* a fascinating compendium of all of the basic statistics on education at all levels. In addition to these full annual reports, the center also supplies a steady flow of timely statistical and interpretive bulletins. The quarterly sourcebook series New Directions for Student Services is invaluable for comprehensive treatment of current issues in the profession. It is published by Jossey-Bass and is currently edited by Margaret J. Barr.

References

Adelman, C. *From Reports to Response.* Washington, D.C.: U.S. Government Printing Office, 1986.

American Association for Counseling and Development. *Monthly Membership Report.* Alexandria, Va.: American Association for Counseling and Development, Mar. 1988.

American Council on Education, Commission on the Student. *Involvement in Learning.* Washington, D.C.: American Council on Education, 1949.

Astin, A. W. *Minorities in American Higher Education: Recent Trends, Current Prospects, and Recommendations.* San Francisco: Jossey-Bass, 1982.

Bloland, P. A. "Student Affairs' Brass Ring: An Allegory. Part I." *ACPA Developments,* 1986a, *13* (3), 1.

Bloland, P. A. "Student Affairs' Brass Ring: An Allegory. Part II." *ACPA Developments,* 1986b, *13* (4), 1.

Bloom, A. D. *The Closing of the American Mind.* New York: Simon & Schuster, 1987.

Bose, C. E., and Rossi, P. H. "Gender and Jobs: Prestige Standings of Occupations as Affected by Gender." *American Sociological Review,* 1983, *43,* 316–330.

Boyer, E. L. *College: The Undergraduate Experience in America.* New York: Harper & Row, 1987.

Breland, H. M., and others. *Demographics, Standards, and Equity: Challenges in College Admissions.* Washington, D.C.: American Association of Collegiate Registrars and Admissions Officers, 1986.

Burns, J. A. *Symposium '86.* Ogden, Utah: International Higher Education Marketing Symposium, 1986.

Cahalan, M., and Farris, E. *College Level Remediation.* Washington, D.C.: Center for Education Statistics, U.S. Department of Education, 1986.

Carnegie Foundation for the Advancement of Teaching. *Missions of the College Curriculum: A Contemporary Review with Suggestions.* San Francisco: Jossey-Bass, 1977.

Center for Education Statistics. *The Condition of Education: A Statistical Report.* Washington, D.C.: U.S. Department of Education, 1986a.

Center for Education Statistics. *Digest of Education Statistics, 1985–86.* Washington, D.C.: U.S. Government Printing Office, 1986b.

Center for Education Statistics. *Residence and Migration of College Students, Fall, 1984.* Washington, D.C.: U.S. Department of Education, 1986c.

College Board. *Trends in Student Aid, 1980–81 to 1986–87.* Washington, D.C.: College Board, 1988.

Congressional Research Service. *Children in Poverty.* Washington, D.C.: U.S. Government Printing Office, 1985.

Council for the Advancement of Standards. *CAS Standards and Guidelines for Student Services/Development Programs*. Iowa City, Iowa: American College Testing Service, 1986.

Delworth, U., Hanson, G., and Associates. *Student Services: A Handbook for the Profession*. San Francisco: Jossey-Bass, 1980.

El-Khawas, E. *Campus Trends, 1987*. Washington, D.C.: American Council on Education, 1987.

Fenske, R. H., and Huff, R. P. "Overview, Synthesis, and Additional Perspectives." In R. H. Fenske, R. P. Huff, and Associates, *Handbook of Student Financial Aid: Programs, Procedures, and Policies*. San Francisco: Jossey-Bass, 1983.

Fenske, R. H., and Scott, C. S. *The Changing Profile of College Students*. Washington, D.C.: American Association for Higher Education, 1973.

Fenske, R. H., Scott, C. S., and Carmody, J. F. "Recent Trends in Studies of Student Migration." *Journal of Higher Education*, 1974, *45*, 61–74.

Hansen, J. S. *Student Loans: Are They Overburdening a Generation?* Washington, D.C.: College Board, 1987.

Hansen, W. L., and Stampen, J. O. "Balancing Quality and Access in Higher Education." Unpublished paper prepared for Wisconsin Center for Education Research, University of Wisconsin, 1987.

Harnischfeger, A., and Wiley, D. "The Marrow of Achievement Test Score Declines." In L. Lipsitz (ed.), *Test Score Decline: Meaning and Issues*. Englewood Cliffs, N.J.: Educational Technology Publications, 1977.

Hauptman, A., and Hartle, T. "Tuition Increases Since 1970: A Perspective." *Higher Education and National Affairs*, 1987, *36* (4), 5–8.

Heilman, M. E. "High School Students' Occupational Interest as a Function of Projected Sex Ratios in Male-Dominated Occupations." *Journal of Applied Psychology*, 1979, *64*, 275–279.

Hirschorn, M. W. "Freshman Interest in Business Careers Hits New Level, and Money Remains a Top Priority, Study Finds." *Chronicle of Higher Education*, Jan. 20, 1988, p. A-31.

Hodgkinson, H. L. *Guess Who's Coming to College: Your Students in 1990*. Washington, D.C.: National Institute of Independent Colleges and Universities, 1983.

Hodgkinson, H. L. "The Changing Face of Tomorrow's Student." *Change*, 1985, *17* (3), 38–39.

Hossler, D. *Enrollment Management: An Integrated Approach.* New York: College Entrance Examination Board, 1984.

Kaufman, P. *Growth in Higher Education Enrollment: 1985 to 1987.* Washington, D.C.: Center for Education Statistics, U.S. Department of Education, 1987.

Knefelkamp, L. L., Widick, C., and Parker, C. A. (eds.). *Applying New Development Findings.* New Directions for Student Services, no. 4. San Francisco: Jossey-Bass, 1978.

Korb, R. A. *Occupational and Educational Consequences of a Baccalaureate Degree.* Washington, D.C.: Center for Education Statistics, U.S. Department of Education, 1987.

Lenz, E., and Myerhoff, B. *The Feminization of America: How Women's Values Are Changing Our Public and Private Lives.* Los Angeles: Tarcher, 1985.

Miller, T. K., and Prince, J. S. *The Future of Student Affairs: A Guide to Student Development for Tomorrow's Higher Education.* San Francisco: Jossey-Bass, 1976.

Mohrman, K. "Unintended Consequences of Federal Student Aid Policies." *Brookings Review,* Fall 1987, pp. 24–30.

National Commission on Excellence in Education. *A Nation at Risk.* Washington, D.C.: U.S. Government Printing Office, 1983.

Pfeffer, J., and Davis-Blake, A. "The Effect of the Proportion of Women on Salaries: The Case of College Administrators." *Administrative Science Quarterly,* 1987, *32,* 1–24.

Rawlings, H. R. "The Basic Mission of Higher Education Is Thwarted by Academic Departments." *Chronicle of Higher Education,* Oct. 14, 1987, p. B-2.

Rigol, G. W. "Men and Women and the SAT: A Look at the Issue of Sex Bias." *College Board News,* 1987, *15* (4), 3.

Saddlemire, G. L., and Rentz, A. L. *Student Affairs: A Profession's Heritage.* (Rev. ed.) Alexandria, Va.: American College Personnel Association, 1986.

Sanford, N. *The American College.* New York: Wiley, 1962.

Stamatakos, L. C. "Student Development: The New Orthodoxy." *ACPA Developments,* 1987, *14* (3), 1.

Stampen, J. O., and Fenske, R. H. "Financial Aid and Ethnic Minorities." *Review of Higher Education,* 1988, *11* (4), 337–353.

Study Group on the Conditions of Excellence in American Higher Education. *Involvement in Learning.* Washington, D.C.: U.S. Secretary of Education, 1984.

Touhey, J. C. "Effects of Additional Women Professionals on Rating of Occupational Prestige and Desirability." *Journal of Personality and Social Psychology,* 1974, *29,* 86–89.

U.S. Department of Commerce. *Fertility of American Women: June, 1983.* Washington, D.C.: U.S. Government Printing Office, 1985a.

U.S. Department of Commerce. *Household and Family Characteristics: March, 1984.* Washington, D.C.: U.S. Government Printing Office, 1985b.

Western Interstate Commission for Higher Education. *From Minority to Majority: Education and the Future of the Southwest.* Boulder, Colo.: Western Interstate Commission for Higher Education, 1987.

Whiteley, M. A. "The College Mathematics Experience and Changes in Majors: A Structural Model Analysis." Unpublished doctoral dissertation, Division of Educational Leadership and Policy Studies, Arizona State University, 1986.

Chapter Twenty-Three

New Opportunities:
How Student Affairs
Can Contribute
to Outcomes Assessment

T. Dary Erwin

The call for outcomes assessment and evaluation in colleges and universities is widespread across the country today. The profession of student affairs too has the responsibility to respond to the issues raised about the competency and value of higher education. In addressing questions about the quality of higher education, the emerging trend of assessment may require new strategies and directions for our future.

Numerous reports about the declining quality of the educational experience have appeared regularly in the past few years. For instance, the Association of American Colleges (1985) chastised educators who have been concerned more about the length of college education than its content and purposes. William J. Bennett, the former Secretary of Education, has spoken of the declining quality of the undergraduate experience and the need for colleges to "do a more conscientious job of stating their goals, of gauging their own success in relation to those goals" (1986, p. ii).

Although these criticisms have been leveled primarily at academic programs, they pervade student affairs and other areas of higher education as well. Questions remain unanswered about the role, the scope, and the benefits of student affairs programs for students. The adoption, or mandate, of assessment programs (Boyer, Ewell, Finney, and Mingle, 1987) has been the legislative and coordinating boards' response to questions about academic quality. In turn, assessment has become a very powerful mechanism for encouraging institutions to review what they are doing and to demonstrate how well they are doing it. Will assessment become a similar mechanism for ensuring quality in student affairs programs?

Several state legislatures have mandated that public colleges and universities document their performance. For instance, the state of Tennessee was an early entrant into outcomes assessment, designing a model that links funding with delivery of educational services (Bogue and Brown, 1982). Regional accrediting associations such as the Southern Association of Colleges and Schools (SACS) (1984) have also implemented new criteria for reaffirmation that include both a statement of specific educational goals and documentation of how well students are meeting those goals. In most cases, institutions have the flexibility to determine their own educational objectives and assessment methods but must provide evidence of program quality. In contrast to the decentralized approach of the accrediting associations is the statewide comprehensive outcomes assessment program in New Jersey. Four areas have been targeted for evaluation of colleges and universities at the state level: student development, student learning, faculty activities, and institutional impact (Morantes, 1987).

The appropriateness of outcomes assessment is equally pertinent to student affairs programs if one believes that these programs contribute to the educational development of students. If student affairs professionals directly affect the development and learning of students, then the student outcomes movement in higher education represents an opportunity for student affairs divisions to become more closely allied with the central mission of the institution—educating students. Moreover, divisions of student affairs can benefit students by specifying and documenting those aspects of social and personal development believed to be significant in an undergraduate institution. Students, academic staff, administrators, and the public can then have a clearer understanding of the purposes and value of student affairs programs. Forward-thinking institutions should begin the assessment process in student affairs before it is thrust upon them from the outside (if this has not already happened). Progressive divisions of student affairs may be able to influence future directions and uses of assessment in their areas only if they have an ongoing assessment program in place.

This chapter discusses the role of student outcomes assessment for student affairs and outlines steps in the assessment process for institutions considering the initiation of a student outcomes assessment program. Three general components of assessment will be explained: the outcomes to be measured, the factors affecting the development of these outcomes, and the assessment procedures and methodological considerations.

Specifying Student Outcomes

The first step in the assessment process is to identify the outcomes or objectives that will be measured later. In particular, departments of student affairs must first define their educational goals in order to know what to assess. What are the goals for students toward which student affairs professionals work? What benefits are expected for students who are affected directly by student affairs professionals? How does an institution decide on its outcome goals?

The process of defining student developmental goals should occur at least at two levels. At one level, a college or university should establish an institution-wide committee to discuss and define specific developmental goals common to all students at the institution. Moral development, tolerance of diversity, autonomy, and interpersonal relationships are good examples of global goals to which both student affairs and academic affairs contribute. This committee should include faculty, but there should be a greater representation of student development professionals. The involvement of faculty will help sell developmental goals as a component of general education and a partner in outcomes with liberal studies. The task of this committee is similar to the task of defining liberal studies that many institutions are undertaking. From this perspective, outcomes of liberal studies and of student development are two different but similar components of general education outcomes. Kuh, Shedd, and Whitt (1987) write of the goals of student affairs and liberal education as essentially overlapping. In practice, liberal studies committees often focus on the core curriculum and do not also consider personal and social development.

The other level at which developmental goals should be established is the student affairs departmental level. What are the developmental goals that a particular department enhances with its programs and services? The personnel in each student affairs department should discuss what they do to promote directly the education of the student. Some institutions may also define student development goals for the entire division before defining departmental goals; however, it is important that student affairs departments still outline in detail the developmental constructs to which they contribute. Some departments may contribute to outcomes to a greater extent than others, and departmental goals may overlap with those of other departments or committees. As will be discussed later in the chapter, these student development goals are not the programs or services of the department, but the attitudes or developmental aspects of the student that are to be enriched.

The literature suggests several conceptual frameworks that student affairs educators should consider before determining their institution's goals. Widick, Knefelkamp, and Parker (1980) discuss the major student development theories and approaches, which are generally psychological in nature. For example, some of the theories that are reviewed are those of Chickering (1969), Perry (1970), and Heath (1977). Lenning (1977) completed a comprehensive review of educational outcome concepts published between 1918 and 1977. These concepts range from simple lists of educational goals and objectives to taxonomies and theoretical frameworks. Yet another approach was undertaken by Kuh (1984), who tried to broaden the thinking of student affairs professionals to include areas beyond student development. He discussed approaches from anthropology, sociology, and political science that can be used. Bloland (1986) also challenged the practice of limiting educational goals for students to developmental impacts.

Delineation of student outcome goals for student affairs depends on the mission of your institution, the philosophy of the student affairs staff, and the orientation of the student affairs programs. In constructing particular goals and objectives, it is important to recognize the uniqueness of an institution and a department of student affairs. For example, an institution with a religious affiliation has a special mission in addition to that of a public university. Also, the formulation of student outcome objectives should not be just an adoption of a single set of dimensions from a single theorist. For example, choose two or three vectors from Chickering's scheme, depending on the relevance of the vectors to your student affairs goals. Moreover, most conceptual approaches or theoretical frameworks are too broad for many divisions of student affairs. For example, the fostering of moral development is probably shared by many programs within an institution. The combination of student services offered and the training of the staff are other influences on the composition of outcome goals.

It is also helpful to conceive of *global* and *specific* outcome objectives. Many of the dimensions or constructs reviewed by Widick, Knefelkamp, and Parker (1980), Lenning (1977), and Kuh (1984) are too broad to be useful in practice. Lenning (1980) and Hanson (1982) refer to the problems of vagueness of student services goals (Lenning, this volume, Chapter Twelve). For example, a particular division of student affairs might choose leadership as an outcome, but this construct is too vague and broad to be measured as a single outcome. Leadership can be interpreted as assertiveness, speaking effectiveness, independence, and so on. Which aspect(s) of leadership is the intended, measurable outcome? In the process of determining outcomes, list global goals first; then elaborate and define them to create specific objectives. Failure to specify goals can weaken the effectiveness of outcome assessment or evaluation programs.

It is also important to distinguish between types of outcomes. Educational and developmental outcomes must be separated from resource management functions (Erwin and Tollefson, 1982). Examples of resource management objectives are those of service activities, such as the number of students registered, residence hall rooms filled, and students admitted. These functions are vital to any institution's operations but do not directly enhance students' education. Lenning (Chapter Twelve) makes a similar distinction between outcome goals and process goals. Outcome goals focus on program results; process goals refer to how the goals will be achieved. Too often emphases are shifted from what a program is supposed to accomplish to how it will be accomplished.

Finally, consider possible overlap between student outcomes specified by student affairs educators and those specified by academic affairs educators. For instance, many institutions select cognitive development as a desirable educational objective. Is this objective in the domain of student affairs or academic affairs? It is important for staff to specify only those objectives to which they contribute directly. Although disagreement abounds in the profession about appropriate student affairs concerns (Bloland, 1986; Barr, 1986; Kuh, Bean, Bradley, and Coomes, 1986), the professionals of each institution should determine the goals for which they feel themselves accountable.

Environmental Factors Affecting Student Outcomes

The second step in student affairs assessment is to delineate the influences of the campus environment. What aspects of the campus environment might produce personal and social change in the students? What happens at your institution to accelerate positive student change or promote student growth? What programs and services influence the development of students? Although this step may be the most difficult one for our profession, it may also be the most necessary.

Certainly, this step is now receiving significant attention. Huebner (Chapter Six) and Banning (Chapter Eleven) have discussed the general influence and importance of campus ecology. Accrediting associations such as SACS now charge institutions with explaining the link between goals and assessment. They are asking what produced the results shown by the assessment and how the results can be improved.

In an attempt to answer these questions, Micek and Arney (1974) describe several global environmental variables that might be considered: the instructional and research environment, the physical environment, the economic environment, the social environment, and the organizational environment. Of course, these variables are too global to be directly useful, but student affairs educators might isolate components within these five for which they are responsible. The following examples from this author's outcome research illustrate ways that economic, social, and organizational environments may be conceptualized and studied in relation to students' development.

To illustrate the concept of the impact of economic environments, two instruments—the Scale of Intellectual Development (SID) (Erwin, 1982) and the Perceived Self Questionnaire (PSQ) (Heath, 1968)—were administered to a sample of freshmen and readministered to them several years later when they were seniors. Students were divided into four groups according to the amount of their total college expenses they personally contributed over the four years: none, about 25 percent, about 50 percent, or more than 75 percent. Controlling for freshmen's SID or PSQ levels, seniors who financed at least 75 percent of their college education were less dualistic or rigid in their thinking, were more committed to their life's goals, had a firmer sense of direction and of stability, and were more able to express their values and thoughts than seniors who did not contribute toward their college expenses (Erwin, 1986). In an alternative definition of an economic environment, another longitudinal study (Erwin and Love, forthcoming) examined the impact of financial aid packages on development in autonomy. In that study, the economic environment was defined as the effects of receiving a scholarship or grant, a loan, or work-study or part-time employment. Controlling for entering freshmen's autonomy, juniors who worked part-time or were on work-study had higher autonomy scores than juniors with loans or no financial aid. In both studies, the impact of the economic environment was defined and then studied in relation to developmental change over a four-year period.

A study that illustrates an operational definition of a social environment in student affairs looked at the impact of roommates in a residential hall (Erwin, 1983). On the basis of the PSQ, students were defined as being high or low in maturity and were assigned roommates according to this maturity categorization. Three groups, or types of social environments, were studied: rooms with two high-maturity students, rooms with two low-maturity students, and rooms with high- and low-maturity students. A roommate then was conceived as a part of the social environment and studied as an influence in the students' change in maturity over a semester.

A last example illustrates the concept of organizational impact on development. As Astin (1984) hypothesized, the degree of a student's involvement in cocurricular activities should be related to personal development. In two other studies (Erwin, 1983; Erwin and Marcus-Mendoza, 1988), the degree of participation in community groups or campus activities was related to differences in motivation and intellectual development. Operational definitions of the impact of organizational structure involved categorizing students into the following groups: those who held three or more major offices, those who held one major office, those who participated but held no office, those who belonged but did not participate, and those who did not belong or participate at all.

These studies are merely examples of defining categories of environments. Institutions can easily define their own categories of campus environments that may affect students' development. Institutions that wish to gauge student perceptions with a standardized instrument should refer to Pace's (1984) College Student Experiences Questionnaire (CSSQ), which measures student involvement in a variety of environmental areas. These CSQ subscales range from clubs and organizations to the student union to experiences with faculty. Particularly valuable are the norms associated with each of the fourteen subscales for research and doctorate-granting universities, comprehensive colleges and universities, selective liberal arts colleges, and general liberal arts colleges. These norms allow an institution to compare students' perceptions about their campus environments to similar institutions.

Assessing Student Outcomes

After specific objectives have been selected, it is time to consider the following assessment steps: selecting instruments, designing new instruments, collecting assessment information, analyzing the information, maintaining the information, and using the information. Measurement terms will not be covered here; the reader should refer to Lenning (Chapter Twelve).

Selecting Instruments. The first step in the assessment process is to review existing assessment instruments. Student affairs professionals should examine existing instruments because the time, resources, and training needed to design new instruments are considerable. Using the guidelines mentioned above, focus on reliability, validity, method, and type of score reporting (norm or criterion-referenced) in making a selection. A particularly important factor is content validity. Does the instrument match with the stated outcome objectives? Will the instrument give the information that is sought? In addition, consider the costs and training associated with purchasing, administering, and scoring the instruments selected. For example, at Alverno College, which has fewer than 1,000 students (Mentkowski and Doherty, 1984), it may be feasible to interview students and rate their responses to the Moral Judgement Instrument (Kohlberg, 1981); at a large public university with thousands of students, Rest's (1987) Defining Issues Test, which is objectively scored, may be more appropriate. Lastly, in the selection or design of instruments, consider cultural, gender, and handicap differences that may bias the results of the assessment. For example, in the design of the Erwin Identity Scale (Erwin and Delworth, 1980), it was important to eliminate any items that caused handicapped persons to score lower on the Conceptions about Body and Appearance subscale.

Unfortunately, few instruments are available that purport to measure student development. A fine source was compiled by Mines (1982). More recently, Hood (1986) has prepared a volume describing instruments designed to measure Chickering's (1969) seven vectors of development. Many of the instruments are listed with brief descriptions of their history. Although not based on developmental theory, another excellent resource was prepared by Robinson and Shaver (1973), who listed numerous attitudinal surveys. The traditional *Mental Measurements Yearbook* (Mitchell, 1985) describes other measures of typical and maximum performance.

In an example of instrument selection at one institution, four developmental instruments were selected by an institutional committee charged with exploring development at James Madison University. These four instruments were the Defining Issues Test (Rest, 1987), which measured constructs of principled moral consideration and the utilization of concepts of justice; the Erwin Identity Scale (Erwin and Delworth, 1980), which measured constructs of confidence, sexual identity, and conceptions about body and appearance; the Scale of Intellectual Development (Erwin, 1982), which measured constructs of dualism, relativism, commitment, and empathy; and the Student Development Task and Lifestyle Inventory (Winston and Miller, 1987), which measured constructs of purpose, interpersonal relationships, academic autonomy, intimacy, and salubrious lifestyle. As described earlier, this committee sought to identify developmental goals for the typical student and examined a wide array of student development instruments. These goals were conceived as being enhanced not only by the division of student affairs but by academic affairs as well. At James Madison University, assessment activities in development are undertaken by both academic and student affairs personnel. For instance, since the director of student assessment works with the academic departments, each academic program is requested to include one or two developmental goals among their program objectives. The enhancement of student development is viewed as a shared responsibility between student affairs staff and academic faculty.

Designing New Instruments. There is a great need for the design and study of new instruments and methods for assessing student development (Hanson, 1982). The process is involved and lengthy and requires technical expertise. Consult Wesman (1971) and Henryssen (1971) for suggestions and procedures for instrument construction if you are considering designing in-house instruments.

In this process, the use of environmental referents to gather initial perceptions is a very helpful technique. Aulepp and Delworth (1976) provide information on environmental referents and other environmental assessment techniques.

Collecting Assessment Information. When, where, and how should student information be collected? It has been demonstrated (Erwin and Delworth, 1980, 1982) that the freshman orientation period is an optimal time for initial developmental assessment because students change developmentally even during their first few days of college. Assessment during the orientation produces a base line that can be used both in comparison with follow-up measurements and for referring students to planned programmed interventions on the basis of developmental level (Erwin and Miller, 1985).

When studying the impact of environmental influences, it is critical to follow students for later retesting. Recently, Astin (1982) popularized the notion of value-added education, or the study of educational growth between an initial assessment and a post-experience assessment. Value-added assessment is essentially a longitudinal design study, which has been advocated by student-life study researchers for years (Hanson, 1982). It is the study of what happens to the student over a designated time, rather than the absolute level demonstrated at a particular time. Although the value-added approach has been applied primarily in academic contexts (for example, Northeast Missouri State University, 1984), it also lends itself well to student affairs interventions. Collect an initial assessment, apply the intervention, assess the student again with the same measure, and examine any gains or losses between assessments.

Although the concept of post-test minus pretest scores is inherently appealing, it is also fraught with statistical problems (Linn and Slinde, 1977). Change scores are essentially unreliable measures, and a measurement specialist should be consulted for appropriate data analysis techniques if this approach is being considered.

If an institution plans a broad-based assessment program, it would be wise to collect cross-sectional information. Sampling freshmen, sophomores, juniors, and seniors furnishes information regarding typical performance at the four educational levels. Cross-sectional information cannot be used to infer the results of particular environmental experiences, but only of the impact of the institution as a whole.

New-student orientation periods have already been mentioned as a time to collect as well as to dispense information, but what are other appropriate times? Some institutions are currently considering setting aside an ''assessment day'' to administer a comprehensive battery of learning and development tests. Outcomes measures may also be administered to exiting seniors to glean a final assessment of the college experience.

In addition to student affairs staff, it is important to include input from students themselves at all phases of the assessment process. This is particularly essential when data are being collected over time. A major problem at most institutions now establishing outcomes assessment is the students' motivation to participate. Although assessment may be required of students, it is not possible to require that the students participate cooperatively and produce valid responses. Students' participation in the planning and explanation of the assessment process is crucial in overcoming this problem.

Analyzing Information. Information will be best used if it is analyzed by the people to whom it pertains. If information has been collected to evaluate the impact of a particular environmental program, professionals responsible for that program should be heavily involved in the analysis of that information. Technical consultants and student affairs professionals from other areas should be a part of the evaluation team, but results are more likely to be understood and used in future programs if the personnel have a personally vested or "stakeholder's" interest in the results.

Hanson and Lenning (1979) and Pascarella (1987) have presented several designs for analyzing the impact of student affairs programs. In general, developmental measures serve as the dependent variables and environmental groups as the independent experimental variable under study. Although sophisticated research expertise is needed, it is statistically advantageous to employ multivariate statistics because of the multidimensionality of students' development (Kuh, Bean, Bradley, and Coomes, 1986). Such statistical techniques may be more likely to be utilized in summative evaluation studies, while more informal assessment methods are used in formative evaluations (Hanson, 1982).

Maintaining Information. Chapter Nineteen by Kalsbeek on computerized student information systems (SIS) covers these methods of maintaining information very well and should be consulted. Such centralized systems are now commonplace in higher education; however, most SISs have been designed for resource management, not student development (Erwin and Tollefson, 1982).

Using Information. The key to any evaluation study is how the results will be used. As mentioned earlier, the persons responsible for programs should also participate in their evaluation. If the study was intended to be formative, then the results can be used for program improvement. If the study was summative, then program continuance becomes an issue. A precedent already exists in higher education for linking outcome information to budgets. In the state of Tennessee, institutions are monetarily rewarded for demonstrating student gains on various outcome measures (Bogue and Brown, 1982). Again, the academic departments are the primary focus of these practices, but basing funding on the evaluation of student affairs programs is a realistic possibility for some states.

In spite of external demands for summative evaluation, educators should use outcomes assessments for diagnostic and formative feedback to students. As Miller and Prince (1976) have indicated, self-understanding serves as a fine stimulant for growth, and it would be regrettable not to use reliable outcomes assessment data in this way.

Brown and Citrin (1977) have advocated implementation of a student development transcript, which would contain developmental information. Included should be not only course grades but also developmental scores and ratings and reports of environmental experiences. The recording of students' participation in student activities, programs, and services to enhance development can serve both the students and the institution. Students obain a record of their involvement (Astin, 1984), and institutions gain information for accountability and evaluation.

Future of Outcomes Assessment

The call for increased assessment and evaluation in student affairs is not a new one (Hanson, 1982). Although a well-defined assessment plan itself generates institutional improvement as much as empirical implications (Ewell, 1984), assessment activities are still uncommon in student affairs. Perhaps unfortunately, this need for evaluation is being transferred from the institutions to external agencies that now require proof of the value of education. At least one-fifth of the states currently require some form of outcomes assessment, with the number likely to increase (Boyer, Ewell, Finney, and Mingle, 1987). On the other hand, the student outcomes movement represents an opportunity for the student affairs profession to join with academic affairs to demonstrate the contributions it makes to students' lives. Whatever direction divisions of student affairs take, the student outcomes assessment movement is sure to be a part of their future.

Educators warn and the public agrees that education should be broad, including personal and social development as well as narrower vocational purposes. The claims of the student affairs profession for the promotion of the global goals of personal and social development now have a more attentive audience.

To make use of these opportunities will require adjustments and modifications in practices and attitudes. First, it will require us to state a clearer definition of what we do in student affairs and for what purpose. Our dual roles as educators and resource providers will lead to further debate. Divisions of student affairs that choose the role of educator may require closer cooperation with divisions of academic affairs. Increased competency of student affairs staff will also be required in assessment methods and in handling information by computer. If a division of student affairs does not currently support an assessment person, it would be wise to consider such a position. Otherwise, the duties of evaluation might be placed in another area of the university. Students will be provided with objective information about their personal growth and development that may become a part of a broader transcript. Students need feedback about their development for self-improvement and as a gauge for how the institution is assisting them in this development. Environmental interventions of demonstrated worth may become a part of the core curriculum for students. Educational interventions may no longer be limited to classroom work but also may include other types of group experiences sponsored through student affairs. Such proof will enhance the credibility of higher education as well as of student affairs.

Steps for Action Assessment

After considering the issues about assessment discussed in this chapter, the student development administrator may still be trying to decide what to do. This section is a reiteration of the steps for initiating and launching an assessment program. Although these points may be best directed to the vice-president for student affairs, it is also appropriate for other student development professionals to reflect on them to enhance both their own work and the profession's future.

1.   Is it a mission for the division of student affairs to enhance students' development? If the answer is no, outcome assessment or documentation of student growth should not be an activity for the division; stop here.
2.   Specifically define the student developmental goals for the division of student affairs. Most importantly, have members

of the student affairs department define the department's developmental goals they particularly enhance for students.

3. Identify the programs and services that are believed to enhance the department's developmental objectives.

4. Select or design instruments that measure those developmental goals and environmental components.

5. Collect developmental and environmental information.

6. Analyze assessment information. Are students who participate in the programs and services demonstrating greater development? Are the programs and services accomplishing their goals?

7. Share the assessment information with students. Keep a record of their developmental scores over time.

8. Reexamine the above steps and revise any component as necessary. Developmental goals, and particularly environmental programs and services, will evolve on the basis of assessment information.

This chapter was intended to persuade readers of the importance and longevity of student outcome assessment and to describe briefly several steps for getting started. At this phase of the movement, any contribution—no matter how technical—can give impetus to assessment in student affairs. There is much need and much opportunity to direct the future of student affairs and of general education as a whole.

References

Association of American Colleges. *Integrity in the College Curriculum.* Washington, D.C.: Association of American Colleges, 1985.

Astin, A. W. "Why Not Try Some New Ways of Measuring Quality?" *Educational Record,* Spring 1982, pp. 10–15.

Astin, A. W. "Student Involvement: A Developmental Theory for Higher Education." *Journal of College Student Personnel,* 1984, *25,* 297–308.

Aulepp, L., and Delworth, U. *Training Manual for an Ecosystem Model.* Boulder, Colo.: Western Interstate Commission for Higher Education, 1976.

Barr, M. J. "Should We Be Surprised?" *Journal of College Student Personnel,* 1986, *27,* 304–305.

Bennett, W. J. "Foreword." In C. P. Adelman, *Assessment in American Higher Education.* Washington, D.C.: U.S. Government Printing Office, 1986.

Bloland, P. A. "Student Development: The New Orthodoxy? Part II." *ACPA Developments,* 1986, *13* (4), 1, 22.

Bogue, E. G., and Brown, W. "Performance Incentives for State Colleges." *Harvard Business Review,* 1982, *59,* 123–128.

Boyer, C. M., Ewell, P. T., Finney, J. E., and Mingle, J. R. "Assessment and Outcomes Measurement—A View from the States." *American Association for Higher Education Bulletin,* 1987, *39* (7), 8–12.

Brown, R. D., and Citrin, R. S. "The Student Development Transcript: Assumptions, Uses, and Formats." *Journal of College Student Personnel,* 1977, *18,* 163–168.

Chickering, A. W. *Education and Identity.* San Francisco: Jossey-Bass, 1969.

Erwin, T. D. "The Scale of Intellectual Development: Measuring Perry's Scheme." *Journal of College Student Personnel,* 1982, *24,* 6–12.

Erwin, T. D. "The Influence of Roommate Assignments upon Students' Maturity." *Research in Higher Education,* 1983, *19,* 451–459.

Erwin, T. D. "Students' Contribution to Their College Costs and Intellectual Development." *Research in Higher Education,* 1986, *25,* 194–203.

Erwin, T. D., and Delworth, U. "An Instrument to Measure Chickering's Vector of Identity." *National Association of Student Personnel Administrators Journal,* 1980, *17,* 19–24.

Erwin, T. D., and Delworth, U. "Formulating Environmental Constructs That Affect Students' Identity." *National Association of Student Personnel Administrators Journal,* 1982, *20,* 47–55.

Erwin, T. D., and Love, W. B. "Selected Environmental Factors Associated with Change in Students' Development." *National Association of Student Personnel Administrators Journal,* forthcoming.

Erwin, T. D., and Marcus-Mendoza, S. T. "Motivation and Students' Participation in Leadership and Group Activities." *Journal of College Student Personnel,* 1988, *29,* 356-361.

Erwin, T. D., and Miller, S. W. "Technology and the Three R's." *National Association of Student Personnel Administrators Journal,* 1985, *22,* 47-51.

Erwin, T. D., and Tollefson, A. L. "A Data Base Management Model for Student Development." *Journal of College Student Personnel,* 1982, *23,* 70-76.

Ewell, P. T. *The Self-Regarding Institution: Information for Excellence.* Boulder, Colo.: National Center for Higher Education Management Systems, 1984.

Hanson, G. R. "Critical Issues in the Assessment of Student Development." In G. R. Hanson (ed.), *Measuring Student Development.* New Directions in Student Services, no. 20. San Francisco: Jossey-Bass, 1982.

Hanson, G. R., and Lenning, O. T. "Evaluating Student Development Programs." In G. D. Kuh (ed.), *Evaluation in Student Affairs.* Cincinnati, Ohio: University of Cincinnati, 1979.

Heath, D. H. *Growing Up in College: Liberal Education and Maturity.* San Francisco: Jossey-Bass, 1968.

Heath, D. H. *Maturity and Competence: A Transcultural View.* New York: Gardner Press, 1977.

Henryssen, S. "Gathering, Analyzing, and Using Data on Test Items." In R. L. Thorndike (ed.), *Educational Measurement.* Washington, D.C.: American Council on Education, 1971.

Hood, A. B. (ed.). *The Iowa Student Development Inventories.* Iowa City, Iowa: Hitech Press, 1986.

Kohlberg, L. *The Meaning and Measurement of Moral Development.* Worcester, Mass.: Clark University Press, 1981.

Kuh, G. D. "A Framework for Understanding Student Affairs Work." *Journal of College Student Personnel,* 1984, *25,* 25-31.

Kuh, G. D., Bean, J. P., Bradley, R. K., and Coomes, M. D. "Contributions of Student Affairs Journals to the Literature on College Students." *Journal of College Student Personnel,* 1986, *27,* 292-304.

Kuh, G. D., Shedd, J. D., and Whitt, E. J. "Student Affairs and Liberal Education: Unrecognized (and Unappreciated) Common-Law Partners." *Journal of College Student Personnel,* 1987, *28,* 252–260.

Lenning, O. T. *Previous Attempts to Structure Educational Outcomes and Outcome-Related Concepts: A Compilation and Review of the Literature.* Boulder, Colo.: National Center for Higher Education Management Systems, 1977.

Lenning, O. T. "Assessment and Evaluation." In U. Delworth, G. R. Hanson, and Associates, *Student Services: A Handbook for the Profession.* San Francisco: Jossey-Bass, 1980.

Linn, R. L., and Slinde, J. A. "The Determination of the Significance of Change Between Pre- and Posttesting Periods." *Review of Educational Research,* 1977, *47,* 121–150.

Mentkowski, M., and Doherty, A. *Careering After College.* Milwaukee, Wis.: Alverno College Productions, 1984.

Micek, S. S., and Arney, W. R. *Inventory of Institutional Environment Variables and Measures.* Boulder, Colo.: National Center for Higher Education Management Systems, 1974.

Miller, T. K., and Prince, J. S. *The Future of Student Affairs: A Guide to Student Development for Tomorrow's Higher Education.* San Francisco: Jossey-Bass, 1976.

Mines, R. A. "Student Development Techniques." In G. R. Hanson (ed.), *Measuring Student Development.* New Directions for Student Services, no. 20. San Francisco: Jossey-Bass, 1982.

Mitchell, J. V., Jr. (ed.). *The Ninth Mental Measurements Yearbook.* Vols. 1 and 2. Lincoln: University of Nebraska Press, 1985.

Morantes, E. "A Statewide Comprehensive Outcomes Assessment Program." Paper presented at fifth annual Regents' Conference of the State University and Community College System of Tennessee, Nashville, 1987.

Northeast Missouri State University. *In Pursuit of Degrees with Integrity.* Washington, D.C.: American Association of State Colleges and Universities, 1984.

Pace, C. R. *Measuring the Quality of College Student Experiences.* Los Angeles: Higher Education Research Institute, University of California, 1984.

Pascarella, E. T. "Some Methodological and Analytic Issues in Assessing the Influence of College." Paper presented at joint meetings of the American College Personnel Association and the National Association of Student Personnel Administrators, Chicago, 1987.

Perry, W. G., Jr. *Forms of Intellectual and Ethical Development in the College Years.* New York: Holt, Rinehart & Winston, 1970.

Rest, J. *Guide for the Defining Issues Test.* Minneapolis, Minn.: Center for the Study of Ethical Development, 1987.

Robinson, J. P., and Shaver, P. R. *Measures of Social Psychological Attitudes.* Ann Arbor: Institute for Social Research, University of Michigan, 1973.

Southern Association of Colleges and Schools. *Criteria for Accreditation.* Atlanta: Southern Association of Colleges and Schools, 1984.

Wesman, A. G. "Writing the Test Item." In R. L. Thorndike (ed.), *Educational Measurement.* Washington, D.C.: American Council on Education, 1971.

Widick, C., Knefelkamp, L., and Parker, C. A. "Student Development." In U. Delworth, G. R. Hanson, and Associates, *Student Services: A Handbook for the Profession.* San Francisco: Jossey-Bass, 1980.

Winston, R. B., Jr., and Miller, T. K. *Developmental Task and Lifestyle Inventory Manual.* Athens, Ga.: Student Development Associates, 1987.

Chapter Twenty-Four

Future Directions:
A Vision of Student Services
in the 1990s

Ursula Delworth
Gary R. Hanson

The chapers in this book represent an implicit statement concerning who we are. It is time to make this statement explicit. We are a profession committed to and expert in the integrated development of college students. We view student development as the product of person-environment interaction (Layton, Sandeen, and Baker, 1971) and are thus concerned with the nature and effectiveness of institutions of higher education as they affect and are affected by students. Singly or in combination, we are service providers, administrators, teachers, and researchers. Each of us may choose to play only one or two of these roles during his or her professional lifetime, yet our professional training (as graduate students and thereafter) must prepare us to understand, communicate, and to some extent participate in all these functions.

What, then, constitutes a profession? The dictionary states that it is "an occupation requiring . . . advanced study in a specialized field." It is this "specialized" that matters. To call ourselves a profession, we must make explicit what our specialty is.

Some definitions of our profession assume a body of theory, knowledge, and practice that is uniquely ours, and some of our colleagues assert that we possess this. We do not. We view our theory as coming mainly from the core behavioral and social science disciplines of psychology and sociology and the emerging field of organizational development. Our practical knowledge is shared as well with psychologists, organizational consultants, social workers, management specialists, and others.

If our theory and practice are not unique, can we be a profession? We believe the answer is yes, but such a self-definition requires us to articulate and adhere to a viable definition of our specialty.

In this chaper, we outline and discuss what we see as the core components that define the structure of the student services profession. We describe in depth each major component and then discuss its implications for the student services profession. In particular, we consider the curriculum implications and present a model curriculum incorporating and integrating these essential components.

Structure of the Profession

In the first edition of this book (Delworth, Hanson, and Associates, 1980), we delineated five major, related components that define the structure of the student services profession. We now add the area of ethics and standards as a sixth component, and acknowledge our lack in doing so earlier. Thus the components, as shown in Figure 1, are history and philosophy, relevant theories, models of practice, professional competencies, management and organizational competencies, and ethics and standards.

It is no accident that these components form the first five sections of this book, history and philosophy being combined with ethics and standards and related topics. We view these as fixed, essential, core components in the profession. However, we also believe that the content of each component will and should change over time. For example, being able to train para-

Figure 1. Structure of the Profession.

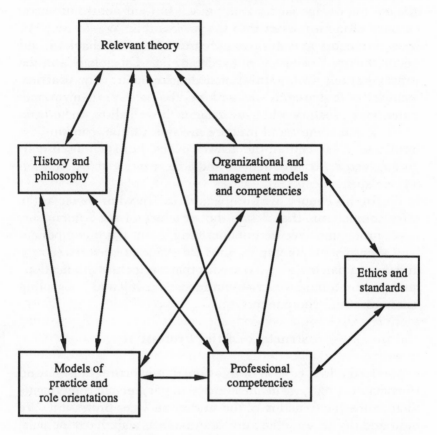

professionals is perhaps less central currently and has been omitted as a separate chapter. External developments and an evolving consensus within the profession dictate core philosophy, theory, models, and so on at any given point in time. The components are generic and form the rationale and basis; the models change as needed.

The earlier sections of this book have demonstrated the existence and relevance of each of these six components. The compelling reason for considering each of them essential is found in their relationship and in the gap left by omitting any. As Figure 1 demonstrates, each feeds into the next. That is, just as models of practice necessarily feed into professional competencies, so too competencies feed back into clearer definitions of practice models or even into the evolution of new models.

We can apply this basic idea to a more detailed discussion of the components. The material in Part One amply demonstrates that our profession does indeed have a history, one that includes both thought and action. We have also developed statements of ethics and standards, and we live in a world in which we must interact with the legal system. On a day-to-day basis, our ideas and attitudes have evolved out of our history and philosophy. In building or choosing theories to use, we rely on ideas and concepts provided by our philosophy. As we develop or borrow and adapt theories, we can use them to develop role orientations or models; that is, we can better describe and define roles, functions, and ways of operating in our day-to-day practice. Our models, therefore, provide a bridge between theory and day-to-day practice. Successfully implementing these roles or models requires particular competencies. Naturally, different roles demand different combinations of competencies. Thus, there is a direct link between the role orientations we assume and the skills we employ. The way we use our competencies in our professional activities leads to a particular style or mode of operating, which we refer to as the management or administration of the profession. Embedded in the concept of management and administration is the value of self-assessment and self-evaluation. The administration and management of our services is one example of the loop back to the competency component. These six building blocks of our profession, then, form a template to guide the future direction of student services.

As we consider these six components, we see progress and change over the past decade. Our ethics and standards statements are more specific, and educational materials are available. Our philosophy continues to be debated—we hope a healthy sign! Legal issues are more predominant and worrisome, especially for administrators. Many of us have developed some basic computer literacy and are striving to work with the newer constructs of information processing and enrollment management. We do not seem to know much more about evaluation, but we continue to consider it important. We are just beginning, along with our academic colleagues, to take outcome assessment seriously. Theory, which began to focus on person-environment interaction in the 1970s, in the 1980s has discovered that not all persons are similar. There is increased interest in women's (as different from men's) "ways of knowing," and we are starting to look at the multiple ways in which diversity of gender, ethnicity, and age can change both our theory and practice. Fenske and Hughes (Chapter Twenty-Two) document well the changes in society and in our students that have prompted our own shifts in the profession. We are seeing that there is much to be taught, and much to be learned, in both our preparation programs and our professional development experiences. What direct implications does all this have for the curriculum?

Curriculum for the Profession

Through the years, a number of models of graduate education have been discussed in the literature (for example, Meabon, Bailey, and Witten, 1975; Shaw, 1985), most of them focusing on master's-level preparation. Most recently, the multi-organizational Council for the Advancement of Standards (CAS) has developed and implemented standards and guidelines for student services and development programs (Council for the Advancement of Standards, 1986). These standards cover a number of topics, such as faculty, in addition to specifying the curriculum at the master's level. The CAS standards have been widely distributed and discussed and are currently used to accredit preparation programs. Basically, the standards propose a choice of one of three emphases in master's programs: counseling, development, or administration. There is substantial overlap among the three in terms of areas such as higher education theory and practice, knowledge regarding college students, and research basics. Each emphasis, however, focuses on course work and practice relevant to its own mission.

Our conceptualization of the curriculum takes a somewhat different approach from that of the CAS standards. We mandate curriculum areas but allow student (or program) choice within these areas. Our proposals can easily be modified slightly, however, to meet the requirements of the CAS standards, at least for the developmental and administrative emphases. The counseling emphasis proposed by the standards seems too similar to a generic counseling program to fit with our model of graduate education in the profession of student services and student development.

Goals. Before describing the nature of a model curriculum for student services, it is important to review our purposes. A curriculum plan can be used to set professional standards, assess current status and facilitate intentional change in the profession, select and manage staff, and establish our academic legitimacy. A brief explanation of each aspect shows why we must develop a curriculum that can be used for these purposes.

Standards of excellence are important to a profession because they allow us to state our ideals, hopes, and goals. By building a strong curriculum at the graduate level, we can introduce ideas of excellence early and implant expectations of how we ought to think and act as professionals. The day-to-day delivery of student services is guided by standards introduced through the curriculum.

In planning a curriculum, we cannot avoid assessing who we are and dreaming about who we might become. Teaching others what we do demands that we carefully examine our practice to become more aware of what we do well and what we do poorly. Planning a curriculum allows us to define our role. To become a "specialized" profession, we need to plan for the future by carefully developing the graduate curriculum. As we plan, we can anticipate both the direction and the role of our professional growth. A good curriculum allows us to introduce new ideas, concepts, and models of practice. We then evolve with a sense of purpose and direction, not by default.

The curriculum of a graduate program in student services can also be used to guide staff selection and management. As new staff join us, we can review job descriptions in light of the curriculum each new professional has experienced. We believe the curriculum presented in the next section will result in professionals well prepared to deal with the demands facing student services not only today but also in the future. As new staff join us, we must compare them with existing staff in terms of the knowledge, competencies, and attitudes they bring with them from their graduate programs. The curriculum we propose not only serves to guide preservice education but can also be used for staff development training to build new strengths in existing staff.

A solid curriculum is essential to any profession. Like it or not, our right to exist as professionals depends to a certain degree on how legitimate, rigorous, and substantial our thinking is. When we compete for dollars to implement our practice, we state that what we have to offer is valuable. We are judged against others. If we can establish that our profession has academic legitimacy, we will be able to convince decision makers in higher education that what we do is based on good thinking, rigorous evaluation, and careful management. The foundation for these activities is a comprehensive curriculum.

In summary, all these purposes serve a common goal— to perpetuate and enhance our profession through the education of competent professionals. We can achieve this goal only through clearly delineating appropriate curriculum. As they examine our proposed curriculum, we ask readers to keep in mind current professional practice as well as ideas and visions for the next decade and beyond.

The Model. We recommend a curriculum model that seeks to produce generalists at the master's level and specialists at the doctoral level. The field is too fluid to assume that master's-level specialists will always find appropriate employment. More to the point, most entry-level positions require a range of understanding and skills that can be gained only in a broad core curriculum. What this curriculum needs to do is prepare the student to enter the field successfully, not to function as a chief student affairs officer. Therefore, the focus is on "plus one" strategies, or helping the student to function at the next level, or the first professional job. Across courses and field experience, a focus is needed on three basic competency areas: critical thinking, diversity of reading and writing skills, and understanding of institutions of higher education. Consistent development in these areas is often more essential than the content of the course itself. Through the curriculum, the student comes to understand that he or she is entering a profession based in higher education and focused on academic pursuits. The student must be able to enter this world as a peer and colleague, even in an entry-level position. This requires skill in thinking through problems in a critical manner and the ability to communicate ideas in both oral and written form. Effective writing requires many formats. Hence, the student will need to learn how to write brief administrative memos as well as papers to back up an idea for a project.

What we are saying here is that the curriculum cannot be simply a collection of somewhat related courses. Each instructor should explicitly state how the basic competencies of critical thinking, diversity of reading and writing skills, and understanding of higher education institutions will be taught and practiced in each class.

Master's Program: Curriculum Components. These curriculum components follow our outline of components of the profession, with the following additions:

1. *History and Philosophy.* A minimum of one course in the history, organization, and philosophy of higher education and student services is recommended.
2. *Theory.* We advise a minimum of two courses in this area; one should be in theories of human development.
3. *Models of Practice and Role Orientations.* One course is recommended. It should examine relevant role orientations and discuss patterns of organization and specific agencies in student services in light of these models and roles. Professional ethics and standards can also be covered in this course.
4. *Core Competencies.* A minimum of four courses, each dealing with one specific competency, is advised. At the present time, they should include assessment and evaluation (with some focus on outcome assessment), consultation, instruction, and counseling and advising. Each course should include relevant theory and models and both a didactic and an experiential skills component. The counseling course should include basic group skills unless a separate core course is offered in group work.

5. *Specialized Competencies.* At least one course in this area should be offered. Ideally, students should have a choice of two or three. We see program development and environmental assessment and redesign as the key current specialized competencies, probably with program development as the priority course for most preparation programs.

6. *Administration and Management.* At least one basic course should be offered. This should include some theory but should focus on specific management tools needed by the professional in entry-level or intermediate positions.

7. *Practicum or Field Work.* A minimum of one year of practicum in at least two selected student services agencies is recommended. Students, faculty, and on-site supervisors should determine a training plan that ensures experience and supervision in at least two core competencies in each placement. In addition, at least one practicum should include experience in a specialized competency area, and at least one should involve some basic management tasks. A weekly seminar with a faculty member, required of all students enrolled in practicum, should focus on integrating practical experience with previous and concurrent course work.

8. *Additional Theory and Tool Courses.* Each student should select a minimum of one additional theory course and one course that will provide additional tools or skills. A requirement of two courses in each of these areas would be highly desirable. These courses may be offered through the student services program but are more likely to be offered in the behavioral science or business departments. Theory courses might include organizational or social learning theory or be focused on a specific population, such as adult learners or women. Skill courses include elementary statistics, testing, business law, and computer technology.

Master's Program: Organizational Considerations. The organization and sequencing of the model curriculum depends, of course, on such factors as the subdivisions of the academic year (such as semesters or quarters); the philosophy, competencies, and size of the faculty; and the specialized goals of the preparation program. The basic curriculum components presented above can be arranged in a pattern of forty to forty-five semester hours or three to four semesters of graduate work. However, other patterns may be preferable. Both core and specialized competencies lend themselves well to an intensive workshop format. A number of topics can be dealt with in a seminar format, especially models of practice and history and philosophy. Self-paced modules using written, audio, and audiovisual materials might be especially useful in presenting at least some aspects of the theory component as well as portions of the core and specialized competencies. Preparation programs that emphasize a competency-based approach can combine formal class work with a variety of more individualized approaches. Whatever organizational pattern is adopted, it is essential to include some experiential work near the beginning of the program and to schedule the first formal practicum or field experience during the first year.

Professional identity is a nebulous component that is nevertheless essential in any viable preparation program. In developing a professional identity, students must address issues of ethics, professional behavior and expectations, and professional organizations as well as the material identified as core curriculum. How the knowledge, attitudes, and skills that constitute professional identity are integrated into the program is best left to each group of faculty and students. Some programs may find it useful to schedule a "pro-seminar" during all or part of a student's first term in order to introduce these issues. Others may design a seminar late in the program, and still others may decide to integrate this material into several courses and practicum experiences. Our recommendation is simply to take this area seriously and to design its inclusion with care and commitment.

Doctoral Programs. All doctoral students should complete the equivalent of our entry-level professional curriculum, either before or early in their doctoral program. Following that, the core of doctoral training in the profession should be:

1. Demonstrated competence in both the understanding and the production of relevant research.

2. Demonstrated mastery of core and specialized competencies that are essential for leadership in at least one of the role orientations or models of practice. Mastery of two models would be more desirable, but one can be set as a minimum.

Research competence certainly involves course work in statistics and design, as well as a dissertation. Beyond these basics, however, real comfort with and appreciation of research is acquired only through systematic involvement in relevant research projects over a period of time. We recommend the early and continued involvement of doctoral students in research projects being conducted by faculty, researchers in student services, or other appropriate persons and groups. This apprentice approach is the most effective way to facilitate both skills in and commitment to research in doctoral students.

The apprentice model is also highly relevant in the area of core and specialized competencies. Advanced course work lays a solid foundation, but mastery depends on the opportunity to work closely and over an extended period of time with one or more experts in the specific competency.

Doctoral training is training for leadership in the profession. Students should have the opportunity to experience themselves as emerging leaders by participating in professional organizations and meetings, publications, consultation with entry-level professionals, exchanges with other programs, and whatever additional methods are feasible.

In-Service Programs. Strong, effective in-service programs are essential because staff turnover is declining. We predict a continued increase in well-conceptualized and well-organized staff development programs during the next decade. We recommend that such programs do the following things:

1. Assess needs in terms of the core training components presented earlier.
2. Set priorities on those areas that develop competencies immediately needed in student services or the institution and contribute most clearly to the mission and goals of the student services division and specific agencies within it.

3. Use resources such as faculty from student services and higher education preparation programs and behavioral science departments; literature, especially monographs and sourcebooks that can be read quickly; and experts in the community or at nearby institutions.
4. Facilitate and reward participation by staff members.

Caveats. Whatever curriculum model is chosen, it is essential to remember that ours is a young profession. Changes in the focus of our work must inevitably follow changes in the nature of society, higher education, and our students. We are at our best when we can be on the front line of such change, providing leadership for new directions in meeting the needs of our students and our institutions (see Erwin, Chapter Twenty-Three, for an example of such leadership in the area of outcome assessment). Our curriculum, however conceptualized, must be responsive to these shifts and must prepare professionals who can provide both service and leadership in emerging paradigms and models. We believe that our proposed model, which mandates education in core components as opposed to specific content, meets this criterion well. However, it is also necessary for faculty to keep abreast of changes in the field and sensitively alter courses and develop new courses to meet these shifts. In our field, perhaps more than in more established professions based on one academic discipline, each faculty member must assume the role of acute sensor of the environment and talented curriculum developer. To do otherwise is to exclude our students from the prime action in higher education and thus to doom our profession to less than equal partnership in our institution.

Visions

What do we see ahead for the profession? We agree with Fenske and Hughes (Chapter Twenty-Two) that the dual challenge for higher education is to improve the quality of academic programs while maintaining access for underserved populations. We would broaden "academic programs" to "educational experience," for, as Erwin (Chapter Twenty-Three) notes, positive outcome is related to both in-class and out-of-class experiences.

The challenge is exacerbated by financial pressures on institutions and made more complex by lack of knowledge regarding students (especially underserved populations) and how they learn, and by such traditional, artificial barriers as those between academic and student affairs and between academic departments. As Fried (Chapter Thirteen) notes, there is a tremendous amount of important knowledge regarding students and how they learn and develop that is simply not available to or known by the majority of academic faculty in our institutions. At a time of tremendous increase in the numbers of both women and returning adult students, little attention is paid to the unique characteristics of these populations, to "women's ways of knowing" (Belenky, Clinchy, Goldberger, and Tarule, 1986) and the "mattering" so essential to our adult students (Schlossberg, Lynch, and Chickering, 1989). Rawlings (1987) addresses the ways in which artificial barriers between academic departments trap students into an overspecialized undergraduate experience and militate against the achievement of a meaningful liberal education.

In the face of these obstacles, we maintain a vision that we as student services and student development professionals (by whatever name) can make a difference. To do that, several things must occur. We must see ourselves as allied with the mission of our institutions and be able to both articulate and produce programs, services, and research that make a difference. We must insist on being full partners in this endeavor with other institutional staff, and we must be able to demonstrate our ability to function effectively in this role. We must become more skilled at demonstrating that student development is not just a nice, humane concept, but the very basis of what we do in education—facilitating the cognitive development and educational achievement of students. To do so, we have to know the diverse ways in which students learn, what developmental, gender-specific, and other factors hinder or facilitate such learning, and how such factors can be addressed both in the formal curriculum and in the larger campus environment.

This role, moreover, is open to professionals working at all levels. We think of Erwin (Chapter Twenty-Three) working on outcome assessment at an institutional level. We think also of one of our graduate students, who, while working with student groups regarding selection of members and staff, has taught these groups the basis of human development and important gender differences.

One key to our increased influence is the quality and effectiveness of both our graduate preparation programs and continued professional development efforts. We cannot, obviously, share with others what we do not know. And we must be able to use an appropriate and effective process in this sharing. Perhaps the most important step we can take in this regard is to ensure that our educators, both of graduate students and in professional development settings, are clearly the most competent, committed, and knowledgeable persons in our field. To the extent we are able to achieve this goal, our future looks more secure.

Another key is our acceptance of a model for our profession that delineates core components and that can be interpreted to our colleagues in higher education. We and the authors in this volume have presented and discussed what we believe to be the relevant components in such a model. Further, we have offered guidelines for ensuring that they will be effectively integrated in our work. Only you, as readers, can decide if our model for the profession provides you with the vision necessary to make a difference in the lives of students and the future of our institutions.

References

Belenky, M. F., Clinchy, B. M., Goldberger, N. R., and Tarule, J. M. *Women's Ways of Knowing: The Development of Self, Voice and Mind.* New York: Basic Books, 1986.

Council for the Advancement of Standards. *CAS Standards and Guidelines for Student Services/Development Programs.* Iowa City, Iowa: American College Testing Service, 1986.

Delworth, U., Hanson, G. R., and Associates. *Student Services: A Handbook for the Profession.* San Francisco: Jossey-Bass, 1980.

Layton, W. L., Sandeen, C. A., and Baker, R. D. "Student

Development and Counseling." In P. H. Mussen and M. R. Rosenzweig (eds.), *Annual Review of Psychology*. Vol. 22. Palo Alto, Calif.: Annual Reviews, 1971.

Meabon, D. L., Bailey, W. R., and Witten, C. H. "The Competent Student Activities Administrators: A Model for Training." *Journal of College Student Personnel*, 1975, *16* (2), 100–106.

Rawlings, H. R. "The Basic Mission of Higher Education Is Thwarted by Academic Departments." *Chronicle of Higher Education*, Oct. 14, 1987, p. B-2.

Schlossberg, N. K., Lynch, A. Q., and Chickering, A. W. *Improving Higher Education Environments for Adults: Responsive Programs and Services from Entry to Departure*. San Francisco: Jossey-Bass, 1989.

Shaw, W. "Student Affairs Education and the Small College." *National Association of Student Personnel Administrators Journal*, 1985, *22* (3), 44–46.

Name Index

Subject Index

A

189–190; as relativists, 361; remedial concerns of, 381–383, 388, 395; staff development benefits to, 536–537, 544; unclear concerns of, 383, 386–387; whole person concept of, 35–38, 271, 285, 575, 576; women as, 557, 558–560

Students for a Democratic Society, 88

Study Group on the conditions of Excellence in American Higher Education, 568–569, 575, 583

Suicide, and counseling issues, 382–383, 389

Support and challenge, in classroom management, 362–363

Support system: for consultation, 412–413; and counselors, 276–277; for stress, 195

T

Taliferro v. *State Council of Higher Education,* and civil rights liability, 101, 109

Teachers Insurance and Annuity Association, 20

Teaching and training: aspects of competencies in, 353–370; assessment and evaluation in, 365–368; background on, 353–355; classroom management in, 363–363; clinical, 363; and cognitive complexity, 359–362; conclusion on, 368; and course content, 363–365; curriculum for, 608–615; distinction between, 355–356; and ethical issues, 395; for information resources, 504–505; and learning and teaching styles, 356–359; process of, 355–363; and professional associations, 273; and program development, 432–433, 436–437. *See also* Staff development

Technical competence, as management skill, 505

Technology, unclear, in organized anarchy, 224, 226

Tennessee: immunity in, 96; outcomes assessment in, 585, 596; program assessment in, 569–570

Territoriality, and person-environment interaction, 174–175

Texas: enrollment trends in, 557, 561; zero-base budgeting in, 481

Theoretical bases; aspects of, 113–242; background on, 113–115; functions of, 113–114; of organizations, 209–242; of person-environment interaction, 165–208; of student development, 117–164

Thinking-feeling, in typology, 151, 153–154

Third Article of Compact, 10

Tinker v. *Des Moines Independent School District,* and free speech, 87–88, 109

Title VI, 93

Title VII, 93

Title IX: of Education Amendments, 93; of Higher Education Act, 86

Toll v. *Moreno,* and immigration, 103, 109

Torts, liability under, 96–97

Training. *See* Teaching and training

Transaction, construct of, 177

Transactional approach, to person-environment interaction, 169–170

Transactional relationship, with interaction, 180

Truman Commission, 14, 15, 23

Trustees, and organizational structure, 448–449

Typological theories: aspects of, 149–154; concept of, 121, 149; type characteristics in, 152–154

U

Unconditional positive regard, in helping relationship, 373

Unit budgeting, characteristics of, 485–487

United Kingdom, influence of, 5, 8, 32, 36, 118, 143, 353

U.S. Department of Commerce, 561, 583

U.S. Department of Education: and data bases, 521, 579; and enrollment trends, 557; and program assessment, 570; and record keeping, 102